BOOK SALE
$1.00

*G. C. McClintock*

Louis S. St. Laurent at his desk; Prime Minister's Office, Ottawa,
winter 1956-7.

# Louis St. Laurent : Canadian

Published on the occasion of the Centennial of Canadian
Confederation. The preparation of the manuscript was subsidized by the Centennial Commission.

Ouvrage publié à l'occasion du Centenaire de la Confédéra-
tion Canadienne et redigé grâce à une subvention de la
Commission du Centenaire.

*Also by Dale Thomson* Alexander Mackenzie: Clear Grit

# Louis
# St. Laurent:
# Canadian

Dale C. Thomson

1967
Macmillan of Canada
Toronto

Library of Congress Catalogue Card No. 68-11107

Printed in Canada for The Macmillan Company of Canada Limited by the T. H. Best Printing Company Limited

# Contents

# Photographs

# Preface

This is a study of the political career of the Right Honourable
Louis S. St. Laurent, Prime Minister of Canada from November
15, 1948, until June 21, 1957. It is not an 'official' or 'authorized'
biography, and has not been subsidized or subjected to control
by the St. Laurent family or any interested parties. During the
period of research and writing, the St. Laurents, including Louis
St. Laurent himself, were models of circumspection and co-
operation, providing information but never seeking to impose
their views or alter the author's judgement. He can only hope
that their great trust in him will be found to be justified.

The author's debt of gratitude for advice and assistance during
the preparation of this book is large indeed, and the limitations
of space make it impossible to acknowledge all those who have
contributed to the process. Very welcome financial assistance was
received from the Centennial Commission, the Canada Council,
and the Canadian Institute of International Affairs. Over two
hundred persons submitted to interviews, including such busy
men as former President Dwight D. Eisenhower, former Prime
Minister Harold Macmillan, and the late Prime Minister Jawaharlal Nehru. A special word of affectionate thanks must go to
two members of the St. Laurent family, Miss Lora St. Laurent,
who did much to persuade her brother to allow his biography to
be written, and Mrs. Madeleine Veitch, who helped gather material, particularly regarding her father's early life. Dr. W. Kaye

Lamb, Dominion Archivist, and his staff rendered their usual efficient and courteous service in making available archival material. The Honourable J. W. Pickersgill, whose knowledge of the subject of the book is unsurpassed, was particularly helpful.

The chapter on the Suez crisis owes much to Mr. Terence Robertson, whose excellent book, *Crisis: The Inside Story of the Suez Conspiracy*, contains much valuable material not available elsewhere. His friendly co-operation was much appreciated. Mr. Patrick Daniel of Ottawa read the manuscript and made many helpful suggestions. Last, but far from least, Miss Elizabeth Richards of Montreal rendered very great assistance by proofreading the manuscript at several stages and checking points of detail. Without her painstaking efforts, the final product would certainly be of lesser quality.

# Louis St. Laurent : Canadian

# 1

## Call to Duty

When the St. Laurents took their seats at the supper table on the evening of Thursday, December 4, 1941, the meal seemed just another pleasant and familiar feature of their well-ordered family life. As on thousands of other occasions over the years, the distinguished-looking lawyer – then fifty-nine years old – had been driven shortly after six o'clock by his chauffeur from his down-town office to his Upper Town home on Quebec City's Grande Allée. His wife had been ill, but she was now sufficiently recovered to supervise the details of housekeeping again, and under her direction the cook and maid were bustling about, putting the final touches to the food.

The number of places around the table had diminished with the years as Louis and Jeanne St. Laurent's five children had grown up. Three of them, Marthe, Thérèse, and Jean-Paul, were married but still living in Quebec; with World War II in its third year, Renault, the eldest son, was a lieutenant in the Royal Canadian Navy, and Madeleine, the youngest of the family, was an officer in the Canadian Women's Auxiliary Corps. There were eight grandchildren already, and the three-storey house echoed with their cries and laughter on Sundays; but it was becoming an increasingly quiet, even lonesome, place during the week. That evening, however, they were five at table, for Renault was stationed at the local naval base, H.M.C.S. *Montcalm*, and had

1

come home for supper; Jean-Paul, whose wife was in hospital expecting a child, had returned rather than eat alone; and Aunt Lora, Louis St. Laurent's spinster sister, had come over from Compton to do her Christmas shopping.

The scene was similar to that taking place in other homes right across Canada. The head of the family carved and served the meat, and his wife served the vegetables, all the while making conversation with the others, and exchanging bits of news. The meal was well advanced when, in the Canadian capital, 280 miles away, a lonely and harried bachelor, too preoccupied to think of food, picked up the telephone in his study and interrupted the pleasant family gathering. He did much more; he disrupted, once and for all, the comfortable pattern of the close-knit family's life.

As the others exchanged glances of curiosity, Jean-Paul left the table to answer the telephone, then came back to announce that it was a long-distance call from Ottawa for his father. Louis St. Laurent rose with a gesture of impatience at being disturbed at supper, and left the room in turn. Soon he could be heard repeating at intervals the words, 'Yes, Sir.'

'That must be the Prime Minister,' Renault commented as they all strained to hear more; 'he is the only person Dad would say "Sir" to that often.'

Jean-Paul blurted excitedly what they were all thinking, but dared not express. 'He's asking Papa to join the cabinet to replace Ernest Lapointe as Minister of Justice.'

The expression of curiosity on the faces of Jeanne St. Laurent and her sister-in-law was transformed into one of dismay. When the head of the family returned to the dining-room, he confirmed that the call was from Prime Minister Mackenzie King, and stated that he was to go to Ottawa at once. He had not been told the purpose of the summons and had not felt it proper to ask; he had simply agreed to take the night train that was leaving in a few hours.

One reason St. Laurent did not ask was that he suspected the answer already, and did not want to hear it. Mackenzie King's chief Quebec lieutenant for some twenty years, Ernest Lapointe, had died eight days earlier and an anxious search had been going on for a successor who could hold the support of French-speaking

Canadians for the government, and assure their maximum participation in the war effort. Completely bilingual and one of Canada's leading lawyers, he had been mentioned in the press, along with several others, as a possible choice. In fact, he had been so concerned about the speculation that, after attending the funeral mass in Quebec City for Lapointe, he had not gone on to Rivière-du-Loup, where the final service was to be held, for fear of attracting the attention of those who were looking for a new minister.

The small family group resumed their meal, but tense excitement and concern had replaced the relaxed atmosphere of a few minutes earlier. Back at the head of the table, St. Laurent warned that the decision soon to be taken would affect the lives of all of them.

'Don't forget,' he stated, in part to suppress the eager enthusiasm of Jean-Paul, who was already conjuring up visions of his father as the greatest figure in Canada, 'if I accept, you will suffer enormously, and you will certainly not benefit from the move.'

His wife was still more emphatic. Devoted almost exclusively to her home and her family, she realized instinctively that the call to duty was a direct threat to her whole way of life, and she reacted sharply against it. Her husband already had his share of duties to perform as head of the family and the law firm, she protested, and his place was in Quebec City, not Ottawa. Besides, she went on somewhat petulantly, he knew nothing of politics, and the Prime Minister could find any number of people equally well qualified to replace Lapointe. Lora St. Laurent supported her sister-in-law. Their own mother had taught them always to put their family first, she reminded her brother, and their father had kept out of politics for that very reason. She herself had lived by the same precept, serving as housekeeper for their late brother, Nil, when he was a country priest, and later raising the children of their other brother, Maurice, when his wife died. Now, with Jeanne still convalescing from a serious illness, and Renault in uniform, she argued, Louis was needed more than ever at home.

Sitting quiet and erect in his dark, gold-braided uniform, Renault represented by his very presence the other side of the argument. The bonds between him and his father were close and strong; the younger man's greatest ambition was to emulate his parent in manner, word, and deed; Louis St. Laurent's ambition had long been to pass on to his eldest son the leadership of the family and of the law firm that bore their names. Yet they, too, had disagreed sharply just a year earlier on the same subject of service, the day that Renault had announced his intention to join the Navy. At that time, Louis St. Laurent himself, fearing for his son's life, had advanced with considerable vigour the argument that the first call of duty was at home. When Renault persisted in his plan, relations between them became strained, and only after he had reported for duty in Halifax did his father act to repair the breach. 'Man is a strange animal,' St. Laurent commented in his first letter in early 1941, after referring to his attitude of the previous months. 'I was and I am so proud of you and your sense of the responsibilities imposed on us. . . . My friends congratulate me in referring to you. And I would congratulate the father of any other son who acted like you. But that is the voice of reason, and "le coeur a ses raisons que la raison ne comprend pas." '

Now Renault was back in Quebec City, serving as an example to other French-speaking Canadians, and encouraging them to enlist as well. It was he who had led the tri-service funeral escort through the streets of the city when the final tribute was being paid to Ernest Lapointe. In a sense, the relationship between him and his father was reversed now: the older man was faced with a difficult decision and it was the younger one who had set the standards of conduct.

'Now, Mother,' Renault said firmly, but kindly, as the ailing woman's agitation grew, 'we all have to do what we can to help Dad make the right decision.'

Whenever the St. Laurents had been faced in the past with a problem of common concern to all of them, a council of all members of the family had been called, and the subject had been thoroughly thrashed out before any action was taken. Clearly, such a meeting was needed now, and, as soon as the meal was finished, Marthe and her husband, Mathieu Samson, and Thérèse and her husband, Frank Lafferty, were asked to come over. Also included, at the suggestion of one of the boys, was Wilfrid Edge, a local notary of their father's generation who had become a close confidant and friend of the male members of the family during their many fishing, hunting, and golfing expeditions together.

With only Madeleine and Jean-Paul's wife absent, the council was soon convened and it deliberated until the time arrived for Joseph Dion, the family chauffeur, to drive them to the station. They were unanimous in preferring to remain together in Quebec, but all realized that the call to duty could not be refused merely on that basis. As Quebec co-chairman of the War Savings Campaign, St. Laurent had spoken out frequently in recent months in favour of the war effort, urging his fellow Canadians to support with their money a cause for which so many young people were risking their lives. The pride and confidence of the children in their father made it easier for them than for their mother to accept the prospect of his being called to Ottawa; Jeanne St. Laurent could only see that her comfortable, happy home life was being disrupted by politics, a word with an unpleasant connotation in the St. Laurent household. No firm decision was taken before the train left, largely because the purpose of the trip was still not definitely known. However, the troubled lawyer declared to his wife at the last moment: 'Jeanne, I don't know why Mr. King wants to see me, but if it is to ask me to enter politics, I will tell him that at sixty years of age it's too late.' As he climbed aboard the train, the little group looked more like a group of mourners than a family preparing to keep an appointment with destiny.

Prime Minister Mackenzie King had not arrived lightly at his decision to summon Louis St. Laurent to the capital. Finding a suitable replacement for Lapointe was one of the more crucial steps in his long career, each one of which had been planned with great care. He and Ernest Lapointe had been political partners ever since he had inherited the leadership of the Liberal Party after Sir Wilfrid Laurier's death in 1919. As different in their private lives as in their physical appearance, they shared the same concepts of Canada and Canadian politics, and had managed to keep their party in office for fifteen out of the twenty-two years that they had worked together. More important, they had succeeded in large measure in healing the rift between French- and English-speaking Canadians caused by the issue of conscription in World War I, and had obtained an unequivocal mandate from the Canadian people in March 1940 to lead them in World War II. However, with the Quebec electorate clearly in mind, the government had promised to conduct the war effort without resorting to conscription for overseas service, and already pressure was building up in other provinces to repudiate that stand. The issue of conscription was a Damocles' sword hanging over the administration, and was threatening to divide it on ethnic lines if a shortage of volunteers developed. In the event of a crisis, a man like Lapointe would likely be indispensable in working out a policy acceptable to both groups. The Prime Minister was not exaggerating when he confided to his diary in early November 1941, on learning that the Minister of Justice had entered a Montreal hospital, that the prospect of losing him was 'a grave one indeed'.

The seriousness of the situation was increased by the weakness of the rest of the French-Canadian representation in the cabinet. In the late 1930s a team of great orators, Ernest Lapointe, Arthur Cardin, Fernand Rinfret, and C. G. 'Chubby' Power, held the province in their sway. Since then, Rinfret had died in 1939, Cardin had been struck down in early 1941 by a heart attack, and now Lapointe was seriously ill. Furthermore, Cardin was a taciturn and highly individualistic person with whom the Prime Minister was not on close terms, and who shone more as a hustings orator than as an administrator. As for Power, he was highly popular and competent, but, his fluency in French and his Irish origin notwithstanding, he was considered a *Canadien anglais* and was thus excluded from the list of possible successors to Lapointe as Quebec leader in the cabinet. In addition, he disappeared periodically from Ottawa on prolonged drinking bouts, to the displeasure of the abstemious head of the government. Finally, there was Senator Raoul Dandurand, but he was eighty years of age, and had himself, as it turned out, only a few months to live.

On November 14, Mackenzie King was advised that Lapointe's case was hopeless, and the next morning he travelled to Montreal to receive the report of the three-man medical team that had made the diagnosis. The sick man's son-in-law, Roger Ouimet,

met him at the railway station. 'You don't know what a loss this is for Canada and for me,' the Prime Minister commented mournfully, and he went on to explain that he had been thinking of appointing Lapointe to the Senate and naming him President of the Privy Council, to enable him to continue to advise the government without tiring himself unduly. Suddenly, the Prime Minister eyed the young lawyer intensely and asked: 'What do you think of St. Laurent?' He had begun the search for a successor.

At Notre Dame Hospital, he was shown the X-ray plates, which indicated a rapidly spreading cancer; it was only a matter of days. In the sick room, the two long-time political partners chatted naturally, but their conversation soon turned to the matter most on both their minds: the succession. Foremost on the list of names mentioned was that of Adélard Godbout, the premier of Quebec, and undoubtedly the leading Liberal in French Canada after Lapointe. Some ten days earlier, Mackenzie King had already raised the matter with Godbout, but the latter had replied at once that he did not feel qualified for the post, particularly in view of his poor knowledge of English and lack of legal training. Other names were mentioned, including that of Louis St. Laurent whom both Mackenzie King and Lapointe considered the sort of person who would lend strength and authority to the government. However, St. Laurent had always rejected overtures to draw him into politics, and it seemed doubtful whether his services could be obtained. They finally agreed that Godbout should be persuaded to move to Ottawa.

On November 19, Mackenzie King called at the hospital again on his way to St-Lin, where he was to take part in celebrations for the centenary of Sir Wilfrid Laurier's birth. Godbout was also taking part in the ceremonies at St-Lin, and Mackenzie King succeeded in isolating him in the tiny kitchen of Laurier's birthplace long enough to tell him that he must come to Ottawa, that Lapointe had agreed that he was 'the only man to take his place'. The Quebec premier resisted manfully but he had to agree that there was an urgent need in Ottawa for someone able to 'speak with authority on the whole Quebec question'. By the time they left the tiny village, the matter seemed about settled, at least in Mackenzie King's mind; the Prime Minister interpreted their hand-shake in front of the tablet they unveiled to Laurier's memory as symbolic of 'the combined leadership which is likely to follow'.

Another person who took an active part in the search for a suitable successor to Lapointe was Chubby Power. Taking the position from the outset that he was excluded by his ethnic origins from the key role, he canvassed his Liberal friends for an acceptable name. There was the brilliant and outspoken Aimé Geoffrion, generally considered the leading lawyer in Quebec, but he had always disdained to give up his lucrative practice and his epicurean ways for bondage to the public whim. 'My God, Geoff, in the middle of the war, we've got to have a good mind from Quebec,' the worried Power had protested when they discussed the problem in Montreal. He was sorry, the great lawyer remarked, that he did not have sufficient *noblesse* to place himself on the sacrificial altar of politics; however, Louis St. Laurent just might be induced to accept; 'I think the poor devil has a streak of nobility in him that might make him fall.' A former premier of Quebec, Alexandre Taschereau, was also a possible choice, but he was advancing in years, and his political star had been dimmed in the 1930s by accusations of scandal, and by defeat at the hands of Maurice Duplessis. Moreover, another former Quebec premier, Sir Lomer Gouin, had once tried a second career in Ottawa, and the experience had not been a success; Taschereau's friends advised him against it. Then there was Philippe Brais, Montreal lawyer and business man, and a member of the provincial cabinet, but he was identified more with the English-Canadian financial community than with the French-Canadian population, and his anglicized French bore witness to that fact. Another provincial minister, T. D. Bouchard, was also mentioned, but he was approaching the end of his career and his prestige was waning. In addition, he had become embroiled in an argument with a group of priests over the payment of taxes, and had become tagged as anti-clerical, the kiss of death in Quebec politics. The first choice of most Liberals was undoubtedly Adélard Godbout, to whom no one had any objection, except that he was perhaps not big enough for the job, and that he was needed in Quebec. And, finally, St. Laurent's name recurred frequently, but most people felt he was not available. Power reported to Mackenzie King on his soundings in Montreal the day the St-Lin celebrations were held. The Prime Minister concluded from their conversation that he was 'all for Godbout', and that the only problem was to make sure that Cardin concurred in the choice.

Ernest Lapointe died on November 26; the funeral was held in Quebec City three days later and was followed the same day by a second ceremony in Rivière-du-Loup, some hundred miles farther down the St. Lawrence River. During the train trip, Mackenzie King found an opportunity to broach the subject of the succession to Cardin. Still looking very frail as a result of his heart attack, and, in Mackenzie King's words, as if he 'might easily go at any time', the Minister of Public Works agreed that Godbout would make a good appointment, then asked, having evidently been thinking over the matter as well: 'Why do you not get St. Laurent? He is a distinguished figure; very able lawyer; carries great authority.' The Prime Minister noted the comment carefully and was impressed. 'I feel that he is perhaps the very man most needed,' he confided to his diary a few hours later. However, he and Lapointe had agreed on Godbout, and the bid for the premier's services was already made; he would continue his efforts in that direction.

Louis St. Laurent's precautions to avoid attracting attention at Lapointe's funeral were in vain; his name cropped up several times that day. Adélard Godbout had been consulting his political friends about the proposed move to Ottawa and had encountered almost unanimous opposition to the plan. On the return train journey from Rivière-du-Loup to Quebec City, he insisted that he would be of more service by remaining in Quebec City, and continuing to lead the Liberals there. The choice of a successor in Quebec would be very difficult, he pointed out, and dissension among the provincial Liberals would also affect Canada's contribution to the Allied strength, besides opening the door to Maurice Duplessis and the Union Nationale Party, who were opposed to an all-out war effort. However, Godbout's first reaction to St. Laurent as a possible alternative was rather negative. While he felt that the Quebec City lawyer was certainly a man of fine character, he doubted whether someone without political experience could have much influence in the province of Quebec. Moreover, St. Laurent's aristocratic bearing, his professional activity as the legal representative of 'outside' business interests, particularly in the pulp and paper industry, and his limited experience in dealing with the public, made him an unlikely leader of the masses. Certainly no one, commented one of Godbout's ministers, thought of calling him 'p'tit Louis'.

On the train, Mackenzie King referred confidently in conversations with other Liberals to the new 'Mackenzie King–Godbout team', but he was still trying to convince the modest premier, and, at the same time, to sound out the reaction to such a political formula. As the train bore him back to Ottawa the following day, he felt more and more strongly that there was no other solution. He spent a good part of that day, and of the next, composing a letter that could not easily be refused. In his four-page appeal he stated:

> If ever the finger of destiny pointed to a man who was meant to succeed Laurier and Lapointe, in the representation of Quebec East, and of his province in the federal arena, that man, viewed from whatever side you will, is most clearly and obviously yourself. In my leadership of the Liberal party – over more than twenty-two years – I have never before, that I am able to recall, begged of any man to become a member of any government of which I have been the head. I do not hesitate, however, to urge you just as strongly as I possibly can to come to Ottawa, and that at once. Unless you do, the situation at any moment may so develop that neither you nor I, for the remainder of our days, will be able ever to see it adequately met.

There was only one loophole in the passionate appeal. 'If you can name for me any other man who is in a position to meet that need as effectively as yourself, I shall not say another word.' However, to him there seemed to be no such person in sight.

Mackenzie King read the contents of the letter to Godbout by telephone on December 1, and they agreed to discuss the matter in Ottawa three days later. The following day he received a visit from Rodrigue Cardinal Villeneuve, who called to express his sympathy at the loss of Lapointe. The Prime Minister confided to him his concern with finding a suitable replacement for the deceased minister and mentioned his plan to bring Godbout to the federal capital. The church leader appeared surprised, but did not oppose the idea, and commented that they 'saw things pretty much the same way'. Mackenzie King was touched, feeling that he had a valuable and understanding ally in dealing with Quebec.

In the meantime, Godbout called a special meeting of his cabinet to discuss the situation. At first the other provincial ministers saw the Canadian Prime Minister's urgent request as an impressive honour difficult to refuse, but the future difficulties it implied for themselves soon became evident. They knew of no other man who could hold them together as a team, and stand up against their opponents as well. They opposed the move, and joined in the search for an alternative choice.

Backed by the views of his colleagues, Godbout was more determined than ever to resist the pressure of the Prime Minister when he arrived in Ottawa. He repeated the argument that his English was not sufficient for the federal arena, and that his departure would leave the provincial government divided and exposed. He suggested T. D. Bouchard instead, but Mackenzie King rejected that proposal summarily. After a preliminary discussion, the two men met with Cardin and Dandurand to canvass suitable names. It was Cardin, according to Mackenzie King's diary, who 'brought forward that of St. Laurent as the outstanding man from Quebec, likely to be most helpful in the federal arena'. Godbout agreed that St. Laurent commanded great respect, but questioned his ability as a political leader; Dandurand declared himself satisfied that the Quebec City lawyer was suitable for the post. The Prime Minister recalled that Power, who was not in attendance, had said St. Laurent was 'the best man in the province to run', and 'could easily be elected in Quebec'. But, ever cautious, Mackenzie King listed his disadvantages as well: he had been the representative of 'English' financial interests in Quebec, and his alleged views in favour of a total war effort, perhaps even in favour of conscription, might hurt his image among French Canadians – all the political warts were exposed. Nevertheless, when the examination was finished, there was still no one whose name produced the same degree of unanimity. Mackenzie King concluded that 'he would be the most fitting, next to Godbout, of any successor.' Later in the day, he telephoned him in Quebec.

When the train drew into Ottawa's Union Station shortly before noon on December 5, St. Laurent was still torn between his sense of duty to his family on the one hand, and to his country on the other, and was hoping that it would not be necessary to choose between the two. The Prime Minister's principal secretary, Walter Turnbull, met him and they drove straight to Laurier House where Mackenzie King worked in his third-floor library in the forenoon.

Although he had served the Liberal government as legal counsel many times, the Quebec lawyer scarcely knew Mackenzie King; they had met briefly on a few social occasions, but had never discussed matters of public interest. However, from the moment he entered the library, and was greeted by the words, 'Oh, Mr. St. Laurent, how good of you to come,' he began to fall under the influence of the Prime Minister's charm and sincerity.

The two men had a quiet lunch, during which they chatted casually, all the while assessing one another. The Prime Minister began his campaign of persuasion by referring to the earnestness of the war situation, the need for unity and sacrifice, and the importance of winning through to victory in order to meet the challenge of Canadian nationhood. 'When he had gone through that sequence,' one of his staff remarked later, 'only a perfect heel could refuse his call to duty.' It was not until they were back in the library that Mackenzie King referred directly to the purpose of the interview. At that juncture of the war, he declared, it was all-important to get the best men that could be secured for government service, and he was 'particularly anxious to get someone who would be a worthy successor in Quebec East constituency to Sir Wilfrid Laurier and Lapointe'. He believed that St. Laurent was the person to fill the role and to enter the cabinet as Minister of Justice.

Although the Prime Minister had struck his Achilles' heel in appealing to his sense of duty, St. Laurent did put up some resistance. He realized that in such critical times every man should be prepared to do what he could to help the country, and he was anxious to follow that precept, but he was not sure that he was the right man for the position; there were others who could better fill the post. He advanced the same arguments against his appointment that had been submitted to the Prime Minister by others. Quebec East, a working-class section of the city, was not the kind of constituency where he would have much popular appeal; in addition, there would be some prejudice against him because of his association with 'the big interests'; his name might command more respect in legal circles outside Quebec than at home. Mackenzie King replied that he would not except Quebec, and argued that his guest would be an excellent person to 'interpret the Quebec point of view to the [other] Provinces'. The Prime Minister recounted his efforts to persuade Godbout to enter the government, his failure in that regard, and the unanimous view of Dandurand, Cardin, and Godbout that St. Laurent was 'the best appointment that could be made from Quebec at this time'. St. Laurent endorsed Godbout's view that the Quebec premier would render better service by remaining in Quebec City at the moment, as 'it would be a fatal thing if Duplessis ever again got hold of the Government there'. The Quebec premier was greatly respected, St. Laurent pointed out; he worked well with the Cardinal, and could do more to influence the people than anyone else. St. Laurent asked particularly about Godbout's attitude toward the proposed appointment and said he would like to discuss the matter both with him and with the Cardinal. Mackenzie King remarked confidently that he could count on the support of both men.

After the elaborate search and the careful campaign of persuasion, the Prime Minister's victory was almost effortless. St. Laurent was evidently motivated purely by a sense of public service, Mackenzie King reflected afterwards, and made it clear that he would not want to stay longer than the duration of the war. The government leader assured him that 'of course' this could be as he wished. If he felt later that he wished to stay on, or return to his practice, or even take another post, this could be settled 'in the light of circumstances'. No promises were asked beyond that, and none was given. The two men discussed the progress of the war, and the Prime Minister confided that he had information from Winston Churchill to the effect that peace might come as early as 1942, thus implying that the Quebec lawyer's tour of duty might be as brief as one year. St. Laurent made a more conservative estimate of two years, in order to avoid disappointment. It all depended on when the United States entered the struggle, he remarked; when they did, they might well conscript men for overseas service, and then 'it might become necessary to do the same'. Thus, almost incidentally, the political novice put his finger on the issue that was to harass them both for three and a half long years. But it was not a factor in their negotiations.

It was a sad and worried man who returned to Quebec City on the late afternoon train to make his final decision. If he accepted the urgent invitation to join the cabinet – and he could see no alternative – he would be putting his duty to his family second, and that was contrary to the whole pattern of his life. He would be making his wife unhappy, and that, too, was something he had tried hard to avoid ever since he had met her as a beautiful and temperamental girl thirty-five years earlier. It would mean abandoning his law practice for the duration of the war, and at a time when Renault, who was to succeed him eventually as head of the firm, was also absent. And, as he had told the Prime Minister, it was not an easy matter to abandon a law practice at nearly sixty years of age, and then take it up again later.

Financial considerations were the most worrisome of all. Over the years, he had built his income from a mere fifty dollars a month at the outset to around fifty thousand dollars a year, and the prospects for further expansion were excellent. It had not been easy; he had worked harder than most men, allowed himself few holidays, had been stricken once with tuberculosis, and had lost precious savings in the Wall Street crash of 1929. In fact, he had only begun in recent years to recoup his losses, and pay off the debts incurred at that time. He was in the process of building up a valuable portfolio of directorships, and just that year one of the choicest, that of the Bank of Montreal, had come to him. He had refused invitations to join law firms in Montreal, where the really big money was to be made, because he and his wife preferred to live in Quebec, but he did spend about one day a week as special counsel for a Montreal firm, and so he had an office there as well. His family had become accustomed to a high standard of living, with domestic servants, a chauffeur, holidays in Europe, and memberships in the best clubs. Although he and his wife did not entertain frequently, he had an excellent wine cellar, and his wife was known for her fine cuisine. A provident person, he had accumulated thirty-three insurance policies, which alone cost him several thousand dollars a year. A minister's salary of twelve thousand dollars a year would not even pay his current expenses, let alone enable him to build up his reserves again.

These thoughts were still running through St. Laurent's mind when Joseph Dion met him at the railway station, and drove him home to his anxious wife. The next three days were busy and difficult ones. The family was still far from unanimous, the women being still unconvinced that such a sacrifice was called for at his age. Voices rose as he insisted that he could not refuse the call to duty, and that their very lives depended on an Allied victory. It was true that he had considered the 1914-18 war a purely European quarrel, he conceded, and that he had felt no obligation to take part in it personally, but he was convinced that this time the entire free world was involved; French Canadians had to be made to realize that fact, he argued, and persuaded to make the greatest possible contribution to the war effort. But these were intellectual arguments, and as he himself had commented not long before, 'le coeur a ses raisons que la raison ne comprend pas.'

On Saturday, St. Laurent discussed the situation briefly with his law partners, then rushed off to consult Cardinal Villeneuve and Premier Godbout. He was determined to have the approval of the church leader before accepting the task; if the Cardinal felt, like so many other French-speaking Canadians, that the war did not require such sacrifices, he would have no hesitation in refusing his services. However, any hopes he cherished in that respect were doomed in advance; Mackenzie King had already taken the precaution of enlisting Villeneuve's support; St. Laurent was encouraged to assume the heavy responsibilities. As for Godbout – having participated in the choice, he naturally encouraged St. Laurent to accept and promised his co-operation. Another eminent citizen whom St. Laurent consulted, Chief Justice Albert Sévigny, a former class-mate and long-time friend, took the same view, but tempered his advice with a word of warning drawn from his own experience. A Conservative in politics, Sévigny had been a member of the Borden cabinet when conscription was intro- duced in 1917, and his house in Quebec City had been stoned by irate fellow residents. 'You enter politics at the summit and with- out experience,' he warned St. Laurent. 'You will see that politics is a capricious woman. When all goes well, everyone is at your feet; when the tide changes, everyone will be against you.'

With each interview, even the illusion of having a choice seemed to disappear. Later in the day St. Laurent called at a local hospital to visit his latest grandchild, Jean-Paul's daughter, who had been born during his trip to Ottawa. 'I may be making a mistake for myself,' he mused as he stood over the crib and con- templated the tiny red face, 'but perhaps in the long run this child will benefit.' By the time they went to mass the next morning, the decision was no longer in doubt. As he left the church, he met a fellow lawyer, and told him somewhat gloomily that he had been asked to succeed Lapointe, and did not see how he could refuse. The family was gathered together for Sunday dinner in the Grande Allée home when the news broke upon the world that Japanese forces had attacked Pearl Harbor. That meant full American participation in the conflict; there seemed no longer any possibility of arguing, as many French-speaking Canadians had done, that it was 'just another imperial war' in which North American interests were not involved. Louis St. Laurent's decision was confirmed.

Events continued to follow one another rapidly. He spent Monday clearing up business details and transferring files to other members of the firm, then caught the night train once again to Montreal, and repeated the performance in his office there. It was from Montreal that he telephoned his decision to the Prime Minister, and agreed to take office the following day. With none of the secretiveness so customary on such occasions, he discussed his situation openly. Meeting two Montreal lawyers in front of the massive Royal Bank building on St. James Street, he stopped long enough in the bitterly cold wind to tell them that 'Mr. King has asked me to take Mr. Lapointe's place, and I don't see how I can refuse.' Much as they admired his gesture, the other men wondered what kind of politician someone would make who discussed such matters with casual acquaintances – one of them a staunch Tory! – on a street corner.

St. Laurent had breakfast on December 10 in the Windsor Hotel with his former law partner, Mr. Justice Antonin Galipeault, who had tried in vain on many occasions to interest him in politics, when Galipeault himself was a provincial minister. Now the roles would be reversed; St. Laurent would be the politician, Galipeault the non-partisan jurist. Fate, they agreed, played strange tricks with men's lives. Shortly before noon, he was in the Prime Minister's East Block office in Ottawa. Other men were giving their lives in war service, St. Laurent told the government leader with evident emotion, and in the circumstances he could not refuse the request being made of him. However, he recalled the prediction of Winston Churchill that the war might end suddenly in 1942, and expressed the hope that he would not have to serve more than two years. It was wishful thinking; Mackenzie King himself had commented in his diary that the attack on Pearl Harbor 'made it look as though it might be several years'.

The Prime Minister was elated as he entered the Council Chamber a few minutes later to inform the cabinet of the new colleague he had recruited. Jealous of his prerogatives, he was pleased that the negotiations had been kept secret, even from most of the other ministers, that he had reached his own decision on the matter rather than having his hand forced, and that he had made the appointment 'over and above all the lower order of political considerations'. The swearing-in ceremony took place at Rideau Hall before the Governor General, the Earl of Athlone, in the early afternoon, and then the Prime Minister escorted St. Laurent to his new office in the Justice Building, explaining that he wanted to visit once more the room occupied by his long-time friend and companion-in-arms, Ernest Lapointe. On the walls were the portraits of all the ministers of justice since Confederation, beginning with Sir John A. Macdonald himself. Through the Gothic windows they could see the Parliament Buildings, a few hundred yards away, and, off to the north across the Ottawa River, the Gatineau Hills of Quebec.

As soon as the Prime Minister had left, St. Laurent was introduced to the office staff by Benoit Godbout, the Quebec premier's nephew, who had served Lapointe as assistant private secretary. After making it clear that he intended to make no changes in personnel, since he was only in Ottawa on a temporary basis, the new minister asked if there were any matters requiring his attention at once. Since his predecessor had left the office for the last time several weeks earlier, there were, in fact, a great many; within a few minutes, he and Godbout were seated at the huge desk, examining the pile of documents that had accumulated. They had already cleared up the most urgent matters before members of the Parliamentary Press Gallery arrived to meet the new minister. St. Laurent told the curious newspapermen, most of whom had never seen him before:

> Last Thursday, Mr. King asked me to come to Ottawa at the earliest convenient time, and I was here the next day. He told me it would be helpful if I would accept the responsibility of this office. I replied that I could not shirk any duties which those responsible for the government of Canada felt I should perform. I look upon myself as just a good average Canadian, and I am going to try to do the kind of job good average Canadians want done. When I took the oath of office to-day I felt that oath to be identical in effect to the oath taken by many thousands of Canadians at this time. This is a war job.

When St. Laurent stressed the temporary character of his commitment, one astute political observer commented: 'We shall see.' Politics is a demanding mistress who does not release her suitors as long as they can serve her purposes. But that was a matter for the future. One newspaperman summed up the general impression in his column that evening with these words: 'If ever there was a case of a job seeking the man, this is it.'

# 2

---

## Eastern Townships Boy

Louis St. Laurent was an eighth-generation Canadian; his lineage could be traced to a settler who landed in Quebec around 1660, and beyond him to a merchant family in Burgundy. That adventurous ancestor was called Nicolas Huot, but, perhaps because his father's first name was Laurens, or because of some particular association with the majestic river, he soon added the name St. Laurent to the ones given him at birth. The archives of the old fortress city record the gradual evolution of his signature from Huot to Huot–St. Laurens, and then to Huot–St. Laurent. An educated man according to the standards of the time, and with good connections in the young colony, he found employment as sheriff in the court-house. In addition to seeing to the administrative details of justice, he prepared legal documents in a clear and polished hand. With such a position, the adaptation to life in New France appears to have been relatively easy; he was on hand when the Sovereign Council was created in 1663, and assisted Monseigneur Laval in establishing the Seminary of Quebec, later to become Laval University. When he married a Parisian girl, Marie Fayette, in 1662, two titled members of the colony attended the ceremony.

In the best tradition of the tiny community, the couple had ten children, and lived in large part off the land. After residing in Quebec and in near-by Beaupré for eighteen years, Huot abandoned his position to join in founding a new parish down-stream, on the present site of Ste-Anne-de-la-Pocatière. Only in 1693, the year of his death, did the family return to the Quebec City area. The eldest of their three sons, Laurent-Etienne, may have been the first settler of another new parish, St-Nicholas, some ten miles above the capital on the south shore. He and his teen-aged wife were typical settlers – hard-working, pious, and il-literate; they signed the marriage register with a cross. Succeeding generations of the family moved west along the river; when the British took over the colony in 1759, they had reached Nicolet, across the St. Lawrence from Trois-Rivières. Since they were peasants and labourers, the change of masters had little direct impact on their lives. Inevitably, some members of the family were attracted to the commercial and administrative centre of Trois-Rivières, and it was there that Louis St. Laurent's grand-father was born in 1812. Like his forefathers for four generations, Louis-Etienne St. Laurent* did not learn to read or write, but he must have moved in the better social circles, for he married into one of the oldest families of the town. His bride was Marie-Louise Parent, a direct descendant of the Scottish pilot Abraham Martin, known as one of the first two farmers in Canada (his fields were later to become famous as the Plains of Abraham). Another of her ancestors, Louis Guimont, was tortured and killed by Indians, and was accorded a prominent place on the list of Canadian martyrs.

Trois-Rivières was prosperous during the 1830s, and boasted a population approaching five thousand souls, its own newspaper, and its own local administration. His want of education notwith-standing, Louis-Etienne St. Laurent succeeded in establishing himself, in partnership with a friend, as a storekeeper, and made a comfortable living for himself and his family. For the first time in many years, a St. Laurent had time to take an interest in the political life of the community. Supporters of Louis-Joseph Papineau and Robert Nelson in the 1837 uprising against the colonial administration, he and his wife were members of a group

---

*His name was inscribed at birth as Louis-Clovis, but he was known throughout his life as Louis-Etienne.

Louis St. Laurent with his brothers and sisters, circa 1894. Left to right: Maurice, Louise, Lora, Louis, Kathleen, Nil.

Birthplace of Louis St. Laurent, and his father's store; Compton, Quebec.

Louis St. Laurent at about twenty years of age.

who decided to burn a certain Judge Martineau in effigy to protest his attitude during the struggle. Petite nineteen-year-old Marie-Louise was lowered with a rope through an opening in the judge's roof to steal his robe and cap for the purpose. Having become urban dwellers, the members of the family were more exposed, not only to the political, but also to the economic, winds sweeping the colony. Trois-Rivières was hit hard by the economic depression that began in 1858; the normally busy harbour was stilled; workers were idle; and stores like St. Laurent's verged on bankruptcy. Louis-Etienne suffered an additional misfortune; his business partner absconded with their remaining funds. Virtually penniless, St. Laurent, his wife, and their eight children moved to the new and more promising town of Sherbrooke, forty miles from the United States border.

Sherbrooke was the commercial and political centre of the Eastern Townships, an area settled first by immigrants from the United States and later by British immigrants brought across the Atlantic by the British and American Land Company. When Louis-Etienne St. Laurent and his family arrived, only a quarter of Sherbrooke's population of four thousand was French speaking. Wrote a contemporary historian:

> This mixed population lives harmoniously together, the French Canadians co-operating and harmonizing with their British-born brothers. Differences will be found in the habits of life and tone of thought of a people so diverse in race, in social habits, and in creed, but these differences do not lead to strife, they tend rather to soften the manners, and it has been remarked by careful observers, not themselves Canadians, that the tone of the society shows traces of refinement due to a mixed population.

In the following decades, the close contact between members of the two founding groups of Canadians, living and working together in the pleasant and peaceful countryside, was to produce a type of person known as the 'Eastern Townships man' — one who respected both cultures, took pride in the dual heritage of Canada, and drew on them to enrich his own life.

Forty-six years of age, and with practically no money, Louis-

Etienne did not find it easy to make a new start. However, his eldest son, Jean-Baptiste-Moïse, already nineteen years old, was able to share the burden of supporting the family, and his wife, a practised seamstress, added to their income by taking in work at home. Together, they succeeded in opening a new store. Jean-Baptiste-Moïse was a tall, broad-shouldered young man with dark, piercing eyes and black, wavy hair. The first member of the family in several generations to have attended school, he could read and write, had some knowledge of mathematics, and spoke English, albeit with a heavy accent; well groomed and well mannered, he became one of the most attractive young men in Sherbrooke. On one occasion, his appearance very nearly caused an international incident. He had been sent to Montreal to order supplies for the store just at the time when the world was shocked by the news of Abraham Lincoln's assassination. The assassin, John Wilkes Booth, had escaped, and there were rumours that he had fled to Montreal, a city considered by many to be a centre for Southern spies and conspirators. Any stranger was suspect to the excited population, and, shortly after Jean-Baptiste-Moïse arrived, he was arrested on suspicion of murder. He spent several hours locked in a hotel room before being identified by two acquaintances from Sherbrooke and released.

Storekeeping was his life, and in January 1872 Jean-Baptiste-Moïse, thirty-two years old and still a bachelor, joined with a friend in opening a haberdashery across from the market-place on Wellington Street. The enterprise prospered, and when Jean-Baptiste-Moïse St. Laurent took over the business in his own name in June 1875, the stock on hand was valued at ten thousand dollars, and was described in advertising as 'one of the best collections in the Eastern Townships'. In addition, he was able to dabble in property speculation, held mortgages on other lots of land, and even found time to take an interest in local politics. But, once again, misfortune struck the family in the form of an economic depression; Jean-Baptiste-Moïse St. Laurent was in Halifax early in 1877, on the first leg of a trip to Europe, when he received word that his credit had been suspended. He returned home and was forced to sell his entire stock for 'fifty cents on the dollar'. Later in the year, his brother Louis-Philippe, in business as a tinsmith, had to close shop as well, and he moved to Manitoba. The third brother, David, who had worked with his eldest brother, was obliged to hire out as a clerk in another store. The family was back where they had started on their arrival in Sherbrooke twenty years earlier.

One man's bad luck is occasionally another's good fortune. In the little village of Compton, fifteen miles away towards the American border, a storekeeper named F. T. Authier had also gone bankrupt about the same time, and a second store had burned down. Looking about for new opportunities, J.-B.-M. St. Laurent visited the small community and was attracted both by the economic opportunities and by the pleasant rural existence of the three hundred inhabitants. Although it had only two streets running at right-angles to one another, Compton was in the heart of one of the most prosperous agricultural areas in the country. The Coaticook River, hardly more than a stone's throw from the village, and Moe's River a few miles to the east provided abundant water, and their valleys were ideal for grazing. Some of the larger farms had been founded as early as the beginning of the century and were renowned for their fine herds of horses and cattle. In addition, there were some fifty sawmills in the township. Most illustrious among the residents of the area were Colonel J. H. Pope, one of the Fathers of Confederation, and Senator M. H. Cochrane, who raised pedigree livestock just outside the village. Compton had no railroad station, since the residents had not allowed the Sherbrooke-Coaticook line to be built through the tiny centre, but Compton Station was just two miles away. On the other hand, there were three churches – Anglican, Methodist, and Roman Catholic – and representatives of other religious groups called frequently to care for the spiritual needs of their faithful. To the forty-year-old St. Laurent, weary of the quest for fortune in Sherbrooke, the small community offered the hope of a new and more peaceful life. In 1879 he arranged to take over Authier's former store and the adjoining house, and hung out his shingle in foot-high letters:

J. B. M. ST. LAURENT.    GENERAL MERCHANT.

The arrival of the well-groomed business man, with his ample sideburns and moustache, heavy dark brows, and large brown eyes, caused a ripple of excitement in the village, particularly among the unmarried ladies. Referred to as 'the new Beau Brummell', he was observed carefully, to see who would be the object of his attention. It turned out to be the local schoolteacher, a red-haired Irish Catholic named Mary Ann Broderick. They were married in April 1881.

Although the child of immigrant parents, Mary Ann could claim roots in the area as old as the community itself. The farm on which she was born, five miles out of Compton on the Coaticook road, had been settled by an American couple named Wyman around the turn of the century. They had left it to their only daughter, Phoebe, and her husband, an Irish-Catholic school-teacher, John Ford. Without children of their own, the Fords had persuaded one of John's nieces and her husband, Bridget and Stephen Broderick, to come out from County Galway, Ireland, and join them in working the land. The Brodericks had arrived in Compton in 1847 with forty cents to their name. It was a happy arrangement. The young immigrants had two children, whom they called Phoebe and John, and a third was expected in 1852, when Stephen decided suddenly to join the California gold-rush, and try to make enough money to buy a farm of his own. The expedition was a combination of good fortune and tragedy. Broderick and his travelling companion, a neighbour named Quartz Bliss, found work easily, at excellent wages, but living costs were equally high. Potatoes cost seven dollars a pound, and were hoarded as a special luxury for St. Patrick's Day. Nevertheless, they managed to save a good part of their earnings, and, after about two years, were ready to set out for home again. Then their ship was wrecked off the California coast, and they lost every-thing. Bliss gave up and returned home, but the strong-minded Broderick went back to the gold-fields and began again. He was absent from Compton a total of four years, but when he returned he was able to buy an adjoining piece of land, and he set himself up as a farmer in his own right.

During Stephen Broderick's absence, his third child, Mary Ann, had been born, and she was three years old on his return. The childless Phoebe Ford had become very attached to her, and, when the two families separated, she persuaded the younger couple to leave the little girl in her care. Thus Mary Ann was raised by a devout Puritan born in the United States. There was only one restriction on the old woman's authority; Mary Ann was to be raised as a Catholic like the other children. When the child was twelve years old, John Ford died, and her parents and brothers and sisters – six by now – moved back into the old home, but Phoebe Ford continued to raise her. When she had finished the local Protestant school, she was sent as one of the first pupils to the new Roman Catholic convent in Coaticook, where she completed her education. Phoebe Ford lived long enough to see her graduate and take up her duties as a schoolteacher in Compton.

With a rare combination of Irish wit, Roman Catholic religious fervour, and Puritan self-discipline, Mary Ann Broderick exercised her profession for nine years and established a reputation as a demanding but just teacher, before fate knocked on her door in the form of the elegant new storekeeper. Jean-Baptiste-Moïse St. Laurent courted her in English spoken with a noticeable French accent; she responded with definite traces of an Irish brogue. On their honeymoon, she did venture to speak a few words in her husband's native tongue, but she abandoned the attempt when he laughed at her accent, and swore indignantly that he would never hear her speak French again as long as he lived. She kept the vow, but not only because of the flare of Irish temper. 'I married a Frenchman,' she confided to a visitor in later life, 'and I knew that if I spoke French there would not be a word of English spoken in the house, so I was firm about not saying one word of French, and not letting them speak French to me.' As a result, her children were to become perfectly bilingual in their own home.

Orderly and punctual in everything she did, the new bride settled quickly into a routine that was to vary little throughout her life. Her day began shortly after 6 a.m. with communion at the white-painted St. Thomas Aquinas Church, where they had been married. Almost invariably clad in an ankle-length grey or black dress trimmed with a high white collar and button-on cuffs and covered by an ample apron, and wearing her red hair parted precisely in the centre and wound into a bun at the back of her head, she created an impression of severity reminiscent of her upbringing by Phoebe Ford. However, she was a cheerful soul, and bustled about her home from early morning until late at night, devoting herself single-mindedly to her domestic duties. She sewed her own clothes, baked bread, made her own butter, and raised her own vegetables. When the day's work was done, she sat in the living-room and told her beads. It was clearly understood from the outset that, while 'St. Laurent', as she always called her husband, was master in the store, she was in charge of the home.

Providence was kind; the children started arriving promptly, and at regular intervals. The first, a boy, was born on February 1, 1882. Two days later, while his mother was still confined to bed, he was carried to the church and baptized by Father Maurice Beaudry in the presence of his proud father and his grandparents. Mary Ann had agreed that his first name should be Louis, in honour of his grandfather in Sherbrooke, Louis-Etienne St. Laurent, and Stephen (by happy coincidence the English translation of Etienne) in honour of her father. In her absence, father and priest inscribed both names on the birth certificate in French; thus, the boy became officially Louis-Etienne St. Laurent. But, to his mother, he remained Louis Stephen, and so he became known to the world.

The St. Laurents had seven children in all, and, except for one who died in infancy, they thrived in the uncomplicated society of rural Quebec. Motor cars were still unknown there, and the tranquillity was disturbed only by the occasional building project, or the sound of horse-drawn vehicles moving along the unpaved streets. Each family had its own barnyard and garden, so that it was hard to tell where the countryside began and the village left off. Although both hotels held liquor licences, drunkenness was rare; and one of the first acts of the citizens when they received a municipal charter was to impose prohibition.

The St. Laurent store was equipped with a pot-bellied stove, around which were distributed several chairs, and within spitting distance of each chair was a spittoon. The store was a favourite meeting-place for the men, who lingered frequently while making their purchases, exchanging gossip and hearing the latest news. J.-B.-M. St. Laurent was a well-informed man whose regular reading included the *Montreal Star*, the *New York Catholic News*, and both the French and English newspapers from Sherbrooke and Coaticook; a willing talker, he drew both French- and English-speaking Canadians to listen to him, to do business with him or with one another, and to enjoy each other's company; his roof provided a meeting-place for the members of the two ethnic groups. About the time he went into business in Compton, a stream of French-speaking Canadians began to arrive from Beauce County, a hundred miles to the east. Dirty and weary after the long trek, they turned up at the church or at the St. Laurent store for help and advice. 'They told me to come and see you, that you are an honest man and can talk to the English,' one declared when he appeared at the counter. Priest and storekeeper worked hand in hand to assist them, suggesting lands that might be purchased, helping to negotiate a fair price, translating and mediating, and initiating the new arrivals into the unwritten rules of the bilingual society.

Young Louis did not understand the complexities of French-English relations during his early life. He knew that his mother spoke to him in one way, his father in another, but assumed that all parents did so; only when he started school did he discover that he had been speaking two distinct languages. At table, the children asked for objects at their mother's end of the table in English, at their father's end in French. In the house and garden they played together in English, but as soon as they stepped into the store they switched into French, according to their father's demand.

Louis's principal playmate was his sister Lora, a year and a half his junior. Louise, Maurice, Kathleen, and Nil were all so much younger that his attitude towards them was more that of the protective big brother than of an equal. Although he was basically a serious and sensitive child, he did occasionally get into mischief; on one occasion he filled Lora's long red hair with thistles in the guise of a crown, and once he almost suffocated her by burying her in the sand, Sunday clothes and all, until she was completely out of sight. For her part, she once tossed his cap over the wood-pile, and made him so indignant that he set out in the dead of winter through the snow for Coaticook, where their parents had gone on business, to report the incident. Fortunately, his grand-father Broderick saw him trudging past the farm, having covered almost half the distance, and drove him back home. One of the tragedies of Louis's young life occurred when their St. Bernard dog tried to snatch a fresh roast off a neighbour's windowsill, where it had been set to cool. The infuriated housewife seized a pan of boiling water and threw it over the animal, scalding it so severely that it had to be put to death. The boy was grief-stricken, and refused to become attached to another pet.

As he grew older, Louis found other playmates in the village, such as the two sons of the tailor, 'Père' Drolet, and Xénophile Lalumière, son of a local labourer. But, most of all, he liked to spend his time in the store, exploring the boxes and barrels and crates, with their strange contents and strong smells. When cus-tomers entered, he would withdraw and sit, half-hidden, on a box, listening to the grown-up conversation. He was filled with pride and respect as he watched his father dispense wares and advice with equal facility, help arrange financial deals, and play the role of peacemaker between the customers. Sometimes, he and the other children would play at storekeeping in the carriage-house, and he would imitate his father, distributing goods, counting the receipts, and settling the disputes that arose. In later years, he recalled fondly his father's role in assuring 'the peace of Compton'. 'I learned in that small community,' he once recalled, 'not by precept but merely by example, that it is possible for people of goodwill to live and let live without being called upon to sacrifice any of those essentials to which any group desires to hold firm.'

Life in the St. Laurent household was well ordered, comfort-able, and full of love. J.-B.-M. St. Laurent was a stern disciplina-rian, determined that his children should be at least as well behaved and well dressed as those of other parents. His wife applied to them the same strict code of life that she practised herself, but with more of a velvet glove. While Louis admired his father, he adored his mother, and he accepted unquestioningly her basic philosophy that the most important thing in life is to do one's duty thoroughly from day to day without dreaming of reward or more glorious occupations. Sundays were observed more strictly than in most Roman Catholic families, and for a particular reason: the St. Laurents lived next door to the Methodist church, or meeting-place, commonly called 'la mitaine' in French,* and the members of that congregation, adults and children, spent much of the Sabbath, dressed in their best clothes, in prayer. Mary Ann St. Laurent was determined to prove that her children were as well brought up as the little Methodists; instead of letting them play with their friends after mass, she kept them in their finery, and made them spend the day at home.

Louis did not begin school until he was eight years old, probably because, as he commented later, his mother thought she herself could do as good a job as the teacher, and also because she wanted him to have a solid grounding in her language. Thus he learned to read and write English before he did French, and acquired a basis in arithmetic that gave him an advantage over the other children. The Roman Catholic separate school was situated in a one-room wooden building next to the church, and run by a French-Canadian girl named Corinne Choquette, sister of the local priest. Under an unusual financial arrangement, the Board of Protestant School Commissioners collected all the school taxes and passed a portion of them along to Father Eugène Choquette for the education of the twenty-odd Roman Catholic children. Louis St. Laurent was a direct beneficiary of that close co-operation between the two religious groups.

From the outset, he was an outstanding pupil. Because of his shyness and his fear of being scolded, he prepared his lessons carefully; as a result, he was consistently at the head of the class. A mother's, and a teacher's, pet, he might well have incurred the jealous dislike of his class-mates if he had not been so modest and unassuming; despite his success in school, his careful dress, and his reserved manner, he seems to have been a popular boy. Only

---

*Meaning 'mitten', but in fact a corruption of the English word 'meeting'; apparently the strange word was written as it sounded.

one tough youngster described him in later years as 'the sort of kid you'd like to punch in the nose'. Father Choquette recognized his outstanding qualities and took a particular interest in him. Fascinated by the uses of electricity, the priest had a collection of electrical instruments in the rectory, some of which he had built himself, and he invited the young lad to join him in his experiments; they spent many hours together delving into the new field of knowledge. Louis was not particularly adept with his hands, but he was thorough and tenacious and would not rest until he understood the working of each piece of apparatus. One of his greatest thrills during that period of his life was to hear his mother's voice on a phonograph they had assembled. From the priest's collection, his interest spread to mechanical instruments, and he began tinkering with locks, clocks, and other devices. One elderly widow always had some new challenge for him when he called with food parcels from his mother, and her kitchen clock must have been the most frequently dismantled and reassembled in the village. On the other hand, he was notably clumsy with larger tools such as the axe, hammer, and saw.

Father Choquette exploited this young talent by collecting broken toys and enlisting Louis's help to repair them. Twice a year an auction sale was held at which the only currency accepted was paper money issued in class in lieu of prizes. The children vied keenly for the precious bits of paper during the year, and hoarded them for the day when their cherished objects would come under the hammer. Of course, Louis was always in the strongest position, but he used his financial strength carefully and with a strong sense of family solidarity. He observed the bidding carefully, and whenever one of his brothers or sisters had reached their financial limit he stepped in and secured the item for them.

Reading was from an early age the boy's principal interest, and he raced through the small family library indiscriminately, from the complete works of Dickens to the serialized stories of Robert Louis Stevenson in the *Family Herald* magazine. Most of his reading was in English because, except for the few text-books in school, French-language material was not available. To feed his appetite for the written word, he (and Lora) saved soap coupons, and sent away to the United States for the cheap, paper-back books that were given as premiums. When electricity was installed in their house, J.-B.-M. St. Laurent had a switch placed at the foot of the stairs so that he could make sure his eldest son did not read in bed. Normally obedient, Louis used to hide a candle in his room so that he could go on reading after the light was turned out.

His antipathy for piano practice led him to similar subterfuge. His aunt, Kathleen Broderick, who lived with them for a time, was assigned to teach him music, but when she left him alone in the parlour to practise, he propped a book in front of the music score and played with the keys while he read. The resulting noise was hardly convincing, and he was scolded frequently for his indifference; to make matters worse, he once forgot to remove the book at the end of the period. The trick was discovered after he had gone to bed; 'Aunt Kit' made him return downstairs and complete his practice under supervision. He resolved not to inflict such torture on his own children.

Sports and other forms of physical exercise held little attraction for him. He did go fishing with other boys near the covered bridge below the village, but was forbidden to go in the water because the growth of his uncle, Tom Broderick, had been stunted in his youth and it was suspected that he had caught some germ in the Coaticook River. The boys wandered across the fields to Moe's River, but the swimming-hole was small and shallow, and Louis never learned to swim as a boy. He played baseball occasionally in summer, tobogganed on the slope behind a neighbour's barn in winter, and played lawn croquet behind the store with his father, but did not demonstrate any particular enthusiasm for outdoor activities. Even less appealing to him were the chores assigned by his father. Before breakfast, he had to open the heavy shutters on the store windows, sweep the rough floor, clean the pewter spittoons and, because his hands were small, remove the soot from the narrow glass chimneys of the coal-oil lamps. Other tasks, such as caring for the horse and cow and pig, he usually managed to avoid.

Among the advantages of being raised in a bilingual home was that Christmas Day was celebrated in English style, with turkey, plum pudding, presents, and visits with the Brodericks, while

New Year's Day, a more significant occasion for French Canadians, was also treated as an important feast day and was often spent in Sherbrooke. Louis's grandfather St. Laurent died when the boy was only six years old, but his grandmother lived until he was eleven, and the whole family gathered occasionally at her home on Windsor Street, near the bridge over the St-Francis River. His uncle Dave worked in the nine-cent store at the upper end of town and had a key to the front door. One of the greatest thrills for the St. Laurent children was to be taken into the deserted building, to be allowed to wander between the counters, and to pick their own presents; Louis collected several revolvers on these annual expeditions. During the trips to Sherbrooke they also visited Aunt Phoebe Reilly, their mother's sister; she had several children of about the same age as themselves, and they had pleasant times together.

One of the most providential happenings for the storekeeper's son during his formative years in Compton was the appointment of a new teacher. Dorilla Têtu's prettiness belied her strong personality and her exceptional intelligence; a tiny person, she succeeded in striking fear into boys much larger than herself; at the same time, she took a particular interest in the diffident yet obviously clever young St. Laurent. At the age of fourteen, he would be eligible to attend a *collège classique*, the stepping-stone to a professional career or the priesthood. No French-Canadian boy from the village had ever taken that important step; she determined that he would be the first. For five years she was almost his private tutor. However, while she showered him with special attention, she also demanded special results and refused to allow him to coast through classes on his superior ability. When he had finished the usual exercises, she gave him more advanced ones, and by the time he graduated he was solving problems in algebra that were on the curriculum of the fifth-year *collège classique* course. She also introduced him to geometry, physics, and even astronomy, none of which was in the elementary school program. From her he learned to enjoy mathematics, and he spent many hours searching for solutions to difficult problems with the eagerness of a bridge or crossword-puzzle addict. Above all, she imparted to him intellectual curiosity and made him aware that there is always more to learn and to understand. The clever young woman's efforts were not in vain. In 1896, Louis passed the entrance exams to St. Charles Seminary in Sherbrooke almost effortlessly, and one of his teachers there was to remark that he was the best-prepared pupil in his class.

The years in Compton also provided an introduction to public life. Louis was eleven years old when the village received municipal status; Albert Pomroy, a local farmer, became the first mayor, and J.-B.-M. St. Laurent the first secretary-treasurer. The following year, the storekeeper became secretary-treasurer of the new school district as well. Louis was keenly interested in his father's new duties, and, with his ability in mathematics, was soon doing most of the bookkeeping, with only an occasional helping hand from his father. J.-B.-M. St. Laurent was becoming a person of some importance in the area, and his support was solicited for a variety of projects. In May 1891 he was the only French-speaking Canadian, and the only Liberal, in a delegation that travelled to Quebec City to persuade the Liberal provincial government to build an agricultural college in Compton. The mission did not succeed completely, but a model farm was established just north of the town two years later. Although Compton was recognized as a Tory stronghold, and had never sent a Liberal either to Ottawa or to Quebec, the village storekeeper remained faithful to the Liberal cause and looked forward to the day when the balance would change in favour of his party. In the federal elections of 1881, the English-speaking citizens did give a majority of their votes to the Liberal candidate, but the French Canadians clung to the old dictum, 'le ciel est bleu, l'enfer est rouge', and voted largely 'Bleu'.* However, Wilfrid Laurier's accession to the Liberal leadership in 1887, Prime Minister Sir John A. Macdonald's refusal to prevent the hanging of Louis Riel in 1885, and Laurier's eloquent rebuttals of the charge of anti-clericalism, were all hopeful signs. In his store, J.-B.-M. St.

*In Quebec, Conservatives and Liberals are identified in popular terms as 'Bleus' and 'Rouges' respectively; 'Bleus' were considered at that time closer to the Church, 'Rouges' more revolutionary.

Laurent did what he could to promote Liberal fortunes. The lively debates around the stove provided Louis St. Laurent with his first contact with politics.

J.-B.-M. St. Laurent did not restrict his political activities to trying to convert his customers; in 1894, he contested the Liberal nomination for a provincial by-election in Compton constituency. It was the first time that a French-speaking Canadian's name had been put forward there, constituting a direct challenge to an understanding that English Canadians should represent the area with French-Canadian support. The move annoyed some of the local Liberals, who accused him of encouraging rivalry between the two ethnic groups, and they succeeded in having him defeated. The move had been premature, but the storekeeper's zeal for the Liberal cause was not diminished by the setback; when Laurier visited Sherbrooke in the summer of 1896, during the election campaign, St. Laurent took his eldest children to hear the Liberal leader. His attitude was in strong contrast to that of the local bishop, Monseigneur Racine, who refused to receive the Liberal leader personally. Louis was impressed by Laurier's speech, but even more impressed when the great man stopped after the meeting to shake hands with them, and to call his father by name. Later in the campaign, they also heard Prime Minister Sir Charles Tupper and one of his principal lieutenants, Thomas Chapais, but the fourteen-year-old boy was not swayed by their oratory, and he was confirmed in his father's political faith. On election night he joined the crowd of men who had gathered in the store to hear the election news relayed to them over the wall telephone from Sherbrooke. It was an excited youngster who went to bed in the early morning, realizing that his father's cause had triumphed, and that he, himself, had shaken the hand of the new prime minister of Canada.

When Louis St. Laurent set off for Sherbrooke at the beginning of September 1894 in his father's buggy, it was generally assumed that he was taking the first step towards the priesthood. About a third of Quebec's college students entered the church after the six-year course, and both his mother and Father Choquette hoped that he would do the same. With that goal in mind, the parish priest persuaded the church authorities to waive the tuition fees, and even loaned him part of the hundred-dollar fee for a year's board and lodging.

St. Charles Seminary was situated on a promontory of land above the town. It was a bilingual institution and offered, in addition to the six-year classical program, a three-year commercial course designed primarily for the more business-minded English-speaking members of the community. Most of the 180 students were residents, who lived in the dormitories on the upper floors of the red-brick, four-storey building; a few boys with parents or close relatives in Sherbrooke had permission to live at home. Since the college had its own laundry, infirmary, book-store, and chapel, it was considered unnecessary for the boys to leave the premises during the school year except for the New Year's holiday or for occasional visits to relatives in town. As winter exams were held immediately after Christmas Day, and only those who had passed in every subject were allowed the mid-term holiday, that was one of the busiest periods of all.

Under a system described officially as 'paternal', discipline was severe and protocol strict. Tardiness was considered a serious offence, and the hour for returning to the college after a holiday was absolutely rigid. Smoking and drinking were, of course, forbidden, and some of the older students were sent home during Louis St. Laurent's years there for having, in the classical language of the school, practised the cult of Bacchus. Less severe forms of punishment included strapping, learning Latin verses by heart, and copying Latin texts while other students enjoyed a few precious hours 'outside'. It was a Spartan régime, with the emphasis on hard work, cleanliness, regular habits, and economy. Parents were advised to send spending money to the college authorities for distribution as the latter saw fit, and to follow the precept, 'the more moderate the supply, the better in general'. Stress was placed on proper dress and behaviour; ties were mandatory in classrooms and each student was required to have not only proper choir dress but also a special school uniform for Sunday wear, the latter composed of black trousers, a peaked black cap, and a knee-length, bell-bottomed frock coat. The young men were expected to conduct themselves as gentlemen, and to address one another as *monsieur*, and in the formal *vous* rather than the comradely *tu* normally employed by youngsters of their age.

The day began shortly after 5 a.m. with the ringing of the bells in the tower above the dormitories; at that signal the students sprang out of bed and got down on their knees for the first prayer of the day, washed, dressed, and made their way to the classrooms for an hour of study before breakfast. Mass was celebrated at 7:30, followed by breakfast at 8, and then the day's work began in earnest. During the daylight hours, classes alternated with recreation periods, but every minute was accounted for until vespers had been said at 7 p.m., following which, except for very special occasions, the boys were sent back to their dormitories.

In appearance, at least, the fourteen-year-old lad from Compton differed little from his new class-mates. He was of average size, well groomed, and had a heavy shock of wavy dark hair that he took pains to keep in place. Perhaps it was his obvious shyness and his consistently orderly appearance that distinguished him most from the others. Seeing him standing apart and ill at ease the day of his arrival, a second-year boy, Léon Marcotte, approached him and asked him his name. 'Louis St. Laurent,' he replied in a deep voice that betrayed his embarrassment. In a spontaneous gesture, the older boy asked him if he would be his friend; Louis accepted gratefully, and they shook hands. The incident had a prominent place in his first letter home. It was easier to establish relations with the English-speaking students than with the French-speaking group because his cousin, Clifford Reilly, was taking the commercial course, and introduced him to other members of the class. Most of them were Irish Canadians like Louis's mother, and he was soon identified as one of them. He discovered that the father of one boy, John Hackett from Stanstead, knew his own parents, and, in fact, had given his mother her teacher's certificate many years earlier; John and Louis also became close friends.

The professors, a mixture of French- and Irish-Canadian priests, were a stimulating lot, and Louis was soon attracted to several of them. Tall, bespectacled Abbé A. Maltais was not nearly as severe as he looked, and proved to be a passionate admirer of La Fontaine, most of whose fables he could recite by heart. Sharing the teaching of philosophy with Maltais was large, jovial Father Simard, who delighted in provoking a lively discussion in class. The science and mathematics professor was Abbé B. A. Bégin, a rather distraught man who had some difficulty in maintaining discipline and was referred to somewhat irreverently out of earshot of the authorities as 'Whiskers'.

The first year passed quickly. Grateful for the opportunity to continue his education, and anxious to prove his worth, Louis applied himself diligently in every class. Still so shy that he burst into tears whenever he was spoken to sharply in class, he strove for perfection, not to attract praise, but to avoid being scolded. When given a choice, he wrote and spoke in English, but his marks in French grammar and composition were also excellent. At the end of the first year he was awarded a record twelve prizes, plus an honourable mention in singing, one of the few subjects in which he was considered by his family to be almost a dunce! Success came perhaps too soon. With a new self-confidence, he found another challenge to test his mettle. Father Maltais was an ardent chess player, and his enthusiasm was contagious; in the winter of 1897-8 a chess craze swept the college; home-made boards appeared as if by magic, and the contests took on epic proportions. As soon as the recreation bell sounded, the priest would appear in the recreation hall, looking for a suitable challenger. Louis distinguished himself in this field as well, and he was chosen frequently to defend the honour of the students. As with everything else, he prepared himself carefully, studying the game and planning every move like a general on a field of battle. He became so proficient that he entered a contest in a Montreal newspaper, and some of his solutions were published. As a result of these new activities, however, his exercises appeared less frequently in the *cahiers d'honneur*, and he received only passing mention at the year-end ceremonies. When he returned home, his father told him sternly that he had to choose at once between a career as a chess player and some other occupation. He promised to do better in the future.

Although he grew rapidly into a tall, well-built young man, Louis St. Laurent seldom took part in the games played in the courtyard during the recreation period. For exercise, he walked vigorously around the perimeter in a somewhat awkward gait, his long feet pointing outwards and his weight too far back towards his heels. He enlisted as one of the first members of the school cadet corps that was formed a year after his arrival, and took the rudimentary military training as seriously as he did everything else. Dressed in their school uniforms, and bearing a motley collection of rifles, bayonets, and swords donated by the regular militia, the boys were soon leading parades through town, presenting arms for visiting dignitaries, and taking part in the funeral procession whenever one of their fellow students died. One of their most memorable performances was a march to the railway station in 1901 to be reviewed by the Duke of Cornwall and York, later to become King George V. St. Laurent was lieutenant of the troop at that time and second in command; he finished his brief military career as captain and commander of the unit. The experience helped him to overcome his shyness, and on one occasion he even climbed on a table to make a speech of commendation to his men after a successful parade.

In keeping with the tradition in *collèges classiques* in that period, he took an active part in literary programs. At sixteen he became the first secretary of the Académie St-Barthélémi, a literary association founded by the *belles-lettres* students; and in 1900, he became vice-president of the Académie St-Pierre, the most important student organization. Following the example of the Académie Française, the Académie St-Pierre had ten chairs bearing the names of illustrious literary figures; Louis St. Laurent's chair bore that of the great French-Canadian historian, François-Xavier Garneau. He made his contribution to the literary life of the college in both French and English, and even in Latin. On St. Patrick's Day, he spoke English with the best Irish brogue he could muster, on one occasion making a stirring address in memory of the Irish patriot Daniel O'Connell. If his delivery was hardly reminiscent of that of the great orator, the words at least were well chosen. He recommended the career of 'the uncrowned king of Ireland' as a 'glorious example of manliness, of integrity, and of virtue', sang the praise of both 'the sacred cause of religion' and 'the sacred cause of nationality', and denounced the treatment accorded by the British to his mother's people. His speeches and essays in French covered a wide range of subjects, including history, poetry, and philosophy. Occasionally he took part in dramatic productions, even playing female roles, since girls were not allowed on the premises. He also took an active interest in the model court, which operated under the supervision of Father Simard; during his senior years he played nearly all the key roles, including that of judge, crown prosecutor, and defence attorney.

Louis St. Laurent's various speeches and essays, his reports as recording secretary of the two literary associations, and his contributions to the college *Chronicle*, reveal much about his personality during that period. In French or English, his style was simple and straightforward, with few of the embellishments that marked the writings of most of the other students and that were so characteristic of late nineteenth-century writing. He was generous in his assessment of others' efforts, but he had a dry, sometimes biting wit and a tendency to damn with faint praise. 'Monsieur Chaput did not attain perfection, it is true,' he remarked once, 'but he gave proof once again of his good intentions.' 'Then the President came and offered us a mess of pottage, but it was too much,' he teased his friend Biron; 'we had already had our fill, and we preferred to digest the prayer that ended the meeting.' Sometimes he turned his caustic pen on himself. 'St. Laurent chronicler?' he sighed as he began his turn at keeping the college diary. 'Fate and the President have conspired against me. But to do them justice I must say that they had no choice, it was me or nobody. And, well, as the saying goes, when one can't have what one loves, one loves what one has.' Of a practical bent, it was not easy for him to find subjects he considered worth recording in the well-ordered college life. 'At recreation period this evening the students were so dull that you would think they were getting ready to go to confession,' he complained after a New Year's holiday. His 'Chat with the *Chronicle*' on Thanksgiving Day, 1900, written in English, revealed a nice combination of piety and wit. 'What do we have to be thankful for?' he asked, and then replied to his own question by referring to their religion, their Canadian nationality, and the education they were receiving. But, he went on, they should be thankful for other things for which they sometimes failed to return thanks.

> We should thank our lucky stars that we are not allowed newspapers for if we were we would know all about what is going on at the present time and our memory would be so filled with the doings of the day that we would not be able to remember the remarkable events of prior centuries; now, no one with a drop of common sense would consent to make such an exchange. We all know that the doings of our contemporaries have not the least importance whatsoever, and will not have until they are a few hundred years old and our great-grand-children have to learn them out of a revised history. We should be thankful that we are closeted up out of harm's way where we are not tempted to meddle in politics, steal apples or kisses or commit any of those petty crimes of youth. We should be thankful that we have someone to wake us up at 20 minutes after 5 in the morning . . . because if we didn't, we might not wake up ourselves.

As he grew older, St. Laurent felt the confinement of residential life more severely. He was a recognized member of a group of Liberals that gravitated around Abbé Maltais, an ardent Liberal who boasted a personal acquaintance with Wilfrid Laurier, and the two of them discussed political questions frequently. Far from being a Quebec nationalist, he defended Laurier's concept of a united Canada. On one of the most sensitive political topics, the Boer War, St. Laurent defended Laurier's policy of allowing volunteers to join the British units in South Africa, and argued that the British policy of suppressing the uprising was justified. He also supported the United States in driving the Spanish out of Cuba, in 1898, on the grounds that the Americas belonged to the Americans, not to the Europeans.

When Laurier visited Sherbrooke in January 1900, as prime minister, he had no difficulty being received by the bishop; he was even able to call at the seminary and to speak briefly to the students. Several non-resident students were able to attend his meeting in the evening, and they brought back newspaper reports of his address. 'For my part,' he declared as the new century began, 'I have devoted my political career to a single concept. . . .

Whether I succeed or fail, when I will have been laid in my tomb I will have won the right to have inscribed on my monument the words: "Here rests a man who sought to make of the French-Canadian and English-Canadian families a single family, united and living in harmony under a single flag." ' Laurier went on to comment on the difficulties of serving that cause. 'In Ontario and the other English Provinces they say, Laurier hasn't done this or that. He is a Frenchman. In Quebec they say: Laurier does too much, he is *un Anglais*, an Englishman. Because I do my duty, placing myself above considerations of race, party and faith, I am exposed to attack on the basis of every prejudice from either side.' He concluded with a stirring appeal for a 'truly national, truly British, truly Canadian policy'. They were words that Louis St. Laurent was to endorse without hesitation, and even to echo in the future. When the Liberal leader returned to Sherbrooke during the election campaign in October 1900, excitement ran so high in the seminary that blows were exchanged between 'Bleus' and 'Rouges' in the recreation hall. On polling day, November 7, St. Laurent arranged with a day-pupil to write the results on bits of paper as they arrived, and to place them in a pail that he lowered on a rope from the dormitory window. There were cries of jubilation in the darkened dormitory from the 'Liberal committee' as another victory for Laurier became evident.

During his last three years of college, Louis St. Laurent matured rapidly and found a reasonable balance between his studies and his other activities. His professors were increasingly impressed by his ability. Father Bégin allowed him to remain in the science laboratory after class to carry out more advanced experiments; he also encouraged his interest in mathematics by setting particularly difficult problems for him to solve. After he had submitted an essay on Molière's play *Le Misanthrope*, Father Maltais sent him out of the classroom on the pretext of an errand, and told the other boys that no better composition had ever been written at the college. He went on to predict to the hushed group that if St. Laurent entered the church, he would certainly become a bishop, and if he entered politics, he would become prime minister. The bright young man's relationship with Father Simard was an especially happy one. The heavy-set, jovial priest delighted in stimulating a discussion in philosophy class, and he succeeded so well with St. Laurent that the latter was soon disrupting lessons with his penetrating observations. Thinking to curb his zeal, Simard ruled that he must put all his remarks in Latin; the handicap proved to be merely an additional challenge, and St. Laurent spent many hours preparing his arguments for each class. Out of the contest of wills grew a lasting friendship. His academic excellence and his lack of interest in sports notwithstanding, Louis St. Laurent seems to have been popular also with his fellow students. He was so modest and considerate that it was almost impossible to take offence when he was praised repeatedly by the professors and given prize after prize.

While St. Laurent's personality did not change during the six years of college life, his plans for the future were altered; he decided to become a lawyer and not a priest. The scanty introduction to the field of jurisprudence through the model court struck a responsive chord. Many of the young men who opted for the law had in view a career in politics, but for Louis it held rather an opportunity for further study. A B.A. degree, he felt, was simply an indication that one was capable of continuing to learn, and the law was the field of learning that attracted him most. Politics he rejected because, he stated later, 'those who got into politics appeared to be putting themselves forward'. Abbé Simard encouraged him in his new ambition, and made a special trip to Compton to persuade his parents to accept the change in plans, even if it meant that there would be only five future priests in the twelve-man graduating class instead of six. Louis's mother was disappointed, but she accepted the plan and postponed her dream of offering a son to the church.

As his family looked on with pride, Louis St. Laurent received his degree in the main hall of the seminary on June 20, 1902. Bishop Laroque, the official head of the college, presented him, in addition to the parchment, with a series of prizes, including his personal award for the best scholar. At twenty years of age, Louis had justified the confidence placed in him, and he was to be given the opportunity to become the first professional man in the family since Nicolas Huot arrived in Canada two and a half centuries earlier.

Freed from the restrictions of seminary life, Louis St. Laurent spent a pleasant summer, exchanging visits with John Hackett, playing host to Léon Marcotte, who had opted for the priesthood, and helping his father with his various sets of accounts. While he had obtained his college degree and his parents' consent to continue his studies, he still faced the problem of financing a three-year law course. It was his sister Lora who provided the solution. After the Liberals assumed office in Ottawa, J.-B.-M. St. Laurent had become the village postmaster, and had placed his daughter in charge of the small post office. A devoted admirer of her brother, Lora offered him part of her salary to help him carry out his ambitious plan. The choice of universities was also dictated in part by financial considerations. His academic record made him eligible to have his fees waived at Laval University, but no such arrangement existed with McGill University in Montreal. In addition, the law students in Montreal had a reputation for being more interested in fun than in study; J.-B.-M. St. Laurent felt that his son would be safer in Quebec City. The deciding factor was an offer by John Hackett's father, who had been a minister in a previous Conservative government of the province before becoming a judge, to introduce him to what he declared to be the best law firm in the old capital, that of Drouin, Pelletier, and Baillargeon. It was a solidly Conservative firm, L.-P. Pelletier having served as attorney general in the Conservative provincial government of E. J. Flynn. The opportunity to article in such a well-established office was accepted with gratitude despite the difference in political colour.

In the autumn of 1902, Louis St. Laurent took a room above a tobacconist's shop on Quebec City's Côte de la Montagne, a ten-minute walk from the university, and arranged to take his meals in a home near by. University life reflected the class-consciousness that prevailed in local society. The business and professional life of the city, including the legal fraternity, the university, and even, to a large extent, the church, was dominated by an élite made up of the oldest families of the two ethnic groups, who got on well together despite differences of language and religion. The teaching staff of the Faculty of Law was made up almost entirely of practising lawyers or judges who lectured as a public service and because of the prestige associated with a university appointment. Thus young St. Laurent learned civil law from Superior Court Justice Charles Langelier, political economy from Lieutenant-Governor Louis Jetté, constitutional law from the distinguished notary, L. P. Sirois, and Roman law from the Leader of the Opposition, E. J. Flynn.

The student body of the faculty fell naturally into two groups – the members of the *bonnes familles* from the city, and the others. After class, each group went its own way, the local gentry climbing up to their comfortable homes, the outsiders returning to their modest furnished rooms; only rarely were the latter invited to a home for a meal. Louis St. Laurent did not resent this class distinction and had little desire to penetrate the more select social milieu. He felt that many Quebec City students were narrow in their outlook, particularly in religious matters, compared with the residents of the Eastern Townships. Because of this situation, Louis St. Laurent found his friends among his fellow 'outsiders', including Albert Sévigny, Jules-Arthur Gagné, and Thomas Vien.

As in Sherbrooke, Louis St. Laurent's life soon fell into a regular pattern, largely circumscribed by the triangle between his lodgings, the university, and the law office. He was never seen in female company, and his relaxation consisted mainly of reading English literature or walking on the Plains of Abraham. It was obvious from the outset that he had made a wise choice in opting for a legal career. With his usual thoroughness, he grasped the deeper significance of each subject. While many students considered the Civil Code a series of rules to be learned by heart, he saw in it rather a series of solutions to specific problems of human relations, all of them based on a set of general principles about what constituted proper behaviour in an organized society. They were the same principles, he discovered, that had been gradually clarified and defined since the beginning of the Roman Empire. He was intrigued by the parallel development of Common Law in England, and spent many hours reading the works of Blackstone, the greatest authority on the subject. As a result, he acquired a thorough grounding in both systems. He also took a keen interest in constitutional law, and was careful not to miss a lecture on that subject.

The Faculty of Law was a hot-bed of politics, and, in fact, a training-ground for Quebec politicians. St. Laurent made it clear that, although he was articled to a Conservative firm, he was a Liberal. To prove his political allegiance, he joined the campus Liberal Club, and even served as a minister in the Liberal government of the law students' mock parliament. He was sufficiently interested in the debates in the Legislature to obtain a press card from a Sherbrooke newspaper, in order to have a good seat from which to observe the proceedings, but he wrote no articles on what he saw and heard. On one occasion he took an Englishman, to whom he was giving conversational French lessons, to hear Henri Bourassa explain his disagreement with Laurier. They admired the oratorical talent of the French-Canadian nationalist, but did not share his views.

It was Louis St. Laurent's own father who precipitated him into active politics. The Liberals of Compton County were increasingly confident of ending the Conservative monopoly there, and the French-speaking element of the population was anxious to have a representative in Ottawa and Quebec. A pact was made among the Liberals to run a storekeeper named A. B. Hunt from the eastern end of the county as the federal Liberal candidate, and to have J.-B.-M. St. Laurent run in the provincial campaign that was expected to take place at about the same time. By helping one another, it was reasoned, the two men stood a good chance of election. J.-B.-M. St. Laurent was hardly an enthusiastic candidate, as he did not relish the prospect of spending part of each year in Quebec City; on the other hand, he had long argued the necessity of breaking the Conservative hold on the constituency and could not refuse to do his part. The two candidates were chosen without opposition at a Liberal convention in the town of Bury on September 30, 1904, the *Sherbrooke Daily Record* correspondent declaring that there was not a more popular man in all the county than the Compton merchant.

The federal campaign was scheduled to begin first, and six days after the Bury meeting Prime Minister Laurier arrived in

Quebec City and received the members of the University Liberal Club in his suite in the Château Frontenac Hotel. Scanning the youthful faces, he declared: 'As I look at you, I am trying to pick out the one who will be my successor.' It seems most unlikely that anyone thought of the studious, self-effacing young man from Compton for that role, least of all St. Laurent himself. Shortly afterwards, the Minister of Justice, Sir Charles Fitzpatrick, spent an evening with the students in order to fire their enthusiasm and enlist their support. Louis St. Laurent found his partisan appeal, and his lesson on political tactics, of doubtful propriety for the holder of the justice portfolio, but he agreed to help with the campaign. He and another student were assigned to make a series of speeches one Sunday in Champlain County, between Quebec City and Trois-Rivières. On the appointed day in late October, he was waiting on the steps of St-Narcisse Church when mass was concluded, and as the crowd emerged he made his plea to give the Laurier administration a third mandate. When he had finished, he rushed over to neighbouring St-Prosper parish and repeated the performance. The two young men spent the entire day campaigning, ending up at the home of the candidate to report on their activities.

Meanwhile, J.-B.-M. St. Laurent was campaigning hard throughout Compton County on behalf of his federal running-mate. The joint effort was successful; thanks to the Scottish vote in the eastern end of the constituency, Hunt emerged victorious with a majority of 250. Louis spent election day as polling officer in Compton Station. On the national level, Sir Wilfrid won another majority, taking fifty-four of the sixty-five seats in Quebec.

Three days after the federal victory, Liberal Premier S. N. Parent dissolved the Legislature with the obvious intention of exploiting Laurier's victory and riding to office for another term on the Prime Minister's political coat-tails. The manoeuvre seemed hardly necessary, the Liberals having already sixty-four seats compared with their opponents' ten. Caught off guard, Opposition Leader Flynn and his Conservative organizer, Louis-Philippe Pelletier, to whom Louis St. Laurent was indentured, denounced the move as rank political opportunism and refused to participate in the campaign! It was the turn of the Liberals to be embarrassed. A province-wide acclamation on election day would mean an assembly without an opposition, and they would be accused of making a mockery of parliamentary government. Fortunately for them, Conservative Party discipline was not perfect, and a few candidates refused to accept the decision of their leaders; one of them was A. W. Giard, the sitting member for Compton. Grasping at the oportunity to extricate themselves from the ludicrous situation, the Liberal bosses decided not to contest the seats where the rebels were running.

Now it was the Liberal ranks that split. In Compton County, J.-B.-M. St. Laurent and his political friends had spent weeks campaigning for Hunt on the understanding that every effort would be made to send a French-speaking Liberal to the Legislature; they did not intend to become mere pawns in a power play and have victory snatched from their hands by their own leaders. At his father's request, Louis called on the provincial treasurer, who was responsible for party matters in the Eastern Townships, and on Senator Raoul Dandurand, the federal organizer, to protest the decision – but in vain. He was told that neither money nor other forms of support would be forthcoming if they went ahead with the contest. They ignored the warning. With limited resources, everyone's contribution was welcome; Louis was allowed to return home to lend a hand. He and his cousins, John Reilly from Sherbrooke and Armand Thibault from Montreal, toured the constituency with a horse and buggy, holding meetings wherever possible and calling on the voters to support the Liberal Party. More fluent in English than the candidate, they concentrated their attention on the eastern side of the constituency, where someone labelled the law student 'Daddy's phonograph'. According to the practice of the time, the two candidates appeared at a nomination meeting on November 18 in Cookshire, and presented their arguments for election. Since no cabinet minister would come into the area, the Liberals had persuaded a former Conservative organizer from neighbouring Brome County to address the crowd. His presence provoked the Tories, and they heckled him so much that his message was all but inaudible. In addition, he became involved in a scuffle on the platform with one of the joint chairmen over the speakers' list. 'Unparliamentary language followed,' reported one journalist, 'and some tight squeezes, a few rushes and one or two touch-downs.' St. Laurent and Giard received a good hearing, however.

The Liberal campaign ended in Compton the day before the election, and on November 25 the voters gave their verdict. The Liberals received a majority of ballots in the area around the village, but too few in the French-Canadian settlement around La Patrie, where Giard lived. In the federal campaign, they had spent considerable money to bring lumberjacks out of the woods to vote on election day; in the second contest, no funds had been available for such purposes. The St. Laurents and their friends went down to defeat by a margin of 148 votes. J.-B.-M. St. Laurent advised his son never to become involved in politics again, and the younger man agreed heartily; it was far too dirty a game for his taste. On December 4, 1904, the *Sherbrooke Daily Record* carried the laconic note: 'Mr. Louis St. Laurent has returned to Laval University, Quebec.'

The brief excursion into politics was a relatively minor incident in the law student's well-ordered existence; it did not affect his determination to master the law, or his good relations with strong Conservatives such as Pelletier, and his friend and class-mate Albert Sévigny. He went quietly about his daily tasks, ignoring the card parties, dances, and concerts that were a large part of Quebec's social life. The assignments he did for his professors were of uniformly high standard, not only because assiduity and thoroughness were part of his nature, but also because he appreciated the opportunity to attend university. Although the St. Laurents were a relatively undemonstrative family, they were deeply attached to one another, and Louis's career was important to each one of them. While at Laval University, he developed the practice of writing to his mother on his birthday to express his gratitude for all she had done for him. The birthday letter became part of the family tradition; until the end of her days, the devout little Irish-Canadian woman waited eagerly for the postman to call on February 1 with her son's letter, and could not bring herself to begin her housework until she had read it. His visits to Compton were happy occasions. He took an interest in the activities of every brother and sister, and they were flattered by his attention. Parting was always a sad experience. At the end of one visit, when they were all at table, Nil, a warm-hearted, spontaneous lad whose admiration for his brother, ten years his senior, was almost unbounded, blurted out suddenly: 'This is Louis's last dinner.' They finished the meal in a pall of sadness and suppressed emotion.

Some twenty-five students sat for the final law exams at Laval University in the spring of 1905. On June 17, the list of all successful candidates appeared; it began: 'Louis St. Laurent de Compton, LL.L. (avec grande distinction)'. It was the highest rating that could be obtained. The university rector, Monseigneur Olivier Mathieu, was heard to remark that 'the young St. Laurent will go far.' Two days later the degrees were presented by the Governor General, Lord Grey. It was one of the most important social occasions of the year, and the upper echelon of Quebec society was well represented. J.-B.-M. St. Laurent and Lora were also present, but not Louis's mother. Although she was pleased and gratified at her son's achievement, she seldom left her home any more, and feared she would be out of place in the French-speaking milieu.

As the names were read in Latin, the graduates advanced to the Governor General's chair to receive their parchments and a word of congratulation. For Louis St. Laurent there was a triple presentation: he was also handed the Governor General's personal medal for the best student in the class, and the Prix Tessier, a twenty-dollar gold piece. The important occasion did not pass without a minor incident. As he passed Lady Grey's chair, the large sleeve of his gown caught in the arm of her chair, and pulled him up short. There was a sudden silence, and then a titter ran through the crowd as he struggled to disengage himself. The embarrassing incident lasted only a few seconds, but long enough to cause him to leave the platform red-faced and confused. In the audience, an eighteen-year-old girl from Beauceville named Jeanne Renault felt a surge of compassion for the intelligent but awkward young man. She was to recall it later.

The news of Louis St. Laurent's accomplishment reached Compton in a matter of hours. The *Sherbrooke Daily Record* carried a special dispatch entitled, 'Compton Boy wins high honours at Laval'. A French-language daily in Montreal proclaimed him 'perhaps the most brilliant scholar that Laval University has had for some time'. When he arrived home, he was received as a returning hero. A collection was taken up, and a roll-top office desk was presented to him at an all-male banquet in the church hall. Still shy and withdrawn despite his successes, but genuinely moved, he managed to stammer out a few appropriate sentences in reply. J.-B.-M. St. Laurent, by then a white-whiskered, somewhat portly sixty-five-year-old, made no attempt to conceal his pride.

# 3

## Up the Ladder

When he decided to study law, Louis St. Laurent intended to return to the Eastern Townships and open an office in Sherbrooke. He loved the rolling countryside, dotted with white-painted wooden houses, and he felt at home in the tolerant, bilingual atmosphere. With his father growing old, he wanted to be near his family and to accept his responsibilities as the oldest son. In 1905, these reasons still seemed valid to him. Lora was doing her share in the post office, but Maurice was taking the commercial course at St. Charles Seminary, Louise was a novice in a convent at St-Pie-de-Bagot, and Kathleen was about to graduate from the new academy for girls in Compton. Even thirteen-year-old Nil was expected to leave for St. Charles Seminary in a year. There was one obstacle to his plan: another young law graduate, Jacob Nicol, had opened a law office in Sherbrooke not long before. Since he had served as secretary to the provincial treasurer, Nicol had excellent political connections in both Quebec and Ottawa and had a corner on legal patronage in the area, a type of work almost indispensable to a small-town lawyer until a regular clientele was established. At any rate, there was hardly enough work in Sherbrooke for two ambitious men of the same generation.

St. Laurent discussed his problem with Louis-Philippe Pelletier, but the latter was spending little time in politics since the 1904 election, and did not need another junior associate. However, he had come to like the young man and to respect his ability; he offered him a desk and chair beside the secretarial staff, and fifty dollars a month for his services, until a better opportunity could be found. St. Laurent was disappointed at finding no better market for his training, and returned rather unhappily to discuss the situation with his father; J.-B.-M. St. Laurent told him firmly to take the job. It was not so important how much he earned or what title he had at the outset, the aging storekeeper pointed out, but rather how much he would learn in the first few years of practice; working under one of the best lawyers in the province could not be a waste of time. Louis St. Laurent accepted the offer, and returned to Quebec City for the next stage of his education.

The two men soon developed a pleasant and fruitful working relationship. Pelletier had a wide knowledge of jurisprudence, and a sharp instinct for finding solutions to tough problems, but he cared little for research; St. Laurent enjoyed delving into legal tomes for precedents and rules to prove a point of law. They discussed each new case thoroughly, then the older man decided on their general approach, and left his young assistant to find the arguments to prove their point of view. The comments of his Liberal opponent notwithstanding, Pelletier proved to be an upright and kindly man. On one occasion they spent many hours on a case in which a tinsmith was suing for fifty or sixty dollars. After having visited the shop several times, St. Laurent asked impatiently if it would not be better to settle out of court since so little money was involved. The distinguished lawyer rejected the suggestion. 'Oh no,' he replied. 'This matter is very important to our client. We must always do our best, no matter whether the cost is big or little.'

The bond of trust between the two men grew, and after about a year Pelletier decided that it was time for St. Laurent to try his own wings. An appearance was scheduled in an arbitration case concerning a bridge over the St. Lawrence River near Quebec City, and they were being opposed by Alexandre Taschereau and G. G. Stuart, both outstanding lawyers. St. Laurent prepared the case with his usual care, and looked forward to observing the legal contest. The evening before it was to be called, Pelletier telephoned to say that he had to go out of town, and that the younger man would have to take the case alone. Apprehensive at the prospect of facing such skilled opponents by himself, St. Laurent protested vigorously, but Pelletier assured him that only an incidental procedure was involved, and not a final judgement. With strong misgivings, St. Laurent appeared as required the next day, and was struggling valiantly to present his side of the case, when he noticed his superior standing at the back of the room, calmly watching the proceedings. As soon as the ordeal was over, he went over and asked with some indignation, 'Why did you do that?' Pelletier laughed. 'Well, you know, you won't learn to swim unless someone throws you in.'

It was 1907 before Louis St. Laurent pleaded a case himself. It involved a claim by one of his closest friends, Marius Barbeau from Beauce County, who felt that he had been deprived of a legacy from his grandmother by a priest who made her sign a new will on her death bed. The new will substituted the priest's name for Barbeau's as sole heir, and, if probated, would have wiped out a ten-thousand-dollar inheritance. Marius Barbeau was also a graduate in law, but he was something of a rebel against the staid Quebec society, and inclined to question its norms; the incident made him indignant, and he determined to have the final will disallowed. St. Laurent was hesitant to become involved in such a delicate matter, but he responded to the call of friendship and consulted Pelletier. Together, the three of them found a promising precedent and decided to proceed. At the preliminary questioning, St. Laurent interrogated the priest, and drew out enough information to persuade Pelletier to go further. The case was scheduled to be heard in the autumn of 1907 before Mr. Justice François Langelier. Shortly before the day arrived, they learned that three nuns had called on the judge and complained that it was 'odious' to be attacking a village curé in that manner. Aroused at the attempted interference with the course of justice, Pelletier took over the cross-questioning and subjected the priest, as well as the nuns, to a severe tongue-lashing. When he lost the case, he became still more furious and insisted on appealing the decision. During the request to appeal, a sharp exchange took place between Pelletier and the vicar of the parish where the old woman had lived, during which the lawyer was called a liar, and he, in turn, demanded that the vicar be made to leave the court-house. As it turned out, Pelletier was handling a case before the Privy Council in London when the appeal was heard, and St. Laurent had to deal with it largely on his own. In a two-day performance, he was able to prove to the satisfaction of Chief Justice Taschereau that undue pressure had been exerted in obtaining a new will, and that the woman had been too feeble mentally to understand what she was being asked to sign. The appeal was successful.

Marius Barbeau was already a student at Oxford University when he received the good news. Louis St. Laurent had played a part in making that possible as well; he had been offered the first Rhodes Scholarship to be granted to a Laval University student, but had refused because he was anxious to get on with his legal career. Since Barbeau was more preoccupied with the larger subject of the origin of man than with fine points of law, St. Laurent suggested that he apply for the scholarship, which would give him an opportunity to spend two or three years seeking answers to the questions that concerned him. The proposal appealed to Barbeau, and he received the award. Together, the award and the legacy gave him the opportunity to begin a new career, and, in fact, started him on the path to becoming one of the leading anthropologists in Canada.

For Pelletier, the case had less pleasant consequences. In order to take it to the Court of Appeal, the proceedings in the Superior Court had to be published, including the bitter exchange between himself and the vicar. The document became available just as Pelletier decided to re-enter active politics, and the Liberals used it to portray him as anti-clerical. He was defeated first as a provincial candidate in Lotbinière constituency, and then as a federal candidate in Dorchester constituency; once again he vowed to give up politics for good. Louis St. Laurent did not escape criticism completely. Although he attended church regularly, and his personal conduct was of a high standard, rumours continued for many years that he was not a good Roman Catholic. (A quarter of a century later he was crossing a beach in Old Orchard, Maine, when someone cried out in French, 'What a pity that such a brilliant man, with such a fine physique, should have no faith!' St. Laurent continued on his way, removed his dressing-gown, crossed himself, and entered the water.)

Louis St. Laurent had proved a valuable friend to Marius Barbeau and soon had cause to be grateful to him. A skilled musician, and a popular guest at the card parties, musical *soirées*, and picnics where the young people of Quebec met, Barbeau urged him to modify his rather one-sided existence, and join the social circuit. During the 1906 Carnaval season, Barbeau took him along to a party, and St. Laurent found himself playing cards opposite a young lady who he soon decided was the most attractive he had ever met. Her name was Jeanne Renault, and she recognized him as the brilliant student who had caught his sleeve in Lady Grey's chair during the graduation ceremonies the previous spring. As soon as the game was over, they began to talk, and when the party ended Louis even summoned up enough courage to escort her to the house where she was staying. They both decided that evening, without saying so to one another, that they had found a mate.

The backgrounds of Louis St. Laurent and Jeanne Renault were strikingly similar. The girl's father, P.-F. Renault, was a storekeeper in Beauceville, where he had arrived about the same time that J.-B.-M. St. Laurent moved to Compton. However, he had found a larger market awaiting him, particularly among the lumber companies along the upper reaches of the Chaudière River, and as a result he had built a large business, with three departments and some twenty employees. A huge man who weighed three hundred pounds in his prime and wore an ample black beard, he presided over his business dressed in a morning coat, silk tie, and gloves, greeting each client personally and making sure he was directed to the section that interested him. The Renaults had eight children, seven of them girls, whom they raised in relative luxury in a turreted, three-storey house next to the store. They were a talented musical family, P.-F. Renault himself singing in the church choir in a rich bass voice, and his wife serving as the church organist. All the girls but Jeanne played musical instruments, and they put on concerts frequently in their home. Jeanne, perhaps the most beautiful and certainly the most temperamental of the Renault girls, declared early in life that she wanted a good husband who would enable her to have a fine home and family of her own; other matters were relatively unimportant to her. Like the other girls, she had received her education at the local school and at the Ursuline Convent in Halifax, where they were all sent to learn English, music, and other attributes of refined society.

The day following the card party, Jeanne was to visit friends in near-by Lorette; Louis mentioned that he was in the habit of taking an evening stroll with a comrade and asked if he could meet her at the station on her return. She agreed, and when he met his current walking partner, Oscar Morin, another former class-mate, he confided to him that he had met 'a very charming young lady' the previous evening, and, while she didn't seem very interested, 'she may be the one I will marry'. For her part, she had already announced to her friends that he was her 'ideal', but had been warned that he would not be an easy catch, since he spent practically all his time with his books. Even with such serious intentions, they did not succeed in bridging the gap of reserve on that second evening, and St. Laurent escorted her to her friends' home again without even making a further appointment.

Once again, Barbeau played a useful role. Although he himself was one of Jeanne's several admirers, he helped them to meet again the following summer, first at a picnic near the town of Beauceville, then at a bazaar in the town itself. On the second occasion, Jeanne was busy helping to serve the dinner to the visiting dignitaries, but she asked Louis to go over to the house and introduce himself to her mother. The courtship was becoming serious. The two young people began to correspond. Seeing one of the letters, Renault decided that if the young man had anything to communicate to his daughter he should do so openly, and not in sealed envelopes; they were ordered to carry on their correspondence by postcard. Despite the restriction, the romance continued to grow. Observing his daughter's increasing attachment for the twenty-five-year-old lawyer, Renault took advantage of a trip to Quebec City to clarify the situation. 'You are corresponding with my daughter,' he stated bluntly. 'What are your intentions?' Although taken aback by the directness of the question, St. Laurent managed to assure him that his intentions were serious and upright, and that, in fact, he had marriage in mind.

The next step was to arrange a meeting of the two families. At Louis's request, the St. Laurents invited Jeanne and her father to visit Compton. Jeanne had stated that her beau was the most handsome man in Quebec City; Louis prepared the ground at home by saying she was the most beautiful girl in the old capital. The news that he was courting a girl from Beauce County hardly impressed the other members of his family, who thought of the residents of that area as the 'jarrets noirs'* and the butt of jokes because of their distinctive accent. Louis's sisters were particularly on guard against the person who had captured the heart of the brother they admired and adored. Happily the meeting went off well. The two prospective fathers-in-law discovered that they had many common acquaintances among the local population, and soon they were out with the horse and buggy calling on them. The fact that one was a Conservative, the other a Liberal, did not hinder them from establishing a pleasant relationship. The ladies got on equally well; while the St. Laurent girls rejected their brother's claim that Jeanne resembled their sister Louise, they noted with approval that she had little in common with the Beauce farmers they knew, and conceded that she was, in fact, very pretty. The engagement took place during the Carnaval season of 1907. With Mme Renault as chaperon, Louis escorted Jeanne to concerts, light operas, card parties, and other activities, drawing the line only at dancing, which he swore he could never learn.

The only remaining obstacle to the marriage was Louis St. Laurent's meagre income; he was still on a subsistence salary of fifty dollars a month, far too little to support a woman accustomed in her own home to a full-time cook, a full-time seamstress, and two or three maids. While he was considering ways of improving his financial position, he attracted the attention of another bright young lawyer, Antonin Galipeault, who had opened a law office

---

*'black garters', a reference to the fact that the residents of the Chaudière Valley often had muddy feet and legs because of the low-lying land.

on rue St-Pierre, not far from the Pelletier firm. An ardent Liberal, Galipeault had become president of a local branch of the St. Jean Baptiste Society, and then a member of the Quebec City Council. Clearly marked for a political career, he was looking for a law associate in order to free himself to some extent from his legal practice. He had observed St. Laurent pleading in court, and had noticed that, while his style was far from brilliant, his arguments were so carefully prepared that they could seldom be refuted. In addition, his knowledge of English was a considerable asset in dealing with commercial cases. Galipeault decided that they would complement one another well; he offered him a salaried position, and added the argument that St. Laurent should get out of a Conservative office before he became 'corrupted'. The political consideration did not impress St. Laurent, but he was attracted by the prospect of sharing the list of clients Galipeault had built up, and obtaining a base for further expansion. They finally agreed to form a partnership.

The wedding took place in Beauceville on May 19, 1908. Louis St. Laurent cut a dashing figure with his broad moustache, his thick hair plastered down in an orderly series of waves, and his three-quarter-length morning coat, tight-bottomed trousers, and grey spats. Beside him, Jeanne looked petite and elegant in a high-necked white dress, moulded carefully to her narrow waist, and then fluffed out over her hips with the help of numerous petticoats. Following the religious ceremony, the twenty-six-year-old bridegroom smoked a cigar, replied to the toasts, and, generally, gave the impression of enjoying the occasion. Before leaving by train on their honeymoon trip, the young couple descended into the cellar of the Renault home and burned the bread-box full of postcards that had marked their courtship. Then, Jeanne dressed in a high-stacked hat and a travelling shawl, Louis in a broad white Stetson hat, double-breasted suit, and patent leather shoes, they set out for the Mecca of newly-weds, Niagara Falls.

The honeymoon trip was shorter than originally planned because a provincial election had been called, and Pelletier was a candidate again; he asked St. Laurent, who had not yet left to join Galipeault, to limit his holiday to one week. As a result, the young couple had to spend the first three weeks after their honey-moon in a boarding-house on rue St-Cyrille, waiting for their new apartment to be redecorated. In late June they moved into their first home, an eight-room flat near the Anglican Church on rue St-Jean. Furniture had figured prominently among the wedding presents, and they were able to make most of the space habitable. They also had maid service from the beginning; Louis was determined to keep his wife in the manner to which she was accustomed.

Success came rapidly to the young law partners. Stimulated by the new challenge, and impressed by the responsibilities of founding a family, St. Laurent worked harder than ever. He arrived in the office promptly at eight in the morning, returned home for a brief lunch, and then went back until six o'clock. Most evenings, he worked a few more hours at home. When he had finished his self-imposed evening assignment, he and Jeanne played cards; their social life was restricted to visits from their families and a few select friends. The children began arriving in rapid succession. Marthe was born in March 1909, Renault in September 1910, Jean-Paul in April 1912. Since Jeanne objected to going to a hospital, all were born in an improvised delivery room at home. The choice of so large an apartment proved to be wise foresight.

Antonin Galipeault was elected a member of the Quebec Legislature for Bellechasse constituency just a month after the partnership began. However, the demands of political office were still relatively light in those years; even the premier continued to practise law, and sittings of the Legislature were often arranged to fit the schedule of the courts. The most time-consuming part of a member's life was dealing with patronage, and, in particular, receiving the many people who appeared at the law office in quest of political favours. In addition, politics often determined a lawyer's clientele; a member of the Legislature was frequently obliged for political reasons to handle minor cases even though it meant passing up more remunerative ones. Despite their disparity of interests, the two men got on well and worked out an effective team relationship. While Galipeault was undoubtedly the more effective court-room performer, particularly before a jury, St. Laurent won the attention of judges by his thoroughness and sincerity. Although his speaking style was still hesitant, and the nervous habit of shrugging his shoulders was somewhat distracting, he created the impression of trying to establish the truth, rather than merely to score a debating point. Even though he appeared at times to be playing into the hands of his adversaries by making more admissions than necessary, the weight of his arguments more than compensated for his apparent want of tactical skill.

Louis St. Laurent's bilingualism proved to be a major asset in his career. By seeking precedents in both legal systems, adopting alternatively the deductive Latin and the more pragmatic Anglo-Saxon approach to problems, and examining the meaning of legal concepts in both languages, he was able frequently to add a new dimension to a legal argument, and give his clients an advantage. Moreover, French-speaking lawyers whose English was weak retained him to plead for them, and English-language firms engaged him to do their French legal work. In this way he came into contact with the largest English-language legal firm in Quebec City, Pentland, Stuart, and Brodie. G. G. Stuart, who counted among his clients some of the largest firms operating in Quebec, took a particular interest in him, and even offered him a junior partnership, but St. Laurent declined, since he did not feel he could leave Galipeault so soon. In poor health, Stuart sent him work he could not undertake himself, and they worked together on many cases.

St. Laurent's first trip to Ottawa was also a result of his bilingualism. Galipeault was asked by the mayor of Quebec, Sir Georges Garneau, to look after the expropriations required to restore the site of the Battle of the Plains of Abraham. Since the expropriation procedure had been laid down in the charter of the Quebec Battlefields Commission, a document drawn up in Ottawa by English-speaking legal experts, the matter was passed on to St. Laurent. He decided that it was unnecessarily complicated, and should be amended. Garneau was impressed by the advice, and decided to consult the Minister of Justice, Sir Allen Aylesworth, one of the great legal figures in Canadian history. He and St. Laurent appeared before the minister in Ottawa in the spring of 1910. After listening carefully to their viewpoint, Sir Allen turned to Garneau and said: 'I think the young man is right; we will have this Charter amended and have the ordinary law apply to the Battlefields Commission.' Within a matter of weeks, the legislation was passed, and the expropriations began that autumn.

Not all of Louis St. Laurent's cases were that important; in building up his practice he was obliged to deal with a great variety of minor matters, and to work for very small fees. Whatever the nature of the case, or the fee involved, St. Laurent was as thorough as Pelletier had insisted on being in the tinsmith's case. When he represented a client in a dispute between musicians, he spent so many hours studying musical instruments that he not only won a verdict, but impressed his family with his knowledge of a subject in which they had written him off entirely. In another field, several engineers were heard to say that they liked him as their lawyer because he understood their trade so well.

St. Laurent's big break-through came in 1912. He had just received some publicity in the local press for winning a damage suit against the Canadian Pacific Railway in a case involving compensation to an injured fireman. At that moment, representatives of the daily newspaper the *New York World* were in the city negotiating the purchase of extensive timber lands in Quebec from the Canadian magnate D. A. Pennington. When agreement had been reached, the Americans inquired about a lawyer to represent them in drawing up the necessary documents, and to advise them on the Quebec law. When Pennington mentioned that his lawyer was G. G. Stuart, they asked if he wasn't the man who had just lost the case reported in the newspapers. Pennington conceded that he was. 'Then we'll take the winner,' one of them declared. That was the wedge that opened the door of opportunity wide. As a result of his handling that large deal, others were brought to him; soon he was specializing in corporation law, travelling to the United States to visit his clients, and representing them in Canada. When Stuart died early in World War I, Louis St. Laurent took over many of his clients, including the important pulp and paper company of Sir William Price. He played an active part in founding the Quebec Forest Industries Association, which gave him, incidentally, contacts with all the firms that were members of that organization.

As a result of this rapid expansion, the Galipeault–St. Laurent partnership soon had more business than the two men could handle. They invited the veteran politician Senator P.-A. Choquette to join them; and in 1914 two younger men, Alphonse Métayer and Hector Laferté, joined the firm as well. St. Laurent was the mainstay of the team and the most productive member. His reputation was built on reliability rather than originality; he preferred 'equitable solutions' to victories wrung from adversaries by wit and guile, and argued that, if it was possible to reach a fair agreement by negotiation, the time and expense of a court case should be avoided. Occasionally corporation officials found him over-zealous in adhering to prescribed practices, but, on reflection, they usually realized that their business was safer in his hands than in those of someone who had less respect for the law.

As they became more prosperous, the St. Laurents began planning a house of their own. Since P.-F. Renault wanted to hand over his business to his son Henri and retire to Quebec City, the two families agreed to purchase adjoining lots on Grande Allée, a broad street in Upper Town near the Plains of Abraham and almost out in the country. Unfortunately, the joint venture did not materialize. In April 1912, the Chaudière River overran its banks and inundated both the store and house in Beauceville, causing damage estimated at one hundred thousand dollars. Although in failing health, P.-F. Renault worked to salvage what he could of his property, but the strain proved too much for him, and he died of a heart attack. His widow decided to stay and help their son rebuild the business. Louis and Jeanne St. Laurent took over both lots in Quebec, and built a fifteen-room, three-storey house astride the two of them. In 1913, they moved in, together with their three children, Marthe, Renault, and Jean-Paul; Thérèse was born there two years later, and Madeleine in 1917. With those additions, the family was complete.

During the same period, misfortune struck in Compton as well. In 1910, J.-B.-M. St. Laurent suffered a stroke that left one side of his body paralysed. Thereafter, he was forced to spend most of his day seated by the old stove in the store, leaving Maurice to carry the main burden of running the business. In 1915, he had another attack – this time a fatal one. Thus, the man who had arrived in Compton almost a penniless bachelor thirty-five years earlier died a respected elder citizen, known to his neighbours as 'the peacemaker'. Louise soon followed her father to the grave. While still a novice in the convent, she hurt her leg; when the injury failed to heal, she was sent home and eventually the ailment was diagnosed as tuberculosis of the bone. She became a permanent invalid. Her mother refused to let her go to a sanatorium, insisting that no one could give her better care than her own family. For eight years Louise lived on, her physical strength ebbing gradually away, but her beauty, kind disposition, and spiritual faith increasing in inverse proportion. She died in April 1917.

In the meantime, the other members of the family had grown up. Maurice had married and was running the store, Kathleen had joined a religious order, and Nil had become a priest. With her youngest son's ordination, Mary Ann St. Laurent's most fervent prayer had been granted. Advancing steadily on his chosen path, Louis St. Laurent was not affected greatly by the fall of the Laurier government in 1911, nor by the outbreak of World War I three years later. He considered the fighting across the Atlantic a purely European quarrel, and thought it would be settled before long by negotiations; at any rate, he was too busy, and had too many responsibilities, to feel personally involved in the conflict. In 1914 the law firm moved into larger quarters in the new Imperial Bank Building on rue St-Pierre, and St. Laurent succeeded his former employer, L.-P. Pelletier, as Professor of Law at Laval University. In 1915 the university awarded him the degree of doctor of law. In a sense, the professorship and doctorate marked his ordination into the legal aristocracy of Quebec. In 1917 his acceptance was confirmed when he was invited to become a member of the exclusive Garrison Club. More important to him, his income was over ten thousand dollars a year. At thirty-five he had won success, and solely by his industry and competence.

Although he worked harder than most men, Louis St. Laurent was a devoted family man and never hesitated to put his private responsibilities first. He still spent most of his evenings in a big chair surrounded by his legal books, but he never failed to interrupt his work to solve one of the children's problems, dry a tear, or say an affectionate good-night. He forbade physical fighting, but did not, like his mother, assert that physical punishment was unnecessary; all of his children had occasion to feel the sting of his hand. However, the experience was as upsetting for him as for the child, and he preferred to maintain order by glowering over his glasses, or by employing cutting sarcasm, a method at which he was particularly effective. Sending a child to bed without supper was a common form of punishment in the St. Laurent household, but he usually relented before long, took a glass of milk and a sandwich to the offender's room, and made peace. On some subjects he was adamant; he demanded punctuality, and refused to condone aspersions on one or other of Canada's main ethnic groups. When Renault returned from play and repeated some uncomplimentary remarks he had heard about English-speaking Canadians, he was sent to his room. When another child referred to a neighbour as a 'French Canadian', she was told firmly that there were no French Canadians or English Canadians, only Canadians who spoke English or French, and that they should be referred to as 'English-speaking' or 'French-speaking' Canadians. He identified his family with the French-speaking group, but insisted that they learn English as well, and, in order to give them practice, certain meals were conducted entirely in English. In French, the St. Laurent children were taught to address their parents as *vous* rather than the more familiar *tu*, a rare practice in Quebec, but more common in the upper strata of society in France. The children loved and admired their father, but they also came to recognize his imperfections. Although less volatile than their mother, he displayed a hot temper if aroused; whenever they saw his dark eyes flash, the red colour mount his neck and flush his face, they realized that he would brook no questioning of his authority. And they knew, as soon as he acquired his first car, that he was one of the worst drivers in the world.

The McLaughlin touring car was ordered through the Renault store in Beauceville, and the St. Laurents picked it up at near-by Valley Junction at the beginning of the 1916 summer holiday; Henri Renault agreed to accompany them to Compton, and to teach his brother-in-law to drive on the way. Like all automobiles of the period, it had high narrow wheels for maximum clearance, a gas light near the driver's seat, and a squeaky horn that startled everyone and everything within hearing range. It was a memorable trip. With their father watching carefully every move their uncle made as he negotiated the rutty road, the children, crowded into the back seat with their mother, gave a running commentary on all that flashed by on the way. The journey was made in a single day and they arrived in Compton dusty and weary, but happy with their new experience. When Louis St. Laurent took the wheel himself, things did not go as smoothly. He started off invariably with a tremendous jerk, alarming all his passengers, and seemed so frozen to his seat that he could not adjust the speed or avoid objects in his path. Whenever the children became noisy, he would stop the car, turn around, and give them a lecture on the importance of remaining absolutely quiet so that he could concentrate on driving. The nerves of even the youngest became frayed, and they were all relieved when the outing was over. In Quebec City, he drove to work for a time, but proved something of a threat to other motorists and pedestrians. On one occasion, he struck a streetcar as he was pulling out of his driveway; another time, he gave himself a bad scare by narrowly missing a cyclist. Other members of the family urged him to leave the car at home, or to let someone else drive. Finally, he hired a chauffeur, who doubled as handyman, but he persisted in trying to master the art of driving for several years, knocking down gate-posts and scraping fenders in the process.

Just when St. Laurent's future seemed assured, he developed a swelling of the glands in his neck. His doctor suspected that he might have contracted tuberculosis from his sister, and ordered complete rest and fresh air. Suddenly the carefully erected structure of his professional and private life seemed about to collapse; a lengthy absence from his office meant losing many of his important clients. So serious was the situation that he considered abandoning his law practice altogether, and taking up farming near Compton; however, his brothers and sisters laughed at the thought of his earning his living by physical labour, and his wife had no desire to exchange her comfortable city home, staffed by two maids and a chauffeur, for a farm-house that might not even have running water. St. Laurent concluded that the only solution was to get well and to continue in his profession. In the spring of 1917, the family moved to Métis on the Gaspé coast. There he applied himself with his usual single-mindedness to overcoming the illness by bathing in salt water, taking walks along the rugged shore, playing the occasional game of golf, and, above all, resting a good portion of each day. When the time arrived for the children to return to school, the swelling in his neck had begun to decrease; they moved back to the city, but he continued to concentrate on restoring his health. Only gradually did he resume his work. The cure was complete.

One result of Louis St. Laurent's illness was the renewal of his interest in outdoor life. A member of the firm, Alphonse Métayer, was an enthusiastic sportsman and liked to recount his fishing and hunting trips with Wilfrid Edge, a long, lanky notary who had an office near by. One day, St. Laurent asked him rather hesitantly if he could go along with them some time. Métayer and Edge could hardly imagine the rather distant and serious intellectual as a congenial companion in a primitive camp and were reluctant to accede to his request; when they did, it was mainly for want of a good reason to refuse. St. Laurent prepared himself with the usual meticulous care, and on the appointed day they took a train to the village from which the hike to the camp was to begin. The other men smiled as he set out resolutely along the narrow path with his rather awkward gait, a packsack of provisions on his back. Their scepticism turned to admiration as he covered mile after mile without any sign of faltering. However, he was so uncommunicative, maintaining silence except when spoken to, and answering comments mainly in monosyllables, that Métayer and Edge decided that something had to be done or the trip would be spoiled. Edge finally agreed to tell him a salty joke from his large repertoire, to see if he could break the ice. He made his choice carefully, in order not to shock the English-Canadian lawyer – for so he considered St. Laurent – with his Gallic humour. St. Laurent listened quizzically, then burst into a guffaw of laughter; the three continued on their way excellent companions.

Almost overnight, St. Laurent became a fishing enthusiast, and joined no fewer than three clubs north of the St. Lawrence River.

From fishing, his interest spread to hunting; however, his ardour for that sport was dampened when he killed a female deer, and its twin fawns leaped out of the undergrowth just a few yards away from him. The sight of the two beautiful young creatures, whose mother lay dead at his feet, upset him deeply; it was his last deer-hunting expedition. Sometimes the entire St. Laurent family went on fishing trips to the Club des Laurentides, north of Rivière-à-Pierre, where they shared a camp with Edge. Each such holiday was a major undertaking, involving a train journey, a long hike or horseback ride, and a canoe trip with numerous portages; after the group arrived, there still remained the problems of looking after the city-bred children, and initiating them to camp life. Wilfrid Edge, still a bachelor at that time, proved a valuable friend, and won the lasting affection of both generations, but particularly of Renault and Jean-Paul who admired his skill as a woodsman. The isolated site provided an ideal opportunity for the St. Laurent children to get to know their father better. Far from the preoccupations of his office, he relaxed, explained the wonders of nature to them, showed them how to fish, and told them stories by the fireside while the loons called to one another out in the darkness.

For a few years in the 1920s, the St. Laurents owned a small farm on the Ile d'Orléans, just below Quebec City. The property contained a roomy farm house, a large garden, a stable with two horses and a pony, a croquet lawn and a tennis court, and a stretch of beach on the St. Lawrence River. The family spent several pleasant summers there, Louis St. Laurent commuting by ferry to and from his office. On week-ends he played golf, and sometimes he took his children for an outing on the river in a rented motor cruiser. Unfortunately, the house burned down in 1928, and they did not rebuild it.

St. Laurent's illness proved to be only a minor setback in his rise to legal eminence. Beginning with a widely diversified practice, he found himself, more by chance than choice, dealing increasingly with commercial law. From that field he moved into constitutional law, in which he also became a recognized authority. He pleaded his first case before the Supreme Court of Canada in

1911, and was back more than sixty times over the next thirty years. In 1920 he made his first appearance before the judicial committee of the Privy Council in Great Britain, the highest tribunal in the British Empire, and returned there almost annually until World War II broke out; one year he made the trip three times.

In 1923, he and Galipeault dissolved their partnership and set up separate firms. The parting was amicable; their interests had simply become so divergent that there was little point in remaining together. After a term as Speaker of the Legislative Assembly, Galipeault had become Minister of Public Works in the Gouin administration, a portfolio that involved an immense amount of detailed work, including much of the government's patronage. The waiting-room of the law office was filled from early morning until late evening with favour-seekers. As he walked through, St. Laurent shook his head at the thought of all the lucrative cases that had to be refused because precious time was being spent on that aspect of politics that he found so distasteful. Another factor in the decision to end their long and fruitful association was that they had, between them, five sons of about the same age; the firm could not absorb that many at once; each father decided he would have to make a place for his own.

St. Laurent matched his skill with most of the great lawyers of the period, including the knowledgeable and gentlemanly Eugène Lafleur, and the tumultuous, dazzling Aimé Geoffrion. A generation older than St. Laurent, Lafleur was generally recognized as the leading personality of the Quebec Bar from the beginning of the century until his death in 1932. Thus, when he remarked in 1920 that Louis St. Laurent was 'one of the coming men in Quebec', the prediction was noted carefully. Geoffrion was a towering, slender man with a drooping moustache and a cultivated arrogance designed to demonstrate that no man was his master. He had a staccato delivery that made judges and opponents alike strain to follow his line of reasoning. St. Laurent confessed readily that he had to listen carefully to the arguments of the colourful Montrealer, but he felt the effort was worth while, as close analysis revealed a well-constructed, almost indestructible line of reasoning. Like Lafleur, Geoffrion was not long in recognizing St. Laurent's talent. A contemporary at the Quebec Bar once described Lafleur, Geoffrion, and St. Laurent as follows: 'Lafleur was neat in his thinking but not as nimble as Geoffrion. . . . St. Laurent was solid, sound, pleasing to his courts, and established an intimacy with them. He had a human touch despite his technical detail and thoroughness.'

In his years as a practising lawyer, Louis St. Laurent appeared in many important cases, and made a significant contribution, through his legal arguments, to the interpretation of Canadian law. For instance, in 1922 he argued before the Supreme Court – albeit unsuccessfully – that salaries received from a provincial government were not subject to a federal income tax. In 1926, he represented the Jewish community of Montreal in a test case concerning the right of Jews to be represented on the Montreal Protestant Board of School Commissioners. The question had arisen because the law only made provision for Catholic and Protestant schools; for educational purposes, the Jews were equated with Protestants and paid taxes to support the Protestant school system, but they had no legal right to be represented on the Board. St. Laurent argued that they must either be given such representation, or allowed to have their own schools. The principle of Jewish schools was accepted, and while a compromise arrangement made it unnecessary to create them at that time, the legal interpretation marked a step forward in assuring the rights of an important minority group in Canada. During the Depression, St. Laurent was called upon to deal with many bankruptcy cases, and this experience led him to make suggestions to the federal government for sweeping changes in bankruptcy legislation. His suggestions were enacted at a subsequent session of Parliament. In the field of constitutional law, he was retained sometimes by the Quebec government to present its argument against the federal government; sometimes he found himself on the federal side.

Politics had little or nothing to do with St. Laurent's assignments; the Bennett government employed him frequently; when the Liberals returned to power in 1935, they did so even more often. This transgression of the traditional practice that legal patronage should be reserved for members of the party in power led to a protest by Liberal member Jean-François Pouliot, who asked the Minister of Justice indignantly what services St. Laurent had rendered to the Liberal Party to deserve such favours. Lapointe ignored the query. When the Bennett government introduced legislation that left large discretion to the Tariff Board in fixing duties, St. Laurent was able to convince the Supreme Court, on behalf of the Quebec government, that such powers surpassed the functions of an administrative body, and constituted a usurpation of the functions of Parliament. In 1934 he argued before the Supreme Court that the Dominion Companies Act of 1927, passed by the Liberals, infringed on provincial rights; in that case his argument did not prevail. When the Liberals returned to power in Ottawa in 1935, they found on the statute books several pieces of legislation enacted in the last months of the Conservative administration and known as Bennett's 'New Deal' measures. Hurriedly drafted shortly before the 1935 election, and designed as a bold attack on the economic crisis and its consequences, they were considered by some lawyers to infringe provincial rights. Prime Minister Mackenzie King decided to test their validity in court. St. Laurent spent a large part of two years representing the federal government in presenting the important cases before the Supreme Court and the Privy Council; the result of the litigation was that much of the legislation was declared *ultra vires*.

The first case that St. Laurent took to the Privy Council concerned a new Quebec succession duty, to which there was objection on two grounds: first, that it was an indirect tax, and contrary to the provision of the constitution that a province can only impose direct taxes; and, second, that a succession duty could not be imposed on property situated outside the province though owned by residents of Quebec at the time of decease. In an earlier test case, in 1914, this argument had prevailed, but the Quebec government had amended the legislation subsequently. Several appeals were entered again, and the Gouin government distributed them among a number of leading law firms. St. Laurent realized that the first lawyer to get a decision from the Supreme Court would be sent to test the new legislation before the Privy Council; keen to make the trip overseas, he proceeded as quickly as possible and succeeded in obtaining the assignment. In the spring of 1920 he and Joseph Gravel, another Quebec city lawyer on a similar mission, together with their wives, sailed across the Atlantic on the White Star liner S.S. *Megantic*.

Following the usual practice, the Deputy Attorney General of the province, Charles Lanctôt, also appeared in the case, and they engaged a brilliant member of the London Bar, Sir John Simon, later British Foreign Secretary, to advise them on English practices. The hearings took place in a relatively small room on the corner of Downing Street and Whitehall, just a few steps from the Prime Minister's offices and official residence, and within five minutes' walk from the Houses of Parliament. Although obliged to wear a wig and gown, the Canadians found the atmosphere of the court less formal than in many courts at home. The judges, who included such celebrated jurists as Viscount Haldane and Lord Buckmaster, gave the impression of engaging in an interesting intellectual exercise, and the proceedings took the form of a quiet, almost leisurely conversation. Louis St. Laurent's court-room style was well suited to this atmosphere. Averse to sensationalism, he seemed as anxious as the judges to find the right answer to the legal problem before them. The case was heard over a period of four days. St. Laurent and his associates argued that Quebec had preserved the right existing before Confederation to 'impose a duty upon a succession within its territory to movables locally situate outside that territory', that the right was not limited 'provided that the taxation was direct and for provincial purposes', and that the succession duty was indeed a direct tax. Their arguments were accepted on all counts, and the validity of the Quebec legislation was upheld.

As soon as the hearings were over, the two couples set out to see London, St. Laurent preparing their daily program with the same method and care as he applied to all aspects of his life in Canada. From London they moved on to Paris, and then to Rome where Nil was carrying out advanced study. On the whole, it was a rather typical first tour of Europe by North American couples, and they reacted no differently from most, being impressed by the accomplishments of the past and shocked by the dirt and misery of the present. They were thrilled to visit the land of their ancestors, but realized they belonged on the other side of the Atlantic. They were happy to sail for home.

Jeanne St. Laurent was sea-sick on the trip, and, in any event, she preferred her home to other places; she let her husband go without her on most of the trips to the Privy Council that followed. St. Laurent enjoyed matching his skill and knowledge with the members of the judicial committee of the Privy Council, and while he had great respect for them, he realized that they did not know the details of all the legal systems within the British Empire. Occasionally, he found himself instructing them on points of Quebec law. After one of his appearances before them in 1928, in which he was representing the federal government in a conflict between the federal Bankruptcy Act and the Quebec Civil Code, the judges noted in their written conclusion the precedents to which 'St. Laurent in an able argument called their attention', and agreed with him that the 'bankruptcy and insolvency' clause of the B.N.A. Act gave priority to federal legislation in that field. The case not only marked another victory for him; it earned him a rare commendation; compliments to counsel are very seldom recorded in Privy Council decisions.

The most important cases in which Louis St. Laurent appeared in London were those relating to the New Deal legislation passed in the last session of the Bennett régime. At issue was not only a series of laws enacted by a previous administration, but Canada's future, for if no solutions were found to the economic and social problems resulting from the Depression, internal tensions and disorder seemed likely to disrupt the country before a sense of unity was ever achieved. Most of the provinces were represented by counsel, and the hearings, which lasted several months, brought together one of the greatest arrays of Canadian legal talent ever to meet outside the country. Three of the items submitted to the Privy Council were designed to give effect to conventions adopted by the International Labour Organization, and approved by the Parliament of Canada, concerning hours of work, minimum wages, and weekly rest periods. The legislation marked a new initiative in Canadian labour legislation, a field generally considered until that time as within provincial jurisdiction. The Statute of Westminster of 1931 established Canada's position as a sovereign nation, and made it possible for her to enter into treaty obligations; however, doubts existed concerning the power of the federal government to carry out such obligations in areas of provincial jurisdiction. The purpose of the test cases was to decide that question.

As counsel for the federal government, St. Laurent and his associate, C. P. Plaxton, of the Department of Justice, based their argument on Article 132 of the B.N.A. Act, which granted the Parliament of Canada in 1867 'all powers necessary or proper for performing the obligations of Canada or of any Province thereof . . . arising under Treaties between the Empire and Foreign countries'. With the evolution of Canada to independence, they asserted, the federal government possessed not only its previous right to carry out treaty obligations in the fields of federal and provincial jurisdiction, but also the right to negotiate treaties in the same areas. This view, they pointed out, had already been endorsed by Chief Justice Sir Lyman Duff of the Supreme Court of Canada. Nevertheless, the members of the Privy Council rejected it on the grounds that the possession of treaty-making powers by Canada was 'an uncontemplated event' in 1867, and that Clause 132 could not be stretched to cover it. Impressed by the 'compact theory' of Confederation, they saw in the additional powers an instrument to permit Ottawa 'to undermine the constitutional safeguards of Provincial constitutional autonomy'. They rejected as well the argument, accepted in other federal countries, that matters which had become of concern to the country as a whole should come under the authority of the central government. 'While the ship of state now sails on larger ventures and into foreign waters,' they declared, 'she still retains the watertight compartments which are an essential part of her original structure.' The three acts were declared *ultra vires*; a basic problem in the operation of Canadian federalism remained unsolved.

The second series of Bennett legislation also raised the matter of federal-provincial relations. The Employment and Social Insurance Act, 1935, had provided for a national employment service and a national insurance fund. St. Laurent and Plaxton argued that the federal government had been given responsibility in 1867 for problems that were national in scope, and that unemployment not only was nation-wide, but could only be dealt with effectively at that level. Moreover, Ottawa could raise taxes 'for the public purposes touching the peace, order, and good government of Canada', and that broad clause certainly embraced the critical employment situation. In any case, they maintained, the legislation did not propose to regulate property and civil rights, an acknowledged field of provincial jurisdiction, but rather 'a social and economic condition of national concern relating to the peace, order and good government of Canada and its trade and commerce' that was not even considered when the British North America Act was drawn up. The judgement in that case was delivered by Lord Atkin, and was again unfavourable; the legislation was an insurance act, he declared; as such, it affected civil rights and was invalid. Once again, the solution of a major problem was postponed.

St. Laurent was more successful in defending other items of the New Deal legislation. A series of amendments to the Criminal Code designed to prevent restrictive trade practices was upheld on the grounds that the legislation fell squarely within the definition of criminal law, and did not deal with property or civil rights. A companion piece of legislation, the Dominion Trade and Industry Act, 1935, also designed to restrict unfair trade practices, was accepted as being within the scope of 'the regulation of trade and commerce'; and the Farmers' Creditors Arrangements Act, 1934, was considered 'genuine legislation relating to bankruptcy and insolvency'. The Natural Products Marketing Act, 1934, on the other hand, broke on the rock of provincial rights. St. Laurent argued that, while marketing was a provincial matter, the federal government was responsible for interprovincial and international trade, and the intervention of the two levels of government was required to solve the current marketing problems. 'It would seem to be a reasonable construction of the powers of the two legislative authorities,' he maintained, 'that having between them the whole of the powers they should be able to exercise them in such a way as is proper for the good administration of the inhabitants.' The court agreed that cooperation might well be necessary, but stated that a solution would not be achieved 'by either party leaving its own sphere and encroaching upon that of the other'. The act was annulled.

The decisions taken by the judicial committee of the Privy Council with regard to the various items of legislation did not facilitate the solution of Canada's serious internal problems, but they did provide a fresh interpretation of the division of powers, and thus a basis for a renewed attack on them. As counsel for the federal government, St. Laurent came to realize that some effective steps had to be taken by whatever level of government could best deal with the consequences of the economic depression. The history-making cases also won him recognition as one of the leading authorities on constitutional law in Canada.

St. Laurent made his last appearance before the Privy Council on July 31, 1939. Already the war clouds were hanging low over the city; Prime Minister Neville Chamberlain had abandoned his cherished hope of 'peace in our time'; and the ancient city of London was being made ready to withstand the expected attacks of the German *Luftwaffe*. He arrived home just two weeks before World War II began.

During the inter-war years, St. Laurent rose not only to prominence in the legal profession but also to relative affluence. By the end of the 1920s his fees for individual cases were frequently in the thousands of dollars. He followed the stock market closely, and had a considerable portfolio of shares when the Wall Street crash came; in a few hours his assets, like those of so many others, were transformed into almost useless pieces of paper, and his potential wealth into obligations. The fruits of years of hard labour were wiped out; he had to begin again. A relatively small commercial centre, Quebec City did not offer the same potential for a corporation lawyer as Montreal or Toronto, and, as business stagnated, he found himself taking cases he had considered too small for his attention not long before. He even contemplated moving to Montreal, where he had been invited to join a larger firm, but decided against the change because his family was well established and happy in the old city, and because it would have meant abandoning his own firm. At the same time, the economic crisis was not a completely unfavourable situation for a practising lawyer; he found himself occupied with bankruptcy and insolvency cases that would not have arisen in normal times, and all three levels of governments hired him to deal with matters directly related to the distressing economic and social conditions. By the mid thirties he was as busy as ever, and his earnings were climbing once again. Although he maintained his decision to remain in Quebec, he accepted an arrangement to spend one day a week as special counsel to a Montreal firm at a fee of around five hundred dollars a day. By the time the war broke out his earnings were in the fifty-thousand-dollars-a-year bracket, and he was rapidly recouping his losses.

While St. Laurent's career made it necessary for him to spend more and more time away from home, he continued to view his family as his first responsibility. He was determined that his children should have the same loving care as he had received in Compton, plus the additional advantages that his financial position could provide. None of his children was sent to hospital; a room in their own home was transformed into an operating room or sick room as required so that the patient would have the best possible combination of love and medical science. When Marthe broke her leg while a student in Montreal, he was so worried about a repetition of his sister Louise's tragic fate that he forbade the nuns in the convent where she was in residence to call a bone-setter, and rushed over himself to see that she got the best X-rays and hospital treatment. When she broke a leg again while sliding on the Plains of Abraham, and it did not heal properly, he persuaded a famous American orthopaedic surgeon, who happened to be on a visit to Montreal, to come to Quebec and perform another operation. Fortunately, it was a success.

When Renault and Jean-Paul were in their teens, he and Wilfrid Edge took them on several excursions along the lower St. Lawrence River, where they fished for sea trout from a small yacht. Each trip was treated as a major undertaking, and prepared with great detail; St. Laurent wanted the boys to remember these expeditions as the best times in their lives. The youngest members of the family also received their share of attention. As little girls, Thérèse and Madeleine took their places in the front window every evening and tried to guess which car would turn into their driveway and deliver their 'Papa' to them. On Thursday evenings their excitement ran particularly high, since that was the day he brought the latest comics in his big briefcase. After supper they were allowed to climb up on his lap and listen to him read the adventures of the Katzenjammer Kids and other legendary figures, adding a generous portion of moral lessons as he did so.

As part of their education, all the children were given trips to Europe. When she was eighteen, Marthe spent six months with a family in Paris, returning home, to the displeasure of Jean-Paul, with a Parisian accent. Renault and Jean-Paul crossed the Atlantic with him one summer while they were students at St. Charles Seminary in Sherbrooke, and he showed them London and Paris. Thérèse and Madeleine's turn came in 1936. Before they left Quebec, he took them to a reliable shoe store to have sturdy black Oxfords made for them, and insisted that they have tweed suits and coats made on their arrival in London. His wife and Renault were along that year, and they all watched proudly when he pleaded a case before the Privy Council. As soon as he was free, he assumed the role of guide, just as he had done for Marthe, and then for the boys. Guide-book in hand, he led them systematically through London, and then through Paris, undaunted by the sighs and groans of his children and wife, who would often have preferred a quiet hour at a sidewalk café or a browse through a department store. He had planned Christmas for them in Rome, but he was recalled to Canada to look after the affairs of an important client, and Renault took his mother and sisters to Italy in his place. Their disappointment was tempered by a sense of relief that they would not have to maintain the same rigorous schedule during the remainder of their stay in Europe.

After his father's death, Louis St. Laurent assumed the position of head of the entire family; in that role, he encouraged all the members to stand together, and make whatever sacrifices were necessary to help one another. For instance, when Nil was assigned a parish in an isolated corner of the Eastern Townships, he argued that Lora should go and keep house for him there. Then, when Maurice's wife died, leaving him with three small boys, he insisted she return home again, and raise the youngsters in the family home. Mary Ann St. Laurent, by then in her sixties, fell in with the plan, and even began to learn French, since the boys spoke no English. Lora found herself with an adopted family; she was to have none of her own.

In 1930, misfortune struck the family again. Nil had been appointed to the staff of the Bishop's Palace in Sherbrooke as chaplain of the Catholic trade union and of the local prison. In the spring of that year, he was chosen to lead a pilgrimage to Carthage, on the north coast of Africa. Lora and Marthe were with the group, and, when they arrived in Carcassonne in southern France after a long bus trip from Versailles, the three took a walk through the old town; then Nil retired to his room to do some work and recite his breviary. A few minutes later he was found in his chair, dead of a heart attack. The two women turned around and escorted the casket home. The loss of her priest-son was a heavy blow to Mary Ann St. Laurent, seventy-eight years old, and stooped and grey with age. Nevertheless, she continued her regular, pious existence, rising as usual at six a.m. to go to communion, and supervising her household. Known by then as the chatelaine of the village, she went out seldom, but neighbours called regularly to pay their respects, and her grandchildren were always sure of a warm welcome. In late 1932 she fell ill and the doctor diagnosed an incurable cancer. As soon as he realized that her end was near, Louis St. Laurent cancelled all his engagements and returned to Compton. For several weeks he stayed by her side, sharing the vigil with Lora. She died on April 8, 1933, serene in the knowledge that she had done her duty, and had taught her children to do theirs. As her strength ebbed she found happiness in the knowledge that three of her children had entered the Church, Lora was sacrificing herself for the family, Maurice was carrying on the store, and Louis had risen to the top of his profession without abandoning the principles she had taught him.

Within his own immediate family, Louis St. Laurent continued to exercise the same careful supervision. When the boys graduated from St. Charles Seminary, they were enrolled in the Laval Faculty of Law, again following in his own footsteps. They were articled to the family firm, but received only $2.25 per week, instead of the usual five dollars paid to legal clerks; St. Laurent's reasoning was simple: the less money they had, the less they would go out; and the less they went out, the better they would succeed in their studies. The results justified the means; Renault won several prizes, and Jean-Paul, too, graduated with quite respectable marks. Both entered the firm as soon as they became members of the Quebec Bar.

With the girls he was more careful still. He allowed young men to call, but they had to be out of the house by 11 p.m. The visitors came to know the signs well; when St. Laurent put aside his reading in the front room and turned out the light by his chair, the evening was over; within a few minutes, hasty good-nights had been said, and the family was on the way upstairs to bed. If a young man was late in calling on one of his daughters, St. Laurent answered the door himself and announced that she had made other plans; a man who was not punctual, he argued, was neither well mannered nor trustworthy. On two occasions, he refused appointments to the Supreme Court of Canada, partly because of the low salary paid to judges, but, more important, because it seemed less likely that the girls would find suitable husbands in Ottawa than in Quebec City. In 1931, Marthe married a young doctor, Mathieu Samson. She was a beautiful, popular girl, and her marriage was an event of some importance, in part because of her personal qualities, but also because of the position the family had attained in local society. The St. Laurents had become accepted as one of the *bonnes familles.* In 1936, Jean-Paul was married as well. By the time World War II broke out, Louis St. Laurent was a grandfather several times over.

# 4

---

## In Public View

Although St. Laurent made no effort to attract attention, his success at the Bar drew him inevitably into public view. He had, of course, firm opinions on many issues. For instance, he deplored the divergence of views between English-speaking and French-speaking Canadians over relations with Great Britain, and saw the fall of Laurier in 1911 before the combined forces of Borden's Conservatives and Bourassa's Nationalists as a backward step. He regretted still more the disagreement during World War I over the advisability of imposing conscription and was inclined to condemn both sides for their intolerance. When a delegation from Ontario, including the car manufacturer R. S. McLaughlin and Queen's University professor O. D. Skelton, arrived in Quebec City in October 1916 to encourage a *bonne entente* between the two ethnic groups, he was invited to attend a banquet in their honour. Unimpressed by the flow of compliments and expressions of good will, he reacted sharply when called upon without warning to speak, and delivered a heated lecture on the importance of respecting one another's views. Taken aback at first at the unexpected outburst, the organizers of the meeting soon became convinced that he was needed in the *bonne entente* movement. He was persuaded to take part in a return visit to Toronto in January 1917. With the war in a crucial phase, there was little that the well-meaning group of men could do to alter the course of events. Conscription was approved by Parliament in July 1917. In Quebec City, the residence of Louis St. Laurent's friend Albert Sévigny, who was Minister of Revenue in the federal government of Robert Borden, was stoned by an irate mob, and he was denounced as a traitor to the province. He was defeated in the general election held later that year.

During that critical period for Canada, Louis St. Laurent was struggling to regain his health and preoccupied with providing for his wife and five children; those were excellent reasons for remaining on the political side-lines. At the same time, he felt strongly about the split between the two groups of Canadians, and when the war ended he was anxious to see unity restored. His opportunity to contribute to that goal came through the Canadian Bar Association, of which he had become a founding member in 1914.

Patterned on the American counterpart, the Canadian Bar Association was formed to provide a forum for more frequent contacts between lawyers practising in the different provinces, and to work towards a greater degree of uniformity in the law, within the limits of the federal system. Since the members of the legal fraternity were frequently leaders in the political, economic, and social life of the country, it was hoped that closer communication between them would also contribute to national unity. A Conservative member of Parliament from Manitoba, James Aikins, became the first president, Eugène Lafleur became Quebec vice-president, and Louis St. Laurent became one of the council members from Quebec. In deciding to play an active role in the association, St. Laurent adopted an attitude contrary to that of many fellow members of the Quebec Bar, who feared that any attempt to make the law more uniform throughout Canada would endanger the Quebec Civil Code.

Little could be done during the war, but, in June 1920, Aikins, who in the meantime had become Sir James Aikins and had been appointed Lieutenant-Governor of Manitoba, visited Quebec City and appealed for greater participation in the association. He had high praise for the qualities of French-speaking Canadians, and stressed the common interests of the two groups. Confederation, he argued, was a design to solve problems among Canadians, and to ensure their protection and freedom; only by Canadians' remaining united could those goals be assured. He appealed for an immediate end to the split caused by conscription. As one of the hosts at the dinner-meeting given for Aikins, St. Laurent was called upon to speak, and responded warmly to the hand of friendship extended by the visitor. With his dual ancestry, his knowledge of both systems of law, and with the conscription crisis still fresh in his memory, he welcomed the conciliatory gesture and developed Sir James's theme of co-operation and unity still further by pointing out how much the two systems of law had to offer one another. Struck by the positive response to his remarks, Aikins asked St. Laurent to repeat the statement at the next meeting of the Canadian Bar Association.

Accordingly, Louis St. Laurent, then thirty-eight years of age, delivered his first address to a national audience in Ottawa in September 1920. He was introduced by the Alberta vice-president, R. B. Bennett, as 'one of the younger and most distinguished members of the Bar of Quebec'. After making it clear that he considered himself a member of the French-speaking community, he declared his intention of speaking English to prove 'our sincere desire to encourage closer and more cordial relations with our fellow lawyers from the other provinces'. The Civil Code of Quebec was not merely a book of rules, he stated, but rather 'the historical synopsis of what has been, in the past, well-ordered human behaviour, and, as such, is indicative of those undying principles to which well-ordered future human behaviour should conform'. Complaints that the code was excessively rigid arose from the fact that lawyers confused principles with practices, he argued, and forgot that, while principles remain stationary through time, practices have to be adapted to changing circumstances. In addition to its intrinsic value, St. Laurent continued, the Civil Code was the cherished heritage of one of Canada's oldest and largest provinces, and, in the struggle to create in Canada a much-needed 'national spirit', such legitimate pride had to be taken into account. 'A national spirit cannot attach to the soil alone; it must comprise the men who dwell upon it, the institutions which make them a body politic, and also the private laws which crystallize their attitude towards each other and their

methods of realizing human progress.' Canadians were 'pre-
ordained partners in a necessary society', he asserted, and, while
they might prefer to be a more homogeneous people, the different
groups were 'the only material out of which a Canadian nation
can grow'. Consequently, the growth of a common national
consciousness depended on the existence of 'a widespread feeling
that in spite of such differences, perhaps even at times because of
such differences, all these things are good to conserve, are worthy
of mutual respect, constitute something for the whole nation and
for each individual to take pride in and which enriches the
national heritage'. In that spirit, he urged Canadian lawyers to
try to recognize in the two great systems of jurisprudence inherited by them 'some of the good that is in us and in them both,
and find that good sufficient to outweigh the misgivings we are
too prone to feel for that which is not of ourselves and our own
surroundings'.

The reaction to the speech was immediate and enthusiastic,
French-speaking lawyers seeing in it an eloquent defence of the
Civil Code, English-speaking lawyers a surprisingly positive viewpoint; the audience rose in a spontaneous gesture of approval and
gave an unprecedented three cheers for the speaker. Delighted
with the reception accorded to the man he had 'discovered' in
Quebec, Sir James declared the address to be of national importance, and moved that it be distributed as a pamphlet to all lawyers in Canada. A member from Toronto seconded the motion.
Louis St. Laurent had made his début on the national scene.

The sudden success resulted in other invitations to speak, including one from the Empire Club of Toronto, an organization
that was, to most French-speaking Canadians, the very heart of
hostile territory. On November 25, 1920, St. Laurent repeated
his message in the Queen City, and expanded on the theme of
national unity. It was important to emphasize the positive factors
in English-French relations, he urged, and to increase the areas
of understanding, 'not because you or I expect to derive any
immediate benefit from it, but because we both hope that those
who come after us may avoid some of the petty quarrels we have
had'. Canada had a great future, he prophesied, but also a great
heritage, and the country would be the richer 'by counting in its

assets the traditions and cultures of two great races, the institutions and private laws of two great civilizations, and . . . the two great languages through which these traditions, this culture, these institutions and these laws have been turned down to us'. The message was not new, but it was expressed frankly and clearly without either the recriminations or the meaningless embellishments characteristic of so many contributions to the great Canadian debate. In short, it was a statement that English-speaking Canadians could understand and appreciate. 'Good may come out of Quebec,' declared the Toronto *Globe* in a rather equivocal headline when reporting the speech.

While Louis St. Laurent's appeals to reason were not isolated incidents, neither were they typical of relations between the two ethnic groups. The rancour of the conscription crisis remained in Quebec, and the Conservative Party was identified there with that measure. In the 1921 federal election, the Liberals took every seat in that province, and their new leader, William Lyon Mackenzie King, was able to form a minority government. During the 1925 election campaign, the self-proclaimed 'Liberal organ' *Le Soleil* carried a cartoon in which the Conservative Leader of the Opposition, Arthur Meighen, was described as 'the trafficker in human flesh', and shown crying 'aye, aye, ready' as he passed by a Canadian soldier, held in the grip of bloody, long-nailed hands marked 'Imperialism'. When Arthur Meighen succeeded in forming a government in 1926 and dissolved Parliament almost immediately following a defeat in the House of Commons, a large portion of the population was quite ready to believe the assertion of *Le Soleil* that a *coup d'état* had been perpetrated by Meighen in collusion with Governor General Byng. The election that followed was fought in Quebec almost exclusively on the issue of whether the Governor General was justified in granting dissolution to Meighen after having refused one to Mackenzie King a few days earlier.

St. Laurent followed the public debate with interest, more attracted by the constitutional issue than by the political power struggle. His Liberal allegiance ranged him on the side of Mackenzie King and the latter's chief lieutenant in Quebec, Ernest Lapointe, whom he knew on a professional basis, but his ties with the party were so nebulous that some people considered him a Conservative. In fact, when Meighen was called upon to form a government in June 1926, one of the leading Conservatives in Quebec sounded him out discreetly to see if he would accept a portfolio in the new administration. St. Laurent had made it clear that he was not interested in a political career. If he had desired to go into politics at that time, something he refused even to contemplate, it would have been on the Liberal side.

To make his political affiliation clear, Louis St. Laurent agreed to address a meeting on behalf of the Liberal candidate in his constituency, C. G. Power, just three days before the 1926 election. He was presented by Mme Ernest Lapointe as 'one of the best-known members of the Quebec Bar'. It was hoped that he would support the Liberal argument that the Governor General and the Tories were conspiring to thwart the processes of true democracy in Canada. From that point of view, his speech was a disappointment. Lord Byng was perhaps the most likeable Governor General Canada had known, St. Laurent stated, but the position he had taken with regard to dissolving Parliament seemed to be a step backwards; however, the real responsibility in that matter lay with his advisers. 'If a head of a government gives bad advice to a Governor, and in the present case it is the Conservative party leader who has given the bad advice, it is up to us to dismiss him.' In addition to a strong attachment to constitutional practices, a clearly distinguishable vein of Canadian nationalism ran through St. Laurent's remarks. Canada was rich enough to stand on her own feet, he asserted, and her interests need not be subordinated to 'all the splendour of the British Empire'. 'We have the right to demand the respect of our constitutional liberties, not losing sight of the fact that the king should reign, but not rule.'

Seated on the platform, Power realized that the distinguished lawyer might be able to impress the judges, but that he was not likely to win many votes for the Liberals. As soon as the speech was over, he took the floor himself and put on the more colourful type of performance to which the audience was accustomed. Power won another easy victory, and the Liberals were returned to power in Ottawa with a small majority.

Apart from his family and his law practice, St. Laurent was occupied mainly in the years between the wars with his association
with other members of the legal fraternity. He took an active
interest in the work of the various groups, from the local Junior
Bar Association to the national organization; paternalistic by
nature, he helped many younger lawyers at the outset of their
careers, frequently giving them free legal advice for which he
might well have charged a substantial fee. When he became
*syndic* of the Quebec Bar,* he set high standards of conduct, but
he also showed understanding when members found themselves
in difficulties and took considerable pains to help them solve their
problems. In 1927, he became a life member of the Canadian Bar
Association, and in the following year he replaced Eugène Lafleur
as its vice-president for Quebec. In 1928, he represented Ernest
Lapointe, the federal Minister of Justice, at the annual meeting
of the association in Regina. The occasion marked his first trip
west of Ontario.

Once started, the climb up the ladder of the professional organizations was rapid. In May 1929, he was elected *bâtonnier* or
head of the Quebec district Bar, in June *bâtonnier-général* for the
whole province. The double occasion was marked by banquets
in Montreal and Quebec, and eulogies in the press. One of his
former professors, Sir François Lemieux, Chief Justice of the
Superior Court, paid tribute to 'the dignity of his life, the wisdom
of his character and the sureness of his reason'.

As Quebec vice-president of the Canadian Bar Association,
St. Laurent was not only responsible for arranging the meeting
in Quebec City in September 1929, but was also called upon to
preside over the main events when the president, Wallace Nesbitt
of Toronto, became ill. The theme of his remarks was the same as
in 1920; the gathering together of Canadians from all parts of the
country 'tends to make us better Canadians, and, as such, better
associates in that great Commonwealth of Nations, proud of
their allegiance to the Imperial Crown'. Among the speakers at
in Quebec City in September 1929, but was also called upon to

---

*The officer responsible for standards of conduct and discipline.

Borden, who had received harsh treatment at the hands of French-speaking Canadians for his part in introducing conscription in 1917. In his years of retirement, Borden had made a considerable effort to get to know Quebec better, and as a result he had developed a deep attachment for French Canada. In his address, he spoke of the rich double heritage of Canadians, extending back over a period of three centuries, and he illustrated, by references to history, the community of interests and the interrelationship between the two groups. The founding of Quebec by Champlain had prevented the St. Lawrence valley from being colonized from New England, he pointed out, and thus from being integrated into the present United States of America; and in 1635, the year of the French explorer's death, an Englishman named John Hampden was establishing the right of the people's representatives in Parliament to refuse taxation by royal decree. 'Shall not Canadians look back with thankful memory to John Hampden, pioneer of our freedom,' Borden asked, 'and with grateful recognition to Samuel Champlain, pioneer and founder of our heritage?' The two ethnic groups would remain distinct, the former prime minister asserted, but they were 'much nearer to each other than either seems to imagine' and it was 'desirable to emphasize their points of sympathy and contact rather than their divergence of temperament and outlook'. St. Laurent was much impressed by Borden's speech and he was to quote from it on many occasions, partly to further the cause of national unity, and partly to redress what he concluded had been an injustice to a patriotic citizen.

St. Laurent's busy schedule as host to his fellow lawyers proved to be but a preliminary step towards greater responsibilities. When Eugène Lafleur refused to accept the association presidency on grounds of age, the post was offered to the retiring Dominion vice-president, R. B. Bennett. However, the Calgary lawyer had become leader of the Conservative Party and was preparing an all-out attack on the Mackenzie King administration in the 1930 elections; he wished to avoid the additional responsibilities. Finally, Bennett agreed to become president, if St. Laurent became vice-president. St. Laurent's attitude was reflected in his acceptance remarks.

> This association has now reached the point where what it is
> doing for the Canadian people is of such importance that the
> honour and the responsibility of high office are things which no
> member can contemplate without very considerable reluctance
> and trepidation. . . . Our association has become an important
> instrument in welding together elements which are moulding
> the mentality of the Canadian citizen.

A month after the Bar Association meeting, St. Laurent found
himself playing host, in his capacity of president of the Canadian
Club of Quebec, to the annual conference of the Association of
Canadian Clubs. His message to the delegates was similar to the
one he had delivered to his fellow lawyers. The 'broad national
spirit' that the Canadian Clubs aimed to develop must be based
on a legitimate pride in the accomplishments of the 'two parent
races of the Canadian people', plus a common pride in the national wealth they shared. However, the very magnitude of Canada was an obstacle to the development of a common Canadian
mentality, and thus to the development of the immense national
treasure-house. In keeping with his plea for Canadians to get to
know each other better, St. Laurent presented a detailed description of life in Quebec City, complete with statistics of the number
of masses celebrated in the old capital every Sunday, the number
of religious communities, school attendance, real estate values,
and taxes. 'We are your partners in the work of developing a
common national spirit,' he explained, 'but we want you to know
us as we really are, just as we want to know you as you really are.'

In the early summer of 1930, Galipeault ended his political
career by accepting an appointment to the Court of Appeal. The
Liberal organizers in his constituency, Bellechasse County, tried
to persuade St. Laurent to run in his place, but even the prospect
of a provincial cabinet portfolio could not induce him to enter
politics. In late July 1930, many residents of Quebec were astonished and even alarmed to learn on waking up one morning that
the Liberals had been turned out of office in Ottawa, and that
R. B. Bennett would be called upon to form a new government.
Louis St. Laurent was also surprised, but not particularly concerned; he knew Bennett better than he did Mackenzie King,
and he had never believed the vicious propaganda against the

Tory party. Moreover, he felt it would be a healthy development for Canada if both major parties could win the confidence of Canadians in every part of the country.

Bennett was already prime minister when the Canadian Bar Association met in Toronto in August 1930, and Louis St. Laurent had to replace him as presiding officer. He found it strange that a French-speaking Catholic should be welcoming the foreign guests to Canada. He commented:

> Perhaps . . . it will seem an anachronism [to our guests] that in these days a Canadian of French origin and living in Quebec should feel it unusual to find himself occupying the chair at a function like this in the City of Toronto, but I can assure them that it has by no means become an everyday occurrence, and that the Canadian Bar Association is well in the forefront in disseminating the ideal that the whole of Canada is the Canada of all the Canadian citizens, and that their hereditary interest in their country and its institutions applies to the whole of Canada, and to all its component parts.

Before the end of the meeting, his fellow lawyers chose him to succeed the Prime Minister as their national president, making him the first French-speaking Canadian to hold that position. He accepted the post, partly because of his pride in his profession, but, more important, because he felt he would be proving that discrimination was at last being vanquished in Canada and that all citizens had a chance of attaining such positions of nation-wide significance. His only regret was that the choice was motivated to some extent by a desire to have a president from Quebec. 'Geographical considerations still loom very large,' he noted in his acceptance speech, and he expressed the hope that 'some day we will outgrow them, and not have them as restrictions when we are choosing the officers of the Association'.

One of Louis St. Laurent's first functions as president of the Canadian Bar Association was to lead a delegation of members to attend the annual meeting of the American Bar Association in Chicago. He was accompanied by his wife, and by Marthe and Renault, and addressed the huge assembly of lawyers from every part of the continent. Just as the peoples who overthrew the

Roman Empire finished by adopting its laws because of their great value, he stated, so the Americans had maintained the essence of the British legal system, and the Canadians in Quebec had preserved the French system. Laws and language were no longer the monopoly of a single state but a common heritage, he went on, and each country could share in them, every citizen 'glorying ... in his own and each other's untrammelled freedom, yet conscious of his ... responsibility to pass down to the generations yet unborn the same great heritage of common social traditions and common social ideals'. The Quebec press revelled in the knowledge that a French-speaking Canadian had risen to such heights, and had spoken for all of Canada at an international gathering. That autumn, he received an honorary doctorate from Queen's University; he was indeed becoming a person of national stature.

The 1931 meeting of the Canadian Bar Association was held in Murray Bay, on the north shore of the St. Lawrence River, some hundred miles below Quebec City. In his presidential address, St. Laurent referred to the economic depression that had been paralysing Canada for nearly two years, and made it clear that his sympathies lay with Prime Minister Bennett, who had asked for special powers for the purpose of 'relieving distress, providing employment, and, within the competence of Parliament, maintaining peace, order and good government throughout Canada'. In a scarcely veiled reply to those Quebec politicians who saw in such a step a greater danger than the ill it was designed to correct, he argued that the economic situation 'and the dangers which it may portend' justified emergency action, which could be taken 'without ceasing to look upon ourselves as an actual democracy... and without fearing that as a deviation from principle it might be setting a dangerous precedent'.

In the same speech, St. Laurent also dealt with a topic of considerable interest to lawyers at the time – the legal ramifications of Canada's increasing independence of Great Britain. The sovereignty of the Dominions had been recognized by the Balfour Declaration of 1926, and their new situation was about to be translated into law by the Statute of Westminster. Doubts existed whether appeals to the Privy Council would be abolished automatically. Since the Privy Council had decided in 1927 that much of the vast wilderness between Quebec and the Labrador Coast belonged to Newfoundland, dissatisfaction had been growing in French Canada with that body. At Murray Bay, Louis St. Laurent rejected the view that Canada's new status would terminate the appeals automatically, but commented that it would no doubt empower the federal Parliament to do so in its field of jurisdiction and the provincial legislatures in theirs. He did not urge such a step, merely pointing out that, if the appeals continued, it would be 'not in any spirit of subordination, nor because we will be compelled by any authority outside of our own Dominion to do so, but merely because we may of our own free choice, continue to find it convenient to avail ourselves of such advantages as the tribunal offers'. He himself felt that the Supreme Court judges were as likely as the British legal experts to reach sound decisions on Canadian matters, but, he conceded, there were still people who regarded the Privy Council as the ultimate court of appeal. He asked:

> Is that fact, and its soothing effect upon the outraged feelings
> of a disappointed litigant, sufficient to justify the expense and
> delay of sending learned counsel on an enjoyable visit to
> London? I have no doubt that some day it will be found that the
> inconvenience outweighs the conveniences, and ordinary clients
> will be satisfied to let us stay at home, and to accept their fate
> from our own Canadian courts.

As for constitutional disputes between Ottawa and the provinces, he preferred to see them all submitted to the Supreme Court of Canada, and its decisions 'looked upon as binding both on that Court and on the Privy Council in all future similar cases'. Such a practice would lead automatically to recognition of the Supreme Court as the highest tribunal in the Canadian legal system.

St. Laurent's vast knowledge of the law, his personal, almost old-world, charm and dignity, and his sincere, straightforward manner made him a popular president; he was asked to accept a second term. Only Sir James Aikins had served more than one year in that post. He accepted the new mandate as a gesture of goodwill towards the members 'who belong to my race'.

The last meeting of the Canadian Bar Association under St. Laurent's presidency was held in Calgary, Prime Minister Bennett's home town. In his presidential address, he returned to the subject of the Quebec Civil Code, which he had analysed with such success twelve years earlier. It was not a reproduction of the Napoleonic Code, he pointed out, the latter being only 'the pattern to which the Commissioners were to cut our Canadian cloth'; in fact, the differences between the two legal systems within Canada were not much greater than those between English and Scottish law, and were not a greater obstacle to a common loyalty to one King, one flag, and one country.

> It has been my experience [he stated] . . . that these meetings, far
> from showing that we should achieve uniformity of legislation
> in civil matters to foster a broad Canadian nationalism, have
> demonstrated that we are fostering it more quickly and more
> surely by the better realization that this broad Canadian
> nationalism is in no wise incompatible with the retention by
> each of us of social institutions and legal forms which are so
> intimately a part of the civilized status we have inherited from a
> revered and worthy ancestry.

In the single sentence, he summed up his concept of Canada: unity, founded on diversity, and based on mutual respect.

Louis St. Laurent's reaction to the Great Depression and the social and political ferment it fostered reflected his respect for law and order and his strong sense of responsibility. He deplored the inclination of many Canadians to blame their political system for their unhappy state, viewing with equal concern the demands in English Canada for increased federal powers to deal with the situation and the opposite tendency in French Canada, to withdraw within the borders of Quebec. He was sharply critical of young political extremists in Quebec, but even more critical of men in responsible positions like the historian Abbé Lionel Groulx, who encouraged dissatisfaction by his blunt criticism of existing institutions and added fuel to the ever-present flames of anti-English sentiment in Quebec. Addressing a meeting of the St. Charles Seminary alumni in June 1933, St. Laurent said:

Let us not throw the blame on others, but, rather, accept it ourselves. I believe that it is going a bit far to assert as Abbé Groulx does that the present situation is not acceptable to the coming generation and will not be accepted by it. I have little patience with the fits of anger, the impetuousness of the new generation who complain with bitterness of the heritage of their elders. . . .

At the same time, he was prepared to accept his share of responsibility. Referring, in the same speech, to Groulx's complaints that Quebec's economy was falling increasingly into 'foreign' hands, he declared:

I admit that the capital stock of our province is largely controlled, directed and owned by those who are not of our race; but whose fault is that? . . . we have encouraged the others and neglected our own [companies]. . . . Let us support our own businesses and we will succeed in transforming our economic system.

St. Laurent had been impressed by the steps taken by the Gouin administration, which held office from 1905 to 1920, to develop the economic potential of Quebec, but recognized that the Liberals had lost momentum under Gouin's successor, Alexandre Taschereau.

On the national scene, Louis St. Laurent displayed the same genuine concern, strongly tinged with realism, in seeking solutions to the problems that beset Canadians. He believed in 'the progressive results of gradual evolution', he told a graduating class of the University of Manitoba, when receiving an honorary degree from that institution in May 1935; those who wanted to reshape Canada had to remember that the Fathers of Confederation had accepted a certain arrangement because circumstances dictated it, and it was still important to take these facts of Canadian life into account. 'If you do not,' he remarked, '. . . you may have a pretty theory but you cannot make it work.' Rather than by tinkering with the B.N.A. Act, or increasing the powers of the central government, progress towards a strong Canada could best be achieved, he suggested, by making sure that 'every citizen, in every part of Canada, can confidently feel that he has nothing to fear for what he regards as his natural rights of free citizenship from the action of any possible majority'.

As the economic depression continued, the restlessness of the Canadian population grew. In 1935, the Bennett administration was defeated at the polls and Mackenzie King and his fellow Liberals were returned to office in Ottawa; in 1936, the forty-year Liberal reign was ended in Quebec, and Maurice Duplessis, formerly the leader of the Conservative Party in Quebec, became premier under the new banner of the Union Nationale. A group of more extreme Quebec nationalists, including such articulate young men as Paul Bouchard, Pierre Chaloult, and Jean-Louis Gagnon, demanded 'un état libre français en Amérique', in their right-wing weekly newspaper La Nation, and adopted Abbé Groulx as their spiritual leader. Confederation was 'breaking up on its own and . . . nothing can save it from its fate', wrote the priest in a letter to Chaloult early in 1936. Bouchard ran as an 'independent nationalist' candidate in a by-election in Lotbinière constituency in late 1937, predicting another world war and asserting that the Liberals would force overseas service on French-speaking Canadians. Lapointe, once again Minister of Justice, entered the fray and stated unequivocally that 'the government of which I am a member will never apply conscription'. C. G. Power, who had won the Military Cross in World War I, declared: 'I went, I returned, I will not go back and I will send no one.' Reassured, the Lotbinière electorate gave the Liberals a decisive victory.

Watching the political contest from the side-lines, Louis St. Laurent was doubtful of the wisdom of the no-conscription promise; he had learned long ago not to make commitments in advance, particularly when circumstances could not be foreseen. He reacted still more strongly against the separatist declarations of the young firebrands. 'Let us not be preoccupied with building walls around the province of Quebec,' he advised the students of St. Charles Seminary in May 1938. 'We have our well-defined national character, our customs and our faith; all that is a sufficient moral barrier.' The interest of French Canada, he declared, was to proclaim that 'everywhere in Canada, we are chez nous'.

Back in office, the Mackenzie King government had to devise

some way of dealing with the consequences of the prolonged economic crisis. Western Canada was in the most desperate plight, and the three prairie governments were on the verge of defaulting on their financial obligations. In August 1937, a royal commission was formed to re-examine 'the economic and financial basis of Confederation' and 'the distribution of legislative powers in the light of the economic and social developments of the last seventy years'. N. W. Rowell, Chief Justice of Ontario, was named chairman; the other members were Thibaudeau Rinfret of the Supreme Court, John Dafoe, editor of the *Winnipeg Free Press*, H. Angus, University of British Columbia political economist, and R. A. Mackay, political scientist at Dalhousie University in Halifax. St. Laurent's name had been mentioned as a possible commissioner, but he had made it clear that his heavy commitments to his clients and his personal financial situation would prevent him from accepting such an appointment. However, he realized the importance of the commission's assignment, and agreed to serve, with J. M. Stewart of Halifax, as legal counsel.

The commission had not yet begun its work when Rinfret withdrew for reasons of health. Lapointe consulted St. Laurent, who suggested that one of his closest friends, Joseph Sirois, a Quebec City notary and professor of constitutional law at Laval University, would be the most suitable replacement. While he had travelled little outside his own province, and had scarcely any practical experience of the working of Canadian federalism, Sirois brought to the commission the prestige of one of the oldest legal firms in Quebec City, and, in a sense, the seal of approval of the Quebec élite. While he had no particular interest in the work of the commission at the outset, he allowed himself to be persuaded by St. Laurent that it was a duty he should accept; St. Laurent assured him of his close support.

The hearings began in Winnipeg on November 29, 1937, with the frail but erudite Rowell conducting the proceedings as if in his Chief Justice's chair in Toronto. Looking very much the highly-paid eastern Canadian lawyer, in his well-cut conservative suit, his dark hair greying at the temples, and his salt-and-pepper moustache neatly trimmed, Louis St. Laurent took an active part in the proceedings, questioning witnesses closely and becoming involved in lengthy debates on their briefs. It soon became apparent that the problems facing Canada were far more of an economic and financial than a constitutional nature, as many people had presumed. Premier John Bracken of Manitoba declared bluntly that if Ottawa did not come to the rescue of his government soon it would not be able to keep afloat financially, and he suggested that it might be necessary to amalgamate the three prairie provinces in order to reduce expenses and create a more viable economic unit. The Government of Manitoba brief was prepared largely by an American economist from the University of Minnesota, and presented by the Provincial Treasurer, Stuart Garson. It advocated vastly greater federal intervention in the fields of fiscal and economic policy, including manipulation of the value of the dollar to maintain Canada's competitive position in the world market. Such proposals went far beyond anything that St. Laurent had contemplated; he was taken aback both by their radical nature and by the plea of the provincial authorities for an increase in the activities of the federal government. He also came into direct contact for the first time with the prevailing sentiment in western Canada that the prairies are the milch cow of eastern Canada, and that since most of Ottawa's policies are designed to serve the East, they are inevitably harmful to the West. When St. Laurent argued that maintaining the exchange rate of the dollar had not helped eastern Canada very much, he was told that 'if it . . . weighed heavily on the West, then it must have benefited the East.' The situation in Saskatchewan proved to be even worse than in Manitoba. Over 50 per cent of the population was receiving government relief, the commission was informed, and there were neither funds to continue aid to the unemployed nor prospects of jobs to enable them to look after themselves. The brief presented by the Saskatchewan government urged a system of federal grants on a per-capita basis, a universal old-age pension for persons over sixty-five years of age, and an extensive list of other federal measures; in return, the brief suggested that the provinces abandon completely the income, corporation, and succession tax fields. To St. Laurent, it was a revolutionary proposal, and directly opposed to his concept of Confederation, with each government autonomous in its own field of jurisdiction and paying its own way.

Under Rowell's direction, the commissioners and their staff formed an efficient team. 'This is a hard-working Commission...,' commented J. B. McGeachy in a series entitled 'Confederation Clinic' in the *Winnipeg Free Press*. 'Witnesses are examined in brisk style and are not encouraged to be long-winded.' He described St. Laurent's examinations as 'a model of concision'. In one exchange with T. C. Davis, the Saskatchewan Attorney General, St. Laurent questioned a statement that no more money could be raised by taxes, and was told that 'there is no hope of soaking the rich in these parts, because there are no rich'. 'Have you ever thought of soaking the farmers?' St. Laurent retorted, still clinging to the Easterner's view that many western agriculturalists drove Cadillacs and spent their winters in California. 'After a remark like that, of course, Mr. St. Laurent couldn't get elected as a dog-catcher anywhere in Saskatchewan,' the *Free Press* correspondent commented in reporting the incident.

The revelations of that western trip troubled St. Laurent deeply, and forced him to reconsider many of his views on Canada. As a boy, he had heard Laurier state in Sherbrooke that the West was the land of the future, with limitless possibilities, and he had accepted the statement at face value; forty years later, the area was apparently already overpopulated, and dependent on outside support. The demands he heard for state medicine, a national system of unemployment insurance, old-age pensions, and the transfer to Ottawa of provincial debts seemed tantamount to remaking the federal system; on the other hand, he realized that a situation could not be allowed to continue in which municipalities could not even raise enough taxes to feed people who were starving. There was no doubt that the decisions of the Privy Council had limited 'deplorably' the powers of the Dominion government in certain fields, he told members of the Cercle de la Pensée Française in Winnipeg before returning home for Christmas. 'It seems likely that our constitution will have to be amended if Confederation is to survive.' How the important changes demanded in the West were to be reconciled with the

Quebec government's special responsibility to protect the rights of French-speaking Canadians, he did not know. In his capacity as commission counsel, he was brought face to face with the greatest dilemma of Canadian politics.

When the commission began its hearings in central Canada, it ran into serious difficulties. Although Rowell had been assured by Maurice Duplessis, shortly after the commission was created, of the 'entire co-operation' of Quebec, reports began to circulate early in 1938 of a plan by Duplessis and Ontario Premier Mitchell Hepburn, a Liberal but at odds with Mackenzie King, to frustrate its work, on the grounds that it was investigating subjects of provincial concern. The two premiers had much in common: they were both extroverted, hard-driving, hard-drinking men who revelled in the prestige and power of their offices, and were united in their opposition to Ottawa. During a series of visits at Hepburn's farm outside of Toronto, and at Duplessis's bachelor suite in the Château Frontenac Hotel in Quebec, they frolicked and fraternized, and agreed to stand together against the common foe. When the commission began its hearings in Toronto in May, Hepburn appeared before it, but only to castigate it with a brutality that deeply shocked the gentlemanly chairman. The Ontario premier insisted that provincial autonomy be respected, that the financial resources of the provinces be increased rather than decreased, and that an interprovincial conference be called to discuss constitutional changes. His stand was tantamount to a boycott of the commission.

Everyone who noticed Duplessis's rumblings about the 'centralizing tendencies' of the Liberals in Ottawa suspected that the attitude of the Ontario premier was but a preview of what was awaiting the team of investigators in Quebec. Beside himself with worry, Rowell collapsed with a cerebral attack, thus ending his contribution to the vital study. When the commission began its hearings in Quebec on May 12, Joseph Sirois was in the chair. The role of St. Laurent took on added importance in the delicate situation. Besides trying to obtain the co-operation of the Union Nationale government, he had to bolster the spirits of his friend Sirois, who was horrified at being precipitated into the centre of the controversy, and concerned over finding himself at odds with an important segment of Quebec opinion. In fact, it was only after much persuasion from St. Laurent that he accepted the temporary chairmanship. St. Laurent was hardly the ideal person to deal with the Quebec premier. He had shown his distaste repeatedly for Duplessis's political tactics, and they had clashed openly at meetings of the Private Bills Committee of the Quebec Legislature. On one occasion when Duplessis was attacking the chain stores as 'exploiters' of the common man and a 'band of thieves', he had dared the Union Nationale boss to repeat his charge outside the committee room, where he would not be protected by parliamentary immunity. The challenge went unanswered, but the feeling of animosity between the two men remained.

In his opening statement, Sirois tried to set a conciliatory tone by declaring that the commission had no authority to change the constitution but was merely instructed to gather information from all interested parties 'on the ways of improving and harmonizing relations between the Dominion and the provinces', and was directed to stay 'within the strict limits of the federal constitution'. His efforts were in vain; Maurice Duplessis did not even appear, but his legal counsel, Emery Beaulieu, read a statement denying the right of the commission to carry out a unilateral investigation of federal-provincial relations.

> To recognize the authority of your Commission would be, in a way, to recognize the supremacy of the federal authority in matters of provincial jurisdiction [he declared]. . . . Despite the very clever choice of expressions in the Order in Council, it is clear that the government of Canada intends to use the report, if your conclusions are appropriate, to introduce a measure aimed at amending the constitution in the direction of an ever greater centralization.

Under the circumstances, the Quebec government refused to take any further part in the proceedings.

Other submissions had been prepared, and, while they were being received, members of the commission continued to hope that the Quebec premier would have a change of heart. St. Laurent issued specific invitations to Beaulieu and several senior civil servants to testify, but they went unanswered. On the final day of the week-long hearings, he put on the record a series of twenty-three questions he had intended to ask. They provided an opportunity to elaborate on criticisms made by the Quebec government of the existing federal system in fields such as federal subsidies to the provinces, federal-provincial conferences, over-lapping services, unemployment insurance, social and labour legislation, the delegation of powers from one government to another, human rights, and the treaty-making power of Canada. The views of the provincial administration would have been invaluable in seeking answers to questions it itself had raised; Duplessis preferred to play the role of champion of French-Canadian rights by abstaining, rather than by trying to convince the commissioners of his point of view, and perhaps influencing their conclusions.

The aloofness of the Union Nationale leader in public was in marked contrast to his attitude behind closed doors. At a lunch-eon reception given by Lieutenant-Governor Patenaude, he met the commissioners and their staff, and, after a few drinks, decided to invite them to his office at the end of the day. Anxious to oblige, and hoping he was having a change of heart, they hastened to accept. Duplessis was in high spirits when they arrived, and received them with boisterous good humour and large quantities of champagne. Although Dafoe was a teetotaller and Sirois and St. Laurent very moderate drinkers, they went along with the spirit of the occasion. Eventually the premier declared in a loud voice to a member of the commission staff that he thought they were a fine bunch of fellows, and that he was inviting them all to dinner in the Château Frontenac. Once again, the group submitted to his will. As they had been bidden, they assembled in the hotel lobby promptly at eight o'clock to meet their host, and to be taken to a private dining-room. The minutes passed, and then the quarter-hours, but Maurice Duplessis did not appear. About 8:45 p.m., as they were debating whether to try to find a meal somewhere else, he burst through the revolving doors, fol-lowed by a string of acolytes. Flushed and unsteady, he glowered at them, and snorted that he wished people from Ottawa would learn to keep appointments on time when they came to a provincial capital. Then, having delivered the reprimand, he laughed uproariously at his own humour, and led the way to the elevator. At table, he continued to enjoy himself at their expense, proposing frequent toasts and insisting that those he drank with call him by his first name. He took particular delight in poking fun at the more sober members of the group. Dafoe was his favourite target, and the great newspaperman was subjected to such rudeness that both Sirois and St. Laurent were embarrassed as residents of Quebec at the treatment accorded him, but all three managed to maintain their composure. As soon as the meal was over, and it was obvious that the really serious drinking was about to begin, they withdrew with a tremendous sense of relief. The party continued for several hours, champagne being brought in by the case; when one brand was found to be of inferior quality, it was tossed through the fire-escape door. As the drunkenness increased, the bawdy good humour turned to rowdiness, and glasses, dishes, and other movable objects soared through the room. An ardent baseball fan, Duplessis proved expert in knocking out electric light bulbs with champagne glasses. One man was hit by flying glass, and had to be escorted down the fire escape and through the front door of the hotel to give the impression that he had been hurt in a street accident. Some time in the early hours of the morning, the secretary of the commission, Alexander Skelton, was huddled behind a chair, peering through the bars, determined to witness the end of the spectacle. He was the last of the visitors to have direct contact with the Quebec government before the commission moved on to the Maritimes.

By the autumn of 1938, the hearings were completed and the commissioners sat down to prepare their report; since St. Laurent was not directly involved in writing the final document, his contribution might have ended there, except that a disagreement arose concerning the recommendations to be made as a result of the study. The commissioners and their advisers had been impressed by the evidence that most of the provinces could not look after their unemployed, and there was a strong feeling that, for both humanitarian and financial reasons, the responsibility for unemployment insurance, a field of provincial jurisdiction, should be transferred to the federal government. It was also felt that income, succession, and corporation taxes should be collected by Ottawa in order to ensure a uniform tax structure, and that subsidies should be paid to the provinces on the basis of need – need to be judged on the ability to provide services according to a national average. While the other commissioners agreed on that position, Sirois saw in it a serious departure from the provisions of the B.N.A. Act, and from the principle that there should be a clear delimitation of responsibilities and financial powers between the two levels of government. He was convinced that the proposed changes would be unacceptable in Quebec. After long consideration, he finally decided he would have to differ, and began to prepare a minority report.

The situation was serious. A dissenting opinion by the chairman of the commission, and the only member from Quebec, would not only constitute a failure of the whole investigation but would emphasize the differences of opinion that it was hoped to resolve. In a desperate move to avert such a disaster, St. Laurent and his fellow legal counsel, Stewart, were called in again. They arrived in Ottawa shortly before noon, were briefed on the situation over a light lunch, and met the commissioners and their staff at two o'clock. 'I was never prouder to see legal minds at work,' one participant declared later; 'they were like two tennis players batting the ball back and forth with ease and style.' A couple of years earlier, St. Laurent would have had more sympathy for the Quebec-Ontario point of view, but he had travelled across the country and seen the situation for himself. Canadians were in need in every part of the country, he argued, and only the national government could give them effective aid. A problem so obviously of national dimensions as unemployment insurance required action at the national level. By five o'clock, the critical meeting was over; Sirois continued to ponder the issue for a day or two, but he eventually rallied to the majority point of view. 'Sirois is rather cross with me,' St. Laurent commented afterward, 'but he'll get over it because the decision is right.'

World War II broke over the world in early September 1939, and Canada entered the conflict on September 10, after a decent period of waiting to convince reluctant citizens, particularly in Quebec, that the action was no headlong plunge to follow the

British lead, but the decision of a sovereign nation. Maurice Duplessis did not wait long to exploit the situation; he called a snap provincial election for October 25 on the grounds that he needed a clear mandate to prevent the Liberals from using the war as a pretext to centralize power in Ottawa and to impose conscription for overseas service.* A provincial government led by local Liberal leader Adélard Godbout, he asserted, would be a mere puppet régime doing the bidding of Anglo-Saxon-dominated Ottawa. The real Liberal leader in Quebec was Ernest Lapointe, Duplessis declared, and he challenged the Minister of Justice to do battle with him on the hustings.

The Union Nationale leader's strategy of choosing the federal government as his principal target, and of condemning the provincial Liberals by association, seemed almost foolproof at first glance; observers chuckled at the prospect of the Liberals' being beaten by the stick of conscription that they had used on Duplessis's own party when he had been a Conservative. Godbout fought back as best he could. 'Liberalism is a rampart against conscription,' he declared after consulting Lapointe, and it would never be introduced under a Liberal government. 'I pledge on my honour, weighing each of my words, to leave my party and even to oppose it if a single French Canadian is mobilized against his will between now and the end of the war by a Liberal administration or even a temporary administration including Ministers in the King Cabinet.' Four days later, Lapointe picked up the gauntlet thrown down before him by Duplessis. The provincial election was 'an act of national sabotage', he stated in a radio broadcast on October 9, and he and his colleagues would stake their careers on its outcome. Following Godbout's example, Ernest Lapointe, Public Works Minister Cardin, and Postmaster General Power pledged that 'we will never consent to conscription, that we will never be members of a government that tries to introduce it, and that we will never support such a government'. Maurice Duplessis's tactics backfired; Godbout emerged victorious with over three-quarters of the seats in the Quebec assembly. In March 1940, Mackenzie King called a federal election. It was hardly an

*Compulsory military service *within* Canada was never an issue; it was introduced early in the war.

interesting contest. The anti-conscription pledge was repeated throughout Quebec; Mackenzie King won the greatest victory of his career, and left the Tories with but one seat in 'la belle province'. The political scene appeared to be set for the duration of the war.

When St. Laurent rushed back from London in August 1939, he was in some ways a very different man from the one who had shrugged his shoulders at World War I as none of his business. Twenty years of contact with the world outside Quebec had made him realize that a community of interests existed, not only with other Canadians, but with other peoples as well. The fall of France in 1940 disturbed him deeply, and he followed the news of the Battle of Britain almost with a sense of direct involvement, convinced that, if the British were also obliged to surrender, North America would be directly threatened. He was already in his late fifties, and there seemed at first little that he could contribute personally to the war effort. Early in 1941, he responded to a call from Finance Minister James L. Ralston to assist with the Victory Loan Campaign. As co-chairman of the Quebec campaign committee, he spent a large part of the spring of 1941 touring the eastern part of the province, urging his fellow citizens to put their money into Victory Bonds. 'We have to face the facts,' he advised a huge crowd in Quebec City on June 1, 1941, after watching a parade of 7,500 troops, 'and admit that the war is being fought to prevent the enslavement of the world by dictators.' Canada was at war, he told the Montreal Rotary Club a few days later, and on the outcome of that war depended 'the very existence of Canada and of Canadian institutions and the life and freedom of the Canadian people'. To encourage subscriptions, Cardinal Villeneuve wrote an open letter to St. Laurent, urging Roman Catholics to support the campaign 'as a sacred duty' and warning of 'the deadly danger to our beloved Canada'. Premier Godbout threw his support behind the campaign as well, urging French-speaking Canadians to realize that the outcome of the war was of vital interest to each one of them, and warning that 'we would be the first to be affected if the Empire were to fall'.

The Victory Loan Campaign in Quebec was a success, not only in terms of dollars, but also in improving the image of the province in the rest of Canada. The mayor of Montreal, Camillien Houde, had been interned in August 1940 for advising the population not to register with the government, rightist leader Adrien Arcand had been arrested, and a group of young men in Montreal were openly hostile to an all-out war effort. St. Laurent was pleased to be able to demonstrate that such people did not represent all of French Canada. 'The unanimity demonstrated during this campaign augurs well for the future,' he stated proudly in thanking contributors on June 25, 1941. 'Our country will come out of this conflict stronger and better prepared to face the promising future; the recent weeks have shown that the Canadian people are capable of great achievements.' Then, having given a major part of his time over a period of three months to the savings campaign, St. Laurent returned with a sense of relief to his own business, to his family. The next call from Ottawa was to disrupt his private life for a much longer period.

# 5

## Conscript

Conscription was among the subjects discussed at the first cabinet meeting that Louis St. Laurent attended, on December 10, 1941. Mackenzie King escorted him into the Council Chamber, introduced him to the ministers around the heavy oval table, and installed him in Ernest Lapointe's former chair on his immediate right. The choice of seat was significant since it suggested that St. Laurent was to be the principal representative from Quebec, a role he had no desire or intention to assume, and he feared that the gesture would arouse jealousy among the other ministers. Most of his new colleagues were strangers to him; he knew Ralston and Power, but he had only a superficial acquaintance with the other Quebec ministers, Senator Raoul Dandurand and Arthur Cardin. It is hardly likely that Dandurand recognized him as the Laval law student who had asked him in 1904 for the party's support to help his storekeeper father get elected as a provincial candidate.

The United States and Japan having entered the conflict a few days earlier, James Ralston, who had become Minister of National Defence in July 1941, presented a new and expanded army program for the global struggle that lay ahead. A thoroughly upright man, he stated frankly that he did not know whether enough men could be obtained by voluntary enlistment, and that he might have to inform Parliament accordingly when it met in a few days; if sufficient volunteers were not available, he felt that conscription would have to be introduced. The dreaded word was pronounced. The Prime Minister warned of the dangers of such a step, both to the country and to the Liberal Party. Cardin, still frail from his heart attack, supported him with the blunt prediction that there would no longer be a Liberal Party worthy of the name in Canada if conscription was introduced, and warned that he was not simply going to renounce all that he and Lapointe had done to encourage the province of Quebec to play its full part in the struggle on a voluntary basis. St. Laurent observed the debate with keen interest, both because of the importance of the issue, and for the opportunity to assess his new colleagues. On the subject of conscription, they seemed to fall into three groups. A hard core of English-speaking Canadians, including Ralston, Minister of Defence for Naval Services Angus Macdonald, Minister of Mines and Resources T. A. Crerar, and Minister of National Revenue Colin Gibson, were ready to insist on conscription if it was necessary for a total war effort. The anti-conscriptionists were led by Cardin, and included Agriculture Minister James Gardiner and the Prime Minister himself. Between the two extremes was a more heterogeneous group, less committed to a firm viewpoint, and seeking a compromise solution. In this category was C. G. Power, who was committed to oppose conscription, but who, as Associate Minister of National Defence and Minister for Air, could also appreciate the viewpoint of those who advocated conscription if necessary. He suggested that the entry of Japan into the war would justify calling up much larger numbers of men for home defence, thus releasing those who were willing to go overseas. Mackenzie King accepted the suggestion eagerly, warning that Japanese bombings, and even landings, had to be anticipated, and that the need was for strength at home. Ralston was not convinced; the necessity, he insisted, was for troops to serve abroad, where the fighting would take place.

Even though he was gone, and his successor appointed, Ernest Lapointe's influence was still felt in the Council Chamber. What position would he have taken, ministers wondered, and would St. Laurent assume his no-conscription pledge as he had his portfolio and his chair? In his last letter to the Prime Minister, Lapointe had declared that he was 'ready to fight very strongly, if conscription became an issue', and he had repeated that view shortly before he died. On the other hand, he had been devoted to national unity, and it seemed conceivable to some who knew him well that if he were convinced that conscription was essential to Canada's survival, he might have accepted it. As for St. Laurent, he had always had doubts about the wisdom of making the commitment not to introduce compulsory military service; such major problems, he felt, should be decided on their merits at the time when a decision had to be taken. Following a practice developed over a period of forty years, his contribution to the four-hour discussion consisted of a series of penetrating questions and comments designed to present the issue in the clearest possible light. Mackenzie King was pleased with his new minister's initial performance, recording later in his diary that St. Laurent 'took his place in a moment among those present', and 'entered into the debate . . . to good effect'.

The first cabinet meeting was merely a preliminary contact with government business; before getting down to serious work as a member of the team, St. Laurent had to obtain a seat in Parliament. That same day writs were issued for by-elections in Lapointe's former constituency of Quebec East, where he was to run, and in three other constituencies – Montreal–St. Mary; Welland, Ontario; and York South, in the Toronto area. Another new member of the cabinet, Minister of Labour Humphrey Mitchell, was to stand in Welland; the contest in York South resulted from the resignation of a Conservative member to make way for Arthur Meighen, who had agreed to return to the House of Commons from the Senate to replace R. B. Hanson as Leader of the Opposition. The 'father of conscription', as Meighen was known in Quebec, was returning to do battle with his long-time foe, Mackenzie King, and, almost certainly, to lead the fight for compulsory overseas service.

Although the comments of both Liberal and Tory press throughout Canada on his appointment were highly laudatory, St. Laurent was not at all certain of the reception he would receive from the Lower Town residents of Quebec City who would be asked to elect him as their representative in Parliament. While he had felt obliged to join the cabinet, he was determined not to have recourse to the methods usually associated with Quebec politics in order to obtain a seat in Parliament. It was his duty to offer his services; if his offer was rejected, he could return to private life with an easy conscience. Such were the thoughts running through his mind as he arrived at the railway station in Quebec City on December 12 in company with his daughter Madeleine, who had just been promoted to the rank of captain and was being transferred to a new post in her home town. A large crowd, led by Adélard Godbout and Oscar Drouin, the provincial Minister of Commerce, Industry and Municipal Affairs, were on hand to meet him, and in his address of welcome the eloquent little premier proclaimed him 'the powerful man who will be the authorized spokesman of our nationality'. Flushed and moved as he was called on to make his first political speech on his own behalf, St. Laurent mounted a bench in the hall of the station, and told the enthusiastic audience in a voice filled with emotion that he was proud of the reaction across Canada to his appointment; 'proud for myself and proud for my family naturally, but proud, too, for my city, my race, my province; proud that people know from one end of the country to the other that in this old French city of Quebec anyone can be asked to perform any service of which he is believed capable, and he will answer: here I am, what am I to do?' In the hour of crisis, one thought dominated all others, he went on. 'We are Canadians, we have remained Canadians for three centuries. We remember our ancestors and we think of our descendants.' The speech-making lasted an hour; it was almost midnight before his family managed to get him into the car and take him home.

The following morning, St. Laurent began looking into the matter of getting elected. Having been briefed by Power before leaving Ottawa, he knew that one of the persons directly involved was Oscar Drouin, who in addition to being a minister in the Godbout cabinet, and the provincial member for Quebec East, was also president of the federal constituency organization and chief local organizer. A strong French-Canadian nationalist, he represented the most determinedly anti-conscriptionist wing of

the provincial cabinet, and had taken at face value Ernest Lapointe's promise that compulsory overseas service would never be
introduced by the Liberals. He soon made it evident that he
expected the new minister to give a similar undertaking. The
other key men in the constituency were Colonel Oscar Gilbert,
owner of the Lower Town Hôtel St-Roch, an establishment of
somewhat dubious reputation, and Jean-Marie Dessureault, a
leading lumber merchant, alderman, and local Liberal Party
treasurer. Both Gilbert and Dessureault had given valuable assistance to Lapointe and had some reason to hope for recognition
in return, in the form of the Quebec East nomination, a senatorship, or some other political reward. Their hopes formed part of
the heritage left by Ernest Lapointe. Since he was merely asking
to be elected for one term to perform a patriotic service, St.
Laurent was determined not to become involved in party affairs
there any more than was absolutely necessary. For the moment,
however, he needed some help, and he chose Dessureault as the
person most likely to provide it on terms he could accept. On his
first day back in Quebec City, he spent much of the afternoon in
the lumberman's office near the harbour, urging him to act as his
official agent. He knew nothing of politics, St. Laurent insisted,
and had no idea how to proceed. Dessureault acceded to the
request.

The official invitation to accept the Liberal nomination was
presented shortly before Christmas by a delegation of Liberals
from the constituency led by Oscar Drouin and the mayor of
Quebec, Lucien Borne. In an obvious attempt to bind the new
minister's hands, Drouin declared that the population wished the
policies followed by Lapointe to be continued. St. Laurent ignored the suggestion; he had no intention of replacing Lapointe,
he stated, but he could promise 'as sincere and patriotic a devotion as his'. 'We French-speaking Canadians have been here for
three hundred years, . . .' he told the delegation. 'This land
belongs to us . . . and we must continue to live here. . . . We are
only 2 per cent of the North American population but we are
as good as the others and our race can obtain perfect equality
with the best of them.' The Prime Minister had told him that it
would be an irreparable loss for Canada if the French-Canadian

influence in Ottawa were to decrease. 'I told him that such a statement did him honour . . . and I promised him my support because he knew he could count on the word of a French-speaking Canadian.' When the little group of Liberals filed out of the office, they were impressed by the sincerity and the elevation of the reply they had received, but far from convinced that they had picked a political winner in Quebec East.

The St. Laurents spent a dismal Christmas. Tense and pre-occupied, the head of the family sat silently in his living-room chair throughout most of the festive season, listening to every radio news report, and refusing to be drawn into the usual family activities. His wife and children tried to make him relax, remarking that he need not feel he had taken on personal responsibility for the entire war, but he appeared to be conjuring up visions of Canadians dying on the battlefield because of his decisions. St. Laurent could not tell them the main cause for his concern: before he left Ottawa, he had learned that a large unit of Canadian troops had landed in Hong Kong, that the Japanese had attacked the tiny British colony within days of their arrival, and that it seemed unlikely that any would escape. In view of his depressed mood, his family was almost relieved when he returned to the capital to hear Winston Churchill address a joint session of the Canadian Parliament on December 30. The family life they cherished had, in truth, been suspended for the duration of the war.

Early in the new year of 1942, Power installed himself in a Château Frontenac suite and took charge of the election preparations. Drouin was still officially the local organizer, but was displaying an evident reluctance to act until the candidate's stand on conscription was determined. On January 12, St. Laurent toured the constituency with Power, visiting the different Liberal organizations such as the Club Lapointe and the Club Ouvrier Libéral, and meeting the party workers whose personal efforts were essential to his election. It was impossible to have a French-speaking Canadian as head of the government at the moment, he told one group, and, in the circumstances, there was no one who deserved their confidence more than Prime Minister Mackenzie King. Questioned on the subject of conscription, he repeated the government's official statement that the mobilization law would not be amended without first consulting the Canadian people. St. Laurent's reference to consultation was more significant than his audience realized. Although hardly any Canadian troops had seen battle, pressure was building up in the other provinces in favour of conscription, and Mackenzie King was finding his promise increasingly embarrassing. Meighen was campaigning vigorously in Toronto in favour of compulsory overseas service, and there was a real possibility that the Conservatives would introduce an amendment to the Speech from the Throne to that effect when the new session of Parliament began in February. Fearing that an open debate on the issue would divide the country and perhaps even the government, the Prime Minister suggested to the cabinet that a referendum might be held to test public opinion. If the result was an even split, he reasoned, it would be obvious to all Canadians that compulsory military service could not be introduced; if there was a firm majority in favour of such a step, the government's hands would no longer be tied, and the Liberals could still argue that it would be better for them to administer the country's war efforts than to let the responsibility fall into other hands. The English-speaking ministers approved the suggestion, and Cardin and Dandurand also found merit in it at first, but after thinking it over during the Christmas holiday they began to fear that it would be interpreted in Quebec as a sly manoeuvre to pave the way for conscription. St. Laurent adopted the attitude that he was not bound by any previous commitments, and he joined Mackenzie King in seeking a workable solution to the dilemma. The worried Prime Minister noted his attitude with keen appreciation. In the end, Cardin and Dandurand fell in line, and the cabinet agreed on a plebiscite to 'seek . . . release from any obligation arising out of past commitments restricting methods of raising men for military service'.

As Cardin had predicted, the announcement of the plebiscite sent an almost visible shudder of alarm through French Canada. The Liberal newspaper *Le Soleil* warned that Mackenzie King was not remaining true to Sir Wilfrid Laurier; Premier Godbout came under such heavy pressure from cabinet colleagues that he felt obliged to state that conscription for overseas service would be a crime, and to express the conviction that Mackenzie King would never take such a step. Oscar Drouin demanded that St. Laurent declare his opposition to conscription categorically, and, when the Minister of Justice refused, he resigned as constituency organizer. Jean-Marie Dessureault agreed to take his place. Fearing a general revolt among Quebec Liberals, Mackenzie King thanked Arthur Cardin in caucus for agreeing to the plebiscite, and asked him formally 'to take his place at my right side . . . as Leader of his Province'. With Godbout being referred to by *Le Soleil* as 'le chef du Canada français', Louis St. Laurent might well have wondered why he had been given Lapointe's seat in the Council Chamber; such matters were of little importance to him; he was only a temporary politician.

Since something of a moratorium had been declared on federal politics since the 1940 election, the Liberals were hoping that St. Laurent would be elected by acclamation in Quebec East. However, as soon as the plebiscite was announced, Paul Bouchard, the right-wing Quebec nationalist who had run in Lotbinière County in 1937, and extracted from the Liberals the no-conscription pledge, announced that he would run under the banner of a new party, the Parti Canadien. He soon attracted support from politicians of a variety of political hues, including Conservatives, Union Nationale members and rebellious Liberals; among the most active and outspoken were the Liberal member of Parliament Liguori Lacombe and the Independent Conservative member Sasseville Roy. A third candidate also appeared, but dropped out before the end of the race. Meanwhile, in Welland constituency, an all-out conscriptionist candidate was chosen to stand against Humphrey Mitchell.

Chubby Power decided that the election of St. Laurent in Quebec East must be clearly distinguished from the plebiscite, or the Minister of Justice might be in serious trouble. His fears were confirmed when the chairman of a small meeting of Liberal workers at the Salle Laprise agreed to support the new minister, but stated flatly that he would fight 'to the end' against conscription. The by-election was the immediate question to be settled, the organizers were told; the plebiscite was another subject, and would be discussed in due course.

The day following his sixtieth birthday, St. Laurent made his first appeal to the electorate by radio. He had lived in Quebec City for nearly forty years, he told his listeners; he had a wife, children, and grandchildren, as well as sincere friends and clients who placed their trust in him. Why should he abandon all that to go to Ottawa and work fifteen hours a day at a crushing job that would not enable him even to pay his taxes and the insurance premiums to protect his family? Because the payment of insurance premiums was not enough to guarantee his family and other Canadian families against the danger that hung over them. 'There is no heroism about it,' he declared, 'it is simply a realization, cold, calculated, selfish, if you want, of the peril that threatens us, and of the price that must be paid to avoid it.' Referring to the forthcoming plebiscite, he gave the assurance that 'the Prime Minister will not repudiate his promises if you do not agree to cancelling them'. At the same time, he left little doubt that the government would ask to be freed from its commitment, and that he himself would join in making that request. 'If you elect me I will support Mr. King,' he stated, but if Mr. King should disappear, 'I will support no other government leader who does not have the confidence of my province.' So much for high statesmanship; St. Laurent's advisers had impressed on him that a politician must appeal to the voters on a level they could understand. With strong misgivings, he had made some concessions in that regard in preparing his address. The Prime Minister conceived of Canada as a sovereign nation, he went on, and in the words of the late Governor General, Lord Tweedsmuir, 'The first duty of a Canadian is not toward the British Commonwealth, but toward Canada and its King, and those who dispute that render a bad service to the Commonwealth.' The attitude of the Conservative leader, Arthur Meighen, in contrast, was characterized by 'a blind, sentimental, arrogant, and intransigent attachment to England. . . . For people like him Canada has never been and will never be anything but a conquered colony.' There was more to come. 'I know that the word "conscription" brings back memories of 1917,' St. Laurent remarked in conclusion. 'Let us not place ourselves in the position where a Meighen government could come and impose it on us with bayonets and machine guns.'

There could hardly have been a greater contrast between two candidates than between Louis St. Laurent and his Parti Canadien opponent. St. Laurent was a gentleman, Paul Bouchard conceded in opening his campaign on February 2, but he belonged to the 'ring of two hundred', the 'little group of financiers and bankers from Toronto who control the economy and all the riches of the country'. As for the Liberals, the only reason they did not form a union government as in 1917 and impose conscription was that they wanted all the patronage for themselves. A 'political police' was operating in the area under the authority of the Minister of Justice, he charged, and had threatened to put him in a concentration camp. 'Can you see it, a Justice Minister elected by acclamation because he made his opponent disappear!' Posing alternately as the Eamon de Valera and the George Washington of Canada, Bouchard offered to lead the country into republican status after the war.

St. Laurent's biggest test of the campaign came on February 5, when he spoke to a small crowd in the Limoilou parish hall, in the heart of the constituency. The area had been the scene of rioting in the 1917 crisis, and it was assumed that the working-class population was solidly opposed to conscription. On the previous evening, the Godbout cabinet had discussed the issue hotly until well after midnight, and some ministers had only agreed to attend the meeting 'for appearances' sake'. There was a noticeable reluctance among local Liberal dignitaries to occupy the chairs on the platform. Premier Godbout was the first speaker, and he appealed for party unity, in order 'not to open the door to the conscriptionists'. Oscar Drouin followed, and declared categorically that, while he supported St. Laurent, he would fight against the federal government in the coming plebiscite campaign. The audience cheered him enthusiastically. Other speakers followed, including Power, who tried valiantly to warm up the audience by a humorous attack on Bouchard. Then St. Laurent was introduced, and, fitting his pince-nez into place, he began to read his prepared text, glancing only occasionally at his listeners. It was a competent statement for a court-room, or a directors' meeting, but it found no echo in the Lower Town hall. The other men on the platform, and the audience, were as relieved as he was when it was over. As soon as he had finished, he put aside his papers, removed his glasses, straightened his shoulders, and began again. 'And now,' he stated, with an intensity that made the audience snap to attention, 'I want you to know what Louis St. Laurent is made of.' He remembered with horror the sound of machine-guns in the streets of Quebec in 1917, and felt it would be a catastrophe if that happened again. 'I don't hesitate a minute to say that I am against that kind of conscription, but I am in favour of French-speaking Canadians doing what is necessary along with the others to defend our dear country. It is the privilege of nations to defend themselves, and to pass on to coming generations the advantages they have enjoyed.' The crowd tensed, sensing that something important was happening. 'For my part,' he continued firmly, 'I will probably come and ask you to vote "yes" on the plebiscite. You can listen to me or not; you will be free to do what you want.' He would do his duty as he saw it, he declared, and accept their verdict. No one doubted the sense of his words; he would support conscription if he felt it was necessary. St. Laurent's heated outburst lasted only two or three minutes; then he sat down. In the heavy silence that followed, Power leaned over to Renault St. Laurent, beside him on the platform, and whispered, 'It takes a brave man to say that.' In the audience, André Taschereau, a junior law partner, commented to Marthe Samson, 'Your father is beaten.' Then, like a burst of thunder, the clapping and cheering broke upon the room. As the men on the platform stared in disbelief, someone leaped up and began singing the victory song: 'Il a gagné ses épaulettes'. It was a happy crowd that jostled its way out into the street. 'At least that one doesn't try to shoot us a line,' a burly worker was heard to remark.

One of the main difficulties faced by Power was to find speakers to support the candidate. Usually eager to demonstrate their support of a minister, local Liberals hung back, afraid of compromising their own careers. Sarto Fournier, member of Parliament for Montreal-Maisonneuve, was on the way through Ottawa to help Humphrey Mitchell in Ontario when he learned of the problem. The situation was 'terrible', Power complained to him dejectedly; 'no one will move', and 'St. Laurent doesn't understand anything' about campaigning. Fournier offered to speak in Quebec East instead of in Welland. 'Come along if you feel like getting into the furnace,' the minister told him, but he warned that Bouchard was a dangerous opponent with strong appeal among members of the younger generation. Fournier accepted the challenge. The only other outside speakers were Senator Léon Mercier Gouin and Robert Laurier, an Ontario cabinet minister and nephew of Sir Wilfrid Laurier. A few radio broadcasts were made from Ottawa.

As the campaign progressed, St. Laurent's oratorical style improved; he abandoned his prepared texts and spoke directly to the crowds as he would to his own children. Even his organizers were surprised to discover that under the imposing surface was a warm-hearted and uncomplicated human being. On the whole, he was, in their eyes, a 'good' candidate; that is, he accepted the schedules prepared for him, turned up on time for appointments, and listened carefully to Power's advice. In Ottawa, Mackenzie King followed the contest closely, telephoning frequently to Power and Dessureault for detailed reports, and exhorting them to ever greater efforts. He was so anxious for a victory there and in York South that he dared not let himself believe the optimistic reports from the two constituencies. The Liberals did not run a candidate against Arthur Meighen, but they spread the word among the electorate to vote for the C.C.F. candidate, Joseph Noseworthy; they also advised the Socialists on tactics, organized polls, and helped prepare campaign literature. In Quebec East, Paul Bouchard put on a vigorous campaign, asserting that St. Laurent was already a member of a secret cabinet committee created to organize conscription, and that preparations had been made for his own arrest for denouncing Canadian aid to Britain. A man of vivid imagination and violent temperament, he was convinced of the iniquity of the Liberals; he suspected them of distributing gifts in large quantities to buy votes, of using the Hôtel St-Roch as a centre for prostitutes imported from Montreal, and even of turning the large hot-houses before the Legislative Buildings into dressing-rooms for the girls to use between calls on recalcitrant voters. Thousands of ballots, he was sure, were placed in the ballot boxes before the polling began.

On election day, February 9, St. Laurent toured the constitu-

ency, calling at Liberal committee rooms and encouraging volunteers by his presence. Bouchard maintained his feverish pace;
ever suspicious, he received a report in mid-afternoon that his
opponents were operating a 'telegraph' system from a secret headquarters on rue de la Couronne; in other words, names of people
who were not going to vote were being compiled, and staunch
Liberals sent to cast ballots in their place. The Parti Canadien
candidate gave instructions to have the place raided by a group of
paid thugs, to wreck everything, seize any evidence, and toss the
wrongdoers, purported to include two cabinet ministers, into the
street, 'shirt-tails in the air'. One of his associates warned him
that such an act would be illegal, and persuaded him to request
a proper mandate from the police. When the document was
obtained, a gang of men rushed to the address, only to find a
nearly empty office and no evidence of the activity that had been
reported. The disappointed candidate was convinced that the
Liberals had been warned and had flown the coop.

The result of the contest was almost an anticlimax. Surrounded
by his family and the principal party organizers, St. Laurent sat
in his living-room and listened to the results on the radio, hoping
for a victory because of the job to be done, but determined that
he would not be disappointed if he was told by the electorate to
remain in Quebec. He took an early lead, and defeated Bouchard
by a comfortable four thousand votes, some sixteen hundred less
than Lapointe had obtained in 1940. Whether the result was
simply a vote on party lines, the product of an efficient electoral
machine, or a personal vote of confidence in St. Laurent was not
clear; he took it as a confirmation of the Prime Minister's request
for his services. Elsewhere the news was also good for the Liberals;
they were winning in Welland and Montreal–St. Mary, and
Meighen was trailing in York South. As soon as victory was
certain, the entire family was driven down to Limoilou Hall, the
scene of his political début, where they were greeted by a happy
crowd waving posters bearing his photograph, and singing 'Il a
gagné ses épaulettes'. Even Oscar Drouin came forward to express
his congratulations. 'I am a conscript,' St. Laurent told them
seriously. 'I will serve where I am told to serve, and in the best
interest of my compatriots. . . . I will follow the policies I have

outlined.' Long after midnight, the St. Laurents were still in their sitting-room, talking over their new and exciting experience. At one point, a relative who had been helping in the campaign recounted that she had spent the day driving a group of people from one poll to another: she asked the victorious candidate what was their purpose in visiting the different stations. Until that moment, St. Laurent had been convinced that an honest decision had been taken; suddenly he suspected that his own family might have been used to carry out election tactics he had always condemned. He was furious, but it was too late to turn back; nevertheless, it was a sour note on which to end a happy evening. In Ottawa, the Prime Minister was drawing his own conclusions from the contest; St. Laurent had proved himself already as a 'worthy successor to Lapointe and Sir Wilfrid Laurier', he wrote in his diary.

Louis St. Laurent was greeted as a conquering hero by enthusiastic Liberals and screeching bagpipes when he arrived in the nation's capital on February 10. On February 19, the Prime Minister and Power escorted the new minister into the Commons Chamber, and, following tradition, asked permission for him to take his seat. To the members of the St. Laurent family sitting in the gallery, he looked more like a lamb being led to slaughter than a conquering hero. At the same time, he seemed to fit naturally into the parliamentary atmosphere, bowing to the Speaker with an easy grace, and then moving to his place on the government side as if he had been long trained for the job.

From the outset, St. Laurent set himself a rigorous fifteen-hour-a-day schedule, examining documents with the same rapidity and sureness that had enabled him to accomplish such huge amounts of work in his own legal firm. His advisers soon learned that they were dealing with a man who knew the law as well as themselves, who could take decisions without the usual detailed briefing. They also learned that he was determined that political considerations should not influence the course of justice. His deputy minister, F. P. Varcoe, found him so unaware of political realities that he felt obliged to give him advice on that aspect of the matters submitted to him.

One of St. Laurent's main responsibilities as Minister of Justice was for the internal security of the country. The Royal Canadian Mounted Police came under his jurisdiction, and he had to apply many war-time controls such as press censorship and anti-sedition regulations, designed to curb activities harmful to the war effort. Many of the matters brought to his attention required a fine appreciation of the borderline between personal freedom and the public interest. On February 26, 1942, he had the disagreeable duty of ordering the removal of thirty thousand persons of Japanese origin from the Pacific Coast area, and the confiscation of their motor vehicles, cameras, radios, and firearms. In later years, the forced migration seemed cruel and unnecessary; however, the attack on Pearl Harbor had occurred only a few weeks earlier; on February 24, a Japanese submarine had shelled Santa Barbara, California; and British Columbians were convinced that Canada was about to be invaded. Rumours were widespread that a fifth column existed in the Japanese Canadian community, and that the Asians would rise to support the invader at a given signal. In the circumstances, the drastic step seemed a wise precaution.

The main preoccupation of the federal government in those early months of 1942 was the plebiscite, scheduled for April 27. Although Mackenzie King stressed that the vote was not on the issue of conscription, but that he was merely asking for a free hand to meet all eventualities, eleven Quebec Liberals, including Ernest Lapointe's son Hugues, had voted against the Speech from the Throne to express their opposition to any change of policy. In March, Raoul Dandurand died, and Cardin was becoming increasingly reluctant to ask for a firm 'yes' in the plebiscite. St. Laurent's presence in Ottawa took on increasing importance. 'Before you vote on April 27, ask yourself this question,' he urged in a broadcast on March 24. 'If Hitler could vote in my place today, how would he vote? Without a doubt, he would vote "no". So the enemy dictates the answer. I have to vote "yes".' Cardin rallied and spoke in the same vein, but some Liberal members from Quebec campaigned openly against the government position. Jean-François Pouliot, member for Témiscouata, toured the province with a recording of one of Ernest Lapointe's last speeches, in which the deceased minister had repeated his no-conscription pledge. If the situation was difficult for Mackenzie King, it was still more so for Adélard Godbout, who was almost alone in his cabinet and in the Quebec Legislature in supporting the Ottawa administration. With some of his colleagues urging the public to vote 'non', and others 'oui', he was obliged to take an ambiguous stand that his opponents described derisively as 'noui'. In the end, the plebiscite did not really decide anything. The total vote was 64 per cent in favour of relieving the government of its promise not to impose conscription for overseas service, 36 per cent against; however, the latter figure included 72.5 per cent of the Quebec electorate, and probably about 90 per cent of the French-Canadian vote. In St. Laurent's constituency, the government's plea was rejected by seven to one; the deep split in the Canadian population was merely confirmed. While the government in Ottawa proclaimed it had won a victory, the Prime Minister concluded privately that 'to keep Canada united, we . . . have to do everything in our power [to keep] from reaching the point where necessity for conscription would arise.' St. Laurent agreed that the government could be considered to have been freed of its engagement, but he insisted that every step taken towards conscription should be approved in advance by Parliament.

The scene of the debate shifted once again to the Council Chamber. The conscriptionist and anti-conscriptionist wings were as far apart as ever; members first of one group and then of the other seemed on the point of resigning, and at times Mackenzie King himself threatened to quit if they did not reach an agreement. St. Laurent worked hard to keep the team together, arguing with Cardin that disruption of the cabinet would merely result in handing the country to the conscriptionists, and with Ralston and Angus Macdonald that their departure might well precipitate an election that would paralyse the war effort for months, and probably make a further French-Canadian contribution to it impossible. To both groups he counselled calm realism, and unity around Mackenzie King as the only man who could ensure a maximum war effort. On May 8, the Prime Minister presented in cabinet a compromise proposal to repeal the section of the National Resources Mobilization Act restricting compulsory service to Canada, but to take no further action for the time being. St. Laurent threw his support behind it, and pleaded with Cardin to do the same, on the grounds that Parliament would have to be consulted before any other step could be taken. His efforts were in vain; the Minister of Public Works resigned, leaving him, just three months after his election, the only French-speaking Canadian in the cabinet.

In deciding to remain in the cabinet, St. Laurent realized that he was placing himself at odds with a large sector of public opinion in his province, even within the Liberal Party there. On May 12, *Le Soleil* published an editorial entitled 'Mr. King Imposes Conscription', suggesting that other French-speaking Canadians should follow Cardin's example. Various Liberal organizations, and many individuals, urged the Minister of Justice to resign. 'There is no question of imposing conscription at the moment,' he replied to one correspondent, 'and I am sure that the present government would never consent to such a step except for our proper well-being.' He urged Liberals to desist from making public statements against the government. 'I am here in Ottawa, and I am aware of the facts; you are in Quebec where you hear all sorts of rumours; do you really think you are in a better position to decide what is in our best interest? . . . Our cause will not be helped by such publicity.'

Impressed with his new colleague's firm stand, the Prime Minister appointed him to the War Committee, the small group within the cabinet with special responsibility for the war effort. 'He is so sensible, so straight, and so exceedingly able,' Mackenzie King wrote in his diary after the two had met with Ralston and the Chief of Staff. 'St. Laurent is a complete match for Ralston on the legal side, and speaks out with a vigour for Quebec that none of the Quebec Ministers seemed able to do through sensitiveness of their position and being in the minority. St. Laurent does not suffer in any way in that particular.'

The debate in the House of Commons to amend the National Resources Mobilization Act was opened by Mackenzie King on June 10, 1942, with his clever if rather ambiguous slogan, 'conscription if necessary, but not necessarily conscription'. Cardin followed the next day, giving vent to his long-pent-up feelings in a bitter attack on his former colleagues, accusing them of betraying Quebec and preparing to introduce conscription surreptitiously. From the reception accorded him, it was clear that he had the support of practically all the other French-speaking members. The reply of English Canada was given by freshman member John Diefenbaker, who suggested that Canada's motto should be: 'Everything mobilized to prevent everything being lost'.

As the critical debate proceeded, St. Laurent's time was divided between listening to the various speeches, preparing his own statement, and striving to prevent further resignations, this time from the conscriptionist wing of the cabinet. The Prime Minister and the Minister of Defence were in complete disagreement over the procedure to be adopted in the event that conscription for overseas service was found necessary, Mackenzie King insisting that Parliament be consulted first, Ralston arguing that the step be taken by order in council, leaving Parliament to discuss the *fait accompli*. The two men wore down each other's nerves, and, after a particularly difficult discussion in cabinet on June 12, the Minister of Defence announced that, since they could not find common ground, he would have to resign. The Prime Minister, his celebrated resourcefulness and ability to manoeuvre in troubled waters almost exhausted, resolved to accept the resignation if it was offered, even if that meant losing both the principal advocate and the principal opponent of conscription. When Ralston asked for a further appointment, Mackenzie King called St. Laurent to explain the situation; the Minister of Justice objected that English-speaking Canadians would gather the impression from such a development that conscription was really necessary; he urged his leader to continue the negotiations. When Ralston called, Mackenzie King managed to win time once again.

St. Laurent's long-awaited first major address in Parliament was delivered on June 16. He spoke mainly in English, because, he explained, 'I have some things to say about the relations between English-speaking and French-speaking Canadians which I would not like any of my English-speaking colleagues to feel that I would express more freely in French. . . .' The division of public opinion was regrettable but it was 'one of the inescapable consequences of the situation in which Providence has placed the citizens of this nation'; two groups had been installed side by side, 'and stern reality, without taking from them any of their racial traits, has forced them to work together towards the building up of a new nation.' The word 'conscription' had come to symbolize for many French-speaking Canadians not a form of service, he pointed out, but 'a theory that they can be forced to enrol, train, fight and die for some other cause than that of their own country'. The Empire-first view of many English-speaking Canadians 'seems to many of us in Quebec to be characterized by a blind sentimental, proud, and even arrogant attachment to England, and to ignore Canada's evolution to sovereignty in her own right'. 'We feel that Canada is in this war on its own, in its own interests,' he declared, and that the country's contribution should be determined, not by 'the memories and fancies' of some citizens, but by the most efficient use of available manpower.

While most French-speaking Canadians were patriotically supporting the war effort, there were extremists in Quebec as well, St. Laurent conceded, and even those who dreamed of separation from the rest of Canada. However, he had counselled them in a recent broadcast to lay aside 'that chimerical dream' and he had been assured that nationalist leaders were not looking to the establishment of a sovereign French state in North America, 'not at least during the life of anyone living today'. French-speaking Canadians neither could, nor desired to, dominate others, he assured the attentive House, but Canada was their home and they wished to be recognized 'as full partners and full citizens anywhere and everywhere in Canada'. No thinking person could have any objection to the government's resorting to conscription in the event of absolute necessity, he argued; the point at issue was whether members had confidence in the present government to do so only if and when it was essential. That was a matter each man had to decide on his own; as for himself, in spite of the difficulties that might face the government in the future, he felt that it was his duty to carry his share 'of whatever responsibility may be involved'. He had based his decision on the view that the two groups of Canadians could get along together, and that 'there is more in each group worthy of admiration, worthy of being conserved, than there are things which might make one group offensive to the other'. While that fact might not be apparent to everyone, 'the attempt to make it apparent to all Canadians seems to me to be a task worthy of the best efforts of all true Canadians', and he hoped to be of 'some assistance' in accomplishing 'as much . . . as is possible in our day and generation'. It was a simple but eloquent statement of faith in Canada, and the well-filled Chamber was silent except for his voice until St. Laurent resumed his seat; then, applause and desk-pounding broke forth from all sides. The Prime Minister rose, walked over to his seat, shook his hand and thanked him warmly. Others followed; it was an experience none would soon forget. The handshake was 'a symbolic meeting', Mackenzie King wrote in his diary that evening, and demonstrated that he had found 'a colleague from Quebec who was a worthy successor of Lapointe and Sir Wilfrid Laurier'. In a letter to Godbout not long afterwards, the Prime Minister expressed his thanks to the premier for recommending 'without a doubt the best man in the Cabinet . . . and I don't exclude myself in making that statement'.

If the speech won many plaudits, it attracted criticism as well. Wilfrid LaCroix, Liberal member for Quebec-Montmorency, replied to it for many French-speaking members later the same day in prophesying that 'the province of Quebec is to be deceived once again'. Outside Parliament, the National Committee of the Imperial Order Daughters of the Empire condemned St. Laurent's concept of loyalty as 'selfish and without soul', and added that 'Canada is best served by serving the Empire as a whole'. Ralston's threat of resignation hung over the heads of Mackenzie King and St. Laurent throughout the debate, but the Minister of Defence had still not made the final break when second reading of the bill was approved by a heartening 158 votes to 54. With that assurance that the government could carry on for a time, St. Laurent continued to insist that the Minister of Defence should not resign, since such an act would split the party and make an election necessary after all. The behind-the-scenes negotiations continued. By the end of July the bill had become law, and Mackenzie King and Ralston had reached a *modus vivendi* that was the result more of exhaustion than of agreement. In effect, it was a victory for Ralston, for the Prime Minister acknowledged that, having made no explicit commitment to Parliament to consult it before-hand, conscription could be imposed by order in council when the government deemed it necessary. At the same time, Mac-kenzie King made no commitment to do so, merely conceding that, if he did not accept his minister's advice at a later date to introduce conscription, Ralston would have cause to resign. The first conscription crisis was over.

During his first months in office, Louis St. Laurent was involved in another issue of crisis proportions. Following the capture of the Canadian contingent in Hong Kong, the government was ac-cused of sending ill-trained and ill-equipped men into a veritable trap. Responding to pressure from the opposition, the Minister of Justice persuaded Sir Lyman Duff, Chief Justice of the Supreme Court, to act as a one-man royal commission to inquire into the circumstances surrounding the expedition. Since Duff was gener-ally recognized as one of the greatest legal minds in Canada's history, his appointment seemed to be an effective answer to the charge that the facts were being concealed. Lt.-Col. George Drew, the dynamic and outspoken Leader of the Opposition in Ontario, was appointed counsel for the federal Conservative leader. The investigation was carried out under an oath of secrecy, and the Duff report was submitted to Parliament on June 5, 1942; apart from minor criticism, it found the expedition neither ill con-ceived nor badly managed. Drew, however, took strong exception to the conclusions; in a letter to the Prime Minister, he attacked both the report and the commissioner in violent terms. To im-pugn the highest legal authority in the land was a serious matter; worse still, he included in his letter secret information communi-cated by the United Kingdom government to the commission. As Minister of Justice, St. Laurent retained a Toronto lawyer, D. L. McCarthy, as special counsel to advise on appropriate action to deal with the breach of security. McCarthy advised that legal proceedings be instituted against Drew for a violation of the De-fence of Canada Regulations. The minister accepted the advice, and the preliminary steps were taken; but, before the case was called, McCarthy had second thoughts, and reported that the evidence was not strong enough to obtain a judgment. Furious at being placed in an embarrassing position, St. Laurent had no alternative but to inform the House of Commons that the proceedings had been discontinued. The Conservatives were jubilant, and subjected him to a torrent of criticism in Parliament that he was not soon to forget. He took the reproaches manfully until he was accused by one member of 'lacking in frankness'; then the blood rushed up to his face, his eyes flashed, and his stubbly moustache seemed to bristle as he leaped to his feet and demanded an immediate withdrawal. Surprised at the sharpness of his reaction, the offending member withdrew the imputation. The House went on to other matters, but the incident had revealed a side of his character that few people in Ottawa knew; in the conscription debate, he had presented the image of cool-headed reasonableness; when aroused, he could evidently be a dangerous opponent.

The matter did not rest there. In late July, the *Vancouver News-Herald* carried a story purporting to describe the contents of Drew's secret letter to the Prime Minister and to quote from it. The Minister of Justice was guilty of 'a shameful prostitution' of the Royal Canadian Mounted Police, the Ontario Conservative leader was reported to have written, by using it 'to obtain statements which obviously were very much in keeping with the wishes of one department of that government'. Drew had allegedly urged that the Minister of Justice 'be called to account without delay'. The news report gave rise to a House of Commons debate, during which Dr. H. A. Bruce accused the Minister of Justice of using the R.C.M.P. to get evidence 'to destroy the character and reputation' of George Drew. Stirred by the new charge, St. Laurent vigorously denied any personal involvement in the matter. When the press report of the letter reached him, he had made inquiries, he stated in the House of Commons, and found that the R.C.M.P. had been asked to obtain the opinion of longshoremen in Vancouver about an assertion that more military vehicles could have been loaded onto the ship bound for Hong Kong if they had arrived in time; he had concluded that it was quite proper for the R.C.M.P. to comply with such a request. The subject was dropped in the House of Commons, but it had provided an unpleasant first contact between Drew and St. Laurent. 'He just isn't a politician, that's all,' concluded one newspaperman in assessing the new Minister of Justice. 'His handling of the Drew case . . . demonstrated that.' On the other hand, St. Laurent's performance shortly afterwards in piloting the estimates of his department through the House revealed that he was a first-class jurist and administrator. His first session ended on a more positive note.

During his first months in office, St. Laurent made the seven-hour train journey to Quebec City almost every week-end to spend Sunday with his family. Since the only accommodation he could find in Ottawa was a two-room suite in the Roxborough apartment hotel on Laurier Street, his wife preferred to remain in Quebec City. On her occasional visits to the capital, she had to prepare breakfast on a bedside table with the aid of an electric kettle and stove; the home-made jams and preserves she brought along were kept under the bed. In the circumstances, the short reunions in their comfortable Grande Allée home simply served to remind them of the pleasant life they had abandoned. The Sunday-night farewells at the station were so mournful that finally one of the daughters suggested that if they could not enjoy their brief hours together, the head of the family would have to stay in Ottawa until the end of the war.

Even with the session over, Louis St. Laurent maintained his heavy schedule, walking up to the Hill before nine every morning, still puffing on his after-breakfast cigarette, crossing over to the Rideau Club on Wellington Street, or to the Château Laurier Hotel, for lunch, and returning to work until well after the civil servants had gone home for the evening. He usually ate alone at night in the Roxborough dining-room, and spent his evening going over documents in the tiny apartment. One of the tasks in which he was most interested was the appointment of judges. He was determined that any recommendation he made should be based on one consideration only, the necessity of maintaining the highest possible standards in the Canadian judiciary; patronage was to be banished as long as he was responsible for filling vacancies. He followed Lapointe's policy of trying to increase the

proportion of French-speaking Canadians in positions of responsibility, but insisted that the appointments be made on the basis
of competence, and not on a mere ethnic ratio. His advisers
soon learned that to suggest a name on any other grounds would
provoke an outburst against the 'cry-babies' who were not willing
to prove their ability to compete with their fellow citizens. More
delicate and disagreeable was his task of enforcing the war-time
laws and regulations. There were some ten thousand draft-
dodgers in hiding in mid-1942; as the minister responsible for the
R.C.M.P., St. Laurent had to order that they be tracked down
and put into service. He also had to check on statements and
activities that seemed likely to harm the war effort. Rumours
abounded in Quebec, and each one had to be investigated. One
had it that Lapointe had been shot, and that the story of death by
cancer was invented by English-speaking Canadians to hide the
truth. Another asserted that twenty ships had been sunk in the
St. Lawrence; still another claimed that a prominent Quebec
business man was supplying fuel and supplies to German U-boats.
According to one widespread story, French-Canadian girls were
being forced to work in munition factories where they would
become sterile. One of the newspapers most frequently on the
verge of illegality was Le Devoir; St. Laurent's personal acquaintance with the editor, Georges Pelletier, whom he had known at
Laval University, enabled him to settle many problems without
applying the full force of the law.

With Parliament adjourned, the Prime Minister was able to
give his attention to finding replacements for Cardin and Dandurand. With his keen sense of political balance, he decided to
admit to the cabinet, as an example to the others, one man who
had remained true to him during the recent debate and one who
had not done so but was now prepared to support the government
even if it had to introduce conscription. For the first category he
picked Ernest Bertrand, member for Montreal-Laurier, appointing him Minister of Fisheries; for the second category he chose
Alphonse Fournier, member for Hull, who was given the Public
Works portfolio in return for an assurance of allegiance. The
previous Minister of Fisheries, J. E. Michaud of New Brunswick,
was promoted to Cardin's old portfolio, the Department of

Transport. Another French-speaking Canadian, General L. R.
Laflèche, was promoted from the post of Deputy Minister of
National War Services to Minister of that department. None of
the new cabinet ministers held great promise as administrators or
political leaders, but the cause of Canadian unity necessitated
their presence at the Council table. In contrast, St. Laurent's role
became more important than ever. Not only was he 'the ablest
man in the government', Mackenzie King confided to Joseph
Atkinson, publisher of the *Toronto Daily Star*, but 'he would be
my choice [as successor] in a moment were he not of the minority
in both race and religion'. Ironically, every transgression of the
normal rules of politics that St. Laurent committed made him
more attractive to the Liberal king-makers. His appeals for a
non-partisan approach to the war effort, his refusal to condone
political favouritism in making appointments, and his indifference to political power, all militated against his return to Quebec
at the end of the war. While he was unaware of the fact, the
mantle of leadership was being fitted on him from the day he
took his oath of office.

In addition to carrying his heavy administrative load, St. Laurent made an average of a speech a week, spreading his dual message of a maximum war effort and national unity. Co-operation
and understanding were the essential basis of both international
and national affairs, he told members of the Canadian Club of
Quebec on October 21, 1942; 'the unhappy fate of nations that
placed their faith in isolationism . . . offers us examples of catastrophe that we have no right to ignore.' Roman Catholics had as
much interest as other Canadians in thwarting Hitler's plan 'to
destroy Christianity and substitute for it the cult of force and of
the all-powerful totalitarian state'. The war had to be, and would
be, won, he stated, but victory would not solve the problems
facing Canada or mankind as a whole. In the post-war world,
men must strive not only for collective, but also for individual
security.

> What a bitter irony that our economic system only managed to
> provide jobs for the unemployed as a result of the war! . . . To
> win the war, the interests of the whole community are given

priority over those of individuals and groups. Could not a
similar approach, by the state, employers and workers together,
assure individual security, and a greater degree of well-being
and satisfaction after the war?

It was an unlikely statement for a corporation lawyer and member of the Quebec upper class, but it reflected St. Laurent's basic
simplicity and social consciousness. A few days later he went even
further. 'If, after victory is achieved, the government is unable to
provide employment for everyone,' he told the Hull Chamber of
Commerce on October 29, 'we will have to replace it by another
government.'

Pleasant as it was to speculate about the post-war world, the
immediate fact remained that Canadians were seriously divided
in the face of the greatest threat in their history. In those dark
months of the war, St. Laurent came to realize the full significance
of Laurier's plaint that he had to fight extremists on both flanks.
In Toronto, he was baited by the *Globe and Mail* for telling
French-speaking Canadians they should join in the war effort because Canada's interests were at stake, not because Great Britain's
interests were at stake. At the same time, when General Laflèche
stood for election in Montreal-Outremont constituency, the
Liberals were opposed by twenty-six-year-old Jean Drapeau, who
presented himself as 'the candidate of the conscripts'. 'We are in
favour of the war effort for Canada,' the ardent young Quebec
nationalist declared, 'but we don't give a damn about the war
effort for England.' Drapeau's organizer, Marc Carrière, boasted
that he had received his call for military service but had ignored
it; he was to spend several months in jail for his defiance of
authority. Drapeau was supported as well by a new Quebec
nationalist movement, the Bloc Populaire, founded by Liberal
M.P. Maxime Raymond, and by the Ligue pour la Défense
du Canada, of which André Laurendeau was the self-styled
'mainspring'. Laurendeau tried hard during the campaign in
Outremont to make an issue of Camillien Houde's internment,
publishing letters to St. Laurent in *Le Devoir*, and accusing him
of holding the former mayor illegally. The Minister of Justice rejected the volatile young newspaperman's charges and continued

to apply the regulations. Laflèche was elected without difficulty.

During his second session of Parliament, which began late in January 1943, Louis St. Laurent's political education continued and occasionally his patience was severely tried. When he released Communist leader Tim Buck from internment after the latter had signed an undertaking not to hinder the war effort, he was charged by friends of Camillien Houde with having more sympathy for the Communists than for his own people. When he was asked to comment on a statement by former member of Parliament Agnes McPhail that she had 'never met a progressive judge', and that they were all 'political heelers', he retorted angrily that he would draw the attention of the censors to the dispatch, to see if publicity for such statements could not be prevented. It was a sincere, well-meaning, but dangerous statement, and the outburst did not go unnoticed by his opponents. 'Though perfectly bilingual, he does not understand the language of liberty,' commented newspaperwoman Judith Robinson in the *Vancouver Province*.

While St. Laurent had long been convinced of the importance of avoiding controversy between the two principal groups of Canadians, he had not fully appreciated before entering the government how difficult it is to keep from wounding sensitivities or giving extremists fuel for attack. In introducing in the House of Commons a proposal to amend the B.N.A. Act in order to postpone redistribution of federal constituencies until after the war, his intention was to prevent discord in so critical a period. A more seasoned politician would have tried to reduce the debate to a minimum by shortening his own remarks; St. Laurent, however, proceeded to answer in advance most of the arguments that could be raised by either side, and to raise fresh topics such as the need for a Canadian flag, recruiting in Quebec, and bilingualism. On the latter subject, he expressed confidence that 'the day will come when, if not all those who sit in this House, at least its leaders and those who grace the Treasury benches and those who sit immediately opposite, will find it to their advantage to be bilingual.' Conservative House leader Gordon Graydon objected to the assertion, and the report soon spread through English Canada that the Minister of Justice wanted to force French on the whole country. Nor did he succeed in assuring French-speaking members. Cardin condemned the postponement of redistribution as a violation of the 'sacred contract' entered into with the provinces at Confederation; a newly-elected Independent Conservative member, Frédéric Dorion, supported the former minister and read into the record a protest by the Quebec Legislative Assembly at the failure to consult it. Jean-François Pouliot accused St. Laurent not only of 'pouring oil on the fire' of disunity by postponing redistribution but of 'adding straw to the fire, in fact lighting the fire of prejudice throughout the country'.

St. Laurent entered the debate again, denying that Confederation was a pact between the provinces. Neither Quebec nor Ontario existed in the period before 1867, he pointed out, there being only one province, Canada, from which both were created; the federal arrangement had been worked out by 'responsible prominent leaders of the population' who agreed that provincial governments would be established to deal exclusively with certain matters, while others would be a joint responsibility and still others would be dealt with by 'the representatives of the inhabitants of the provinces who sit in this Parliament'. Since the redistribution of seats in the House of Commons fell in the last category, any opinion expressed by members of the Quebec Legislature must be in their capacity as individual citizens, and not as members of a group responsible for dealing with the subject. The bill had a relatively easy passage, but in the process St. Laurent had found himself at odds with both French- and English-speaking Canadians.

As the months of 1943 passed, political partisanship increased. Premier John Bracken of Manitoba became leader of the Conservative Party, renamed the Progressive Conservative Party, and began attacking the Liberals for their conduct of the Canadian war effort. In an Ontario provincial election, a marked swing of Liberal votes to the C.C.F. Party enabled George Drew to form a minority Conservative government. An opinion poll indicated that the Socialists had become the most popular party in Canada; in the fourth year of the war, the people were restless for a change. The Mackenzie King government lost a series of four by-elections, two of them in western Canada to the C.C.F. Party, and two in

Quebec. Shocked into action, the Prime Minister called an end to the phony war-time political truce, and ordered a meeting of the Liberal Party's National Advisory Council for late September. He himself launched the counter-attack at the party gathering, castigating his opponents for exploiting popular discontent with the war-time controls. A series of far-reaching proposals were unveiled under the slogan 'planning for peace', calling for 'full employment and maximum production', a labour code, housing and health programs, family allowances, steps to assure Canadian national sovereignty, and national unity based on 'the partnership of the two great races and respect for the historic rights of minorities'.

Louis St. Laurent not only endorsed the proposals but adjusted to the more partisan political atmosphere. In the face of mounting opposition, he was more than ever convinced that the team of which he was a member was the best suited to bringing the country through the war and placing it on the road of peace. The plebiscite had proved to be a 'wise and useful measure', he told members of the Montreal Reform Club on November 13, 1943, but it had 'put a little too much wind in the sails of the nationalist barge' in Quebec; still, he prophesied, none of the would-be captains would likely be able to muster 'an ocean-going crew'. The same speech contained what was perhaps his first definition of the Liberal Party and its objectives. 'We are and shall remain the party of progress,' he declared after referring to the increase in C.C.F. strength, 'the party desiring the greatest good for the greatest number, the common weal for all rather than individual privileges for a few; however, unlike our opponents [on the left], we mean to bring about this progress, adjust real grievances, eliminate and prevent notorious abuses without tearing up the Constitution.' It was Laurier Liberalism expressed in the words of a responsible, realistic man who disapproved of radicalism but favoured reform.

In April 1944, St. Laurent had an opportunity to express his views in another area when Mackenzie King made a trip to Great Britain, and appointed him Acting Secretary of State for External Affairs; Ralston became Acting Prime Minister. The Prime Minister's decision to entrust St. Laurent with the External Affairs portfolio was recognized as a mark of special confidence, for the veteran politician had always clung tenaciously to it himself. Although the Minister of Justice had no practical experience in diplomacy, the government leader was convinced that he would be 'ideal' for the job; the web of responsibility was being drawn tighter around the war-time 'conscript'. Making his first speech in his new role before a French-speaking audience in Hull, Quebec, on May 21, he commented that, since he would be relieved of those duties automatically as soon as the Prime Minister arrived back from London, it was 'perhaps the first and last occasion I will have to speak in public in this capacity'. His attitude to Canada's foreign policy, he explained, was that Canada was a sovereign nation and could not allow others to determine her attitude in international affairs; at the same time, Canada must refrain from 'an egotistical and unrestricted nationalism', described by the Catholic philosopher Jacques Maritain as 'the great danger that the world will have to avoid tomorrow'. He believed in the usefulness of the Commonwealth, but felt that it should not form a separate bloc, or limit the freedom of action of its members. World peace depended on the application of universal principles to all nations, St. Laurent declared firmly; the war had proved once again that there could be no national security in isolation, but only in international co-operation. He proposed that Canada follow a middle road between 'extreme nationalism' and 'exaggerated internationalism'.

Mackenzie King was so pleased on returning to Canada at the way St. Laurent had handled the Department of External Affairs that he increased rather than decreased his colleague's responsibilities in that field. Canada's contribution of a billion dollars' worth of war material to Britain earlier in the war had been severely criticized by Quebec nationalist elements as a 'gift' to the mother country; a new proposal to provide relief and rehabilitation in newly-liberated countries of Europe was coming under equally heavy attack. As a French-speaking minister, St. Laurent was well placed to reply for the government, and did so to good effect. He also spoke on behalf of the government when General Charles de Gaulle, commander of the Free French Forces, visited Ottawa, declaring with more than a trace of wishful thinking

that 'all Canada is united in support . . . of the Allied nations.'
The French leader replied with an appeal for 'real international
co-operation' and announced that France intended 'no longer
to divide, but to . . . play her full part in this universal task' of
assuring world peace.

Another matter in which St. Laurent played a useful role for
the government was the introduction of family allowances in
Canada. Conceived largely as a means of putting a floor under the
incomes of poorer families, and of maintaining the purchasing
power of Canadians in the event of a post-war economic depression, the quarter-billion-dollar scheme aroused protests on two
counts; in English-speaking Canada it was condemned as a bribe
to Quebec, in Quebec as an intrusion into a field of provincial
jurisdiction. To St. Laurent fell the responsibility for dealing
with the second charge. Fifteen years earlier he himself might
have had serious reservations about such legislation, but the
experience of the economic depression, his activity as legal counsel in connection with the Bennett 'New Deal' legislation, and
particularly his work with the Rowell-Sirois Commission had
broadened his views and developed his social consciousness. Just
as he had become convinced of the necessity for a federal system
of unemployment insurance, so he felt Ottawa must assist in
assuring a basic standard of living throughout Canada. Thus,
when the proposal was submitted to the House of Commons, he
endorsed it enthusiastically as 'an epochal proposal for the better-
ment of conditions in this country'. Since the legislation had
been drafted in the Department of Justice, and under his close
supervision, he was well able to deal with arguments concerning
its constitutional validity. The Employment and Social Insurance
Act of 1935 had been declared invalid not because it provided
that grants be made to individuals, he recalled, but because
conditions had been attached to them, and recipients were not
completely free to accept or refuse the money. However, both
Chief Justice Duff in the Supreme Court and Lord Atkin in the
Privy Council had declared in discussing that case that the federal
government could raise money by taxation and distribute it to
individuals, provided that it did not regulate matters within provincial control. Since the family allowances legislation imposed

no obligation, even to accept the money, and affected no rights already established, there was no basis for declaring it unconstitutional. The federal government was justified in introducing such measures because of its responsibility for the general economic activity of the country, St. Laurent argued, and in addition it had 'some moral obligation' to do so. Since the 'ordinary labourer' could not earn enough money under the existing economic system to provide adequately for himself and a family, Ottawa had a duty when devising an economic policy that was in the interests of the majority 'not to allow it to bear too harshly on individuals without giving some consideration to alleviating the harshness with which it bears upon those individuals'. The dual purpose of the bill, he explained, was to bring about 'some nearer approach to equality of opportunity for the children of the nation' by aiding them in a situation which was not of their making, and to provide 'for the continuance of the Canadian economy'. He rejected as 'contrary to the principle of ministerial responsibility' a suggestion that the moneys involved be turned over to the provinces.

While some Conservative members of Parliament were unenthusiastic about the legislation, they hesitated to oppose it openly for fear of jeopardizing their party's chances at the next election, particularly in Quebec. One of the less cautious, Dr. H. A. Bruce of Toronto, declared that it was 'a bribe of the most brazen character, made chiefly to one province and paid for by the taxes of the rest'. Premier George Drew described the 'baby bonus' bill in a radio broadcast as 'iniquitous', and 'the penalty of appeasement'. Nevertheless the measure was voted into law by an overwhelming majority.

As 1944 advanced, St. Laurent's range of activities widened. Mackenzie King was drawing him more and more into the field of international affairs; he spent most of July attending the United Nations Monetary Conference at Bretton Woods, New Hampshire. At the same time, he was becoming involved increasingly in Liberal Party activities, and identifying himself with the new program. When the Conservatives made a strong assault on Ilsley's budget in the early summer, he came to his colleague's support with a vigorous defence of both the war record and the post-war program, and declared that 'when the time comes around for an election I intend to go before the constituents of [Quebec East] . . . and I do not expect to face destruction.' Eyebrows were raised, even by occupants of the Treasury benches, at the news that the 'conscript' was planning to meet the electorate after the war. In one important instance, he would have been glad to play an active partisan role, but was unable to do so. The Quebec Legislature was dissolved in late June, and Adélard Godbout was fighting for his political life against Maurice Duplessis. In 1939, Lapointe, Cardin, and Power had thrown their prestige and their considerable oratorical talent into the balance, and had been largely responsible for the Liberal victory. Now only Power was left of the powerful team, and the newer ministers, including St. Laurent, were no match for the fiery Union Nationale leader. Godbout and his fellow candidates asked them to keep out of the campaign in order to give Duplessis as few opportunities as possible to identify the provincial Liberals with the less pleasant aspects of the war effort.

One of the federal government's measures that proved embarrassing to Godbout was a directive from the federal Department of Labour ordering employers to check the registration cards of their employees, and to report the names of all men who had not conformed with the National Selective Service Regulations. Since farmers and the heads of family firms were included under the directive, this meant that fathers were ordered to denounce their own sons, if the latter were draft-dodgers. Maurice Duplessis attacked Godbout for not being able to prevent 'this system of delation'; and André Laurendeau took up the fight against 'these dictatorial rules . . . that make espionage a duty and cruelty a virtue'. The Quebec Premier complained to St. Laurent that most of his colleagues, as well as the vast majority of the population of the province, were revolted by the Department of Labour directive, and urged that the terms be modified; no father would denounce his own son, he argued, and, probably, none would be prosecuted for not doing so. The Minister of Justice refused to be moved; there were far more French-speaking Canadians than English-speaking Canadians who were trying to escape their duty, he replied, and it was part of the duty of parents to instil in their children a sense of respect and obedience for laws that were considered in the best interest of society by the competent authorities.

Worse still for the Liberal image in Quebec than the Department of Labour directive was the shooting of a young French-speaking army deserter during an R.C.M.P. raid. The law officers had not aimed directly at him, but the bullet had ricocheted and he had been killed instantly. The reaction in Quebec was immediate and violent. Laurendeau condemned 'the policemen of Mr. King and Mr. St. Laurent' and declared that the victim's only crime was that he took seriously the Liberal promises not to impose conscription. Godbout and his colleagues tried to direct the public's attention to their new and sweeping program of economic and social reform; their efforts were in vain; all other considerations paled before the 'assassination of a conscript'. Maurice Duplessis was carried to power on a wave of indignation against Ottawa; Godbout was the unhappy scapegoat. Elsewhere that summer, T. C. Douglas defeated the Liberals in Saskatchewan, and formed the first C.C.F. government in Canada; and in Alberta, the Social Credit Party won its third election victory in a row. The tide still appeared to be turning against the Liberals, and the most critical period of the war was still ahead.

# 6

---

## Conscription

The month of September 1944 was one of the most pleasant of the war for Mackenzie King and his colleagues. The Prime Minister spent a good part of the month in Quebec City as host of the second Quebec Conference, and his frequent appearances with Churchill and Roosevelt enhanced his prestige. The fighting in Europe was expected to be over in three or four months, and the negotiations of the Allied leaders centred largely around the coming struggle against Japan in the Pacific. Neither Great Britain nor the United States was keen on a Canadian contribution to the final phase of the war, but it was generally agreed that at least a token force would have to be sent to satisfy public opinion in English Canada. With St. Laurent's support, Mackenzie King was able to persuade the more zealous members of the cabinet to limit Canada's contribution to units from the Royal Canadian Navy and the Royal Canadian Air Force. The spectre of conscription seemed about to be banished from the Canadian political scene. At a closed luncheon meeting in the Quebec Reform Club on September 14 the usually cautious Prime Minister was in such high spirits that he predicted that all Canadian soldiers who served overseas in World War II would be able to boast that they had enlisted voluntarily. The reaction of his Liberal audience was instantaneous; a burden they had carried for five years was lifted suddenly from their shoulders; the meeting broke up in a heady atmosphere of enthusiasm and hope.

Preparations were going ahead swiftly for the approaching peace. On October 13, 1944, Brooke Claxton, one of the most dynamic and imaginative young men in the Liberal Party, was sworn into office as Canada's first Minister of National Health and Welfare; Ian Mackenzie was appointed to the new portfolio of Veterans' Affairs; and C. D. Howe accepted the key post of Minister of Reconstruction. As Minister of Munitions and Supply, Howe had earned an excellent reputation in every Allied country, including the Soviet Union, for transforming the stagnant and inefficient pre-war Canadian economy into a highly productive machine; however, it was feared that he would be bored with normal peace-time administration, and that he would soon return to the construction industry, where he had made a fortune before the war. Louis St. Laurent and C. D. Howe got on very well together. Both had entered politics from a sense of patriotism rather than from partisan considerations or personal ambition. They shared a feeling of disdain for men who played politics with war issues; and they both preferred blunt honesty to the circumspection so often imposed on them in what they considered to be their temporary public-service careers. At the same time, they admired the Prime Minister for his ability to pilot the Canadian ship of state through the war-time shoals, and felt that his idealism outweighed his instinct for political self-preservation. For his part, Mackenzie King was anxious to keep them in Ottawa as long as possible. After he had persuaded St. Laurent to remain through the election, he enlisted his help in urging Howe to stay on and convert to peace-time uses the huge industrial complex he had done more than any other man to create. Howe allowed himself to be persuaded by St. Laurent to accept the new task. The two men's careers were not only parallel in some respects; they were becoming closely interrelated.

Mackenzie King also made contact with Cardin again, with a view to preparing his return to the cabinet, since the problem of conscription had apparently disappeared. Some members from Quebec urged that the former minister be recognized as Lapointe's real successor, in order to close completely the breach over compulsory overseas service, and to enable the party to pre-

sent a united front at the forthcoming election. Sounded out by
Power on the subject, St. Laurent told them to go ahead 'by all
means', as he had no political ambitions. The Prime Minister
was not of the same opinion; he was willing to have Cardin back
in the fold for reasons of party unity, but he was more than
satisfied with his new Quebec lieutenant.

Preparations for demobilization had begun, and the possibility
of disbanding the units conscripted for home defence was under
consideration, when reports began appearing in the Canadian
press that reinforcements were inadequate in Europe. On September 23, Ralston flew across the Atlantic to investigate the
situation. He discovered that the reports were only too true; the
Canadian forces had suffered heavier losses than anticipated
following the invasion of Normandy on June 6, the pools of
reserves in Italy and western Europe were nearly empty, wounded
troops were being returned prematurely to the front lines, and
army morale was suffering as a result. Returning to Ottawa on
October 18, the Minister of Defence reported to the cabinet that
an additional fifteen thousand men were needed in Europe by
the end of the year, and that they could only be obtained among
the units conscripted for domestic service. The optimism of recent
weeks had been premature; the conscription issue was still very
much alive.

As soon as the Prime Minister received the first intimation of
the new crisis through a telegram dispatched by Ralston from
London, he consulted St. Laurent, and the two men agreed that,
at such a late stage in the war, more harm than good might well
result from attempting to impose overseas military service. With
such support, Mackenzie King braced himself to resist another
onslaught by the conscriptionists. On October 19, Ralston and
General Kenneth Stuart, army Chief of Staff, outlined the situation to the war committee of the cabinet, and Stuart submitted a
written report that concluded with a recommendation that, if the
number of men required could not be obtained from among the
general-service personnel in Canada, N.R.M.A. personnel* should
be sent overseas. The Prime Minister was quick to note that the

*Men conscripted for domestic service under the National Resources Mobilization
Act.

general did not exclude the possibility of finding sufficient volunteers, but the Minister of Defence pressed for immediate conscription. When St. Laurent's turn came to speak, he agreed that the situation was very serious and expressed concern over the bitterness developing between the men overseas and those at home, but he did not take a firm position. The other ministers present asked for further time before stating their views. The following morning Mackenzie King and St. Laurent went over the situation together. They both felt that there was no necessity for conscription in order to win the war in Europe, and that the only result of introducing it would be to alienate all of Quebec. Determined to avoid such a situation within a year of the time limit for another election, the Prime Minister outlined a clever alternative plan to the Minister of Justice. If Ralston insisted to the point of tendering his resignation, it would be accepted, and General Andrew McNaughton, Canada's best-known senior officer and an opponent of conscription, would be named to take his place. McNaughton had commanded the Canadian troops overseas from the beginning of the war until late 1943, when he had a serious disagreement with both the Imperial General Staff and with his Canadian superiors, including Ralston; he was persuaded to retire from the key overseas post for reasons of health, and had been living quietly in Ottawa since his return. When St. Laurent learned of the plan, he gave it at least tacit approval, commenting that everyone had great confidence in the general, and would accept his view of what was, or was not, necessary. Since he was very much aware that appointments to the cabinet were the prerogative of the head of the government, he did not feel that he could go any further.

Although he had never committed himself to opposing compulsory overseas service, the view of the Minister of Justice might have been summed up as 'conscription only as a last resort'. Of primary concern to him during the difficult days that followed was the morale of the troops in Europe; if they did not feel adequately supported at home, he reasoned, they might be more vulnerable to enemy attack, and casualties might be greater. If they suffered reverses, or if they were withdrawn, the desperate Nazis might exploit the fact for propaganda purposes by asserting that the Allied forces were crumbling.* While the Germans could not possibly win the war, the argument might serve to keep up the bloody struggle for a while longer. Whichever way St. Laurent examined the situation, adequate reinforcements seemed essential; the only question was how to obtain them. Conscription might well turn out to be the least efficient solution, he argued with himself, as it would engender such resistance in Quebec that the total war effort might be diminished. He joined with his cabinet colleagues in trying to devise other ways to find more men. Special inducements should be given to the N.R.M.A. men who volunteered, he suggested, and disadvantages imposed on those who did not. There were 120,000 volunteers stationed in Canada, and 90,000 more in Britain, he and other ministers pointed out; surely it was possible to get 15,000 of them into action. Ralston clung to his view that there was no alternative to sending conscripts overseas, and threatened to resign if his recommendation was not accepted without delay; it seemed likely that he would take Ilsley, Macdonald, and perhaps Crerar and Gibson with him. Mackenzie King countered with a similar threat if his colleagues did not support him.

From October 18 to October 30, the cabinet virtually lived with the dilemma, meeting nearly every day for several hours, then adjourning without visible signs of progress. In addition to the time they spent in the Council Chamber, St. Laurent and Ralston, who maintained their mutual high regard, discussed the problem privately on several occasions; Mackenzie King and St. Laurent met frequently as well. By October 26, the press was aware of the crisis, and speculating on its ramifications. In a final attempt to reach a compromise agreement, Mackenzie King and St. Laurent met Ralston on October 30. Earlier in the war, he might well have supported conscription, St. Laurent told the Minister of Defence, but he could not do so within months, perhaps weeks, of the end of the conflict, particularly before all other means of obtaining the reinforcements had been tried. When the Prime Minister had employed the expression, 'conscription if necessary', it was meant to signify 'necessary to win

*The Canadian conscription crisis was indeed taken into account by the German military leaders in preparing the Ardennes offensive in late 1944.

the war', and not necessary to meet the army's requirements, he argued, and, since the war was going to be won regardless of the decision taken, there was no need to invoke the promise. The Prime Minister was beyond such rational argument; approaching pathos, he complained that conscription would mean the defeat of the government, and the end of the Liberal Party and of his own career; he saw in the insistence of the single-minded Minister of Defence a plot to ruin his health, to destroy him politically, and to take vengeance for his life-long devotion to the interests of 'little' Canadians. Once again, the discussion was in vain.

His irrational outbursts notwithstanding, Mackenzie King was not so close to the end of his resources as he appeared; the next day, the Prime Minister reminded St. Laurent of their conversation about McNaughton, and when the Minister of Justice commented that it might be for the best to bring him into the picture, the general was summoned to Laurier House. To the Prime Minister's delight, McNaughton still took the position that conscription would work irreparable harm to Canada, and that it was unnecessary in order to win the war. With renewed hope, the Prime Minister offered him the defence portfolio. McNaughton accepted; it was agreed that he would take personal charge of an appeal for volunteers, and that any decision concerning conscription would be postponed until after the results of the appeal were known. Simultaneously, every effort would be made to release volunteers in Canada and Great Britain for front-line duty.

When the cabinet met on October 31, St. Laurent was the only person present, besides the Prime Minister, who knew of the impending move, and he wondered if the proposed cure would not prove more drastic than the disease, since Ralston's departure might precipitate other resignations. After two or three hours of discussion, the area of disagreement had been narrowed, and St. Laurent had the impression that the Minister of Defence had not yet made up his mind to resign, when Mackenzie King declared that the time had arrived to reach a decision. The Minister of Defence had no solution to the reinforcements problem, except to impose conscription, the Prime Minister declared, but there was a person, General McNaughton, who felt that *he* did, and who was ready to try; Ralston had in the past stated his readiness to resign, and the time had come for him to make room for his successor. Taken by surprise, the Minister of Defence said he would, of course, go, uttered a few words of farewell, shook hands round the table, and left. No one else moved. The following day, McNaughton took his place immediately on the other side of the Prime Minister from St. Laurent.*

While St. Laurent's personal inclination had been to continue the search for a formula acceptable to all the ministers, he supported his leader loyally. Speaking in Quebec City a few days later, he stated that Ralston was 'a great Canadian who is worthy of the admiration of all Canadians', but that his recommendation would have dealt such a destructive blow to national unity that 'it might have taken decades to rebuild it'. The fifteen days of agonizing search for a solution to the problem had confirmed his view that 'we of Quebec Province have the right to have confidence in a group of Canadians who are not of the same racial origin as we but who, like us, are Canadians before anything else'. At the same meeting, Godbout paid a fervent tribute to Mackenzie King and St. Laurent as the saviours of Canadian unity. Elsewhere, the reaction was very different. A *Globe and Mail* editorialist described the government's policy as 'Quebec shall rule, or the national house shall be destroyed', and declared bitterly: 'We beyond Quebec are in truth a subjugated people – sold into bondage for political power.' The Minister of Justice was roundly condemned in English Canada as the ringleader of an alleged group of French Catholics who controlled the Prime Minister. In actual fact, St. Laurent had still not committed himself irrevocably on the conscription issue. 'I trust you will believe that if I felt conscription would be the right thing at this time I would not hesitate in saying so,' he wrote sharply on November 15 to one Conservative who had criticized him in the press, 'but I do not think that is the case ... and General McNaughton also thinks there are [other ways].' On November 12, Ralston gave his version of the crisis to the press, provoking a sharp increase in anti-government sentiment in English Canada.

*For a more graphic description of this scene, see R. M. Dawson, *The Conscription Crisis of 1944*, p. 41 ff.

Inside the cabinet, the remaining conscriptionists stiffened in their resistance once more, and made it clear that they regarded the voluntary recruiting campaign as a doubtful experiment that would have to be followed by conscription if it failed to achieve results in a limited period of time. The government had been given a mere respite, not a reprieve. Mackenzie King summoned Parliament to meet on November 22; the final show-down could not be delayed much beyond that date.

In his harassed state, the Prime Minister leaned more and more heavily on St. Laurent, calling him frequently to his study in Laurier House for special consultations. The calm and reasonable approach of the Minister of Justice was a balm to his frayed nerves, and he found strength in St. Laurent's quiet confidence that right was on their side. Within the cabinet, the Minister of Justice had a similar moderating influence. Respected and liked by all his colleagues, he never once exchanged bitter words with those who differed with him, whereas the disagreement between the Prime Minister, on the one hand, and Ilsley, Macdonald, and Crerar, on the other, became almost a personal feud. By his very presence he curbed anti-Quebec sentiment, since it was difficult to accuse of bigotry and want of patriotism a group of people represented by such a man. By his loyalty to the Prime Minister, he set an example that it was difficult for the others not to follow. Unfortunately, perhaps, the solution to the problem lay outside the Council Chamber – specifically, in the army camps from which the necessary volunteers would have to be drawn.

On entering the government, General McNaughton was convinced that there were enough volunteers already available, but that they had been wrongly deployed and needed to be taken out of less essential posts in order to be sent to the front. Since such an operation required more time than was available to him, he decided to tour the whole country in a nation-wide appeal for volunteers. After receiving a very indifferent reception at meetings in Arnprior and Ottawa, however, he abandoned that plan. Many of his senior officers were convinced that the recruiting campaign could not succeed and were determined to prove that they were right; Major-General G. R. Pearkes even allowed officers in his Pacific Coast command to criticize the government's policy in a meeting with the press in Vancouver. They found eager allies in the Tory party and the English-language press. Faced with such obstruction, the recruiting campaign never got off the ground; in the first three weeks, only 694 N.R.M.A. men volunteered for overseas service. On November 20, two days before Parliament was to meet, Ilsley, Macdonald, and Crerar indicated in cabinet that they favoured conscription and were prepared to resign if it was not introduced; on the following day, Mackenzie King suggested to his colleagues that a definite time limit should be set, and if an adequate number of men had not been acquired by then he would resign, leaving his successor to introduce compulsory military service. Once again, the government was on the brink of disaster. A period of intense silence followed the ominous declaration, and then ministers began rallying to the Prime Minister's support. The four French-speaking Canadians and Agriculture Minister Gardiner declared that they would follow him if he left; soon it was apparent that the out-and-out conscriptionists were in a minority, and it was their turn to talk of resigning. His confidence enhanced, Mackenzie King renewed his appeal to avoid a break-up of the cabinet. In the end, it was agreed to wait another two weeks for the results of the recruiting campaign; meanwhile, they would present a solid front to Parliament, and ask it to approve a vague resolution supporting the government in 'its policy of maintaining a vigorous war effort'. After the meeting, the government leader and St. Laurent went over the whole situation again, and discussed the various situations that might arise when Parliament met the next day; then Mackenzie King returned to the solitude of Laurier House, recorded in his diary that the Minister of Justice had been 'very helpful', and went to bed. St. Laurent dined that night by chance with the Minister of National Revenue, Colin Gibson, who also lived in the Roxborough Apartment Hotel. A firm conscriptionist, Gibson assumed that a majority of members in the House of Commons would demand some form of compulsory military service, and that the French-speaking ministers would all resign, thus making way for a cabinet willing to introduce such a measure. The two men chatted amicably about the situation, then said a regretful good-bye, realizing that by the end of the following day they might no longer be cabinet colleagues.

Neither man reckoned with the extraordinary resilience of the Prime Minister. On the following morning, less than four hours before Parliament was to meet, General McNaughton telephoned to inform him that, according to the military headquarters staff, the voluntary system would not get the required men; worse still, one military district commander had resigned, and if others followed his example the whole military machine might disintegrate. A less seasoned politician might have panicked or collapsed; Mackenzie King saw in the new situation a way out of the dilemma. He had never closed the door irrevocably on conscription, but had merely demanded to be convinced of its necessity; the latest advice from General McNaughton could not be questioned; having done everything possible to avoid it, he could introduce compulsory overseas service with a clear conscience. With a sense of relief, he began to prepare the radical change in course. St. Laurent spent the morning in his office, clearing his desk in anticipation of spending most of the coming days in the Commons Chamber, and completely unaware that the government's policy had been altered. The Prime Minister arrived on Parliament Hill just in time for the opening of the House of Commons, took his place in the Chamber, and proceeded with the business as if nothing unusual were to happen. As soon as Mackenzie King had read the letters exchanged between himself and Ralston concerning the latter's resignation, Opposition leader Graydon moved, seconded by John Diefenbaker, that '... all trained troops in the Canadian defence army should immediately be dispatched for reinforcements overseas'. In their zeal, the Tories ran afoul of the rules of Parliament; the Speaker refused to accept the motion because the required forty-eight hours' notice had not been given. The Prime Minister then proposed to allow General McNaughton, not yet a member of Parliament, to address the House the next day; after some bickering over procedure, the proposal was accepted. With that, the sitting was adjourned. Before going to his office, Mackenzie King found time to ask Angus Macdonald to delay the resignation he had threatened to submit that day, and sent word to his supporters that the cabinet would be meeting later to discuss 'further information' he had received. Only then did he send for St. Laurent, who was as mystified as everyone else at the vague allusion.

Louis St. Laurent was deeply perturbed on learning of Mc-Naughton's advice that the voluntary recruitment campaign had failed, and even more so by the picture presented to him of a possible open conflict between the civil and military authorities. In his eagerness to win the support of his leading Quebec colleague, Mackenzie King may well have exaggerated the gravity of the situation. St. Laurent's first reaction was one of indignation at what appeared to be an attempt by the army to intimidate the government, and he was determined not to submit to what was tantamount to rebellion. It was the Prime Minister's turn to counsel moderation, and they soon agreed that neither the country nor the cabinet could stand further disagreement. While he was still convinced that the war could be won without imposing conscription, the Minister of Justice was aware of the importance of maintaining the strength of the infantry units in Europe, both for purposes of morale and because of their special importance in the final stage of the fighting. He realized, too, that the very existence of the government might depend on his decision, and that the real choice before him was whether it should survive to introduce a modest measure of compulsory overseas service, or whether it should fall and be replaced by a government committed to the all-out conscription that Graydon and Diefenbaker had demanded. He had kept his hands free in order to meet just such a situation; now, with the pessimistic comment that it might cost the Liberals every seat in Quebec, he rose to the occasion and told the Prime Minister that he would support limited conscription for overseas service.

While St. Laurent was making his crucial decision, six cabinet colleagues–Ilsley, Crerar, Macdonald, Howe, Gibson, and Mulock – were pondering their own future in a near-by office. The policy of voluntary recruitment was no longer defensible, they agreed, and they had no alternative but to resign, even if the government fell as a result. Thus, while Mackenzie King was struggling to prevent an anti-conscriptionist revolt, the conscriptionists were preparing to desert him for a policy he had already abandoned!

Only one other minister was informed of the new situation before the cabinet met that evening. Chubby Power had been in hospital in Quebec during the critical previous weeks and had missed most of the difficult discussions; the Prime Minister filled him in briefly on the new situation and appealed for his support. The veteran politician grasped the hard facts in a few minutes and agreed that some change in policy had become inevitable, but concluded that he personally would have no choice but to resign if the no-conscription promise were broken. St. Laurent's attitude became more important than ever.

The cabinet meeting was almost an anticlimax. The Prime Minister and McNaughton explained the situation, and recommended that 16,000 N.R.M.A. men should be sent overseas. Caught by surprise, both sides in the disagreement remained silent. The Prime Minister went on to discuss how the men would be chosen, and how the new policy would be presented to the country. St. Laurent's contribution was limited mainly to insisting that the Quebec members be warned in a caucus meeting before the policy was announced. Only at the end of the meeting was the word 'resignation' pronounced; Power said he would have to go, and Gardiner declared immediately that he would too, if others did. The Prime Minister intervened forcefully to say that if anyone resigned, he would have to do so himself, and begged them to stay together. As soon as he could end the discussion, Mackenzie King returned to his room and sent for St. Laurent, Bertrand, and Fournier, thanked them for standing by him, and pleaded for their continued support in order to keep the country together and make it possible to carry out all the social reforms they had planned together. In something of a state of shock, the two junior ministers found little to say one way or another. Following the meeting, St. Laurent returned dejectedly to his own office, where some of his staff were waiting. 'It's happened,' he burst out in response to their inquiring gaze. 'I told the Prime Minister to invite me to celebrate the holiday season here, because my people won't have me at home.' There was no need for further explanations; everyone knew that conscription had arrived.

Mackenzie King spent an hour the following morning explaining the decision to caucus, and appealing for continued unity.

The French-speaking members listened in glum silence, with the haunted look of animals at bay. Ralston explained his position, but there was no demonstration of support for him. The meeting was adjourned as soon as possible to allow the cabinet to discuss the order in council that would bring the fateful measure into being. Power handed in his resignation in the Council Chamber and then left; St. Laurent continued to discuss the order, indicating that he was remaining on the team; no one else moved. When the limited conscription was announced in the House of Commons after lunch, most of the Liberals applauded the statement; former Conservative Party leader Hanson cried, 'Surrender!' Later in the day, Charles Parent, member for Quebec West, and Jean-François Pouliot, member for Témiscouata, announced that they were abandoning the government; the following morning Wilfrid LaCroix, member for Montmorency, followed suit. Public Works Minister Fournier was noticeably absent from his seat for the next few days, but no further defections occurred.

The most important unknown factor was the reaction in Quebec. Would French-speaking Canadians accept from the Liberals what they would certainly not have accepted from the Conservatives? Both Godbout and Duplessis denounced the move; Cardinal Villeneuve told Mackenzie King privately that he was sorry it had become necessary, but would still try to be helpful. St. Laurent never wavered. 'I came here to do a war job and because it was felt by the Prime Minister I could be of help,' he stated in a letter on November 23. 'I feel I have no right to quit, whatever may be the increase in the difficulties of the task, so long as it is apparent to me that these difficulties arise out of facts that have a bearing on the service of those who fight for us on the front lines.' He had become convinced that the men in Europe needed more support than was available through the volunteer system, he told one resident of Quebec, and that Canada itself was in danger of falling apart because of the gravity of the issue; both critical situations would be aggravated if he resigned, while by staying on he might at least be able to limit their seriousness; in the circumstances, his sense of duty left him no alternative but to carry on whatever the consequences to himself. At a two-and-a-half-hour meeting with the Quebec caucus, he and Mackenzie King managed to persuade the other French-speaking members to stick with the ship as well, but one of them summed up the general sentiment with the comment: 'I would not dare to go back to my constituency [after supporting the government], I would be stoned to death.'

The first few hours following the announcement of the new policy were the most critical; if they could be survived, calmer spirits would likely prevail. At St. Laurent's suggestion, a secret session of Parliament was held on November 25 in order to put as many facts as possible before the members. During the day, a frantic message arrived from pro-conscriptionist Major-General Pearkes that 1,600 N.R.M.A. men in Terrace, B.C., had seized control of their camp, and that 'the situation . . . can now only be considered as mutiny.' If similar incidents occurred in Quebec, the possibility of civil war seemed real. Tension was increased still further when it was learned that Pearkes had ordered an R.C.A.F. demonstration flight over the base as a warning to the rioters; if the planes were fired upon, as was feared, other troops would have to be sent in, and Canadians would begin killing Canadians. Fortunately, word was transmitted in time to the camp that the R.C.A.F. aircraft were not going to attack, and there was no shooting as they passed over; McNaughton was able to prevent a repeat performance; by the end of the following day, order was restored. The dangerous incident illustrated still more clearly to the government the importance of St. Laurent's staying at his post to calm excited spirits on both sides and to assure respect for the forces of law and order. In correspondence and in conversations, the Minister of Justice worked hard to prove that the government had no choice but to impose a limited measure of conscription, and that the decision was motivated by recent information from Europe, not by pressure from conscriptionist zealots. It was simply a matter of reducing casualties to the minimum, he argued repeatedly; the campaign to recruit volunteers had failed because of the counter-propaganda of those who opposed it, and the Prime Minister could not allow men to die at the front because of political considerations at home. Even if most people in Quebec disagreed with the decision, he hoped that they would continue to believe in the honesty and sincerity of those who took it, and that thoughtful persons would realize that the lesser evil had been chosen. It seemed almost a vain hope; except for a few faithful friends, St. Laurent appeared to be almost universally condemned by his own people.

As the debate proceeded, it became evident that while practically all French-speaking Liberal members opposed the new policy, and would vote against it, no more would cross the floor. Since LaCroix and Pouliot were well known as political mavericks, their action would not be interpreted as significant; more serious was the attitude of Public Works Minister Fournier, whose absence from the Commons Chamber was becoming a matter of speculation, and even of opposition questions. Under heavy pressure from the Ottawa newspaper *Le Droit* and from close friends to resign, the minister hesitated for several days. St. Laurent countered pressure with pressure, and, finally, on November 29, was able to pass along word to the Prime Minister that Fournier was going to stay with the team. The government was not to lose a single French-Canadian minister; it was a greater achievement than most Liberals had dared to hope for.

As each day passed, the government's position grew stronger. Ralston subjected McNaughton to a penetrating inquisition, but stated that he would support the government's new policy in order to assure the expedition of reinforcements to Europe as quickly as possible. Gradually the Quebec members began to participate in the debate, and, while they criticized the resolution, they carefully abstained from attacking either Mackenzie King or St. Laurent; even Cardin gave no intimation that he was about to leave the Liberal Party. It remained to be seen, however, how they would vote; the combined opposition of the all-out conscriptionists and the anti-conscriptionists could bring down the government. On December 1, Joseph Jean, parliamentary assistant to the Minister of Justice, moved an amendment asking that the war effort be pursued vigorously but 'without resorting to conscription for overseas service'. The amendment had been drawn up to give the French-speaking members an opportunity to express their opposition to conscription, and then to support the cabinet's policy as the only other acceptable alternative; Jean was chosen to move the amendment because, as St. Laurent's parliamentary assistant, his prestige was great enough to give the appearance of a strong protest, but insufficient to endanger the government. He had warned his minister in general terms that an amendment would be proposed, and had sent to the Prime Minister his resignation as parliamentary assistant only minutes before he rose to speak. As they watched the strategy unfold, the Conservatives began to realize that once again they were being out-manoeuvred.

As he observed the debate, St. Laurent asked himself how he could help most effectively, and at what point he should intervene in the debate. In a discussion with Godbout in Montreal, he was glad to learn that the former premier understood his position, and regretted having to condemn the government's action himself; to have failed to do so would have precipitated a deluge of more violent declarations from Quebec Liberals. The Minister of Justice never faltered in his support of the Prime Minister; the only doubt in his mind was whether he could exercise any effective influence on his fellow citizens and convince them that, on the basis of facts he could not divulge, they should continue to place their trust in the government. Mackenzie King had no such doubts. 'The more I see of St. Laurent, the nobler soul I believe him to be,' he wrote in his diary after one chat during the critical days. 'One of God's gentlemen if ever there was one.' He advised the Minister of Justice to wait until most of the other Quebec members had spoken and then intervene to pour oil on the troubled waters. The timing was, in fact, determined by Hugues Lapointe. As the son of the late minister, and an army colonel on leave of absence, his attitude was important in determining the success of the government's resolution. Since half of the artillery company that Hugues Lapointe had commanded during the D-Day operations had become casualties, the Prime Minister presumed that he would understand the situation, and help to rally the other members to the government's stand. Mackenzie King made a special plea for his support, but his efforts were in vain; shortly after their conversation, the handsome young officer declared in the House of Commons that he would oppose the measure as he 'would rather withdraw from public life than have it be said by any man who had placed his faith in me that I had failed to keep the word I had given'. At the same time, he conceded there was no one else he wanted to see as head of the government, and he expressed the hope that national unity, to which the Prime Minister had dedicated his life, would survive the current crisis.

The tribute was touching, but the defection of Ernest Lapointe's son on the vital issue was still serious; Mackenzie King decided that the moment had come for St. Laurent to redress the balance. St. Laurent's intervention was considered so important that he was asked to read his notes beforehand in cabinet, where they were endorsed with only one or two suggestions for minor improvements. The speech was delivered on December 6. Brief, concise, and direct, it resembled in many respects the pleas he had made so often in court over the years. Until the evening of November 22, he explained, he had sincerely believed that the voluntary system 'under which over nine hundred thousand of our bravest and best men have offered their services in this great cause' was the best means of supporting the men in action. However, the new situation had forced him to reconsider his view and to ask himself if the lack of reinforcements would increase the level of casualties. He realized full well what the reaction would be in his province if he agreed to any measure of compulsion for overseas service,

> but I came here to do a war job, and because it was felt by the Prime Minister, rightly or wrongly, that I could be of some help. I feel that I must still go on, whatever may be the increase in the difficulties of the task, so long as it is made apparent to me that these difficulties arise out of facts which have a bearing on the security of the men who are doing so much more for us than we can do for them.

He paused, turned directly towards Mackenzie King, and declared: 'I decided I would stand or fall with the Prime Minister. . . . The all important fact is that the reinforcements will be neither insufficient nor delayed.' It was a straightforward, almost matter-of-fact statement, but it released a torrent of desk-pounding; the Prime Minister broke into a happy smile. He presumed that the government's resolution would be approved,

St. Laurent went on. 'The will of the majority must be respected and it must prevail.' At the same time, he hoped that 'the majority will always, as it is doing in this case, assert that will only after giving due consideration to the feelings and views of the minority . . . and then only to the extent to which the majority is sincerely convinced that the general interests of the whole body politic require that it be thus asserted'. Once again, he ended with a plea for unity. Now that the members had all the facts before them to prove the necessity for the resolution, he urged, they should 'unite and . . . assert to the men overseas that this nation, from one ocean to the other, stands pledged to a victory that will be decisive and that will endure'.

Mackenzie King was almost beside himself with delight. The speech was 'magnificent', he declared later – 'magnificent in the sense that it was forthright, honest, sincere, straightforward and true. . . . He is indeed a sterling character.' There was only one word to describe the performance, another cabinet minister wrote in a note of congratulation, and 'that word is "guts" '. Opposition leader Graydon twitted him for having changed his mind so radically, but not a single French-speaking member criticized the speech, although several ignored it in making their own. On the following evening, the amendments proposed by both Jean and Graydon were defeated by large margins, and the main resolution was approved by a vote of 143 to 70; 23 French-speaking Canadians supported the government, 34 opposed it, and 9 were absent. Amazed at the size of the majority, and relieved after the long days of tension, the Liberals broke into cheers. The rest was anticlimax; at two o'clock the next morning the House adjourned until the end of January 1945.

The reaction across Canada to St. Laurent's stand was generally very favourable. The *Montreal Star* described him as one of the 'great Canadians, who without surrendering one iota of their pride of race, put country ahead of party, duty before self-interest'. The Conservative Quebec *Chronicle Telegraph*, a few days earlier a bitter critic, paid tribute to his 'courage, honesty, and disinterested public service'. On the other hand, the Toronto *Globe and Mail* described his speech as a 'nauseating performance' and denounced the 'bare-faced partisan manoeuvre' of men who cried politics, and wailed about the injury to national unity. And in Quebec, the man who had presided at St. Laurent's first political meeting wrote to tell him that he had proved himself once again 'more imperialist than Canadian'. One of the most heartening messages that he received came from Captain Pierre Sévigny, son of his long-time friend, the Chief Justice of the Quebec Superior Court, Albert Sévigny. The young officer wrote from overseas to express 'all the admiration felt for you by the French Canadians overseas', and their general conviction that 'as long as you are on guard at home our fate is in good hands and our interests will be protected'. To St. Laurent the letter was ample reward for the long and difficult days he had just passed through; as long as the brave men whose welfare was always foremost in his mind approved his conduct, the criticism of others was without significance. The Prime Minister himself assessed the role of St. Laurent in a public statement two years later, made in Quebec City:

> I shall always believe that it was the firm and statesman-like stand taken, in that hour of crisis, by the Minister of Justice that ensured the continuance of the government and averted an appalling disaster. I am perfectly certain that had Mr. St. Laurent withdrawn his support of myself, or indeed, wavered in that support, I should have had no alternative but to tender my resignation and with it the resignation of the Ministry.

In that month of December 1944, the citizens of Quebec were not yet able to appreciate his services; recalling the incidents of 1917, a police guard was placed on his house on Grande Allée, and he was advised for his own personal safety to keep away from Quebec City until the strong feelings against him and his colleagues had subsided.

The government had survived a vote in the House of Commons, but the people of Canada seemed less likely to give them a favourable verdict in the general election that had to be held within a few months. The compromise on conscription that had been hammered out on Parliament Hill left both English- and French-speaking Canadians with a feeling of resentment at having their will thwarted, and Gallup polls were running strongly against the Liberals. The first test of public opinion after the conscription debate was a by-election in Grey North, on Georgian Bay in Ontario, to obtain a seat for General McNaughton. The government had hoped that the former commander-in-chief of the troops overseas would be allowed into Parliament by acclamation, but both the Conservatives and the Socialists were keen to test their strength, and a bitter three-way contest developed. The government's situation was made more difficult by the fact that about one-third of the N.R.M.A. men chosen to go overseas had failed to report after being granted Christmas leave. The continuing wrangle over conscription was both unfortunate and unnecessary; casualties in Europe in previous weeks had been much lighter than anticipated, and the 16,000 men who were under way seemed sufficient for the army's needs. Nevertheless, General McNaughton was defeated by the all-out-conscriptionist candidate of the Conservative Party. St. Laurent found some consolation in the thought that rejection of the Liberals in Ontario might lessen animosity towards them in Quebec. During the same period, however, an ugly incident occurred in Drummondville, some seventy miles east of Montreal, that aroused passions in French Canada once again as well. One Saturday night in late February, a joint squad from the R.C.M.P. and the military police descended on the town and began a search for draft defaulters and deserters. A riot broke out, and in the ensuing mêlée several people on both sides were hurt. The fighting lasted several hours, and at one stage the situation was so serious that the army base at Sherbrooke was alerted to prepare to send reinforcements. Almost miraculously, the incident ended without any loss of life, but public indignation was once more directed against the government in Ottawa. On the one hand, the new provincial Bloc Populaire leader, André Laurendeau, condemned the federal government for its 'barbaric' and 'iniquitous' tactics; and the *Globe and Mail* declared the riots to be the result of the 'cowardly leadership' of the Mackenzie King administration. As the minister responsible for the R.C.M.P., St. Laurent issued a bland statement, expressing confidence that the force had 'proceeded with their usual careful methods in carrying out the job they had to do'. The unhappy event underlined the importance of the government's delaying the election until the fighting in Europe had ended; but with its five-year mandate due to expire in mid-April there was cause to wonder if time was not going to run out for it too soon.

Far more agreeable and stimulating to Louis St. Laurent than the domestic political situation were the preparations being made for peace. He was keenly interested in the proposal to create a new international body, similar to the League of Nations but without its numerous defects. Just as he felt that a sentiment of Canadian nationalism would serve as a rallying-point for English-and French-speaking Canadians, so he felt that the two groups would accept a Canadian foreign policy based on active participation in an effective world organization. Thus the quarrel between those who saw in the British connection a tie with the motherland and those who saw in it an instrument of imperial domination would be outdated, and Canada could play a useful role on the international stage. With this goal in mind, St. Laurent urged the Prime Minister to attend the founding conference of the United Nations Organization scheduled to begin on April 25 in San Francisco; for his part, when Mackenzie King began to prepare the delegation early in 1945, he placed his Minister of Justice high on the list of those whom he would take along.

By early March, the Liberal election strategy was prepared; Parliament would meet on March 19 and sit for a month, and be dissolved just before the legal limit of its existence was reached. Voting would take place on June 11, by which time, Providence and Lady Luck willing, the fighting in Europe would be over and the victory jubilation would dim memories of the struggle over conscription; in the new atmosphere of relief and hope, the government could ask for a mandate to help build the brave new world. In fact, the session went pretty well according to the Liberal plan. The session of Parliament ended on April 16, and the following day the cabinet was shuffled to conform to the post-war image. Five ministers – Crerar, Macdonald, Michaud, Laflèche, and McLarty – tendered their resignations and were replaced by Douglas Abbott as Minister for Naval Services, Lionel

Chevrier as Minister of Transport, Paul Martin as Secretary of State, D. L. McLaren as Minister of Revenue, and J. J. McCann as Minister of War Services. In addition, Joseph Jean became Solicitor General, a post that had been unfilled for many years.

Of all his responsibilities, St. Laurent found preparations for the political contest the most baffling. Three and a half years earlier, he had protested to the Prime Minister that he knew nothing of politics, and now he was supposed to organize the entire campaign in his province. Power was the logical person to undertake the task, but he felt he must remain on the side-lines as long as the war was on, and, in addition, he was proving temperamental in his relations with the Prime Minister. To make matters worse, a group of disconcerted Quebec Liberals were planning to form a new party with Cardin as their leader, and the popular former Minister for Air had been approached as a possible member. In an interview with Mackenzie King, Power conceded readily that St. Laurent was the ablest man in the government, but predicted that he would probably not be able to get re-elected in Quebec East, and suggested that he should not make any speeches outside his own constituency since he might hurt the chances of other candidates. St. Laurent's problem was to make any appearances at all, since the Prime Minister insisted that they both attend the San Francisco Conference, and it was not likely to end before election day. When it became evident that Power would not place his considerable organizational talent at the party's disposal, St. Laurent called Joseph Jean to his office, and told the Solicitor General that he would have to look after the campaign in Quebec as best he could; Jean's only instructions were to try to find Liberal or Independent Liberal candidates for every riding. With that vague directive, St. Laurent set off with the Prime Minister for the founding meeting of the United Nations Organization.

The goals of the Canadian delegation at San Francisco were relatively modest, since Mackenzie King was hardly an enthusiastic internationalist and was more preoccupied with asserting Canada's sovereignty than with working towards a form of world government. St. Laurent was more enthusiastic about the possibilities of the new organization than his leader, and more anxious to have Canada do her full part to make it effective. In that respect, he felt closer to the senior staff member of the delegation, L. B. Pearson, Canadian Ambassador to Washington, whose imagination was stirred by the possibilities of the new world body. Recalling the inability of the League of Nations to prevent aggression, both St. Laurent and Pearson were convinced of the importance of putting teeth in the United Nations Organization by creating an international police force under its command. On one point they agreed emphatically with the Prime Minister: the organization must be truly international in character, rather than a tool of a few great powers. With that consideration in mind, the Canadians worked to assure the effective representation of the middle-sized powers like Canada in the Security Council, and to make sure that they took part in making all decisions in which their own armed forces were involved.

It soon became evident that the attempt to limit the authority of the major powers was doomed to failure; Churchill, Stalin, and Roosevelt had agreed at Yalta that each major power should have a permanent seat in the Security Council, and a veto over all questions of substance, except when a party to a dispute. In behind-the-scenes discussions, the British and Americans urged that the veto power was the necessary price of obtaining Soviet co-operation, but St. Laurent gained the impression that the two Western powers were as anxious to obtain it as the Russians. In the end, he concluded reluctantly that the Yalta formula represented the greatest possible measure of agreement that could be obtained among the great powers themselves on this subject, and that it was not too high a price to pay for a world organization that held so much promise in other respects. The world was still imperfect, St. Laurent concluded after observing the negotiations, and so the organization would have to be imperfect as well. With time and practice, he hoped that the habit of co-operation would grow, and that a situation would eventually evolve where nations conformed automatically to the rules of conduct that would be outlined in the United Nations Charter, thus making the veto, and even armed force, superfluous.

Still feeling a novice in international politics, Louis St. Laurent was content to play the role of a useful member of the Canadian delegation, addressing the assembly on topics assigned to him, and serving on committees such as the one charged with drawing up the provisions for the new International Court of Justice. He was consulted frequently, particularly by the Prime Minister, and his distinguished, even courtly, appearance, his fluency in English and French, and his forthright attitude, leant prestige and weight to the Canadian team. One of the most vivid experiences of St. Laurent's stay south of the border was a visit with the Prime Minister to Oakland harbour to welcome a group of Canadian missionaries and relatives of missionaries being repatriated from a Japanese concentration camp in the Philippines. Some of them were White Nuns from the monastery across the street from his own home in Quebec City. Their tattered clothes, he recounted later, were hanging as loosely on their emaciated frames as on a clothes-rack. The two men met the widow of a Protestant missionary who had died from the privations of camp life; with her were her seven children, the eldest just fourteen years of age. She told them that life had seemed almost unbearable to her when she was first left alone with such a heavy responsibility, and no resources except her two knees to pray on, but they had all survived, and no one would ever be able to make her doubt the effectiveness of prayer. Her story touched St. Laurent deeply, and he saw it as an illustration of the need for courage in striving to establish world peace.

The Canadian delegation had been in San Francisco only a few days when they were informed that victory in Europe was at last imminent, and would probably arrive in early May, about half way through the federal election campaign. If the electorate could be made to realize that a near-miracle had been accomplished in bringing the country through the war intact, that they had made a very creditable contribution to the Allied victory, and that they now faced a future with limitless possibilities, they would scarcely condemn the government that had been the instrument of such success. Mackenzie King spent much of his time fretting over his victory broadcast to the Canadian people; St. Laurent prepared a similar message in French. They were delivered on VE Day, May 8, direct from San Francisco. St. Laurent called on all Canadians to unite in the celebration of victory, and in giving thanks to God 'for saving us and all the other peoples of the United Nations'. But, he warned, there was still another war to be won, 'the war against war itself'; out of the furnace of the great conflict had come a desire to assure security in the world, and at San Francisco the nations were 'trying to assure for all peoples on the earth, generations still unborn, the benefits of a more secure and fuller life'. That achievement alone, he declared, would be a fitting monument to commemorate the accomplishment of the free nations in the terrible war that was being brought to an end.

With the fighting in Europe over, and the election date approaching, the Prime Minister was impatient to return home to begin his cross-Canada speaking tour. The reports he had been receiving until VE Day were still pessimistic, and he was even advised that he had little chance of being elected in his own constituency of Prince Albert, Saskatchewan. In Quebec, Joseph Jean had thrown himself into the task of finding candidates but he had encountered a general reluctance to run on a straight Liberal ticket. To make matters worse, Cardin announced the formation of a new party, the Front National, a federal counterpart of Duplessis's Union Nationale. Almost simultaneously, Camillien Houde, freed from internment and welcomed as a hero in Montreal, made it known that he, too, was forming a new party in order to assure 'the survival of the French Canadians as an ethnic group'. Also campaigning in Quebec were the Bloc Populaire, led by former Liberal M.P. Maxime Raymond, and a group of independents under the rather tenuous leadership of Frédéric Dorion, a close associate of Maurice Duplessis. Against such an array of anti-conscriptionists, Jean feared that the Liberal Party would be crushed once and for all. On the morning of May 8, he arrived in Sherbrooke to begin again the thankless task of trying to persuade a group of local Liberals to choose a candidate. The former member for Sherbrooke, Maurice Gingues, had announced his intention of retiring, and party officials had all but decided to let the seat go by default. The Solicitor General worked hard during a luncheon meeting to stir them out of their lethargy, but he was about to abandon the struggle when the news broke suddenly upon the world that peace had been declared in Europe. Immediately, the atmosphere in the town changed;

people ran out into the streets to announce the glad tidings, faces lit up, and a fresh resilience was evident in everyone's step. The contagious cheerfulness swept over Jean and his luncheon companions, and suddenly they were filled with a new feeling of hope for the Liberal cause. The discussions began again, but this time on a more positive note; by mid-afternoon Gingues had been persuaded to accept the nomination, and preparations were under way for a convention to confirm the choice. By early evening the streets were filled with gay, carefree people bent on celebrating the return of peace. The political meeting had already begun before a small audience when a cloudburst struck the city, and torrents of rain poured down upon the revellers. Someone suggested taking cover at the Liberal meeting, and in a few minutes there was not even standing room in the hall. Rising to the occasion, Jean made the best speech of his life, proclaiming an end to the discord between Canadians, and the dawn of a new era. The candidate was chosen to a chorus of roars of approval; his victory was certain even before the crowd swept out into the streets again to continue the celebrations.

The VE Day festivities were hardly over when Cardin began experiencing difficulty in finding candidates to run under his new party's banner; even some of the men who had already agreed to do so were returning to the Liberal fold. Promises of financial support evaporated. At the opportune moment, Jean let Cardin understand that if he abandoned the plan to form his own party he would not be opposed in his own constituency; the ailing old warrior agreed to stand as an 'Independent Liberal' which meant, for all practical purposes, his reintegration in the party. After that, Jean's difficulties in finding candidates were over. When Mackenzie King and St. Laurent arrived in Vancouver on May 16, they were greeted by a report in the Vancouver *Sun* declaring that 'Liberals all the way from Halifax to Victoria are confident now that Quebec is safe for Liberalism'.

Leaving the Prime Minister to conduct his nation-wide campaign, St. Laurent rushed home to look into the situation in his own constituency. Dessureault reported that his prospects of success in Quebec East were improving rapidly despite strong opposition from Independent candidate Noël Dorion, younger brother of Frédéric Dorion. With that assurance, St. Laurent went on to Ottawa to attend to official business. His first campaign speech was a radio address in French on May 23, just two weeks before polling day. Its most remarkable feature was that he did not once pronounce the word 'Liberal', but described the work going on at San Francisco, and Canada's role there as 'a young, but completely adult, nation, mistress of all her own decisions, both domestic and international'. In a second broadcast two days later, he faced the conscription issue squarely. He had entered the cabinet only because he felt Canada was in danger, he recalled, and he had been careful from the outset not to commit himself to anything except to working in the best interest of Canada. It would have been easy for the Liberals to take a stand against conscription; had they done so, they would have swept the province of Quebec and held it for at least a generation. However, they would have sown in Canada 'a crop of hate and conflict so serious and so venomous that no one could foresee with certainty the consequences for the Canadian nation'. Turning to the charge that the government had broken its promise with regard to conscription, St. Laurent declared that the Prime Minister's undertaking in 1939 not to impose compulsory overseas service without prior consultation had been given to the whole country, and not merely to Quebec, and that he had been relieved of it by the vote of the Canadian people in the plebiscite. In the circumstances, the Minister of Justice stated, 'I cannot admit Mr. King broke any promise that bound him when the Order in Council was passed last November.' He described the conditions leading up to the measure for partial conscription, and related the warning the government had received that casualties would be greater if reinforcements were not made available promptly. 'Could we refuse to do anything possible to reduce the danger to our soldiers fighting so bravely overseas?' he asked in conclusion. That was the question the public would have to decide, and he would submit to their verdict.

On June 3, Mackenzie King and St. Laurent appeared together for the first time on a political platform. Before an audience of 12,000 people in the Montreal Forum, the Prime Minister turned to his Quebec lieutenant and declared that 'no man could possess a truer friend . . . no leader could have a more loyal colleague; no Prime Minister could have an abler counsellor.' If St. Laurent had not agreed to enter the government in 1941, he told the huge crowd, 'I very much question if I would be speaking to you tonight'. His listeners reacted enthusiastically to the tribute to a fellow French Canadian; the wildly successful meeting leant credence to reports that the tide was running in favour of the Liberals. There were additional indications. Sarto Fournier, a Front National candidate not long before, spoke fervently in favour of Mackenzie King. In Rivière-du-Loup, Jean-François Pouliot appeared at the railway station with a large crowd and gave a rousing reception to 'his' Prime Minister. At the Prime Minister's meeting in Quebec City, the platform of the Palais Montcalm was filled with local Liberals, including Adélard Godbout, Hugues Lapointe, and Wilfrid LaCroix; even Power had been persuaded to return from the Gaspé Peninsula, where he had been sulking during most of the campaign, and to introduce the party leader. In his first appearance in the old city since the conscription crisis, Mackenzie King received one of the best receptions of his career; he responded generously, paying tribute to Godbout and Power, and appealing for St. Laurent's re-election, that he might continue to have him at his side.

Once again, the St. Laurent family gathered in their living-room on election night to hear the results. The first bulletins from the Maritime provinces were discouraging, but as soon as the figures for Quebec began to arrive, spirits rose quickly. In Quebec East, St. Laurent took the lead at once, and he was soon heading for a crushing victory of more than 10,000 votes over Noël Dorion. He interpreted the result as an endorsement of his stand during the war, and a vote for national unity. The province of Quebec gave the Liberals 54 out of 65 seats; on the national level, the government won a narrow majority of 125 out of 245 seats. The Conservative and C.C.F. parties received 67 and 28 seats respectively. The Prime Minister lost his Prince Albert seat, but he had the satisfaction of knowing that he had brought the country, and the party, through one of its severest tests, and that he had thwarted his political foes both on the right and the left, in English- and in French-speaking Canada.

# 7

---

# The Brave Post-War World

When St. Laurent returned to Ottawa two days after the election, his main concern was similar to that of many thousands of other Canadians – to see how soon he could get his release from war service and resume his peace-time way of life. The war with Japan was not yet over, but the British and Americans had made it plain that they wanted no more than a token Canadian force in the Pacific, and volunteers would suffice for that purpose. He had helped to hold the country together during the struggle in Europe, to establish Canada's position in the international community of nations, and to obtain for the Liberals a further mandate to carry out their post-war program. There was only one task left to complete; for about a year he had been a member of a committee formed to prepare a federal-provincial conference on reconstruction, that was scheduled for midsummer. When that meeting was over, he could retire from politics with the feeling that he had done his duty. In February, his daughter Madeleine had married Hugh O'Donnell, his former associate in the Montreal law office, and Renault had married earlier in the war. Louis St. Laurent was anxious to resume his place at the head of the family in Quebec before he became a stranger there.

Following a post-election cabinet meeting, Mackenzie King took St. Laurent home to his farm in the Gatineau Hills for a quiet dinner and chat. During the previous months and years they had spent many hours together, but usually under conditions of stress when urgent problems had to be solved. In the relaxed atmosphere of Kingsmere, the seventy-year-old Prime Minister found him not only a colleague whose judgement could be trusted, but also a delightful companion. They discussed the election again, examined the problem of finding replacements for McNaughton and McLaren, the two cabinet ministers who had been defeated, and considered the future prospects of the government. They spoke of Mackenzie King's own position, without a parliamentary seat, and the government leader suggested that, since St. Laurent had won such an impressive vote of confidence, he might be the one to take over the leadership. Whether the remark was seriously intended or not, it was met by an unequivocal refusal. Later that evening, St. Laurent assured Renault that they would be back in the law firm together within six months.

Mackenzie King and St. Laurent flew to San Francisco on June 22 to sign the United Nations Charter, then rushed back to throw themselves into the summer program of work. The Minister of Justice became chairman of the committee charged with preparing the federal-provincial conference, and spent many hours putting the government's views and recommendations into a document that became known as the Green Book proposals. In brief, they suggested that the war-time agreements to centralize tax revenues in Ottawa be continued for a further period in order to enable the federal authorities to carry out a far-reaching program of reconstruction and social welfare. Specifically, the federal government would continue to occupy the personal income tax, corporation tax, and succession duty fields; in return, it would make grants to the provinces to assist them in providing a reasonable level of services, and would accept wide responsibilities for old-age pensions, unemployment assistance, health insurance, public works, and the development of natural resources. While such proposals were in line with the Prime Minister's views as a social reformer, with those of Brooke Claxton, the indefatigable work-horse of the government, and of senior officials such as Deputy Minister of Finance Clark, Alexander Skelton, John Deutsch, and R. B. Bryce, they seemed out of character at first sight for a Quebec corporation lawyer. However, St. Laurent felt strongly that the federal government had a responsibility to avoid another economic depression, and the human suffering it would entail.

> Thirty years ago I didn't think the individual was entitled to anything else but a fair share of the national resources of the land and what it provided, and that each one had the responsibility of making his own way [he was to comment later], but now I've had to revise my views in that respect and I've had to realize that because of the way the economy has evolved there are situations . . . that occur when under certain circumstances individuals cannot cope adequately themselves.

That realization, and an increased understanding of economics, had led him to accept the principle of national spending programs that would redistribute the nation's earnings in order to ensure a basic level of services in all areas. He had also become convinced that the federal government must use its fiscal powers to maintain economic activity, engaging in deficit financing when unemployment threatened, and draining off excess money through surpluses and taxes in the event of inflation. Federal intervention to make the wealthier provinces assist the poorer ones seemed as logical to him as strong people assisting the weak, or the more fortunate assisting the less fortunate. Members of the same national family, Canadians shared great natural wealth bestowed upon them by a generous Providence; they had a duty to develop it together, and to share it equitably.

The federal delegation was not going to present its proposals on a 'take it or leave it' basis, Louis St. Laurent stated shortly before the federal-provincial meeting, but, 'if the Dominion comes to the conclusion that it is essential things must be done, we will have to do them notwithstanding [provincial opposition]'. Newspaper forecasts of a clash between Ottawa and the two largest provinces proved all too accurate. Mackenzie King tried to set an elevated and conciliatory tone in his opening statement on August 6, but Premier Drew replied immediately with a harsh, uncompromising attack on the federal government. Maurice Duplessis, in turn, began by professing his desire to 'collaborate and co-operate' with Ottawa, then followed Drew's lead with a vigorous denunciation of the federal proposals. Centralization was an evil principle of government, he declared. 'Hitler is the prototype of the centralizer. Centralization always leads to Hitlerism.' Giving vent to the frustrations and trials of the long war years, the premiers enumerated their grievances at length, alternately charging Ottawa with being power-hungry and demanding greater federal intervention. The spectacle of a series of provincial premiers advancing parochial and often irreconcilable viewpoints, and agreed only in their disapproval of the national government, was a disheartening commentary on Canada's national unity, as the country entered the long-awaited post-war era.

The most stirring moment of the conference came when Mackenzie King announced, just before lunch on the first day, that the world's first atomic bomb had just been dropped on Japan. Except for C. D. Howe, everyone present was taken completely by surprise. The news provided only a temporary distraction, and in the afternoon the acrimonious negotiations were resumed. When St. Laurent sought to elaborate on the federal government's proposals, an hour's wrangling over procedure took place before he could even get the floor. On the second day, the meeting was continued behind closed doors in the hope that the participants would be less likely to play to the gallery; but the atmosphere did not improve, and alert newspapermen were still able to report serious dissension. After the morning session of the third day, the federal team learned that Drew and Duplessis were lunching together, raising the possibility of a new Ontario-Quebec axis reminiscent of the Hepburn-Duplessis alliance that made the work of the Rowell-Sirois Commission so difficult. Despite keen lobbying by the federal ministers and intense efforts by committees of experts, it was evident by the fourth day that there would not be unanimous agreement to Ottawa's proposals. Fearing it would simply formalize differences of opinion by making separate agreements with the different provinces, the federal government proposed an adjournment and suggested that the officials of the two levels of government continue to exchange information until another full-scale meeting was convened. In brief, the first stage of the negotiations had failed.

The new Parliament had been summoned to meet on September 6, and the ministers went on almost immediately to prepare for the first post-war session. On August 12 Japan surrendered, and the guns of World War II fell silent. Mackenzie King made some further adjustments in his cabinet, replacing McNaughton with Douglas Abbott as Minister of National Defence, switching Bertrand to the Post Office Department, naming a New Brunswick member, H. F. Bridges, Minister of Fisheries, and appointing McCann to the Revenue portfolio.

All was in readiness for the session when a frightened little man in Ottawa triggered a crisis that was to set a pattern for the post-war years. Igor Gouzenko, a twenty-six-year-old cipher clerk at the Soviet Embassy, turned up at the offices of the *Ottawa Journal* on the swelteringly hot evening of September 5 with a package of documents, and explained to a man on the city desk that he had evidence of a Soviet spy ring in Canada extending into the most secret branches of the federal administration. With a curt, 'Sorry, I'm busy,' he was told to take his story to the R.C.M.P., or to return in the morning. Frantic at the prospect of other members of the embassy staff discovering that the documents were missing, the Russian crossed over to the Justice Building on Wellington Street, and told the commissionaire at the door that it was 'desperately necessary' that he speak with St. Laurent right away. Once again, he was told to come back in the morning. He returned home and, after spending a fear-filled night, appeared again at the Justice Building, this time with his wife and small daughter, only to find that St. Laurent had gone straight to the Parliament Buildings; they trudged over there. Once again, they were to be frustrated. A secretary spoke to St. Laurent on the telephone in his inner office, then sent them back to the Justice Building. There they waited for two agonizing hours, only to be told in the end that the minister could not see them. 'We had diplomatic relations with Russia,' St. Laurent explained later, '. . . and I felt that I couldn't take the responsibility of seeing someone who had left the embassy, and claimed to have taken papers away from the embassy with him.' In the circumstances, he told the secretary to 'just keep him off for some time' while the Department of External Affairs was consulted on what action was appropriate. Beside himself, Gouzenko said he would return to his flat, and that suicide was the only alternative open to him. The Minister of Justice reported the situation to Norman Robertson, Under Secretary of State for External Affairs, and went into the Commons Chamber for the opening ceremonies of Parliament.

After the Speaker had been chosen for the new Parliament, Mackenzie King and St. Laurent met with Norman Robertson to discuss the situation. Canada, like most other Western nations, was anxious to have harmonious relations with the Soviet Union, and the three men wished to avoid any incident that would stir old suspicions and animosities. At the same time, they could not ignore the possibility that the man's story was genuine, and that he might be in mortal danger. The threat of suicide was also worrisome. They decided not to communicate with the Soviet Embassy for the moment, but if he should turn up again, to have the man directed to Robertson, who was the person authorized to receive staff members of local embassies. Later in the day, St. Laurent was attending a reception when Soviet Ambassador Zaroubin approached him. Angus Macdonald was also present, and, to make conversation, asked if Zaroubin had been out practising his favourite sport of fishing recently. The Russian replied in the negative, then turned to the Minister of Justice and asked pointedly, 'Has Your Excellency found the fishing good today?' St. Laurent stammered a non-committal reply, but was amused by the cool-headed remark.

In the meantime, the Gouzenkos continued their wandering through the streets of Ottawa. Back in the *Ottawa Journal* offices, they were told that 'nobody wants to say anything but nice things about Stalin these days'. Acting on a suggestion that they should take out Canadian naturalization papers, they went to the Crown Attorney's office, only to be told that the application process would take several months. They finally succeeded in getting an interview with a local newspaperman, and even managed to impress him with their story, but he felt it was 'much too big', and 'a matter for the police or the government'. He, too, was 'sorry'. The weary little family returned to their apartment. Frightened for their lives, they persuaded a neighbour on the same floor to take them in for the night. Shortly before midnight the chief secret-service official from the Soviet Embassy and three other men appeared and knocked at the door of Gouzenko's apartment; a neighbour told them that the Gouzenkos had gone away. The four men left, but returned soon, and forced open the door. The Ottawa police were called, and two constables soon arrived. The Russians said that they had come to get some documents left by Gouzenko 'who happens to be in Toronto tonight', and who had given 'his permission to look for them'. When the constables asked if he had also given permission to break the lock, they argued that it was Soviet property. A police inspector was called, who confirmed that they could not be arrested since they had diplomatic immunity. Finally, both police and Russians left, and the house fell silent once more. However, the wheels of justice and order had at last been set in motion. The Ottawa police telephoned the R.C.M.P. to report that Gouzenko wanted to make an important statement; thus the federal authorities were requested by a third party to intervene and could do so without the breach of protocol that would have occurred had they acceded directly to the request of a staff member of a friendly government to denounce his superiors. Gouzenko was taken to R.C.M.P. headquarters and questioned for five hours. At the end of the day the family was placed in protective custody; his courageous act had succeeded, and proprieties had also been respected.

The revelations of the stolen documents came as a shock to Mackenzie King and St. Laurent, since they indicated a spy network extending into the cipher room of the Department of External Affairs, the most secret laboratories of the National Research Council, and even into Parliament itself. This was a very different image of the Soviet government from the language of idealism and co-operation that had marked the San Francisco Conference a few weeks earlier. They had evidently been seeking, and possibly had obtained, the secret of the atomic bomb. Suddenly the dream of peace began to fade once more.

The session was only a few days old when Louis St. Laurent found his responsibilities increased still further. The Prime Minister was showing signs of tension and fatigue that reflected the crushing war-time burden he had carried, and the continuing strain of the post-war era. The federal-provincial conference had been a disappointment to him, and while the spy affair was still a well-kept secret, it added greatly to his worries. He decided to take advantage of invitations from the new U.S. President, Harry Truman, and the new British Prime Minister, Clement Attlee, to spend a few weeks away from his office. The first colleague he informed of his decision was St. Laurent, who urged him to go if his health was in danger. Mackenzie King took advantage of the conversation to repeat that he would like the Minister of Justice to succeed him when the time arrived to retire, but was told once again that it was out of the question. He was already sixty-three, St. Laurent argued, and the party needed a younger man, since it would probably go into opposition after the next election, and a new leader would need the time to fight his way back into power. The Prime Minister conceded that the reasoning had some validity. Anxious to keep his commitments to a minimum, St. Laurent even refused to become acting prime minister during his leader's absence, pointing out that Ilsley had filled that role well in the past and suggesting that he be given the task again; nor would he act as House Leader, proposing Ian Mackenzie, the senior Privy Councillor in the House of Commons, for that post. He did agree to look after the External Affairs portfolio again in the interim. The conversation revealed that the Prime Minister was leaning on him even more than during the war, and was not ready to accept his early return to Quebec.

As long as he remained in Parliament, St. Laurent was bound to have an important role there. The Progressive Conservatives reflected the feeling of a large body of public opinion weary of restrictions when they attacked the administration for maintaining many of the war-time controls for the period of reconstruction. Replying for the government, St. Laurent conceded readily that the controls were a source of increasing irritation to a people anxious to return to normal peace-time conditions, but argued that they were necessary during the transition period. During the debate, he congratulated a new member, twenty-nine-year-old Davie Fulton, for speaking a few words in French, a rare gesture by an English-speaking Canadian, and encouraged him to continue his efforts as a contribution to national unity. He also jousted good-naturedly with his old friend John Hackett, who had been elected in June as the member for Stanstead, and, as such, was the only Conservative member from Quebec.

In mid-October, St. Laurent made his first comprehensive statement to Parliament on international affairs when he presented the United Nations Charter for approval. 'Peace is not the absence of war,' he stated. 'It is a positive condition in which nations can co-operate for the common good.' In the years ahead, the world would be experimenting with forms of international co-operation, and the charter would have to be adapted to changing conditions. Unfortunately, the five major powers insisted on a veto power that made amendments difficult; it could only be hoped that they would not use this special prerogative to give the charter a rigid character.

> If there is to be an effective United Nations Organization, the great powers must remain united under the strain and stress of the post-war period [he warned]. At the same time it is essential that the middle and smaller powers should be accorded a voice in the peace settlement proportionate to the contribution which they have made in winning the war and which they are willing to make to the problems of peace. . . . The coming of the atomic bomb has opened our eyes to the appalling possibilities which may face the world if the United Nations should fail to achieve international co-operation.

During a debate lasting several days, the principles he outlined were endorsed by a wide range of members, including Bloc Populaire leader Maxime Raymond and the lone Communist member, Fred Rose. The only assurance asked for by M.P.s, and it was given readily, was that any proposed military contribution to the United Nations should be approved in advance by Parliament. When he concluded the debate, St. Laurent appealed for unanimity, in declaring to the world that 'Canada is prepared to take whatever risk may be involved in joining this organization, because the other risk, that of not having an international organization, is something of such consequence that one dare hardly envisage it.' The resolution approving the United Nations Charter was accepted without a formal vote.

A government motion to set up a joint Senate and House of Commons committee to suggest a design for a distinctive Canadian flag gave rise to the first in a series of debates on that subject extending over nearly twenty years. The Red Ensign had been flown on the flagstaff of Parliament on VE Day at the direction of the Prime Minister, and on September 5, 1945, the day before the new Parliament met, it had been designated by order in council as the flag to be flown at 'whatever place and occasion make it desirable to fly a distinctive Canadian flag'. A new flag was among the proposals contained in the Liberal post-war program. Most of the ministers preferred adopting the Red Ensign as the official flag, or, at least, the Red Ensign with a maple leaf in place of the coat of arms. About the only point of disagreement among them was the colour of the leaf, some feeling it should be green, others, including the Prime Minister, preferring the brilliant hues of Canadian autumn. Rather than risk being accused of imposing a design on Parliament, the cabinet decided to form a parliamentary committee and allow a consensus to develop through open discussion. The debate on the motion to create a committee illustrated how little agreement existed among Canadians on the subject. Some members proposed that the Red Ensign be adopted; others argued passionately in favour of the Union Jack; still others recommended with equal fervour a truly distinctive design. John Diefenbaker demanded a 'solemn pledge' that, regardless of the committee's recommendation, the Union Jack would have 'a prominent place' in a new flag, and forecast that any unanimous proposal from the committee would be, 'at the best, a bizarre and hybrid design'. In a moderate and non-partisan reply, St. Laurent endorsed a recent statement by the Prime Minister that it was unthinkable for a Canadian flag not to contain the Union Jack. 'The Union Jack is a symbol which represents much that is best in the heritage of all those who derive their traditions and their culture from Western Europe,' he argued. '. . . The crosses that are now part of the Union Jack represent much of what we in Canada, from whatever race we spring, all honour as precious and good in our heritage.' Rather than a symbol of conquest or subjugation, he continued, the British flag was the emblem under which 'the institutions of this

Canadian nation have grown and developed', and Canada had become 'an autonomous state, subject in no phase of its domestic or external affairs to any other authority than this Canadian Parliament'. In his view, the movement for a flag was not simply an excuse to discard the Union Jack, but was the reflection of a feeling by Canadians that their nation had reached a stature in the family of nations that required a distinctive symbol. St. Laurent's attempt to present a viewpoint that all members could adopt did find wide support, but a hard core on either side remained unmoved. In agreeing to the formation of the committee, opposition leader Bracken warned that his party would oppose any recommendation that did not include the Union Jack; several Liberal and Independent French-speaking members made clear their determination to oppose any design that contained it.

While St. Laurent was becoming increasingly adept at winning his way with a soft, reasonable approach, he revealed at times a stubborn determination, and an ability to counter-attack, that delighted Liberal back-benchers. Shortly after the Prime Minister's return to Canada on November 19, it fell to him as Minister of Justice to ask Parliament to extend the government's war-time emergency powers for another year, in order to prevent a sharp rise in the cost of living during a period of great consumer demand and limited supplies, and to ensure a fair distribution of goods and services. The opposition parties launched a vigorous attack on the proposal, Diefenbaker protesting that 'liberty will become a legend in this country for a period of one year if Parliament abdicates its powers'. Faced with such strong resistance, St. Laurent gave the assurance that Parliament would be able to discuss with a minimum of delay any order in council passed under the authority of the legislation, but the charges that the government was power-hungry continued. While Diefenbaker's sweeping denunciations annoyed St. Laurent, it was Hackett who succeeded in making him lose his composure by asserting that the government did not have 'the nerve to remove controls and give Canada back to democracy and democratic institutions'. His blood rushing up into his neck and face and his eyes flashing, he snapped back that 'this government has not got the nerve to take off controls and make opportunities at the expense of the mass of the population. . . . It is regrettable that the circumstances are such that controls are required; but they are required, and this government has the nerve to come to the country and say it intends to see that they are maintained as long as they are required.' To most members, accustomed to the urbane, conciliatory approach of the Minister of Justice, the blunt riposte and the heavy irony came as a distinct surprise. The Liberals pounded their desks with glee. The flare of temper had one result that St. Laurent deplored; suddenly, politicians, newspapermen, and members of the general public saw him, not as a war-time 'conscript', but as a post-war politician. 'It was told of Mr. St. Laurent at first that his heart was not in Parliament,' an *Ottawa Journal* writer recalled, 'that he had given it irrevocably to Blackstone. . . . Has he changed? Politics, public life, has charms; it has more than once become the mistress of men, who, late in life . . . succumbed to its enchantments.' Another writer went still further and declared: 'It may be a good guess that Mr. St. Laurent may be the next Prime Minister of Canada.'

While the Prime Minister made no open attempt to keep St. Laurent in the government indefinitely, he always seemed to find one more task for him to accomplish that could hardly be refused. Thus, at Christmas time in 1945, instead of celebrating his final release from politics, the reluctant politician found himself preparing to sail for London as head of the Canadian delegation to the first session of the United Nations General Assembly. The assignment drew attention once again to his rapid rise to political prominence; speculation increased concerning his future when his name appeared in the King's New Year's Honours List with that of J. L. Ilsley, as British Privy Councillors. St. Laurent himself was not particularly impressed by the award, interpreting it with some justification as a gesture to French Canada, and recognition of the need to maintain an ethnic balance in such matters. In fact, he was becoming more and more useful to the government; the immediate problem, however, was not how to keep him in Ottawa, but how to make best use of him during the period he would agree to stay. The Prime Minister was thinking of making him the first full-time Minister for External Affairs, and Ilsley suggested that he take over the Finance portfolio.

While Mackenzie King was convinced that St. Laurent should succeed him, he was also grooming a younger man for the prime-ministership. Lester B. 'Mike' Pearson, Canadian Ambassador to the United States, called at Laurier House early in 1946 to discuss his own future. There was a possibility that he might be offered the secretary-generalship of the United Nations, and he felt inclined to accept the post, but wanted the government leader's advice on the implications of such a step for an eventual political career. Mackenzie King felt that a five-year absence from Canada might have an adverse effect on such a plan, and commented that Pearson would have been well advised to obtain a seat in Parliament at the last election. Like St. Laurent, the clever diplomat was motivated less by personal ambition than by a desire for service, and international affairs held greater attraction for him than domestic politics; he returned to his post in Washington without having made a firm decision in favour of one field of activity or the other.

The United Nations meeting in London was held in an atmosphere later to be described as the 'cold war'. British Foreign Secretary Ernest Bevin and U.S. Secretary of State James Byrnes, on the one hand, and Andrei Vishinsky of the Soviet Union on the other, argued bitterly from the outset, and the assembly seemed destined to become a forum where Communists and non-Communists would display to the world their propaganda wares. Voting soon resolved itself into manoeuvring blocs of delegates, and the goal of attempting to reach a consensus on world problems was relegated to a place of secondary importance. In that context, Pearson's chances of becoming secretary general were doomed in advance, Vishinsky arguing that North America had already obtained the permanent site of the world organization and threatening to use the veto power to block the appointment; the important post went to Trygve Lie of Norway. Canada also failed to win the non-permanent seat in the Security Council reserved for a Commonwealth member, St. Laurent announcing after Australia took the lead on the second ballot that his country was withdrawing to avoid embarrassment between the two countries. By the gesture, he not only assured Australian support for Canada when the seat became vacant; he also gave the delegates a salutary lesson in international co-operation. Speaking at the plenary session of the assembly on January 18, he outlined Canada's position in positive terms. World society should move towards a system of law courts and peace officers as in the internal affairs of member nations, he argued, rather than leave the weak at the mercy of the strong. As at San Francisco, he voiced his concern over the veto power, and reminded the great powers that, in signing the charter, they had signed 'a firm pledge [to] . . . use their privileged position only as a sacred trust for the whole of mankind'. The warning had no noticeable effect on the men engaged in the new power struggle.

St. Laurent took advantage of his stay in London to discuss Gouzenko's spy revelations with Prime Minister Attlee and Foreign Secretary Bevin, and to make plans for co-ordinated action by the two governments when the moment arrived to make arrests. He also discussed the continued stationing of Canadian troops in Germany. The Canadians were willing to maintain troops there, he told the British authorities, but as an autonomous unit, and not as a mere component of the British force. The Attlee government hoped to use the Canadian troops to relieve some of their own for duty elsewhere, but St. Laurent had no intention of freeing troops that would hold down other peoples in the Commonwealth, and he made it clear that the Canadians would soon be repatriated to fill the nearly two hundred thousand civilian jobs waiting for them at home. Then, at the earliest possible moment, he flew home himself to attend to his other duties.

Four days after leaving London, St. Laurent was in his place as chairman of the co-ordinating committee of the federal-provincial conference. Since the plenary session in the previous August, negotiations had continued, and Ottawa had increased the unconditional grants it was willing to pay the provinces as rent for the three main fields of direct taxation. Mackenzie King and St. Laurent were inclined to go further, and to give the assurance that they only contemplated occupying the tax fields in the event of an emergency, but Finance Minister Ilsley and his advisers insisted that the federal government needed a completely free hand if it was to take effective action in the event of the economic recession that was generally anticipated. In the circumstances, the federal ministers appeared to be holding to a rigid position, whereas they were, in fact, the rather unwilling mouthpieces of Dr. Clifford Clark, Bank of Canada Governor Graham Towers, and other experts before whose superior knowledge of financial matters they felt obliged to bow. The result was a stiffening of the attitude of Drew, Duplessis, and other premiers, and the meeting was adjourned without any real progress having been made.

Two days after the conference ended, an American journalist broke the news of the Soviet espionage network. The R.C.M.P. planned to pick up all suspects in a co-ordinated series of raids as soon as St. Laurent returned from London, but the federal-provincial meeting had delayed the move. Suddenly, immediate action became imperative; the whole cabinet was informed of Gouzenko's flight, and a royal commission, composed of Supreme Court Justices Robert Taschereau and Roy Kellock, was appointed to examine his revelations. Early on February 15, fourteen federal civil servants were taken into custody. St. Laurent signed the orders for the arrests, but insisted that the raids be held in daylight, and not in the dark of night as originally planned; to pull people out of their beds at gun-point seemed to him to smack of totalitarianism. Later in the same day, the Canadian people were informed that 'secret and confidential information' had been disclosed to 'unauthorized persons, including some members of the staff of a foreign mission in Ottawa', that several persons had been detained, and that a royal commission was already investigating the situation.

In the atmosphere of growing tension between the Soviet Union and the West, the Canadian government's main concern was to avoid precipitating a wave of panic that would still further prejudice the hopes for peace. When the American press learned that the spy ring extended into the State Department, a veritable witch-hunt could be expected, and even demands for a final showdown with Russia. Mackenzie King and St. Laurent shuddered to think of the possible consequences of their acts, and conjured up visions of a third world war in which Canada would certainly be the principal battle-ground. When they released the commission's first report to the press on March 4, their worst fears seemed likely to be realized; Ottawa became the focus of attention for the sensationalist press of the whole Western world. To add to the government's concern, protests poured into Ottawa because the persons arrested were held incommunicado during their inter-rogation; as Minister of Justice, St. Laurent was accused of in-fringing human liberties and of using police-state measures. The steps taken were doubtless radical and unorthodox, and St. Lau-rent realized that the persons arrested could not be held for long without charges being laid against them; at the same time, he realized that the security of the free world was at issue, and that all precautions must be taken to prevent other members of the spy ring from being warned in time to escape. His position was difficult and unpleasant; after forty years of defending the rights of his fellow citizens he had too much respect for the law to contravene it lightly, but when asked bluntly if he was prepared to accept the responsibility for at least partial failure of the care-fully planned counter-measures because of his qualms, he realized that he had to put the national interest first, and authorize the unusual procedure. While the criticism mounted in the press, he urged the commissioners to complete their investigations rapidly so that formal charges could be laid, or the detained persons released.

The Prime Minister's strength continued to ebb, and he leaned more and more on his hard-working, systematic Minister of Jus-tice. Under heavy pressure from opposition parties and from the press to appoint a full-time Minister for External Affairs, Mac-kenzie King finally overcame his reluctance to abandon personal control of Canadian foreign policy, and began considering likely candidates. Brooke Claxton was keenly interested in the post, but he could not be spared from his duties as Minister of National Health and Welfare and as the member of the cabinet primarily responsible for Liberal Party affairs. Pearson's name was also con-sidered by the Prime Minister, but he had been outside Canada for some time, and Mackenzie King felt he should first reintegrate himself in the Ottawa scene by taking on for a while the post of Under Secretary of State for External Affairs. The third possi-bility was St. Laurent, and at the end of February the Prime

Minister asked him to take the portfolio, at least for a short period. St. Laurent objected that he must absolutely leave the government by the end of 1946, already a year later than he had intended; such an appointment, he protested, would encourage the speculation that he was planning to try for the party leadership. The two men were unevenly matched when it came to such negotiations; Mackenzie King was charming and understanding, but he was also tenacious; by the end of the discussion, St. Laurent had agreed to serve as acting minister during the Prime Minister's proposed trip to attend the Commonwealth Conference in London and the Peace Conference in Paris, in the spring and summer.

The second report of the Taschereau-Kellock Commission was transmitted to St. Laurent on the very morning that Parliament was to reassemble, and it contained startling news: Fred Rose, the Labour-Progressive member for Cartier constituency in Montreal, was implicated in the conspiracy, and would have to be arrested. The Minister of Justice conjured up visions of more newspaper sensationalism if the arrest was made as the Communist member arrived on Parliament Hill, or worse still, if he shut himself up in the Parliament Buildings, where he enjoyed immunity from arrest. It was decided to wait for an opportunity to take him into custody discreetly. When St. Laurent arrived in the Commons Chamber, he noticed that Rose was in his place, seemingly unaware of impending events. The Prime Minister tabled the first report of the commission, but withheld the second on the grounds that it had not yet been presented to cabinet. Opposition leader Bracken demanded a statement on 'the extraordinary procedure . . . in holding certain Canadians incommunicado', but was turned away with the soft answer that a statement would be made the following day. Rose was watched all day by the R.C.M.P. officers; still unsuspecting, he left the Parliament Buildings late in the evening, and was arrested as he reached his home. Only the following morning was the Canadian public informed of this dramatic development.

When he spoke in the Throne Speech debate, John Bracken repeated the charge that the government was falling into 'totalitarian' ways, and cited the handling of the Gouzenko affair in support of his assertion. St. Laurent had stated in the previous December that 'no secret orders [in council]' existed, and yet the documents tabled with the first royal commission report included one such order dated October 6, authorizing the arrest of the persons suspected of spying activities. 'We were misled,' the Leader of the Opposition charged, and accused the government of using 'Star Chamber methods' in conducting the investigation. The Prime Minister succeeded in heading off a debate on the spying itself, but the attacks continued on the procedure that had been adopted. The Gouzenko case would soon be forgotten, declared Conservative member Arthur Smith from Calgary, but 'the people of Canada will always regret and will never live down the fact that we threw aside and abrogated the rights and liberties of our citizens'.

Stung by the charge, St. Laurent insisted on replying at once. When he had been asked to sign the order to interrogate the spy suspects, he had at first refused on the grounds that it was not proper in peace-time to have such powers, and that 'no one should be detained, even for interrogation, without there being some form of intervention of the judicial authority'. However, he had been made to realize that he was faced with a choice between the exercise of powers under his jurisdiction for the security of the state, and the desire to avoid 'some political discredit'. In the circumstances, he had taken the advice of commission counsel and signed the order. It was always difficult to act on information that could not be disclosed to the public for the moment, he commented, but he had done what he considered right in similar circumstances in 1944, and had been vindicated at the polls; he hoped that the public would one day agree that in this instance 'we took the right course, the courageous course, the only course . . . to [assure] . . . the safety of our form of government in this country'.

The rebuttal was effective, but there remained the matter of the secret order in council to explain. It had been passed as a precautionary measure, he stated, and had not yet been used when he had declared that no such orders existed; as a result, it had slipped his memory. The opportunity to harass the government was too good for the opposition to miss, and Diefenbaker ridiculed St. Laurent for forgetting an order 'that swept aside Magna Carta and the Bill of Rights'. The incident illustrated the corrupting influence of power, he stormed in his highly effective court-room style, and, pointing his finger across the aisle, he asked, 'I wonder how many other secret orders the Minister of Justice has forgotten? . . . Where is the rule of law? It is flouted by the government.' Caught in error, St. Laurent had no choice but to sit and take his punishment. As soon as possible, he obtained a letter from the commission counsel, stating that the order was no longer required; it was revoked on April 1.

Parliament took a long Easter holiday to enable the ministers to continue their negotiations with the provinces. The federal team had raised to fifteen dollars per capita the rental fee it offered to pay for the income tax, corporation tax, and succession duty fields, but continued to insist on sole occupation of these three important sources of revenue. Drew and Duplessis maintained their positions as the champions of provincial rights. Mackenzie King and St. Laurent were increasingly doubtful of the wisdom of increasing subsidies to the provinces rather than handing back taxation powers to them, but Ilsley and Claxton strongly supported the team of advisers, and the government's position was maintained. As an additional inducement to the richer provinces, Mackenzie King offered on April 29 to abandon the gasoline and amusement tax fields in return for a suitable *quid pro quo*. Drew virtually ignored the offer, arguing that definite fields of taxation should be allocated exclusively to the provinces. Duplessis followed with another denunciation of the federal administration for its 'contempt for sacred pacts'. Finance Minister Ilsley went one step further by offering to abandon pari-mutuel taxes, then, after pointing out that seven of the nine provinces had all but accepted the federal proposals, he appealed for unanimous agreement. Drew rose at once to denounce the statement as a 'take-it-or-leave-it' position; Duplessis followed suit and announced he was leaving for home that evening. The Union Nationale leader returned to Quebec City but was back on the following Monday to hear a final plea for reason from St. Laurent. At his conciliatory best, the Minister of Justice pointed out again that the federal government's need for additional taxes was a result of the war, and argued that in the circumstances it was only logical to continue the war-time agreements for a further period. Reminding the delegates that no precise counter-proposals had been made, he suggested that the provincial delegations meet to draw up specific views on the whole problem of tax sharing. If they put forward a joint statement of the rental payments they required, he assured the conference, Ottawa would not adopt 'a stubborn attitude that could make agreement difficult'. Without saying so directly, he held firmly to the position that a rental agreement was the only solution the federal government could accept. The appeal fell on barren ground. Duplessis complimented him on being 'a remarkable and adroit lawyer, especially when pleading a bad case', and described Ottawa's attitude as being 'I take the best share because I'm the lion'; both he and Drew maintained their previous positions. The following day, after eight months of work, the conference adjourned indefinitely. Maurice Duplessis was welcomed as a hero by his supporters on his return to Quebec City. After a century as defenders of provincial rights, the Liberals were firmly identified in the public mind as 'centralizers'. The absence of an agreement with all the provinces made it impossible to proceed with some far-reaching proposals outlined in the Green Book, including the establishment of a nation-wide health insurance system.

One of the matters that St. Laurent had agreed to look after before retiring was the redistribution of parliamentary seats that had been postponed during the war. It was a delicate matter, since the government proposed to abandon the fixed number of sixty-five seats to be allocated to Quebec under the B.N.A. Act, while maintaining the principle that the number of seats in the other provinces should be proportionate to those in Quebec. Eighty years after Confederation the figure of sixty-five seats no longer corresponded to reality, St. Laurent argued in presenting the government's plan to the House of Commons on May 28, and numerous exceptions had led to a deviation from the principle of representation by population; by choosing a new quotient of just under 50,000 voters in each constituency, the total number of seats could be increased to 255, with Quebec receiving eight more, Ontario one, and British Columbia two, while Saskatchewan would lose one. According to such a formula, the guarantee given to Quebec of a fixed proportion of the total seats would be maintained, and the province would, in fact, increase its representation in Ottawa. Taking issue with Duplessis's argument that the provinces must be consulted on any change in representation in the House of Commons, St. Laurent declared that 'the people of the provinces are represented in this Parliament, and for the purpose of such matters as are confided to the jurisdiction of this Parliament it is by those representatives here that the people of the provinces speak'. He rejected the thesis that the Canadian Parliament derived its authority from the provinces, pointing out that both the English-speaking and French-speaking Fathers of Confederation from the Province of Canada sat in the same legislature before 1867, and continued to do so after July 1, 1867, as members of the Parliament of Canada. In other words, the members of Parliament, and not the members of the provincial legislatures, were the direct political heirs of the men who had negotiated Confederation, and the B.N.A. Act authorized them specifically to legislate on the manner in which Canadians were to be represented in Ottawa.

Speaking on behalf of the official opposition, John Diefenbaker demanded that the provinces be consulted on the change in representation in Parliament, thus adopting a position clearly at odds with that of his party since Confederation. Independent member Frédéric Dorion took a similar position, while C.C.F. leader Coldwell aligned himself with St. Laurent, and Social Credit chief Solon Low sought refuge in ambivalence. Freshman member Jean Lesage threw his full support behind the government's proposal. To consult the provinces, he argued, would merely mean risking the refusal of the ones who enjoyed special privileges through the departure from 'principles of the compact'. When he intervened to answer the first series of speeches, St. Laurent took up the 'abstract question' of whether Confederation was a compact, a treaty, or a contract.

There was no doubt a solemn agreement reached on some definite principles by those individuals who, in fact, purported to represent and to act for the two major groups of the

population [he conceded readily], ... and that agreement is one
we, their descendants, are in honour bound to respect; but ...
it would be entirely wrong to believe that in 1867 there was
set up by a voluntary act of autonomous pre-existing states
a union which derived its substance from those who made the
agreement. ... They did not have the powers which they could
transfer to the central power.

As a matter of fact, he pointed out, the resolution drawn up at
Quebec in 1864 to authorize the provincial legislatures to determine or alter the electoral districts was dropped, and Parliament
was granted that responsibility specifically under Section 51 of the
B.N.A. Act. His conclusion was unequivocal. 'The central power
does not derive its existence and its authority from the provinces
and it does not need to go back to the provinces in order to say
what Canada shall be in the future'; the Conservative position
would make Parliament 'the mere creature of or delegate of
sovereign provincial states', and destroy the concept of Canada as
a national entity.

Having dealt with the principal subject on which there was
disagreement, St. Laurent allowed himself to be drawn onto
more treacherous terrain. Earlier in the debate, Arthur Smith of
Calgary had asked whether, in the minister's view, the authority
of Parliament to alter Section 51 of the B.N.A. Act concerning
representation implied similar authority to change Section 133
concerning the use of French and English in Parliament and in
the courts. A more cautious politician would have side-stepped
the question, but St. Laurent responded as a man attracted by a
difficult problem.

Legally I say it can [he stated thoughtfully]; the situation
appears to me to be this. There are persons and nations who
reach a high estate in the affairs of men, and the high estate they
reach imposes upon them high obligations. ... I feel – and I
believe my fellow Canadians of my race and religion can feel –
that a better guarantee than anything that might be found in
Section 133 is to be found in that respect of those who have been
formed under the principles of British freedom and British
fair play, to protect what are our essential rights.

It was not likely that the heirs of such a long tradition would 'do things which the conscience of mankind would regard as dishonourable', he observed; 'humanity at large' would condemn them if they did. His confidence in his English-speaking fellow citizens was shared by few residents of Quebec. Cardin rose in turn to express the more general view held there that a change on such a vital matter should not be made without consulting the provincial authorities.

Before the debate was concluded, John Hackett intervened to appeal for the support of French Canada on behalf of his party, arguing that the amendment proposed by Diefenbaker demonstrated the Conservatives' good will towards Quebec. The government's proposal, he warned, would end for all time the right to consider the B.N.A. Act as a pact or a treaty, and would make it 'the merest statute which can be torn to shreds whenever the exigencies of a political party . . . exact it'. While sympathizing with his friend's attempt, as the lone Conservative member from Quebec, to attract French-Canadian support to his party, St. Laurent scoffed at the dire prediction that the bill was a threat to the survival of French Canada. 'I feel that my people, those of my race, can stand on their own feet,' he declared in concluding the debate, 'and if they get in the Parliament of their nation the right to be represented by a number of elected members proportionate to their own numbers they will be very well taken care of and they will have no occasion to complain of any unfairness.' Drawing an analogy from the international scene, he recalled that 'this veto business is something which is proving very difficult in the assembly of the United Nations'; if the government's proposal had the effect of ending forever 'the contention that the constitution of this nation cannot be amended in respect of certain national matters unless the proposal be subjected to the veto of the great powers who sit in the provincial capitals, then I think this is a happy day for Canada'. Diefenbaker's amendment was defeated decisively, with only three French-speaking members supporting it; St. Laurent's motion had a still easier passage. Outside Parliament, however, the debate was far from over. Duplessis sounded the battle-cry against St. Laurent's view that Parliament could change its system of representation without consulting the provinces, denouncing it as 'the antithesis of democracy', and 'the indispensable foundation of Communism, Bolshevism, Fascism, and Hitlerism'. In Ontario, Drew declared his opposition to any plan to set up 'a form of dictatorship by centralizing power in one centre far away'.

Rushing to complete his remaining assignments as a politician, Louis St. Laurent went on to introduce amendments to the Combines Act and the Judges Act, became involved in a debate on the subject of divorce, and took part in the quest for a flag design acceptable to all Canadians. The discussion on divorce procedure was initiated by C.C.F. member Stanley Knowles, who complained of the limited grounds for divorce recognized in Canada, and of the burden imposed on Parliament for granting divorces in Quebec, where dissolution of marriages was not recognized. Replying as Minister of Justice, St. Laurent revealed both his strong religious views and his preoccupation with devising practical solutions to recognized problems. Roman Catholics maintained that the Bible does not provide for divorce on any grounds, St. Laurent reminded members of Parliament, and even Protestants were in agreement that it does not provide for divorce on any other grounds but adultery. To admit other grounds 'meant either to deny the existence of a divine law or to say that the human law can over-ride the divine law'; this he was not prepared to do, because 'the indissolubility of marriage is of such value that its public value outweighs the inconvenience to which a certain number of individuals are put and the suffering which is put upon them through no fault of their own'. Although he opposed divorce himself, he recognized that many Canadians held other views, and that Parliament had a responsibility to legislate in that field. To avoid the burden of investigating the many requests for divorces, he suggested that Parliament might refuse to consider any applications except when a decree of separation based on finding of adultery by a Quebec court could be produced; passing the bills would then be a mere formality. If, in addition, the Quebec legislature could be induced to give both men and women equal access to a separation, the citizens of Quebec would be placed in a situation comparable to that of other Canadians. St. Laurent's suggestion was welcomed in the

House, Knowles even conceding that it was better than his own. It had one fatal flaw: the Union Nationale government could never be induced to make divorces easier to obtain. The matter was dropped once again.

The search for a distinctive Canadian flag was no more successful. The co-chairman of the flag committee, Walter Harris, was instructed by the Prime Minister to push hard for agreement on a design by the end of the session, and Mackenzie King made clear his own preference for the Red Ensign with a gold maple leaf in place of the coat of arms. The basic disagreement in the committee centred around the advisability of including the Union Jack, French-speaking Canadians arguing vociferously against it, English-speaking Canadians demonstrating an equally emotional attachment to it. Finally, a compromise was made by reducing the size of the Union Jack from its dimensions on the Red Ensign to less than a quarter of the total space, and changing the colour of the background from red to white. With those modifications, the Prime Minister's design was approved on July 11 by all but one member of a sub-committee, and endorsed by a majority of committee members. The Prime Minister had been out of the country for several weeks, but had returned in late June; both he and St. Laurent accepted the modified design, and possible strategy was discussed to get the necessary legislation through Parliament without precipitating an acrimonious debate. St. Laurent suggested that the simplest and most effective way would be to bring the flag into existence by passing an order in council based on the committee report, and then let the members debate the *fait accompli*, the government to stand or fall on the outcome. While the solution seemed simple to a temporary public servant about to return to private life, to the experienced Prime Minister it was fraught with danger, as it implied using the English-speaking majority to force a flag on Quebec. Mackenzie King's fears were confirmed when Jean Lesage and about ten other Quebec members appeared in his office and warned him bluntly that they would vote against the design, even if it meant bringing down the government. In the face of the threatened revolt, the Prime Minister wavered. Late in the evening of July 11, he called Harris to his office and told him not to bring in the report of the committee. It was the turn of the committee chairman to resist; he had worked for months to obtain agreement, and he insisted on going ahead. The following day, he made his report to the House of Commons. However, the next move was up to the government; it alone could propose action on the recommendation with any hope of success. Mackenzie King refused to act; Canada was to wait another generation for a distinctive national flag.

In mid-July, Mackenzie King left Canada again to attend the peace conference in Paris. Ilsley was so exhausted from the heavy duties of Minister of Finance that he could not accept temporary leadership of the government, and was assigned to lead a Canadian delegation to a meeting of the United Nations Relief and Rehabilitation Administration in Geneva. As a result, St. Laurent found himself with the triple responsibility of the acting-prime-ministership and the External Affairs and Justice portfolios. Fortunately, he had competent assistants to help him to carry the tremendous burden; J. W. Pickersgill in the Prime Minister's Office and Hume Wrong, Associate Under Secretary of State for External Affairs, were accustomed to a minimum of direct supervision, because of Mackenzie King's practice of spending much of his time at Laurier House. Since Pickersgill and Wrong both admired the Quebec minister greatly, the three men proved to be an efficient and harmonious team. With his numerous functions, St. Laurent was the dominant personality in Ottawa during the summer of 1946. On one typically busy day, August 6, he introduced to the House of Commons a set of trade agreements with Mexico and Colombia, proposals to create a World Health Organization and a United Nations Educational Scientific and Cultural Organization, and legislation concerning the national capital area; in addition, he took part in a debate on war crimes, and by the end of that day he was working on a draft prepared by Pickersgill for a speech to the Canadian Teachers' Federation. A few days before the session ended, House Leader Ian Mackenzie left for a trip to Scotland, and St. Laurent took over his duties as well. Attempting to work as a team with the other parties, he showed a readiness to accept opposition suggestions that surprised observers and disarmed his adversaries, but proved effective in terms of legislation approved. He reported that a concerted drive was being made to reduce the number of war-time orders in council still in effect, assured the House that the government was as anxious to dispense with the emergency powers legislation as other parties, and even accepted a Conservative amendment setting the date of its expiry. By such conciliatory tactics, and by exceptionally long hours of sitting, the session was brought to an end on the last day of August. Opposition spokesmen paid tribute to his leadership in the House, C.C.F. member Angus McInnis declaring that he had displayed 'so much ability, tact and fairness that I think he has impressed all of us, and that, particularly, as he is a relatively new man in the House'.

While most of the other members rushed home to enjoy what was left of the summer, St. Laurent went straight on to other duties. The very next day he was in Montreal to meet the Prime Minister on his return to Canada, and to report on his stewardship. As they rode back to Ottawa together in the private railway car, Mackenzie King noted with interest that St. Laurent had not only managed well, but had enjoyed the challenge of coping with the opposition in Parliament, and had quickly established a good working relationship with his associates. Encouraged, the government leader again spoke of the future. If St. Laurent would agree to remain in public life, he would certainly be chosen as the next party leader, the Prime Minister declared, and he offered to do everything possible to that end. St. Laurent remained adamant. He would be sixty-five in February, he pointed out, and the strain of his current pace would break his health; moreover, it would be difficult to regain his law practice if he waited any longer. Finally, the veteran politician revealed his immediate objective: he wished St. Laurent to take over the External Affairs portfolio. The move had been suggested by Brooke Claxton, who was also at the Paris Peace Conference, as a way of persuading the Quebec minister to stay in politics a while longer, and to gain time to weave the web that would keep him there as the next party leader. For the Minister of National Health and Welfare, it was a self-effacing suggestion, for he himself had long hoped to become Minister for External Affairs; but he placed the party's, and the nation's, interest before his own. St. Laurent's first reaction to the proposal was that his Quebec followers would think he had agreed to remain in public life, and he did not wish to create such a misleading impression; in fact, he was hoping the Prime Minister would transfer the Justice portfolio to Ilsley, for whom the burden of the Finance Department had become too great, thus leaving him completely free to return to Quebec. Mackenzie King countered with the suggestion that St. Laurent and Ilsley should simply change portfolios. The discussion continued until the train rolled into Ottawa's Union Station at nearly midnight, and the two men stepped onto the platform to meet the crowd of politicians, newspapermen, and other citizens that had assembled to welcome the Prime Minister home.

After Mackenzie King dropped him off at his apartment building that night, St. Laurent continued to reflect on the subject of their unfinished discussion, but he was as determined as ever to resist the appeal to stay on in Ottawa. His wife had never become reconciled to living in Ottawa, and spent much of her time alone in the Grande Allée home. Renault and Jean-Paul were carrying on in the law firm, but it was a headless organization, and he felt that his presence was required there. In addition, Aimé Geoffrion had died a short time earlier, and his former clients were looking about for other counsel. For nearly five years, St. Laurent had been drawing on his financial reserves in order to serve his country; he now saw a last opportunity to recoup his losses, including those that still hung over his head from the Wall Street crash, and to build up a fund for his rapidly approaching old age. He discussed the situation with his wife by telephone in Quebec and she implored him not to delay his return any longer. Thus, he was determined to be firm with the Prime Minister when he arrived at Kingsmere late the following afternoon to continue their discussion. The two men set off for a walk across the gently undulating countryside. Tenacious, resourceful, and persuasive, the Prime Minister marshalled his arguments carefully, and advanced them with the adroitness of the master strategist he had long ago proved himself to be. St. Laurent had agreed to lead the Canadian delegation to the United Nations session beginning in October, he recalled, and should have the title of Minister for External Affairs for purposes of prestige. It could be made clear that the appointment was only temporary, and that a full-time minister would be chosen before Parliament reassembled; the interim arrangement would provide time to work out a more permanent solution. Once again, St. Laurent succumbed to the appeal to be of service. If he could help out in that way during his last months in Ottawa he would be only too ready to comply, he assured his leader. Relieved, the Prime Minister suggested that the change be made the following day. That evening St. Laurent telephoned his wife in Quebec City. 'What kind of impression did you make?' she asked apprehensively. 'Too good, I'm afraid,' he replied sheepishly, and informed her that he had agreed to become Minister for External Affairs.

Louis St. Laurent was sworn in as Secretary of State for External Affairs on September 5, 1946; the same day it was decided that L. B. Pearson should return from Washington to become his under-secretary, and that Norman Robertson should become High Commissioner in London. The reaction to his appointment was even stronger than he had anticipated. He tried in vain to explain to his colleagues and other close associates that he was just making the Justice portfolio available for Ilsley, and giving the Prime Minister time to find a more permanent Minister for External Affairs; his many admirers were encouraged to increase the pressure on him to remain in Ottawa. Negotiations were about to be undertaken to bring Newfoundland into Confederation, the removal of the Department of External Affairs from the Prime Minister's cautious direction opened up the possibility of new initiatives in Canadian foreign policy, and several items of legislation that would shape the country in the years ahead were being prepared for the new session of Parliament. The new challenges were interesting to him, and the argument that he could play a uniquely useful role again proved irresistible; he acquiesced once again. When he informed the Prime Minister that he would remain throughout the session, the older man was so relieved and delighted that he had difficulty in finding words to express his appreciation. 'It is as noble a sacrifice as one can make,' Mackenzie King commented later. 'It reminded me of the staunchness of Ernest Lapointe and of his friendship.'

St. Laurent spent much of the closing months of 1946 at the

United Nations in New York, occasionally rushing back to Canada to look after particular responsibilities, then returning to resume his place as head of the Canadian delegation. Under his direction and that of Pearson, Canadian foreign policy became more venturesome, and also more flexible. Rather than attempt to impose a distinctly Canadian viewpoint, they bent their efforts to find reasonable solutions to problems that divided other members of the world organization. On October 29, St. Laurent made his maiden speech as Minister for External Affairs before the United Nations General Assembly. Earlier in the day, Soviet Foreign Minister Molotov had surprised delegates by abandoning the truculent hostility toward the West that had characterized his earlier statements, and making a sweeping proposal for disarmament. Hoping eagerly that the speech marked the beginning of a new era of co-operation, St. Laurent had gone over to the Russian spokesman, shaken his hand warmly, and assured him that there was no reason why Canada could not live on as amicable terms with her neighbour across the Arctic as with her neighbour to the south. In his own relatively short address, he expressed regret that the Security Council had not yet agreed on establishing an international peace force, and reiterated Canada's readiness to contribute her share of troops in order to put 'world force behind world law'. He urged as well 'compulsory jurisdiction of the International Court of Justice with a minimum of restrictions', and 'the progressive development of international law and its codification'. With the Security Council already frustrated by the veto power, it was more important than ever to 'beware of recriminations, of charge and countercharge', he warned, and to apply 'good will, patience and forbearance . . . in the interests of peace and understanding'. Coming immediately after the sensational Soviet proposal, the statement seemed bland and modest; it corresponded more to the aims and the needs of the world organization, however, than still another eloquent but unproductive speech. In the various committees, the Canadians maintained a similar approach, attempting to reconcile differences rather than impose solutions. In that spirit, St. Laurent opposed a move to censure South Africa for racial discrimination, drawing attention to Prime Minister Smut's conciliatory attitude; and he discouraged an attempt to outlaw the Spanish régime of General Franco, arguing that interference in that country's internal affairs might tend to worsen conditions rather than improve them. In general, he aimed to set an example of conduct for other nations to follow, fully realizing that even the major powers, who had the primary responsibility for world peace, were inclined to put their own interests before those of mankind as a whole.

One of the quick trips that Louis St. Laurent made home to Canada from New York was to attend a banquet in his honour at Quebec on November 29. Announced as a tribute for past services, the occasion was designed in some people's minds as part of the subtle campaign to keep him in public life. For Mackenzie King, it was an opportunity to tell French Canada of his ever greater esteem and affection for his colleague. Speaking after a glowing tribute by Adélard Godbout, the Prime Minister declared that he would not have been able to continue to lead the government in 1941 'if St. Laurent had not responded to the call of duty, and entered the Ministry when he did'. After paying homage to Arthur Cardin, who had died a few weeks earlier, he went on to refer to the conscription crisis, telling the largely French-speaking audience:

> I do not know that it has ever been realized how near we came, in November 1944, to having no government at all in Canada, and no party that could form a government with any hope of being able to carry on while our armed forces were facing the last terrible ordeal of battle at the front. . . . I am perfectly certain that had Mr. St. Laurent withdrawn his support of myself, or, indeed, wavered in that support, I should have had no alternative but to tender my resignation, and with it the resignation of the Ministry.

After heeding 'the stern voice of duty' during the war, the government leader went on, St. Laurent had been persuaded to extend his term of service several times; now he was in the same position as the soldier in an American Negro regiment who pleaded for his release on the grounds that he had only enlisted for the duration of the war. 'Yo po' niggah,' his sergeant had replied, 'Yo enlisted fo' de duration of de war. De war may be ovah, but de

duration am just beginning.' 'Please, Mr. Minister,' said the
Prime Minister, turning towards his colleague, 'do remember
that "de duration am just beginning." ' The crowd roared with
delight; and the members of the St. Laurent family beamed
proudly, but their happiness was tinged with concern as they
began to realize that the alleged farewell gesture was really part
of the campaign to keep the head of the family in Ottawa.

In his reply, St. Laurent, too, referred to the conscription
crisis:

> Not for a moment was I able to hesitate as to the line of conduct
> that I was duty bound to follow, but that line of conduct was
> indicated to me by facts known to me and that I could not
> communicate to my friends. I, therefore, found myself in the
> painful necessity of following a line of conduct which many of
> you, my friends, sincerely and honestly felt to be wrong.

The course had been a difficult one,

> but it was not nearly as hard as that which was accepted by the
> hundreds of thousands of young Canadians who joined the
> colours . . . who volunteered to go and fight, to be wounded, to
> be crippled, perhaps even to die so that we might live and so
> that the Canadian nation might continue to live.

The burst of applause that followed the forthright and moving
statement indicated clearly that his conduct was forgiven, if not
fully approved. Having dealt with the war, St. Laurent suddenly
adopted a more partisan tone. Still indignant at the criticism he
had received in Quebec for first postponing the redistribution of
parliamentary seats, and then failing to consult the provinces, he
recalled that some people had said he might be a good enough
lawyer, but he knew nothing about politics. 'I confess that I know
nothing about a certain kind of politics,' he stated, his eyes flashing defiantly. 'Not only do I confess it, but I glory in it.' Before
the courts, he had learned to submit 'the truth, the whole truth,
and nothing but the truth', and that had proved to be 'a pretty
successful system'; when he entered politics, he was too old to
change, so he 'continued to respect the intelligence and the good

faith of my new judges, and quite frankly, I am under the impression that it is a system which they do not dislike'. He recounted how, during the debate on the redistribution bill, he had been asked if Parliament could modify the provisions of the constitution concerning the use of the French language in its deliberations. 'One of those experts in political strategy might have avoided giving a clear answer to such a question'; but he had been asked a legal question and he gave a legal answer. As a result, he had been attacked by Premier Duplessis even after he had written and explained the circumstances. Similarly, in the field of federal-provincial relations the Union Nationale leader had made 'pompous declarations' in public of his willingness to co-operate with Ottawa, but refused either to accept Ottawa's proposals or to make any of his own. That might be clever political strategy, St. Laurent commented indignantly, but it was 'not the way I understood telling the truth, the whole truth and nothing but the truth'. A bit more and he would have been calling the Quebec Premier a liar; in any event, it was certainly an unusual statement from a man making his valedictory political address. Although it was almost midnight before he sat down, his fighting words were received with great enthusiasm, and they had the effect of encouraging the campaign to keep him in public life. The *Montreal Star* reminded him of his statement in 1941 that 'there are times in the lives of men and in the lives of nations when strict individualism might well be looked upon as selfishness'. Even Conservative papers expressed the hope that he would continue his service to Canada. The reluctant politician had cause to wonder if he had not once again proved himself a poor strategist.

On December 10, Louis St. Laurent was back from New York again, this time to hand over the Justice portfolio to James Ilsley, after having run two departments for several months while other aspects of the cabinet shuffle were being worked out. On that day Douglas Abbott became Minister of Finance, Brooke Claxton Minister of National Defence, Paul Martin Minister of National Health and Welfare, and Colin Gibson Secretary of State. St. Laurent was clearly the second most important member of the team. 'The task [of leadership] will be easy as long as I have you at my side,' the Prime Minister wrote to him at Christmas time. 'What may come thereafter I feel may well be left to the Providence which united our paths at a moment of crisis over five years ago.' The old man's great faith would not prevent him in the coming year from using his remaining energy and his great talents to shape future events. The St. Laurent family, enjoying another Christmas together, were determined to influence Providence in the opposite direction.

# 8

---

## Re-conscripted

Louis St. Laurent adapted easily to the field of international diplomacy. The career diplomats who worked under him were impressed by his ability to grasp the essentials of each subject they submitted to him, and appreciated his open-mindedness in examining their proposals, in contrast with the cautiousness, bordering on distrust, displayed by the Prime Minister. While he seldom initiated new policies, he worked closely with his officials, establishing his authority by his competence, and suggesting, rather than ordering, changes that he felt were necessary. Under his direction, morale soared in the department, and it became an exciting place to work. He also displayed an ability to reduce complicated negotiations to simple terms. 'When he returned from Lake Success and gave us a report on what was going on, even we understood him,' commented one cabinet colleague with a combination of humour and seriousness. At the same time, he never forgot that he was but one member of the cabinet, and that the Prime Minister had the final responsibility for government policy. He not only deferred to the views of Mackenzie King, who continued to look upon Canadian foreign policy as his special prerogative, but accepted a degree of surveillance, even interference, that a more ambitious and self-centred man would have resented.

In many respects, St. Laurent's attitude towards foreign affairs was merely an extension of his views on domestic matters, and certainly it was based on his assessment of Canadian politics. One of the basic considerations of Canadian external policy was that it should not be harmful to national unity, he told an audience at the University of Toronto in early January 1947, for 'a disunited Canada will be a powerless one'. This preoccupation need not prevent Canadians from playing a positive role on the international scene, he continued, for there were attitudes and values in human society with which they could all identify themselves. For instance, both English- and French-speaking Canadians shared the same concept of political liberty, the same respect for the supremacy of law, the same basic values of Western civilization 'which lay emphasis on the importance of the individual, on the place of moral principles in the conduct of human relations, on standards of judgement which transcend mere material well-being'. Finally: 'Our common experience has led us to accept . . . that security for this country lies in the development of a firm structure of international organization.' With such a common set of principles, Canadians could make a useful contribution to international society within the limitations of a secondary power, particularly if their government was careful to obtain the support of all political parties for each particular policy.

In addition to emphasizing the importance of domestic realities in determining Canadian foreign policy, Louis St. Laurent's statement in Toronto outlined a new approach to world affairs. Prior to World War II, Canadian Conservatives had been inclined to view the nation's external relations within the context of an imperial or Commonwealth policy, while the Liberals practised a rather negative form of nationalism inspired by Mackenzie King's scepticism of the League of Nations. Attempting to encourage Canadians to rise above less important considerations, St. Laurent asserted that relations with the Commonwealth, the United States, and France remained important, but the highest priority must be given to 'the establishment of a world order based on principles of freedom', and that other relationships must be subordinated to that goal. While the new policy represented the thinking of his closest advisers in the Department of External Affairs far more than that of the public at large, or even of the

Prime Minister, it was to remain the guide-line for Canada in the decade to come.

In the session of Parliament that began on January 30, 1947, St. Laurent tried to restrict his contributions to international affairs, but the Prime Minister fell ill with pneumonia after two weeks, and when he had recovered sufficiently, left for a month's holiday in the United States. Once again, the willing work-horse found himself Acting Prime Minister and House Leader. Occasionally, he was stirred into undiplomatic outbursts and even to setting aside his preoccupation with assuring bi-partisan support for Canadian foreign policy. When Conservative member Howard Green from Vancouver suggested that Canada would exercise more influence in the world by strengthening the British Empire, and making her voice heard through a common imperial policy, St. Laurent retorted, 'I'm not prepared to recommend to this House that we go back to the pre-Statute of Westminster days.' As far as the Liberals were concerned at least, he stated, Canada was going to have a foreign policy of her own, and was not going to be 'merely the instrument to carry out a foreign policy made up for us elsewhere'. He proved equally sensitive over what he considered the rather cavalier attitude of the major powers towards smaller nations like Canada, particularly in neglecting to give them more than a symbolic role in negotiating peace treaties. Twenty-five nations had signed the Atlantic Charter in 1942, he pointed out in the House of Commons, and had pledged not to make a separate armistice or peace with the enemies; yet two years later, at Yalta, the three major powers had agreed on the occupation of Germany, and had left no function there for the other member countries. 'Canada was proud to share the fortunes of war with her Allies,' he stated with a trace of bitterness; 'she expects to share with them also the task of making a just and lasting peace.' Events of the past two years had justified the fears expressed at San Francisco that the most powerful nations would try to dominate the post-war world. St. Laurent's passing reference to Germany prompted Gordon Graydon to ask why the Canadian force had been withdrawn from Europe. On his feet in a flash, the minister snapped angrily, 'The occupation force in Germany was withdrawn because we were left out.' Reporting the exchange, one newspaperman used the words 'we were kicked out'; the incident was blown into a sensational story. While the expression 'left out' described the situation more accurately, the stronger language corresponded to St. Laurent's sentiments. Once again, he had proved himself too blunt and forthright to be judged a good politician.

Mackenzie King returned to Canada at the end of April feeling much stronger, but torn between asserting his leadership and merely exercising a general control from Laurier House while he tackled the problem of finding a suitable successor. St. Laurent remained his clear personal choice as the next Liberal leader, both on the basis of personal qualifications and because he felt it would be poetic justice to hand back to a French-speaking Canadian the mantle he had inherited from Sir Wilfrid Laurier. As the spring of 1947 arrived, he began to prepare the final campaign to that end. In view of the Prime Minister's infrequent appearances on Parliament Hill, St. Laurent's schedule was not lightened greatly by the old man's return. Inside the House of Commons he continued to play a leading role, and outside he was continually in demand as a public speaker.

In May, he received an honorary doctorate from Dalhousie University in Halifax, in June another from the University of Ottawa. On both occasions, he repeated his plea for national unity and world peace. In contrast to the Prime Minister, he was optimistic about the ability of mankind to survive the dangers of the atomic age and the confrontation between capitalism and communism. The Soviet Union would not initiate a war because it could not maintain its high level of military strength, he argued; but neither could it disarm unless the West did as well; that was the explanation of the sudden and sweeping Soviet disarmament proposal. He could also sense the rising tide of nationalism in economically underdeveloped parts of the world, and, within individual nations, the 'surge ... to further eliminate privilege and class and bring about a more even distribution of opportunities and of well-being, and a wider participation in the control of the means of production'. Those, he argued, were the real challenges to mankind in the post-war years.

The first serious disagreement between Mackenzie King and

St. Laurent occurred over the evolution of India to full national status. Although the Prime Minister had contributed much to Canada's growth to independent nationhood, he feared the consequences of a similar step for the Asian sub-continent, arguing that, once independent, India would certainly leave the Commonwealth and perhaps even unite with other Asian countries against the West in a bloody power struggle. In late May 1947, the Canadian government was informed by the British that India was soon to achieve independence on such generous terms that she was expected to remain within the Commonwealth, and Canada's view was requested on certain aspects of the plan. A very positive reply was prepared in the Department of External Affairs, endorsing the idea of full equality for India as a sovereign nation, and St. Laurent produced it in cabinet to obtain the approval of the other ministers. Mackenzie King was going through one of his recurring periods of resentment at the way power was slipping from his hands, and was endeavouring to reassert his authority; when he learned the nature of the document he snatched it out of St. Laurent's hands, pointed out that the original communication must have been addressed to him as head of the government, and commented acidly that he was still Prime Minister and entitled to answer his own correspondence. He was horrified, he went on, at the thought of an Asian majority dominating the Commonwealth, and objected to Canada's offering advice on matters it knew nothing about. Before his outburst was over, he was almost predicting that Canada would be precipitating another world war by becoming involved in the delicate situation. To the surprise of the other ministers, St. Laurent took the rebuke in silence. Why, several asked themselves, particularly since he had probably not been scolded by another man since his youth? The explanation was partly that St. Laurent understood Mackenzie King's condition perhaps better than the old man understood it himself, and also because he knew the Prime Minister was right in asserting that the reply was his prerogative. Really at fault were Pearson and other officials in the Department of External Affairs who had acted without consulting their superiors closely enough; St. Laurent accepted the blame in their stead. The Prime Minister revised the Canadian reply, removing all references to Indian independence within the Commonwealth. When Prime Minister Attlee announced the plan for Indian self-government on June 3, Mackenzie King made it clear in the House of Commons that Canada had not been consulted, but had been informed of the impending development and been asked for an opinion. The incident was closed, but rumours circulated in the corridors of Parliament Hill that relations between Mackenzie King and St. Laurent had become strained, and that St. Laurent was more determined than ever to leave the government before the end of the summer.

One of the most challenging subjects with which Louis St. Laurent had to deal during 1947 was a proposal to bring Newfoundland into Confederation as Canada's tenth province. Representatives of the island colony had participated in the negotiations to enter Confederation in 1864 and 1865, but the terms of union had never been presented to the local legislature. Further negotiations just before the turn of the century had proved equally inconclusive. Subsequently, Newfoundland had become an autonomous dominion in her own right, but became financially insolvent during the Great Depression; with the approval of the Newfoundland legislature responsible government was suspended in favour of a Commission of Government appointed by the United Kingdom, which guaranteed the island's finances. It was understood that the people of Newfoundland would have the right to decide on their future when solvency was restored, and this occurred during World War II, thanks largely to United States and Canadian military expenditures there. Accordingly they had to choose among several alternatives: the restoration of responsible government, continuation of the Commission of Government, union with Canada, even union with the United States. Both the British and Canadian governments were strongly opposed to allowing the strategically important area to fall into American hands, and preferred incorporation into Canada, but the record of past negotiations made them wary of announcing their views, lest the Newfoundlanders take umbrage at such interference in the affairs of the island. In 1946, a national convention was elected in Newfoundland to draw up proposals for the future status of the colony, and on April 1, 1947, a delegation was chosen by it to go to Ottawa for the purpose of discussing possible terms of union; a proposal to send a similar delegation to Washington was defeated.

As Minister for External Affairs, St. Laurent was directly concerned with the negotiations, and became chairman of the cabinet committee responsible for them. With his strong sense of Canadian nationalism, he was favourable to the union from the outset. As a resident of Quebec, he had a further interest; a disagreement existed over the location of the border separating Labrador, the continental part of Newfoundland, and the largely uninhabited northern portion of Quebec. The question had been submitted to the Privy Council after World War I, and that body had largely accepted the Newfoundland contention that the boundary followed the watershed between the Atlantic slope on the one hand, and the St. Lawrence and Hudson Bay slopes on the other; the Quebec argument that the border should run just inland from the Atlantic Ocean was rejected. In the eyes of many French-speaking Canadians, their province was deprived of a large portion of its legitimate and natural hinterland; they accused the British Privy Councillors of partiality on the grounds that Newfoundland was still directly under British rule, and began agitation to abolish appeals to the Privy Council. St. Laurent had shared the view that Quebec was the victim of a bad decision and he hoped, in bringing about the union, to rectify the situation, or at least reduce its consequences. Duplessis warned him bluntly that he expected to be consulted, and insisted that no decision be taken without the 'indispensable agreement' of the province of Quebec. In the circumstances, the presence of a French-speaking Canadian as head of the Canadian team took on added significance. The talks with the Newfoundlanders were bound to be delicate on other grounds as well. While the head of the Newfoundland delegation, Gordon Bradley, and the secretary, J. R. Smallwood, were known to be outspoken advocates of union with Canada, the business and professional community of St. John's was almost unanimously opposed to it. So strong was the anti-union sentiment in the convention, that the delegation was authorized merely to inquire whether a basis for union existed, but not to negotiate. Thus, the Canadian team had to avoid carefully appearing over-anxious, while at the same time holding out considerable financial inducements, and accepting the prospect that the underdeveloped area would remain an economic liability for many years to come. It seemed doubtful whether sufficiently favourable terms could be offered without stirring up an adverse reaction among the richer provinces, and precipitating demands from the poorer ones for similar treatment.

In that context, the discussions began on a cordial but cautious note. At a dinner for the visitors at the Ottawa Country Club on June 24, Mackenzie King stressed that the question of the colony's future was one for the people of Newfoundland themselves to decide and not a matter in which either the people of Canada or the government of Canada would wish to interfere. Bradley was equally circumspect, pointing out that he and his colleagues were only a committee of the national convention, and were authorized merely to ascertain what fair and equitable basis of federal union was possible. St. Laurent was chosen as chairman of the discussions which were to extend, with frequent interruptions for the purpose of obtaining additional information, over several months. Ilsley, Howe, Claxton, and Walter Harris, St. Laurent's parliamentary secretary, also took an active part, while the federal officials included J. W. Pickersgill, J. R. Baldwin, R. A. Mackay, and Mitchell Sharp. It soon became evident that integration of Newfoundland as the tenth Canadian province was more complicated than most people had imagined, since it had very different legislation in a large number of fields, including a complicated system of denominational schools. In addition, the estimated cost to the federal treasury of extending federal services to Newfoundland, and of assuring a level of provincial services comparable to those in existing provinces, seemed startlingly high to some members of the federal team. Much as he desired to assure for Canada the physical dimensions foreseen by the Fathers of Confederation, St. Laurent wondered if a majority of his fellow Canadians would pay such a heavy price to make that vision come true. At one stage, he considered a suggestion from the federal officials that Canada purchase Labrador at a price sufficient to provide Newfoundland with a substantial reserve fund, and give the new province an assured basic income. The proposal offered the tempting possibility of assuaging feelings in Quebec over the border between that province and Labrador, for while the huge area would be incorporated into the Northwest Territories, it would belong to all of Canada. However, it soon became evident that Newfoundland would not contemplate such an arrangement, and it was dropped.

The Newfoundland talks were carried on concurrently with equally delicate ones concerning the Liberal Party leadership. Several members of the Prime Minister's immediate entourage were deeply disturbed over the estrangement between Mackenzie King and St. Laurent that had persisted since the incident over India's future, and feared that their plan for the succession would be thwarted because of it. When approached on the subject, St. Laurent thrust out his chin and stated that he had carried out the terms of service agreed to in 1941, and that he was going home to make some money. Mackenzie King, for his part, merely shrugged his shoulders and commented that he had done his best to have the popular minister stay, and that he could do nothing more. Once again, it was Brooke Claxton who took the initiative in the matter. The Minister of National Defence found a few minutes to discuss the situation with St. Laurent at the annual External Affairs picnic in early July, and gained the impression that he could still be persuaded to remain in Ottawa if the right kind of pressure could be brought to bear on him. Next Claxton tackled the Prime Minister himself. Uncertainty about the succession was having an unsettling effect on Liberals across the country, he told the seventy-two-year-old Prime Minister in a private interview on July 7, and the Conservatives were exploiting the situation; the best way to minimize the consequences of the inevitable change of leaders was to persuade the one person best qualified and most generally acceptable as the next leader, to remain in Ottawa. Canadians in every part of the country had spoken of St. Laurent's outstanding qualities and fine personal character, and he personified the partnership of the two ethnic groups that Mackenzie King himself had so often referred to as the key to the successful administration of Canada. Only the Prime Minister himself could convince him that he should stay on, Claxton urged; in doing so, Mackenzie King would unite the party, enhance Liberal fortunes, and crown his career with one of his greatest accomplishments. Anxious to prove his own good will, Mackenzie King protested that there was no one he would rather have as his successor, and that if St. Laurent insisted on leaving in the autumn, he, himself, might go at the same time.

After Claxton had taken the initial steps, the campaign picked up speed. On July 11, two influential Quebec Liberals arrived in Laurier House, and asked the Prime Minister if it was true that he wanted St. Laurent to stay on in public life. Mackenzie King told them that he would like very much to have him as his successor, and that the party as a whole would support such a move, but that he had heard from several sources that St. Laurent was determined to leave Ottawa. Once again, the old man repeated his threat that if St. Laurent left he would have to go too, as he could not carry the burden alone. The two visitors left, deeply shaken at the prospect of losing the two leading personalities in the party at the same time, and determined to do their utmost to avert such a serious situation. On June 17, Mackenzie King had a chat with C. D. Howe, to find out if the latter would be willing to remain in the government provided St. Laurent became Prime Minister. In characteristically blunt style, Howe told his leader that in his place he would get out of the government at once while he was still on the top of things and before the break came in the favourable political climate. As for St. Laurent's assuming the Liberal Party leadership, the Minister of Reconstruction remarked that there was not a member of the party who would not welcome such a move. Following his talk with Howe, Mackenzie King finally concluded that he should give up the leadership the following year at the latest, and that he must take the necessary steps to have St. Laurent chosen as his successor. He arranged to have dinner with him alone at the Ottawa Country Club the following evening.

In some ways, the meal resembled the luncheon at which they had become acquainted in early December 1941. Mackenzie King was, as always, the perfect host, inquiring affably about the various members of the St. Laurent family, and about his guest's own well-being. St. Laurent, for his part, was still the same straightforward, earnest person; the principal difference was in his attitude: five and a half years earlier he had realized that he could not refuse the call to duty; now he did not feel the same moral obligation. When the Prime Minister asked him what he really wished to do in the years ahead, his answer was ready; he realized that Mackenzie King would be going to England in the late autumn for Princess Elizabeth's wedding, and that it would be convenient to the government for him to stay on during that period, but he would leave at the end of the year. Mackenzie King countered immediately with his principal weapon, the threat to resign at the same time. To govern Canada it was necessary to have a leader from Quebec as well as one from Ontario, he argued, and he had always tried to respect that rule. On the defensive, St. Laurent remarked that the system of dual leadership had not always been necessary, and pointed out that neither Sir John A. Macdonald nor Sir Wilfrid Laurier had followed that practice. The Prime Minister replied that in those instances there were several strong ministers from each group. Trying another tack, Mackenzie King then referred to his health, remarking that while he had been feeling better in recent weeks, he would soon break down if he continued to carry so much responsibility. The Minister for External Affairs revealed that he was as vulnerable as ever to that type of appeal. He had been concerned whether people would feel he was doing the right thing in getting out, he conceded, and he had discussed the matter with Sir Lyman Duff, but the retired Chief Justice of the Supreme Court had assured him that, with his record of service, no one would blame him if he put his personal interests first. Mackenzie King interrupted to endorse that opinion. At the same time, he made it clear that the opportunities for service were not over.

Judging the time right, the government leader made his final plea. He would like to have it definitely understood that St. Laurent would succeed him as prime minister, he stated, and he was willing to give up that office at any time that St. Laurent would take on its duties; he himself had but one further ambition, to exceed Sir Robert Walpole's record as prime minister, and that would be accomplished in April of the coming year. Surprised to see how far the schedule had been established in Mackenzie King's mind, St. Laurent stiffened in his resistance and declared that he could not, on any account, think of taking on the office. Laurier's career was an exception that proved the rule, he asserted, and it was highly unlikely that a French-speaking Canadian would again be accepted as prime minister. Sir Wilfrid's fifteen years in office constituted a pretty good record for a man who was merely an exception to the general rule, Mackenzie King replied, and asserted that St. Laurent was capable of doing just as well. When other arguments failed to discourage the persistent Liberal chieftain, the Quebec minister raised more personal considerations. The fact of the matter was that he could not afford to remain in public life, he explained; friends had offered to help him financially if he remained in politics, but he was very reluctant to accept such assistance, because it might appear to imply some sort of obligation towards the donors. Once again, Mackenzie King had a ready reply: if *he* had not been helped by friends, he would not have been able to remain in public life either, and he had never felt any embarrassment on that score; in fact, nearly every political leader received financial aid to compensate for the loss of revenue resulting from his public service.

By the end of the evening, St. Laurent had exhausted the list of objections; he found himself discussing the time required to organize a convention, and then for the new leader to establish himself before meeting the electorate. Still he clung stubbornly to his position. Must it be taken then that nothing would induce him to stay on? the Prime Minister asked. No, he replied firmly, he did not feel he could. Mackenzie King appeared to resign himself to the situation, and they went on to discuss possible alternatives, as well as party strategy for the coming period. However, he had not accepted the decision as final. They could just regard the conversation as the first in a series, he commented when they said good-night; St. Laurent had not succeeded in closing the door once and for all. Once he had completely accepted the idea of retiring, the Prime Minister did not let the matter rest. In late July, he wrote a letter to all his ministers, asking them to be on hand in September to discuss a leadership convention. He also raised the subject at a cabinet meeting on July 31, stating that he had only been able to carry on because St. Laurent and Ilsley had agreed to postpone their departure, and that a new leader might have to be chosen before the end of the year.

Despite the preoccupation with the party leadership, the nation's business had to be carried on as usual. Since St. Laurent could not leave the capital for more than a few days at a time because of the Newfoundland negotiations and his other duties, other ministers asked him to stand in for them; sometimes he found himself holding half a dozen portfolios on a temporary basis. Although the Prime Minister spent most of his time at Kingsmere, the two men continued to consult together frequently. Mackenzie King was concerned that the federal representatives would offer such generous terms to Newfoundland that they would be rejected by the Canadian public and by some provincial administrations; countering, St. Laurent reminded him that, according to a recent Gallup poll, 80 per cent of the population was in favour of the proposed union. One of the reasons for Mackenzie King's uneasiness was a by-election in New Brunswick made necessary by the death of the Minister of Fisheries, Frank Bridges, earlier in the summer. The Liberal Premier of New Brunswick, John McNair, was a strong advocate of increased federal aid to the provinces, and could be expected to lead a wave of protest if Newfoundland came in under more advantageous conditions than he had been able to obtain. Mackenzie King and St. Laurent met McNair in Ottawa in late August, and the premier was invited to enter the federal cabinet himself. He declined, and recommended instead Milton Gregg, a World War I Victoria Cross winner, and president of the University of New Brunswick. Although a political novice, Gregg had been Serjeant-at-arms in the House of Commons for several years, and was highly respected; he was appointed to the cabinet on September 2, and the by-election was called for October 25. Since Bridges had won the seat by less than a thousand votes in 1945, the Prime Minister asked St. Laurent to delay announcing an agreement with the Newfoundland delegation until the contest was over.

On a quiet, sultry evening in midsummer, Louis St. Laurent was sitting at his desk in the almost deserted Parliament Buildings, sorting out the papers that had accumulated over almost six years, when John Hackett walked in through the open door. Asked what he was doing, the minister replied simply that he was cleaning out his desk before going home. 'No, you won't be able to go to Quebec,' his friend commented, 'they won't let you.' 'They can't keep me here by force,' St. Laurent retorted, his temper beginning to rise. 'No,' the other man conceded, 'but they are going to convince you that it is your duty to stay.' 'How?' 'Well, you'll see,' Hackett answered. 'And if they do choose you as leader, and you are at the head of the party at the next elections, we poor Tories won't have a chance. You'll sweep the country.' St. Laurent protested that there was no call for such exaggerated statements, but was assured that the opinion was genuine, and not mere flattery. The two men sat across the desk from one another and began to discuss the situation frankly. They both knew of the feeling in Quebec that Laurier's accession to the prime-ministership had been a matter of chance, Hackett began, and that English Canadians would never again allow a French-speaking Canadian to occupy that position; that sentiment was erroneous, but it was an obstacle to the cause of national unity they were both trying to advance, and it was high time to disprove it once and for all. St. Laurent listened carefully; he had rejected that same argument when advanced by cabinet colleagues, on the grounds that they were interested in perpetuating the Liberal Party in power; he could not reject it when it was expressed by a Conservative, and a man he had known for over forty years. By the time they said good-night, he was beginning to reassess his position.

When Hackett's view was discussed at the next family reunion in Quebec, Renault and Jean-Paul agreed that it could not be dismissed lightly; the women clung to their position that the head of the family had done his share, and should return to their midst. In Ottawa, cabinet ministers, senators, and members of Parliament called to urge St. Laurent to stay and lead them. C. D. Howe offered to remain in public life if St. Laurent would accept the Liberal Party leadership. Paul Martin, whose heart had been set since childhood on becoming prime minister, also pleaded with him to do so; St. Laurent advised the ambitious young minister that he was making a mistake, for even if Canadians accepted one French-speaking Catholic as prime minister, they would certainly not accept two in a row, and the result might well be that he would never realize his ambition, but Martin maintained his position.

The final factor in making St. Laurent change his mind was a message that, without consulting him, a group of wealthy admirers had joined together to wipe out his pre-war losses, and to strengthen his financial position in a way that left him under no obligation whatsoever towards the donors; he was asked to accept the arrangement as a gesture of appreciation for past services and sacrifices on behalf of Canada, and as a contribution towards enabling him to continue to serve his country. Overcoming St. Laurent's reluctance to accept the generous move was one of the most difficult parts of the campaign to enlist him for another tour of duty, but he eventually conceded that he would have earned more than the amount in question if he had returned to Quebec in 1945, and that he would be creating no obligations by going along with the plan. In the early part of September, just before leaving for New York to attend the United Nations session, he told the Prime Minister of the arrangement, and informed him that he now felt that he could stay on for the duration of one Parliament. By then, he would be seventy years old, he remarked, and he did not feel he should try to carry on after that. Delighted at the news, Mackenzie King refused to discuss such remote considerations. They chatted about Howe's role in a new team, and St. Laurent suggested that the Minister of Reconstruction should be given responsibility for industrial development and the utilization of natural resources in order to provide him with a challenge proportionate to his great talents; already a St. Laurent –Howe team was in the making.

Under St. Laurent's direction, Canada's foreign policy changed from a rather indifferent, at times even sceptical, attitude towards the United Nations to a positive determination to make the world organization work and to commit Canadians to it as the cornerstone of their relations with other countries. He and Pearson established a fruitful working relationship based on mutual trust and admiration. Less concerned than the Prime Minister with the domestic political implications of foreign policy, St. Laurent allowed his officials a greater degree of freedom in seeking solutions to the serious problems of the cold war; Pearson, for his part, was careful not to abuse that confidence, and kept his minister well informed of day-to-day developments. So close was their co-operation that it was difficult to distinguish the contribution of each one to a particular decision. The more positive Canadian attitude emerged just as many people were once again beginning to despair of peace. In March 1947, a meeting in Moscow of the foreign ministers of the major powers to decide the future destiny of Germany had ended in failure, and in Eastern Europe Soviet-supported Communist parties were seizing power in one capital after the other. In Western Europe, the Communists had been expelled from coalition governments in France and Italy and were trying to upset the tottering régimes there by every possible means; in Greece, they were waging a bitter guerilla warfare. The Russians and Americans were deadlocked over the fate of Korea, the uses of atomic energy, and the control of conventional armaments, and Moscow had spurned an offer to share in the benefits of the multi-billion-dollar Marshall Plan to aid the economic recovery of Europe. Despite Mackenzie King's strong reservations, Canada chose that critical juncture in international affairs to accept the seat in the Security Council being vacated by Australia after a two-year term. Announcing the decision in Ottawa on September 8, St. Laurent stated:

> We are standing for membership in a body with a discouraging record . . . [because] in spite of its shortcomings, we in this country continue to believe that the best hope for mankind lies in the establishment of a world organization for the maintenance of peace . . . [and] if we wish to enjoy the benefits of such a development we must also accept its responsibilities.

With this recognition that it was impossible to achieve status without responsibility or security without commitments, a quali-fied observer has commented, Canada may be said to have reached maturity in international affairs.

St. Laurent outlined the Canadian position in greater detail in his statement before the General Assembly on September 18. While the other branches of the world organization were functioning satisfactorily, he declared, the record of the Security

Council had confirmed the fears expressed in 1945 that the veto power would prevent it from operating effectively. The world would not accept indefinitely, he warned, 'voting procedures and practices which, in the name of unanimity, underline disunity; and which reduce agreement to a lowest common denominator of action that in practice often means inaction'. If forced to do so, the West might 'seek greater safety in an association of democratic and peace-loving states willing to accept more specific international obligations in return for greater national security'. The reference to a new association was the first public indication of a plan being discussed by Western diplomats, and probably originating in the office of the British Foreign Secretary, Ernest Bevin, for a Western defensive alliance to be known in history as the North Atlantic Treaty Organization.

From the beginning of the United Nations session, the Canadian delegation concentrated its efforts on increasing the effectiveness of the world organization. Pearson was named chairman of a sub-committee to recommend ways of expanding the functions of the General Assembly. Another Canadian, Escott Reid, became chairman of a committee that succeeded in improving the rules of the assembly, in order to allow it to do its work with greater dispatch. When the Korean question was referred to the General Assembly over the objections of the U.S.S.R., Canada supported an American resolution calling for free elections in the whole country, rather than separate polls in North and South Korea, dominated by the Soviet Union and the United States respectively. After the proposal was accepted, Canada was appointed to a temporary commission to deal with the elections. In the Palestine question, the Canadians, and particularly Pearson, played a key role in reconciling British and American policies. On major issues, the Canadian delegation usually supported the American policies, but this was often to be explained by the fact that the Canadians had exercised a telling influence behind the scenes in elaborating them. On less vital questions, Canada took a strongly independent position. Despite some rather lively exchanges, the Canadian role remained, in the view of one competent analyst, 'essentially that of a constructive critic and conciliator... helping to break deadlocks or to effect compromises which did not sacrifice general principles'.

Still carrying a heavy load of domestic responsibilities, St. Laurent shuttled back and forth between Ottawa and New York, leaving J. L. Ilsley in charge of the delegation during his absence. On September 29, he was back in the capital to preside over the final discussions with the Newfoundland delegation. The visitors left for home much more enthusiastic than when they had arrived, and determined to press for approval of union in the national convention, as well as in the referendum that was to follow. From Ottawa, the Minister for External Affairs went on to Quebec City to address the Chamber of Commerce on the international situation. It was an important occasion, since he had to prepare public opinion in French Canada for a further period of international tension, and forestall a new withdrawal within the frontiers of Quebec, the instinctive reaction of French-speaking Canadians in times of stress. Once again, he referred to his *bête noire*, the veto power of the major powers. Even though the assurance was given in San Francisco that the veto power would not be used 'except in the interest of the United Nations as a whole', he declared, the Soviet Union had used it over twenty times, and had made the Security Council 'practically unworkable as the main instrument . . . to secure and maintain peace'. It had become 'perfectly clear' that the aim of Soviet policy was to destroy 'what it calls capitalistic régimes', and to establish 'Communist totalitarianism' everywhere. St. Laurent stated firmly:

> We will go to the most extreme limits to make the United Nations work as a universal one-world organization, and I still hope we can do it. . . . But if theory-crazed totalitarian groups persist in their policies of frustration and futility, we will not, for very much longer, allow them to prevent us from using our obvious advantages to improve the conditions of those who do wish to co-operate with us.

Not only was this forthright warning the first announcement to the Canadian people that the country would be taking a firmer stand in the cold war, but it was made in the heart of Quebec, from which most resistance to such a policy was bound to come. No other Canadian could make the important statement with such hopes of a favourable reception; St. Laurent was pursuing his task of national unity by enlisting the support of all Canadians for the new, dynamic foreign policy.

Mackenzie King left for Britain on October 30 to attend the royal wedding, and St. Laurent once again became acting prime minister. His activities were increased still further by his view that if he was to remain in politics, he could not continue to refuse invitations to speak in public; his agenda soon became crowded with engagements outside Ottawa. On November 6, he released the proposed terms of union with Newfoundland. The total cost to Canada of obtaining a tenth province might be around $180 million over a ten-year period, he commented, but he shrugged off the objection that it was a pretty expensive acquisition with the comment that the sum was 'peanuts according to present-day financial standards'. Labrador was to be included in the new province; without being able to say so, he conceded implicitly that his efforts to meet at least in part the Quebec view on that point had failed. The provinces would not be consulted on the agreement since 'the Government will be consulting the representatives of the people who live in the Provinces in bringing it before Parliament for approval'. As was to be expected, Premier Duplessis protested both the arrangement with regard to Labrador, and what he considered a violation of the 'pact' theory of Confederation, which implied provincial consultation in making so important a change in the Canadian federal system.

Relations between Mackenzie King and St. Laurent from the time the latter agreed to remain in public life until he actually became Liberal leader were not always comfortable for either man. Pleased as he was to have picked his own successor, the old warrior could not repress an occasional feeling of resentment as he realized that power was already passing into someone else's hands. St. Laurent took considerable pains to avoid the impression of presuming on the decision of the leadership convention, but he could not help planning the future with that eventuality in mind. When the Prime Minister returned to Canada on December 4, he was once more determined to exercise personally the authority invested in his office until he actually retired. He was concerned about the initiative taken by the Canadian delegation at the United Nations, and feared that Canada might become implicated in situations that bore the seeds of a third world war. Before leaving for London, he had prevented Pearson from accepting an invitation to become chairman of the U.N. Palestine Commission, and had insisted that it be made clear that the Canadian who was chosen as a member, Justice Ivan Rand of the Supreme Court, would participate as an impartial investigator, and was not bound by instructions from Ottawa. He was just as reluctant about Canadian participation in the U.N. temporary commission formed to supervise elections in Korea. On his arrival back in Ottawa, he expressed his concern at the part Canada had agreed to play in both matters. St. Laurent had some sympathy for the Prime Minister's point of view, and had tried to dampen the zeal of the more enthusiastic internationalists in the Department of External Affairs, but for rather different reasons. Quite apart from the fact that Canada was already considered favourable to the Jewish cause, he felt that a prominent role in the Palestine Commission would imply complete neutrality, and might lead to requests for Canadian troops in the disputed area, or even risk a clash with Britain and other powerful friends. He had given careful thought as well to the advisability of participating in the Korean Commission, but had concluded that, as it was a temporary assignment with less direct implications for Canada, the importance of exercising a wholesome influence at the United Nations outweighed the disadvantages.

Throughout December 1947, the international scene looked increasingly sombre. In the middle of the month, a meeting of the foreign ministers of the major powers broke up after failing to agree on the future of either Germany or Austria; while the Soviets moved to consolidate their control over Eastern Europe, the United States, Britain, and France prepared to strengthen Western Europe by increased economic and military aid. The last vestiges of co-operation between the Communist and non-Communist camps were torn away; World War III seemed a very real possibility. Against that disheartening background, St. Laurent found himself recommending to cabinet Dr. George

Patterson as the Canadian member of the U.N. Commission on Korea. Still upset about the commitment that had been made in his absence, and conjuring up visions of Canada's being crushed in a conflict between the United States and the Soviet Union, the Prime Minister declared heatedly that a great mistake had been made, and that he could not support the recommendation. The Minister for External Affairs listened to the outburst in silence, then replied in a moderate tone that, while there was general agreement about the seriousness of the world situation, Canada was still a member of the United Nations and occupied a seat in the Security Council; unless she decided to withdraw from the world body, there were certain obligations of membership that she could not ignore. Mackenzie King retorted that the United Nations was a useless organization that had merely served as a forum for Soviet propaganda, and, in any event, Canada was not in a position to save the world like some latter-day Sir Galahad. Pressing his viewpoint, he learned that Canadian participation on the commission had been recommended by Pearson, authorized by St. Laurent in his capacity of Acting Prime Minister, and communicated to the United Nations by Ilsley as interim leader of the Canadian delegation in New York; however, the matter had not been submitted to cabinet as a whole. Strengthened by that revelation, the Prime Minister refused to sign the order in council appointing the Canadian representative. Being personally involved, Ilsley defended the action that had been taken, and the tension mounted in the Council Chamber. Finally, Mackenzie King realized that too much heat had developed to permit a rational appraisal of the situation, and he postponed further discussion; the ministers left the East Block, troubled and in bad humour.

By the time the matter was raised again on December 22, both sides had stiffened in their resistance. The Prime Minister argued that Canada was being placed in a position where she might be drawn into a war with the U.S.S.R.; St. Laurent argued that the only point at issue was whether Canada should boycott the commission. Ilsley interpreted any criticism of the decision as a reflection on himself; the other ministers were divided. Working himself again into a state of excitement, Mackenzie King declared that he would resign rather than sign the order; in an exchange reminiscent of the conscription debate, Ilsley countered with his own threat of resignation. St. Laurent remained outwardly calm, but he was equally determined not to give way. It was finally agreed that the United States should be informed that, in the light of recent international developments and information gained in Europe by the Prime Minister, Canada wished to reconsider her position. There the matter rested over Christmas, but each of the principal actors in the drama spent considerable time during the holiday season reflecting on the situation. St. Laurent readily acknowledged the Prime Minister's right to approve every government policy, but he also realized that a public disavowal of a decision taken by Ilsley, Pearson, and himself would destroy confidence in them, and lead inevitably to their resignations. To the delight of some members of his family, he began once again to envisage the possibility of returning to Quebec.

On December 30, the Prime Minister, St. Laurent, and Pearson met to discuss the situation again but they soon found that they were still in disagreement. The message to Washington had been framed in such a way that the American authorities realized the Prime Minister was being difficult, and that the other ministers most interested in international affairs still favoured participation in the work of the Korean Commission; it practically suggested that the President intervene to persuade the government leader to be more reasonable. Mackenzie King's mood was not improved by receiving a letter from the United States Under Secretary of State, urging that the original policy be maintained. He repeated his threat to resign. It was St. Laurent's turn to be firm. If the Prime Minister resigned, a Liberal-Conservative coalition would be formed, he commented, and that was hardly a preferable alternative. Changing his tone rapidly, the government leader protested that it was ridiculous to think of the government breaking up over a matter that did not concern Canada directly. In the calmer atmosphere that followed, St. Laurent suggested that Pearson go to Washington and speak to the President and to Secretary of State Marshall, and offered to go himself later on if it proved necessary. Mackenzie King accepted the proposal, and the under-secretary left on his mission immediately after New Year's Day; however, since he was more interested in persuading the Prime Minister than the President to change his mind, his trip resulted only in a letter from Truman urging again that the original commitment be accepted. On January 7, the determined old government leader sat down to prepare a reply, in which he proposed to refuse for the first time a direct request from a United States president. Alarmed, Pearson showed the draft to St. Laurent, who consulted Ilsley, then telephoned the Prime Minister and asked for an appointment. He was invited to dinner at Laurier House.

The evening began with a pleasant talk over the meal, and then Mackenzie King and St. Laurent withdrew to the third-floor study. In a quiet, chatty tone, St. Laurent recalled that six years earlier they had been sitting in the same room when he had agreed to enter the cabinet. Now, he had come to the conclusion that, unless the position that had been adopted publicly on the Korean Commission was maintained, he and Ilsley would both have to leave. While they recognized the Prime Minister's right to repudiate their action in New York, he explained, to do so would make it appear that they had foolhardily endangered the nation, and their influence would be destroyed. In addition, they had entered into an undertaking on behalf of Canada which could not simply be ignored. Once again, Mackenzie King countered with his own resignation threat; St. Laurent replied that such an action would destroy public confidence in the ability of the Liberal Party to steer a safe course in international affairs. Once they had established that neither man wanted the other to leave, the search for a compromise solution began again. They were in disagreement, they established, in their assessment both of the world situation and of the political scene at home. St. Laurent argued that, the present tension notwithstanding, he did not expect ever to see another war in his lifetime, nor did he think one would come in the next fifty years. Mackenzie King clung to his view that a world conflagration was highly likely at any time. On the domestic scene, St. Laurent asserted that Quebec would give solid support to participation on the Korean Commission because it was a United Nations undertaking and bore no taint of British imperialism; the Prime Minister was convinced that four-fifths of Canada would oppose the move, and that every member of Parliament from Quebec would speak against it if given the facts. For the first time, they examined the proposed task of the commission, the Minister for External Affairs pointing out that the assignment was to observe how the election in Korea would be carried out, and not to impose it on people against their will. St. Laurent offered to state in Parliament, if the matter was discussed there, that as he understood the U.N. resolution creating the commission, that body should only act over the whole of Korea, or in other words, with the consent of both the Soviets and the Americans. The Prime Minister leaped at the opportunity for an agreement on those terms. With that position asserted, he replied, his grounds for refusing to sign the order in council no longer had any weight, and, in fact, the Canadian stand would be rendered even stronger by making it clear that action would be taken only with the consent and co-operation of both the Soviets and the Americans. Both men were immensely relieved to have found a way out of the impasse, and to put an end to their most serious disagreement in six years of constant collaboration. None of the persons involved in the clash of wills was soon to forget the incident, and they remained sensitive on that subject for some time. Mackenzie King continued to have serious reservations about the attitude of the Department of External Affairs, and he began to realize that the difference of viewpoint between him and most of his ministers on international affairs was very wide; he concluded that he should not remain in office much longer.

Mackenzie King announced his retirement plan on January 20, 1948, at a meeting of the National Liberal Federation; the date for the leadership convention was set for August. Heralding the new era, Ian Mackenzie was appointed to the Senate, Milton Gregg transferred to the Department of Veterans' Affairs, and at St. Laurent's specific request C. D. Howe was made Minister of Trade and Commerce. The Minister for External Affairs left the party meeting early. He had never visited the prairies as a minister of the Crown, and yet from there, some people felt, would come the strongest reaction against a French-speaking Catholic leadership candidate; he had agreed to address a meeting of the Manitoba Liberal Association in order to give party members in that province an opportunity to assess his qualifications for the post.

When he arrived in Winnipeg, St. Laurent had no intention of announcing his availability for the leadership, but he had been in the city only an hour before a reporter asked him bluntly how he felt about taking on the job. 'If it was something which would further rather than retard Canadian unity, I don't see how I could refuse,' he answered frankly. 'On the other hand, if there was any indication of a split on religious or racial lines I would not like to be a party to such a split.' His address to the Liberal gathering the same evening was hardly the type of spell-binding oratory usually expected of a candidate for the top political post in the land. He began with a sound and solid defence of the government's policies in the manner of a competent administrator, then went on to reveal something of his political philosophy. Both the Conservative and Liberal outlooks held the promise of much good, but also of much evil, he declared.

> The Conservative who defends his centuries-old institutions may do much good but he may also do much evil if he is obstinate in maintaining abuses which have become intolerable. The Liberal who contends against these abuses and who after long efforts succeeds in extirpating them may be a public benefactor, just as a Liberal who lays a rash hand on hallowed institutions may be a scourge not only for his own country but for humanity at large.

Over the years, Canadian Liberalism had become a philosophy of 'progress, but orderly and measured progress'. Among the reforms still to be carried out under its banner were the achievement of national unity, and, as a prerequisite of that unity, 'a situation of absolute equality' among all citizens, 'equality not only in the text of our constitutional laws but practical equality in the daily application of these texts, in the real situation of each individual'.

For the attentive reader, newspaper reports of the five speeches he delivered in less than three days – four in English and one in French – provided a well-rounded picture of his personality and his views on the issues of the day. To most Canadians, the impression was highly favourable, but the Prime Minister was distressed over his frank admission that he was available for the leadership, and his equally frank reference to his religion and ethnic origin. When St. Laurent returned to Ottawa, he was advised to leave references to his religion and language out of his speeches in the coming months.

One of the first persons who came to see St. Laurent on his return to Ottawa was J. L. Ilsley. With his health restored since abandoning the Finance portfolio, the fifty-three-year-old Nova Scotian had watched with interest the popularity polls, and noted that he and St. Laurent had about the same appeal throughout the country as a whole. A hard-working man of unbending integrity, he would have been in many ways an ideal English-speaking Protestant leadership candidate, and he was undoubtedly attracted by the post, but he was also a realist. After examining the situation objectively, he concluded that St. Laurent had a better chance of winning the leadership, and, having reached that decision, he made up his mind to retire, and he informed the Prime Minister and St. Laurent accordingly. The government leader received the news with a sense of relief, St Laurent with a feeling of regret that he would not have his competent and experienced colleague with him in a new ministry. Just as one leading Liberal announced his withdrawal, another burst anew on the political scene with a sensational article in *Maclean's* Magazine. Chubby Power, increasingly restless under the cautious leadership of Mackenzie King, denounced the government for 'travelling in the ditches of expediency', abrogating 'every human right founded upon the Magna Carta', and turning 'from being Labour's friend to being Labour's provoker'. It was not clear whether he was expressing his personal frustration or making a leadership bid. While St. Laurent appreciated the former minister's viewpoint, and maintained his feelings of friendship for him, the Prime Minister was merely strengthened in his determination to choose his own successor.

Parliament re-convened on January 26, 1948, and the leadership question was forced largely out of St. Laurent's mind by his day-to-day occupations. At an early stage, Frédéric Dorion raised the matter of the disposition of Labrador under the proposed terms of union with Newfoundland. The federal government had not 'the legal power to dispose of a territory belonging to the province of Quebec', the Independent member declared, founding his argument on the assertion that Quebec had not been consulted when the border question was submitted to the Privy Council in 1927, and, in any event, that body, as part of the British government, was one of the interested parties. Finally, he argued, the Privy Council had not handed down a decision, but merely reported on a 'reference' and no proper action had ever been taken to give it the force of law. Having taken a keen interest in the matter from the outset, and having accepted the inclusion of the disputed area as part of the proposed new province, St. Laurent replied at once to the charge. The government of Quebec had designated Aimé Geoffrion and Deputy Attorney General Charles Lanctôt to represent it in 1927, he recalled, and the two men had been retained as joint counsel for the federal and the provincial governments; Geoffrion had made it plain during his appearance that he was acting for the Quebec government. The verdict of the judicial committee of the Privy Council had been 'very disappointing' to both the federal and the provincial administrations, but Ottawa was bound to treat it as a valid decision, and it was so doing in its negotiations with Newfoundland. St. Laurent's intervention did not put an end to criticism in Quebec, but it did place the facts on record and reassured the members of the national convention in Newfoundland who were still making up their minds about union.

In the field of foreign policy, St. Laurent carried on as best he could with the Prime Minister pulling in one direction, Pearson and his staff in another. The Communist *coup d'état* in Czechoslovakia in early March, followed by the suicide of Jan Masaryk, the country's greatest statesman, served to spur to action the Western statesmen and diplomats who had been discussing a possible anti-Communist alliance over the previous six months. The day after Masaryk's death, British Prime Minister Attlee sent a telegram to Ottawa underlining the need for the free nations to present a united front, and suggesting a meeting of United

Louis and Jeanne St. Laurent on their wedding day; Beauceville, Quebec,
May 19, 1908.

Mackenzie King congratulating Louis St. Laurent on his being chosen as Leader of the Liberal Party; Ottawa Coliseum, August 7, 1948. Between the two men: Jeanne St. Laurent.

Prime Minister Louis St. Laurent and his new cabinet, together with the Governor General, Viscount Alexander, and the retiring Prime Minister, Mackenzie King; Rideau Hall, Ottawa, November 15, 1948. Left to right: *first row*: J. G. Gardiner, C. D. Howe, L. S. St. Laurent, His Excellency Viscount Alexander, W. L. Mackenzie King, J. A. MacKinnon, C. Gibson; *second row*: R. Winters, R. Mayhew, P. Martin, J. Jean, L. Chevrier, A. Fournier, B. Claxton, D. C. Abbott, J. J. McCann, H. Mitchell, E. Bertrand, M. Gregg, S. Garson.

Louis St. Laurent as 'Uncle Louis', with a young Canadian, Doris Roper;
Dresden, Ontario, April 21, 1950.

States, Canadian, and British officials to plan the formation of an Atlantic regional security organization. St. Laurent had referred to such a possibility in the United Nations the previous autumn, and he, Defence Minister Claxton, and Pearson supported the suggestion. If Britain and the United States were drawn into a war with the Soviet Union, Canada would be destroyed whether she was a participant or not, the three men argued in a meeting with the Prime Minister; the only way of escaping such a fate was to join with the two most powerful Western nations in trying to preserve peace through discouraging further Communist aggression. In the moment of real crisis, Mackenzie King proved still able to rise to the occasion; he cast aside his preoccupation with politics and his isolationism, and agreed to send an affirmative reply to London. The following week, Harry Truman announced the reintroduction of compulsory military service in the United States. A shudder ran through the crowd of parliamentarians that listened to the President on the radio in a room adjoining the Commons Chamber; the spectre of conscription was back to haunt them after a scant three years. At a hastily convened cabinet meeting immediately after the broadcast, the advisability of compulsory service was discussed, but Claxton gave the assurance that the Chiefs of Staff were not thinking of making such a recommendation for the moment. St. Laurent pointed out that the real problem was to decide how Canadians could best contribute to maintaining world peace, and expressed his confidence that they would be ready to do their full part, just as they had in the past. There was no doubt in the minds of any of the men listening to him that his comment implied the reintroduction of conscription if necessary to resist the current threat. Later in the day, the Prime Minister assured the House of Commons that Canada would 'play her full part in every movement to give substance to the conception of an effective system of collective security by the development of regional pacts under the Charter of the United Nations'.

St. Laurent's situation as Minister for External Affairs became increasingly difficult as international tension continued to grow, and the divergence of views between his advisers and the Prime Minister was accentuated. His own position was usually much closer to Pearson's than to Mackenzie King's, but he recognized that the latter had the final word in determining the government's policy, and he hesitated to differ with a man who had so much more political experience. In his public statements, however, St. Laurent continued to warn Canadians of the Communist threat, and to urge firmness and unity in resisting it. The proposal to set up a 'self-defensive union' did not mean that a third world war was considered inevitable, he pointed out at Kitchener, Ontario, on March 24, but was based on the premise that the best way of preventing such a war was to confront the forces of Communist expansionism with an overwhelming preponderance of moral, economic, and military force on the side of freedom; the mistake must not be repeated of allowing a potential aggressor to believe that the democratic nations were too lax and disorganized to resist attack. In presenting the estimates of the Department of External Affairs to the House of Commons on April 29, he described the *coup d'état* in Czechoslovakia as 'a frightening case history of Communist totalitarianism in action', and announced that Canada would be willing to associate herself with other free states in creating 'appropriate collective security arrangements which may be worked out under Articles 51 and 52 of the [United Nations] Charter'. Such an organization, he asserted, would be 'a dynamic counter-attraction to Communism – the dynamic counter-attraction of a free, prosperous and progressive society as opposed to the totalitarian and reactionary society of the Communist world'. Notwithstanding the Prime Minister's concern, no other government had gone so far in publicly committing itself to participation in the proposed pact.

The statement made banner headlines. The *Winnipeg Free Press* declared it to be 'perhaps the frankest statement of foreign policy ever made in the Canadian Parliament'. On the other hand, a writer in *Le Devoir* denounced it as an incitement to war, and declared St. Laurent 'a half-French Canadian showing himself more bellicose and imperialistic than the people of the [Montreal] *Gazette* and the [Toronto] *Globe and Mail'*. Even the vigorous campaign of the Vatican against the Communist threat could not overcome the instinctive resistance of many French-speaking Canadians to participation in any foreign struggle.

Ironically, St. Laurent found himself being criticized in Quebec as too soft on Communism for refusing to ban the Labour-Progressive Party, and too belligerent for preparing to resist any attack by the Soviet Union.

With a provincial election near, Duplessis did not hesitate to use the issue of Communism to attack his Liberal opponents, and he found a ready-made occasion in a rather bizarre case of a collection of Polish art treasures that had been moved to Canada early in World War II by the Polish government in exile in London. The Canadian government had agreed to provide storage space for them on the Central Experimental Farm, but only on the clear understanding that it would assume no responsibility for their safekeeping. After the fall of Nazi Germany, a Communist régime was installed by the Russians in Warsaw, and it asked for the return of the paintings as the property of the Polish state; an investigation revealed, however, that they had been removed. The Canadian government agreed to have the R.C.M.P. conduct a search to ascertain their whereabouts, and they were traced to the Hôtel Dieu Hospital in Quebec City, where the Mother Superior showed them to two constables. At about the same time, the Mother Superior found herself with two requests to hand them over, one from the persons who had brought them, and one from a man representing himself as the 'agent' of the new Polish government. Concerned over becoming involved in an international controversy, she informed Premier Duplessis of the situation, and he ordered them transferred to the provincial museum. Suddenly the federal government found itself being attacked by the Polish Foreign Ministry for holding the treasures illegally in Canada, and by the Quebec Premier for violating a cloister in its search for them. 'With Stalin and his satellite atheist governments, Mr. St. Laurent uses all the procedures of diplomacy and diplomatic protocol,' Duplessis told the press, 'but with a noble and admirable religious order of Quebec, he uses the Mounted Police.'

Nothing could have illustrated better than Duplessis's attack on him why St. Laurent had kept out of politics for so many years, and why he still had moments of doubt about his decision to remain in public life. A comment by one newspaperman during that spring of 1948 offered him another foretaste of the treatment he was likely to receive in his native province. Roger Duhamel wrote:

> After Laurier, the Liberals want another French-Canadian to betray his own people, to be the slave of the party, and the faithful servant of foreign interests. Mr. St. Laurent is the worthy successor of Laurier; he flatters himself that he is simply a Canadian, that is, that he has disavowed his French origins. . . . It won't take much of an effort. . . . Let it not be forgotten Mr. St. Laurent is much more *Stephen* than Louis.

In the final weeks before the Liberal convention, St. Laurent refused steadfastly to solicit support; he had agreed to offer his services as leader, provided no split along ethnic or religious lines would result from his candidacy. At the same time, he made it clear that he would be just as pleased if the delegates decided to let him return to Quebec at once. In the meantime, he was still Minister for External Affairs, House Leader, and the Prime Minister's principal lieutenant from Quebec; those responsibilities were sufficient to occupy him full time.

He received some criticism in the Canadian press when it was learned that the Canadian member of the Korean Commission, Dr. George Patterson, had specific instructions not to participate in preparing elections in South Korea after the Communists had refused to allow a vote throughout the whole country; the election preparations went forward regardless of the Canadian attitude. On the Palestine question, that commission recommended partition of the area, and Pearson won high praise at the United Nations for his skill in working out a compromise plan, but within a week of its approval by the General Assembly fighting broke out between the Arabs and Jews, and the plan could not be applied. On May 14, the Jews announced the *de facto* partition of Palestine by the formation of the state of Israel.

The first test of strength in the cold war between the Soviet Union and her former Allies occurred in Berlin. In response to a U.S.-British-French plan to unify control of West Germany, the Russians blockaded West Berlin; an airlift was created to feed its population, and the British government raised the possibility of Canadian participation in the dramatic project. Mackenzie King once again reacted instinctively against acceding to the request, arguing that it was tantamount to involving Canada in World War III without her prior consent. Despite the gravity of the situation, St. Laurent continued to believe that a general war would not occur, and that the best way of preventing it was to present a united front against the Communist threat. The Prime Minister was much more pessimistic, and asked Claxton to make as many preparations as possible in the next two weeks. That placed his estimate of the possible time of the outbreak precisely during the week of the Liberal convention! Louis St. Laurent maintained his attitude of calm determination, insisting that the North Atlantic alliance, with the United States, Great Britain, and Canada as its solid core, was the best assurance against the catastrophe. With his full support, Pearson and his officials pressed for an early conclusion to the negotiations going on in Washington to set up the new security pact.

Political developments in Canada in the weeks before the convention were far from encouraging for the Liberals. Premier George Drew's government was re-elected in Ontario on June 7, but there was a movement within the Progressive Conservative Party to have him replace John Bracken as national leader, and it was likely that he would be Leader of the Opposition at the next session of Parliament. Having clashed with St. Laurent as early as 1942, and denounced the Mackenzie King administration frequently since becoming premier of Ontario, it seemed likely that he would prove a dangerous opponent.

In Quebec, Maurice Duplessis called an election for July 28. Since St. Laurent had agreed, at Godbout's urgent request, to take part in the provincial contest, the outcome would indicate his influence in French Canada. Realizing that in the previous four years the Union Nationale leader had consolidated his position and built a highly efficient electoral machine, many Liberals viewed the test of strength with alarm. Maurice Duplessis had succeeded in winning strong support among the Roman Catholic clergy, the English-speaking financial barons of Montreal's St. James Street, and the broad mass of the French-speaking population. The long-standing practice of patronage was refined into a powerful instrument to buy votes, even in the most remote areas of the province. Presiding personally over the Private Bills Committee meetings, the premier was able to direct the expenditure of public funds on a vast number of small projects. Communities were warned openly that if they did not support the Union Nationale Party they could expect no favours; business men were informed that if they did not contribute to the party fund their prospects of making money in Quebec were dim. Two months before the election, members of the Quebec press gallery were given a free trip to New York, and they received a fee for reporting on Union Nationale meetings. 'We didn't invent a new system,' explained one of Duplessis's intimates; 'the only thing we can really be accused of by the Liberals is of taking over their system and making it more efficient.' During the campaign, Duplessis displayed the new Quebec flag chosen by the last legislature, and shouted that he was leading French Canada in 'a fight for survival' against the 'centralizing' Liberal administration in Ottawa, of which Godbout was a mere vassal. The entry of Newfoundland into Confederation was a plot to bring three hundred thousand more 'Britishers' into the country, he warned. Referring to the billion-dollar Canadian loan to Britain and the post-war aid to Europe, he charged that the Liberals had 'billions' of dollars to give the 'foreigners', but none for Quebec. The Communist threat was fully exploited as well, the Union Nationale leader recounting his version of the story of the Polish treasures to illustrate Ottawa's complicity with the enemies of the Catholic faith, and alluding to secret Communist camps with 'thousands of machine guns' in the woods of northern Quebec.

Neither Louis St. Laurent nor Adélard Godbout was a match for such a combination of oratorical talent and political astuteness. When he addressed a Liberal meeting in Quebec City's municipal stadium on July 15, St. Laurent revealed his delicate situation by declaring that he was speaking, not as a member of the government in Ottawa, but simply 'as a citizen of Quebec, interested like all of you in the good administration of our province'. The remark was tantamount to admitting defeat in advance, and trying to minimize the consequences for the Liberal team in Ottawa. While most of the audience sympathized with his appeal for 'frank co-operation' between Quebec and Ottawa, and admired' his high-minded attitude, they were disappointed at not being treated to the usual Quebec political performance. At meetings in Montreal and Sherbrooke, St. Laurent repeated his message, but the only significant result was to draw to himself the fire of Godbout's opponents. 'The worst thing that could happen to us would be for him to become Prime Minister of Canada,' declared Independent candidate René Chaloult, for he was 'of English mentality', 'a capitalist, and, moreover, a colonial, there-fore an imperialist, and his heart is in London'. Montreal Mayor Houde denounced him as the leader of a 'nest of traitors', and predicted that the Communists were going to vote Liberal and that St. Laurent would impose conscription. In Quebec East constituency, Duplessis repeated that 'we, the Government of Quebec, protected the Sisters against Mr. St. Laurent's police'; de-clared that St. Laurent had said Quebec had only the right to 'the leavings of Ottawa', and that the Canadian Parliament could abolish the French language in Ottawa. The crowd booed the name of their federal representative. By the end of the campaign, it was apparent that the Liberal slogan 'a vote for Godbout is a vote for St. Laurent' had misfired badly. On July 28, Duplessis made good his boast that 'never yet has the St. Laurent overflowed the St. Maurice' in defeating his opponents by eighty-two seats to eight. Less than two weeks before the leadership convention, St. Laurent had been repudiated in his own province; Houde called gleefully for his resignation.

In private, St. Laurent confessed that he felt discouraged by the results of the contest, but in public he merely commented that he still believed 'in the usefulness of the Liberal Party to the Cana-dian nation'. Anxious to prevent him from seeking to withdraw his name at such a late date, Mackenzie King minimized the significance of the Union Nationale victory, and argued that Du-plessis would not be able to influence a federal contest. Although the Prime Minister had let it be understood that he would be neutral in the leadership contest, he had no intention of having his choice thwarted, and as the delegates arrived for the con-vention he began to exercise his influence quietly behind the scenes, counselling St. Laurent on matters of detail and making known his personal preference. By August 1, the names of three candidates, St. Laurent, Gardiner, and Power, were known, but only the Minister of Agriculture was campaigning actively for the leadership. Paul Martin was reported to be torn between putting his name forward in order to at least establish his position for the next convention, or throwing his support openly behind the almost certain winner. On August 4, Mackenzie King decided to intervene more directly and telephoned C. D. Howe to suggest that he should allow himself to be nominated, and then withdraw in favour of St. Laurent. Abbott, Claxton, Chevrier, Martin, and Premier Garson of Manitoba received similar 'suggestions'. Later that evening Paul Martin made one of the most heart-wrenching moves of his life, and announced his support for St. Laurent, because of his 'great admiration of his great integrity, and . . . intelligence and industry'. Other delegates suspected of sympathy for Gardiner received more or less veiled warnings to fall in line; one western M.P. was made to understand that the senatorship he hoped for would not be forthcoming if he persisted in supporting the Minister of Agriculture.* By midnight of the day prior to the convention, St. Laurent's victory was as certain as anything in politics can be, and he had not lifted a finger in his own behalf.

Caught up in the excitement of the contest, all the adult members of the St. Laurent family arrived in the capital and joined in the round of receptions and dinners that are part of a political gathering, but refrained from soliciting the support of delegates. Gardiner, on the other hand, campaigned actively, receiving delegates in a Château Laurier suite, chatting with them on a first-name basis and putting heavy pressure on the undecided. Power campaigned as well, but, while he did not exclude the possibility of becoming a compromise choice, he was mainly interested in the opportunity to put his views before the large Liberal gathering. Throughout the busy round of activities, St. Laurent retained his usual poise, but he was plagued by a deep sense of uneasiness. He fretted about the text that had been prepared for him to use the following day, worried lest his

*He resisted the pressure, and received his reward from St. Laurent all the same.

candidature should cause a vote on ethnic lines, and wondered whether he was making the biggest mistake of his life. His son Renault kept close by him, bolstering his spirits and reminding him that he was about to plead his greatest cause. 'You are pretty well responsible for the predicament I find myself in today,' he commented almost reproachfully to his son as they left the last reception about midnight on the day prior to the voting. 'If I am,' Renault replied, 'it is the greatest compliment you can pay me.'

On the afternoon of August 6, nine names were placed in nomination, St. Laurent's being proposed by Stuart Garson and seconded by House of Commons Whip Leonard Tremblay; then Howe, Martin, Claxton, Chevrier, Abbott, and Garson dutifully withdrew, and announced that they were supporting the Minister for External Affairs. Lots were drawn among the remaining three, and Power led off with a vigorous appeal to return to the principles of Liberalism. Warning against 'a whitewash of the past and a blank cheque for the future', he called for a wide range of reforms, and a greater responsiveness to the will of the people. He summoned the delegates to join in a struggle against 'autocracy, complacency, and inertia', and proposed to 'canadianize Canada . . . regardless of opponents, internal and external'. Still a highly popular man, the former minister was given tremendous applause.

In contrast, St. Laurent's speech was disappointingly mundane. He had no intention of participating in an oratorical contest in order to win votes, he began, or to put forward a personal program. He was 'a Liberal by inheritance' who had become a Liberal by conviction. To him the Liberal Party was 'a party of progress, of true progress, of the kind of progress that can be based upon understanding and co-operation between men of good will'. Like Power, he argued that it was also 'the party of the people'. Having made that declaration of party faith, St. Laurent devoted the rest of his allotted twenty minutes to his life-long theme of national unity. 'Our nation was planned as a political partnership of two great races,' he told the six thousand men and women before him; 'it was planned by men of vision, of tolerance, as a partnership in which both of the partners would retain their essential characteristics, their religion, their culture.' The destruction of national unity would do a 'grave injury' to Canada, and also to the rest of the world. 'If the world is ever to have peace, if the nations are ever to live in harmony, that condition will only come about through the achievement of genuine understanding and tolerance, and the development among nations of the world of the kind of partnership which we have been able to develop in Canada and which has made Canada a nation.' At the same time, national unity did not consist merely of 'the absence of friction' between the two groups, he pointed out, but also 'the promotion of . . . social security and social justice', 'the maintenance of the constitution', 'the maintenance of . . . the right of the people to control the Parliament . . . and through their Parliament all the executive and administrative branches of government', and 'the respect of the constitutional rights of the provinces'. The Liberal Party was traditionally the party of provincial rights, he recalled, and must not depart from that tradition. 'I do not think it has; I am sure it never intended to.' But it also stood for federal-provincial co-operation, 'believing that without both the preservation of the rights of the provinces and co-operation between all governments, all Canadians, Canada cannot fail to have less unity and less strength.' St. Laurent delivered the last portion of his speech in French, stressing again the theme of provincial rights, but asserting that the government of Canada was 'the government of all Canadians', even if some people considered it 'a foreign and even a hostile government'.

As the third and last speaker, Gardiner based his appeal on his reputation as a political organizer in Saskatchewan, and offered his services as the 'spark-plug' needed to revitalize the party. While he had always considered himself a friend of French-speaking Canadians, and had demonstrated that sentiment by his opposition to conscription in 1944 and his isolationism in foreign policy, he had not taken the trouble to learn French, and found himself at a serious disadvantage in competing with the other two candidates for the votes of Quebec delegates. In addition, he had little support among English-speaking Canadians outside of the farming population. His main assets were his great personal courage and his superior oratorical style, on which he counted heavily to influence doubtful voters at the last moment. Unfortunately for him, there were few people in that category by the time the convention began.

On the whole, the three speeches merely confirmed the delegates in the opinions they already held. Power retained their affection and their appreciation for remaining true to his principles. Gardiner lived up to his reputation as a doughty fighter, but failed to demonstrate the breadth of understanding and culture of a national leader. Although St. Laurent's statement was easily the worst delivered of the three, he inspired confidence, admiration, and, above all, trust. The delegates made him their new leader on the first ballot with 848 votes, compared to 323 for Gardiner and 56 for Power. Caught by surprise, not at the choice they had made but at its decisiveness, the crowd rose as one man to hail their new chieftain. Shouting above the din, Gardiner and Power declared the choice unanimous. It was just 6 p.m. on that August 7 as St. Laurent advanced from his seat at one end of the platform to receive the congratulations of Prime Minister Mackenzie King and other personalities who rushed forward to shake his hand. As the noise subsided, he moved to the rostrum again, and stood there, face flushed, eyes glistening, and shoulders shrugging occasionally in embarrassed self-depreciation. When he was allowed to speak, his voice betrayed the strong feelings welling up within him, feelings less of pride than of humble gratitude for the gesture of confidence and awareness of the heavy responsibility it implied. Above all, he was moved by the realization that so many English-speaking Canadians would accept a second French-speaking Roman Catholic as their leader. During his childhood in Compton, and later as a lawyer, he had learned to admire the best traits of both English- and French-speaking Canadians, he stated, and he had found throughout Canada 'an immense reservoir of good will which was more than sufficient to dissipate any feeling of mistrust which we inherited from our traditions and from our ancestors, who during centuries were rivals and even enemies'. That reservoir of good will was 'large enough to stamp out these prejudices . . . and to enable us to admit, deep in our hearts, that we can find more admirable things about one another than nasty traits to arouse our suspicions'. By their votes, the English-speaking Canadians present had shown their 'desire to extend an open hand'; as a French-speaking Canadian, he replied to that gesture by stating that 'we wish to grasp this hand and co-operate in the expansion of this great country which Providence has entrusted to us.'

When he had finished, he turned and saw that his wife had been brought to the platform, and was sitting beside Mackenzie King. Once again tears came to his eyes as he bent and kissed her. The crowd roared with delight, realizing that after thirty years of being led by a lonely bachelor they would have a family man at their head. In turn, Jeanne St. Laurent was led to the battery of microphones to express her thanks for the 'honour and trust' placed in the man she had chosen as her 'ideal' more than forty years earlier. The rest was anticlimax. Joyful at having carried off his last, and one of his greatest, political manoeuvres, Mackenzie King took the rostrum a final time in order to share his feelings with the audience. When Lapointe had died, he had felt that his own time to give up had almost arrived as well, he recounted. On the way back from the funeral he had asked 'our good friend, Chubby Power' who was the best person to replace 'our late dear friend'. Without a moment's hesitation Power had answered: 'The man you should try to get is Louis St. Laurent.' And so it had come to pass. The explanation was wanting in accuracy, but the exaggeration of Power's role was harmless, and in the spirit of the occasion; even in his most unguarded moments, Mackenzie King remained a consummate politician. It was over an hour before the St. Laurents were able to leave the hall and make their way back to the seclusion of their apartment.

# 9

## 'Uncle Louis'

'When a man seeks an office it isn't news, but when an office seeks a man it is.' The newspaper comment reflected the reaction of political observers that a statesman, and not a politician, had been chosen to administer the nation's affairs, and, almost incidentally, to lead the Liberal Party. An analysis of the ballot revealed that St. Laurent had received a larger percentage of the votes from Ontario than from Quebec, and that his fears of dividing the delegates on ethnic or religious lines had been exaggerated. Most French-speaking Canadians took pride in their distinguished representative in Ottawa; English-speaking Canadians saw in him that rare phenomenon, a French Canadian who thought like them and possessed the qualities they admired. There was less unanimity about his role as a party leader, some observers wondering whether his inexperience and naïvety would make him a tool of the professional politicians and a blind for their less creditable activities. Doubts also existed about his attitude towards the very progressive, even left-wing, program that had been drawn up at the convention under the slogan, 'the fighting faith'. It seemed evident that, as a positive Canadian nationalist, he would endorse the resolution on national unity, the call for 'an exclusively Canadian flag' and for abolition of appeals to the Privy Council; but could he endorse the demand for further social legislation, subsidized low-cost housing, and the various other Green Book

241

proposals that had not yet been carried out? While he was dedicated to correcting injustices, promoting economic development, and moulding the Canadian population into a harmonious unit, Louis St. Laurent seemed hardly the man to lead the more impatient members of the party in what they considered was the true orientation of Canadian Liberalism, a sustained campaign of progress and reform. On the other hand, he enjoyed tackling new problems and devising solutions to them, and, as long as he could be convinced that proposals made to him were responsible and feasible, he was willing to espouse them. He believed in free enterprise as the most efficient means of assuring a high level of employment and prosperity, but at the same time he felt strongly that the government had a responsibility to make sure that the economic machine worked smoothly and that individual citizens did not suffer unduly as a result of its malfunctioning. In that context, he favoured the use of public investment, including public-works projects, to provide jobs and maintain productivity, and he accepted social welfare legislation as a means of caring for the weaker members of society and assuring a more equitable distribution of the national income. On one point he felt particularly strongly: he insisted that the State should not play favourites, and that any government program should be available on the same basis to all citizens.

St. Laurent's influence on federal-provincial relations was also a matter for speculation. Many English-speaking Canadians hoped that he would counter the influence of Maurice Duplessis and other Quebec nationalists, encouraging his fellow French-speaking Canadians to identify themselves with Canada as a whole, and to accept nation-wide programs in fields of common interest. Autonomy-minded Quebec citizens were concerned about that very possibility, fearing that many French-speaking Canadians might vote for him on the basis of sentiment, and accept by so doing the 'centralizing' program adopted at the convention. 'It would be inconceivable for the province of Quebec to abandon its autonomy ... for the simple reason that a French-speaking prime minister of Canada asks it to,' commented a newspaperman in the *Action Catholique* shortly after the meeting. 'It is not a question of sentiment, it is a matter of vital interest.' Finally, in foreign affairs, there was some uncertainty whether he would prove to be really an internationalist or would reflect the isolationist views of his native province. In Commonwealth matters, would his sentiment of Canadian nationalism lead him to loosen still further the links with Great Britain, or would he play an important role, as Laurier had done, in adapting that organization to new conditions? With regard to the United States, would he, as the former legal counsel of important American firms operating in Canada, encourage greater integration of the two countries, or would he strive to reduce the danger of eventual absorption of Canada by its more powerful neighbour?

St. Laurent himself was full of doubts and questions in the days following the convention. More than ever, the world of politics seemed to him a strange and unfriendly place, and he felt totally unqualified by temperament and training to occupy the top position in the Liberal Party hierarchy. When he expressed his concern to Mackenzie King on August 11, the old man reminded him what someone had said about the pyramids: from a distance they seemed impossible to climb, but as one drew nearer a series of steps could be discerned; it was in that light, the Prime Minister remarked reassuringly, that he would have to view his future responsibilities. Anxious to concentrate on learning his new job, St. Laurent wished to avoid any trips outside the country for a few months, particularly to Great Britain, since his opponents in Quebec would interpret a visit to London as proof that he was a tool of British imperialism. Having already agreed to remain head of the government for a few more months, Mackenzie King undertook to attend the Commonwealth Prime Ministers' Conference, and a United Nations meeting in Paris, both scheduled for that autumn. It was decided that J. W. Pickersgill, special assistant in the Prime Minister's Office and an ardent admirer of St. Laurent, would remain in Ottawa to help ensure a smooth transfer of power. The formal change of prime ministers would take place in mid-November, shortly after Mackenzie King's return.

One of the very first matters to be settled by St. Laurent following the convention was the composition of the new cabinet. In his view, competence and the ability to work as a member of a team were the primary considerations in selecting ministers. Basically a pragmatist in his approach to public affairs, he paid little attention to ideological factors, feeling that if ministers were sincere in their desire to give the country the best possible government they could agree on the means of doing so. Before he was chosen leader, he had made sure of having the services of C. D. Howe as a sort of general manager of the Canadian economy. One of his first acts after the convention was to arrange for Pearson to enter the cabinet as Minister for External Affairs. The fact that Howe and Pearson were poles apart in their political philosophies was of little concern to him; each was the most competent man in his field. Mackenzie King was delighted with Pearson's entry into politics, and forecast that he would be the next leader of the Liberal Party. The loser under the new arrangement was Brooke Claxton, who had long wished for the External Affairs portfolio. In 1946, the Minister of National Defence had put aside his personal interests and suggested that St. Laurent take the post as a means of keeping him in public life; now he was to miss it again, in part at least because of his own role in choosing the new leader.

Another post that had to be filled soon was the Justice portfolio, held by D. C. Abbott until a new appointment could be made. For some time, sporadic negotiations had been going on with Premier Stuart Garson of Manitoba to have him replace J. A. Glen, who had suffered a heart attack, as the representative of Manitoba in the cabinet. He agreed to become Minister of Justice in November. Among the younger members of the Liberal caucus were several promising men whom St. Laurent also hoped to bring into the government as soon as opportunities presented themselves. They included Robert Winters, a protégé of C. D. Howe; Walter Harris, his own parliamentary assistant in the External Affairs Department; and Hugues Lapointe. Outside the cabinet, but at his right hand, he was anxious to have J. W. Pickersgill, whose wide knowledge of Canadian politics and government and seemingly boundless energy and initiative made him an invaluable assistant.

On August 19, St. Laurent returned to Quebec City, to be welcomed again at the railway station as a conquering hero. In the crowd of several thousand people were Power, Mayor Lucien Borne, and many other persons who had greeted him shortly after he entered public life, in the darkest days of the war. 'What we are celebrating tonight is not so much the homage of Quebec to St. Laurent,' he told them with his usual modesty, 'but the homage of the Canadian nation to the French section of this country.' By choosing him as the successor to Mackenzie King, 'without regard for race, religion or language', the Liberal convention had struck an important blow for national unity, and Canada offered to the world a salutary example 'where two great races have joined in making one great nation'. The statement was exaggerated, but pardonable in the joyous circumstances; for the moment, the ideal of his life seemed more attainable than ever before, and he was to have his greatest chance to make it a reality. His only other trip outside Ottawa during August and September was to Toronto where he spoke on International Day at the Canadian National Exhibition and urged Canadians to support the proposed 'North Atlantic Security System'. The goal of the collective arrangement, he declared, was to discourage Communist aggression while some basis of coexistence with Communist régimes was being worked out, 'if only . . . that of mutual toleration'. Apart from those two brief excursions, Louis St. Laurent remained at his desk in Ottawa, preparing to take over the heavy burden of directing the nation's affairs.

Even before the Liberal convention took place, the Progressive Conservatives decided to change leaders as well. Besides losing the 1945 general election, John Bracken was frequently outshone in Parliament by other party members such as John Diefenbaker and Gordon Graydon, and outside Ottawa by George Drew. According to some speculation, the Conservative organizer for Quebec, Yvan Sabourin, was being considered as a possible choice on the grounds that he would be the best counter-weight to St. Laurent, and because of his close connections with the Union Nationale administration. The Ontario Premier was a clear favourite from the outset, however; he was highly popular in Ontario and was also reported to have excellent relations with Maurice Duplessis. The weakness in Drew's armour lay in statements he had made in earlier years, which were bound to return to haunt him. He was reported to have urged, in 1935, a return to a single strong government instead of 'the costly inefficiency of ten governments doing, in most cases, the job of one'. During the war he had been an outspoken conscriptionist, and he had denounced the family allowances program, in 1944, as an 'obvious bribe' to Quebec. As the fighting in Europe drew to an end, he had embarked on an ambitious plan for a massive wave of immigration from Great Britain as 'the one thing that can keep the French-Canadian pressure within bounds'. On the other hand, he and Maurice Duplessis joined forces in attacking the Mackenzie King administration in Ottawa after the war, and in March 1948 he declared that he 'would be happy to walk arm in arm with Mr. Duplessis'.

The other candidates for the Progressive Conservative Party leadership were John Diefenbaker, who had been defeated by John Bracken in his first try for the post, and forty-three-year-old Donald Fleming, the small but aggressive member for Toronto-Eglinton. Fleming belonged to that small group of English-Canadian politicians who had taken the trouble to study French, and his efforts to speak that language were highly appreciated in Quebec. From French-speaking audiences he drew enthusiastic applause by denouncing St. Laurent for suggesting that the French language could be banned from Parliament. As a result, he became the darling of the Bleus in Quebec, and Camillien Houde referred to him fondly as the 'member from Toronto who answered Mr. St. Laurent in French'. With John Diefenbaker's support limited largely to his native western Canada, and Fleming still a relative novice in politics, the result of the contest was almost a foregone conclusion; on October 2, George Drew became the new national leader of the Progressive Conservative Party. Since it seemed likely that Drew would be his leading opponent during the rest of his political life, the convention's choice gave Louis St. Laurent little reason for satisfaction. The two men had clashed over the Hong Kong investigation almost as soon as he had arrived in Ottawa, and Drew's attitude during the federal-provincial negotiations did not augur well for their future relations. Mackenzie King did nothing to lessen his apprehension by sending a telegram of sympathy from Paris, forecasting that he would have to fight all over again Sir Wilfrid's battles against racial prejudice and divisive concepts of Canada. Putting aside his misgivings, St. Laurent followed the dictates of protocol and sent his congratulations to Drew, both on being chosen as Conservative leader, and on 'the opportunity for service to Canada that comes with that position'.

The new Liberal chieftain had little time to contemplate the political struggle that lay ahead. On October 5, he welcomed to Ottawa the Newfoundland delegation charged with negotiating the final terms of union with Canada. A few days later he dashed up to Algoma East constituency in northern Ontario, where Pearson, sworn into office as Secretary of State for External Affairs on September 10, was making his first bid for election. Since Pearson was a political novice, and St. Laurent was still untried as a political leader, the by-election was observed with interest to see if the two men would have as much success there as on the national and international planes. The Liberal leader asked for support on behalf of his new colleague on the basis that a man should be chosen for his ability to serve his country, and not on any other considerations.

St. Laurent's plan to work himself into his new duties during Mackenzie King's absence was disrupted when the Prime Minister fell ill in London just as the Commonwealth Conference was about to begin. Fully occupied with his appeal to the voters of Algoma East, Pearson could not leave the country; St. Laurent had no choice but to put aside his misgivings about the reaction in Quebec, and fly to London. He arrived in the British capital on October 14, shortly after the meeting had begun. As on other aspects of Canada's external affairs, he had not always agreed with Mackenzie King concerning the Commonwealth. The older man's views were coloured by a suspicion that under the guise of free co-operation between autonomous units, the British leaders, regardless of party, were still seeking to establish a single imperial policy in accordance with their own interests; with advancing age, he also found it difficult to accept the proposals of the Labour government to transform the Commonwealth into a multi-racial organization. As a French-speaking Canadian, St. Laurent shared to some degree Mackenzie King's suspicion of British intentions, and, like many other people, was sensitive to what is generally considered outside the United Kingdom as the British attitude of superiority. On the other hand, he was attracted by the prospect of transforming the Commonwealth into an association of free peoples of different races and from different continents that could become a precious instrument of international co-operation. With such considerations in mind, he had supported actively the steps taken by the Attlee government to divest the organization of the last vestiges of its imperial past, by, for instance, changing the name of the Dominions Office to Commonwealth Relations Office in 1947, and had participated in revising the Letters Patent defining the functions of the Governor General in order to bring them into line with those of the King in Great Britain. As the occasions presented themselves, the word 'Dominion' was replaced by 'Canada' in official documents in order to conform to the new concepts of the Commonwealth and of Canadian national sovereignty.

Shortly after the Liberal convention, Sir Norman Brook, Secretary of the United Kingdom cabinet, had visited Ottawa to discuss the possible position of India, Pakistan, and Ceylon within the Commonwealth. Burma had already left the organization, and since Jawaharlal Nehru, chairman of the Indian Congress Party, was committed to making India a republic, he was bound to follow suit unless a formula could be found to reconcile republican status with Commonwealth membership. The British government was anxious to devise some such arrangement that would be acceptable to both India and the other Commonwealth countries. In their discussions with Brook, Mackenzie King and St. Laurent agreed in principle on the desirability of keeping India and the other Asian colonies within the Commonwealth, but were reluctant to espouse any particular formula.

The British official continued his tour of Commonwealth capitals, but called at Ottawa again shortly before the Commonwealth Conference was due to begin, this time with more specific proposals; by the time Mackenzie King arrived in London in early October, he had been won over to the idea of taking the necessary steps to build a multi-racial Commonwealth. Accordingly, one of his first acts on reaching the British capital was to seek out

Nehru and his sister, Mrs. L. Pandit, both somewhat apprehensive over their first meeting with other Commonwealth leaders,
to assure them of Canada's good will towards India; the gesture
was much appreciated and marked the beginning of a close friendship between the leaders of the two countries. Still more convinced than Mackenzie King of the importance of using the
Commonwealth as an instrument to assist the peoples of Asia in
their great adventure of nation-building, and to prevent a cleav-
age of the world into two parts on a racial basis, St. Laurent on
his arrival in London reiterated Canada's desire to be helpful in
any way possible, and invited Nehru to visit Ottawa with a view
to working out possible forms of co-operation. The invitation
was accepted with alacrity.

The conference presented the usual opportunity for a survey
of international affairs, and, in particular, for delegates from
other countries to hear an appraisal by British leaders of recent
developments. The picture painted by Foreign Secretary Bevin
was anything but a cheerful one; Communist puppet régimes had
been installed by the Soviet Union throughout Eastern Europe,
East Germany was being re-armed by the formation of 'police'
units, and Communist guerillas were still attempting to take over
Greece. If the British and American troops were withdrawn from
Western Europe, that area was bound to fall before the Communist advance, just as all the nations of Eastern Europe had
done. The only encouraging signs were that the Berlin airlift was
proving a complete tactical and psychological success, and that
Western diplomats were making progress in setting up a North
Atlantic defence organization.

Making his first contribution to a Commonwealth meeting,
St. Laurent endorsed the British statement generally, and pointed
out that if the industrial potential of Western Europe fell under
Soviet control, the imbalance between the two blocs would be
very serious. On the other hand, he felt that the Soviet leaders
were very realistic, and if they were confronted by the united
power of the Western Hemisphere, it was unlikely that they
would risk further aggression in Europe. It was important, therefore, he argued, to convince Western Europeans that participation in a Western defence system was a feasible answer to the

threat hanging over them, and would call for fewer sacrifices than the alternative of another war. In that context, St. Laurent declared, Canada supported enthusiastically the proposals for both a European political union, and a North Atlantic organization for military and other forms of co-operation. At the same time, he resisted British proposals to establish closer military co-operation between Commonwealth members on the grounds that regional defensive arrangements should have priority. The Canadian Prime Minister designate listened with interest to Nehru's view of the international situation, and particularly to his plea to approach the current problems from a moral and humanitarian rather than a purely military point of view. The Indian leader saw the conflict as a power struggle between the Soviet Union and the United States that neither could win; the Commonwealth, he argued, had a useful role to play in making sure that democratic freedom survived and continued to grow despite the difficult circumstances.

The other delegates, for their part, observed St. Laurent carefully, noting with approval his rather unusual combination of Gallic warmth and Anglo-Saxon reserve, of idealism and common sense. His conservative appearance belied his progressive views, and he soon became identified more with the Asian leaders than with the prime ministers of Australia, New Zealand, and South Africa, who had greater reservations than he about the changing character of the Commonwealth. Clement Attlee and his colleagues were delighted to find in the future Canadian prime minister a man of such progressive views, and were grateful for his support of their proposals, particularly with regard to India's status. With the decision to allow India to remain in the Commonwealth on becoming a republic, the door was opened to major changes in the character and role of that organization. The final communiqué revealed nothing of that historic step since the agreement had still to be approved by the governments of the member countries.

Louis St. Laurent arrived back in Canada on October 24 and threw himself into the task of completing final arrangements for the transfer of power, set for November 15. He and his wife were still living in the same tiny apartment they had occupied during

the war years. Wealthy friends had offered to buy them a more appropriate residence, but he had refused for fear of incurring what
might be considered a moral debt towards the donors, and took
instead a larger set of rooms in the same building. On October 25,
Pearson won an easy victory in Algoma East and the Liberals won
another by-election in Saskatchewan; the conditions seemed right
for the fresh beginning. The swearing-in ceremony took place in
the presence of the Governor General, Viscount Alexander, at
3:55 p.m. on November 15, St. Laurent taking the oath as President of the Privy Council, Robert Winters as Minister of Reconstruction and Supply, and Stuart Garson as Minister of Justice.
The other ministers remained in the same posts.

Following a reception later that same afternoon to celebrate
the birth of a new royal heir, Prince Charles, the new government
held its first cabinet meeting. Postmaster General Ernest Bertrand
marked the occasion by presenting the new Prime Minister with
a cane that had once belonged to Sir Wilfrid Laurier; it was a
symbolic gesture, for the Liberals were hoping for a second period
of national unity and rapid economic development. Seated at the
head of the table, St. Laurent drew out his silver cigarette case,
fitted a cigarette into his holder, and lit it. Other ministers followed suit. That, too, was a symbolic move: under Mackenzie
King, smoking had been forbidden in the Council Chamber. It
was truly the end of an era.

The cabinet meeting was a short one. Louis St. Laurent announced the appointment of Walter Harris as parliamentary
assistant to the Prime Minister, and obtained approval of a more
extensive housing program, to be directed by Winters. Then he
crossed the corridor of the East Block to his new second-floor
office, with its Gothic windows opening onto the lawns in front
of the Parliament Buildings, and the massive fireplace recalling
the days when Sir John A. Macdonald and other predecessors had
occupied the room. He sat at the huge desk for a long time,
working his way through the documents before him and planning
the days ahead. When at last he put on his hat and coat, picked
up his well-filled brief-case, and made his way towards the stair-
way, he found to his surprise that the elevator operator was still
on duty. He asked the man why he had not gone home at the

same time as the other members of the staff. Strict instructions had been given not to leave until the Prime Minister had been taken down to the main floor, he was told. St. Laurent shrugged his shoulders. 'In the future, you go home with the others,' he said; a prime minister could walk down a flight of stairs just the same as everyone else.

In his first address to Canadians as their prime minister that evening, Louis St. Laurent pledged himself and his colleagues to broad objectives: 'a national standard of social security and human welfare', 'a united nation based . . . on equality of opportunity and a deep attachment to a common homeland', and 'complete freedom of Canada as a nation ready to co-operate with other nations to promote the common prosperity of all and to promote world peace'. At first glance, they seemed to be rather abstract goals; the challenge of the immediate future would be to transform them into precise policies. Early in December he was the object of yet another triumphal reception in Quebec City, and was proclaimed the most distinguished citizen of the proud old fortress city in which he had arrived as a shy and rather awkward country boy forty-six years earlier. Now, surrounded by his wife, his children, and several of his twelve grandchildren, the sixty-six-year-old politician declared that he had been unable to refuse the opportunity to prove that Laurier's career was not an exception to any rule and that a French-speaking Canadian could truly aspire to the highest political office in the land. 'There is neither conquered nor superior race in our country,' he stated flatly. 'There are only Canadians. . . . My appointment to the post of Prime Minister suggests that this union of Canadians is a reality.' He developed his concept of Canada further on December 11 in concluding the negotiations for the entry of Newfoundland into Confederation. 'This nation of ours which you are about to enter is based on an equal partnership of . . . two great races,' he told the delegation that was preparing to return to St. John's. '. . . Our country has two official languages and two distinct though closely related cultures. But we are one people.'

Although the Liberals had only a bare majority in the House of Commons, they were full of optimism at year's end. Quebec was obviously proud of its native son; in the rest of Canada, St.

Laurent's first radio broadcast had been well received, and he had succeeded in communicating to listeners the warmth and sincerity that were his greatest political assets. There even seemed to be a danger of people coming to expect too much of him. 'It is not unfair to Mr. St. Laurent to say that no man could be quite as good as his colleagues and the highest echelon of the civil service consider him,' commented newspaperman Bruce Hutchison; '... the present honeymoon period of the St. Laurent régime should not be over-estimated.' Those who expressed doubts about his leadership qualities referred to his unusual frankness and his blunt, politically indiscreet rejoinders when aroused. Then there was his rigid adherence to what he felt was right, regardless of political considerations. Even if a man reached such a high office without compromising his principles, or playing the usual game of politics, some asked, could he stay there for long without doing so? And yet, 'Maybe there's a moral here,' reflected *Maclean's* Magazine correspondent Blair Fraser; 'maybe courage, ability and integrity can bring a man success in politics.' On December 3 Ilsley's former seat in Nova Scotia fell in a by-election to a hitherto unknown Conservative, George Nowlan, despite the fact that St. Laurent had appeared there for a testimonial dinner to his former colleague shortly after becoming Prime Minister. And five days before Christmas, the electors of Carleton County, on the outskirts of Ottawa, chose George Drew as their representative in Parliament with nearly twice as large a majority as his predecessor had received. The fact that Stuart Garson won an easy victory in Manitoba hardly cancelled out the two setbacks in the public mind; the doubts concerning the new Prime Minister's ability as a politician remained.

Louis St. Laurent was at the entrance to the Parliament Buildings, dressed in top hat and morning coat, to welcome Viscount Alexander when His Excellency arrived on Parliament Hill on January 26, 1949, to open the new session of Parliament. For the first time, movie cameras were allowed to photograph the initial proceedings in the Commons Chamber; they recorded the burst of applause from the Liberals as the new Prime Minister took his place, the happy smile of Mackenzie King, seated in the front row just beyond the ministerial section, and the enthusiasm of Progressive Conservative members as their own new leader, looking handsome and vigorous, settled his large frame into the seat directly across the floor from St. Laurent's. Although they seemed at first glance two very different men, St. Laurent and Drew had one very important trait in common; they were both shy and sensitive, one concealing that fact under a cloak of Victorian dignity, the other under an appearance of aggressive self-confidence. The Tory leader's public pose had brought him rapid success in the provincial arena, and he had become a slave to it; the strain of maintaining an image that did not reflect his true personality was to contribute eventually to his downfall. In contrast, St. Laurent fitted naturally into the office of Prime Minister, combining modesty with an impression of authority, and feeling much more at ease in Parliament than his leading opponent.

Eager political observers did not have long to wait for the first clash between the two men. Clearly a pre-election document, the Speech from the Throne outlined a heavy program of work, including approval of Canadian membership in the North Atlantic Treaty Organization and of the terms of union with Newfoundland, as well as legislation for a St. Lawrence seaway, a trans-Canada highway, and the extension of family allowances. Also forecast was the creation of a royal commission to investigate the possibilities of federal aid to the arts, letters, and sciences. In order to meet a March 31 deadline set for the entry of Newfoundland into Confederation, St. Laurent suggested that the Throne Speech debate be postponed after two days in order to approve the terms of union; the Leader of the Opposition rose at once to object to the proposal. The Prime Minister commented mildly: 'We do not mean to adopt a dictatorial attitude,' but his remark merely elicited a series of derisive 'Oh, Oh's' from the benches opposite. Colouring, St. Laurent stiffened, and retorted sharply that 'honourable members can say "Oh, Oh" all they like, but this is the fact. I know the intent of our desires just as well as honourable members who are saying "Oh, Oh".' The battle was joined. Liberal members were delighted at the indication that their new leader was going to stand up to his opponents; they were less pleased, a few minutes later, when he withdrew his proposal in order to avoid a long and probably bitter debate on procedure.

Predictably, the main subject chosen by George Drew for his parliamentary début was federal-provincial relations. Denying that he and Duplessis were responsible for the failure of the federal-provincial conference in 1945-6, he attacked the 'centralization of power' in Ottawa, and called for 'a new and revised system of taxation' that would enable the provinces and municipalities to carry out their responsibilities. Speaking in a loud, clear voice that carried to every corner of the chamber and gesturing just sufficiently to lend an appearance of vigour and combativeness to his performance, he cut an impressive figure. At the same time, it was a humourless speech, and as the recital of charges against the government, supported by frequent and lengthy quotations, continued, the strident tones began to grate on the ears of his listeners; when he concluded with a brief amendment that 'Your Excellency's advisers do not have the confidence of the House,' the end came as a relief and an anticlimax.

When St. Laurent rose to reply, he referred with typically gentle irony to 'what the Leader of the Opposition . . . has taken so long to say'. His own speech was still longer, and having got off to a late start had to be given in two parts, one late on the Friday, the other the following Monday. He teased the former conscriptionist for devoting so little attention to the international situation, and quoted Quebec Conservative organizer Yvan Sabourin's statement that Canada might well be able to remain neutral in a conflict between the Soviet Union and the United States. Even if all but one of the twelve million Canadians desired such a policy, St. Laurent declared, it would be impossible to carry out. Since the proposed defensive arrangement was purely defensive, he went on, 'any free man . . . should have no greater hesitation in having his country become a party to the North Atlantic security pact than he had in having his country become a signatory to the San Francisco charter'. St. Laurent also took up Drew's charge of centralization, challenging him 'to cite a single instance, since the end of the war, where the central authority has attempted to go beyond the limits prescribed by the constitution'. On the contrary, he asserted, 'the whole tendency of this government since the cessation of active fighting has been to withdraw from those fields where during the war it had to invade the ordinary jurisdiction of the provinces'. Warming to his task, he charged the Leader of the Opposition with a 'very substantial distortion' in accusing him of claiming that Parliament could determine the future shape of Canada without consulting the provinces.

> What I said in that debate is quite clear [St. Laurent explained]. I said that there were certain matters which had been confided to the Parliament of Canada, and certain others which had been confided to the provincial legislatures. . . . With respect to the first . . . the people of the Provinces spoke on these matters through the representatives they elected to the Parliament. . . . With respect to the matters which were confided by the constitution to the provincial legislatures, it would be quite impossible for this Parliament to do anything about them without the consent of those having the responsibility.

Leaning forward in his seat, the Leader of the Opposition asked: 'Was it not in the same speech that you dealt with the subject of language and the right of this Parliament to deprive any group in the country of a particular language, if it was felt that should be done?' That was another 'most serious distortion', St. Laurent retorted: he had been asked on that occasion how article 133 could be amended; and he had given 'a truthful answer'. He had spoken of the 'theoretical power to do a thing . . . but, in fact, it was quite inconceivable that it could ever be done'. Drew's subsequent assertion in the Ontario Legislature that the federal government claimed 'the right to change our laws relating to language, to education, and even to civil rights, the control of property and the administration of justice', was 'in every line, in every word and in every letter of each word . . . absolutely false'. Red-faced, the Progressive Conservative leader took the rebuke in silence; the Liberal members pounded their desks with pleasure as they realized that their new chieftain could hold his own against the man who, it had been prophesied, would crush him in debate. Returning once again in his concluding remarks to the theme of national unity, St. Laurent warned the Conservatives against 'making one appeal in one language in one part of the country and a quite different appeal in another language in other parts of the country'. The Liberals, he asserted, had 'always been able to put forward the same policy and to make the same appeal in both languages. There has never been a Liberal government since Confederation which has not recognized at all times in its ranks the principle upon which this nation was really founded, the principle of the partnership of the two races.'

Unhappily, St. Laurent's high-minded plea for true national unity had little immediate effect. In a federal by-election campaign in the Quebec riding of Nicolet-Yamaska that winter, the Bleus continued to accuse the Liberals of war-mongering, and the Rouges urged support for their candidate on the grounds that St. Laurent was 'a French Canadian and a Catholic', while Drew was 'an English-speaking Protestant and an anti-French Canadian'. Although there was no open alliance between the Conservatives and the Union Nationale, the former kept out of the contest, and it became a straight fight between the Union Nationale organization and the Liberals, who went down to defeat before the Duplessis machine. In the House of Commons. Donald Fleming returned on February 3 to the subject of the French language in Parliament, arguing that St. Laurent's comment to the effect that it could be abolished without consulting the provinces was 'a perfectly deliberate and studied remark' and could not be disavowed. In a radio broadcast that evening, the Prime Minister again rebutted the 'silly story' that he recognized 'no written safeguard for the use of the language of my father, and the language of my own family'. Once more he explained his statement; it was no use; the indiscretion would follow him until the end of his political career.

On February 8, St. Laurent introduced a resolution to approve the terms of union between Canada and Newfoundland. While representatives of the C.C.F. and Social Credit groups endorsed the proposal in general, Drew moved an amendment, asking that the provinces be consulted; the amendment was defeated. The Prime Minister also rejected a suggestion by one member that half of the new Senators be named by the province. 'It would be a mistake to have in the other place persons feeling that they had a responsibility to a government of a Canadian province,' he replied, 'National unity demands that all those who form part of the Canadian Parliament feel that their responsibility is to the Canadian people as a whole, and that they are not the representatives of any provincial government or any municipality or other local authority.'

The debate on union with Newfoundland was interrupted to enable St. Laurent to fly to Washington on February 11, for a meeting with President Harry Truman. Although he joked to a group of newspapermen in the American capital who inquired about the purpose of the visit that the President had passed 'his acid test' at the polls, and he had come 'to try to find out, at first hand, Mr. Truman's secret about winning an election', he had much more serious matters on his mind. Foremost among them was the St. Lawrence seaway and power project. The province of Ontario was in urgent need of additional sources of power, he told the President, and Canadians were becoming so impatient with American delaying tactics that the government was under increasingly strong pressure to build it alone. Truman recalled that he, personally, had always favoured the project as a joint venture, even when a Senator, and gave the assurance that he would do whatever was possible to get congressional approval, despite the strong opposition of railway companies, trade unions, and Atlantic seaboard financial interests. In a spirit of understanding and co-operation, St. Laurent expressed the hope that pressure for unilateral Canadian action could be resisted for a while longer.

The two men also discussed trade between the United States and Canada, the President agreeing with St. Laurent's view that the greatest possible freedom from restrictions between the two countries was desirable, but appealing for a gradual approach to that goal in order to overcome opposition and prevent disruption within the two economies. The Canadian visitor went on to argue that the North Atlantic Treaty, almost ready for final approval, should not only be a military alliance, but should also provide for closer economic and social co-operation between member countries. Truman was clearly not as interested in that possibility as in creating a military shield against Soviet Communism extending from Alaska right across the Arctic to Berlin. In that context, they discussed the United States military bases established in New-foundland in World War II under a ninety-nine-year lease. St. Laurent gave the assurance that the British-American agreement authorizing them would not be challenged when the area became part of Canada, and the President reciprocated by declaring that Canada's political independence was in the interest of both nations. In general, the atmosphere of the talks was very cordial and the two men established a personal rapport that augured well for the future. At a press conference, St. Laurent also succeeded in impressing the Washington press corps with his knowledge of Canadian–United States relations, one reporter referring to his 'disarming frankness that covered up the evident caginess of his replies'. The trip was an undoubted success.

In addition to his heavy schedule of work in the capital, St. Laurent accepted an out-of-town engagement nearly every week-end, partly to show himself to as many people as possible, partly to explain the policies he stood for. During a trip to Montreal in March, he inspected a detachment of city police, visited the two universities, attended a Richelieu Club luncheon, a civic dinner, a press conference, five receptions, and a mass, and had a private meeting with members of the local St-Jean-Baptiste Society. A week later he made a whistle-stop tour through a series of small centres west of Toronto, and visited Chatham and Windsor. When he got off the train at Belle Rivière, an elderly woman moved forward to shake his hand, but he put his arms around her and kissed her instead, then drew back, blushing furiously, as surprised as the other persons present at his political audacity. In Paris, one man shouted from the station platform: 'You're better looking than George Drew.' 'I can't compete on that score,' he flashed back. 'Nobody has ever called me gorgeous.' The crowd was delighted with the allusion to Drew's nickname of 'Gorgeous George'. At a reception in Windsor he shook hands with fifteen hundred older people, and in an evident appeal for the support of the workers in the local automobile factories declared before an audience of three thousand persons that he believed 'not only

in the right of labour to organize' but also in its right to a prominent place 'alongside management and alongside investment'. He
rejected the possibility of curbing Communist influence in labour
unions by legislation, as was being done in the United States.
Departing from his prepared text, he declared:

> There are two ways, you know, to fight enemies of freedom in
> one's country; one of those ways is to shout about it until we get
> red in the face and to urge repressive laws, prison terms and
> concentration camps, and in doing so, start down a road at
> the end of which we would lose the freedom we are trying to
> protect. The other way is to protect our faith in our free
> institutions ... by making those institutions work to the
> advantage of the great majority of the community; ... by
> working to spread social justice and to eradicate injustice and
> to eradicate exploitation and oppression whenever it may be
> found.

His simple, straightforward language and his evident confidence
in the judgement of his fellow citizens made a deep impression.

The threat of Communism in Canada was another issue on
which the Progressive Conservatives and Liberals disagreed. In
an address to McGill University students in late February, Drew
declared that Canadians were in danger of losing their personal
and economic freedom 'to the bureaucrats who accept the basic
philosophy of Karl Marx, no matter what political name they
may adopt'. Indignant at the slur on both the Liberals and the
federal civil service, St. Laurent repudiated the charge in the
House of Commons as 'irresponsible and unwarranted', and
challenged Drew to 'name the individuals and produce his proofs'.
The Tory leader retorted that 'the last man in Canada who should
challenge me in regard to the abuse of power is the Prime Minister
himself'; he had not forgotten, he declared, that St. Laurent had
once laid charges against him 'that had no relation to the law',
and then 'had neither the courage nor the decency to apologize'.
In addition, he went on, the government leader had 'used the
power of censorship ... to prevent the publication of a letter
which would have shown improper use of the Royal Canadian

Mounted Police by his department'. When St. Laurent denied the charge 'completely and unreservedly', Drew announced that he would table the letter that he had written to Prime Minister Mackenzie King concerning the Hong Kong inquiry seven years earlier. St. Laurent reminded him that it would be improper to do so since the British government had refused specifically to allow the letter to be released on the grounds that it contained secret information concerning Hong Kong. Unable to obtain consent to table the letter in the House of Commons, Drew handed it to the press. 'Methods of Gestapo. P.C. Leader urges Prime Minister to be called to account for "Prostitution" ' ran the headlines in the Montreal *Gazette* on March 2. St. Laurent protested the breach of secrecy; the relations between the two men took on more and more the appearance of a personal vendetta.

On March 28, the North Atlantic Treaty was presented to the House of Commons and approved in a single day, only two Independent members from Quebec opposing it. A similar degree of unanimity was displayed three days later when Newfoundland became the tenth province of Canada. The simultaneous ceremonies in Ottawa and St. John's marked the final success of three years of delicate negotiations. The major share of credit for the union was undoubtedly due to the small, extroverted newspaperman, J. R. Smallwood, who had led the fight for it in Newfoundland against the commercial interests and the Roman Catholic clergy in St. John's. Through his radio programs, he had persuaded the poverty-stricken residents of the outports of the benefits of joining Canada, and succeeded in obtaining a modest majority in favour of union in the referendum. St. Laurent's influence as head of the Canadian team of negotiators had been considerable, and he had also reassured the Roman Catholic hierarchy in Newfoundland who were distrustful of the Protestant majority and fearful for the future of the denominational school system. Because of their concern, St. Laurent persuaded Sir Albert Walsh, a Roman Catholic and chairman of the commission charged with administering the colony in recent years, to accept the lieutenant-governorship during the first critical months.

Gordon Bradley, it was agreed, would become the Newfoundland representative in the federal cabinet as Secretary of State, and Smallwood the provincial premier.*

Despite the careful planning, the Canadian government was still not certain that on the day set for the official ceremony there would be no demonstrations against union in St. John's, or even that Smallwood could form a cabinet. The concern proved unwarranted. Standing on a platform under the Peace Tower of the Parliament Buildings on March 31, St. Laurent listened to a radio broadcast of Walsh being sworn into office in St. John's, then he in turn spoke to the new citizens of Canada. They were joining 'a good country ... a country with a distinctive character and distinctive qualities', he told them. In becoming part of it, they would not be losing their own personality, as 'our constitution ... assures to each province the preservation of its ancient traditions, its own culture, and all those distinctive characteristics which add variety and colour to our national life.' Following his speech, he took up a stonemason's mallet and chisel and cut the first line of the coat of arms of the new province in the arch underneath the Peace Tower. The insignia of the other nine provinces had been carved into the grey stone many years before and a space had been left vacant for the day when Confederation would be completed in the dimensions envisaged by its founding fathers. That day had come at last; it would be one of Louis St. Laurent's most enduring accomplishments.

Throughout the winter, St. Laurent worked equally hard at directing the nation's business and learning the art of politics. He appeared on time at cabinet meetings, in contrast to the practice of Mackenzie King, who was frequently very late, and he was well briefed to discuss the matters on the agenda. The deliberations were usually brief and to the point, the minister responsible presenting each item of business, and others being invited to make their comments, but irrelevant comments or long-winded interventions were not encouraged. St. Laurent followed the discussion closely, and, as soon as he felt the facts had been made

*Colin Gibson was moved from the Secretaryship of State to the Ministry of Mines and Resources, the latter post in turn being vacated by James McKinnon, who became Minister without Portfolio, and a Senator, on May 9.

clear and the different viewpoints fairly expressed, he summed up the situation in a few words and proposed a decision. It was nearly always adopted at once, and the ministers went on to the next item. Cabinet meetings became shorter and less wearisome, and ministers had more time to devote to their other responsibilities. With his natural dignity and his competence, he had no need to assert his authority or demand respect, and played his role of *primus inter pares* with ease and simplicity. Of his cabinet colleagues, only Howe called him by his first name, and this in private; to the others he was 'Mr. St. Laurent' or 'the P.M.'.

Ministers soon learned that it was to their advantage to submit to him in advance the proposals they wished to make in cabinet, thus making sure that there were no serious weaknesses in them, and that the principles on which they were based were sound. He was particularly patient with junior ministers still apprehensive of making recommendations to such competent and experienced executives as C. D. Howe, and spent considerable time going over their submissions with them in advance. When Fisheries Minister Mayhew arrived in his office one day with a plan to abolish a subsidy to the fishing industry, but worried about the political repercussions of such a step, St. Laurent looked at the proposal carefully, and then asked: 'Do you really think that is the right thing to do?' The minister assured him that he was convinced it was right, but was less certain that it was politically advisable. 'I think it is right too,' St. Laurent said calmly, 'and I think we should do what we feel is right, and then face the political consequences afterward.' The matter went forward to cabinet with his endorsement.

Outside the Council Chamber, morale and efficiency among his closest collaborators were equally high. Norman Robertson, one of Mackenzie King's most trusted advisers during the war, was recalled from London to become Clerk of the Privy Council and Secretary to the Cabinet. Jules Léger was brought home from the Canadian Embassy in Belgium to serve as private secretary to the Prime Minister, and Pierre Asselin, son of the famous newspaperman Olivar Asselin, was also appointed to the staff of the Prime Minister's Office. Watching over every aspect of political and administrative activity, Jack Pickersgill proved an invaluable aide and counsellor. 'Check it with Jack' became a watchword on Parliament Hill. In the Liberal Federation offices on near-by Queen Street, the party's general secretary, H. E. Kidd, and his staff, working under the direction of Claxton and in close liaison with Pickersgill, prepared with enthusiasm for the approaching contest.

On the political plane, the Liberal leader continued his efforts to give Canadians, in his own words, 'some indication of the processes of mind of the man who is their prime minister'. In one of a series of radio broadcasts, he made a special appeal to the women, describing his own 'family circle' and commenting that 'the needs, the aspirations, the joys and sorrows of my dear ones are the needs, the aspirations, and the joys and sorrows of practically all Canadian women'. He invited them to write to him personally, and give him their views on the important matters of peace and social security. Fortunately, he took the precaution of stating that he would not promise to answer every letter individually; he was deluged with so many replies that his staff was kept busy for weeks acknowledging them. It was an encouraging sign that he could 'get through' to a large sector of the voting population.

The House of Commons adjourned on April 8 for a two-week Easter recess, and St. Laurent, accompanied by his wife and his daughter Marthe, left the same evening by train for a tour of the western provinces. 'People vote for men they have confidence in rather than for party programs,' he remarked in Edmonton, on his first stop, and the purpose of his trip was to give as many people as possible the opportunity to decide whether he deserved their confidence. The newspapermen who accompanied him noted that he was most successful in establishing contact with small groups of people, but that even on the platform he was learning to divest himself of his rather stiff court-room manner, and speak directly to individual members of his audience. Rolling through the sparsely settled hinterland of Alberta *en route* to Vancouver, the train stopped briefly at the small town of Edson. The station platform was crowded with children who had been brought down from the local school by their teacher – incidentally a militant member of the C.C.F. Party – to see their Prime Minister at first hand. Touched by their presence, St. Laurent chatted to them about their country, explaining the significance of Newfoundland's entry into Confederation, and telling them in simple terms the meaning and promise of being young Canadians. Thanking them for coming to meet him, he remarked that if it was in his power he would give them a holiday from school for the rest of the day. Immediately there was a huddle of members of the local school board who were present, and, as soon as the Prime Minister had finished speaking, it was announced that the holiday had been granted. A scream of delight welcomed the statement, and the children waved enthusiastically as the train moved out of the station; St. Laurent stood on the rear platform of the last car and waved back happily until they were out of sight. At the next few stops, he made a point of speaking to the children present, and again received an enthusiastic response, both from them and from their proud parents. Deep in the Rocky Mountains later in the day, one reporter from a Conservative newspaper remarked ruefully to another: 'Uncle Louis is going to be hard to beat.' The nickname stuck, and St. Laurent had found his feet as a politician.

The rest of the trip was an unqualified success. In speeches in Vancouver he stressed the government's policy of full employment and social security; in Victoria he declared that Canada had reached 'adult nationhood', with all the advantages and responsibilities that status implied. In Calgary on the return journey, he led a parade through the main streets in an open car waving a Stetson hat and was photographed in full Indian headdress. During his visit to a veterans' hospital there, one patient complained that the patients should not have to pay the federal sales tax on the material for their handicraft work; to everyone's surprise, St. Laurent answered: 'I don't think so either. You write me in Ottawa and I'll take the matter up with Mr. Abbott and see what can be done about it.' In Calgary, then the most Conservative city west of the Great Lakes, he also paid a generous tribute to Viscount Bennett, and to the local Conservative members of Parliament. In Saskatchewan, where the C.C.F. Party was in power, he commented good-naturedly that most of the supporters of the Socialist government were merely 'Liberals in a hurry'. As he moved from one city to another, his self-confidence grew, and with it his enthusiasm. 'It certainly is great to be a Canadian,' he declared in Saskatoon with evident conviction. 'Ours is the happiest country in the world,' he told a group of teachers in Winnipeg. To the same audience he declared:

> Canada is certainly a united country today, but we remain united only by conscious and deliberate policy. . . . If we are to maintain a united nation, if as a nation we are to count for anything in the world, there must continue to be give and take, understanding, tolerance, and a readiness to find solutions to our problems, solutions which satisfy the majority, and which do not exasperate the minorities.

The tour was, by general agreement, a landmark in Canadian politics. The dignified French Canadian, the eastern lawyer, the international statesman, had shown that he had also the common touch. 'In Mr. St. Laurent the public has found at last the stuff of Canada,' wrote a *Winnipeg Free Press* editorialist, 'a French Canadian who is half Irish, speaks English with no trace of French, has a Gallic shrug and gesture, and might have been brought up in Halifax, Winnipeg, or Victoria.' As the train rumbled through northern Ontario on the way back to the capital, St. Laurent concluded that he was ready to face the electorate; when he arrived in Ottawa, he learned that the Liberals in Quebec and the Maritimes were of the same mind. On his first day back in the House of Commons he called the election for June 27.

One of the important tasks that St. Laurent had to delegate while he was testing his political skill in western Canada was the representation of Canada at a special Commonwealth meeting called to approve India's membership as a republic. Since the conference of the previous October, negotiations had continued through diplomatic channels, Canada arguing in favour of as little rigidity as possible, both in establishing machinery of con-sultation and in setting standards of eligibility for membership.

St. Laurent and Pearson were increasingly convinced that the future role of the Commonwealth lay in acting as a bridge between the continents and races of the globe, and in assisting the newly independent nations such as India, Pakistan, and Ceylon to develop the democratic institutions, as well as the economic and social conditions, that would prevent them from falling prey to Communism. Thus, while the original proposal to let former colonies remain in the Commonwealth as republics was not made by the representatives of Canada, they did take an active part in working out a suitable formula. Patrick Gordon-Walker, then Parliamentary Under Secretary of State for Commonwealth Relations in the Attlee administration, was to comment that the triumph of the 'Canadian view' had transformed the Commonwealth even as early as 1947 into the sort of organization 'into which these nations of Asia could fit easily and with spiritual comfort'. Louis St. Laurent's personal contribution towards the modification of the Royal Style and Titles was one of the most significant steps in that direction. He argued that the King was first and foremost the sovereign of the United Kingdom and that the choice of sovereign was properly that of the British people. Other member countries should recognize the King as 'Head of the Commonwealth', but, since they did not participate in his choice as sovereign, they were free to decide whether or not to accept allegiance to him as their own head of state. This interpretation, which was accepted by other Commonwealth leaders, allowed India to remain in the Commonwealth by recognizing the King as head of the organization, while the relations of the other member countries remained unaltered. Before leaving for western Canada, St. Laurent had sent a special message to Nehru, expressing the urgent hope that a way would be found for their two countries to maintain and strengthen their friendly relations within the Commonwealth, and assuring the Indian leader of Canada's good will and understanding. With such careful preparation, the new Commonwealth formula was adopted quickly at the meeting in April, and St. Laurent announced it on April 27 as one of his last acts before the dissolution of Parliament. It was, in the words of a Le Soleil editorialist, 'in the best British tradition, both efficient and illogical'.

In addition to its new leadership, the government went to the country with a sizeable record of accomplishments to its credit. Since St. Laurent had taken office as Prime Minister, Newfoundland had been brought into Confederation, a new International Wheat Agreement had been signed, the North Atlantic security pact created, income taxes eliminated for three-quarters of a million citizens, and old age pensions and family allowances increased. In addition, the high level of prosperity gave the lie to those who were still predicting a post-war economic depression.

Convinced that St. Laurent's personal qualities were the party's greatest asset, Liberal strategists planned his campaign so that he would meet as many people as possible on a person-to-person basis. He himself described his campaign strategy in his opening radio broadcast on May 9 as a series of 'neighbourly visits' to his fellow Canadians, and promised only that, whether he spoke in English or in French, he would 'speak with one voice and make the same appeal'. Since his wife had little taste for such a hectic schedule, his daughter Marthe agreed to accompany him. The nation-wide tour began with a visit to Sherbrooke and Compton. At St. Charles Seminary, he was greeted by his old schoolmates Canon Dolor Biron and Abbé Léon Marcotte; in Compton, the village was decorated with flags, and the whole population gathered in front of the family home to welcome him. Standing beside rough-handed, weather-beaten Xénophile Lalumière with whom he had wandered through the fields many years earlier, he could not repress the tears that welled up in his eyes. Campaign-hardened newspapermen who witnessed the scene were surprised to find themselves dabbing at their cheeks as well. It was great to be a Canadian, he repeated with evident emotion, as he looked at the children crowded at his feet, the adults standing in the middle of the street, and beyond them, the little cemetery where his parents, his brother, and his sister were buried.

> We so often speak of government of the people, for the people, by the people [he commented]. I say, haven't we a demonstration of it right here before us? . . . There is something fine about our democracy, our way of life, that a tiny village such as Compton can produce a man to be Prime Minister of all Canada. This, to me, is democracy at its very best.

If he had one dream, he confided to his former neighbours, it was to spread throughout the world 'the peace of Compton'. When he had finished speaking and had shaken hands with everyone, he sat down on the front step of the old frame house, and chatted for a while with Lalumière about their early years. It was an unforgettable moment, one reporter from Toronto wrote, 'for here was a quiet, humble and certainly unpretentious man, being welcomed home with a fervour and deep feeling of respect that would do credit to a king'.

The visit to his native village set the tone for St. Laurent's entire campaign. From Compton he went directly to the Maritimes, where he motored from one town to another, stopping frequently to shake hands and to exchange a few words with whoever happened to be near him. Once or twice a day he delivered prepared speeches, but at the frequent smaller stops he improvised, and gradually even his major addresses were delivered largely without notes. He seldom referred to Drew or the other party leaders, made few promises, but repeated his message over and over that Canada was more prosperous, and Canadians more affluent, under a Liberal administration.

From the Atlantic seaboard, he moved through eastern Quebec and then on to northern Ontario, maintaining the same neighbourly, almost unpolitical, tone. Recalling his experience in western Canada, he paid special attention to the children, and they responded as if he were truly their 'Uncle Louis'. His interest in them was not a mere political ploy. Still not quite sure of himself as a politician, and embarrassed at asking blatantly for votes, he found in the youngsters a host of precious allies; he talked to them as he would to his own children, and discovered that in doing so he was able to get his message across to their parents as well. As he saw how well he was being received, he realized that he was actually enjoying politics for the first time.

The group of newspapermen assigned to report on his campaign found the experience exhausting and exhilarating at the same time. Ignoring the usual practice of reserving his important statements for the larger meetings, he frequently made newsworthy declarations on the spur of the moment at roadsides, in response to questions, or merely because a particular problem was brought to his attention. Thus, instead of assuming that anything worth reporting would be handed to them in advance by his public relations officer, Bill Munro, reporters had to be available at all times in order to avoid being scooped by their colleagues. Some of the most interesting incidents occurred when St. Laurent invited his audiences to give him their views and to ask him questions. On one such occasion, on the lower St. Lawrence, a grizzled farmer tugged nervously on his pipe, and then finally blurted out, 'We want to vote for you, Mr. St. Laurent, but they tell us the only way we can do it is to vote for the Liberal candidate. We want to know how to vote for you without voting for Philias.' Somewhat taken aback, the Liberal chieftain had to admit that he could see no solution to their difficulty.

George Drew campaigned with his usual forcefulness, receiving valuable support from his wife, Fiorenza, a woman of great personal charm who spoke French fluently. His program included both an attractive list of tax reductions and proposals for increased expenditures, and he attacked the Liberals vigorously as 'arrogant', 'dictatorial', 'socialistic', and 'centralizing'. In Quebec, where Frédéric Dorion had become Tory organizer and a straight Tory candidate, Conservative advertisements proclaimed that Drew was 'in favour of large families' and provincial autonomy, and that he was firmly anti-Communist. St. Laurent, on the other hand, who was usually referred to by his opponents in Quebec as 'Stephen St. Laurent', was denounced as a 'fanatical imperialist', an 'all-out centralizer', 'an Englishman at heart', and 'a temporary leader pending the worst, Pearson'. While Duplessis remained silent, his supporters and even some of his ministers campaigned openly for the Progressive Conservative candidates, and Union Nationale funds were directed into those constituencies where he felt there was the greatest chance of success. Drew and Duplessis appeared together in Quebec City, shook hands in a demonstration of solidarity, and exchanged compliments.

The Liberals replied in kind to the Conservative propaganda, distributing a pamphlet portraying Drew as anti-French Canadian, an ardent conscriptionist, and an opponent of family allowances. Told that his own party was exploiting ethnic and religious issues in Quebec, St. Laurent declared heatedly at a meeting in Owen Sound, Ontario, that he could not believe the charge, but, if it were true, 'they deserve to be reproved in the same manner. . . . If we cannot be accepted by the people of Canada on our worth and because we are looked upon as men who can be trusted and who will not betray a trust we do not want office secured by tactics of that kind.' On a brief visit to his own constituency, he expressed the hope that his organizers were not employing illicit or dishonourable methods to secure votes; he was assured that nothing of the kind was going on.

By the first of June, St. Laurent was adopting a more aggressive tone, attacking the Progressive Conservatives for maligning him in their French-language propaganda, ridiculing the charge that the government was 'old and tired', or 'contemptuous of Parliament', and accusing his opponents of making irresponsible promises. The campaign was entering the final stretch, and he was still looking fresh and cheerful despite his rigorous schedule when he suddenly lost his voice completely. One of his assistants telephoned Claxton, who was directing the entire Liberal operation from a suite in Montreal's Windsor Hotel, and reported the problem. 'Tell him to keep on shaking hands and patting children's heads, but to keep his mouth shut,' the Minister of National Defence ordered. Schedules were hurriedly rearranged, and he was returned to Quebec City with strict instructions to speak to no one, not even his wife. After a week, he was able to take to the campaign trail again. When he toured the Ottawa Valley on June 15, the weather was hot, and he astonished both his staff and his audience by taking off his jacket; if it was a departure from the usual standards of protocol he imposed on himself, the action did no harm to his popular image. Marthe Samson proved equally popular, particularly with the press corps, who were charmed by her quiet graciousness and her friendly smile. At a mass rally in Toronto's Maple Leaf Gardens on June 21, her fifteen-year-old daughter Louise appeared on the platform as well, and reporters re-baptized the Prime Minister 'Grand-papa Louis'.

The strenuous pace of the campaign was maintained until the end. In Newfoundland, Premier Smallwood, who had just won a crushing majority in a provincial election, took St. Laurent in personal charge, and rushed from meeting to meeting in a long car convoy at break-neck speed. The colourful politician outshone him on the platform, but that mattered little, since most of the voters were eager to do their 'Joey's' bidding, and he told them unequivocally to vote for Louis St. Laurent, 'the greatest man Canada has ever produced'. While the exaggerated statement was embarrassing to St. Laurent, there was no doubt that it reflected the strong current of popularity that had been created by his visits across Canada. By election day, he had achieved the astounding feat of visiting 190 of the 260 constituencies, and had given countless thousands of Canadians an opportunity to see him personally. While some people accused him of trying to paper over the cracks in the national structure, many more grasped at his invitation to build a truly united Canada. 'This French Canadian, speaking the same blunt truths to French Canadians as to English Canadians,' commented the traditionally Conservative *Edmonton Journal* in the last week of the contest, 'seems to us to offer all Canadians the first real chance they have had in more than a generation for real national unity.' In a final radio broadcast on June 24, he summed up his message. In every part of Canada he had made the same appeal, and presented the same program, 'to ensure to all Canadians, in every province, of every race and creed, yes, and of all political parties, the closest approach to equality of opportunity and to a fair share of the bounties with which Providence has endowed this favoured land.' Beyond that, he would make but one promise – 'to give you the best service of which I am possible'. With that statement, he rested his case.

For the third time, the St. Laurents gathered in their living-room to hear the verdict of the electorate, and, once again, with mixed feelings. 'If my husband is elected, I won't sleep very much,' Jeanne St. Laurent confided to a newspaperman on election night, before the results began to arrive. 'If he is defeated, I will sleep very well. Then I will go back home.' It was far too late for second thoughts; the Liberals took the lead at once, and at 9:23 p.m., Drew conceded the election. St. Laurent and his colleagues were given a new mandate with a record majority of

190 seats.* The Progressive Conservative forces in Parliament were reduced to 41, the C.C.F. representation to 13, and Social Credit to 10 members. Five Independent members, including Camillien Houde, made up the rest. Only two Conservatives were elected in Quebec, but John Hackett was not one of them; he had declined to run against his life-long friend. In Ontario, the Liberals had beaten Drew on his own ground by more than two to one. St. Laurent's personal victory in Quebec East was four times that of Ernest Lapointe's greatest majority. 'Probably never before in our political history have we Canadians spoken with such a united voice,' commented the *Saskatoon Star-Phoenix*. In his victory broadcast, Louis St. Laurent repeated his vow to work to strengthen 'the spirit of harmony and good will and co-operation between English- and French-speaking Canadians which is the one sure foundation of our unity as a nation'.

*Including Independent Liberals: 193.

# 10

---

## Positive Nationalism

The Liberal victory of 1949 had an uplifting effect on Canadians. A Gallup poll conducted one week after the election indicated that 62 per cent of the population felt St. Laurent had done the best job for his party during his campaign; many of the persons interviewed commented approvingly on the 'dignity' of his performance, and the absence of 'mud-slinging' in his statements. George Drew's tactics had misfired badly; English-speaking Canadians preferred moderation to bombast, and in Quebec the unproclaimed alliance with the Union Nationale had proved ineffective. The C.C.F. leader, M. J. Coldwell, also won praise for his 'dignified' campaign, but both his party and the Social Credit movement remained largely western Canadian political phenomena. 'It may be that Canada has found a man who can really unify and lead her,' commented the London *Economist* on July 2, 'for St. Laurent possesses most of the characteristics which were politically valuable in Mackenzie King, but also qualities of leadership which King never had.'

While he was pleased that he had proved his competence on the hustings, St. Laurent himself remained unimpressed by the praise heaped upon him. 'They are building a very flattering legend around me,' Louis St. Laurent remarked to a senator in early July, 'I hope that the future won't bring too much disillusionment.'

Before tackling the problems that would test his leadership in the months ahead, the victorious politician had one engagement that was very important to him personally: he had promised his family that they would take their first holiday together since he entered public life. Now numbering twenty-nine members, they gathered together in July at Kent Lodge near Bathurst, New Brunswick. Relaxed and confident, St. Laurent fitted back easily into the role of head of the family, surrounded by adoring children and grandchildren. As keen and methodical about his pleasure as about his work, he was out on the golf course early each morning, took several dips a day in the pool, and even decided to learn to swim. In the carefree atmosphere, one of the incidents longest to be remembered occurred when he announced that his pre-war bathrobe had gone out of style, and should be shortened; to the amusement of the others, his wife refused to make more than a modest adjustment, accusing him indignantly of wanting to show off his legs to 'the bathing beauties'. With such matters dominating their conversation, the preoccupations of being Prime Minister were forced far into the background; the summer of 1949 was one of the happiest in their lives. At the end of July, St. Laurent returned to Ottawa, while most of the other members of the family moved up to Cacouna, near Rivière-du-Loup, to continue their holiday. When the first week-end arrived, however, he boarded his private railway car again, and made the four-hundred-mile journey to spend another day or two with them. 'It got lonesome in Ottawa with nothing but politicians around,' he told a reporter who wanted to know the purpose of his trip.

During the summer, St. Laurent shuffled the Quebec wing of the cabinet; Joseph Jean and Ernest Bertrand retired from political life to take up legal appointments; Hugues Lapointe became Solicitor General; and Edouard Rinfret, son of the Chief Justice, was appointed Postmaster General. He also appointed several persons to the Senate, including Adélard Godbout. While the former premier had rendered Canada a great service in 1941 when he helped to choose St. Laurent as Lapointe's successor, he had also paid dearly for that decision; he had not picked an ally capable of supporting him in his struggle against Maurice Duplessis. In fact, St. Laurent had made his task more difficult at times by refusing to meet the Union Nationale leader on his own ground or to make concessions to Quebec nationalism. For his part, Godbout had resisted proposals to pick a quarrel with the federal Liberals in order to dissociate himself from them in the public mind, and was denounced by his opponents as the tool of Anglo-Saxon-dominated Ottawa. In the circumstances, he had little alternative but to acknowledge defeat; George Marler, a fluently bilingual English Canadian, became acting Leader of the Opposition in the Quebec Legislature.

If Quebec provincial politics were a source of continuing concern to the federal government, there were more hopeful signs in Ontario. After a short interim régime under the direction of Colonel T. L. Kennedy, Leslie Frost had become Premier of Ontario in May. While he had been a leading member of Drew's cabinet, he was a quieter, more moderate person, and had never approved of the policy of warring with Ottawa. An admirer of St. Laurent's, he wrote him a warm letter of congratulation on the Liberal victory in June 1949, and took the opportunity to express the view that they should work together closely, since Canada could not be run by a series of governments operating at arm's length and maintaining the nation's business in a state of disorder. Delighted at the overture, St. Laurent telephoned Toronto immediately to assure the Ontario Premier of his wholehearted desire for co-operation. The two men met by chance shortly afterwards in Ottawa at the funeral of a mutual friend, and St. Laurent invited Frost up to the Parliament Buildings for a chat. They soon discovered that they had much in common, including similar views on economic development, social legislation, and federal-provincial relations. The conversation marked the beginning of a new phase in relations between Ottawa and Toronto.

The government was determined to take advantage of its new mandate to act on many matters that had been held in abeyance during the last period of Mackenzie King's leadership and the first months that St. Laurent was in office. Reflecting the spirit of positive nationalism that animated the cabinet, the Speech from the Throne that marked the opening of the new Parliament on September 15 proposed construction of a trans-Canada highway, abolition of appeals to the Privy Council, and authorization for Parliament to amend the constitution in purely federal fields of jurisdiction. A federal-provincial conference would be convened, it was also announced, to seek agreement on an amending formula in other areas.

The constitutional changes were clearly the most important matters on the list, and the government's proposals had been carefully prepared. St. Laurent had rejected the possibility of consulting the provinces on the abolition of appeals to the Privy Council on the grounds that Duplessis would never consent to having the Supreme Court made the final court of appeal; he had decided on similar grounds not to try to obtain agreement to amend the constitution in Canada in joint federal and provincial fields of jurisdiction. While the plan to obtain the authorization of Parliament to amend the constitution in federal fields was merely half a loaf, he felt it was better than none, and, once it was attained, the onus would be on the provinces to secure the rest.

The session began on a temperate note. George Drew had accepted his party's defeat manfully, and surprised many people by his moderation; accepting the verdict of the electorate, he did not propose an amendment of want of confidence in the government. St. Laurent sought to encourage the new attitude of the Leader of the Opposition, and the aggressiveness that had marked their relations in the past began to be transformed into cordiality and respect. The constitutional issues were raised almost at once. Remaining true to his earlier position on federal-provincial relations, Drew insisted that the provinces be consulted. In reply, St. Laurent argued once again that the B.N.A. Act was not a contract between parties existing before Confederation, and pointed out that amendments to the constitution had been made no less than ten times in the past without consulting the provincial authorities. In the circumstances, he declared, 'we feel we have no right to recognize that . . . [they] have any control whatsoever over those matters of public interest and national sovereignty allocated to the federal authority.' On the abolition of appeals

278 LOUIS ST. LAURENT

to the Privy Council, he rejected the implication in some members' remarks that Canadian judges would be less competent or less objective in handing down decisions than the Judicial Committee in London. Notwithstanding his great respect for the British legal authorities, he remarked, 'I believe it is possible for us to find and develop in this country as great jurists as they happen to be.'

As was to be anticipated, the constitutional proposals met criticism from several directions. Conservative member Thomas Church condemned them as 'a separatist movement' and declared that it was not the time 'to give the mother country a black eye'. In Quebec City, Duplessis repeated his argument that the B.N.A. Act was 'a pact concluded between the four pioneer provinces', and demanded that 'the provinces which gave birth to the central authority' should approve the proposed measures. St. Laurent and the Union Nationale leader exchanged a series of letters on the subject, but neither man altered his original position. During the debate in the House of Commons, St. Laurent accepted an amendment by C.C.F. member Stanley Knowles to prevent any change in the rules providing for at least one session of Parliament a year and an election every five years; with those modifications the government's proposal to authorize Parliament to amend the constitution in areas of federal jurisdiction was approved over Conservative opposition. With the abolition of appeals to the Privy Council and the right to amend the Canadian constitution at home, St. Laurent told an audience of young Liberals enthusiastically in late autumn, 'we will be in full possession both theoretically and in practice, of our autonomy. ... We will be masters in our own house.'

One of the important events in Ottawa in late 1949 was the visit of Indian Prime Minister Jawaharlal Nehru, accompanied by his sister, Mrs. L. Pandit, and his daughter, Mrs. Indira Gandhi. The Asian leader arrived from Washington, where he had been urged to accept outside mediation in his dispute with Pakistan over Kashmir; while he had resisted the strong American pressure, he had been somewhat annoyed by it, and, coupled with a divergence of views on the threat of Communism, it had left him somewhat disenchanted with the United States government.

Louis St. Laurent was urged by the Americans to keep up the pressure on Nehru concerning Kashmir, but the Canadian Prime Minister was more preoccupied for the moment with demonstrating Canada's good will towards India with a view to future co-operation. At a private dinner at the Ottawa Country Club, he succeeded in breaking through Nehru's reserve and scepticism of Western motives, and convinced him of Canada's sincere desire not only to understand the challenge facing India, but also to aid in assuring her success. Touched at the warmth and sincerity of his host's remarks, the Indian leader took the small group into his confidence and spoke extempore for over an hour of his country and his concept of its place in the world. It was a memorable experience for those present, and as they listened they could sense a bond being forged between the two countries, so far apart in miles, in culture, and in climate. The old ties of empire were disappearing, but in their place were growing new relationships that could make of the Commonwealth a valuable instrument of co-operation in the critical years ahead. The exchange of views made a strong impression on both prime ministers, St. Laurent seeing in an Indo-Canadian friendship pact an opportunity to assist the new nations of Asia to make democracy work, and thus to extend the reign of freedom and justice in the world.

In an address to a joint session of both houses of the Canadian Parliament, Nehru paid tribute to 'the spirit of understanding' shown by the Canadian government in the discussions of India's future relationship with the Commonwealth, and noted that 'our point of view and Canada's were identical or very near to each other' on almost every topic he had discussed with the Canadian leaders over the previous two years. Canada had been a pioneer in transforming the Empire into 'an association of free and equal nations', he declared; now she was faced with a new challenge, to 'understand our purpose and our motives, and . . . use her growing wealth and power to extend the horizons of freedom, to promote order and liberty, to remove want, and thus to ensure lasting peace'.

The first post-election session of Parliament lasted three months, and was, on the whole, quiet and fruitful. St. Laurent himself piloted through the House of Commons the bills to create three new departments of government – Resources and Development, Mines and Technical Surveys, and Citizenship and Immigration. The Progressive Conservatives continued to accuse the government of being autocratic, and singled out C. D. Howe as the prime target for their attacks. The minister's competence was unquestioned, but his attitude towards his critics was something like that of a giant mastiff being harassed by a terrier pup; accustomed to taking important decisions, he felt that most of the speeches in the House of Commons were a waste of time, and based on either ignorance of the facts or political opportunism. The blunt retorts to criticism appeared to confirm the opposition's charge of arrogance. Occasionally, St. Laurent, too, was stirred into making sharp rebuttals, and into lecturing opposition members in a 'Father knows best' manner that lent weight to the charge of autocracy. On the whole, however, he strove to establish the broadest possible support for the government's actions, and displayed an unusual readiness to accept the suggestions of opposition members. While he was open-minded on almost every topic, he was also a realist, and subjected the proposals of reform-minded Liberals to close scrutiny before accepting them. He agreed in principle to the desirability of choosing a distinctive flag, removing the word 'Dominion' from Canadian statutes, appointing a Canadian governor general, and sending a Canadian ambassador to the Vatican; he was in favour of Senate reform, an immediate start on the St. Lawrence Seaway, and even recognition of the new Communist régime in China. At the same time, he was not prepared to go ahead with any of those measures until he was convinced that it could be accomplished successfully, and that the total effect on Canada would be beneficial. As a result the new administration seemed to some people about as cautious as its predecessor.

The first major task faced by the federal government in 1950 was to try to obtain the agreement of the provinces on a formula to amend the constitution in Canada in matters of joint federal and provincial concern; if that could be achieved, the last obstacle would be surmounted to assuring Canada of full constitutional sovereignty in form as well as in spirit. Unfortunately, when St. Laurent called a federal-provincial constitutional conference for

January 10, 1950, he still had a few illusions about the possibilities of obtaining agreement with Quebec on such an amending formula. When he opened the long-awaited meeting, the Prime Minister summed up what he considered to be the minimum requirements of any amending procedure:

> It must protect minority rights absolutely. It must preserve the federal character of the Canadian nation by preserving the autonomy, within their respective spheres, of the provincial legislatures and of Parliament itself. It must have sufficient flexibility to enable our country with all its great human resources and natural resources to continue to go forward as a dynamic nation.

He and his colleagues were not seeking any alteration in the existing distribution of powers, he emphasized, and felt that such a possibility should not even be discussed. Conscious of the fact that at the 1945-6 federal-provincial meetings Drew and Duplessis had manoeuvred them into making firm proposals, and had then denounced them for adopting a 'take-it-or-leave-it' attitude, the federal ministers refrained from suggesting a specific amending formula, although one had been worked out in general terms in the Department of Justice; St. Laurent merely invited the premiers to 'put forward their views as to the most appropriate form of provincial participation'. He coupled the invitation with the warning that the conference presented 'a very real challenge to the political capacity of the public men of Canada', and that 'sooner or later this challenge will have to be met'.

From the outset of the meeting, it was evident that the Toronto-Quebec axis existed no more. Speaking immediately after the Prime Minister, Premier Frost expressed the view that the problem of amending the constitution would have been better dealt with 'as a whole instead of piecemeal', but offered his complete co-operation in the search for an acceptable formula, and made a series of practical suggestions to that end. Duplessis demanded not only that the whole subject be opened up again, but that they also discuss the financial powers of the different governments, which, he argued, were an essential complement to legislative powers. Of the other premiers, only Angus Macdonald and T. C. Douglas made specific proposals, and those of the Saskatchewan government leader were in direct contradiction to the Quebec government's position. The constitution was not 'sacrosanct', argued Douglas, and to the degree that it prevented the satisfaction of human needs, 'it is archaic and must be changed'. He suggested dividing the clauses of the constitution according to subject matter, one category to be 'entrenched' and only capable of being modified with the consent of all governments, another category to be changed by Parliament plus a simple majority of the provinces, a third category to be dealt with by authorizing the delegation of powers between the two levels of government. He also urged that the federal government be given authority to legislate in the fields of marketing and labour legislation, and to implement international treaties in fields of provincial jurisdiction.

With both St. Laurent and Duplessis refusing to make specific proposals, the delegates finished the first morning's session with a discussion of a possible agenda. In the afternoon, the Quebec Premier repeated his charge that the amendment made at the last session of Parliament to enable it to alter the constitution in the fields of federal jurisdiction was 'a most serious and severe encroachment upon provincial rights'; he suggested again that it be set aside and that the conference 'start anew'. St. Laurent rejected the charge and made the counter-suggestion that the conference try to establish, 'acting in as constructive a way as we know how, . . . the things that we can agree upon as the right results without having as a preliminary to convince either one or the other that the other thing is entirely wrong'. If they could agree that certain rights were going to be respected, he pleaded, it did not matter whether it was 'a result of one's opinion that [the constitution] is a compact or another's that it is the right and moral thing to do'. Duplessis refused to be drawn out, except to concede that there was unanimity on the desirability of having a purely Canadian constitution, and a Canadian final court of appeal. He summed up his position as 'open-minded except that on fundamentals our views are firmly entrenched', and accused the federal government of 'playing hide and seek' by refusing to reveal its 'views or suggestions'. By the end of the day, the only progress that had been made was an agreement that four categories of sections of the B.N.A. Act could be distinguished according to their relative importance to the two levels of government, and that a committee composed of the attorneys general should try to classify them accordingly.

Securing agreement behind closed doors proved much easier than when the delegates were conscious of newspapermen listening to them, and, although Duplessis was a member of the committee in his capacity as Attorney General of Quebec, Justice Minister Garson was able to announce at noon on the following day that unanimous agreement had been achieved on the limited assignment. His report suggested six rather than four categories of subjects, and an equal number of amending procedures, ranging from a simple act of Parliament to unanimous consent; it also recommended consideration of a formula for the delegation of powers between the two levels of government. The conference accepted the report, and thus acquired at least a basis for discussion, but it was evident that no more concrete steps could be taken for the moment; a continuing committee of attorneys general was formed to examine the whole subject in greater detail, and with that the conference was adjourned until autumn. Despite the wrangling that had gone on, and the negligible progress, the meeting ended with a general exchange of compliments. Duplessis made the only exception, commenting wryly to St. Laurent that 'if I were to pay you a compliment, I am afraid so many people would be shocked that some of them might die; and on the other hand it would hurt your humility'. Frost's position was in marked contrast to the Union Nationale leader's. 'There is nothing which cannot be met by a common sense view on the part of the governments and the co-operation and confidence which should exist in a federal system such as ours,' he declared as the meeting adjourned. '. . . And as far as I am concerned, I would like to start right now.'

As they prepared for the next session of Parliament, scheduled to begin on February 16, 1950, Louis St. Laurent and his cabinet colleagues were functioning as an efficient, unified team. The prestige of the government was enhanced further when Robert

Winters and Walter Harris, both competent younger men considered by observers in Ottawa as possible future prime ministers, were named, respectively, Minister of Resources and Development and Minister of Citizenship and Immigration. Their appointments were an effective reply to the opposition assertion that the country was being run by a group of tired old men. At the same time, a Quebec lawyer, Colonel Laval Fortier, was appointed Deputy Minister of Citizenship and Immigration, marking an increase from one to four in a single year in the number of French-speaking deputy ministers. In view of the difficulties in recruiting French-speaking Canadians to fill positions of responsibility in Ottawa, this was no minor accomplishment. Such positive steps were what St. Laurent had in mind when he answered criticism that he was not speaking up sufficiently for French Canada with the retort 'Actions speak louder than words.'

The main concern of members of Parliament as they gathered in the national capital was the marked increase in unemployment that had become evident during the winter. The Speech from the Throne conceded that Canada was experiencing 'a significant amount of temporary regional unemployment' and announced that, in addition to the unemployment insurance program already in existence, federal aid for unemployment assistance would also be introduced. Sensing the public uneasiness that the long-awaited post-war recession was about to manifest itself, Drew launched a vigorous attack, describing the situation as 'critical' and censuring the government for failing to deal with trade and economic problems. He accused the government again of lacking respect for Parliament, of failing to take action against the threat of Communism in Canada, and of riding roughshod over provincial rights. He succeeded in stirring up a heated reaction from the Liberal side of the House; interruptions became frequent, tempers flared, and even St. Laurent replied vigorously to the charges. In a radio broadcast on March 21, the Prime Minister warned the 'gloom-spreaders' that 'nothing is apt to harm us today as much as fear', and that, if they continued to forecast a depression, the country might be talked into one. With Canada's human and material sources, he asserted, and 'with vision and faith', no country had a brighter future. For the moment, however, the uneasiness prevailed, and the government was caught for the first time in a defensive posture, giving the impression that it was hoping for an upturn in the economic cycle to extricate it from its difficulties.

For St. Laurent, the two principal subjects of opposition criticism, the level of economic activity and the struggle against Communism, were closely interrelated. While he felt firmly that any attempt to impose Communism by force, either within Canada or elsewhere, must be resisted by force, he was convinced that it could not be overcome simply by restrictive legislation or police action, or by military means. He deplored the almost hysterical fear of Communism in the United States, and only to a relatively lesser degree in Canada, and was determined to resist the demands of Maurice Duplessis, Social Credit members of Parliament, and some Conservatives for repressive measures. About the time he had assumed the Liberal Party leadership, the government had taken the carefully considered decision not to curb Communist activity within trade unions. The calculated risk that the trade unions would be able to look after the problem themselves paid off, and encouraged him to restrain those who advocated limitations on freedom in Canada. As he told members of the Canadian Club of Toronto:

> The nations of the free world must demonstrate the superiority of our institutions and our way of life to the continued satisfaction of all our own people. And then we must win over those hundreds of millions in Asia and Africa who now feel indifferent and confused and are attached to neither side in the cold war; and ultimately we must convince those other millions behind the Iron Curtain that Communist Imperialism means slavery and that we stand for freedom and peace.

A new dimension of historical significance was added to the problem of dealing with Communism when the Nationalist Chinese government of Chiang Kai-shek was driven from the mainland, and a Communist régime established in Peking under Mao Tse-tung. Diplomatic recognition of Red domination over the most populous country in the world implied acknowledging an enemy victory of dimensions that many people in the Western world, and particularly in the United States, simply could not accept. In assessing the importance of the Communist victory in China, both Great Britain and Canada were influenced strongly by the views of Jawaharlal Nehru, whose combination of Asian origins and Western culture qualified him well to interpret the new situation. As early as February 1949, the Indian Prime Minister had warned against a hostile attitude towards the new Chinese government, arguing that such a policy would merely result in the formation of a huge Sino-Soviet bloc adamantly hostile to the non-Communist powers. He urged a dynamic policy of support for progressive nationalist régimes in South-east Asia as the only effective answer to Communism, and contacts with the Mao Tse-tung government, without commitments on either side, to hold the door open for future negotiations. In December 1949, India extended diplomatic recognition to the Peking régime, and, in early January 1950, the United Kingdom followed suit.

At a conference of Commonwealth external affairs ministers in Colombo, in January 1950, Nehru appealed for massive economic and technical aid to the new nations of Asia, and for recognition by all Commonwealth countries of the Communist government in Peking, as the only means of influencing future developments in China. The delegates were deeply impressed by the Indian leader's argument, and the Canadian Minister for External Affairs, L. B. Pearson, returned home prepared to recommend both his country's active participation in what was to become known as the Colombo Plan for Co-operative Economic Develop-ment in South and South-east Asia, and recognition of Communist China. St. Laurent endorsed Pearson's viewpoint, and the pre-liminary steps were taken, Chester Ronning being chosen to open the diplomatic post, and even receiving instructions to purchase a house in Peking. However, as the weeks passed, the advantages of such a step appeared increasingly dubious. The Communist Chinese reaction towards British and Indian recognition was far from favourable, and led the Canadians to wonder if they would have any real influence in Peking. During the same period, the United States made it clear that they had no intention of recognizing the new government and, within Canada, Maurice Duplessis renewed his charge that the federal government was being dangerously lax in dealing with the Communist threat to the Christian world. Without changing their viewpoint on the principle of recognition, St. Laurent and Pearson decided that the possible advantages were outweighed by the disadvantages within Canada and in relations with her neighbour; the move was postponed.

In his second year as Prime Minister, Louis St. Laurent took in his stride the wide variety of matters brought to his attention. With the orderliness and regularity that were part of his nature, he emerged from his apartment building around nine o'clock every morning and, unaccompanied, walked briskly up Elgin Street to Parliament Hill, lifting his Homburg and saying good morning to all who spoke a word of greeting to him. In his East Block office, or in the other office across from the entrance to the Commons Chamber that he used when the House was sitting, he worked his way through documents, dictated letters, and received visitors at a steady and seemingly unhurried pace that belied the keenness with which he examined each subject. His idealism tempered by years of practical experience, he enjoyed the challenge of examing new proposals, and submitting them to the test of feasibility, and he also took pleasure in devising workable solutions to difficult problems. Always conservatively dressed in a double-breasted suit, heavily starched white shirt, silk tie, and tie-pin, he never appeared so much in his natural surroundings as when he sat at the large desk, against the background of the panelled walls and high Gothic windows.

While he was invariably courteous and straightforward in his relations with persons who worked closely with him, and inspired in them a high degree of loyalty and devotion, there was a lack of personal contact between him and his staff that was difficult to reconcile with his public image as 'Uncle Louis'. Undoubtedly a warm-hearted person, he still maintained something of the shyness of his earlier years, and was unable to make people relax in his company. Light conversation and exchanges of humour seemed more difficult for him than serious conversation. In his private railway car during journeys outside the capital, conversation was disconcertingly spasmodic and interspersed with long and awkward periods of silence, as he dismissed one subject after another with a monosyllable, or a correction of facts, that discouraged further initiatives. Staff members learned that the only way to make him talk was to ask him to explain some particular subject. Since he was almost invariably better informed on most topics than his travelling companions, such subjects were not difficult to find, and he would launch into a careful explanation, during which the time passed quickly and pleasantly.

Interested as he was in every detail of the life of his own kin, and of Canadians as a whole, he knew little or nothing about the personal lives of those who served him as many as fifteen hours a day, and seldom offered a word of commendation for their efforts. After completing a year as one of his secretaries, Pierre Asselin wrote him a note, commenting how honoured he had been to have the opportunity to serve him for that period of time, and expressing the hope that his efforts had been satisfactory. He added the note to the stack of mail that had arrived that morning, placed the lot on St. Laurent's desk as usual, and then withdrew to the neighbouring office to await the reaction. In a few minutes the Prime Minister appeared, holding the piece of paper gingerly in his hand, and asked what was the meaning of the message. Embarrassed, Asselin explained that he had perhaps been feeling a bit sentimental, but it was a happy occasion for him, and he hoped that his feeling of satisfaction was not entirely one-sided. St. Laurent stammered a bit, then blurted out: 'Well, if your work wasn't satisfactory, you wouldn't be here,' and with that, he disappeared again into his own office. On the other hand, he met M. J. Deacey, another secretary, in front of St. Patrick's Church one Sunday morning following mass, bent down to shake hands with the man's little son, and asked, as if referring to a complete equal, 'Do you know that your Daddy and I work in the same office?' He also showed genuine concern about the personal problems of staff members if they happened to be brought to his attention.

Nevertheless, his image as 'Uncle Louis' was no pose. One of his most genuine gestures occurred in the early spring of 1950 when he was touring western Ontario. Less than a mile from the grave of Uncle Tom, the famous Negro who escaped to Canada from American slavery, he saw a six-year-old Negro girl in a crowd of white children; breaking away from the group of dignitaries, he walked over to her, picked her up in his arms, and kissed her. The spontaneous action symbolized his feelings about Canada and Canadians; it also revealed much about St. Laurent himself as a human being.

Among his trips outside Ottawa during the 1950 regular session of Parliament, 'the P.M.', as he was called on Parliament Hill, visited the scenes of the Winnipeg flood, and of the equally disastrous Rimouski and Cabano fires, and paid two visits to the United States to receive honorary degrees at St. Louis, Missouri, and Canton, New York. On the way to St. Louis, he put on a fireman's cap and overalls, climbed into the cab of the Detroit-Chicago train and helped drive it part of the way. Like a boy realizing his fondest dream, he blew the whistle and waved gaily at people along the route. At St. Louis University the following day, he resumed a more serious, and for him more natural, manner to deliver the convocation address. Without referring to Senator Joseph McCarthy by name, he warned the American people against his witch-hunting tactics, and argued that 'the most efficient way to combat Communist infiltration on this continent is not to spread fear and suspicion, but to devote oneself with confidence to the practice of democracy, freedom and justice'. The real danger, he declared, was 'the expansion of Soviet imperialism by means of infiltration in less fortunate continents', and 'it would be falling into a Communist trap to allow ourselves to be distracted from this real danger'. In carefully chosen words, he gave strong support to President Truman and Secretary of State Acheson, two of McCarthy's principal targets, and endorsed unequivocally their policy of 'a strong and interdependent Atlantic community'. At St. Lawrence University in Canton, New York, a few days later, he made a strong appeal for support of the Truman administration in its efforts to win approval from Congress to participate in the St. Lawrence seaway project, warning that Canadians were getting 'rather impatient' about the delay in starting 'a development which will . . . benefit all parts of the continent'.

While St. Laurent was absent in the United States, C. D. Howe introduced in the House of Commons a proposal to establish a prime minister's residence in the Canadian capital. The matter had been under consideration for some years, and there was general agreement that there should be in Ottawa some place like the White House in Washington, or No. 10 Downing Street in London, where the head of the government could live and receive guests in a style appropriate to his position. The only serious resistance to the proposal came from St. Laurent himself, who wished to avoid the impression that he was deriving any special benefit from being Prime Minister, or that his private life was somehow dependent on his public activity. His scrupulousness had already led him to decline an offer from wealthy friends to buy a residence for him, even though a group of Conservatives and Liberals had purchased a spacious house for George Drew and for future leaders of the opposition. In the end, it was pointed out to him that he was blocking an opportunity to solve a long-standing problem, and to render a service to future prime ministers, who might well find the financial burden of the office more difficult to bear than he did. On that basis, he gave his reluctant consent, but insisted on paying five thousand dollars a year, the amount he would save by occupying an official residence and receiving an allowance for running it. Unfortunately, no one was able to persuade him that, in making that stipulation, he was also committing his successors to do the same. As a final concession to his personal sensitiveness, it was agreed that the proposal to establish the residence be debated in Parliament during his absence, and be completely dissociated from his personal case. In a further attempt to avoid ostentation, a proposal to construct a modern building was rejected, and it was decided to restore an old residence on Sussex Street overlooking the Ottawa River that had already been taken over by the Federal District Commission as part of a general plan to develop and beautify the capital area.

The debate on the proposal submitted to Parliament on June

7 revealed that St. Laurent's views were not shared by his fellow parliamentarians; the only serious criticism voiced was related to the five-thousand-dollar annual payment, and the removal of that clause was requested. Howe admitted readily that he did not like the stipulation either, but pointed out that it had been inserted at the Prime Minister's insistence, because the latter wished to be 'in the same position as every other citizen of Canada, namely, that he pay his living costs out of his salary after taxes'. The condition was accepted with reluctance; for once, St. Laurent's personal integrity prevented him from devising the best possible solution to a public problem.

During that spring of 1950, St. Laurent purchased a summer home on the lower St. Lawrence River. Members of the family had found their reunion in New Brunswick the previous summer so pleasant that they urged him to make it an annual affair. The house he chose was in St. Patrick, near Rivière-du-Loup, and just a few doors from a former summer residence of Sir John A. Macdonald. It was a roomy, white-painted structure with a large garden, lawns descending towards the water, a golf course just across the road, and the possibility of fishing near by. All the St. Laurents looked forward to their first summer there as soon as the session of Parliament ended.

Canada's law-makers were within days of finishing their annual deliberations when the news broke over the world on Sunday, June 25, that large-scale fighting had erupted between North Korea and South Korea. Although border incidents had been frequent in previous months, the government of the President of South Korea, Syngman Rhee, was clearly taken unawares, and within hours of the attack's being launched thousands of North Korean troops were across the 38th parallel dividing the two parts of the country. The Canadian government had opposed the partition of Korea, and had withdrawn from the United Nations Temporary Commission on Korea after it accepted separate elections for the southern part of the country; but, later, Canada had recognized the Republic of South Korea as an independent state.

As soon as the news of the fighting reached Ottawa, St. Laurent and Pearson consulted together and agreed that the United Nations must be brought into the picture at once to restore order; since the Canadian plea for an international police force had fallen on deaf ears, it was not immediately clear how the world organization could act effectively. The United States was the only country capable of providing effective military aid to South Korea, but there was a serious danger that if the Americans acted unilaterally, the conflict might be turned into a global struggle between the Communists and the non-Communists. In the circumstances, the Canadians were pleased when the Security Council was called into emergency session, the same day. With the Soviet delegate absent and the Yugoslav delegate abstaining, a resolution was approved unanimously, condemning the North Koreans for 'the armed attack upon the Republic of Korea', demanding their immediate withdrawal, and calling on U.N. member nations to 'render every assistance to the United Nations in the execution of this resolution'.

Speaking in the House of Commons on June 26, Pearson accepted the view that North Korea was guilty of 'an action of unprovoked aggression', and urged support of the Security Council resolution. Through diplomatic channels, he pleaded with the Americans not to intervene in the fighting except as part of a United Nations force and within the terms set out in the United Nations Charter. When word reached Ottawa on June 27 that President Truman was about to announce that his government would provide air and sea support immediately to the South Korean forces, and take Formosa under its protection in order to resist Communist imperialism, he tried to persuade the United States government to delay the announcement until a Security Council resolution had been obtained requesting United States intervention. He also suggested that the fighting in Korea be referred to as a single incident, and not as part of a world-wide Communist strategy. The Canadian viewpoint was received in Washington with understanding, but it did not alter the course of events; the President made his statement at noon on June 27. Fortunately, the Security Council passed another resolution later in the day, requesting just the sort of aid that the Americans had announced. On June 28, Pearson pointed out in the House of

Commons that 'although the United States government has taken this step on its own authority, it is action not only in accordance with the spirit and letter of the Charter of the United Nations, but also in pursuance of the resolution which was adopted by the Security Council'.

St. Laurent called in representatives of the three other political parties to brief them confidentially on the crisis, explaining that the government was ready and willing to recommend Canadian participation in a joint effort to halt the Communist aggression, but only as part of a United Nations operation; he was assured of all-party support for that policy. As an indication of Canada's intentions in that regard, the government decided to divert immediately to the Pacific area some Canadian destroyers about to leave for exercises in Europe. On June 30, the last day of the session, St. Laurent announced the decision, and made it clear that any Canadian contribution would not take the form of 'participation in war against any state', but would only occur as 'our part in collective police action under the control and authority of the United Nations for the purpose of restoring peace to an area where an aggression has occurred as determined under the Charter of the United Nations by the Security Council'. The policy received unanimous support, even Jean-François Pouliot, who had objected to Canadian involvement two days earlier, declaring that he was willing to rely upon 'the wisdom and the foresight' of his leader.

Outside Parliament there was less unanimity. While the English-language press supported the government, isolationist sentiment in Quebec proved to be still stronger than the fear of Communism. In an editorial on June 28, *Le Soleil* denounced the United Nations as 'a screen for the powers who want to dominate the world', and argued that Canada's participation in a joint action would constitute 'a derogation from her position as a free country'. *Le Devoir* declared that the United Nations without Russian participation was merely 'a kind of Western council of war' and described Canadians who favoured participation in a multilateral force as being 'like little dogs who are impatient to show their master [the United States] that they adore him, who need but a gesture and they will throw themselves into the water'.

In view of the critical international situation, Louis St. Laurent had little time to enjoy his new summer home in 1950. He followed the developments from hour to hour, and worked closely with Pearson and senior Canadian diplomats who were striving to ensure that the North Korean aggression would be repulsed but without allowing the conflict to spread. They were concerned that an American policy of protecting all South-east Asia from attack would bring the Communist Chinese into the struggle, alienate India and other members of the United Nations, and perhaps even involve the United States in a drawn-out and almost certainly indecisive land war in that part of the world. In the face of heavy lobbying in Washington by Canadians and other Western diplomats, the Americans gave the assurance that their goal in Korea was only to assist in driving the aggressors back across the 38th parallel, but they insisted that firm action was essential to demonstrate the strength and determination of the free world to resist Communist aggression. The Korean crisis revealed the unpreparedness of Canada to defend itself, or even to participate effectively in an international military operation. Fortunately for Canada, C. D. Howe had been persuaded to remain in public life, and he set out with his usual efficiency and forcefulness to adapt the nation's industrial machine once again to meet the international situation. Keeping Brooke Claxton in charge of the Defence Department proved to be equally fortunate, for even his great energy and initiative were to be severely tested in the months ahead. And it was hard to imagine a man more qualified to hold Canadians together in another period of international conflict than Louis St. Laurent.

Preoccupied with the situation in Asia, it was only with strong misgivings that the Prime Minister agreed to go ahead with a long-standing plan to visit western Canada in the second week in July. He was initiated into the Plains Indians tribe in Saskatchewan as 'Chief Wise Leader', smoked a peace pipe with his hosts, and even joined in a ceremonial dance to the accompaniment of a deerskin drum. In Calgary the next day, he led the six-mile parade that opened the annual Stampede and appeared relaxed and carefree in a gaudy cowboy shirt and ten-gallon hat as he was drawn through the streets by a pair of equally gaily bedecked *percheron* horses. His sombre references to the international situation were in strong contrast to the festive occasion. The United Nations' action in Korea, he told one audience sternly, was designed to make it 'abundantly clear' that the free nations were not going to allow such flagrant aggression 'any more, anywhere'. Western Canadians were given an opportunity to see another side of the personality of the man they had come to know as 'Uncle Louis'.

On July 22, Canadians were shocked to learn of the death of William Lyon Mackenzie King. Since his retirement as Prime Minister he had seldom been seen in public, and had restricted his travels largely to moving back and forth between Laurier House and Kingsmere. St. Laurent had treated him with courtesy and consideration in his last months, consulting him occasionally, and paying him special respect at public functions, but they had had few of the long, confidential conversations of earlier years. The old man had arranged his succession so well that he had become dispensable almost on the day he left office. He had been happy to see his choice confirmed by the electorate in June 1949. Chatting with Pickersgill one day, he had remarked that he had either known personally, or known others who had known personally, every cabinet minister of any consequence since Confederation, and, in his opinion, Louis St. Laurent was the ablest man who ever sat in a Canadian cabinet. At the same time, he warned, the new Prime Minister was ruling over his colleagues with too loose a rein, a practice that could lead him into difficulties. When the Korean War broke out, he recalled that he had foreseen it as early as 1946, and had striven to keep Canada from becoming involved there. He repeated his view that the Middle East was another trouble spot that might set off a third world war.

Louis St. Laurent led the group of mourners who paid a final tribute to the man who had changed his life so completely almost ten years earlier. Mackenzie King had worked 'to strengthen the unity of the nation by scrupulous respect for the rights and the traditions of all elements of the population and by the development of a genuine pride in our common homeland, our common history and our common citizenship,' he told the Canadian people in a radio broadcast on July 23, 'and . . . to give all Canadians a genuine sense of equality of opportunity by the promotion of social justice'. They were goals that he shared, and towards which he would continue to strive.

A few days later, the Prime Minister attended another funeral, this time for his Minister of Labour, Humphrey Mitchell, who had entered public life at the same time he had. Acting quickly to fill the gap in the cabinet ranks, he switched Milton Gregg to the Labour portfolio and made Hugues Lapointe Minister of Veterans' Affairs. The latter was an excellent appointment on several counts; quite apart from the prestige of his name, 'Bob' Lapointe was a competent person, and to have a French-speaking Canadian identified with the men who had served in the two world wars was a clever political stroke. Gregg's new assignment was more questionable. As sterling a character as ever entered public life, he had no experience in industrial relations, and seemed to have few of the qualities required to play a role of intermediary between hard-headed business and labour leaders. He himself readily admitted his shortcomings, but he declared himself ready to serve wherever his chief felt he could be useful. The two appointments reflected the Prime Minister's attitude in selecting candidates to fill positions of responsibility: with only a restricted circle of close acquaintances, and still distrustful of politicians he did not know well, he was inclined to choose those in whom he felt he could place his trust because of their personal qualities.

The government's problems were multiplied during that summer of 1950 by the first nation-wide railway strike in Canadian history. The trouble had been brewing for some time, and in October 1949 Labour Minister Humphrey Mitchell had established two boards of conciliation and investigation. Their findings had been accepted in the spring of 1950 by the railway management, but not by the employees. Further attempts at mediation had proved fruitless, and a strike was called for August 22. To complicate matters, Mitchell died suddenly in late July, and St. Laurent switched Milton Gregg to the Labour portfolio just when the negotiations were in a critical stage.

In view of Gregg's inexperience in labour matters, and the

seriousness of a transportation tie-up at a time when C. D. Howe was reconverting the economy to large-scale defence production, the Prime Minister took personal charge of a last-minute attempt to negotiate a settlement. On August 16, he requested a thirty-day postponement of strike action and offered to appoint a mediator if there was no settlement by the strike deadline. The workers rejected the request for a postponement, but accepted the proposal for mediation. On August 18, Dr. W. A. Mackintosh of Queen's University was appointed to make a last-minute effort to bring about an agreement. After three days, he conceded defeat; the strike began at 6 a.m., August 22; five hours later, St. Laurent summoned Parliament and announced that the government would take the necessary action 'to protect the vital interests of the whole Canadian people'.

While members of Parliament were being flown to Ottawa, the Prime Minister continued his efforts to settle the dispute. On August 26, he, Gregg, and Transport Minister Chevrier met the leaders of the two groups separately, and appealed to them to reach a compromise in the national interest. The strike was perfectly legal, St. Laurent told them, but a prolonged paralysis of rail transportation would be very harmful to the country generally, and would not further their common goal of adjusting the transportation system to modern conditions. When he had visited the scene of the Rimouski fire earlier in the year, he recalled, he had noted that a bridge destroyed by the flames had been replaced by a temporary structure, and a detour arranged to enable traffic to continue to circulate. He suggested that what was needed was a detour that would permit the Canadian economy to function until a more lasting structure of employer-employee relations could be established. At his insistence, the talks were resumed between the two parties to the dispute, but they could only agree to disagree. As the days passed and the transportation tie-up continued, St. Laurent became increasingly indignant at what he considered a stubborn refusal to place the public interest first. His annoyance was directed particularly against the labour spokesmen, since the C.N.R. and C.P.R. presidents had at least accepted the recommendations of Dr. Mackintosh as a basis for further negotiations.

As soon as Parliament assembled on August 29, he cut through the usual time-consuming procedures and placed before it a bill calling for resumption of railway services within forty-eight hours, wage increases on the scale agreed to by railway management, and resumption of negotiations. If no agreement was reached within fifteen days, the two parties were to choose an arbitrator, or, if they could not agree on one, the government would name one. There would be no compulsory arbitration 'in the usual sense', he declared, but rather a 'determination' of the conditions under which the essential services would continue for a further period. When opposition members cavilled at that fine distinction, his temper flared, and he challenged them to vote against the proposal. Drew demanded that an administrator be appointed to operate the railways 'pending final solution of the dispute by the free process of collective bargaining'. C.C.F. leader Coldwell sided more openly with the strikers and called for 'a national transportation policy and a national transportation system, not necessarily entirely publicly owned'. Both amendments were defeated, and the government's bill was approved; the following morning, the railwaymen went back to work. The transportation service was restored, but the Liberal Party's image was tarnished in the eyes of many trade-union leaders.

Having resolved the transportation crisis, members of Parliament went on to other topics. Pearson and Claxton reported on the Korean crisis, the Minister of National Defence outlining measures to recruit 15,000 volunteers in order to contribute a brigade to the United Nations force; Finance Minister Abbott introduced a new budget, increasing taxes on corporation profits and many consumer goods, in order to provide an additional $300 million for defence expenditures. Drew denounced the government for having allowed the country's defences to fall to such a low state of preparedness. Davie Fulton argued that Canada's defence was 'a national obligation which should be distributed equally and fairly among all the people', and demanded legislation to 'raise such forces as would be necessary by the most effective and equitable means'. While he did not mention the words, his remarks could be summed up in Mackenzie King's World War II formula – 'conscription if necessary'. While some English-language newspapers condemned the government's proposal to recruit 15,000 volunteers for service in Korea as picayune, many French-speaking Canadians considered the figure too high. Pointing out that the Prime Minister had said that the Canadian brigade would be composed of only 5,000 men, *Le Devoir* journalist Pierre Laporte accused him of deceiving the public, and he asked, 'Are we to return to the era of Mr. King's lies?' St. Laurent denied the charge indignantly, and explained that there was a difference between the size of a brigade and the total number of men that had to be assembled to provide reinforcements and supporting services. The tenseness and impatience that marked his attempts at negotiating a settlement of the railway strike remained until the adjournment of Parliament on September 15.

Other tests of the Prime Minister's patience were soon to come. On September 25, he met with the premiers in Quebec City in a further attempt to obtain agreement on a formula to amend the constitution in Canada. A standing committee had met in August to try to divide the different clauses of the B.N.A. Act into the six categories recognized by the government leaders at their previous session. They agreed on the classification of 96 out of 147 clauses, and exchanged views concerning the remainder. Legal advisers in the Department of Justice incorporated the partial agreement into a new draft of the constitution, but the cabinet was reluctant to produce it at the conference for fear of being accused once again of trying to impose a formula on the provinces. It was preferable to postpone the whole project, they decided, than to risk an open conflict with the provinces at a time when negotiations for a new series of financial agreements were about to begin. In opening the second session of the constitutional conference, St. Laurent reminded delegates that their ultimate goal was 'to write a new constitution . . . that will be in appearance as well as in effect a truly Canadian document', but, since agreement on a specific formula seemed impossible for the moment, he feared that all they could do for the time being would be to devise 'some method whereby we can, without prejudicing any of the interests that require to be respected, make such amendments from time to time to our constitutional documents as circumstances may require'. In a conciliatory gesture towards Duplessis, he remarked that, whether the B.N.A. Act was founded on 'a compact or on some other basis', a new constitution would be in fact a compact, since it would be based upon 'agreements between the federal government and the ten Canadian provinces'. He also raised the possibility of 'entrenching the rights of the inhabitants of the several provinces in the composition of the central organ', or, in other words, of authorizing the federal government to ensure that human rights were respected.

The speeches of the premiers justified the federal government's scepticism, and St. Laurent's decision to set such modest objectives. T. C. Douglas stated 'emphatically' that he would not agree to entrenching behind a provincial veto the portions of section 92 of the B.N.A. Act concerning 'property and civil rights', and 'generally all matters of a merely local or private nature in the province'. Duplessis declared that he wished to co-operate 'in a friendly way on a fundamental, unchangeable basis'; the rub was that his 'unchangeable basis' was the very one that the Saskatchewan Premier rejected 'emphatically'. Inevitably, the four days of discussion resulted only in an innocuous press release, plus a statement by St. Laurent that there had been 'full and frank discussions' which would be continued by correspondence between the attorneys general. A third session was arranged to follow the federal-provincial conference on fiscal matters scheduled for early December. The negotiations ended on a cordial note; while the meeting was barren of concrete results, St. Laurent had at least the satisfaction of knowing that national unity had not been damaged by intemperate outbursts.

While the negotiations with the provinces were of concern to St. Laurent during the closing months of 1950, they took second place to the international situation. By mid-September General Douglas MacArthur, the commander of the United Nations forces in Korea, had succeeded in turning the tide of battle, and in early October South Korean troops crossed the 38th parallel in pursuit of the retreating enemy. The Canadian government took the position that the United Nations action must not be limited to stopping the fighting, but that a new attempt should be made to unify the country and to hold free elections, the policy that

Mackenzie King had rejected so categorically three years earlier. Backed by a General Assembly resolution 'that all appropriate steps be taken to ensure conditions of stability throughout Korea', MacArthur sent the United Nations troops over the 38th parallel on October 9; a week later, they found themselves doing battle with Chinese units. Since Peking was presumed to be acting with Soviet backing, a major conflict became once more a serious possibility.

With their offices just a few doors apart on the second floor of the East Block, St. Laurent and Pearson met frequently, going over the voluminous dispatches received from other parts of the world, and working out the Canadian policy together. While the Prime Minister allowed Pearson an unusual amount of freedom of action, the Secretary of State for External Affairs never abused that confidence, keeping his superior closely informed of all developments, discussing his ideas with him, and obtaining his approval for any significant initiatives. To ensure public support for the new policies, St. Laurent spoke frequently to groups of Canadians on the new situation. 'We must step up the insurance premium [to maintain peace],' he told a group of underwriters on October 6. '. . . If the worst comes to the worst, and we do not succeed, it will not matter how much we might have saved by skimping.' The Korean 'incident' had proved once again the need to put teeth into the United Nations Organization, he declared, and the Canadian Special Force being trained for action in Korea would remain available for possible future service with the world body. Although he was firm in his insistence that aggression must be resisted, he remained anxious to reduce international tensions, and to bridge the gap between the Communist and non-Communist parts of the world. During a visit to the United Nations in New York in mid-November, he had a chat with Soviet delegate Jacob Malik, and told him that he accepted at face value Moscow's assertion that the people of Russia wanted peace. Few people in the West were prepared to make such an optimistic statement of faith in their fellow men behind the Iron Curtain.

That was the atmosphere when the premiers arrived in Ottawa in early December to negotiate a new set of financial agreements. Instead of the spectre of unemployment that had raised its head the previous winter, Canada's economy was again on a war footing, and the major problem was the scarcity of materials and manpower, resulting in rapidly rising prices. As a consequence, the federal government's system of priorities had to be revised, and the program of economic growth and social security extended over a longer period. 'Unhappily today our main preoccupation is not and cannot be with the maintenance and expansion of prosperity and security within our country, though these continue to be our constant objectives,' St. Laurent stated in his opening remarks at the federal-provincial conference on December 4: 'Our main preoccupation is for the security of our country and its people.' In 1945, the federal government had laid before the provincial premiers 'a comprehensive, integrated series of proposals', but Canada was now faced with 'an entirely new perspective', and it seemed more profitable to 'proceed step by step, discussing the more urgent problems first and endeavouring to work out suitable understandings and arrangements as we go along'. In some fields unanimous agreements between Ottawa and the provinces might be necessary, but in other fields 'something less than universal agreement may be sufficient'.

St. Laurent proposed that the tax rental agreements be renewed for a further five-year period, and that the guaranteed minimum revenues of provinces be increased by some 50 per cent to correspond to the increase in the nation's production and population since World War II. He also announced that the federal government was prepared to establish, in accordance with a recommendation made by a joint committee of the Senate and House of Commons at the previous session of Parliament, a federally financed old-age pension of forty dollars per month for all persons seventy years of age or over; in addition, Ottawa would share the cost of pensions of the same amount for persons in need between the ages of sixty-five and seventy. Implementation of the plan, however, would depend on the unanimous agreement of the provinces, he warned, since the constitution would have to be amended to authorize the federal government to legislate in the first instance, and provincial participation was required in the second one. Inherent in the proposal was the implication that Ottawa had a responsibility to act in areas of national importance, even if they had been assigned to the provinces by the Fathers of Confederation. St. Laurent declared:

> While the federal Government has always recognized and respected the primary constitutional responsibility of the provincial and local authorities in the field of health, and while we certainly have no desire to change that situation, we have recognized the national interest in the promotion of the health of the Canadian people and we have tried to co-operate in a substantial and practical fashion with the provincial authorities.

The negotiations were much less difficult than anticipated. To emphasize the gravity of the international crisis, Pearson addressed the delegates, and warned bluntly that, if the fighting in Asia were to spread to the Chinese province of Manchuria, it was quite possible that a full-scale war with Communist China might result. Claxton followed with an outline of Canada's new defence effort, and Abbott presented, in St. Laurent's words, 'the financial and economic implications of this very gloomy picture'. Leading off for the premiers, Leslie Frost proved himself a model of conciliation and understanding. Even Duplessis, after some introductory remarks such as 'centralization of power engenders autocracy and tyranny', was surprisingly co-operative, even agreeing to a constitutional amendment to authorize Ottawa to set up the proposed universal pension plan.

In view of the more cordial atmosphere, observers began to speculate about a possible *détente* in the struggle between the federal and Quebec governments. In previous weeks, the Union Nationale leader had displayed a desire for more amicable relations, and St. Laurent had grasped eagerly at the hand outstretched, albeit uncertainly, in his direction. Communications between them, and between the spokesmen of the two governments, underwent a notable improvement in tone. In practical terms, however, the change in attitude remained relatively unimportant. While he accepted the pension plan, Duplessis continued to insist that provincial governments should raise their own taxes instead of receiving payments from Ottawa. He was the only premier to refuse to sign a new tax-sharing agreement.

As soon as the premiers had left the capital, St. Laurent returned to his preoccupation with international affairs. Prime Minister Clement Attlee spent a week-end in Ottawa following discussions with President Truman, and brought the welcome news that the Americans hoped it would not be necessary to use the atomic bomb in the Korean War. Also raised during the British statesman's visit was the agenda of the Commonwealth Conference that had been called for early in 1951. The continuing cold war, and particularly the fighting in Korea, had put a strain on relations between the older members of the Commonwealth and the newer ones, particularly India. While he had endorsed the initial United Nations intervention six months earlier to stop aggression, Nehru had disapproved of ordering troops across the 38th parallel, and was alarmed lest the conflict turn into a full-scale war between Asia and the West. Attlee and St. Laurent shared the Indian Prime Minister's view that while it might be desirable to unite Korea under a single democratically chosen government, the most important thing was to halt the fighting before it took on still more serious proportions. They were also concerned over indications that the United States was paying little more than lip-service to the international character of the United Nations operation in Korea, a fact that was not particularly surprising since the Americans were standing virtually alone with the South Koreans against the Communists; the Canadian brigade was not to go into action until February 1951.

The only serious difference of view between the British and Canadian leaders concerned the most effective way of using the Commonwealth to promote peace and international co-operation. Attlee argued that more formal structures were required, and that a common policy should be adopted by all members of the Commonwealth whenever possible. St. Laurent continued to insist that the greatest value of the Commonwealth was as a bridge between democratic nations in different parts of the world, and a vehicle to reduce misunderstandings between them. The mere impression of attempting to interfere with the right of member nations to determine their own policies on particular issues, he pointed out, would reduce the usefulness of the organization.

Shortly before he left for London in an R.C.A.F. North Star aircraft on December 31, St. Laurent reiterated his confidence in the future. 'I have said a good many times since I became Prime Minister that I did not expect to live long enough to see another world war,' he told a press conference buoyantly the previous day, 'and I have not changed my mind'. To prove his point, he noted jokingly that Lloyds of London was offering odds of fifty to one that there would be no war in 1951. In an address to the Canadian Club of London on January 8, he repeated the views on the Commonwealth that he had outlined to Attlee in Ottawa, declaring that:

> The Commonwealth will survive only if we do not try to force too much integration on it. . . . Since it has no central organs of government, there can, of course, be no such thing as a Commonwealth policy as such, though there can be, and most often is, identity of policies among the nations of the Commonwealth.

Community of action by members would be assured in 'all matters of great moment' as long as they shared the same aims, ideals, and interests; if they did not, no formal machinery could make that possible. Under such conditions, there could be no conflict between membership in the Commonwealth and in the United Nations. In fact, he argued, 'I think one would be justified in saying that membership in the Commonwealth tends to fortify our loyalty to the United Nations and to strengthen our support of its fundamental objectives.'

Throughout the ten-day meeting, St. Laurent maintained the same calm, pragmatic approach that he displayed in the Council Chamber in Ottawa. Listening carefully to the views of the other participants, he intervened relatively seldom in the discussions, usually limiting his contributions to clarifying points of detail, or making a specific proposal when he felt a consensus had been established. While his constructive attitude won him respect and admiration, he remained a somewhat remote person to the other prime ministers, who were surprised to find a man of Gallic ancestry cloaked in an appearance of Edwardian reserve. They were interested to hear him, the only Roman Catholic in the group, declare that peaceful co-existence with the Communists was not only possible but essential to the future of mankind. While the Korean War dominated the discussions, many other topics were examined as well, including peace treaties with Japan and Germany, the continuing tension in the Middle East, possible conditions of British entry into a European union, and economic co-operation through the Colombo Plan.

Notably absent from the list was an issue of critical importance to India and Pakistan, the dispute over Kashmir. While the Prime Minister of Pakistan, Liaquat Ali Khan, was anxious to have the question discussed, Nehru refused, and made it clear that he would strongly resent any pressure to change his position. St. Laurent argued against raising the sensitive issue, not because of the merits of the Indian case, but because he felt that more harm than good would be done by forcing Nehru's hand. He did agree to a private and informal discussion of the subject, but withdrew even from that attempt to find a solution as soon as it became evident that no progress was possible. The final communiqué did not mention the topic. With that exception, a considerable degree of unanimity was attained. The prime ministers announced a set of principles for Commonwealth co-operation along the lines enunciated by St. Laurent during Attlee's visit to Ottawa, and urged the conclusion of a peace treaty with Japan, a negotiated peace in Korea, and the establishment of machinery for economic co-operation. A similar measure of agreement was not to be reached again in the immediately succeeding years.

Following the conference, St. Laurent crossed the English Channel for a two-day visit to France. The brief stay in the French capital bore little resemblance to earlier occasions when he had acted as tourist guide for members of his family. As head of the Canadian government, he was the guest of honour at dinners offered by President Vincent Auriol, Prime Minister René Pleven, and Foreign Minister Robert Schuman; he also laid a wreath at the base of the Arc de Triomphe, and attended Sunday mass at Notre Dame Cathedral.

One of the reasons that the trip to the Continent was so short was that St. Laurent no longer enjoyed travelling abroad, and derived little pleasure from the round of official functions associated with the movements of a head of government. He noted with satisfaction the compliments paid to Canada, but felt that those paid to himself were usually highly exaggerated. Entirely absorbed in his public responsibilities, he could seldom be persuaded to go to the theatre, and never to visit an art gallery or a museum. The call of duty was like a magnet drawing him back to Canada, and as soon as possible he ordered the R.C.A.F. crew to fly him home.

Less than two weeks remained from the time St. Laurent arrived in Ottawa until the 1951 session of Parliament was due to begin, and many policy decisions had to be taken before the Throne Speech could be delivered. The United States Congress was still blocking the St. Lawrence seaway project, and Canadians were becoming increasingly impatient with the delay. In the autumn of 1950, St. Laurent had decided that the time had come to force the issue, and had instructed Transport Minister Chevrier to make a series of speeches to prepare public opinion for an all-Canadian seaway. If the Americans reacted in time, he reasoned, then a joint venture would still be possible; if not, they would have had ample warning, and the national pride of Canadians would have been stirred sufficiently to accept the total financial burden of the enterprise.

Another topic of increasing urgency was government assistance to higher education. The National Conference of Canadian Universities had gone on record as favouring federal aid to university education. Education was clearly a field of provincial jurisdiction, but, on the other hand, adequate university training was a matter of vital importance to all of Canada, and the federal government had a direct interest in it, since many of its programs, not the least of them in the field of defence, depended on the availability of competent personnel. The Massey Commission, which was preparing its report, was expected to have some recommendations on that subject. There was also growing public interest in a Canadian bill of rights, but, once again, that was an area of provincial responsibility, and it was difficult to devise a formula that would take into account both the national interest and provincial rights. In western Canada, a demand was growing for a huge irrigation and power project on the South Saskatchewan River. Agriculture Minister Gardiner was one of the dam's most enthusiastic sponsors, and in November 1949 the Prairie Farm Rehabilitation Administration, a branch of his department, had published a booklet in which a specific site was proposed, and the cost estimated at around $66 million.

A further subject that demanded St. Laurent's attention in early 1951 was the nomination of a replacement for Governor General Alexander, whose term of duty in Canada was drawing to a close. He himself had long favoured the appointment of a Canadian to the post, but he was anxious to avoid a split in public opinion, and followed with interest the periodic Gallup polls on the subject. A sounding taken in March 1950 indicated that 45 per cent of the population favoured the appointment of a Canadian, while only 22 per cent preferred another governor general from the United Kingdom. The principal difficulty was to find a candidate who would bring the necessary authority and prestige to the high post. Among other names, that of St. Laurent was mentioned frequently in newspaper speculation, but he had no taste for the ceremonial functions of a titular head of state. In July 1950, a *Le Devoir* editorialist suggested that Vincent Massey would make a suitable occupant of the office; St. Laurent noted the suggestion with interest; it was not often that the Quebec nationalist newspaper endorsed an English-speaking Canadian.

The Korean War and its consequences dominated the third session of the twenty-first Parliament. George Drew launched a two-pronged attack on the government for Canada's low state of preparedness when the fighting in Korea erupted, and for the inflation that had accompanied the scurry to redress the situation. He urged 'a clarion call to service' in view of the serious international situation. Implicit but unspecified in the opposition leader's appeal was the mobilization of Canadian manpower. President Truman had reintroduced compulsory military service in the United States some months earlier, and many Canadians, including military leaders, felt that at least a system of national registration should be introduced, so that men could be called up quickly if conscription became necessary.

Speaking in the House of Commons on his sixty-ninth birthday,

Louis St. Laurent and the Right Honourable Vincent Massey on the occasion of the presentation of the report of Royal Commission on the Arts, Letters and Sciences; Prime Minister's Office, Ottawa, August 9, 1951.

Louis St. Laurent welcoming the Right Honourable Winston Churchill
to Ottawa, January 1952. Between the two men: J. W. Pickersgill.

Louis St. Laurent and
Jawaharlal Nehru; New
Delhi, February 1954.

St. Laurent sought to allay fears of a general conflict, insisting that in his view Canadians would 'not have to indulge in a third catastrophic world war'. Tackling directly the question of conscription, he declared that it was not a matter that should be decided on sentimental grounds. 'Let us be men,' he challenged, 'and let us face realities and do what we think will be the most efficient and the most effective as our contribution to the upbuilding of those international forces.' So far, there was no evidence that conscription was required, he declared, but, if the situation changed, then the government's policy would have to change accordingly, but 'those changes will not be recommended by this government on any sentimental grounds because of any appeals on a racial or religious basis, but on their actual effective value'. The important statement of policy was a far cry from Mackenzie King's position – 'conscription if necessary, but not necessarily conscription'. When Social Credit leader Solon Low advocated 'a complete program of preparedness including compulsory training in the reserve forces for home defence', both Conservative and C.C.F. members joined with the Liberals to defeat the proposal.

The official opposition chose as its fighting-ground the government's proposals to create a new Department of Defence Production under Howe's direction and to enact emergency powers legislation. The two items held out the possibility of baiting C. D. Howe and charging him again with trying to assume dictatorial powers. St. Laurent himself introduced both measures, and did so in as conciliatory a tone as possible. The emergency powers bill was designed to ensure that Parliament was informed immediately of all action taken under its terms, he emphasized, thus affording an opportunity to examine and even rescind such action if that was considered necessary. 'The policy of the government will be not to do anything of major importance without coming to Parliament, and declaring that it is its view that it should be done, and allowing Parliament to disagree with the government if it finds that its policy is not the proper one.' Furthermore, the legislation would expire in a little over a year, and could only be renewed by Parliament after having been debated. The reassurances failed to impress Drew and his followers, the Tory chieftain calling for 'a truly democratic bill' that spelled out more specifically the government's intentions. While he failed to provoke the Prime Minister, he was more successful with C. D. Howe, and the Minister of Trade and Commerce snapped back at his opponent like a huge bear at bay.

Unknown to the general public, a disagreement occurred in March 1951 that set St. Laurent and Howe one against the other in their most serious clash, and threatened to disrupt the cabinet. Under the terms of a wheat agreement signed by Canada and the United Kingdom in 1946, the British were given an option to buy Canadian wheat below the world price, the Canadians hoping in that way to create a reserve of good will in the mother country, for the time when competition became tougher once again; moreover, the purchases of wheat were to be made with part of the billion-and-a-quarter-dollar loan made to Britain after World War II at the below-cost rate of 2 per cent interest. The lower price for wheat had not been easy for Agriculture Minister Gardiner to explain to western farmers, but he had made much of the fact that the Canadians were displaying their loyalty to the mother country, and were also assuring their economic future. Thus, when the British government decided, as was its legal right, not to use the last $65 million available under the loan to purchase wheat as had been expected, he felt betrayed. As the minister responsible for wheat marketing, Howe was not pleased with the British attitude either, but, accustomed to handling multi-million-dollar contracts, he was not prepared to make an issue of it. When Gardiner insisted that pressure be brought on the British government to change its decision, the two senior ministers clashed openly in the Council Chamber. St. Laurent shared Gardiner's sentiment of indignation, but he also shared Howe's feeling of proud independence, and was not prepared to plead with the British for special treatment. Finally, the cabinet agreed to let the Minister of Agriculture fly to England, and try to persuade the Attlee administration to recant; Howe refused scornfully to be associated in any way with the attempt.

Gardiner made his trip in mid-February, and failed completely. On his return, he asked the cabinet to approve the payment to western farmers of $65 million out of the federal treasury as compensation for their losses over the previous five years through selling wheat under the terms of the agreement with Britain. Howe opposed the suggestion. This time, St. Laurent sided with the Minister of Agriculture, pointing out that western farmers had been led to believe by a member of the government that certain marketing conditions had been secured, and that even if the British changed their minds, that did not cancel the cabinet's responsibility in the matter. With farmers' organizations and opposition party members calling for some form of government action, he endorsed a recommendation to add $65 million to the payments made over the previous five years. When the Minister of Trade and Commerce refused to be associated with the plan, St. Laurent declared that he would present it himself in the House of Commons.

The other ministers observed the confrontation with tense interest, realizing that the outcome might well determine the government's future; the Prime Minister had imposed his will on lesser colleagues, and even scolded them on occasion, but he had not previously asserted his authority over the strong-minded 'general manager' of the Canadian economy. If Howe refused to give way, his resignation seemed inevitable; if St. Laurent ceded, his prestige would be seriously affected. In the end, the Minister of Trade and Commerce rose above his personal feelings and acknowledged the Prime Minister's authority; a man who respected firmness and recognized the need for discipline, he could disagree with his leader's viewpoint and still follow him if he was convinced that the leadership was wise and competent on the whole. St. Laurent's and Howe's mutual regard was enhanced rather than diminished as a result of the clash, but relations between Gardiner and Howe were to remain strained for some time.

Always stimulated by a crisis, St. Laurent made a succinct and forceful statement of the government's policy in the House of Commons on March 15, denying publicly that the United Kingdom government had failed to carry out its legal obligations, but agreeing that Canadian wheat growers had 'understandable grounds' for expecting that further purchases would be made. The proposal was adopted, but not before the government was berated simultaneously for letting down the farmers, and, in

Drew's words, for sacrificing to political expediency, 'the good will between the two most important nations in the Commonwealth'.

Outside Parliament, the Canadian political scene was marked in the early months of 1951 by a noticeable *détente* in relations between the federal and Quebec governments. Although he had refused to sign a fiscal agreement with Ottawa, Maurice Duplessis refrained from his customary attacks on the St. Laurent administration. At the beginning of the year, he named Renault St. Laurent a King's Counsel, and made the decision the occasion of a special statement to the press; the St. Laurents were not informed in advance of the appointment. In addition, Renault was named an aide-de-camp to the Lieutenant-Governor. Shortly afterwards, the Quebec Premier told newspapermen that, since St. Laurent had become Prime Minister, 'we find . . . [in Ottawa] a spirit of cordiality and comprehension that did not exist previously'. For his part, St. Laurent added unwittingly to the impression of better relations by declaring in a speech in the House of Commons, in which he vaunted the role of free enterprise in developing Canada's resources, that the Quebec government was to be congratulated for making an agreement with U.S. financial interests to develop the iron-ore reserves of Labrador. On March 17, a correspondent for *Le Devoir* wrote of 'the non-aggression pact' between the two French-Canadian political leaders. One of the most important results of the new political climate was unanimous agreement by the provinces to amend the B.N.A. Act and make possible federal legislation to create a universal old-age pension scheme. Thus the old people of Canada were the first direct beneficiaries of the improved relations between Ottawa and Quebec.

While the indications of improved relations between Ottawa and Quebec City were heartening to most people, they proved embarrassing to the new Liberal leader in Quebec, Georges Emile Lapalme. A former member of Parliament, he was described by Union Nationale partisans as a 'travelling salesman' for the Ottawa administration; now, to add insult to injury, it was said that relations between the two capitals were so good that he was superfluous even in that role! A highly sensitive man, he complained to St. Laurent about the invidious position in which he found himself. To placate him, and to still rumours of a split between them, St. Laurent took advantage of a visit to the Montreal Reform Club in April to declare that 'the so-called St. Laurent–Duplessis axis . . . lacks even the appearance of solidity of a certain bridge we have heard all about'. The reference to a bridge under construction at Trois-Rivières that was to bear the Premier's name, but which had collapsed a short time earlier, was highly appreciated by the partisan audience. The Union Nationale leader found it less amusing.

At the insistence of his family, St. Laurent took advantage of the Easter recess of Parliament to fly to Bermuda for a week; on his return, he and his wife moved into the new prime minister's residence, on Sussex Street. However, Jeanne St. Laurent was determined not to close the house on Grande Allée, even if it meant supervising two households. 'My home,' she told a newspaperman firmly, 'is here in Quebec.' In order to help her pass the time in the capital, friends furnished a basement room in the prime minister's residence as a card room, and a small sitting-room that formed part of the prime minister's suite in the Centre Block continued to be reserved for her as well. The only change in St. Laurent's life as a result of the move was that he had to be driven to and from work by a chauffeur instead of walking the short distance from his apartment building; his work schedule remained the same.

The universal pension legislation was approved in early June with a degree of unanimity that was in stark contrast to many other debates. The opposition parties continued their harassment of the government, and of Howe in particular, and succeeded in badgering him into outbursts that seemed to confirm the charges of arrogance and disrespect for Parliament. During a debate on a new set of trade agreements, the Progressive Conservative member Howard Green complained that the system of Commonwealth preferential tariffs was being systematically whittled away, and remarked that he was 'not too sure that this government would not do away with the preferences entirely if they felt they could get away with it so far as the public was concerned'. His patience exhausted, the Minister of Trade and Commerce interjected: 'Who would stop us? Don't take yourself too seriously. If we wanted to get away with it, who would stop us?' 'That is just typical of the Minister,' Green retorted; 'if he wanted to get away with anything who would stop him? I tell him he is not yet the dictator of this country.' In making his remark, Howe was merely reminding his opponent that the government had received a nearly five-to-one majority over his party at the polls, and that the Conservatives could not impose their will on such a Parliament; nevertheless, the ill-chosen words were to become a nail in the Liberal coffin. A month later, one member complained of the high costs of administering the new Department of Defence Production; Howe replied that, to operate a department with eleven hundred people for a year and do over a billion dollars' worth of business, 'three million dollars is not exorbitant'. An opposition member paraphrased his remarks later as, 'What's a million?' He had not used the words, but they too became permanently associated with his name.

Shortly before the session ended at the end of June, Drew provoked another storm by accusing C. D. Howe of according government contracts to his 'family company'. Howe explained that since he entered politics in 1935, he had had no connections with the firm bearing his name, but that his son and son-in-law had entered it in recent years as two of the team of fifty engineers. He had given some work to the company because no other firm could carry out the tasks, and because it was 'the right thing to do'. Intervening in the discussion, St. Laurent recalled indignantly that the Leader of the Opposition had made a similar insinuation of wrongdoing because the legal firm of St. Laurent, Gagné and St. Laurent had acted as solicitors for a company in Quebec City that had built ships for the government. He challenged Drew to make a specific charge 'in a manly way' so that it could be properly investigated by a House committee. The Conservative chieftain replied that he was not 'as cowardly as the Prime Minister' had proved to be in failing to curb his powerful minister. In the ensuing exchange, Drew insisted that St. Laurent had used the words 'lack of courage'; indignantly each man demanded that the other withdraw the insulting expressions; only on the following day did they do so. Tempers remained at the danger point for two more days, but, as the session was about to end on June 30, Drew rose to the occasion, and admitted that he had used a 'both unparliamentary and inappropriate' expression. St. Laurent replied in his most gracious tone that 'the addition of a little spice to the proceedings of the House does no permanent harm to the tradition of parliamentary institutions'. The session ended on a cordial note.

While the government had cause for satisfaction at the legislation that had been approved, political storm-warnings had appeared as well. On June 25, the Conservatives had won all of four by-elections, three of them in constituencies formerly held by Liberals.* Canadians were evidently becoming restless under the high taxes, rising prices, and shortages resulting from the Korean War, and were responding to opposition charges of arrogance and heavy-handedness. In the contest in Brandon, the intervention of John Diefenbaker had been decisive. A short time earlier, it had been learned that some Canadian-built ships owned by a Hong Kong firm but registered in Canada, and still not completely paid for, had fallen into the hands of the Communist régime in Peking. The Conservatives had demanded that the ships be seized, but even they could suggest no way of seizing them. The prairie lawyer conjured up a picture of the ships flying the Canadian flag, but manned by Red sailors singing 'Our Home and Native Land', while carrying supplies to kill Canadian soldiers in Korea. 'Mr. Howe says we have a lot of money invested in these ships,' he declared, 'but when we criticized another expenditure he said "What's a million dollars?"' It was effective politics, and helped the Progressive Conservative Party to win the seat.

For the first time since entering public life, St. Laurent took a month-long holiday in July. When he arrived in St. Patrick, his family noticed that he was showing the strain of his heavy schedule, and they recalled his statement to Mackenzie King that he would not want to continue in office after he was seventy years old.

*The constituencies: Brandon, Manitoba; Winnipeg South Centre, Manitoba; Waterloo South, Ontario; Queen's, P.E.I.

He would reach that milestone in February, he was reminded, and if he was going to step down in time to give his successor a chance to establish himself as prime minister before another election, he would have to announce his retirement soon. Some members of the family also resented the suggestion that he was being pushed around by Howe, and the personal nature of many opposition criticisms; they sought to protect him from such attacks in the only way possible, by having him withdraw from public life. He had done his share, St. Laurent heard over and over; it was time to return home. On July 16, the Toronto *Telegram* gave the first indication that the campaign was succeeding when it reported that he had had his fill of politics, and was determined to retire in 1952. The story was picked up by other newspapers and carried right across the country. The reaction of Liberals to the news report ranged from disbelief to near-panic. Despite recent setbacks, a Gallup poll in July indicated that 50 per cent of the voters were still favourable to the government, and that the Prime Minister's personal prestige was undiminished. The speculation concerning a possible successor did not reassure the government's supporters; Howe was the most logical choice, at least on an interim basis, but he had become increasingly a target of opposition attack, and his political ability was questioned. There was a whole series of competent younger cabinet ministers, but none with comparable prestige, and, above all, none that could be sure of keeping Quebec in the Liberal fold. The flurry of speculation permitted at least a partial assessment of St. Laurent's career up to that moment. Most of the remarks were highly favourable, even the Conservative *Ottawa Journal* declaring, 'he has been, in truth, a Prime Minister of whom the Canadian people could be proud.' Bruce Hutchison described him as 'our most successful politician mainly because the nation saw him as a man above politics.'

By the time St. Laurent returned to Ottawa at the end of July, he was feeling fit and full of energy once again, and left almost immediately on a trip to western Canada. At a series of picnics to celebrate the fiftieth anniversary of the arrival of the first wave of Ukrainian immigrants to Canada, and on a leisurely automobile trip from Edmonton to Prince Albert, Saskatchewan, where his sister, Sister Maria Teresa,* was principal of a Roman Catholic girls' school, he displayed the same relaxed confidence and vigour that he had shown in the summer following the 1949 election campaign. While he was not susceptible to flattery, he was pleased to note that so many Canadians felt his efforts on their behalf were worth while, and that they wanted him to continue; for his own part, the challenge of the wide variety of problems awaiting his attention attracted him, and he was convinced that it was the most useful way of spending his time and energy.

There was a further factor that influenced him in making his decision: the prestige of the government was evidently slipping, and to leave at such a time would create the impression that he was abandoning a sinking ship; he would not have it said that he had shirked his duty. On September 6, he issued a written statement referring indirectly to the speculation about his possible retirement. 'A distinguished journalist has commented that I am content to do the day's job and leave to the future the things that have to be done then,' he observed. The question of his retirement was 'still a matter for the future, and when the proper time does come, I will make my decision and announce it myself'. The family would have to wait a while longer for him to return to them.

*Baptized Kathleen.

# 11

## Extended Mandate

The principal problem facing the Canadian government in the autumn of 1951 was to reconcile the expensive military defence effort with demands for expenditures in other sectors. On July 10, cease-fire talks had begun in Korea, but they seemed likely to be long and difficult, and in the meantime the fighting continued. In Europe, the North Atlantic Treaty Organization was operating successfully, but the cost was high. Louis St. Laurent assured the Canadian people in a radio broadcast in early September that he and his colleagues were well aware of the problem of rising prices and scarcity of materials, but it was impossible to impose price controls in peace-time without introducing a system of government subsidies. As for reducing the military budget, he was convinced that Canadians wanted to do their share 'to prevent war and to keep this country the right kind of a country for our children and our grandchildren to live in, and they don't want us to scrimp on defence'. When the costliness of certain defence measures was mentioned during a meeting of the defence committee of the cabinet, he leaned back in his chair and declared in an even tone, 'Well, we will do what we consider to be our duty, and the Canadian people can decide if they want to follow us.'

One of the most heart-rending communications he received about the international situation came from a French-speaking soldier with the famous Royal 22nd Regiment in Korea. 'Why so much suffering, so much privation of every sort?' the young man wrote from a camp near the battlefront. 'Why die? For the cause? What cause? . . . Reassure me, Monsieur, I beg of you. . . .' Touched by the appeal, St. Laurent answered at length. He knew of the suffering and hardship that Canada's soldiers were experiencing to defend a way of life and a degree of liberty that were so dear to the free world, he replied, and no one had attacked the Communists as long as they stayed at home. 'We want peace and we respect the freedom of choice between our ideology and others', but we want to show the Communists that it does not pay to resort to force if they decide that freedom of choice is not enough to serve their cause.' 'Be assured, my dear fellow citizen,' he concluded, 'that each in his own way, you as a soldier, and I as Prime Minister, we are working together to ensure a better future for all free peoples in a world at peace.' Less than two months later the young man was killed.

With Parliament due to meet again in October, the government was anxious to announce that a start would soon be made on the St. Lawrence seaway and power project. In conversations with Premier Frost during the summer, St. Laurent had been impressed by the growing need in Ontario for further electrical power, and acknowledged that if the Americans did not agree soon to participate Canada would have to go ahead alone. On September 28, he flew to Washington to discuss the situation with President Truman. Unless the hydro-development aspect of the project was begun soon, Ontario would have to build steam plants to meet its immediate needs, he told the American leader. However, that would be only a palliative, and the Canadian and Ontario governments had already agreed on a cost-sharing formula to harness the resources of the St. Lawrence River. Opposition to the project had almost vanished in Canada, and public opinion would support an all-Canadian seaway and power project; while that was not the most rational solution, further delay would be more expensive than unilateral action. Once again, Truman recalled that he had been favourable to the project for many years, and that he was doing his utmost to have it approved; at the same time, he understood the Canadian position, and if there was no other way of getting it built he would support a purely Canadian initiative. When St. Laurent met the Washington press corps he stated that he was not making a threat, and that he still preferred a joint undertaking, but the time had come for action in one way or another. His return home was marked by a bitter attack in the Toronto *Globe and Mail*, in which he was accused of refusing to stand up to Canada's neighbours because of 'the lure of Yankee dollars', and in order 'to save dollars which nobody asked him to save'. Chevrier's carefully planned campaign to stir up public support for the project was almost too successful, and threatened to boomerang.

The day before Parliament met, twenty-five-year-old Princess Elizabeth and her husband, the Duke of Edinburgh, landed at Montreal's Dorval Airport to begin a Canadian tour. St. Laurent welcomed them there, then rushed back to the capital, where they followed him two days later for a full schedule of engagements. While he did not know the Princess well, he admired the seriousness with which she was preparing to take her father's place; it was an example of devotion to duty that he had been taught to appreciate many years before.

The Speech from the Throne read by Lord Alexander was a positive document, forecasting the creation of a St. Lawrence seaway agency 'to proceed either with the Canadian share of an international undertaking or a solely Canadian development', a causeway over the Gut of Canso in Nova Scotia, an investigation by a royal commission to determine 'whether the economic and social returns to the Canadian people on the investment in the proposed South Saskatchewan River project would be commensurate with the cost', and the implementation of certain recommendations of the Massey Commission report that had been submitted to the government in June.

The session was lively but fruitful. The government tried to stem the criticism of defence expenditures by setting up a committee to give members an opportunity to assess the military budget more accurately. Legislation to create a St. Lawrence Seaway Authority was approved after only a short debate, St. Laurent repeating that United States participation would still be welcomed, but that Canada was not prepared to countenance further delays for that reason. While he continued to preach inside and outside Parliament his doctrine of a distinctive Canadianism, he had occasion to realize that his views in that regard were not yet accepted by all his fellow citizens. Some Progressive Conservative members protested against the policy of replacing the word 'Dominion' with 'Canada' whenever public documents were being revised, and accused the government of systematically cutting the ties with the United Kingdom. St. Laurent intervened in one exchange on November 8 to declare that 'there are some people who rather like the name of Canada', and to point out that 'that was the name given to the new nation by the British North America Act at the time it came into being.' The government took the view that most Canadians felt it was 'a privilege to be a Canadian citizen', he remarked, 'and are quite satisfied to be described as such instead of being described as citizens of a "dominion"'.

The government had planned to finish the session before Christmas, but it ran into strong opposition to a proposal to forbid price-fixing, or the establishment of minimum resale prices. The result of a special inquiry, and of hearings before a special committee of Parliament, the bill was a carefully conceived compromise between the viewpoints of consumers, concerned with rising prices, and manufacturers and retailers, anxious to avoid price controls. Sensing the government's delicate situation between the two groups, Drew accused the Liberals of a lack of courage for delaying action on the problem, but when Justice Minister Garson finally introduced the measure on December 17, Fulton rejected it as ill-considered and proposed a six-month postponement, which would have the effect of killing it. With Christmas only a few days off, members were anxious to leave for home and, on December 20, representatives of the smaller parties suggested extending the hours of sittings. Donald Fleming, however, condemned the suggestion as 'an attempt at applying closure' and challenged the government to 'have the courage to try to apply it'. St. Laurent rose to the bait, and declared heatedly that if the debate was not concluded that day, he intended to give notice that the closure rule would be invoked on December 27. By the time the House of Commons was called to order the following morning, the cabinet had realized that it was lending weight to the charges of autocratic behaviour, and the Prime Minister withdrew his notice of closure; instead, he announced a five-day Christmas recess to begin that evening. The debate resumed on December 27, and after a series of Conservative amendments were defeated, Chevrier finally proposed 'that the question be now put'. Fulton declared that closure was being applied after all 'to prevent the evidence in this matter from coming before the people'. The Conservatives having achieved their purpose, the debate was soon concluded, and members rushed out of the capital in time to spend New Year's Day in their constituencies.

One of the most encouraging developments at the year's end was an agreement with Duplessis to accept a program of federal aid to universities, as recommended by the Massey Commission. The other provinces had raised no objection to the measure, but when the subject was first broached to the Quebec Premier in November, he had denounced it as 'a dangerous usurpation by the federal government of powers reserved exclusively to the provinces', and warned that 'the problems of the universities cannot be solved by intrusions, even gilded ones.' Instead, he proposed that 5 per cent of the revenues from the personal income tax be turned over to the provinces. In an exchange of correspondence, St. Laurent replied that the law did not permit such payments to the provinces, and pointed out that $7 million had been approved by Parliament at the current session for university aid.* He urged Duplessis to accept a provisional arrangement for one year, 'without prejudice to the future', and proposed the creation of a joint committee that would work out a cost-sharing formula as had been done in allocating payments to victims of the Cabano and Rimouski fires a short time earlier. Duplessis accepted the suggestion on condition that the cheques should be accompanied by a certificate signed by representatives of both governments, and indicating that the payments were the result of a joint decision.

*The figure represented payments to universities at the rate of fifty cents per head of population, the amount for each institution to be proportionate to its share of the total student body.

One of St. Laurent's first important actions in 1952 was to recommend to the King the appointment of a new governor general. In the United Kingdom, seventy-seven-year-old Winston Churchill had made still another political comeback, and he wanted Lord Alexander to serve as Minister of Defence in his new cabinet. It was generally assumed that a Canadian would be selected, and speculation centred on the names of Vincent Massey, House of Commons Speaker Ross Macdonald, and General H. D. G. Crerar, but Massey was a clear favourite among both English-speaking and French-speaking Canadians. St. Laurent discussed the proposed change with Churchill when the latter visited Ottawa in early January, and Pearson called on the King to make the formal recommendation. His Majesty and the other members of his family were delighted at the prospect of being represented by a man whose qualities they had learned to appreciate when he was Canadian High Commissioner to London from 1935 to 1946. The Prime Minister made the formal request to Massey in a transatlantic telephone call to London, where the former diplomat was holidaying, and the appointment was announced on January 25. It was received with almost unanimous acclaim, only a few Canadians expressing regret that another tie was being severed with the mother country. St. Laurent expressed his own view at a press conference following the announcement. The King's choice of one of his Canadian subjects to represent him in Canada, he argued, would not weaken the attachment of other Canadians to the Crown. 'I think we should realize that some day we have to grow up and . . . there will be a time when it won't be necessary for us to have apron strings tied to those who have the responsibilities of responsible government.' The appointment of a Canadian as viceregal representative did not imply a firm rule that a Canadian must always be chosen in the future, he warned; it merely indicated that 'no one of the King's subjects, wherever he resides, should be considered unworthy to represent the King provided he has the personal qualities and a position in the community which are consonant with the dignity and responsibility of that office'.

The departure of what was probably the last non-Canadian governor general was a sad occasion in Ottawa, for Lord and Lady

Alexander had been among the most popular figures there. The famous Field Marshal's official relations with the Prime Minister and his other advisers were about perfect, combining the utmost circumspection in respecting St. Laurent's leadership of the government with occasional discreet suggestions, and a constant willingness to assist in making the business of running the country a success. Some of the most pleasant evenings spent by the St. Laurents in Ottawa were at small dinner parties in Rideau Hall. When Lord Alexander's six-year term of office came to a close, the Prime Minister called the first recorded meeting of the Canadian Privy Council, composed of members of both main political parties, as a final mark of appreciation. The departure of the Alexanders from Canada coincided with the succession of a new monarch. On February 6, King George VI died after a long period of poor health, and his daughter Elizabeth took his place on the throne.

As the winter of 1951-2 wore on, a feeling of fatigue and discouragement swept over the Prime Minister. The opposition parties maintained a steady stream of criticism after Parliament reassembled on February 28, and the problems facing the government seemed to increase rather than diminish. The economy was levelling off after the boom associated with the Korean crisis, and patches of unemployment were once again beginning to appear. In western Canada dissatisfaction increased as a result of a bad harvest and an outbreak of foot-and-mouth disease. Premiers Douglas and Duplessis were preparing for provincial elections, and while the C.C.F. leader demanded immediate action on the South Saskatchewan dam project, further aid to farmers, and emergency relief to flood victims in the southern part of the province, his Union Nationale counterpart announced a renewed struggle for 'fiscal independence from Ottawa', thus declaring at least a temporary suspension of the truce with the St. Laurent administration. In May, Norman Robertson returned to London as High Commissioner, and Pickersgill succeeded him as Clerk of the Privy Council and Secretary to the Cabinet. Through the shift in personnel, St. Laurent lost one of his most trusted advisers, for by transferring from the Prime Minister's Office to the Privy Council, Pickersgill disqualified himself from playing the role of political adviser in which he was so valuable. The Prime Minister found himself regretting that he had stated his intention to remain in office. One of his advisers suggested that the general election be held in the coming autumn, thus enabling the weary government leader to retire in 1953; however, the political situation hardly seemed propitious for the government. More important, St. Laurent disliked the idea of asking for another mandate, and then failing to carry it out. He put off the decision, and got on with more immediate matters.

The principal item of business during the session was the readjustment of representation in the House of Commons following the 1951 census. Always a sensitive topic, it gave rise on each occasion to charges that members of the party in power were attempting to reshape constituencies to their own advantage. As a means of putting an end to such practices, C. G. Power introduced a private bill calling for the creation of an independent commission, to modify the electoral map as necessary. The idea appealed to St. Laurent and most of his colleagues, and they examined it carefully; they also studied the possibility of forming ten separate commissions, one for each province. The only serious reservations were that any independent body should not be authorized to decide a matter of such vital concern to Parliament, and that any conclusions of a commission would have to be ratified by Parliament, thus making almost certain a lengthy debate in any case. St. Laurent agreed to put the whole matter before an all-party committee, and let the differences of viewpoint be hammered out there. In presenting to the House of Commons the resolution to create the parliamentary committee, he attempted to dissociate the executive branch of the government from the project, declaring that it was 'a responsibility placed by the constitution on Parliament generally'. He also stressed that he expected members to approach the task as individuals, and not according to their party affiliations. The only recommendations he made to the committee were that representation from any province should not be reduced by more than 15 per cent, that no province should have fewer members than one with a smaller population, and that a second constituency should be created in the Canadian northland. His aim in putting forward those conditions was to prevent Saskatchewan, a province with a decreasing population, from losing more than three seats, instead of the five it would lose under the existing legislation. George Drew demanded that the provinces be consulted on the proposed redistribution of seats in Parliament, but the government's proposal was accepted by the other parties and approved.

With six by-elections called for late May, George Drew put on an aggressive performance in the House of Commons; he repeated frequently his charge of 'dictatorship' and denounced Liberal back-benchers as 'rubber-stamps for the government'. The taunts stirred the Prime Minister out of his lethargy, and he lashed back at his opponent; Drew's attitude was reminiscent of 'performances and outbursts' when he first arrived in Parliament, St. Laurent declared heatedly, 'when it was the privilege of the honourable gentleman to lecture members of this house on the way in which the proceedings of this house should in his opinion be carried out, instead of being carried on as they have been in the long and somewhat fruitful years of the life of this house when the honourable gentleman was not a member of it.' Undeterred, Drew continued his attacks, proposing a royal commission to investigate 'organization and general efficiency of government administration', arguing against renewal of the Emergency Powers Act, and hammering on his theme of arrogance and inefficiency. On May 26, he received his reward when four of the six by-elections were won by Progressive Conservative candidates, two of them in seats held formerly by the Liberals. Two weeks later Premier Douglas defeated the Liberals in Saskatchewan by forty-two to eleven seats; the following day W. A. C. Bennett, a former Conservative, led the Social Credit Party to its first victory in British Columbia, virtually wiping out both the Liberal and the Progressive Conservative forces.* The only consolation for the federal Liberals was that none of the other parties seemed likely to crystallize the sentiment of dissatisfaction throughout the country around its own leader and program. The most significant, but unannounced, result of the Liberal setback

---

*Results of Saskatchewan election, June 11, 1952: C.C.F. 42; Liberals 11; Progressive Conservatives 0; Social Credit 0. Results of British Columbia election, June 12, 1952: Social Credit 19; C.C.F. 18; Liberals 6; Progressive Conservatives 4.

was that St. Laurent put out of his mind for the moment all thoughts of retirement; he would not abandon a sinking ship.

As usual, there was a flurry of activity at the end of the session as members prepared to return home for the summer. On June 17, the new federal-provincial tax-sharing agreements were approved after only a half-day debate, and without a formal vote. The redistribution bill had a rougher passage. Opposition members complained that Liberals had used their voting strength in the sub-committees assigned to deal with individual provinces to increase their chances at future elections. Drew complained that 'the law of the jungle' had been followed in several instances, and demanded a fresh start by a non-political commission. The Liberal majority defeated the proposal. The debate over the new electoral map for Saskatchewan was particularly acrimonious, since the constituency of Lake Centre, represented by John Diefenbaker, was one of the three seats eliminated in that province; it looked like a Liberal plot to get rid of a dangerous opponent. St. Laurent sat silently and ill at ease as the discussion went on about him, clinging to the position that the matter had to be decided by the members of Parliament, and that the government was only involved inasmuch as it had to propose legislation based on the committee report. When Donald Fleming challenged that argument, and called upon him to make a statement of the government's views on the whole matter, he repeated that 'it is the legislative branch of our constitutional set-up that has to do with the definition of the constituencies'. He urged members once again 'not to examine these different boundaries in the light of what they may do for Liberal prospects, Conservative prospects, C.C.F. prospects, or Social Credit prospects, but in the light of what they feel is the proper thing in view of their responsibilities to the public generally as well as to their own constituents'. They must not be influenced by any member of the cabinet in making their decisions, he told them, no matter how honest that minister's opinion may be. Ironically, in his determination to avoid even the appearance of interference by the government in reshaping the electoral map, he left his followers free to practise the very methods he condemned. In spite of his precautions, the government did not escape the charge of gerrymandering.

Another achievement during the 1952 session was the approval of a pension plan for members of Parliament. A proposal had been considered periodically over many years to give some measure of security to Canada's law-makers. It was a delicate matter, for citizens who were disappointed at the failure of Parliament to act on their own requests were bound to complain that members could find money for themselves but not for others. St. Laurent had serious reservations about the advisability of the step, fearing that some members would come to look upon their duties as a career rather than as an opportunity for service that implied a personal sacrifice. At the same time, he recognized that personal responsibilities made it impossible for many well-qualified Canadians to enter public life, and that the general quality of candidates was lowered as a result. Once convinced that action was required, he gave the plan his strong personal support, but made it clear that individual members were free to vote as they saw fit. Only three Conservatives opposed the measure. As anticipated, the public reaction was generally adverse. 'I have for years worked for the Liberal Party . . . ,' wrote one of many people who sent their protests to the Prime Minister, 'but [I]will never vote Liberal again. You in Ottawa are turning people communistic.'

The end of the session came on July 4 as a relief to the ministers, who had been placed on the defensive much of the time. St. Laurent's leadership had frequently been wanting in vigour, and a series of incidents had lent credibility to the charge that inefficiency and extravagance were being concealed behind the huge Liberal majority in the House of Commons. For instance, the committee on defence expenditure had discovered an order for 14,500 carving-forks for an army of only around 100,000 men. It was a minor matter, but it encouraged opposition members to continue their search for evidence to confirm their suspicions. More serious, there were reports of the theft of large quantities of public property at the army base near Petawawa, Ontario, and in April the government had appointed Montreal accountant George Currie to investigate the situation; his report was awaited with eager anticipation by the opposition. In a report on the political situation in early July, Brooke Claxton pointed out to St. Laurent that the Liberal membership in the House of Commons had decreased from 193 to 185 as a result of twenty-eight by-elections over the previous two years, and that the Progressive-Conservative representation had grown from 41 to 49. The situation of the other parties had remained unchanged. He attributed the trend to a natural reaction against the abnormally large Liberal majority, high taxes, and the feeling that the government was becoming increasingly remote from the people. With characteristically blunt honesty and clear insight, he also drew attention to the failure of the Liberals to present a positive statement of party policy, to provide effective leadership in the House of Commons, and to ensure unity among party supporters at the constituency level. The reinvigorated, well co-ordinated team that had propounded a 'fighting faith' during the general election was in danger, just two years later, of becoming a stagnating colossus, crushed and demoralized by its own weight. The most positive aspect of the situation, Claxton reported, was the completely unanimous feeling that the Prime Minister was the party's greatest asset; in the circumstances, the first and most important step required in restoring the situation was an unequivocal statement that he was going to lead the Liberals in the next election. The Prime Minister's reaction was true to form. 'I would like to retire,' he wrote in a short note to Claxton on the day the session ended, 'but if we are in danger of defeat would prefer to be among the vanquished than appear to have run out.' As the members left Ottawa, the word spread quickly that 'Uncle Louis' would definitely lead them into battle again.

Claxton's analysis of the political situation was presented to cabinet on July 15, and the ministers approved his plan for a counter-attack designed to begin at once and carry right through the next general election. Every minister was asked to prepare a summary of the activities in his department since the previous election, with an analysis of expenditures by constituency, and to compile replies to opposition criticism. They were also to visit every constituency for which they were responsible in order to see that young, capable, and popular candidates were chosen whenever possible, to improve relations with newspaper editors and publishers, and to ensure that the views of party workers at the constituency level were communicated to the Prime Minister. A meeting of the Liberal Party's advisory council was called for October to mark the beginning of the counter-offensive.

On the provincial level, the tide continued to run against the Liberals. Maurice Duplessis called an election for July 11, and put on the best-organized and most effective performance of his career. His defence of the free-enterprise system assured him of the support of Montreal's English-speaking financial community, and of the two leading English-language newspapers there, the *Gazette* and the *Montreal Star*. In each constituency he referred in detail to the schools, bridges, and hospitals that had been built there by his administration, and reminded his audiences that it had all been done despite the fact that only 'thirteen cents on the dollar' of taxes paid in Quebec went to Quebec City as against eighty-seven cents that went to Ottawa. Georges Lapalme presented a comprehensive program of reforms, lashed out against the graft and corruption of the Union Nationale régime, and declared that it was 'time for a change'. St. Laurent remained discreetly quiet during the contest, except to denounce as 'absolutely false' a Union Nationale advertisement asserting that taxes had been imposed by the federal government to pay for Lapalme's campaign. The election outcome was a foregone conclusion; a majority of English-speaking and French-speaking citizens united to give Duplessis sixty-eight out of ninety-two seats. In August, the Social Credit administration of Ernest Manning was re-elected in Alberta with a crushing majority.

Keen to play his part in restoring the Liberal Party's fortunes, St. Laurent interrupted his summer holiday frequently for trips to Ottawa and a series of short tours in eastern Canada. In late August, he set out for British Columbia, where the young Liberals were chafing under the leadership of the cabinet minister from British Columbia, Robert Mayhew, whose many fine qualities did not include the ability to reform the party structure. Since he was one of St. Laurent's best friends, and since, moreover, the Prime Minister had a strong sense of loyalty towards his colleagues, the criticism was hardly welcomed in Ottawa. At the end of the session, the two parliamentary assistants from British Columbia, Ralph Campney and James Sinclair, had been urged to continue to work under Mayhew on the understanding that he would retire at the end of the current Parliament. Campney had accepted the arrangement, but Sinclair, more volatile and independently-minded, had submitted his resignation as parliamentary assistant and announced his intention to move his family back to Vancouver; it had taken St. Laurent an hour to persuade him to withdraw his resignation and remain on the team.

Accompanied by his wife and one of his daughters, St. Laurent appeared almost as an interested tourist on his west-coast tour, speaking both on and off the platform in a chatty tone that belied the seriousness of his mission in the eyes of his fellow Liberals. At a Board of Trade dinner in Trail, B.C., on September 1, he recounted the incident of his grandmother being lowered through a roof in 1837 to steal the gown of a judge whom a crowd of irate citizens wanted to burn in effigy. Discussing the international situation, he commented that the basic error of earlier years had been not to make clear that aggression against the democratic nations would be met by force, and that 'no one . . . told Hitler or Mussolini that if they started anything . . . one of them would finish as a suicide and the other hanged by the neck before being strung up by the heels'. In Victoria he outlined Canada's foreign policy in a non-partisan address, and in Prince Rupert he told a Sunday luncheon meeting of the local Chamber of Commerce that the 'one sure road to peace among men' was pointed out in the Biblical story of the Good Samaritan, and in the second commandment: 'Thou shalt love thy neighbour as thyself.' After stops in Alberta and Manitoba, St. Laurent ended his tour in Hamilton, Ontario, predictably on the theme of national unity. Because of the 'sincere efforts of the majority of Canadians to achieve mutual understanding and by their willingness to co-operate in solving the major problems that faced our country,' he declared, an adult nation had been built that fitted the definition of a nation given by St. Augustine as 'an association of reasonable beings united in a peaceful sharing of the things they cherish'. Although a strong contrast with the 'give 'em hell' type of campaign that President Truman had made famous, the two-week trip was an undoubted success. Even the pessimistic Sinclair wrote from Vancouver that it had exceeded his expectations in every way, and that the Liberals there were all proud to say they belonged to the party headed by Louis St. Laurent.

Back in Ottawa, St. Laurent demonstrated a degree of vigour and decisiveness that had been noticeably absent the previous spring. In mid-October, he appointed Mayhew Canadian Ambassador to Japan, replaced him as Minister of Fisheries with James Sinclair and made Ralph Campney Solicitor General. Speaking before members of the party's advisory council on October 28, he made a spirited defence of the administration's record, chiding the Tories for suggesting it was time for a change while remaining themselves 'the same old party which has always opposed changes for the better as long as it dared to'. Replying to charges by George Drew that Canada had erected a 'dollar-sterling road block' to trade with the Commonwealth, he pointed out that the barriers had been erected by the British themselves in order to protect their scarce currency reserves. With regard to the charge of overtaxation, he reminded his audience that the only increases in rates in recent years had been to provide for defence and for the old-age pension, and refused to hold out hopes for a tax cut, except 'as and when the danger of war is reduced'. A special edition of the flashy party review, *The Liberal*, contained an impressive forty-three-page summary of the 'great record of achievement' in the previous four years. It was certainly a creditable list, including the entry of Newfoundland into Confederation, the appointment of a Canadian governor general, abolition of appeals to the Privy Council, provision to amend the constitution in Canada with regard to federal matters, federal aid to universities, beginning of construction on a trans-Canada highway, a universal old-age pension, a 40 per cent rise in national income, trade, and personal incomes, a third of a million new homes, and a new and positive foreign policy. The implication was clear: under the Grits, Canadians could expect more of the same.

St. Laurent needed all his new-found energy to meet the problems that faced him in late 1952 and early 1953. Parliament had been summoned to meet on November 20, when an urgent Commonwealth meeting was called to discuss the critical situation of the

British pound. In addition, rumours continued to circulate about the thievery that had taken place at Petawawa army camp, which George Currie was still investigating. With indications that the Defence Department had become too large for even such a tireless worker as Claxton to manage, it was decided to create the portfolio of Associate Minister of National Defence, and Campney was assigned to fill it. When the session opened, George Drew was in excellent form. He attacked the government for overtaxing Canadians by half a billion dollars or '$100 for the head of a family', supported his charge of waste and extravagance by reporting that the Department of National Defence had purchased over a million pairs of shoes, over a million ties, and thirty thousand teapots for an army of one hundred thousand men, and repeated his charge of centralization in federal-provincial affairs. St. Laurent replied in a relatively low key, conceding that there had been instances of misdemeanours in military camps, but giving the assurance that, where proof was available, prosecutions had been 'conducted with vigour and to a successful conclusion'. He announced that he and Finance Minister Abbott were leaving the very next day for London to discuss the currency problems of the United Kingdom with other Commonwealth spokesmen, but warned that no such meeting could 'by itself solve the problem of making sterling convertible', or, as the Leader of the Opposition had put it, of removing the 'roadblocks in the way of trade'.

St. Laurent's caution with regard to the negotiations in London proved to be warranted; at the end of the conference, a communiqué recognized the complexity of the problem, rejected implicitly the possibility of an exclusive Commonwealth trading bloc, and announced agreement on 'the restoration of the convertibility of sterling . . . by progressive stages'. The Canadian view of maximum free trade had prevailed. In addition to economic and financial matters, the Commonwealth leaders took advantage of their meeting in London to discuss the title of the new Queen, whose coronation had been set for the following spring. It was a complex matter, since Her Majesty was the head of state of some Commonwealth countries, but to others she was simply the symbol of the Commonwealth association. In the end, the problem was settled in typically pragmatic fashion; each country was to use a form suitable to its particular circumstances, but all would include a common element. For Canadians she would be 'Elizabeth the Second, by the Grace of God of the United Kingdom, Canada and her other realms and territories Queen, Head of the Commonwealth, Defender of the Faith'.

During his stay in the British capital, St. Laurent had a private audience with Her Majesty, and assured her of the devoted loyalty of all her North American subjects. The occasion illustrated once again his attitude towards Canadian public affairs. He was neither blindly attached to the monarchy, nor biased against it; rather, he had a keen appreciation of its unifying force, and its potential for exercising an uplifting influence on the population. In particular, he admired the way in which members of the royal family, and particularly the young sovereign, carried out their responsibilities. The fact that Laurier had been scoffed at in Quebec for his eloquent tributes to Queen Victoria and the connection with Great Britain did not prevent St. Laurent from declaring on his return to the House of Commons that he considered his audience at Buckingham Palace to be 'additional evidence of the fact that we have a system of government to which none anywhere in the world is superior', or from paying tribute to 'the manner in which the traditions of the royal family are being discharged by our gracious sovereign of this day'.

While the Prime Minister was still in London, George Currie completed his report on the Petawawa investigations, and one of the first five copies was flown to London for his attention; he read it in the aircraft on the return journey. It was a damning document, referring to 'a general breakdown in the system of administration, supervision, and accounting', as well as 'lax control, poor discipline, and the presence of dishonest personnel', a combination that had 'proved disastrous'. Under such conditions, the report revealed, some 550 tons of scrap metal had been removed from the base and sold by army personnel for private profit, a contractor hired to clear a camp area had used army equipment instead of his own, and 'horses were hired by army personnel and placed on the payroll under the names of non-existent labourers'. Soldiers had also been assigned by their superiors to carry out private projects, including the construction of pleasure boats, and even, in one instance, building a child's rocking-horse. The total amount of money involved was not large, most of the missing goods had been recovered, and remedial action had been taken at once. In the circumstances, Currie concluded, 'it does not fit the facts to indict or to smear the whole army works service personnel because of the sins of a handful of crooks'. He made a series of forty-four recommendations to correct the situation.

As the C-5 aircraft carried St. Laurent westward across the Atlantic, he became increasingly worried. Brooke Claxton was in Paris attending a NATO meeting, and Campney had only been in his new post for a few weeks; he himself would have to take charge of the situation. As soon as he arrived in Ottawa, he sent a telegram to the Minister of Defence, pointing out that the report was bound to create a bad impression, and suggesting that the only course was to make all the information available to Parliament at once. Claxton wired his concurrence, and the Prime Minister tabled the report when he reappeared in the Commons Chamber on December 15. Conceding that 'regrettable offences had occurred', and 'some severe and sweeping statements' made, he stated that the report would be submitted to the committee on defence expenditures, so that it could be examined in detail.

Convinced that they had found the evidence they had been looking for to prove their charges of maladministration, the Progressive Conservatives attacked at once. Noting that the document bore the date of November 26, Drew accused the government of having withheld it from Parliament for over two weeks. The charge was not completely unjustified; the Acting Prime Minister, C. D. Howe, had refused to receive it until copies had reached the Prime Minister and the Minister of National Defence. At the same time, St. Laurent was perfectly accurate in replying that 'everything possible has been done to bring it to the attention of the House within hours after it reached the Minister [of Defence]'. Stanley Knowles made a more serious charge. C.C.F. leader M. J. Coldwell had received a copy several days earlier, he revealed, and there were discrepancies between the two versions. In particular, a charge of laxity and inefficiency 'at or near the top' of the defence structure had been modified to read simply 'higher up'. Who had made the changes? Knowles wanted to know. Taken by surprise, St. Laurent could only agree to investigate the matter. The Liberals appeared as crestfallen as their opponents were jubilant. Later in the day, Pearkes added to the doubts by pointing out that Currie referred to 'interim suggestions' he had made, and which had been acted upon already. The statement appeared to contradict Claxton's repeated assurance that no interim report had been received. Drew demanded that Currie be reappointed 'to conduct an inquiry into every aspect of the organization and accounting methods of the Department of National Defence'. Other members called for Claxton's resignation.

The 'Petawawa scandal' dominated the parliamentary scene and the newspaper columns for several weeks. The picture of horses on government payrolls, and soldiers making children's rocking-horses, had Canadians from the Atlantic to the Pacific chortling at the government's expense. Finding the situation anything but amusing, St. Laurent investigated the charges one after the other, and consulted with Campney on ways of handling the situation. On December 17, he informed the House of Commons that the 'interim suggestions' had been made by Currie to officials of the Defence Department during the investigation, and not in the form of an interim report to the government. As for the changes mentioned by Knowles, the Deputy Minister of National Defence, C. M. Drury, had received a copy of the draft on November 27, and had suggested certain changes, some of which had been adopted, but Campney had not received the report at that time. In turn, the Prime Minister suggested that Knowles 'enlighten the House as to when and how this copy came into his possession'. The C.C.F. member declined to comply with the request. On the following day, Campney made a preliminary reply to the opposition charges, arguing that action had been taken immediately when the reports of misdeeds were received: that four military personnel and eight civilians had been convicted and sentenced and many of Currie's recommendations already put into effect. The statement did not silence the criticism; members of Parliament left for home the same evening to spend Christmas and to continue the debate in their constituencies.

The government had won a breathing space, and they were determined to take good advantage of it. Brooke Claxton returned to Ottawa on December 20, and took charge of the counter-offensive immediately. For the hard-working, imaginative minister, the situation was almost a personal affront, since he had built up Canada's military strength since June 1950 with the same single-minded devotion that he had displayed in supporting Mackenzie King during the war years, in creating the Department of National Health and Welfare, and in contributing so decisively to the 1945 and 1949 Liberal election victories. One of his first steps was to try to ascertain how a copy of the report had fallen into opposition hands; Currie, equally perplexed on that score, launched an investigation. Parliament reassembled on January 12, and almost immediately, Progressive Conservative member Ellen Fairclough raised the matter of the now-famous horses in a question to the Prime Minister. St. Laurent was ready: there were, in fact, no names representing horses on the Petawawa payrolls, he reported; there were only the names of labourers who had been hired as teamsters. What had happened, he explained, was that an army sergeant had hired horses, and also the men to drive them, and had withheld part of their earnings for his personal profit. It was almost a pity to spoil the colourful story.

On the following day, Claxton made a comprehensive statement, rejecting the suggestion of a 'breakdown' in the accounting system of his department, pointing out that Drury had read the report in advance of its release only in order to check errors of fact, and recalling that the total losses in the case had been estimated by the police at 'probably less than $50,000'. The mystery of the copy referred to by Knowles remained unsolved; Coldwell refused to reveal the name of the person who had handed it to him on the grounds that he would be 'betraying the confidence and trust he has seen fit to place in me'. Asked point-blank 'who stole the copy of the report?', Knowles countered with the question: 'May I ask the honourable member if he has stopped beating his wife?' An R.C.M.P. investigation indicated that an additional copy had been put together in the printer's shop by someone employed there. The C.C.F. members of Parliament were in the curious position of protecting a thief, and using the stolen material to accuse the government of improper conduct. 'I would deprecate it greatly,' St. Laurent remarked pointedly on January 15, 'if our politics sank to the level where, in the conduct of our strife with each other, we had to have agents to steal confidential documents.' After a week of lively debate, the report was finally referred to the committee on defence expenditures. The story of horses on the army payroll became part of Canada's political legend; it remained to be seen how effective it would prove at the polls.

St. Laurent remained in good form throughout the session, seldom allowing himself to be provoked into losing his temper, and trying to maintain a high level of debate. He received an encouraging indication of his personal influence on January 29 when he succeeded in averting another railway strike. The negotiations between management and labour that had been continuing for a year and a half had all but broken down, both sides had withdrawn their previous concessions, and the men were to stop work on the following Monday. Once again, the Prime Minister called to Ottawa the representatives of both groups, and, closely supported by Gregg, spent twelve hours in continuous negotiations with them, first discussing possible terms with one side, then with the other. Reasonable men devoted to serving their common country should be able to reach an agreement, he pointed out repeatedly. The appeal was effective; at the end of the day, he rushed into the Commons Chamber, interrupted the debate that was in progress, and announced that the strike had been averted. With tears of satisfaction in his eyes, he said of the negotiators:

> I think they have done a magnificent job, and that it is a credit to Canadian democracy that matters about which there were honest and sincere and pretty widely diverging views could be settled when honest men of good will got together and did their best to discharge their responsibilities to their fellow citizens. . . . I think it is a bright page to be written into the history of labour relations in this country.

While he made no reference to his own role in achieving the agreement, the men with whom he had been dealing paid tribute to him. 'I never understood why people called him "Uncle Louis" until we met him in the series of meetings today,' one union official commented, 'but he was for all the world like an uncle, older, wiser and kinder.' 'He created the atmosphere which made tonight's agreement possible,' remarked a top railway executive. The terms of the settlement were a still more eloquent tribute; the two sides had agreed that he 'personally – not as Prime Minister, not as head of the government', should choose a referee to decide what adjustments in the wage scale should be made, and they agreed in advance to abide by the decision of the referee. He was indeed emulating his father, 'the peacemaker of Compton'.

Another stirring scene occurred a few days later when St. Laurent submitted to the House of Commons the proposed changes in the Queen's title. Her Majesty was the Queen of Canada, not as holder of a separate office, he declared, but 'because the people of Canada are happy to recognize as their sovereign the person who is the sovereign of the United Kingdom'. The words 'by the grace of God' implied a recognition by Canadians that worldly affairs were not determined exclusively by human will, but 'by men and women as agents for a supreme authority'. Similarly, the expression 'defender of the faith' did not refer to a particular church, constituting rather a proclamation by the civil authorities of their 'continued belief in a supreme power that orders the affairs of mere men' and recognizing the sovereign as 'a believer in and a defender of the faith in a supreme ruler'. The new royal title, 'head of the Commonwealth', he went on, reflected 'the realistic genius of the British people' to 'accommodate itself to the requirements of new situations in the lives of men and . . . conserve the essential without having to conserve forms that to some appear to have become so outmoded that they can no longer be accepted'. He stressed particularly the importance of having found a title acceptable to both Western and Asian member countries of the Commonwealth. 'I think it is a magnificent thing that the peoples of India and the peoples of the Occident can look upon each other as human beings equal in every respect,' he declared; just as the founders of the Canadian nation realized that equality must be recognized and practised within a single country, so the founders of the modern Commonwealth realized that true equality must be recognized in international affairs. With that thought in mind, he had told Prime Minister Nehru that he hoped the Indians, 'in spite of the many more centuries of their social experience and civilization', would not consider Canadians their inferiors, and that Canadians, 'in spite of our rapid development of industrial processes and industrial know-how', would not look upon themselves as superior to the Indians. The other members were silent as the French-Canadian Prime Minister, speaking without notes and with evident conviction, outlined his concept of Canada and the Commonwealth in the modern world. 'It was a most moving address,' replied John Diefenbaker for the official opposition. '... As we listened to the Prime Minister without regard to party considerations, this Parliament became cathedral in devotion to our history, to our heritage, and to our common pursuit of freedom.'

The proposed South Saskatchewan dam was aired frequently both in cabinet and in Parliament during the session. In a report submitted in January 1953, the royal commission declared that the project would be helpful to the economy of Saskatchewan, but noted that it would be very costly and that there would likely be more profitable investments in irrigation elsewhere. The conclusions were a severe blow to the proponents of the scheme, and particularly to Gardiner and the other Liberal members who had been counting heavily on having the project approved, in principle at least, before the election. St. Laurent was also disappointed as he had been in favour of some really significant action to bolster the western economy ever since his visit to the prairies with the Rowell-Sirois Commission in 1937; at the same time, he had asked for expert advice on the advisability of undertaking the project, and he could not simply ignore the answer he had received. When the Minister of Agriculture realized that his argument based on the economic feasibility of the dam had been perilously weakened by the commission report, he changed his ground, and urged the government to make an early start on the project for another reason, to fulfil the promise made by the

Louis St. Laurent arriving home from his world tour; Rockcliffe Airport, Ottawa, March 17, 1954.

Louis St. Laurent with Premiers Frost and Duplessis at the federal-provincial conference; Ottawa, December 1950. Left to right: Leslie Frost, Louis St. Laurent, Maurice Duplessis.

Liberals in 1935 to rehabilitate the drought area. Gardiner suggested that the commission should be thanked publicly 'for having strengthened our opinion that the South Saskatchewan project should be proceeded with as soon as possible'.

Outside the cabinet, pressure from advocates of the scheme was equally strong. On February 3, Diefenbaker raised it in the House of Commons as a subject 'of transcendent importance to the people of western Canada', and forced a debate that extended over several days. Drew joined him in demanding that it be started 'right away'. Gardiner sought refuge in enumerating the preliminary steps already taken, and in stating that the commission report had not yet been discussed in cabinet. Challenged by Diefenbaker to state whether the government intended to 'give what we ask for', St. Laurent declared heatedly that he required 'further information' before making a decision. Personally, he had felt that it would be 'a magnificent thing', he said, 'and that the indirect, if not the direct returns . . . would be a permanent addition to the capital value of this great country of ours'. However, the report had suggested that there might be a better use made of the funds in question, and he would now have to be convinced 'to the extent where I can honestly say I believe it to be the best', before he made a favourable recommendation to his cabinet colleagues and to Parliament. John Diefenbaker's resolution was defeated by the government's supporters; Saskatchewan Liberals were left reflecting gloomily on their chances of re-election.

Despite Liberal attempts to keep the political sea as unruffled as possible, issues continued to appear that seemed likely to alienate voters. In Quebec, Duplessis had not returned after his victory of July 1952 to his policy of peace with Ottawa. He not only refused to sign a tax-sharing agreement, but would not renew the arrangement to distribute federal grants to universities in the province. Letters addressed to him by Finance Minister Abbott remained unanswered, and even St. Laurent was unsuccessful in attempts to persuade him to negotiate a new arrangement. In conceding defeat, the Prime Minister stated in the House of Commons on February 16 that the government was 'deeply concerned' with the problem of assisting higher education, but 'we are also deeply concerned with avoiding the doing of anything to countenance this suggestion that we are trying to inject ourselves into the domain of education. No one wants to do that.' The funds that would have been allocated to Quebec universities remained in Ottawa; those destined for institutions in the other provinces were distributed. A request by the National Federation of Canadian University Students for a federal system of scholarships was quietly filed away.

Maurice Duplessis went still further, and created a provincial royal commission on federal-provincial relations, instructed specifically to study 'the intrusions of the central power in the field of direct taxation'. Prejudging the evidence, the legislation setting up the inquiry asserted that 'since 1917, the central power has invaded important tax fields reserved to the Provinces', thus 'endangering the existence . . . of the Provinces' and threatening 'a centralization of powers incompatible with the confederal system' that 'could only lead to a bureaucratic régime and the gradual disappearance of responsible government'. The argument advanced by the Union Nationale leader that his government needed greater revenues to modernize the province was certainly justified, and to blame Ottawa for the situation was undoubtedly clever politics, but other aspects of his strategy were less clear. Why, for instance, did he accuse the federal government of encroaching on a provincial tax field by imposing direct taxation, when the B.N.A. Act specifically authorized it to raise money 'by any mode or system of taxation'?

St. Laurent had an opportunity to comment on the latest development when a delegation of the Quebec Chamber of Commerce appeared in Ottawa on February 25 and asked him to indicate his readiness to accept the conclusions of the commission. In view of the condemnation of his administration contained in the legislation and the instructions to the commission, the suggestion was tantamount to asking him to admit guilt in advance. Clearly displaying his feeling of irritation, St. Laurent recalled the difficulties experienced in the past in dealing with a government that made sweeping statements but refused to state its position with sufficient precision to permit negotiations on particular issues. There was no reason to feel, he argued, as the Quebec

Premier apparently did feel, that any arrangement between two governments must necessarily result in a loss of autonomy by one of them. 'We make arrangements with foreign countries,' he pointed out, 'and no one considers that there is any abandonment of rights implied; there is rather an assertion of national sovereignty.' The federal government could not withdraw from the field of direct taxation since 'the public is exacting and it demands more and more services', but nothing prevented the provinces or municipalities from raising their own personal or corporate taxes, except their own reluctance to do so. Two sets of taxes were obviously what the delegation from the Chamber of Commerce wished to avoid, and why they had thrown their weight behind the Union Nationale administration; they returned home empty-handed.

The spirits of Liberal members of Parliament were bolstered noticeably when Douglas Abbott brought down a budget containing a reduction of $237 million in personal income taxes, and outlining a $361 million cut in government expenditures. Simultaneously, Howe announced an increase of twenty cents per bushel in wheat payments to farmers, and prospects for greater sales abroad. With the economy once again booming, and the effects of the Currie report fading into the background, the government's supporters began to put pressure on the Prime Minister to call an early election. St. Laurent was opposed to an election campaign just before or during the period of the Coronation, and refused to change on purely partisan grounds his plan for a vote in August; Liberal back-benchers could only hope that their opponents would not succeed in digging up new issues in the further time allotted to them because of the Prime Minister's scrupulousness.

The annual request for renewal of the Emergency Powers Act provided the opposition parties with an opportunity to repeat their charge that the government had become accustomed to almost dictatorial powers. During the debate, Drew referred to an order in council that had never been published, and expressed doubts whether it should even exist. Intrigued, other members asked for further information. 'There is only one,' St. Laurent explained, and when it was passed by cabinet 'information was conveyed to the leaders of the three groups in the House.' The Progressive Conservative leader rose at once to emphasize that he had not been consulted beforehand, nor did he know how the powers under the order in council were being exercised. Sensational news reports of the exchange gave the impression that the Liberals had been caught trying to circumvent Parliament and rule by decree. The debate went on sporadically for over a month, and on March 26, the Prime Minister intervened again, volunteering the information that the order enabled the government 'to do what all the other governments and associates in this North Atlantic Treaty Alliance are doing'. He offered to show it to the other party leaders 'confidentially', but confessed that, 'personally, if I were not a member of the Government I would prefer not to see it' as that would imply sharing responsibility for it. St. Laurent's direct, spontaneous intervention had a strong impact on most members; Donald Fleming described it as the Prime Minister 'at his soothing best', but continued to insist that the extension of the emergency powers legislation was a 'measure of parliamentary suicide' and gave the government the power to 'subvert the whole constitution'. The basis for the assertion was unclear since the contents of the order remained secret; the extension of the legislation was approved later in the same day.

There were other sources of embarrassment to the Liberals. The Minister of Trade and Commerce added to the list of 'Howe-isms' being collected by his opponents. 'Nuts,' he interjected disdainfully, in reply to one of Drew's frequent charges. The Department of Defence Production was merely a purchasing department, he stated on one occasion, and 'if the [military] services say they need a gold-plated piano, it is our duty to buy it.' George Prudham, who had become Minister of Mines and Technical Surveys in December 1950, also supplied the opposition parties with campaign ammunition. Unlike St. Laurent, he had not divested himself of his private business interests on entering the cabinet; in March 1953, it was revealed that his firm, Prudham Supplies Limited, had acquired an old Canadian National Railways station in Edmonton without tenders having been called. The matter was raised in the House of Commons, one member declaring that it was 'a strange state of affairs when a minister of the Crown can negotiate directly with a Crown corporation to buy property without benefit of bidding', and called for Prudham's resignation. Prudham denied categorically that any influence had been exercised, 'political or otherwise', in the matter, but refused to choose between his private and public interests.

Two Liberal back-benchers added to the impression of impropriety. Colonel E. W. George from New Brunswick was found to have been paid in 1951 for 204 days of service as a reserve army officer in Moncton, and 224 days as a member of Parliament in Ottawa. When the apparent ambiguity was pointed out, he explained that he had spent much of his time in Ottawa doing work on behalf of his army unit. The fact remained that he had drawn double pay from the federal treasury for a certain number of days; the indiscretion was to cost him his political career. In April, another Liberal, A. E. Dewar of Saskatchewan, was accused of receiving over seventy thousand dollars from a 'government contractor'. Displaying unusual sensitivity, St. Laurent rose in the House of Commons the day after the charge was made in a newspaper report, and stated that Dewar was at home in his constituency but would deal with the matter on his return. 'If there remained anything which might be a cause of embarrassment,' he added meaningfully, the member would certainly 'wish to take the steps required to prevent that embarrassment from being shared by anyone else'. Six days later the Saskatchewan politician told the House of Commons that he had exchanged cheques with a friend in order to help him to finance construction bids, and had cashed the other man's cheques when the projects were completed; there had been no 'intentional wrongdoing', and he had made no profits from the arrangement. He none the less announced his resignation from Parliament. John Diefenbaker made the subject an occasion for a motion of non-confidence in the government. Neither of the issues contained proof of corrupt practices by the government itself, but they suggested the possibility of wrongdoing, and gave hope to the opposition of finding more incriminating evidence if only a thorough investigation could be undertaken.

On May 7, St. Laurent flew to Washington for his first visit with Eisenhower since the latter had become President of the United States. Apart from the usual lobbying for Canadian causes, his purpose was to establish the best possible communications with the new administration, and perhaps even the kind of personal relations that had proved so fruitful in the days of Franklin Roosevelt and Mackenzie King. In some ways, the first months of Republican government had been disappointing to Canada. While Eisenhower had great charm and integrity, he was a political novice, and a likely prey to advisers and lobbyists whose views were frequently in conflict with Canadian interests. During his election campaign, the President had spoken in favour of a St. Lawrence seaway, and after he assumed office in January, the United States Ambassador had called on St. Laurent to ask him to delay commencement of an all-Canadian project, assuring him that legislation for a joint undertaking was under preparation. Reluctantly, and to the disappointment of many Canadians, the Prime Minister had agreed to wait a little longer. More worrisome than the delay with regard to the seaway was the imposition by Washington in early 1953 of restrictions on the importation of Canadian agricultural products to the United States. On the day before he left Ottawa, St. Laurent's hand was strengthened by a resolution approved unanimously by the House of Commons, urging removal of the restrictions as being in violation of the General Agreement on Tariffs and Trade.

The Canadian party were met at the airport by Vice President Nixon, and taken to Blair House, just across the street from the White House, for their two-day stay in the American capital. Eisenhower and St. Laurent had met previously during the President's military career, and enjoyed excellent personal relations. In fact, they were, in some respects, strikingly similar; they both had great personal charm and prestige; they had entered politics late in life, reluctantly and from a sense of duty; they were above the cut and thrust of day-to-day politics; and they ran their cabinets more as committee chairmen than as hard-driving executives aware of the details of their respective administrations. Both were profoundly convinced that men of good will could reach agreement on even the most difficult problems, provided they were prepared to put aside selfish considerations. The talks took the form of friendly conversations rather than serious bargaining. The President listened carefully to the Canadian argument that the new import restrictions would have an adverse effect on the whole North American economic system and on the development of resources on both sides of the border; that point of view appeared to be novel to him and he seemed impressed by it. On the subject of the St. Lawrence seaway project, he reiterated his determination to obtain the approval of Congress for a joint undertaking, pointing out that the Federal Power Commission was already seized of a request with regard to the hydro installations; once again, he asked Canada to wait a little longer before going ahead alone.

In the field of international relations, St. Laurent sought to exercise a moderating influence and to counterbalance the aggressive line being adopted by fervent anti-Communists who were pushing Washington towards a show-down with the Red bloc. Speaking as a close friend and neighbour, he made it clear that Canada accepted American leadership of the free world, but urged patience and caution in order to avoid a third world war. Since the death of Stalin, Soviet foreign policy was less intransigent, he recalled, and he suggested that the new trend might well indicate a permanent shift in Moscow's relations with the rest of the world; any opportunity to relax tensions should be welcomed. In particular, the Canadian Prime Minister warned against a current argument in the United States that the truce negotiations still continuing in Korea should be broken off, and a decisive blow struck at the Communist forces in that part of the world. With regard to North American defence, Eisenhower gave the assurance that any step taken would be conceived on the basis of a partnership, and with full respect for Canadian sovereignty.

St. Laurent repeated most of his arguments at a press conference and before the National Press Club. Canada was devoting 45 per cent of its budget to defence purposes, he told the newspapermen, but, 'like the United States, Canada wants to prevent a third world war, not to fight one'. While military strength was indispensable, it could not alone provide security; Canadians and Americans had to work to ensure in other lands 'the measure of social justice and economic opportunity we have achieved in our own countries, and . . . that basic human equality which is the hallmark of a genuinely free society'. It was 'not very helpful to preach the abstract advantages of freedom to men and women who are suffering from misery and starvation'. On the specific subject of his visit, St. Laurent pointed out that trade was essential to the strength and prosperity of the North American continent, 'the bastion of the free world', and that it was 'of the gravest importance that no retrograde steps be taken' to hamper it. 'We cannot nibble at this corner here and knock out that piece there to protect some special interest', he warned, 'without weakening the entire fabric.' Carefully avoiding threats and recriminations, he explained that his government was 'most anxious to get on with the job' of building the St. Lawrence seaway, since the need for additional electrical energy was urgent; rapid approval of American participation, he urged, would be in keeping with 'the unique relationship between Canada and the United States'. There were no precise achievements to report to the House of Commons when St. Laurent returned from his trip on May 9, but, he stated, he had 'some good reasons to expect that it would bear some fruit'.

The twenty-first Parliament completed its deliberations on May 14, and the closing Speech from the Throne summarized the accomplishments of the four-year period as a handy compendium for Liberal orators on the hustings. St. Laurent described the list in a radio broadcast as instalments in a continuing Liberal policy; George Drew retorted the following evening that the Grits were giving Canada 'larger and larger instalments of dictatorship', and pledged his party 'to restore the supremacy of Parliament'. After that preliminary skirmish, the two men set off to attend the Coronation ceremonies in the United Kingdom. Since his wife had sworn never to fly until, in her words, she had wings of her own, the Prime Minister made the trip on the liner *Queen Elizabeth*, arriving in London on May 26. In a busy two-week schedule of public functions, they took tea in the royal tent at a garden party on the lawns of Buckingham Palace, spent a week-end at the country estate of Viscount and Lady Alexander, dined with the Churchills, and travelled to Oxford where he received an honorary degree. On June 2, the day of the Coronation ceremony, they took part in the procession from Buckingham Palace to Westminster Abbey, but refrained from following the example of the large and beautiful Queen of the Tonga Islands, who, despite the pouring rain, lowered the top of her carriage so that the people could see her. In the Abbey, four Commonwealth prime ministers sat on either side of the Queen, their wives directly before them, throughout the long and impressive ceremony.

Immediately following the Coronation, the Commonwealth prime ministers held one of their periodic conferences. With the ceremony over, St. Laurent was anxious to leave for home, as he had still to announce the exact date of the election. It was in his London hotel suite that he approved the Liberal campaign slogan: 'Don't Stop Canada's Progress – Vote St. Laurent'. Another decision taken there concerned J. W. Pickersgill, who was chafing under the restrictions of his non-political post as Clerk of the Privy Council, and feeling that he could be more useful to the Prime Minister if he were free to accompany him during the election campaign, and advise him again on political matters. It was Premier Smallwood who provided the solution to the problem. He had come to like and admire Pickersgill during the negotiations that led to Newfoundland's entry into Confederation, and suggested that he replace Gordon Bradley, who would be appointed to the Senate, as Newfoundland's representative in the federal cabinet. Although Pickersgill had no direct connection with Newfoundland, he had taken a keen interest in the new province, and with his wide knowledge of national affairs seemed likely to be an effective spokesman for it in Ottawa. Since Smallwood dominated the Newfoundland political scene, there was certain to be no difficulty in having him elected, and he could even spend most of the campaign assisting the Prime Minister. The arrangement was concluded in the Dorchester Hotel in London at a meeting between St. Laurent, Bradley, Smallwood, and Pickersgill.

Leaving his wife and daughter to return by ship, St. Laurent flew back to Canada, and, following a cabinet meeting on June 12, announced at a press conference that the election would be held on August 10. Asked how long he intended to remain Prime Minister if re-elected, he recalled that he had been in Ottawa for over twelve years, which was much longer than he had expected when he arrived; he hoped to continue 'for quite a long time', but he was still following the advice Cardinal Villeneuve had given him in 1941 to 'do the things that have to be done from day to day as wisely as you can do them, and then take the consequences'. As for the results of the contest, he would only say: 'I am hoping and expect to get returned.' And the issue? 'Good government.' The Liberals were going to make no promises, they were going to run on their record, and on their leader's image. Even the team was to remain almost the same; apart from Pickersgill's appointment, the only cabinet change was the retirement of Public Works Minister Alphonse Fournier to take an appointment on the Exchequer Court.

At seventy-one years of age, Louis St. Laurent looked and felt as fit as when he had assumed the Liberal Party leadership, although, as he admitted readily, 'the years do leave some mark upon one'. His face was still ruddy and he held himself as erect as ever, but his hair and stubbly moustache were completely white, and he was heavier than four years earlier. Since the previous election, 'Uncle Louis' had become 'Grandfather St. Laurent'.

George Drew opened his campaign first with a meeting in his home town of Guelph, Ontario. In a sixteen-point manifesto, he repeated his charges of arrogance, waste, and irresponsibility, promised to reduce taxes by at least half a billion dollars a year, to ban Communism in Canada, to introduce a health insurance program, to expand trade, and to revise the federal-provincial tax system. Two days later, St. Laurent followed with a huge rally in Windsor, Ontario, and the same evening, a nation-wide radio appeal. His only promise was, as in 1949, to 'speak with one voice and make the same appeal' in French or English, and in every part of Canada, since the policies he stood for were 'designed to benefit all Canadians in all parts of Canada'. After outlining the developments in the country over the previous four years, he emphasized that the government was not claiming credit for them all but added, 'I think most responsible people will agree that such spectacular developments do not occur under a weak government or a bad government.' Nor did he hold out the prospect of carefree times ahead; there were 'apt to be difficulties', and Canadians would need 'both wise foresight and experience' in their government to overcome them. On an almost pained note, he took up the charges of waste and extravagance in the defence program, describing the evidence produced as 'certainly not very impressive' and the complaint that information was being withheld as 'just not true'. 'No opposition in our history has ever been given such complete and detailed information about what a government has been doing,' he stated.

On the whole, St. Laurent's campaign was a slightly more relaxed version of his 1949 performance. From Windsor, he moved through western Ontario, making as many as eight chatty speeches a day, congratulating the Canadian people on their achievements in the recent past, and promising not to emulate his opponents in making promises he was not sure of being able to keep. For each evening meeting he had a prepared address, but he departed frequently from it, dropping the recitals of facts and the sharper attacks on the other parties. Children again played an important role in his appearances, Liberal organizers making sure that they appeared in large numbers along his route. In Windsor he was photographed with a small Chinese boy, in Kitchener with a two-year-old tot in a cowboy suit. Noticing a girl in a wheel chair at St. Jacob's, he went over and told her that 'the fact that you are here and looking so happy tells me that you are a very brave girl, and by your example, you will cheer many others.' Newspapermen noted that the 'Uncle Louis' charm was as potent as ever.

The clearest issue of the campaign was federal-provincial relations. In Quebec, Drew criticized the tax-sharing agreements as further evidence of the Liberals' policy of centralization, and in the rest of the country as proof that they were power-hungry autocrats. Duplessis avoided identifying himself openly with the Progressive Conservative leader, but Frédéric Dorion, once again a candidate and Conservative organizer, proclaimed Drew and Duplessis 'two great patriots . . . [who] will save the pact of Confederation'. Without the Union Nationale leader's personal intervention, the argument had little weight; besides, French-speaking Canadians were not unhappy to have one of their own number at the head of the Quebec government, another at the helm in Ottawa, and the two fighting for their support. The word was spread quietly to vote 'bleu au Québec, rouge à Ottawa'. In the other provinces, the issue of federal-provincial relations was still easier for the Liberals to handle. In Ontario, St. Laurent pointed out that even Premier Frost had signed a tax-sharing agreement, thereby implying approval of the federal policy. In New Brunswick, he declared that a clear separation of federal and provincial sources of revenue would be disastrous for the poorer provinces, and assured his audience that 'everything we have done . . . has been designed to place them in a position to perform for themselves, in the way their own people want them performed, the functions assigned to the provinces by the constitution'.

While he stuck to his position that he would only make one promise, 'to do our best to serve the people of Canada to the best of our abilities as long as they want us to serve them', he conceded that 'the people want to know and they have the right to know what policies we have for the future'. Taxes would continue to be reduced 'just as much as possible', he stated in his second radio broadcast on July 9, the Liberal Party still believed that the constitution should be amended at home, construction of housing would be continued at a rapid pace, and a contributory health insurance plan would be established if agreement with the provincial governments was possible. Trade should be expanded, he continued, floor prices on agricultural and fishery products maintained, full employment assured, and great improvements made in transportation, the most spectacular of which would be the St. Lawrence seaway. In Alberta, where tremendous reserves of natural gas had been discovered in recent years, he spoke of an 'all-Canadian' pipeline north of the Great Lakes to eastern Canada, that 'would be comparable with the pushing across this continent of the first transcontinental railway as a bold but sound project in nation-building'.

Inevitably, the South Saskatchewan dam project was raised when he visited Saskatchewan. Candidates for the three other parties were endorsing it enthusiastically, and Liberals were anxious to know how he would deal with the subject. His prepared text for a meeting in Regina contained no reference to it, but, shortly before he was to speak, he decided to meet the issue head on, and scribbled a few notes on a sheet of paper. He had almost finished delivering his prepared statement when, to the surprise of the other persons on the platform, he tensed noticeably, and plunged into the controversial issue. 'I am not going to make any promises,' he declared almost defiantly, '. . . but I do want you to know what our stand is in this matter, and I don't want anyone to go around saying that when I came to Saskatchewan I was afraid to even mention a matter which is undoubtedly of great interest to the people who live in this province.' Because he felt that 'it would be bad for the unity of this country if one section of it felt it was being unjustly treated,' he had taken a political risk in obtaining the $65 million additional wheat payment the previous year, and also in supporting the proposal to reduce the number of constituencies in Saskatchewan by only three instead of five. As for the dam, he had long felt that the provision of additional water would be of more benefit to the people of the area than anything else, but there was no agreement on costs, and there were other aspects still to be clarified. Until all the outstanding questions were settled, he would not feel justified in saying 'Yes, go ahead' and he would not attempt 'to do what I consider to be buying your votes by promising you this project right now'. The scene was reminiscent of his first public meeting in Quebec East constituency, when he faced the conscription issue squarely, and declared that he wanted the audience to know what kind of stuff he was made of; the audience appeared to be impressed, but it remained to be seen what the result would be.

In other parts of the country, he used the same direct approach. Faced with Progressive Conservative candidates in Quebec demanding an ambassador to the Vatican, he told a French-speaking crowd in Thetford Mines that the time was not right for such an appointment, as it would simply provoke a religious dispute at a time when Canadians were forgetting their differences and attaining a high level of national unity. He and his colleagues favoured the creation of a distinctive Canadian flag, he stated on the same occasion, but opinion throughout the country was divided on the issue, and it was 'better to institute those things which will be received wholeheartedly by the whole nation rather than cause dissensions by forcing things which a portion of the population does not want to accept'.

The Liberal campaign was oriented almost entirely around the leader's personality, huge photographs portraying him in a dignified, well-groomed pose, gazing directly into the eyes of his fellow citizens with an expression of quiet competence. His name was given priority over party labels; Canadians were urged to 'vote St. Laurent', and to choose 'a great leader for a greater Canada'. Liberal candidates were described as 'the local St. Laurent candidate'. Generally, his meetings were orderly and pleasant gatherings. Early in the campaign he managed to kill the 'Petawawa scandal' as an issue by joking about the horses that turned out not to be on the government payroll after all. He joshed Drew good-naturedly for promising to reduce taxes by half a billion dollars, and then promising much larger sums in new expenditures; if C. D. Howe's slogan was 'What's a million?', he suggested, the Tory leader's should be 'What's a billion?'. Only occasionally was he heckled; in Edmonton, two men screamed that he was an 'old goat', and told him to 'go back to Quebec'; and in Newcastle, New Brunswick, an old man interrupted to say that he had been 'kicked to one side like a dog' when he tried to get government assistance. The second incident caused St. Laurent to reply heatedly that the laws could not be tailored to fit every individual, but that 'there is no law which provides that anyone in Canada is going to be kicked around like a dog'. The Liberals were delighted with such outbursts, and one newspaperman described him as 'Papa with a punch'.

Once again, St. Laurent's campaign ended in Toronto's Maple Leaf Gardens. Standing under a huge banner bearing the message, 'For the best years in your life, vote Liberal', and with his wife, a daughter, and two grand-daughters by his side, he repeated before a crowd of ten thousand people his simple, non-partisan declaration of faith in Canada. The charges of arrogance and dictatorship seemed somewhat incongruous after such a performance. In his final radio broadcast, he was much more 'Grandfather St. Laurent' than a party chieftain, advising:

I suppose that if you conscientiously believe that it is more important to Canada to have a strong opposition than a strong and stable government you will vote for an opposition candidate, and if you feel that way about it, it is still your duty to get out and vote. But if you feel as I honestly do that in these dangerous times, Canada needs a strong and stable government, the way to be sure of it is to vote for the Liberal candidate in your riding on the tenth of August.

The argument that only the Liberals could assure continued progress and prosperity was an effective one. One of Canada's most distinguished authors, Hugh MacLennan, wrote in an early August issue of *Maclean's* Magazine:

> I wish I didn't have to vote for the Liberals, those cautious inhibited trustees. . . . Yet how else can I vote this summer? Assuming that my ballot indicates that the party I vote for is the one I think could govern the country well, what other vote can I cast but a Liberal one?

On August 10, Canadians opted for more of the same. The Liberals were returned with 173 seats, including two Independent Liberals; the Progressive Conservatives won 51; the C.C.F. 23; and Social Credit 15. Three Independent members were elected in Quebec. St. Laurent himself was returned in his own constituency with an even greater majority than in 1949; not a single one of his ministers went down to defeat. In his victory statement, he pledged to continue to pursue his highest ambition 'to contribute something to the strengthening of the harmony and good will and co-operation which is the one sure foundation of our unity as a nation'.

# 12

---

## World Statesman

The 1953 election result was as important to Louis St. Laurent personally as the previous one. Four years earlier, his colleagues had been given a vote of confidence and an opportunity to show what they could accomplish; now, they had received a vote of approval for their conduct of the nation's business. He interpreted the verdict as a specific rejection of the opposition cry that it was 'time for a change', and as a new mandate for 'good government', steady material progress, enlightened nationalism, and, above all, national unity. As for himself, he felt that, despite his seventy-one years, his fellow citizens had directed him specifically to continue to lead them as long as he was able. When Solon Low had asserted during the campaign that the real issue was who would be prime minister after the Liberals were returned to power, he had reacted indignantly to the implication that he was not going to carry out the mandate he was asking for, and he was determined to prove the Social Credit leader wrong. The fact was that he had identified himself with the whole Canadian family, and not merely with his own, and the geographical focal point of his life had shifted from Quebec City to Ottawa.

Louis St. Laurent spent several weeks following the election shuttling back and forth between the national capital and St. Patrick, and alternating busy days in his East Block office with golfing, fishing, and swimming with members of his family. Even when outside Ottawa, he spent part of his day dealing with the documents sent on to him by his staff, and answering correspondence. One of the letters he received was from a twenty-one-year-old crippled girl who had heard him describe the social security program during the campaign, and, inspired by his 'paternal understanding', wrote to ask why there was not some form of assistance for persons in her situation. Touched by the plea, he replied at once that he agreed with her, and expressed the hope that before long 'a practical solution' would be found. The same day he wrote to Minister of National Health and Welfare Paul Martin that 'this is something about which we should try to get an agreement with the provinces', and telling him that he would like to see it dealt with at the next session of Parliament. On September 17, he brought into the cabinet the bright and hard-working, but mercurial, Jean Lesage as Minister of Resources and Development, shifting Robert Winters from that portfolio to the Department of Public Works.

His most sensational decision during that pleasant autumn was to undertake a world tour in early 1954. In recent years, St. Laurent had received several invitations to visit other Commonwealth countries, but had not felt he could leave Canada for a long enough period of time. When Jawaharlal Nehru repeated his invitation during the Coronation ceremonies, he agreed to consider the matter seriously, if he 'got through the elections all right'. As soon as the Liberal victory was announced, the Indian leader reminded him of his promise. The Canadian High Commissioner in New Delhi, Escott Reid, endorsed the proposal enthusiastically, and particularly Nehru's suggestion that a visit to India should be long enough for him to see something of the country and its people, and not the usual state visit restricted to the capital and one or two other centres. With the post-election session of Parliament likely to be quiet, St. Laurent decided that he could and should make the trip. When he arrived in Ottawa from St. Patrick one Monday in early September, he surprised one of his secretaries who met him at the station by asking him how he would like to take a trip to Asia. When he revealed his plan to the Ottawa press corps a few days later, he made it clear that he had no intention of trying to influence the Asian leaders in their attitude to the two power blocs, or to interfere in problems such as the dispute over Kashmir; he planned rather to carry out a good-will mission, and hoped to strengthen the ties of friendship and understanding between North America and Asia.

Louis St. Laurent was in excellent form as he prepared for the opening of the first session of the new Parliament on November 12 and a state visit by President Eisenhower scheduled for the same week. He took a personal interest in a wide variety of matters that were brought to his attention, and dictated personally much of the correspondence that was normally dealt with by his staff. In early November he sent a message to all Liberals through a party newsletter, warning that 'after the recent decisive victory at the polls we must be careful not to relax into a state of complacency', but rather should pursue 'the policies for which we stand'. The atmosphere was cordial in the House of Commons as the new team of legislators prepared to take up their duties. Dapper, clever René Beaudoin was chosen as presiding officer to an accolade of praise from all parties, Drew paying tribute to his 'impartiality and good judgement', Coldwell predicting that he would be remembered one day 'as a distinguished occupant of this historic chair'. Already the letter from the crippled girl to the Prime Minister had produced some results, and the Speech from the Throne forecast the program of aid to totally disabled persons; a plan was also announced to transform the Department of Resources and Development into a department of 'Northern Affairs and National Development', to correspond to the government's new preoccupation with development of the country's resources, particularly in the Canadian northland.

President Eisenhower's visit went off smoothly, with the usual exchanges of compliments and good wishes. Joint construction of the long-awaited seaway was 'inevitable and certain', the American leader declared, and would be a tangible expression of the 'Canadian-American partnership'. As a further indication of those close ties, he referred to a new joint ministerial committee formed to solve economic and trade problems between the two countries. For his part, St. Laurent declared that the relations between the two countries 'prove to the world that a great power and a lesser power can work in harmony without the smaller

being submerged by his larger neighbour'. The American influence in the world was 'an influence for good', he stated, 'and we
welcome it'. In the balmy days of late 1953, Canada's future as a
sovereign nation seemed assured once and for all.

Parliament began its deliberations in the same moderate key.
George Drew's most dangerous opponents were within his own
party, for a significant number of Conservatives were beginning
to grumble about his ineffective leadership after two consecutive
defeats at the polls. Feeling a surge of sympathy for the Leader of
the Opposition, who was being attacked simultaneously from
front and rear, St. Laurent interpreted Drew's aggressive stance
as inspired more by his need to impress his followers than by any
serious charges he had to proffer against the government. In fact,
the Prime Minister had come to like the Progressive Conservative
leader, and felt that there was little disagreement between them
on basic issues. In replying to Drew in the Throne Speech debate,
he agreed generally with what his opponent had said on the need
to expand trade and to reduce the dangers of an atomic war, and
even refused to take issue with Drew's description of the government's policy as 'socialism in a silk hat'; he and his colleagues still
believed in 'competitive free enterprise', he commented with
good humour, and the proof was that when they did make a bow
to socialism, they did so precisely as the Tory leader had said,
with a silk hat. So successful was he in dissociating himself from
partisan politics that Conservative member Léon Balcer suggested that when the post of governor general became vacant
again, the Prime Minister would be a suitable candidate for that
high office.

The session was adjourned in mid-December for a month-long
Christmas recess, leaving St. Laurent more time to prepare for his
world tour, scheduled to begin in early February. Since his wife
maintained her refusal to fly, two of his children, Madeleine
O'Donnell and Jean-Paul, were chosen to accompany him, in
addition to a staff of seven civil servants. As he was flying
through Europe, the Prime Minister wanted to visit the Canadian
forces serving as part of the NATO shield there, and that implied
visiting the governments of Germany and France, where the men
were stationed. While he dropped Australia and New Zealand

from his original plan, twelve countries were eventually included for one reason or another, and his time in India, the country he most wanted to visit, was reduced to a single week. Furthermore, although Canadian diplomats had firm instructions to reduce official functions to a minimum, it soon became evident that his periods of relaxation would be restricted largely to the flight-time of the R.C.A.F. aircraft between national capitals. The voyage was prepared with no specific diplomatic goals in mind, but the possibility of strengthening relations between Orient and Occident was the most important consideration in drawing up the schedule. As a Western nation with neither a record of colonial expansion nor the potential for future aggression, Canada was not suspect in Asian eyes; on the contrary, a certain bond of sympathy and understanding had been created by the Canadian government's friendly attitude towards India, Pakistan, and Ceylon, visits by Pearson and Sinclair to those countries, and the Canadian contribution of $25 million a year to the Colombo Plan. In the language of international politics, a reserve of diplomatic credit was being established that could prove valuable in maintaining harmonious relations between Asia and the West.

A Canadian diplomatic initiative seemed particularly opportune in early 1954, since the new United States foreign policy, enunciated by John Foster Dulles, of containing Communism had received an almost universally unfavourable response in India. Nehru, like several other Asian leaders, saw it as a form of neo-colonialism that would impose United States leadership on them, and increase rather than diminish the risk of a third world war. The Indian Prime Minister was particularly indignant over the military security pact that Dulles had negotiated with Pakistan; while it was clearly designed to protect Pakistan against the Soviet Union, the practical effect was to supply American weapons that could be used against the Indians in Kashmir. Both Richard Nixon and Dulles had visited New Delhi in an effort to reassure the Indian leader, but without success. Many people in Ottawa and in other capitals felt that St. Laurent, who enjoyed cordial personal relations with both Eisenhower and Nehru, might be able to reduce the feeling of mistrust and perhaps even serve as an intermediary between them. The Canadian Prime

Minister had no aspirations to play a major role in the international chess game, but he was willing to do whatever he could
to improve the situation.

St. Laurent's departure from Ottawa on February 4, just two
days after his seventy-second birthday, was marked by expressions
of support and good wishes from all parties. He was not setting
out with the ambition of changing the course of history, he
stressed in a final radio broadcast, but he hoped to obtain a better
picture of 'the problems which all of us have to face together'.
Decisions taken in Asia, and the welfare and happiness of Asians,
had become of real concern to Canadians, and it had to be
realized that the peoples there also had 'a rich contribution to
make to the general welfare of the free world'.

The first stop was London, where St. Laurent lunched with
Prime Minister Churchill and received a simple but valuable
tip from the Commonwealth's greatest statesman. He had made
several such trips, the great old man confided, and he had found
that the schedule was almost invariably overcrowded and exhausting; as a result, he made it a practice when travelling never to
walk when it was possible to ride, never to stand when it was
possible to sit down, never to sit when he could lie down, and
never to miss an opportunity to visit a washroom, as there was no
knowing when the next opportunity would occur. It was not
advice of high international import, but it was none the less useful. The visits to Paris and Bonn went off smoothly, the traveller
declaring at a press conference in the German capital that 'from
this time on the relations between the peoples of Canada and
Germany have entered a new stage', and that Canadians wished
'to confirm our co-operation with Germany as a partner in a free
world, as a partner of a greater co-operative community in order
to come nearer to our final aim, namely peace on earth to all
people of good will'. There had been long and bitter conflicts
between English- and French-speaking Canadians as well, he
recalled, 'but finally we became convinced that it was better to
look forward into the future than backwards into the past, that it
was better to search for the qualities of the other, and not so much
for his faults and deficiencies'. As a result of this change in
attitude, it had been possible to establish a pattern of life in

Canada that resulted in 'mutual benefits for both sides'. When the Canadians arrived in Rome, Pope Pius XII was ill, and an audience with him had to be cancelled. Monsignor G. B. Montini, later to become Pope Paul VI, received them in his place.

The tour began in earnest when the aircraft touched down at Karachi airport in West Pakistan on February 12, and the travellers were welcomed by Prime Minister Mohammed Ali, a former Pakistani High Commissioner in Ottawa. Asked at a press conference if he had come to mediate the quarrel with India over Kashmir, St. Laurent replied quickly, 'Oh no. . . . I want to leave better relations with Canada and the countries I visit than I found before I attempted the visit.' None the less he pointed out that, after centuries of hostility, the two main groups in Canada had come to accept one another, and in the same way, Canadians had learned to live in peace and friendship with their American neighbours. One newspaperman countered bluntly by asking whether the United States had forcibly occupied any part of Canadian territory. The question indicated that he was right in his resolve to keep away from controversial issues. Running through all of his statements was the message that Canadians recognized and respected the much older civilization of the Asian peoples, and were anxious to deal with them as equals. His country's contribution to the Colombo Plan was but a 'small return for what the West owes the East', he told a group of teachers and students at the new Peshawar University. After being driven up the Khyber Pass to the Afghanistan frontier, he approached the barrier, shook hands with the heavily armed guard on the other side, and told him: 'I hope we can always live in friendship and be mutually helpful to each other.' When the message was translated, the other man responded, 'We are all brothers and this border does not stand between us.'

The R.C.A.F. C-5 aircraft landed in New Delhi on February 21, a full seventeen days after leaving Canada, but the principal challenge of the trip was only about to begin. Under the Asian sun, St. Laurent looked more than ever the old Western gentleman, while Nehru, in Eastern dress, appeared very much the Asian independence leader. As they chatted together, there was reason to question whether the two men could bridge the gap between the continents and races they represented.

On the morning following their arrival, the Canadians attended a sitting of the Indian Parliament during which Nehru reiterated his feeling of concern over the American military aid to Pakistan, and over the fighting between the French and the nationalist forces in Indo-china. On February 23, St. Laurent addressed a joint session of the two chambers of the Indian Parliament with what was designed to be the most important statement of his trip. The Commonwealth was proving its usefulness in 'enabling its Western members to keep in touch with three great Asian nations', he declared, and in making it possible for Canada and India to work together as 'good companions in the broad endeavour to find realistic solutions to world problems'. Canadian foreign policy was based on a realization that a 'world-wide partnership' of all peoples was evolving, based on the interdependence of mankind in every part of the globe. The great differences between the two countries notwithstanding, their similarity of outlook was striking, St. Laurent declared. Canadians were particularly attracted by the Indian approach of seeking 'material progress through the free effort of the people', and welcomed Nehru's statement that his people had 'decided to build India according to democratic methods because, ultimately, we feel that democracy has something of the highest human value.'

St. Laurent had not travelled half-way around the world merely to flatter his hosts; he wanted to put to use the Commonwealth bridge between East and West. Aware that most of his audience, including Nehru himself, felt that the North Atlantic Treaty Organization was an instrument of American 'neo-imperialism', he pointed out that it was a perfectly legitimate collective defence arrangement within the terms of the United Nations Charter, and, more important, the structure around which a Western 'community' could be built that would contribute its own 'creative vitality' to the world. He paid a forthright tribute to the United States as the leader of the NATO group:

> As we see it . . . the readiness of the United States to assume the responsibilities of a major power has been of very great benefit

to the free world. We who live alongside of that great and
dynamic nation know from our own long experience that the
United States is the most unselfish country ever to play this role
and that it has no other ambition than to live and let others
live in mutually helpful intercourse.

He rejected 'the false charges sometimes levelled at the United
States' of using NATO to further expansionist designs. 'Does anyone really believe', he asked, 'that the United States could bring
about aggressive or provocative collective action by the countries
associated with it?' Despite the evident refutation of the Indian
viewpoint, the statement was received with close attention and
respect. Once again, St. Laurent had rendered an important
service by meeting squarely an issue that many men would have
circumvented.

At a banquet that evening, Nehru commented on the 'kinship'
of spirit between his country and Canada. He could not explain
it, except to say that 'there was some kind of deeper understanding, deeper attempt to understand and a successful attempt to
understand even though perhaps in some matters we could not
wholly agree'. After co-operating with Canadians over several
years, Indians had come to appreciate 'this friendly outlook of
Canada . . . which holding fast to her own beliefs and convictions,
can understand others' viewpoints and where possible adapt itself
to others' viewpoints'. As for St. Laurent himself, he had made
a 'deep impress' at their earlier meetings as a man 'of high
integrity, of high purpose and high endeavour'. The cordial
atmosphere and the exchange of compliments in public were
undoubtedly genuine, but they did not reflect, as many people
assumed, still more intimate private discussions. Among their
common traits the two men counted reserve and discretion. Each
found it difficult to break through the other's natural defences;
and they were cautious about touching on subjects that might
lead to disagreement. As a result, their conversations were limited
to more general topics, and interspersed by lengthy periods of
silence. After one such session, a Canadian diplomat remarked in
disappointment, 'These two men haven't got anything to say to
each other after all.'

In public, St. Laurent continued to make an excellent impression. When he received an honorary doctorate at the University of New Delhi from the hands of the Vice-president of India, Dr. Radhakrishnan, he praised the attitude of 'mutual toleration' that was so prevalent in Indian history, and drew another parallel with Canada in referring to the 'unity in diversity' which was the essential characteristic of both nations. Towards the end of the week, he met the local press corps, reputed to be one of the toughest to face in the world. The Indian and Canadian officials who were concerned about the outcome did not reckon with his frankness and humility; he refused to side-step questions, and freely confessed his lack of knowledge when he was unable to reply. Asked if he supported Nehru's appeal for a cease-fire in Indo-china, he replied that he did so 'without any reservation or hesitation whatsoever', since 'nobody wins anything by a war', and political settlements were 'apt to be more permanent than whatever results can be obtained by killing each other off'. He repeated that the North Atlantic Treaty Organization was an instrument of security and not of aggression and denied that it implied the protection of colonies of member countries, such as Goa and Pondicherry on the Indian sub-continent. On the subject of military security, one newspaperman inquired whether he felt it would be 'reasonable, desirable, understandable and expedient for India to arm herself in parity with Pakistan'. After hesitating an instant, St. Laurent replied that he did not know; the room filled with laughter. 'Really, I don't know,' he protested, half embarrassed, half indignant. 'It is not that I want to evade the question, but I don't think I have the kind of information or knowledge that would make an opinion of mine justifiable.' He refused to be led into either criticizing the Americans or differing publicly from Nehru concerning American politics. 'I have travelled quite extensively throughout the United States and I think that in the main the United States citizen is not very much different from the Canadian citizen,' he commented. 'He wants peace; he wants to raise his family under peaceful conditions.' The suggestion was without foundation that the United States was 'deliberately creating tension' by giving military aid to Pakistan, he stated firmly; not one per cent of the American public

366 LOUIS ST. LAURENT

would go along with such a policy. Pushed further on the subject, St. Laurent finally snapped, 'You are free to criticize the United States government. I am not going to do so.' The strong feelings that had been building up suddenly evaporated as laughter broke out once again.

Questioned on the representation of China at the United Nations, he went further than he had done previously, observing:

> At the present time it is not the Nationalist government in Formosa that represents the great mass of humanity that constitutes the people of China, and whether I think that the government is the kind of government China should have or not does not change the facts. . . . I think we have to be realistic and admit that . . . they will some day have to be represented by those that they consider the government that represents them in fact.

The influence of Nehru was obvious behind the declaration. Since a truce had been signed in Korea in 1953, the Indian Prime Minister had argued in their private talks, there was no further obstacle to recognition of the Red régime; not to do so, he asserted, would mean treating the Communists as outcasts from international society, and strengthening them in their opposition to the capitalist world. St. Laurent let himself be convinced; half-way around the globe, he forgot the practical limitations of Canadian politics. When the press conference ended, the journalists gave him an enthusiastic round of applause, a rare tribute in the Indian capital.

By the time his stay in New Delhi drew to an end, St. Laurent had explained Canada's position on the current international issues, and learned more of the Indian viewpoint, but relations between himself and Nehru were still disappointingly distant and formal. On his second-last day in the Indian capital, their daughters, Indira Gandhi and Madeleine O'Donnell, discussed the situation and decided to intervene. That evening each told her father that he was jeopardizing the success of the visit by his reluctance to take the other man completely into his confidence. The two women proved more successful than the politicians and diplomats had been; before the Canadian party flew to visit the

Taj Mahal at Agra the next morning, Nehru asked if they could return earlier than scheduled, as he wanted to have some more time with St. Laurent; the Canadian Prime Minister agreed with alacrity. That evening the ice was finally broken, and they had a thorough and uninhibited discussion; the purpose of the trip had been achieved after all. One of the most important accomplishments of the stay in India was the impression created by St. Laurent as a man. 'He is an honest man without guile,' commented a leading Indian diplomat after he had gone. 'He is clearly above the arts of the petty politician.' Prime Minister Nehru assessed the visit several years later in simple terms. 'For most Indians, he was the first Canadian they had seen, and since they liked him, they had a good impression of Canada.'

Although he carried out his schedule with his usual conscientiousness, St. Laurent was feeling the strain of the arduous journey by the time he reached Madras, his last stop in India, and wrote to his wife that he would be glad to be done with the constant packing and unpacking. He was accustomed to a simple diet, and the oriental food upset his stomach; he ate little of the dishes set before him. The heat added to the strain of spending many hours a day at official functions. Ceylon provided some respite because the party visited the old capital of Kandy, high in the mountains, but when the aircraft landed in Jakarta, capital of Indonesia, after a long flight across the Indian ocean, the temperature was 110°F. After less than two days in Indonesia, and an even shorter stay in Manila, the party flew directly to Korea to visit the Canadian troops serving with the United Nations. Faced suddenly with temperatures below freezing-point, St. Laurent pulled an army battle coat over his suit, and toured the truce line by jeep and helicopter with the Canadian commander, Brigadier Jean Allard. It was his first visit to a battlefront, and he was deeply touched at the sight of the rugged landscape where young Canadians had fought and died. 'It is a terrible country insofar as terrain is concerned,' he commented later, 'and one cannot see why any one of those hills that was the scene of such bloody battles was of sufficient importance to justify the kind of fights that were made for their possession.' During his stay in the war-torn country, St. Laurent held discussions with President

Syngman Rhee, and the American commander, General Maxwell Taylor, unveiled a monument to Canadians killed in action there, and spoke at least a dozen times to small groups of Canadian servicemen. When he left Korea, he was in a state of near-exhaustion.

The visit to Tokyo should have been a pleasant finale to a memorable experience, since relations between the two countries were good, and the Canadian Ambassador, Robert Mayhew, was anxious to ensure a warm welcome for his friend. However, St. Laurent had hardly arrived when he had an attack of dysentery, presumably the result of a germ picked up earlier in his journey. The program for the first full day in the Japanese capital called for a ride through the streets in a royal carriage to the Imperial palace, a reception by Emperor Hirohito, and then a meeting with Japan's greatest post-war statesman, Prime Minister Shigeru Yoshida. Not wishing to disrupt the plan, he concealed his illness, and after a sleepless night set out for the palace, waving cheerfully to the thousands of children that lined the route, observing the precise protocol of the ancient dynasty at the palace, and repeating his message of peace and good will. Later he chatted with the crews of three Canadian destroyers that were in Tokyo harbour, addressed the Japan-Canada Society, and gave a final press conference before leaving Asia.

The newspapermen were particularly interested in his views concerning diplomatic recognition of Communist China. His remarks on the subject in New Delhi had received wide attention, and in response to a question by an American correspondent just as he was boarding the aircraft in Manila, he had surprised his staff by launching into a justification of recognition of the Peking régime as the effective government of the Chinese people. A day later, a press report from Seoul quoted him as stating, 'some day we will have to be realistic and admit that the government of China is the government that the people want.' Within hours Pearson was asked in Ottawa if the Canadian position had been changed, and Drew denounced the description of the Communist régime as 'the government that the people want' as 'a travesty of the facts'. The Minister for External Affairs dispatched a message to Japan, asking for a report on what had actually been said. In an effort to clarify the situation, St. Laurent told the Tokyo press corps that in trying to devise solutions to current problems, it was 'the common-sense realistic approach' to accept that 'those who are in effective control of public affairs in China . . . will have to be participating in the negotiations and agreements reached to dispose of those problems'. At the same time, he refused to be dislodged from his position that Canada was the friend both of the Americans and of countries like India who disagreed with them. 'Of course we do not always see eye to eye upon specific points,' he said of the Americans, 'but in a general way we think that they are doing their best and that it is a pretty good best.'

By the time he completed his program in Tokyo, Louis St. Laurent was yearning to be home. The weary travellers stopped briefly in Honolulu, had a short night's rest in San Francisco, and then flew non-stop to Ottawa. As the doors of the aircraft swung open at Rockcliffe Airport at 9:30 p.m. on March 9, the exact time of arrival set when they took off six weeks earlier, a band struck up the strains of 'O Canada'. Standing in the door-way, and waving his hat at his wife, his cabinet colleagues, and the other members of the welcoming party below, the Prime Minister had tears in his eyes. Leading the way down the ramp, he put around his wife's neck a garland of flowers that he had brought along from Hawaii, and kissed her in an unusual public demonstration of affection. Howe, Pearson and Drew led the rush forward to shake his hand. Hardly on Canadian soil, he was asked by a newspaperman to explain his views with respect to Red China. Once again, he tried to explain his position. He had not advocated recognizing the Peking régime 'at this time', he stated, and the use of the expression 'the government the people of China want', might have been 'an unfortunate way of putting it'. However, there were many problems to be settled in Asia, and 'what I had in mind was that if we were going to discuss the possibilities of a settlement . . . it would have to be discussed with the kind of a government that was there, not because we wanted it but because it happened to be there.' With that the matter was dropped for the moment, and he was allowed to get into his car and be driven home.

The scene when St. Laurent took his place in the House of

Commons the next day was just as moving. Speaker Beaudoin described the desk-pounding that marked his entry as a reflection of 'the genuine sentiments of admiration and affection felt in all parts of the House for the Prime Minister'. His face was flushed and his voice rich with emotion as he tried to express his thanks. He had heard 'O Canada' sung everywhere he went, he said, his trace of Irish brogue more in evidence than usual, 'but when I heard it on opening the doors of the airplane last night, I do confess that a lump rose in my throat, because it was a great pleasure to be back in this land, and because the sight of my friends on the field made me prouder than ever that I could as a Canadian come back to my homeland.' In the rambling narrative of a tourist who had not yet sorted out his many impressions, he spoke for half an hour of the countries he had visited, the sights he had seen, and the people he had met. When he had ended, Drew welcomed him home 'with a full heart', and the two other party leaders followed suit.

A few days later, Liberal senators and members of Parliament gave a special dinner to celebrate their leader's return, and presented him with a globe on which his route was traced, and which bore the inscription '. . . in appreciation of his service to Canada in promoting better understanding and good will in the world'. Once again, the scene was charged with emotion as he described, in words he had learned as a small child in Compton, his main objective in making the long journey. He had tried to convey the message that He who is 'Our Father in Heaven' is indeed 'Our Father' to all people the world over, he told the group of politicians, and that Canada hoped His will would truly be done on earth as in Heaven, and that mankind, His children all over the world, would be able so to arrange their affairs that all could live in peace.

There remained the references to Communist China to explain. While President Eisenhower had been delighted with his defence of the Americans in New Delhi, and had sent a message of appreciation, he was disturbed about the apparent change in the Canadian attitude with regard to the Peking régime. The message was not long in reaching Ottawa that under no circumstances would the President consider recognizing the government of Mao Tse-tung, or allowing it to obtain a seat at the United Nations in the near future. Public opinion was not favourable to such a step either. A week after his return, St. Laurent intervened in a debate on the estimates of the Department of External Affairs to refer to 'at least one of the unfortunate results' of his world tour. He would not claim to have been misquoted, he stated, and accepted responsibility 'for any misinterpretation or misconstruction' of his words, but he did not feel he had used the words 'the government the people wanted' as referring to the Peking régime since he 'never had that feeling about the present government of China'. He had used the word 'recognition' in the broadest sense as 'the government that was in control of the forces that we were opposing'. While he did not feel that diplomatic recognition of the Communist government was called for 'under present conditions', Canada should keep an open mind 'as to when if ever conditions may be such that it will be in the interest of peace and stability in the world to recognize diplomatically whatever government happens to be in control of the forces of China'. It was a painful and even confused performance, and his opponents would undoubtedly have made it more difficult for him if they had not realized his distress. His ruddy complexion and his sense of exhilaration at being home concealed a state of mental and physical fatigue that was serious for a man of his age. The world tour had taken a toll that was to become fully evident only in the months and years that lay ahead; it was his greatest hour, but it marked as well the beginning of his decline; as such, it was a turning-point both for him and for Canadian politics.

Happy as he was to be back in Canada, and to resume his place at the head of the government, Louis St. Laurent had little desire to return to the partisan political struggle. The Emergency Powers Act was allowed to lapse, but not before the Progressive Conservatives used it to accuse the Liberals of what Drew termed 'democratic dictatorship'. More worrisome to St. Laurent were indications of a new spate of troubles with Quebec. During his absence from Canada, Maurice Duplessis had introduced a 15 per cent provincial tax on personal incomes, and repeated in the bill his claim that the provinces had a priority in the field of direct taxation. The Quebec Premier placed the onus on Ottawa to avoid double taxation by demanding that citizens of Quebec be allowed to deduct the amount of the new tax from their payments to the federal treasury. When Douglas Abbott presented his budget on April 6, he rejected once again the claim of provincial priority in the field of direct taxation, and pointed out that to accept Duplessis's demand that the federal tax be reduced by the amount of the Quebec tax was equivalent to recognizing the right of the provinces to determine the amount of the federal tax; it would also destroy the basis of the federal-provincial agreements. He repeated his invitation to the Quebec Premier to put forward an alternative tax-sharing proposal, and assured him that he would 'always find the door open for full and frank discussion in the hope of finding a mutually satisfactory solution'.

Participating in the budget debate, George Drew called for a federal-provincial conference to 'overcome these difficulties'; junior minister Jean Lesage condemned as 'absurd' the argument that the provinces had a priority in the field of direct taxation, and compared the Quebec Premier to a little boy who pulled the cat's tail, and replied to his father, who had told him to stop: 'I am not pulling, the cat is.' St. Laurent sat silently through the discussion until the Leader of the Opposition appealed to him directly in early May to call a federal-provincial conference on 'the broad question of taxation'; then he pulled himself together with an obvious effort, and spoke in support of his Minister of Finance. No one pretended that the tax rental agreements were an ideal or permanent solution, he stated, but they were the best that it had been possible to devise, and he did not think that they impaired in any way the constitutional jurisdiction of either Parliament or the provincial legislature; otherwise, he would not have been prepared to recommend them. While the requirements of the federal administration made it impossible to increase the tax rental payments to the provinces, or to allow provincial taxes to be deducted from the federal ones, he was willing to consider any alternative to the current set of agreements, subject to only three conditions: the rights of both the federal and provincial authorities must be respected, any new terms must be available to all provinces, and the federal government must remain in a position to discharge its 'national obligations'. Until some such basis for discussion was put forward, he did not think a conference would be desirable or 'apt to be at all helpful'.

Not without some justification, Drew described the Prime Minister's statement as 'unhappy in content, unhappy in presentation, and unhappy in its consequences'. Six weeks after his return to Canada, the effects of the world tour had struck St. Laurent with full force, and he was in a state approaching physical and mental exhaustion. Only his dogged determination kept him appearing at his office every morning, and in the House of Commons after lunch; he did not even seem able to bestir himself sufficiently to decide to go away for a rest. He felt he should remain at the helm, but his inability to solve the problems facing the government depressed him, and worsened his condition. In short, he had ceased to lead.

To make matters worse, St. Laurent was informed shortly after his return to Canada that three of his most valuable colleagues, Brooke Claxton, Douglas Abbott, and Lionel Chevrier, had decided to retire from politics. Since they were a generation younger than he was, the news came as a complete surprise; he had assumed that he and Howe would be the first to retire. While their decision had the appearance of a jointly conceived plan, the three men had arrived separately at the conclusion that the time had come to leave the cabinet. While Claxton maintained his killing pace of work, he had become a favourite target of opposition criticism; his family pleaded with him to withdraw from the continuous battle and to accept a position in private enterprise before it was too late. Abbott was also influenced largely by family pressure. Although his responsibilities as Minister of Finance obliged him to impose many unpopular measures, he was one of the best-liked men in Parliament, and was considered a possible future prime minister. However, he was too well-balanced an individual to sacrifice all else to political ambition, and, at the urging of his family, he asked the Prime Minister for an appointment to the Supreme Court. As for Lionel Chevrier, he had played the key role in every stage of the preparation for the construction of the St. Lawrence seaway; the final hurdles were almost passed, and a beginning of construction seemed likely before the end of the year; he decided to see the project through to completion, and asked for the presidency of the authority about to be set up for that purpose. If Mackenzie King had been faced with such a situation, it is unlikely that the three ministers would have succeeded in carrying out their plans; they would have been made to feel that to stay in the government was their first duty, and that they must not put their private interests before their country. They might well have been faced with the threat of the Prime Minister's own resignation if they insisted. Louis St. Laurent was not capable of threats or pleas; moreover, he understood the motives of the men who were seeking their release from the bondage of politics. He could only leave them free to judge for themselves what course they should take, and accept the consequences.

The session ground to an end in late June without the Prime Minister having shown any signs of renewed vigour. He spoke seldom in the House of Commons, making only brief answers to questions directed to him, or reading statements of policy. Paul Martin referred to him as the real author of a bill to assist disabled persons that was passed in the early summer, but he himself took no part in the debate. Queried about the creation of a Canada Council, he replied that he had 'not made any attempt to deal with that problem since I came back from my visit around the world'. His conduct added credence to the opposition charge that the government was composed of 'tired old men'. And yet, he managed to go through the motions of carrying out his duties, spending the usual long hours on Parliament Hill, poring over the papers submitted to him, and making the speeches he had agreed to give. On July 1, he announced the cabinet shuffle made necessary by the resignations of his three colleagues. Walter Harris was appointed Minister of Finance, thus lending weight to speculation that the Ontario Baptist was the new crown prince of the Liberal Party. Pickersgill moved into Harris's place as Minister of Citizenship and Immigration. Ralph Campney moved up from the post of associate minister to that of Minister of National Defence. Entering the cabinet for the first time were Roch Pinard, as Secretary of State, and George Marler, former

Acting Leader of the Opposition in the Quebec legislature, as Minister of Transport.

While the new appointments were generally well received, they gave rise to speculation that the cabinet shuffle was merely a preliminary to more important changes; reports had been circulating in the corridors of the Parliament Buildings that St. Laurent was going to have a good rest at St. Patrick during the summer, and would decide in the autumn on the basis of his health if he would ask that a leadership convention be called. The suggestion that he was losing his grip annoyed him, and when he was asked at a press conference on July 1 about his own plans for the future, he replied somewhat testily that his plans were 'to do a day's work every day and there is no time to peer into the future'; in fact, he added, he would be back in Ottawa the following week, because 'there are so many important things to do'. As he was about to leave his East Block office for the railway station, he could not resist remarking with a trace of bitterness to a small group of newspapermen hovering in the corridor: 'When I return I don't think any of you gentlemen will have occasion to refer to me as a "tired old man".'

As soon as he arrived in St. Patrick, St. Laurent turned his attention to recovering his strength with the same assiduity and determination with which he tackled every problem. Adopting a regular schedule, he spent part of each morning with a secretary dealing with the material sent to him from Ottawa, played golf whenever the weather permitted, and swam in the salt-water swimming-pool that Jean-Paul had built beside his own summer house in nearby Cacouna. He did return to the capital periodically, but his trips there became less frequent as he relaxed and began to regain his strength. When he appeared near Cornwall, Ontario, in early August to take part in the sod-turning ceremony that marked the beginning of the St. Lawrence seaway and power project, his face was brown, and he looked like a man at a country picnic as he and New York Governor Thomas Dewey plunged their shovels into the ground on which the long-awaited power installations were to be built. By the second week of August, St. Laurent had not only recovered

his buoyant spirits, but displayed an aggressiveness that astonished all those who knew of his condition a few weeks earlier. Once
again, a railway strike was threatening to disrupt the economy,
this time over a contributory sickness benefit plan and a series of
smaller issues. The Prime Minister was determined that the
transportation system must not be paralysed, and he prepared to
summon Parliament. When the railway workers voted to quit
work, he ordered an aircraft to pick him up in Quebec City, and
on his arrival in Ottawa stated bluntly that there was not going
to be a railway strike. Meeting with representatives of management and labour the same day, he insisted that negotiations
should be reopened 'in the frame of mind of a desire to reach a
reconciliation of differences of view' and with 'a sincere desire
to find a basis for honourable compromise'. He would call an
emergency session of Parliament if necessary, he told them, and
warned that any settlement they could agree to would be preferable to one imposed from outside. The negotiators returned to
the bargaining table, but two days later Frank Hall, chief labour
negotiator, resigned as chairman of the union negotiating committee in protest against the pressure put upon him by the Prime
Minister to reach an agreement; there was no 'essential difference', he complained, 'between compulsory arbitration as contemplated by the government and acceptance of arbitration under
duress'. His resignation was not accepted by his union and the
strike was averted, but the Liberals' image was not improved in
the eyes of an important segment of the population.

In a second important disagreement in the same season, it was
St. Laurent himself who precipitated the crisis. His family was
just as sensitive as he was to the criticism that he had failed to
give adequate leadership in the spring, and he was urged by some
of his children to assert himself or to retire. Jean-Paul had a
growing antipathy for the Union Nationale administration, and
argued that a stand had to be taken against it for the sake of
national unity. At social gatherings, stories of abuses of power by
Duplessis and his colleagues were commonplace, and stirred St.
Laurent's indignation. That same summer, the Laval University
Press published a book written by Maurice Lamontagne entitled
*Le Fédéralisme Canadien*, which supported the federal govern-

ment's policies on federal-provincial financial relations. The author had been director of the Department of Economics at Laval University until the spring, but had then become assistant deputy minister in the Department of Northern Affairs and Natural Resources, on the understanding that he would also serve as special adviser to the Prime Minister. When Lamontagne's book appeared, Duplessis was so infuriated that he forced the rector of Laval University to dissociate himself from its contents.

The Quebec Premier continued his attacks on the Liberals in Ottawa during the summer; they wanted to replace the federal system with a system of 'trusteeship', he charged, and to turn the Quebec government into an 'auxiliary government' dependent on federal 'pensions and subsidies'. Such a situation, he declared, was appropriate for 'drunks, imbeciles and people incapable of looking after themselves', but Quebec was 'dependent on no one'. When Abbott was appointed to the Supreme Court, he commented that the appointment was made 'because of the centralizing ideas he just expressed'. By the beginning of September, St. Laurent had decided that his health was good enough to do battle with Duplessis, and in his own words to be around 'long enough to avoid leaving too heavy an unfinished task for those who would come after me'. The occasion he chose was a luncheon aboard the Cunard liner *Saxonia*, in Montreal harbour. Without warning his cabinet colleagues in advance of his plan, he astonished his fellow guests by declaring that while nearly everyone seemed pleased that Canada's growth and development was giving the country increasing influence in the world, there were two exceptions: 'one is behind the Iron Curtain, the other is in the province of Quebec, which is not showing any enthusiasm because the growth and development of Canada means the increasing influence of the federal government.' The remark was a deliberate provocation, and the reaction was not long in coming. 'The Prime Minister probably knows the opinion of Russia through the Canadian ambassador in Moscow,' retorted Quebec Attorney General Antoine Rivard. 'For our part we should have liked to know the opinion of a Canadian ambassador to the Vatican. . . . We shall continue to think that it is more important to recognize the rights of the province of Quebec than those of Communist China.'

In the third week of September, the Prime Minister returned to the attack at a ceremony to inaugurate the new home of the Quebec Reform Club. Speaking without notes, and in the simple colloquial French he employed in his own family, he talked for over two hours about his conflict with the government of Quebec. There were sincere, honest Quebec nationalists who saw in the growth of the Canadian nation a danger to Abbé Groulx's thesis of 'a French, Catholic State in America that would be autonomous, sovereign, and separated from the "damned Protestants" that surround us', he declared with the irony that was his favourite weapon. He could never accept their point of view.

> You know, whether people like it or not, the men at the head of governments are only instruments to carry out the plans of Providence, and I believe it was planned that there should be another nation in America like the United States. . . . I am convinced that Montcalm and Wolfe were merely the instruments of an all-powerful Providence . . . sent to create a situation where the descendants of the two great races would find themselves together on this northern part of the American continent.

His opponents believed that Quebec could not be 'a province like the others'; well, he was not of that opinion. When he began attending meetings of the Canadian Bar Association, some of his friends said he was endangering the Quebec legal system by associating with common-law lawyers. Forty years later, that fear no longer existed. 'After all, you know, we are as good as the others . . . and I have never been afraid to place someone trained in Quebec alongside people from any other province.' He denied that such an attitude made him a 'centralizer'. 'I have always asserted that we had no right to take away anything placed under provincial jurisdiction without the consent of those who held provincial responsibility. . . . But between true provincial autonomy and autonomy as a blind to prevent discussion of provincial affairs, there is a difference.' The situation in Quebec reminded him of the story of a certain Alcibiades in ancient Greece who was a clever and ambitious politician, but not very scrupulous. He had a fine dog that followed him everywhere. One time people started criticizing his administration, and, just at that time, Alcibiades had his dog's tail cut off. The animal continued to follow him, but people spoke only of the poor dog who had had its tail cut off. One of his friends asked him why he had done such a thing. 'Well, you know,' the politician answered, 'I prefer that they talk of my dog than of my administration.' 'Two thousand years have passed since then,' St. Laurent remarked with a mischievous grin, 'but human nature hasn't changed, nor have dogs, but there are people who study history and profit from its lessons.'

Once launched on his attack, the indignant Prime Minister outlined a whole series of grievances he held against the Union Nationale administration. He ridiculed the claim that the tax-sharing agreements could somehow undermine the system of Roman Catholic schools and the right to practise the Roman Catholic religion, or endanger the struggle for survival of the French-speaking group. He rejected criticism of the appointment of Douglas Abbott to fill the vacancy on the Supreme Court that had been created by the retirement of a French-speaking Canadian, Chief Justice Thibaudeau Rinfret. A year earlier, he had replaced an English-speaking by a French-speaking Canadian in Montreal, he pointed out, and, anyway, he wanted to avoid a set of rules that would make it impossible for an English-speaking lawyer from Quebec ever to aspire to a seat on the Supreme Court of Canada. He was also annoyed that the province of Quebec had refused to take part in building a trans-Canada highway. The offer of the federal government to pay half of the cost of the project still stood, he declared, and Ottawa would even reimburse half of the cost of the portion that the province had built on its own, 'at least the amount that has been spent wisely'; the accounts would have to be examined, for 'after all, you know, even the Union Nationale must be honest about it.' In addition, the Quebec government would have to agree to the granting of future construction contracts for the highway by a proper system of open tenders instead of the usual private deals. 'We are starting a campaign to let the public in Quebec know what we think . . . ,' announced the Liberal leader when he had completed the enumeration of his disagreements with the Union Nationale government. 'We are going to tell them frankly what is the situation, we are going to tell them that we will continue to raise more taxes than we need and to redistribute some of it to others. . . . If the population feels that is a bad policy, it will vote against us and put someone else in our place. But at least it will know what to expect.'

The declaration of political war made headlines across Canada, and newspapermen commented in sensational terms on the battle of the giants. While many Liberals were delighted that their leader had decided at last to reply in kind to the man who represented the antithesis of all he stood for in public life, other Canadians found his belligerence strangely out of character and wondered how it could be reconciled with his frequent appeals for moderation and compromise. 'No solution will ever be found by exchanges of thunder and lightning,' warned the Montreal *Gazette* on September 20. '. . . By seeking answers to these problems in the cannon's mouth, all hopes of an immediate, limited, workable adjustment will be driven to seek shelter at a safe distance.'

Maurice Duplessis gave his reply at a bridge-christening ceremony at Valleyfield on September 26. St. Laurent wanted to wipe out all the hard-won achievements of French-speaking Canadians, and 'return to the days of the English governors,' he charged. If the provinces allowed themselves to be taken in by 'certain dangerous, centralizing manoeuvres of Ottawa', the day would come when there would be a Communist or Socialist government in Canada, 'something that could never happen as long as the province of Quebec keeps its autonomy'. When he heard St. Laurent, 'a compatriot, a man from the province of Quebec, raised in the province of Quebec, coddled by the province of Quebec, a man who has had all the advantages of living with the population of Quebec', declare that all the provinces were similar, he found that statement 'painful', 'distressing', and 'seriously pathetic'. No 'English politician' had ever dared to make such a statement, the Union Nationale leader remarked; 'it had to be a compatriot who proclaimed something as contrary to the facts as to the law.' Quebec could never accept that position; 'it would be like exchanging . . . the invigorating air of our province for a federal oxygen tent . . . our rights as owners, our mastery of our own house in all respects for the title of pensioner and the role of a pensioner.' He could not understand 'why a man loses his self-control to the point of disowning his race, his province, his rights . . . , why he goes to such trouble to turn the other provinces against Quebec. . . .' St. Laurent had admitted that his government raised 17 per cent more taxes than it needed in order to help the poorer provinces, Duplessis pointed out. 'They take 17 per cent to make gifts to others. When we want 15 per cent of our own money to build schools, he refuses, and he calls that a Canadian policy.' The Quebec Premier, too, had an anecdote to illustrate the situation. The Prime Minister's claim that the fiscal arrangements were only temporary recalled the story of the drunkard who protested that he only went on two binges a year, 'when I go fishing and when I don't'. The fiscal proposals of the federal government were like the drunkard's sprees, 'temporarily permanent'. He had always been ready to meet with St. Laurent or with Finance Minister Harris, Duplessis declared, and had offered publicly to do so in Montreal, or on some other 'neutral ground', but his basic position was very clear: 'co-operation always, co-operation between equals, co-operation that is not a one-way street. Affiliation: never. Abdication of fundamental rights: never. Substitution of federal subsidies for essential taxing powers: never. Direct or indirect federal control of our schools by Ottawa: never. Of our universities: never. Of our secondary school system: never.'

In their concepts of Canadian federalism, the two men were still poles apart. For St. Laurent and his advisers, the basic issue was whether the federal government was to have the economic and financial power necessary to maintain the country's growth and prosperity. There were indications that the economy would slow down seriously in the coming months, and some federal officials feared a full-scale depression. The lesson of the 1930s must not be forgotten, the cabinet was warned; the provinces could not use deficit financing systematically to meet an economic crisis because they had no control of monetary policy and only limited borrowing capacity; it was more important than ever for Ottawa to maintain control of the taxing power. Representatives of Canadian labour lent weight to the arguments of the federal government's financial advisers when they booed Labour Minister Gregg at a Canadian Congress of Labour convention on September 27 on the grounds that Ottawa had not taken adequate measures to relieve unemployment. For Duplessis's supporters, on the other hand, the basic consideration was ethnic and religious rather than economic. 'The issue is whether the French-Canadian people will survive with strength, or whether the confrontation will mark its decline into bondage,' wrote journalist Léopold Richer in *Notre Temps*. *Le Devoir* cartoonist Robert LaPalme described the Prime Minister as 'more Stephen than St. Laurent'.

Caught between the two conflicting viewpoints, St. Laurent began to realize the dangers to Canada of an all-out test of strength, and his instinct for moderation and compromise gradually took over. Maurice Duplessis, for his part, was not so much interested in a power struggle with the government in Ottawa as in the more limited objective of asserting his authority in his provincial domain. Notwithstanding their personal animosity, both men protested their desire to negotiate a settlement of the dispute. The man who played the most effective part in arranging a meeting between them was a political novice, Egan Chambers, who was campaigning as the Progressive Conservative candidate in the Montreal constituency of St. Lawrence–St. George, previously represented by Brooke Claxton. He sent telegrams to both St. Laurent and Duplessis, urging them to 'put all other considerations second to the welfare of your fellow citizens', and to resolve the dispute; the texts were handed to the Montreal press as soon as they were dispatched. St. Laurent replied the following day. He had already stated that if the Quebec Premier wanted to have an interview with him or any of his colleagues, and 'would make his wish known to me either directly or through anyone authorized by him to do so on his behalf . . . arrangements could be made very quickly . . . to discuss [the situation] in a serious attempt to reach, if not a permanent solution, at least a tolerable *modus vivendi.* . . .' At the same time, he declared, the federal authorities could not accept, either directly or indirectly, the assertion of provincial priority in the field of corporation and personal income taxes. No conference could possibly reconcile the firm stands on that issue, but there might be some other approach to the problem, and 'we of the federal government would always be prepared to participate in an investigatory conference if the provincial authorities inform us of their desire to have one'. Once again the text was released to the press; Duplessis grasped at the olive branch extended to him, and telephoned St. Laurent to suggest a meeting in Montreal. The Prime Minister was so delighted that as soon as the time and place were fixed, he telephoned personally to the Parliamentary Press Gallery to announce the news. 'This is the Prime Minister,' he stated when someone came on the line. 'Yeah, who are you kidding?' replied the clerk who took the call; then, recognizing the voice, he screamed for a reporter to come and take down the statement.

The much-heralded meeting took place in the Windsor Hotel on October 5. With no one else present, the two men put aside personal considerations, and soon got down to a serious discussion of the factors underlying their dispute. St. Laurent repeated his assurance that he wanted to help the provinces obtain the revenues required to meet their responsibilities, but stated that he could not accept the theory of provincial priority in the field of direct taxation, since it was contrary to Canadian constitutional law. Duplessis minimized the importance of that aspect of the disagreement, and stressed Quebec's rapidly growing need for schools, roads, and other capital expenditures. St. Laurent conceded willingly that some provinces might require more money than they were able to obtain under the existing federal-provincial tax-sharing formula, and declared that he had no objection to altering the 1952 agreements, on condition that any new arrangement would be available to all the provinces. Once it was established that the matter of principle was not an insurmountable obstacle, and that they were really arguing about dollars and cents, an interim agreement for the duration of the current federal-provincial fiscal agreements was easy to reach. After an hour's discussion, the two men agreed that the provincial tax on personal incomes should stand, and that the taxpayers of Quebec should receive a 10-per-cent abatement of the federal tax. To avoid the inconvenience to the public of making two separate payments, Ottawa would collect both, and turn the province's share over to it later. In return, Duplessis agreed to amend the statute asserting the principle of provincial priority in the field of direct taxation. The bargain struck in the Windsor Hotel suite marked a turning point in federal-provincial relations, for it established the principle that two kinds of tax-sharing arrangements could be made between Ottawa and the provinces; the question whether Quebec was a province like the others was avoided neatly by making the compromise formula available to others as well.

St. Laurent emerged first from the meeting, and told the eager newspapermen gathered to learn the results of the confrontation that after discussing the situation 'frankly and very cordially', he and Duplessis had agreed on a course that would protect the respective rights of each government. Although he refused to go into details, the basis of the deal was clear: Duplessis was to get more money, but at the price of withdrawing his claim of provincial priority for direct taxation and dropping the argument in favour of a particular status for Quebec. While the arrangement was heralded in Quebec as an act of statesmanship, it was condemned by many Canadians in other parts of Canada as a shoddy political 'hotel-room deal'. The federal government's financial advisers were generally unfavourable to the settlement, fearing that the dike had been opened for further concessions, and that the bargaining position of the federal government had been seriously undermined. St. Laurent himself was well satisfied; he felt that he had proved again that it was possible to reconcile the national interest and that of French Canada. His satisfaction was somewhat diminished when Duplessis declared a few days later that he still believed that the provinces had a priority in the field of direct taxation, but that he had agreed to amend the tax law 'to avoid any useless clash'.

St. Laurent maintained his regular pace throughout the closing months of 1954. Rising shortly after 7 a.m., he read the Montreal *Gazette* while eating a hearty breakfast, then stepped into the front seat of his Chrysler limousine beside his chauffeur, Gordon

McCartney, to be driven to Parliament Hill. By the time he arrived there, his confidential messenger, seventy-year-old Aldéric Groslouis, had aired and dusted his office, and Pierre Asselin had placed the morning mail on his desk; a staff of forty persons was busy answering routine correspondence, preparing material for statements and speeches, clipping items from two dozen newspapers for his attention, and preparing memoranda on a wide variety of topics. At one o'clock he returned to the official residence for a quiet lunch; from two-thirty to six o'clock he was back in the East Block. About two evenings a week he attended a reception on the way home, usually at the residence of some foreign diplomat observing his country's national anniversary or some similar occasion. His routine on such occasions was always the same; he arrived promptly, took one drink and smoked one cigarette, circulated among the guests until he had greeted everyone, then left in time to watch the 6:45 p.m. news on television at home. His evenings were spent in a small study on the second floor of the Prime Minister's residence, reading the documents he had brought home from the office, or playing cards with his wife. At eleven o'clock he watched the news again, and then went to bed.

The general impression created by the Liberals was one of competent but unspectacular government, with administrative considerations taking priority over political ones. St. Laurent appeared more than ever to be the chairman of an executive committee, exercising a general supervision over his colleagues' activities but seldom intervening directly in their respective fields of responsibility. Most requests made to him by the public were transmitted automatically to the department concerned, to be dealt with by the appropriate civil servants. Even on important matters of policy, the cabinet appeared to take little initiative, and to spend more time explaining why action could not be taken than in solving recognized problems. No imaginative measures were being taken to counter the economic recession. Three years after it was recommended by the Massey Commission, St. Laurent had to admit that creation of a Canada Council was receiving 'very active consideration', but that he still had nothing specific to report. He spent many hours trying to put together a list of 'unorthodox' or non-political Senate appointments that would enhance the prestige of the Upper Chamber, but did not complete the list because of the determined resistance of Liberals to giving up their claim to the available seats, and the reluctance of distinguished Canadians to offer their services. The government would have had more cause for concern about the political future if it had been faced with a stronger and more united opposition; the three other parties represented in the House of Commons were even further from one another than they were from the Liberals. In addition, George Drew, the only serious contender for the prime ministership, was suffering under the double handicap of poor health and disloyalty within his own ranks. In July, the Toronto *Telegram* had called for a leadership convention to replace him, and in September another Conservative newspaper, the *Winnipeg Tribune*, followed suit. Depressed and discouraged, the Tory chieftain spent much of the autumn in Europe; on his return, he was admitted to hospital in Ottawa. In November, the government lost four out of ten by-elections, but three of the seats had been previously in opposition hands, and the other one was a marginal seat that did not indicate a trend. On the surface at least, the Liberals did not seem to be losing ground.

From the outset of the new session of Parliament that opened on January 7, 1955, the unemployment problem dominated the debates. In the Speech from the Throne, the government conceded that 'some unemployment of a regional and seasonal nature' was being experienced, and announced some increased spending to meet the situation, but not the dramatic remedial action that labour unions and other groups were demanding. With Drew still convalescing from his illness, the Acting Leader of the Opposition, Earl Rowe, a former member of R. B. Bennett's administration, returned to the themes of protectionism and Commonwealth preferences as an answer to the economic problem. In his reply, St. Laurent argued in a quiet, reasonable tone that any tinkering by the government with the financial or trade pattern was unlikely to improve the economic situation. The current unemployment resulted from a combination of seasonal and world conditions, he argued; the former would disappear in a matter of weeks; and as for the latter, all that could be done was to reduce their consequences wherever possible. When his turn came to speak, Coldwell drew attention to the contrast between the Prime Minister's statement and one he had made the previous September, that if he and his colleagues could not solve the unemployment problem they should be thrown out of office as incompetent. The observation of the C.C.F. leader was pertinent; after maintaining a vigorous pace and a positive attitude for several months, St. Laurent had begun to show signs of weariness and discouragement again, and the challenges that had stimulated him in the autumn seemed insuperable in early 1955.

On January 28, St. Laurent and Pearson flew to London to attend a Commonwealth conference; the decision to take along the Minister for External Affairs reflected the Prime Minister's feeling of inadequacy to put forward the Canadian position on the items that were to be discussed. Torn between the feeling that he should not leave Canada during the session and his reluctance to shirk his responsibilities towards his fellow prime ministers, he insisted that social commitments be kept to a minimum in London, and that his aircraft be kept in readiness to fly him home as soon as possible. The discussion in the British capital turned largely around the continuing tension in the Far East. The Premier of Communist China, Chou En-lai, had announced that Formosa would be taken by force, and the Eisenhower administration had responded by signing a mutual defence treaty with the Nationalist Chinese government of Chiang Kai-shek. In mid-January 1955, the Peking régime began intensive bombing of the Tachen Islands, two hundred miles north of Formosa, forcing the Nationalists to begin a strategic withdrawal from the exposed area. Observers speculated on when the Americans would begin exchanging shots with the mainland Chinese forces. Prime Minister Nehru had visited China late in 1954, and, consequently, his views of the tense situation were of particular interest. Chairman Mao Tse-tung had stressed in their discussions that China, like India, was an industrially backward country, and needed a long period of peace to develop its economy; for that reason, the new government wished to have peaceful relations with everyone. It was the Americans, the Chinese leader argued, who were creating tension by helping the Nationalists to attack the mainland. When they met in London, St. Laurent and Nehru had a long private conversation about the situation in the Far East, the Indian leader maintaining the viewpoint that recognition of the Peking government was an essential step in reducing tension in that area. The Canadian Prime Minister listened with interest, but explained that Canada could take no initiative in the matter for the moment.

It was Churchill's last Commonwealth conference, and, although very deaf and old, he imposed his personality on the other prime ministers. He was particularly interested in the implications of the atomic bomb on military strategy, and pointed out that it might well mean the destruction of war, not of humanity; that 'safety might be the child of terror and life the twin of annihilation'. Nehru saw the world more as 'hovering indefinitely on the brink of terror'. St. Laurent participated in the discussions on regional defence organizations, outlining Canada's commitments to North American defence and to NATO, but he left much of the detailed discussion to Pearson, who was constantly beside him at the conference table. While the range of subjects that came up for consideration was wide, the only specific decision taken was to approve Pakistan's request to remain in the Commonwealth as a republic. More significant was the degree to which the participants were able to reach, in the words of the final communiqué, 'a broadly similar response to most international problems of the day'. Nehru put aside his suspicion of the North Atlantic Treaty Organization, agreeing that it was a legitimate 'defensive shield', and not an instrument of aggression as the Communists claimed. He even accepted the statement that in regional defence planning, Commonwealth countries needed 'the closest association with the United States'. A year, or even a few weeks, earlier, St. Laurent would have enjoyed the meeting, and been stimulated by the challenge of establishing a common viewpoint on the great issues of the period. Now his zest and resilience had left him, and he went through the motions of carrying out his functions with grim determination. On his birthday, the management of the Dorchester Hotel presented him with a cake, and Sir Winston extended greetings on behalf of all the delegates, but he could not even be persuaded to take the evening off to attend a play with his daughter Marthe, who was accompanying him. One engagement that he could not avoid was a ceremony to present him with the freedom of the City of London. Even then, instead of relaxing and enjoying the occasion, he insisted that the ritual be kept as simple as possible, and that the drive from the hotel be made in a closed car, rather than in the usual royal coach with a military escort. As soon as the function was over, he rushed back to Canada with an ill-disguised sense of relief.

# 13

---

## Vulnerable

George Drew and Louis St. Laurent returned to the House of Commons about the same time. In welcoming the Leader of the Opposition back, the Prime Minister expressed his delight at seeing him restored apparently 'to his usual good health and his accustomed robust vigour', and referred to the 'personal friendship' between them. The cordial remarks revealed the change in their relations during seven years of political battles. St. Laurent hoped that Drew would be able to carry out his duties effectively, and confound his enemies within his own party. The sense of grievance that Drew had developed during the war had long since given way to a sentiment of liking and respect.

Unemployment remained the government's principal problem; in January 1955, the number of applicants for jobs at employment offices was 50 per cent higher than a year earlier. Milton Gregg and C. D. Howe, contrasting personalities, were given the primary responsibility for answering the opposition criticism of inaction. The Minister of Trade and Commerce gave a detailed analysis of the causes of the recession, explaining it largely as a consequence of 'a general business let-down in the United States', and outlining the economic policies that had been adopted to improve the situation. With characteristic optimism, he declared that the economy was demonstrating 'great vigour and resilience' in adjusting to new conditions, and warned that

390

the government must not interfere 'with the attainment of a highly productive low-cost economy' on which Canada's competitive position depended. Opposition parties scoffed at such expressions of confidence and demanded more specific action.

Even as he was being accused of inaction, Howe was trying to get a huge project started that would achieve precisely the objectives his opponents had in mind. A builder all his life, he had been attracted by the challenge of constructing a pipeline to move natural gas from the recently discovered fields of Alberta to Canada's industrial heartland. In 1951, Parliament had granted a charter to Trans-Canada Pipe Lines Limited, a subsidiary of an American company, to construct a pipeline from Alberta to Montreal via an all-Canadian route. Another company, Western Pipe Lines, which was largely Canadian-owned and had the backing of Premier Manning of Alberta, was seeking authority to move gas from the same area to Regina, Winnipeg, and across the border into the distribution system of the Northern Natural Gas Company in Minnesota. A third organization, the Consumers' Gas Company, backed largely by influential Conservatives in Toronto, was endeavouring to obtain distribution rights for Ontario. The Alberta government took the position that no gas should be exported from that province until a surplus in excess of local needs was proved; the federal government adopted a similar attitude concerning export from Canada. Late in 1953, the Alberta conservation authorities declared that a surplus existed, and, immediately, Premier Frost called for action to move the precious fuel to central Canada. C. D. Howe stepped into the picture enthusiastically to see that the huge project was carried out. Faced with one company that had a charter for the route north of the Great Lakes and with considerable, but American, capital, and another company that was more Canadian-owned but wanted to export primarily to the United States, he forced a fusion of the two under terms designed to pool their advantages; the name Trans-Canada Pipe Lines was retained for the new firm. The Consumers' Gas Company was eliminated as a possible builder of the line.

During 1954 and early 1955, preparations went ahead for the huge undertaking. In May 1954 the Alberta Petroleum and

Natural Gas Conservation Board granted the company an export permit, in July the Canadian Board of Transport Commissioners approved in principle the application to construct the pipeline, and in September agreement was reached with the Northern Natural Gas Company on the distribution of gas in the Minnesota area. Finally, hearings were arranged for January 1955 before the United States Federal Power Commission to obtain approval of the plan to move gas across the border. There remained the knottiest problem of all, that of financing the project. By the beginning of 1955, the company had spent some $15 million in arranging to purchase the natural gas in Alberta, and in obtaining sales contracts, rights of way, and other prerequisites to actual construction; it had also signed contracts with three engineering firms that called for completion of the line as far as Winnipeg by the end of 1955. However, the total cost of the project was estimated as $350 million, and Canadian financial houses refused to underwrite a bond issue until enough sales contracts had been signed to cover the carrying charges. Potential customers, on the other hand, refused to sign contracts until the construction of the pipeline was assured and a firm date had been set for its completion. Negotiations with producers in Alberta were held up for similar considerations. As a result, by the beginning of 1955, no firm contract had been signed with either producers, financial houses, or consumers.

On January 7, Nathan Tanner, president of Trans-Canada Pipe Lines Limited, wrote to C. D. Howe, informing him that the assistance of the federal government would be required in obtaining the necessary financing if a start on construction was to be made that year. He asked Ottawa to guarantee the interest and sinking-fund requirements on a first mortgage of $275 million, representing 80 per cent of the total cost, until the company's earnings reached a level sufficient to cover the financial carrying charges. Even the most cautious feasibility studies indicated that the government would not be called upon to pay anything, he pointed out, and that after the fourth year of operation the company would be able to pay interest on its funded debt. C. D. Howe passed the request on to Finance Minister Harris for the comments of his officials and the staff of the Bank of

Canada. There it ran into trouble. The government's financial experts agreed that the company was certain to reap very substantial rewards after a few years of operations, and that the risks of an eventual loss to the federal treasury were extremely small. Nevertheless, they rejected the request on the grounds that the approval of the United States Federal Power Commission had not yet been obtained, that a government guarantee of a 4-per-cent interest rate would undermine the price of outstanding government bonds and jeopardize new issues, and that, in general, the proposal raised 'awkward problems of precedent and past practice'.

When Harris communicated the reply to the company, he suggested that the problem be submitted to the Industrial Development Bank, a subsidiary organization of the Bank of Canada created to provide moderate-sized loans for which normal financing was not available. Although that organization was not equipped to deal with such a large project, Tanner made his submission as suggested. The officials of the Industrial Development Bank proved to be tough, arch-conservative bargainers. They suggested that 30 per cent of the required capital, or $105 million, be raised by the sale of common stock, and the remainder through first-mortgage bonds. The Industrial Development Bank would purchase $35 million worth of the common stock as fully convertible debentures at 6-per-cent interest, and 'stand by' to purchase a further amount at a fee of 2 per cent if necessary; in return, two of its nominees would be made directors of Trans-Canada Pipe Lines – one of them to be a member of the executive committee – and the executive officers would not be changed without its consent. Finally, the company's share of the initial outlay was to be increased to $10 million, and that amount escrowed. The proposal would have placed the Industrial Development Bank in a position to dictate the company's policy, a situation completely unacceptable to executives of the Gulf Oil Company, the firm that was to supply most of the gas in Alberta. Even more important, Canadian investment firms were unlikely to recommend to their customers the purchase of common shares that constituted such a high proportion of the total cost.

Trans-Canada Pipe Lines had ordered the ingot steel required for the line, and was ready to order the pipe itself, when the negotiations collapsed. In a last-minute attempt to save the project, Clinton Murchison, a Texan oilman and one of the principal financiers behind Trans-Canada Pipe Lines, telephoned to Howe on March 8 and made a new proposal. If the bank would commit itself to $70 million worth of securities, he offered, he and his associates would guarantee repayment in five years of all its disbursements, at the risk of forfeiting their total investment. The offer was transcribed by a secretary, and the Minister of Trade and Commerce took it directly to the Prime Minister. For St. Laurent, it was not a matter of choosing between two colleagues, both of whom he valued highly, but of making a responsible decision. On the one hand, he had to consider the need for the project, and Howe's conviction that it was feasible on Murchison's terms; on the other, he had to take into account the advice of the government's officials, and the feeling in some quarters in Canada that the government should not underwrite a project conceived and directed by American capitalists. Perhaps if he had been in better spirits, the Prime Minister would have been able to work out a compromise solution; in his state of health, however, he could only support Howe, or ask him to desist; he chose the latter course simply because he was not convinced that the pipeline would be built under the terms that Murchison proposed.

On March 17, Nathan Tanner announced that the plan to begin construction in 1955 was being abandoned, since 'representatives of the Company have been unable to negotiate a type of financial assistance which does not result in an agency of the Government of Canada being in a position to control the Company, and such an arrangement makes it impossible for the Company to purchase its gas requirements'. The delay was a bitter disappointment to Howe, who had set his heart on seeing the pipeline built as perhaps the last and most important in his impressive list of achievements on behalf of Canada. To him, an undertaking that would be of immeasurable benefit to the country was being thwarted by excessive cautiousness and because of an ill-advised hostility towards American investors. Adding insult to injury, the negotiations were described in the press as a test of strength between Howe and Walter Harris. Even more important than the postponement of construction, a Calgary *Albertan* correspondent reported, was 'the rise in power of Walter Harris and the decline in influence of C. D. Howe'.

As the winter passed, signs appeared of economic recovery; Harris made the government's major contribution to it by announcing a tax cut and bringing in the first deficit budget in several years. At the same time, he announced the creation of a royal commission under the chairmanship of a Toronto chartered accountant, Walter Gordon, to examine Canada's economic prospects over the next quarter of a century. With the federal-provincial tax-sharing agreements due to expire in 1956, a 'preliminary meeting' with the provincial premiers was held in Ottawa in late April to plan a full-scale federal-provincial conference in the autumn. Although the major proposals made to the provinces in 1945 had not been accepted, St. Laurent told the premiers, a 'large proportion' of them had been implemented separately since then, and others had been set aside as inappropriate or impractical. In an obvious attempt to reduce the area of possible conflict between the two levels of government, he announced that the government wished to withdraw one of the 1945 proposals calling for public works projects designed to create employment, since it did not wish to 'get involved in having to make judgements in regard to thousands of public projects of the normal type carried out by provinces and municipalities'. He also suggested that discussions be carried on 'to see if a more flexible formula could be devised or present agreements modified to accommodate provinces not wishing to enter them on the same basis as the others'. Having made that conciliatory gesture towards Quebec, he acknowledged the viewpoint of those premiers who were less fearful of federal intervention in provincial areas of jurisdiction by offering, 'notwithstanding the constitutional responsibility of the provinces', to share the cost of assisting unemployed but employable persons not entitled to insurance benefits under existing arrangements.

In line with his view that federal-provincial relations should be removed from the political arena, Leslie Frost proposed the establishment of a joint 'technical and advisory committee' that would act as a fact-finding and liaison body and prepare the ground for top-level agreements. After his clash with St. Laurent just six months earlier, Duplessis was surprisingly affable. As on every previous occasion, he made no suggestions, merely commenting good-naturedly that the views of the province of Quebec were 'so clear, so consistent, so constant, and so much based on common sense, that it is useless to repeat them', and giving the assurance that 'in the province of Quebec, we are Canadians, true and faithful Canadians inspired by the desire to work for the welfare and prosperity of our country'. The other premiers were more specific: the new Conservative premier of New Brunswick, Hugh John Flemming, referred to his province's need for 'relatively cheap power', Douglas Campbell of Manitoba urged federal assistance to meet 'rapidly rising educational costs', and T. C. Douglas repeated his view that the federal government should intervene in certain provincial fields of jurisdiction that had become of national significance. A list of items was drawn up for discussion at the next meeting; two committees of officials were formed to prepare the discussions on unemployment assistance and on fiscal relations in general. When St. Laurent returned to the House of Commons, he was accused of having withdrawn the Green Book proposals, and thus of retreating from the position adopted by the Liberals in 1945. He did not deny the charge. Had the proposals been accepted ten years earlier, the federal government would have found it 'pretty embarrassing to carry out the commitments that would have resulted', he admitted. They had been drawn up on the assumption that $250 million a year would suffice to provide for the defence of the country, but the figure in 1955 was close to $2 billion, and there was no prospect of being able to reduce it in the next few years.

The main debate of the session took place on a proposal, presented by St. Laurent, to place the Department of Defence Production, created to meet the Korean crisis, on the same basis as other departments by repealing the section that provided for its abolition on July 31, 1956. The implications of the change were much more important than appeared on the surface, for the Minister of Defence Production was granted very extensive powers that were hardly normal in peace-time. The cabinet had discussed the possibility of placing a time limit on the powers, as had been done for the Emergency Powers Act, but Howe had no desire to subject himself to the periodic harassment of the opposition, and had persuaded his colleagues to get the disagreeable business over once and for all. In the 'present state of international affairs', St. Laurent declared in making his introductory statement, those powers were still required to enable Canada to maintain her defensive strength and carry out her undertakings. By adopting that attitude, he merely played into the hands of his adversaries who were looking for an issue to illustrate their charge of arrogance and autocracy. 'These powers', thundered Donald Fleming in reply to the Prime Minister, '. . . could make the Minister of Defence Production the virtual dictator of the whole economy.' The battle was joined.

The discussion on the resolution lasted only a few days, and then the bill was set aside for nearly two months while Howe made a trip to Australia and New Zealand. When it was brought forward again on June 7, day-time temperatures in Ottawa were around ninety degrees, and most members were already planning to return to their constituencies; nevertheless, the Conservatives were determined to put up a fight. Howe's views had not changed during his travels, and he threw his whole weight into the debate. 'I think I can claim to have more experience in defence purchasing than any other man now living,' he declared, and on the basis of that experience, he was convinced that 'the Department must be armed with an Act giving the powers necessary to do the job'. The debate was rancorous from the outset, with George Drew leading his forces into battle with something of the vigour he had displayed when he first arrived in Parliament, and St. Laurent stirring himself out of his winter lethargy to reply sharply to opposition thrusts. The C.C.F. group ranged itself on the side of the government because the powers Howe was so anxious to keep were designed to curb big business in the national interest; the Social Credit members sided with the Progressive Conservatives because of their belief in free enterprise. At the end of nearly two weeks, Howe tried to stem the criticism that he was seeking dictatorial powers by offering to lay on the table of both Houses of Parliament 'at the earliest possible moment after they are

made', all orders passed under the Defence Production Act, and
to provide for a debate within four days on any order at the
request of ten members of Parliament. To the Progressive Conservatives, the conciliatory gesture was merely an indication that
the opposition attack was beginning to produce results, and on
June 20, Drew declared that he was continuing the debate 'with
a good deal of encouragement'. His remark was not without
foundation; bored by the one-sidedness and the predictability of
parliamentary debate in recent years, members of the Press Gallery reported in vivid terms the struggle between the Tory David
and the Liberal Goliath. Across the land, many editorial writers
endorsed the Progressive Conservative stand. Ironically a measure
designed to protect the public interest in an emergency against
a small group of big business men took on the character in the
public mind of an attempt by another group, their elected
government, to seize arbitrary power.

His rugged appearance and caustic interjections notwithstanding, C. D. Howe was a sincere and sensitive man, and the charge
of placing personal pride before public considerations hurt him
deeply. Having abandoned his professional career and sacrificed
his private life for twenty years to serve his adopted country, he
felt that his entire contribution to Canada was being called into
question. On June 28, he revealed something of his sensitivity
in a rare emotional outburst. For sixteen years he had been
responsible for the procurement of defence supplies, he declared
with evident feeling, and he had never had the slightest trouble in
getting the co-operation of the defence industry when he needed
it. Although the department had 'never missed yet', it was
engaged in a program at the moment to develop a supersonic
aircraft that gave him 'the shudders'. Forgetting to address his
words to the Speaker, he looked across the floor and declared:
'Some of you do not know how it feels to be out on a limb for $30
million or more of other people's money and have a serious
doubt cast on the ultimate success of the program. I can tell you
that you do not sleep very well until you get the situation
straightened out.' As soon as Howe resumed his seat, Donald
Fleming scoffed at the remarks as a 'masterpiece of irrelevancy'
and mocked the Minister's personal tone as 'designed to make

all members melancholy and sad, and even to weep'. 'What's a million?' jeered another member. The bitter struggle continued.

By mid-June, the Prime Minister's silence had become a subject of wide speculation, and his staff and colleagues were running short of arguments to minimize its significance. Although he looked well, and spent most of his waking hours on Parliament Hill, he was not offering real leadership, and the dangers of ruling with too loose a rein, against which Mackenzie King had warned, were becoming increasingly evident. In May it was revealed that the Minister of National Revenue, Dr. J. J. McCann, had remained a director of the Guaranty Trust Company after becoming a minister of the Crown. His situation appeared to be particularly equivocal in view of the fact that his department was called upon frequently to negotiate with that company in establishing succession duties; in fact, it was precisely in that connection that the matter had come to public attention. When the subject was raised in the House of Commons, both St. Laurent and McCann remained silent; on behalf of the government, Harris suggested that the subject be referred to the standing committee on privileges and elections. Drew rejected the proposal, arguing that it was not 'a matter for the conscience of the Minister, but . . . a matter for the conscience of the Prime Minister'. Dr. McCann refused to be pressured into even appearing to concede that his situation was irregular; the incident strengthened the impression that St. Laurent was no longer in charge of his cabinet.

It was an event completely unrelated to politics that snapped the Prime Minister out of his doldrums. While on a business trip to Toronto on June 15, his son Renault suffered a coronary attack and was rushed to hospital for emergency treatment. The close relationship between the two men had not altered with the years, and Louis St. Laurent's feeling that he could continue to offer his services to the Canadian people was a direct consequence of the fact that Renault was taking his place as head of the legal firm, and, to an increasing extent, as head of the family. With the heart attack, the responsibilities were shifted back suddenly onto the older man's shoulders; predictably, he put aside other considerations and rushed to assume them. When he appeared in Toronto's St. Michael's hospital two days after his son's attack, he was once again a leader of men, questioning the specialists in charge of the case, making sure that the best possible care was available, and comforting the other members of the family.

As the days passed, and the doctors were able to assure him that Renault's chances of recovery were good, St. Laurent directed his new-found vigour towards the public business. On July 4, George Hees triggered him into action by stating that he was 'showing contempt both for Parliament and for the press of this country' by refusing to take part in the Defence Production debate. St. Laurent's tone was almost apologetic as he began by explaining that he had not spoken earlier because there really was nothing that he could add to a debate characterized by charges of threats to democracy. In 1950, a similar debate had taken place on the Emergency Powers Act, he recalled, and on that occasion a compromise had been worked out; he was ready to follow the same course again, and proposed that an agreement be made to allow a debate on the legislation at any time after three years. If another party was in power by that time, it could, of course, do as it deemed fit. However, he commented meaningfully, 'all of us on this side expect to be here three years from now to carry out any undertaking that we give to the House and to the country'. Asked if he would allow the current debate to be put over until the next session, he replied that Howe had done 'a pretty good job', and that 'we want him to continue to have what he requires as his tools to be able to continue to do that job in the interests of the public'. Earl Rowe replied for the official opposition without rising from his seat. 'That is not much of an answer,' he declared. 'That is no answer at all.'

St. Laurent's remarks that he intended to be around Parliament in three years did not pass unnoticed. Speculation about his possible retirement had become widespread, and Liberal Party officials had even calculated the time required to hold a leadership convention. The main obstacle to such a plan was that he had no obvious heir apparent. Howe was disqualifying himself more every day, Pearson had chosen to remain in charge of a portfolio that gave him popularity but no solid political base, and Walter

Harris had not yet proved himself in a senior portfolio; the other ministers were still less likely successors. Most important, Liberal strategists could not imagine that anyone else would have the popular appeal of 'Uncle Louis', even when he was in less than top form. With everyone about him encouraging him to stay on, he allowed the moment to pass when, as subsequent events were to prove, he should have announced that he was going home at last. On July 6, he dissipated any remaining doubts about his future plans in a television interview. 'I certainly intend to lead the Liberal Party [in the next election],' he declared, 'if I find that the Liberal Party throughout the country has the same feeling that I find among my colleagues of the Government and of the House of Commons. . . . I hope my health is going to continue as it is at present and if it does, this is the job I undertook to do as long as I felt capable of doing it.'

Digging in his heels, Howe declared on July 7, that 'if the Government must sit here until the snow flies', it could not withdraw the Defence Production bill. At the same time, he went on, he and his colleagues were 'not rigid about every clause and condition', and would be willing to consider a time limit on 'any particular section of the bill about which honourable gentlemen opposite feel strongly'. For those who wanted to understand the significance of his words, he was offering to accept a time limit on the controversial powers once the debate reached the committee stage. By that time, emotions were too strong for his adversaries to accept the peace overture; Michael Starr continued to insist on a time limit for the whole bill. Following the defeat of a Conservative amendment later in the day, House leader Walter Harris moved that 'the question be now put' on second reading; cries of 'the guillotine', 'end of democracy', 'gag', and 'can't stand the gaff', greeted his proposal. Ellen Fairclough declared, 'We now face closure in this debate.' Since Harris's motion was itself debatable without a time limit, the filibuster went on.

Having decided at last to assert his leadership, St. Laurent cast about for a way of bringing the acrimonious debate to an end. In cabinet, Howe was urged to make some further concessions to the opposition, but he rejected the suggestion as a sign of weakness. He had made arrangements to spend his week-ends fishing on the lower St. Lawrence, and was quite prepared to let his opponents talk on in Ottawa all summer. Before he left the capital on Thursday, July 7, for a four-day expedition, he discussed possible compromise formulas with the Prime Minister and with Walter Harris, and told the latter in an off-handed manner to do whatever he wanted. On Friday, the Prime Minister decided to act; he telephoned George Drew and told the Leader of the Opposition that the debate had gone on long enough. He was going to St. Patrick for the week-end, he stated, and if Drew would reflect on what might be a reasonable solution of the disagreement and put his suggestion in writing, he would telephone again when he returned to the capital on Monday at noon, and see if they could not reach a settlement. The Tory leader could hardly believe his ears; as soon as he had accepted the suggestion, and the Prime Minister had hung up, he telephoned Grattan O'Leary, editor of the *Ottawa Journal*, and reported the incident in a high state of excitement and disbelief. So suspicious was he of some trickery that he asked O'Leary to be on hand as a witness on Monday when the call came.

St. Laurent spent a pleasant week-end at his summer home, and then sent instructions for Justice Minister Garson and a senior legal adviser to meet him on his arrival in Ottawa at noon on Monday. Drew and O'Leary were lunching outside the opposition leader's residence when the telephone rang. The Prime Minister asked Drew if he had prepared a possible statement, and, on receiving an affirmative answer, asked him to read it. After hearing it, he remarked that he found it quite satisfactory, and accepted it without changing so much as a comma! When the House of Commons met in the afternoon, he announced the peace terms: the Department of Defence Production would be made permanent, but the clauses to which objection had been taken would expire in four years, unless the government at that time proposed to Parliament, and obtained, their extension. The Conservatives were jubilant at having forced the Liberals to retreat despite their vastly superior numbers; they had difficulty in restraining their enthusiasm as their leader accepted the agreement in the same sober, responsible manner as the Prime Minister had displayed. It was George Drew's greatest hour of triumph in the Canadian Parliament. Howe was sitting in a small fishing boat off Baie Comeau when the news was flashed through the radio that the long debate was over. On his return to the fishing camp, a telegram from St. Laurent was waiting for him:

> Defence Production Act passed this afternoon and now before Senate. I told the House which clauses you were prepared to have come up for reconsideration after July 31, 1959, and thereupon motion that question be now put was adopted without further debate, then main motion went through and in Committee your amendment announced on June 13th, and one along lines you had prepared and stated on July 7th as proper to be considered in committee were adopted and third reading by leave was immediately put through.
> Regards to you and members of your party and best of luck.

Although he had given his tacit assent to the terms the previous week, Howe was furious at the concessions that had been made, and on his return to Ottawa, he accused Harris of having made the deal behind his back; when he found that the Prime Minister himself had carried out the negotiations, he accepted the decision. A leader of men himself, he was prepared to accept the leadership of others, provided it was firm and competent.

The last three weeks of the session were much more pleasant. On July 15, St. Laurent travelled to Toronto, had Renault placed on his special railway car, and accompanied him home to Quebec. In words that left no room for doubt, he assured the doctors before leaving Toronto that he would be responsible personally for seeing that their instructions were followed to the letter, and then told his daughter-in-law firmly to put the patient to bed. In Parliament, he demonstrated the same purposefulness. When Drew raised again the matter of Dr. McCann's relations with the Guaranty Trust Company, he rose at once to declare that he would 'never shirk any responsibility for the propriety of the conduct of any member of the Government'. There had been no conflict of interest between the private interests and the public responsibilities of the minister, he stressed, but Dr. McCann had resigned his directorship in June 'out of his respect for the feeling of the members of the House of Commons, that he personally did not share'. The matter was dropped; on July 28, the session ended on a harmonious note.

As other members of Parliament rushed out of the capital, St. Laurent called in the press corps to announce a list of Senate appointments on which he had been working off and on for two years. Questioned in the past about Senate reform, he had replied that he would express his views through his actions; what he had in mind was not a constitutional change, but an injection of new blood that would enhance the efficiency and prestige of the Upper Chamber. Unfortunately, several of his invitations to enter the Senate were refused, and other appointments became impossible when Liberals in various provinces refused to forgo their claims to the security of the Red Chamber. Nevertheless, the list announced by St. Laurent on July 28 contained several 'unorthodox' choices, including Donald Cameron, director of the Banff School of Fine Arts, William Wall, an educator of Ukrainian origin, and Hartland Molson, a member of the old Montreal family that had made a fortune in the brewing industry. Most surprising of all was the appointment of St. Laurent's life-long friend John Hackett; although the choice was justifiable on the basis of merit, it was also a personal gesture, and incidentally, only the second appointment of a member of an opposition party since Confederation. Another innovation was that the new senators were told clearly that they were 'under no obligation to the Government', and that they were expected to take 'an objective view' of all matters brought to their attention, rather than lining up automatically with the Liberal Party. Other appointments were in the traditional pattern: 'Chubby' Power, David Croll, and Jean-François Pouliot, all senior members of the House of Commons, were transferred to the Upper Chamber. On the whole, it was a very modest response to the continuing demand for Senate reform, and certainly a small result compared to the efforts that had been put into compiling the list.

Dressed in a bright sports shirt, pork-pie summer hat, and grey flannel trousers, St. Laurent spent many hours of the month of August on the St. Patrick golf course. Unlike President Eisenhower, he did not take the game seriously, keeping no score, moving the ball out of the rough for a more convenient shot, using any club that was at hand, and displaying an amateurish style that won him the somewhat disrespectful but affectionate nickname among the caddies of 'Wiggles'. On August 19, he flew to the Knob Lake area of Labrador for a few days of fishing, but his pleasure was cut short when he slipped on a moss-covered stone and broke a bone in his lower leg. He was back on the golf course during the last week in August, but with his foot and lower leg in a cast, and using a golf club as a cane.

With his health so markedly improved, even his wife and daughters were less reluctant to have him continue in public life; they, too, had become accustomed to the political limelight. One member of the family, Jean-Paul, was chafing to enter politics in his own right. He had never shared the distaste of the others for party warfare, nor the devotion of Renault to a legal career; much of his law practice consisted of commercial transactions, some of which had been criticized by members of the Union Nationale party as of doubtful propriety, and he was anxious to reply in public to the charges. When Pouliot was appointed to the Senate, he determined to succeed him as the Liberal member for Témis-couata constituency, where both he and his father had their summer homes. Having repeated just a few months earlier that one politician in the family was sufficient, Louis St. Laurent reacted vigorously against the plan, but, to the general surprise, his wife took the opposite view. Jean-Paul was her favourite child, and when he asked for her support, it was granted readily. The topic led to some lively exchanges throughout the summer, and St. Laurent found himself being accused of withholding from his own son an opportunity that he would encourage another quali-fied Canadian to take. His argument that he would not allow Jean-Paul to impose himself on the constituency by using the St. Laurent name fell to the ground when a group of local Liberal organizers assured him that his son was perfectly acceptable to them as a candidate. In the end, for the sake of peace, but with strong misgivings, he gave in and Jean-Paul received the Liberal nomination without opposition. Delighted at the opportunity to do battle with a St. Laurent, Union Nationale organizers took charge of the supposedly Tory campaign there as well as in Belle-chasse and Quebec South constituencies, where by-elections had also been called for September 26.

One of the matters to which St. Laurent devoted a considerable amount of attention while at his summer home was the gas-pipeline project. Following the collapse of negotiations with the Industrial Development Bank in March, Howe had continued his search for an acceptable formula. In June he reported to the government a plan to build a line through the United States south of the Great Lakes, with a second, all-Canadian, line to follow in an estimated three to five years, as soon as the eastern market had been built up sufficiently. Although no public financing would have been required, the proposal was turned down on the grounds that Canadian national sentiment would not permit even a temporary line outside the country. In August, the inde-fatigable minister visited Toronto and western Canada, and returned with still another proposal: the Government of Canada and the Government of Ontario should construct jointly the expensive and less remunerative portion of the line through northern Ontario, and sell it to Trans-Canada Pipe Lines at a later date. St. Laurent received the suggestion in St. Patrick and examined it carefully. It seemed to him to meet three important requirements: it would cost taxpayers nothing in the long run; it would satisfy the exigencies of Canadian nationalism; and it would assure the participation of both the Progressive Conservative administration in Ontario and the Social Credit one in Alberta, thus reducing the likelihood of criticism from those parties in Parliament. As for the C.C.F. members, he realized that they would call for a line built completely at public expense, but that alternative had to be ruled out, at least for the moment, because of the opposition of the Alberta government and the potential suppliers. The Prime Minister spent part of his holiday drawing up a possible contract between the parties concerned. His first appointment when he returned to Ottawa on September 1 was with Howe, Premier Manning, Ontario Treasurer Dana Porter, and officials of Trans-Canada Pipe Lines. Agreement was reached quickly, and he predicted confidently later in the day

that the great project, ranking in importance with the Canadian
Pacific railway, would be started in the following spring.

On September 4, St. Laurent flew to the prairies to take part
in the golden anniversary celebrations of the provinces of Saskatchewan and Alberta. His foot still in a cast, and accompanied by
his sister Lora, his daughter Thérèse, and his grandson and name-
sake, Jean-Paul's teen-aged son Louis Stephen, he presented more
than ever the image of a jovial and lovable grandfather. He
bantered good-naturedly with T. C. Douglas when the witty
Premier of Saskatchewan introduced him to a crowd of school
children before the Legislative Buildings in Regina. But he was
serious as well. It was 'a great privilege, you know, to have this
land and its wonderful resources as our homeland', he told the
young people, and to have as well 'the best system of government
that has ever been devised by human ingenuity for co-ordinating
the joint efforts of free men and women. . . .' In Calgary he
paraded through the streets in an open car waving a Stetson hat,
attended a miniature stampede, and ate buffalo meat at an open-
air barbecue. In Edmonton he rode down Jasper Avenue in the
same landau that Sir Wilfrid had used fifty years earlier to
inaugurate the province. To emphasize his confidence in the
future, he prophesized on every platform that when the younger
Louis St. Laurent returned for the centennial celebrations of the
two provinces, the most optimistic forecasts for Canada would
have been realized. Far from being the tired and discouraged old
man of a few months earlier, he was enjoying life to the full.

Shortly after his return from the west, St. Laurent attended
the wedding of Louise Samson, the eldest of his seventeen grandchildren. She had just been beginning school when he was
'drafted' to Ottawa; soon a whole generation would have grown
up since then, and the life in Quebec that he had abandoned
with such regret was becoming increasingly remote. On September 26, Jean-Paul St. Laurent and his Liberal running-mates
won the election in the Quebec City area, but with sharply
reduced majorities. A fourth seat, Restigouche-Madawaska, in
New Brunswick, fell to a young Progressive Conservative, Charles
Van Horne. The persons most encouraged by the results were
the small group of Quebec Conservatives who realized that if the

St. Laurent–Duplessis feud could be exploited to enlist Union Nationale support in the next general election, their party might well make real gains in French Canada.

The Prime Minister had no time to speculate on such matters; on October 2, the premiers gathered in Ottawa to try to work out with the federal government a new series of fiscal arrangements. Since the preliminary meeting in April, negotiations had continued on Ottawa's new unemployment assistance proposals, and a plan was agreed upon to share the cost of relief for 'unemployed employables' in excess of one-twentieth of the population in each province. In other sectors, St. Laurent was determined to remove every possible source of friction between the two levels of government. When he read a newspaper report in September that Leslie Frost hoped to obtain agreement to create a federal-provincial health insurance plan by 1958, he had written to the Ontario premier, expressing interest and asking if more details could be sent to him on a confidential basis. It was an unusual request to make of a provincial leader, particularly from another party, but it reflected the confidence and friendship that existed between the two men. Frost responded by sending a draft outline of the remarks he proposed to make at the meeting, and St. Laurent reciprocated at once with an advance copy of his own opening statement.

The welcoming address that the Canadian Prime Minister delivered in the Senate Chamber on October 2 was the fruit of long hours of research and reflection by an inter-ministerial committee over a period of two or three years, and was designed to mark the beginning of a new chapter in federal-provincial relations. It bore clearly the mark of Maurice Lamontagne, who had been transferred to the Privy Council Office as a special economic adviser in the previous June, and who had called for the 'clear-headed integration' of Quebec into Confederation. 'It is impossible, particularly in our age, to separate the fields of jurisdiction and the responsibilities of the different governments in a federal state in such a way as to permit them to ignore one another,' St. Laurent stated; intergovernmental relations and meetings were inevitable, and required 'frank collaboration and conciliation' by all participants if the balance between federal and provincial power was not to be destroyed. In an obvious effort to avoid the appearance of applying pressure, St. Laurent assured the premiers that he and his colleagues would 'have no quarrel' with the provincial governments who were not yet ready to sign an agreement concerning the 'unemployed employables', but they would, of course, like to see the plan extended to be fully national in scope. With regard to health insurance, they recognized that the subject fell 'squarely within provincial jurisdiction' and did not wish to see that situation altered, but there were circumstances in which Ottawa would be justified in offering to assist provincial governments in implementing health insurance plans designed and administered by the provinces. If it could be shown that 'the national rather than the local or sectional interest' would be served by such a step, and that 'a substantial majority of provincial governments representing a substantial majority of the Canadian people' favoured such an initiative, the federal government was ready to give 'technical support and financial assistance' to a program of provincially administered hospital and diagnostic services. In accordance with its aim of reducing possible areas of conflict, St. Laurent announced that the federal government intended to limit its contributions to local works projects or compensation for local disasters, and not to share in 'the normal costs of growth of provinces and municipalities'. At the same time, he and his colleagues would continue the search for some more rational co-operative approach to recurring problems such as seasonal unemployment and maintaining the general level of public investment.

The basic problem facing the conference, he reminded the premiers, was to achieve some method of sharing the revenue available from the direct tax field, and 'some reasonable degree of equity and stability' in the revenue of the various provinces. The tax-rental agreements had served very largely the purposes for which they had been conceived, but they had not proved universally acceptable, and, since the federal government had never claimed that they were 'a final, or a perfect or a permanent answer to the problems in our fiscal relationships', it was quite prepared to see them 'modified, improved, or even superseded', if some better formula could be devised. It would take the wisdom of

Solomon, he remarked, to reconcile all the competing objectives that had to be taken into account. While he was still unwilling to put forward a precise plan, St. Laurent did indicate the general guide-lines that the federal government considered important: first, an equalization formula should be devised that would assure to each province, through a system of federal transfer payments, the same level of revenues from the principal sources of taxation; second, each province should be free to raise its own taxes on personal incomes, corporations, or successions, and its citizens should be allowed to deduct up to a fixed percentage of the federal tax; and finally, a 'stabilization guarantee' should assure to each province a minimum level of revenues, regardless of general economic conditions. The new attempt to reconcile national and provincial interests had certain evident merits; it gave the richer provinces a certain freedom of choice, while at the same time placing a floor under the revenues of the poorer provinces, and assuring the possibility of equal provincial services across the country. After twenty years of shifting more and more burdens to Ottawa, the provinces were not only being asked to accept their responsibilities, but were being offered the financial means to do so. The era of centralization was drawing to an end.

In general, the premiers welcomed the fresh approach outlined by the Prime Minister. Leslie Frost advanced the novel argument that the rapid industrialization of Ontario imposed special 'penalties and obligations' on his administration, and suggested that since greater revenues would accrue to the federal government as a result of the industrial growth, it should abandon a larger share of the tax fields to Ontario than to the poorer provinces. He suggested that the provincial share of personal and corporation taxes be increased from 10 to 15 per cent, that Ottawa vacate entirely the succession duty field, and that provincial taxes on the development of natural resources, in particular logging and mining operations, be made deductible from the federal tax. He also called for a joint committee to work out the details of a federal-provincial health and hospital insurance plan. In contrast to the positive and concrete suggestions of the Ontario Premier, Maurice Duplessis persisted in his attitude of coupling bland assurances of co-operation with an inflexible adherence to his traditional position. The Quebec government was imbued with a 'sincere desire to co-operate with a view to the progress and prosperity of the Canadian homeland', he stated with a reassuring wave of his large cigar, but 'with the complete respect for the freedom, prerogatives, and essential rights of the provincial and federal authorities'. His only suggestion was that the taxing powers of the different governments should be 'clarified and defined', and that taxes should be 'simplified' and imposed with 'moderation' in order to reduce the burden on the taxpayers.

With the exception of Premier Bennett of British Columbia, whose province was moving from a 'have-not' to a 'have' position and had, therefore, more to lose than to gain by an equalization of tax revenues, the other government leaders asked for more generous federal assistance. Several of them called for federal assistance in the field of education, in order, in the words of Premier Matheson of Prince Edward Island, 'to equalize educational opportunities across the country'. The strongest criticism of the federal government's new proposals came from Premier Douglas, who expressed the fear that they might mark the beginning of a 'retreat from the achievements of the past fifteen years', and even a return to 'the chaotic tax jungle of pre-war years' with 'all the pitfalls of unrestrained tax competition, double taxation, and overlapping collection machinery'. Premier Smallwood echoed a similar sentiment when he declared that 'you cannot have a great Canada if Newfoundland is not great, and Saskatchewan and Manitoba, and the island province of Prince Edward Island, and Nova Scotia and New Brunswick. These are the weaknesses in the Canadian chain today.'

Delivery of the initial statements began in mid-morning, and was concluded only at ten o'clock in the evening. Three days of closed sessions followed, devoted mainly to attempting to find a common position on fiscal relations. St. Laurent and the other members of the federal delegation worked assiduously to see how large an area of agreement could be established. It was a frustrating task, and the Prime Minister found it difficult to maintain his equanimity as one premier after the other rose, and, in the name of national unity, demanded more favourable conditions for his own province. Even Leslie Frost seemed to him to be putting political before national considerations, and to have abandoned his view that federal-provincial relations should be removed from the partisan struggle for power. In the end, the delegates could only agree to form a committee of officials 'to meet from time to time to exchange information and examine technical problems in the field of federal-provincial fiscal and economic relations', and a committee of ministers 'to consider more in detail the subject of health insurance'. The only positive achievement was an arrangement to share the costs of relief for unemployed employable workers, and it was worked out outside the plenary session. It was decided that the conference would resume 'at a time to be fixed by the Prime Minister after consultation with the premiers of the provinces'.

As the year 1956 began, nothing indicated that it would be one of the most memorable in Canadian politics. Encouraged by his success in the Defence Production debate, George Drew had toured western Canada before Christmas, attacking the Liberal administration vigorously, and promising further tests of strength in the next session. Opinion in the cabinet was divided between a determination not to give him an opportunity to repeat his performance, and the sentiment that he should be shown clearly that he could not push the Liberal majority around. C. D. Howe personified the second point of view; still disappointed over the outcome of the Defence Production debate and the pipeline negotiations, he was in no mood to agree to changes in government policy simply to avoid a clash with his opponents. For instance, he argued against the proposed cash advances on farm-stored grain because this would precipitate similar requests from other primary producers, and it was impossible to support over-production in every field. Similarly, he opposed a proposal put forward by Jean Lesage to share with the provinces the costs of hydro-electric development projects, on the grounds that the government could not subsidize all forms of power. The 'second string' ministers should wait their turn to try out their ideas, he suggested pointedly after one discussion. St. Laurent was not in a more imaginative frame of mind; by early December, he had begun to feel the fatigue that appeared to recur annually, making his burdens seem almost unbearably heavy. On January 7, he had a long discussion with Leslie Frost on federal-provincial relations, including the subject of hospital insurance, a field in which each was blaming the other for lack of action. The two men agreed that political considerations were forcing them to advance too quickly, and that the first priority should be given to increasing hospital facilities; otherwise it would be impossible to cope with the increased demand for hospital care. After the Ontario premier had left, St. Laurent emerged from his office, and commented in a bemused tone: 'You know, Mr. Frost doesn't like hospital insurance either.'

Shortly before Parliament met on January 10, the federal government set aside its fears of being accused of dictating the terms of a new fiscal arrangement, and made a firm proposal to the provinces. In a letter to the premiers, St. Laurent offered a system of 'unconditional tax equalization payments' that would bring their per-capita yield from income and corporation taxes and from succession duties up to the average level of the two provinces with the highest revenues from those sources. In addition, Ottawa would guarantee that the revenues of each province from the three tax fields would be at least as high as under the old agreements. If any province preferred to impose its own taxes, the federal government would rebate the rate of the federal tax by 10 per cent on personal income, 9 per cent on corporation profits, and 50 per cent on succession duties. The proposals were designed, he wrote, to assure the provinces of somewhat greater revenues than under the previous tax system, and a greater measure of financial stability.

Despite his reservations about Jean-Paul's entry into politics, there was an air of paternal pride in St. Laurent's bearing as he escorted his son into the Commons Chamber on the first day of the new session, and introduced him to Speaker Beaudoin. The Speech from the Throne was a relatively short document, proclaiming the year just ended 'the most productive in our nation's history', but acknowledging that 'some sectors of the economy have not fully participated in this increased well-being'. To assist western farmers, the government proposed to guarantee bank loans on farm-stored grain, and to pay storage and interest charges to the Canadian Wheat Board on the abnormally large stocks on hand. It also announced that a gas pipeline across northern Ontario was to be built jointly with the Ontario government, and leased to Trans-Canada Pipe Lines Limited, which was to construct the connecting lines in western and eastern Canada. George Drew attacked at once, charging the government with 'smug self-satisfaction' and 'uninformative platitudes', and promising 'another example of democracy in action'. In contrast, St. Laurent's reply was moderate almost to the point of diffidence: he and his colleagues were prepared to meet the 'vigorous criticism' that had been announced, and to have as vigorous and searching an inquiry as possible into their activities, because 'the more these things are known and publicized the better they will redound to our own credit.' He spent considerable time outlining the new tax-sharing proposals, describing them as 'a new approach' that could become 'the basis of durable arrangements appropriate to a period of peace-time growth'. Even on the theme of national unity, his optimism was tempered by a note of caution. 'We are becoming a Canadian nation,' he asserted, 'and we have to be very cautious that we do not move too rapidly and that all the moves that are made are conducive to the growth and development of that national consciousness and that spirit of solidarity between our people from one ocean to the other.'

As if to confirm the opposition charge of ineptness, the government stumbled almost immediately into a series of contradictions concerning the shipment of arms to the Middle East. A series of border clashes between Israel and its Arab neighbours had given rise to fears of open war, and Pearson was asked in the House of Commons on January 11 if any Canadian aircraft had been ordered by, or shipped to, Egypt; the Minister for External Affairs replied that he knew of none. Five days later, Defence Minister Campney was asked what military equipment, if any, had been shipped over the previous week-end in the vessel *Star of Assuan*, and to what destination; he gave a similar answer. On the following day, Pearson had to report that a permit had in fact been issued during the summer to export fifteen Harvard training aircraft to Egypt, which were, he added, 'of course, not combat aircraft', and that three of them had been on the ship in question. Pressed about their adaptability to combat use, he commented that he did not know 'how you could put a gun-mounting on a Harvard training aircraft'. Twenty-four hours later the press carried a photograph of one carrying military weapons. Sensing the government's embarrassment, Drew demanded a debate on the whole question of arms shipments to the Middle East, and charged that a permit had also been granted to ship twenty-five-pounder shells to that area. The Speaker refused to allow the debate for the moment, but not before St. Laurent had given the assurance that no shipments would be made until a debate had taken place. The following Monday, St. Laurent, too, had to rise and explain himself further; his assurance about halting arms shipments had been imprecise, so he had added the words 'for that area' when he had checked the proof copy of Hansard. Donald Fleming charged both the Prime Minister and the Minister for External Affairs with fumbling, floundering, and evasion. There was still more to come. Howe declared that the order in council authorizing the shipment was dated July 7, whereas Pearson had stated that it had been passed in 'early summer'. Then, three days later, the Minister of Trade and Commerce had to rise and confess that the shipment had not been authorized by an order in council at all, but merely by the 'ministerial concurrence' of three members of cabinet. George Drew denounced the government for its 'incredible record of evasion, mis-statement, backing away from earlier statements, and finally the admission that most of the earlier statements had been wrong'. In shipping aircraft to Egypt, and anti-aircraft guns to Israel to shoot them down, he charged, the ministers were making themselves accomplices to murder.

As the session advanced, St. Laurent's condition worsened. Suffering from stomach pains, he worried about his health, and sleepless nights sapped his strength. When requests were submitted to him to address groups outside of Parliament, he commented that he had nothing to say, and they were declined by his staff as diplomatically as possible. In the House of Commons, he sat hunched in his seat, speaking only when it was absolutely necessary. On March 5, the *Ottawa Journal* commented on his 'strange silence' and asked: 'Is Mr. St. Laurent, acting in this

inexplicable manner, playing the part of a Prime Minister?'
Following the newspaper comment, he was finally persuaded to
see a doctor who discovered that he had an ulcer; he was put on
a strict diet and advised to stop smoking.

Such was St. Laurent's condition when he presided over a
further meeting with the premiers on March 9 to discuss his tax-
sharing proposal. It was a disheartening experience even for a
man in excellent form, since no one appeared satisfied with the
new formula. Hugh John Flemming of New Brunswick declared
that it gave 'no consideration' to the 'special needs' of the poorer
provinces; Leslie Frost complained that it provided a special
payment to all the provinces except Ontario but failed to meet
the 'special need' of his province. In a closed meeting, Finance
Minister Harris pointed out that the new formula implied a 20
per cent increase in federal payments to the provinces, and that
Ottawa was also assuming a billion-dollar burden of social welfare
payments, a field of provincial jurisdiction. The meeting ended
without anyone changing his position, but after the premiers had
returned home the federal negotiating team tried again. In a
letter prepared for St. Laurent's signature, a further attempt to
meet at least the objections of the poorer provinces was made by
offering to increase the floor on federal payments from 90 to 95
per cent of the average of the two preceding years, and giving the
assurance that no province could 'suffer financially' through
accepting the new formula. It was no use; when Harris outlined
the proposals in his budget speech on March 20, Donald Fleming
brushed his explanations aside as 'nothing but a lecture and a
harangue'. Fortunately, under the new plan the equalization
payments were automatically available and required acquiescence
in their receipt but no formal agreement with the provinces.

Shortly before Easter, St. Laurent flew to White Sulphur
Springs, Virginia, for a conference with President Eisenhower
and President Cortines of Mexico. Conceived in Washington as
a North American 'little summit' meeting, it was received with
something less than enthusiasm in Ottawa, where there was no
inclination to have Canada considered on the same basis as the
Latin American country. It was even feared that the Canadian
Prime Minister would be given third place, since he was not a

head of state like the two other leaders. When the invitation was accepted, arrangements were made for separate arrivals, and for a private chat between Eisenhower and St. Laurent. A simultaneous meeting was arranged between Pearson and Dulles, both of whom had visited Asia and the Middle East in recent months.

Once he arrived at the meeting-place, St. Laurent put on a creditable performance, joining in the exchanges of good wishes and statements of hemispheric solidarity, and establishing an easy rapport with the two other men. He was pleased to note how completely Eisenhower had recovered from the heart attack that had almost ended his distinguished career the previous year. He took considerable pains to explain to the President that the tax on advertising in foreign magazines announced in Harris's budget speech a few days earlier was not a manifestation of anti-Americanism, but simply a measure to help Canadian publications survive in the face of competition from mass-produced foreign ones. Dulles's report on his recent trip was of particular interest to the Canadian leader, and his eloquent analysis of the political forces at work in Asia and the Middle East was impressive, even if it did not coincide on many points with the Canadian point of view. On the basis of a trip to the Soviet Union the previous autumn, Pearson repeated his viewpoint that a fundamental change was taking place in Soviet foreign policy under Nikita Khrushchev, and that a common Soviet-American approach to some international problems was possible; the Americans clung to the position that the basic goals and tactics of Russia were still totalitarian, revolutionary, and expansionary, and that she must be contained along her entire perimeter. The United States attitude towards Communist China was, if anything, even more uncompromising. Eisenhower and Dulles were particularly concerned about the tension between Israel and her neighbours, pointing out that, rightly or wrongly, the Israelis were convinced that they were going to be attacked. Pearson remarked that since the Soviet Union had established itself in the area by supplying military aid to Colonel Nasser, its assistance should be sought in reducing the risks of an outbreak of fighting; the suggestion was not received with enthusiasm.

A brief Easter holiday brought no improvement in St. Laurent's health, and he remained a prisoner of his own hesitant, even negative, attitude towards public issues. Reforms he had hoped in earlier months to achieve now seemed either out of reach or purposeless; queries in the House of Commons about the Canada Council, the South Saskatchewan dam project, cabinet representation for the Toronto area or for Prince Edward Island, the pipeline legislation, increased bilingualism in the civil service, and other topics of current interest were brushed off as if they had become disagreeable to him. At the same time, he expressed no wish to retire, and no suggestion came from the Liberal Party that he should do so; his followers were well aware that he was still the best vote-getter in Canadian politics.

One of the requests St. Laurent could not refuse was an invitation to address the founding convention of the Canadian Labour Congress, a million-man trade union created by the fusion of Canada's two largest labour groups. In view of the increasing estrangement between the government and certain sectors of organized labour, the opportunity to improve relations and restore confidence in the administration seemed almost providential to more progressive-minded Liberals. The meeting was scheduled for the third week of April, and since it was to be the Prime Minister's first speech outside Ottawa in several months, preparations were made with particular care. A draft text was submitted to him, portraying the Liberal Party as the labourer's friend, stressing the importance of labour movements in the country's development, and holding out the promise of a real partnership between the new organization and the administration. While he would likely have accepted the proposed line a few years earlier, and delivered the message with conviction, it was completely out of character for him in the spring of 1956; in fact, he was determined to tell the union leaders that power is accompanied by responsibility, and that they would have to avoid selfish attitudes that would detract from the larger interests of the Canadian nation. Filled with satisfaction at having forged such a powerful instrument with which to improve the lot of their followers, the union organizers were in no mood to receive such a lecture. As the date of the meeting drew nearer, St. Laurent rejected at least a dozen drafts, each one less inspiring than the last, but designed to preserve at least some portion of the positive message to the union officials. Gradually every element of reform Liberalism was eliminated, but he was still unhappy over what he should say. Since no valid reason could be found to cancel the engagement, he appeared in Toronto as scheduled, and read his statement in a lifeless style, obviously anxious to get it over. The delegates gave him a polite but unenthusiastic reception. The Toronto *Telegram* summed up the message in the headline: 'Bigger union means bigger responsibilities, Prime Minister tells Convention'. No votes for the Liberal Party were won that day. A few days later he fared somewhat better at a meeting of the National Federation of Liberal Women of Canada. Speaking to a more sympathetic audience, and extolling the value of family life, he revealed something of the 'Uncle Louis' or 'Grandfather Louis' that had won him success in former years. The Liberals took heart, telling themselves that perhaps their leader's magic touch was not disappearing after all.

# 14

---

# The Trans-Canada Pipeline

As the first weeks of 1956 passed, it became clear that the major political battle of the session would take place over the proposed gas pipeline. The issue was an attractive one for the Progressive Conservative and C.C.F. members, for it offered the opportunity to continue the attacks on Howe as the personification of the government's alleged arrogance and lust for power, and also to exploit the anti-American sentiment that was once again becoming a significant factor on the Canadian political scene. Only the Social Credit group could not oppose the project, since Premier Manning, the most powerful man in their party, had endorsed the plan, and a former Social Credit minister in Alberta, Nathan Tanner, was president of Trans-Canada Pipe Lines Limited. John Diefenbaker announced that the Defence Production debate was a mere 'skirmish' compared to what his party was planning, and C.C.F. member Hazen Argue warned that the government 'ain't seen nothin' yet'.

When Howe moved the resolution to incorporate the Northern Ontario Pipe Line Corporation on March 15, a vote was forced by the C.C.F. group even before he could state the purpose of the resolution. Finally allowed to speak, the Minister of Trade and Commerce pointed out that the primary purpose of the billion-dollar pipeline project was to make Alberta gas available in

Saskatchewan, Manitoba, Ontario, and Quebec, and that the various aspects of the plan were simply the best possible means to that end. For instance, Premier Manning had required, as a condition of his agreement, that a market in the United States be obtained for part of the gas, as the Canadian market was considered insufficient for the rapidly expanding gas industry in Alberta. The line was to pass through northern Ontario both to satisfy Canadian national sentiment and to serve the communities there. The Ontario legislature had unanimously approved a $35 million contribution towards the construction of the uneconomical northern Ontario section; Parliament was being asked to establish a Crown corporation to build it, and to provide $80 million as the federal share of the financing. The scheme was designed to make it possible to deliver gas in Montreal 'not later than 1958', Howe explained, and to do so in a way that would enable the governments concerned 'to recover all their investment plus interest without imposing any unnecessary charges that would reduce the return to the producer and raise the price to the consumer'. It would also enable the government to terminate its direct involvement 'at an early stage', and avoid the problems inherent in public ownership of a pipeline. Although the government was not opposed to public ownership in principle, it did not consider 'as do some of our socialist friends, that public ownership is, as a general rule, preferable to private enterprise', and it would be unfair to subsidize one source of power in competition with others. In addition, the administration would find itself caught between the competing claims of producers and consumers. The cabinet had also rejected a more economical alternative plan to sell Canadian gas in the western part of the United States in exchange for American gas that would be imported into Ontario and Quebec, Howe explained, as the arrangement might turn into a permanent commitment, and neither the American nor the Canadian government wished to become dependent on foreign supplies of power. In an attempt to forestall criticism of subsidizing an American-dominated enterprise, he reported that the board of directors of Trans-Canada Pipe Lines Limited had been broadened to assure a majority of Canadians among its members, including the president, a vice-

president, and the secretary; moreover, the shares of the founders
of the company had been reduced to less than one-quarter of the
total by selling 17 per cent of them to Canadian companies, and
the Canadian public was to be offered the opportunity to purchase 51 per cent of the voting shares.

Speaking immediately after Howe, George Drew denounced
the arrangement, declaring that it made Canada dependent on
the whims of the United States Federal Power Commission and
constituted 'another blank cheque' to 'use public funds to assist
financial interests in the United States in establishing effective
control over one of our major resources'. He condemned the
financial arrangements as 'bad in every respect', 'neither fish nor
fowl nor good red herring', and proposed that the whole question
be referred to a parliamentary committee with a view to assuring
that the pipeline would be built by 'an all-Canadian company . . .
and under Canadian control'; if a private company could not
meet those conditions, then it should be built entirely by
public funds and leased 'for operation under Canadian control'.
During his lengthy speech, the Tory leader succeeded in provoking several interjections by Howe, as well as stirring the anger
of Liberal members by referring to the 'vacuous faces' opposite
him, and expressing regret that no Liberals were 'speaking up
for Canada'. Following the Leader of the Opposition, M. J. Coldwell made a more reasoned, but equally critical, statement, and
called for complete public ownership; on behalf of the Social
Credit group, the Reverend Ernest Hansell supported the government's resolution. The lines were thus drawn for the historic
battle.

After the preliminary exchange, the resolution was set aside
until early May, but the debate went forward outside the
Commons Chamber. It was soon evident from the public reaction
that the Progressive Conservatives had chosen excellent fighting
ground, and that the charge of selling out to the Americans was
causing uneasiness in Liberal ranks, even at cabinet level. One
of the persons most sceptical of the arrangement with Trans-
Canada Pipe Lines Limited was the Minister of Mines and
Technical Surveys, George Prudham, who represented Alberta
in the cabinet, and was engaged in a bitter struggle against the

Social Credit administration in that province. Knowing of his views, another group of business promoters led by Frank Mac-Mahon of Calgary submitted an alternative plan through him directly to the Prime Minister. Although they, too, represented both Canadian and American interests, they proposed to organize a company with at least 70 per cent Canadian control, and to obtain a better price than Trans-Canada Pipe Lines Limited for the gas to be exported; the only assistance they requested from Ottawa, they stated, was a rebate on customs and excise taxes. As proof of his sincerity, MacMahon offered to deposit with Howe a personal cheque for half a million dollars. Before Prudham placed the proposal before St. Laurent, MacMahon outlined it in a letter to Howe that was marked 'private and confidential', and began 'Dear C.D.'. The Minister of Trade and Commerce had two meetings with the Calgary oilman in April, but he was unimpressed by the counter-proposal. His doubts turned to anger when he learned that Prudham had gone over his head to the Prime Minister, and that MacMahon's proposal had also been handed to his political opponents. In the House of Commons, Howe denied that he had received any proposal that he could communicate to Parliament; then, following a stormy phone call to MacMahon, he acknowledged having received a letter and explained that he had not been able to do so earlier because of the 'personal and confidential' restriction that had been placed on it by its author. During their telephone conversation, he reported, not only had the restriction on the letter been withdrawn at his request so that he could refer to it publicly, but the whole offer had been dropped by the financial group.

While St. Laurent did not take a prominent part in the negotiations as he would have done if he had been in good health, he continued to support his senior colleague, realizing that Howe had his heart set on carrying out the project, and wishing to make up for the rebuff he had been obliged to deliver to end the Defence Production wrangle a year earlier. Questioned in the House of Commons about the MacMahon proposal after it had been withdrawn, the Prime Minister endorsed Howe's stand, but when pressed by members across the floor, he betrayed his own uneasiness. 'I can assure you that I do not enjoy as much as you do these questions that are constantly being thrown at us,' he burst out unhappily on May 4, 'and I should be very happy to reach a position where they will be no longer looked upon as desirable by those who are asking them now.' As at least some opposition members knew, the delay in proceeding with the original proposal was caused by further difficulties that Trans-Canada Pipe Lines Limited was experiencing in completing its financing. Largely because of pressure from American competitors, the Federal Power Commission had not yet approved the importation of Canadian gas to the United States, and as a result, the company could not obtain the money required to begin construction on the western section of the line in 1956. With the Ontario government urging immediate action, the necessary permits, gas purchase contracts, and sales contracts already obtained, and the pipe ordered, Howe was determined that there should be no further delay. In an emotional appeal in cabinet, he pleaded with his colleagues to allow him to carry out his greatest, and probably his last, project on behalf of Canada, the crowning achievement of his fifty-year career. He proposed that, in addition to constructing the northern Ontario section of the line, the government should advance up to 90 per cent of the cost of constructing the western portion as far as Winnipeg; in return, the company would pledge all its assets and give the government an option on its shares as a guarantee of full repayment, at 5 per cent interest, by March 31, 1957.

If the proposal submitted to the House of Commons in March was likely to have a rough passage, the reception given to the new one was certain to be even worse. St. Laurent realized the political dangers, but he was more impressed by the consequences to the economy of Ontario if the delivery of natural gas was delayed; while the modified proposal was far from ideal, no other could be devised in time to begin construction in 1956, and the pipeline might even be delayed for several years. At a moment when his leadership was needed desperately, he had not the force to assert it, and he sided with C. D. Howe. After much discussion, and with serious misgivings, the cabinet decided not only to go ahead, but to use the closure rule to ram the measure through Parliament in time to get the line started that summer. The fact that it was the Conservatives who had introduced the closure rule in Parliament before World War I to stifle Liberal opposition, and that the Liberals had pointed to it often as an example of Tory abuse of power, indicated how far the small group of men were departing from the traditions of their party. On May 8, Howe explained the modified plan to the Liberal caucus. There would be a few days of keen debate, the back-benchers were told, but the public had quickly tired of Drew's blustering in the past, and would do so again; after a few days the opposition would have talked itself out, the bill would pass, and before long the Canadian public would only remember another great Liberal achievement in building Canada. Seeing the cabinet apparently united, and confident, the back-benchers agreed to present a solid front in Parliament.

In the House of Commons that same afternoon, the proposal had a very different reception. Before the Minister of Trade and Commerce had finished his statement, Davie Fulton described it as 'a treaty of surrender' to the United States. The Leader of the Opposition called it 'an invitation . . . to investors of the United States to come to Canada and be financed to the extent of ninety cents of every dollar'; to Coldwell, it was a 'sell-out' that would result in 'enormous profits for private United States economic buccaneers'. Having learned that the government had set June 5 as the deadline for approval of the legislation, the Progressive Conservatives and C.C.F. members concentrated from the outset on blocking discussion of the project instead of discussing it on its merits. Much of May 9 was spent discussing whether a new resolution incorporating the revised plan could appear on the Order Paper before the old one was withdrawn. May 10 began with a challenge of a Speaker's ruling, and further discussion of procedural technicalities; even the presiding officer's judgement was to be called into question in the campaign to win time. A total of four votes, each taking about half an hour, were held before agreement could even be reached to discuss the resolution at a later sitting of the House. When second reading was called on May 14, three more votes on procedural points were taken before Howe was able to make his explanatory remarks. Speaking from a prepared text, the minister dealt once again with the objections to the plan, and insisted that it was 'a prudent and practical proposal . . . which we must either launch now or see languish for years to come'. When he had concluded the statement, he leaned towards Walter Harris, seated beside him, and asked, 'Do I do it now?' The House leader gave his approval. 'It is obvious that some honourable members prefer to obstruct this motion rather than debate it,' Howe stated solemnly, 'therefore I beg to give notice that at the next sitting of the committee this resolution shall be the first business of the committee and shall not further be postponed.' The government had stepped into the trap. 'Guillotine!' cried Stanley Knowles. 'Dictatorship!' yelled other members. An almost visible shudder ran through the Liberal ranks. St. Laurent looked straight ahead, pale and silent.

When George Drew rose to reply, he acted like a man who had found a worthy cause to defend, and who had all the virtues of democracy on his side. The House had just heard a threat of dictatorship, he began. When the minister moved closure the next day, he hoped that he would not 'shut off the Prime Minister' as well, as the members had been waiting for four months to hear his views on the subject. 'After all, while we know that the real and effective head of this government on this occasion is the Minister of Trade and Commerce, the Prime Minister is the nominal head.' Almost immediately, the debate took on a personal character. The Leader of the Opposition accused Howe of lying, and pointed out, with obvious reference to the minister's American origins, that MacMahon, whose proposal had been rejected, was at least a 'Canadian, born in Canada'. His attack lasted well into the evening; when Coldwell's turn came, he made an equally vigorous speech against what he termed the 'most outrageous' and 'pernicious' plan.

On the following day, the tension and bitterness continued to mount. The Progressive Conservatives tried to prevent one of their own number, Carl Nickle of Calgary, from speaking, because he was known to favour the proposal put forward by the Government. An expert on the oil and gas industry, he condemned his party's stand when he did get the floor as 'political expediency . . . contrary to what I honestly believe are Canada's best interests'. On the Liberal side of the House, George Prudham suppressed his misgivings and declared manfully that the proposal offered 'the only possibility of getting the line under way this year'. After dinner, the galleries were filled to capacity as citizens flocked to Parliament Hill to share in the excitement. Throughout it all, St. Laurent sat silently in his front-row seat, hunched and obviously unhappy. When Earl Rowe referred to him as the 'silent acquiescing Prime Minister' and charged that he was 'afraid to rise and speak in this issue', he replied without moving that he would rather be silent 'than speak like you are doing now'. In accordance with the closure rule, the debate went on until 1 a.m.; however, when the Chairman of the Committee of the Whole House, William Robinson, tried to have the vote taken the obstruction was continued by raising points of procedure, Davie Fulton carrying the tactics so far as to refuse to resume his seat when ordered to do so by the presiding officer. Suspecting that the clever young Tory was trying to be expelled in order to claim the cloak of martyrdom, Harris managed to avoid a vote on his obviously improper conduct. Finally, after seven votes, including two appeals from the chairman's ruling, the resolution was passed without the expulsion having taken place. Dawn was breaking as the sitting ended. 'The pipeline legislation is doing very well,' Howe commented cheerfully to a television interviewer as he left the Parliament Buildings; Drew and Coldwell repeated their denunciations for the general public. The Prime Minister stepped into his car which was waiting at the side door, and went home, still silent and alone. In its comment on the debate, the Toronto *Globe and Mail* published a cartoon depicting the Peace Tower of the Parliament Buildings as a guillotine, with the execution knife falling towards the Book of Remembrance contained in the war memorial chamber.

Mercifully, the debate was not resumed on May 16, but when second reading was called on May 17, the struggle continued with unabated intensity; once again, there was a long discussion on procedure, and an appeal from the Speaker's ruling, before Howe could make his introductory statement. Far more sensitive to their criticism than his opponents realized, the Minister of Trade and Commerce tried again to disprove the charge of selling out Canadian interests to the United States. He had rejected a cheaper route south of the Great Lakes because 'there is a price on Canadian nationhood', he declared, and if the cheapest solution had always been chosen, 'there would likely have been no Canada'. The pipeline would be controlled by Canada, he insisted, 'because it is located in Canada, because it is subject to Canadian laws'. As for the attacks on himself, he resented the 'snide remarks' that he was 'a second-class citizen' because he had been born in the United States. 'I have lived in Canada for forty-eight years,' he declared proudly. 'I have been a citizen of Canada for forty-two years, and I think my record in Canada will stand up with anyone else's.' He was 'by inclination and training . . . a builder', and happy to be a member of 'a building government'. 'It does not matter to you whether you destroy Parliament in the process,' shouted Donald Fleming across the floor. In the days that followed, Hansard was filled with insults coming from both sides of the House such as 'jackals', 'magpies', 'meathead', 'dictator', and 'trained seals'. However, the Progressive Conservative and C.C.F. members found it increasingly difficult to keep the debate going without discussing the proposal seriously, and the galleries began to empty as the unedifying spectacle began to bore the public. Had the government not already made known its deadline, the filibuster would likely have fizzled out before long. Ironically, just when the tide seemed to be turning in the government's favour, Walter Harris announced that closure would be applied again on May 22; the fighting flared anew.

The Prime Minister chose the second debate under the closure rule to break his long silence. Goaded by the remarks of opposition members, and realizing the seriousness of the government's situation, he made a major effort to assert his leadership. In a statement carefully tailored to the twenty-minute time limit under the closure rule, and avoiding the acrimonious tone of George Drew, who had just preceded him, he commented: 'All of us want this to be an all-Canadian pipeline, to be controlled under Canadian law and to be operated for the benefit of the development of Canada at large.' He went over once again the reasons that had brought the government to the decision that Trans-Canada Pipe Lines Limited was 'the instrument that could and should be used' to build the line, and should receive 'a short-term loan made under conditions that can involve no possible loss to the Canadian taxpayer'. On the subject of closure, he confessed 'quite freely' that it was distasteful to impose a restriction on the length of the debate, but, he asked, 'if we believe, as we do, that this is something that should be done now in the interests of the Canadian people, can we shirk whatever distasteful responsibility we have to take in order to get the matter before Parliament in time for it to make a proper decision, a decision that can be implemented?' He had more than once had to face 'disagreeable duties', he went on, and had 'never shirked any duty that appeared to me to be a duty that was imposed upon me by the responsibilities I had undertaken by my oaths of office'. The government had had to decide if the proposal was 'a good thing in the interests of the Canadian people'; if it considered it was, 'it was our duty to bring it to a decision in the House in time to make it possible for that decision to be executed'. If it was not 'a good thing', it should be defeated, and he hoped that any member of the House who felt it was 'a wrong decision to be made in the interests of the Canadian people' would vote against it.

The sight of the Prime Minister on his feet again, asserting his authority in his most reasonable manner, was a much-needed stimulus for the other Liberal members. Unfortunately, the atmosphere in Parliament had deteriorated too far for such appeals to reason and moderation, and the effect of his intervention was somewhat diminished by the impression that he had been thrown into the breach to shore up the government's defences rather than that he was imposing his will as Prime Minister on his cabinet colleagues. Davie Fulton commented immediately afterwards that the Prime Minister had put himself on record as being on the side of those who were ready to use the 'gag and closure' to hand over control of a Canadian resource to American interests. The debate continued on the same low level; by 3:15 the following morning, several more votes had been taken, and second reading of the bill was approved.

May 23 was spent almost entirely on procedural wrangling, Fulton and Knowles employing delaying tactics with great skill in order to prevent a decision being taken before June 5. Seeing the deadline approaching, the government plunged still further

430 LOUIS ST. LAURENT

along the course it had chosen; on May 24, Howe called one clause of the bill after the other, and after speaking a few words on each, moved 'that further discussion of this clause be postponed'. His opponents protested vehemently that the rules called for a discussion before each postponement, and argued that the few words spoken by the minister did not constitute a discussion; Chairman Robinson pointed out that Howe's motion was not debatable; his ruling was appealed and sustained. In their frustration, Progressive Conservative and C.C.F. members turned their indignation against the presiding officer, criticizing him and appealing his rulings repeatedly. Fulton declared in one heated outburst that he was 'not content longer to see our liberties raped by the Government'. With members hurling insults at one another across the floor, the House was on the verge of chaos. St. Laurent remained silent; outside the Chamber, he commented uneasily that the situation was 'very uncomfortable'. The harassment of the chairman continued on May 25. Donald Fleming spoke for half an hour on a mere point of order, then refused to resume his seat on the ground that the thirty-minute time limit did not apply to procedural discussions. He was finally persuaded to sit down, but bobbed up again shortly with a question of privilege, and continued his argument. Robinson's patience was exhausted at last, and he formally directed Fleming to resume his seat. When Fleming refused, he was expelled for the remainder of the day; as he strode proudly out of the Chamber, his fellow Tories pounded their desks enthusiastically, Diefenbaker crying 'Farewell, John Hampden', and Ellen Fairclough draping over his desk a Union Jack that she had arranged to borrow several hours earlier from the House of Commons staff 'for a party'. The expulsion had all the appearances of a planned coup.

The following day was Saturday, and the cabinet had an opportunity to review the worrisome situation. The Prime Minister's mail, newspaper editorials, and public opinion in general were all running strongly against the government; it was evident that the two leading opposition parties had clearly succeeded in transforming the debate from a discussion of a great and much-needed construction project into a battle over parliamentary rights. His strength and initiative returning, St. Laurent joined his colleagues in searching for ways of reducing the dangerous tension, and of bringing the House of Commons back to a discussion of the pipeline proposal. On one aspect of the struggle they could ill afford to give ground; rightly or wrongly, they had committed themselves to getting the legislation approved in time for a start to be made on the project that summer; if they failed to meet the commitment, they would be placing the whole scheme in jeopardy, causing heavy losses to the interested parties and to the country, and seriously damaging their own prestige as a government. Retreat at that late stage could be much more disastrous than a somewhat clouded victory. When the House met on Monday, May 28, the Prime Minister rose at once to 'state emphatically' that as soon as the motion under consideration was disposed of, debate on the remaining stages of the bill could be carried on for the remainder of the week. To opponents of the pipeline, the statement indicated that the cabinet was becoming worried about the public reaction to its tactics, and the possibility of not meeting its deadline; the announcement merely encouraged the obstruction. 'The retreat from Moscow,' scoffed Diefenbaker with evident satisfaction.

Over the week-end the Progressive Conservatives had developed new tactics as well; George Drew demanded the adjournment of the debate to discuss 'the subordination by the government of the office of chairman of the Committee of the Whole House to serve the partisan interests of the government'. Speaker Beaudoin rejected the motion on the grounds that forty-eight hours' notice was required. René Beaudoin was particularly sensitive to the criticism directed at his deputy, because that morning they both had been attacked in a Montreal *Gazette* editorial for unwilling complicity 'in chipping and chopping at Parliament's rights and privileges – all in the interests of stifling the voice of the House'. A proud man, he had applied himself with a perfectionist's zeal to performing the duties of his high office, and had succeeded so well that members of all parties had mentioned his name as a possible permanent Speaker. Thus, when the newspaper editorial was mentioned in the House of Commons later that morning, he reacted emotionally, declaring that, as a family man, he did not want his children 'after they have read the newspaper, to look at me in such a way that I can perceive that there may be doubt as to whether I am performing my duty in an impartial manner'. He asked that his record be placed before the Committee on Privileges and Elections 'at the first opportunity', and that a thorough study be made of it under the direction of his closest critic, Stanley Knowles; whatever the conclusions, he declared, he would 'abide by the report of the committee'. The only response to his earnest request was Fulton's ambiguous comment that the government should 'put the bill before the committee'. The disorder continued with further appeals from the Chair's rulings. During the evening, Howe made his third speech in the debate, attempting to answer all outstanding questions that had been raised. His efforts were largely fruitless; the sitting ended with Howe and Drew arguing over the minister's personal relations with 'Texas buccaneer' Clint Murchison.

On Wednesday, May 30, St. Laurent intervened again to suggest a practical solution to the conflict; the government would agree to sittings that evening, usually a free night, and all day Saturday, he offered, if the opposition would agree to completing all stages of the bill by the following Monday, the deadline set at the beginning of the debate. He gave notice that he would move closure at the next sitting, but expressed the hope that 'an understanding can be reached which will make it unnecessary to do so'. Drew denounced the gesture as 'a complete farce', and Coldwell, almost choking with indignation, described the government's attitude as 'a travesty on democratic procedure, an abomination, an outrageous thing'. He was surprised, the C.C.F. leader declared, that the Prime Minister, for whom he had had 'the very deepest of respect', would make such a proposal.

On Thursday, May 31, Harris rose as soon as the House was declared in session and moved 'that the Orders of the Day be now read', a stratagem designed to eliminate the time-consuming question period. The step was approved by the usual vote on party lines, and then St. Laurent introduced his closure motion. Still playing for time, Fulton spoke for a full thirty minutes on a point of order. When he could get the floor, the Prime Minister made his first effective defence of the government's position. Struggling to resist being provoked by the taunts from across the floor, he agreed with a statement made earlier by Coldwell that the opposition had a right to do everything possible, 'under proper parliamentary procedure', to prevent the legislation being approved. At the same time, he argued, 'the opposition should not question the right of the government, feeling as strongly as we do that this is in the interests of the country, to do everything we can ... under proper parliamentary procedure ... to give every honourable member the opportunity to vote on this measure.' His composure did not last. When Earl Rowe shouted that Sir John A. Macdonald and Sir Wilfrid Laurier would be ashamed of him, he reddened, and snapped back: 'That is the honourable gentleman's opinion. I have my opinion about the propriety of our conduct and I will be prepared to defend that conduct in every quarter where it may be challenged.' 'Let us go to the country and ask the people,' the veteran Tory member retorted. 'We will be going to the country in due course,' St. Laurent answered intensely; in the meantime the government felt it was 'in the interest of the country to get this project started this year'. The squabbling continued, but eventually the Deputy Chairman, E. T. Applewhaite, was able to rule that the Prime Minister's closure motion was in order; that decision from the Chair was also appealed. 'They are all the same,' cried Conservative member George Nowlan. No one was allowed to remain above the bitter dispute.

It was late in the day when Speaker Beaudoin returned to the Chamber to deal with the appeal from Applewhaite's ruling. Pale, distraught, and clearly feeling the strain of the continued questioning of the Chair's authority, he permitted a further lengthy procedural discussion instead of putting the question immediately, as specified by the rules. In the chaotic situation, he even made another ruling on a procedural point, and it, too, was challenged; the evening was well advanced before the first appeal could be settled. As he was at last about to leave the Chair so that the House could transform itself back into committee, C.C.F. member Colin Cameron rose on a question of privilege, and complained that two letters commenting on the debate, which had appeared in the *Ottawa Journal*, were 'derogatory of the dignity of Parliament and deserving of the censure of this

House'. In a state of nervous exhaustion, Beaudoin first declared that he would not allow the matter to be raised 'merely to delay the proceedings'; then, anxious to avoid the impression of siding with the government, he advised that the articles be handed to the clerk in order to be read into the record and supported by a proper motion. His suggestion was adopted, and as soon as the two steps had been taken, Drew rose to declare, with evident satisfaction, that the motion was debatable; the Speaker's action meant that the Prime Minister's motion would be set aside for as long as the debate on the matter raised by Cameron could be drawn out. It was Harris's turn to raise a point of order; he argued that the rules did not allow the procedure that had taken place. The Speaker interrupted, and, in a voice that betrayed his over-wrought condition, declared that the matter referred to by Cameron was a serious one, in which he himself was involved, since he had been referred to in the letters, and in the circum-stances he was determined to be heard on the subject at some stage. Having said that, he obviously did not know what further step should be taken, and he let Drew have the floor until the adjournment hour of ten o'clock arrived.

The next day, June 1, 1956, was to become known in Canadian political annals as 'Black Friday'. Before Beaudoin left the Cham-ber on the previous evening, he knew that he had departed from the rules in allowing any discussion before the appeal from Chairman Robinson's ruling was taken, and that he had erred still more seriously in allowing Cameron's matter of privilege to be debated at that time. In his upset state, and anxious to avoid further attacks on the Chair, he had lost control of the House. The lights in his office were on well after midnight as he tried to find a way of extricating himself from the dilemma. One of the persons he consulted was Walter Harris, who had protested in the Chamber that the rules were not being observed. Beaudoin recognized his mistakes, and asked for suggestions to correct the serious situation. They discussed various possibilities, but the House leader left with the impression that the damage could not be undone, and that the deadline set by the government for approval of the legislation would have to be abandoned; he prepared to drop the pipeline bill and go on to other business the following day. The Progressive Conservative and C.C.F. members would be jubilant, he predicted, and the Liberals would be made a laughing-stock, but once the tension had been transformed into good-natured joking and the deadline had been passed, the pipeline legislation would be approved with relative ease. Since it was the government, and not the construction company, that had set the date of June 5, a start might yet be made during the summer. René Beaudoin saw the situation differently. After an almost perfect record as Speaker, he had made a mistake, and he was determined to correct it. Before he went home he had devised a plan to reverse his earlier position. Early the next morning, J. W. Pickersgill appeared at his home, anxious to learn what state he was in, and, as an expert on parliamentary procedure, to discuss the predicament. Beaudoin stated curtly that he had the situation under control, but refused to elaborate; the minister left none the wiser than when he had arrived.

The House of Commons met at eleven o'clock the next morning, and the Speaker read the daily prayer in a tone of suppressed emotion. As soon as the Orders of the Day were called, Drew rose to continue his speech, but Beaudoin himself remained standing, not even giving the clerk, Léon Raymond, the opportunity to announce the resumption of the debate on Cameron's motion. He had read carefully the articles complained of, he stated, and had come to the conclusion that 'because of the unprecedented circumstances surrounding this pipeline debate and because of the remarks that were made in the House by members themselves', they should not be considered as breaches of parliamentary privilege; had it not been for some of the 'insinuations or attacks directed . . . to the occupants of the Chair', they might not have been written. In the circumstances, he did not consider that they went beyond 'the bounds of fairness', and he ruled Cameron's motion out of order. 'Do honourable members wish to appeal?' he asked. In the general consternation as members sought to grasp the new situation, Drew asked somewhat confusedly if the Speaker was 'prepared to hear any discussion', since the debate on Cameron's motion had already begun. Beaudoin refused. 'It is a matter of privilege,' he stated, referring to Cameron's complaint, and ignoring the fact that he had already accepted a motion based upon it. 'Whether it is privilege or not, it is my responsibility to decide.' Once again, he asked if his ruling was being appealed. The Leader of the Opposition did appeal and the bells began to ring to announce the vote. The cries of protest from the opposition benches were answered with cat-calls from the Liberals, despite Harris's attempts to calm them. 'Why did you change overnight?' called Diefenbaker, '. . . Are you afraid today?' 'What took place in the dark?' shouted Earl Rowe. Perspiration glistening on his cheeks, Beaudoin teetered on his feet, as if about to collapse. Dr. McCann left his seat on the cabinet benches and went up to him, amid opposition cries of protest; he prescribed a drink of water. Another Liberal member, John MacDougall, who suffered from a chronic heart condition, offered him some of his pills. St. Laurent sat as if frozen to his chair, looking small and miserable. When the vote was taken, the members divided on the same lines as on so many previous occasions in recent days; the Speaker's ruling was upheld. While the counting was taking place, George Hees declared, 'Mr. Speaker, I am voting against the dictatorship which you have imposed on Parliament.'

Events continued to move swiftly. Stanley Knowles moved the adjournment of the House; the insults from the opposition benches continued. Beaudoin rose and, speaking slowly, announced the next step in his stategy. 'I want to tell honourable members that I know what my responsibilities are,' he stated, 'and that I am fully conscious of every step that I am taking.' 'I wonder,' interjected one member. He had 'thought very seriously' about the happenings of the previous day, the Speaker went on, and he considered that he had 'made a very serious mistake' when he had returned to the Chamber to hear the appeal from the chairman's ruling, 'in allowing the point of order and the other dilatory motions'. Since he felt that 'the House should not suffer any prejudice or detriment' on his account, he proposed that it should 'revert to the position where it was yesterday when I was brought back to the Chair to receive the chairman's report at five-fifteen'. He called for a vote on 'the situation which I take at the moment'. Once again, cries of protest rose from the opposition benches. 'What are you doing, Mr. Speaker?' Coldwell called out in disbelief. Raising his voice above the din, Drew moved that 'in view of the unprecedented action of Mr. Speaker in improperly reversing his own decision', the House 'no longer has any confidence in its presiding officer'. Beaudoin pointed out that forty-eight hours' notice was required for the motion. Knowles succeeded in getting the floor, and began to argue that his own motion to adjourn the House was in order. The Speaker accepted it, a vote was taken, and it was defeated. With that matter disposed of, the presiding officer tried again to call a vote on his proposal to revert to the situation existing the previous afternoon, but Knowles and Fulton launched into a procedural discussion, arguing that he could not do so at that stage of the proceedings. His strength and determination flagging, Beaudoin retreated and agreed to postpone his proposed action until after the question period. The shredded remnants of control were slipping from his hands.

Nearly an hour later, the unhappy Speaker tried again and, after a further series of exchanges, managed to call a vote. As the bells began to ring once more, Drew, Coldwell, and other opposition members surged into the centre aisle, shouting their protests. To drown their voices, Liberals broke into song, chanting 'Hail, Hail, the Gang's All Here' and 'Onward, Christian Soldiers'. 'Parliament has ceased to function,' proclaimed Coldwell above the din. 'Where is the Prime Minister?' asked John Diefenbaker. 'Is he silent in the face of this demonstration?' 'This is the lowest moment in Canadian parliamentary history,' declared Donald Fleming. 'This is black Friday, boy,' pronounced Thomas Bell. 'Hitlerism,' added Clayton Hodgson. 'You did it; you brought it on yourself,' called back Jean Lesage. Liberal back-benchers continued their demonstration with songs they had devised in recent days: 'There'll always be a pipeline', and 'I've been working on the pipeline'; attempts by Harris to silence them proved fruitless. St. Laurent and Beaudoin sat in their seats, the former flushed and fingering his moustache, the latter pale and perspiring, as chaos reigned about them. It was the low point in both their careers. After what seemed an eternity to observers, the vote was taken at last on the 'course of action submitted by Mr. Speaker'. The Progressive Conservative and C.C.F. members abstained on the grounds that there was no question properly before the House; the proposal was carried, and a luncheon recess was called.

Whatever the price to his personal prestige and the reputation of Parliament, the Speaker had succeeded in returning to the position of the previous afternoon. When the sitting resumed at 2:30 p.m., he proceeded at once to call the vote on the previous day's appeal from the chairman's ruling, ignoring attempts by Fulton and Knowles to start a new procedural discussion. The disorder broke out again. M. J. Coldwell, normally a sensible, calm man, advanced toward the Speaker's chair, shaking his fist and shouting. Drew followed suit, crying, 'You have no right to sit in that chair.' Beaudoin managed to repeat that he took 'full responsibility for what I am doing'. The chairman's ruling was sustained. As soon as the result of the vote was announced, the Speaker fairly fled from the Chair, as Fulton tried to make a new motion; Applewhaite mounted the dais and the members found themselves in committee. Fulton continued to make his motion, which called for the House to adjourn. The deputy chairman pointed out that he had no choice but to call a vote on a matter already before the members from the previous day's sitting of the committee. The vote was taken with members still protesting; Fulton remained standing throughout, and was counted with both the 'yeas' and the 'nays'. He challenged the vote on the grounds that he could not vote both ways!

Further votes were taken on procedural matters, but the tension could not be sustained indefinitely, and eventually a semblance of order was restored. Shortly before midnight, Howe endeavoured to sum up the debate, and repeated his view that the pipeline proposal was valid and reasonable. 'It is not my purpose to close my engineering practice and my public life by undertaking a project that is an improvident project for the government,' he declared, 'a project which will stand to my discredit over the years.' He still felt it was one of which his children would be 'rather proud'. It was too late for such assurances; the pipeline had become of secondary importance. In the atmosphere of bitterness and disillusionment, the debate went on until 1 a.m.; a series of votes sanctioned the committee stage of the bill, and the members filed out of the Parliament Buildings; 'Black Friday' was over at last.

An atmosphere of tension and anxiety pervaded the entire national capital during that first week-end of June as the actors in the historic drama tried to assess their respective positions and the damage that had been done to Parliament. Objectivity had become impossible, even members of the press gallery dividing into bitterly opposed camps. The Saturday edition of the *Ottawa Citizen* carried an article by Douglas Leiterman entitled: 'An Axe Flailing at the Rights of Parliament', in which the newspaperman charged that Beaudoin had taken instructions from Walter Harris and had followed the rules 'until they got in the government's way, then, he threw the rule book in the Ottawa river'. Although the government was certainly guilty of disrespect for Parliament in imposing a deadline before the pipeline debate had properly begun, and in applying the closure rule on the various clauses of the bill before at least a minimum of debate had taken place on them, the charge of dictating the Speaker's conduct was unjustified. Beaudoin had fallen prey, not so much to the cabinet's high-handedness, as to the misconduct of members on both sides of the Chamber, and, in particular, to the readiness of some opposition members to sacrifice the prestige of the presiding officers by appealing their decisions for partisan advantage.

When the House of Commons re-convened on Monday, June 4, its members had begun to realize the damage they had inflicted, not only upon one another, but upon the institution of Parliament itself. Nevertheless, the opposing forces had embarked on their respective courses of action, and there was no turning back. Still determined to prevent the pipeline legislation from being approved by the June 5 deadline, George Drew rose at once and made a motion of non-confidence in the Speaker. He placed the blame for the unhappy situation squarely at the feet of the Prime Minister, and stated that only an election would 'restore the dignity, honour and traditions of Parliament'. Coldwell supported the proposal, but Victor Quelch of the Social Credit Party took the opposite view, and denounced the Progressive Conservative and C.C.F. members for attempting to impose their will on the majority in Parliament. As soon as the spokesmen of the opposition parties had expressed their views, St. Laurent took the floor. Never had his moderating influence and his ability as a peacemaker been more necessary. In a tone of almost judicial calm that was in marked contrast to the atmosphere of recent days, he submitted that the Speaker still had 'the affectionate consideration and regard' of most members. On the previous Friday, 'very unfortunate occurrences' had taken place, he remarked, and they were to be regretted 'as are to be regretted all examples of defiance of constituted authority'. At the same time, he could not accept the consequences to Parliament of a situation in which a minority group could hold up the business before it 'by making a challenge in respect of their confidence in the procedure followed by the presiding officer of the House'. The Speaker's plight, he stated, was 'a direct result of the firm determination at which the minority had arrived in trying to prevent by every means possible there being time in the House to reach a point where a decision of the House could be made upon the various phases of this legislation'. He 'absolutely repudiated' the suggestion that Beaudoin had subordinated the rules of Parliament to the will of the government, and asserted vigorously that there was a large majority of members 'on both sides of the House' who still had confidence in the Speaker. However, to take a vote on that point in the current atmosphere would not be a 'happy situation', he went on, and members were 'entitled to some time for the consideration of what should be the ultimate disposition of this motion'; accordingly, he moved the adjournment of the debate. The next four lines in Hansard record the reaction to his proposal.

> Mr. Fleming: Another closure!
> Mr. Knowles: The guillotine again.
> Mr. Fulton: That is your answer to everything; chop it off.
> Mr. Diefenbaker: That is the epitome of Parliament.

Compromise and reasonableness were impossible; the pipeline battle had to run its destructive course. St. Laurent's motion to adjourn the debate was approved and, following the question period, he himself gave notice that he would move the application

of closure on third reading at the next sitting. While the vitupera-
tion continued, the members managed to get through the day
without a repetition of the disgraceful scenes of 'Black Friday'.
On June 5, President Sukarno of Indonesia, in Ottawa on a state
visit, and already profoundly sceptical of western forms of democracy, watched the final act of the ugly drama from the diplomatic
gallery. The obstruction and the appeals from the Speaker's
rulings continued, and the pipeline itself received scant attention
from participants in the debate; the main issue had become the
rights of Parliament. The talking ended early the next morning
and the pipeline bill was approved; the deadline set by the
government for approval of the legislation was overshot by only
a matter of hours.

The tragic tale was not yet complete. Just as the House was
about to resume the debate on the Speaker's conduct on June 6,
one of its most likeable members, John MacDougall, fell dead of
a heart attack. Although he suffered from both diabetes and a
heart condition, he had been much in evidence during the late
sittings, cheering his fellow Liberals with his witticisms, and
bantering good-naturedly with his opponents; however, insulin
injections and heart stimulants had not been sufficient to bring
him through the critical period. On hearing the news, members
were reminded that three other men had been hospitalized in
recent weeks. At St. Laurent's request, the House adjourned for
the rest of the day; political pundits were too shocked to speculate
what would have been the consequences if his death had occurred
before the pipeline bill had been passed.

The debate on Drew's motion of non-confidence in the Speaker
was resumed on June 7 in an atmosphere of sorrow and exhaustion. Beaudoin had to preside at his own trial with no opportunity
to defend himself. Hailed just a few months earlier as one of the
most brilliant and competent presiding officers in Canadian
parliamentary history, he was condemned by some of the very
men who had once sung his praise. Knowles asserted as 'a known
fact' that Harris had visited the Speaker in his office on the
evening preceding 'Black Friday', and suggested that Beaudoin
had not come 'independently' to the decision to reverse his
position on Cameron's motion. George Nowlan charged that

Harris had been sending notes to the Speaker during the crucial sitting, and intimated that they contained instructions on the conduct of the debate. The Minister of Finance denied the suggestion forcefully; beyond the usual practice of notifying Beaudoin of persons chosen by the whips to take part in the debate, he declared, the only advice given by the government was Dr. McCann's suggestion that the Speaker take a glass of water to keep from fainting. The denial was not accepted by Fulton, who insisted that the government had been directing the Speaker, and that the only reason its plan had been thwarted was that on the previous Thursday Beaudoin was 'so fully engaged' that he 'missed the signal'. The debate went on for a day and a half; then Drew's motion of non-confidence in the presiding officer was defeated by a vote on the usual party lines.

The official opposition had one more important card to play. The estimates for the new fiscal year had not yet been approved, and the interim supply of funds voted a few weeks earlier was all but exhausted; the government had to ask for money to meet current expenses. If another filibuster was staged on that debate, it seemed likely that the badly shaken cabinet might yet be forced to dissolve Parliament. There was, of course, a calculated risk that the opposition would be accused of mere obstructionism, but the only way of exploiting fully the popular reaction against the Liberals was to force an early election. Consequently, when St. Laurent raised the matter of interim supply in the House of Commons on June 8, his supporters awaited with genuine apprehension the reaction of the Leader of the Opposition. Fortunately for the Liberals, the Progressive Conservatives and Socialists were also exhausted; interim supply was granted without a struggle; the government was safe.

In the view of more objective eye witnesses, no one emerged from the pipeline debate with his credit enhanced. While he asserted himself in the final stages, St. Laurent had failed to provide the leadership demanded by his high office; the Toronto *Telegram* summed up the general impression in the words: 'The Prime Minister loses his grip.' C. D. Howe got his pipeline, but the record he had wanted to round out so gloriously was tarnished, and he was to be remembered not only as Canada's greatest builder but as a man who had ridden roughshod over Parliament. The star of Liberal crown prince Walter Harris began to descend from that time on as well. As for the Liberal Party in general, it was a badly battered fortress, with its principal defences, the images of 'Uncle Louis' and 'C.D.', torn away. The other parties fared little better; the actions of Drew, Coldwell, Fulton, Knowles, Fleming, and others during the pipeline debate had contributed to the degradation of Parliament. Most tragic of all, Speaker Beaudoin was a broken man. Attacked openly by the Tories and Socialists, he was condemned in private by his fellow Liberals. On one conclusion all were agreed: Parliament had been dealt a serious blow.

One of the side-effects of the pipeline debate was to distract attention from provincial general elections in Saskatchewan, New Brunswick, and Quebec. In all three provinces, the governments, facing Liberal opposition, oriented their campaigns against the national administration, hoping to prove their local opponents guilty by association. T. C. Douglas complained of the failure to construct the South Saskatchewan dam and to provide cash advances on farm-stored grain; Hugh John Flemming called for greater federal aid to develop New Brunswick's sparse mineral and power resources; Duplessis campaigned as usual on the issue of provincial rights. Having called off the crusade against the Union Nationale that he had announced at the Quebec Reform Club in 1954, St. Laurent maintained his rule of not participating in provincial contests, but other federal members of Parliament, including Hugues Lapointe and Jean Lesage, campaigned actively for the provincial Liberal leader Georges-Emile Lapalme. Unknown to all, it was Maurice Duplessis's last campaign: even more than Louis St. Laurent, he had become a tired old man. In fact, when the report of the Royal Commission on constitutional problems had been delivered to him earlier in the year, he had been too weary to read it; the material it contained in support of his views on provincial autonomy went unused during the contest. The Union Nationale election machine was still the most effective in Canadian history; he could afford to ride it to power once again, repeating his attacks on the Liberal 'centralizers'. Predictably, his government was re-elected with 72 out of 93 seats. The Liberals were defeated in New Brunswick and Saskatchewan as well. The results were disappointing for Louis St. Laurent; not only would he have to co-exist with the Union Nationale government for a while longer and observe it continue to tarnish the image of Quebec in the rest of Canada, but the bonds of national unity were bound to be weakened by further attacks on the federal government.

Of more immediate concern to the Prime Minister was a Commonwealth conference scheduled to begin in London on June 22. Less anxious than ever to be outside the country while Parliament was sitting, and increasingly preoccupied by domestic matters, he would have preferred to send Pearson in his place, but once again, he felt he could not shirk his responsibility. As on the previous occasion, he asked the Minister for External Affairs to make the trip as well. On the whole, St. Laurent's contribution to the ten-day meeting was not significant. Although he worked almost continuously on the documents submitted to him, and listened carefully to the views of the other prime ministers, he displayed little initiative in seeking solutions to international problems, and allowed Pearson to carry on the more detailed discussions. Sir Anthony Eden reported on the recent visit to Great Britain of Soviet leaders Bulganin and Khrushchev; the question of recognizing Communist China was raised once more and the explosive situation in the Middle East was also examined. The British inquired about the possibility of a Canadian initiative in seeking a settlement of the Kashmir dispute, but St. Laurent rejected the suggestion on the grounds that Nehru would resent any interference by other Commonwealth countries. The precise achievements of the conference were very limited, and disappointing to those who did not understand the nature of the Commonwealth. As St. Laurent explained in his report to Parliament later:

> The purpose for which we meet is the important and
> constructive one of exchanging information and opinions
> in the hope that thereby the Governments and Parliaments of
> member countries can and will make wiser decisions.

The conference does not seek to take any collective decisions and actions itself, but hopes to assist in bringing points of view closer together.

On that basis, the meeting was an undoubted success. The Canadian Prime Minister took advantage of a private audience with the Queen to invite her to preside at the opening of the St. Lawrence Seaway, when that great project was completed. The invitation was accepted with enthusiasm.

St. Laurent's uneasiness about being absent from Ottawa so soon after the pipeline debate was not groundless. The battle had been inconclusive, and had left a deep feeling of resentment on both sides; tempers flared in Parliament at the slightest provocation, and the exchange of insults continued. Beginning to regret that he had not maintained the pressure on the government, Drew took advantage of a supply motion on June 25 to reopen the pipeline debate and to demand the dissolution of Parliament. Later in the same week he was given a still better opportunity to keep the issue before the public. In reply to a letter from Alonzo Cinq Mars, a newspaperman in Montreal, René Beaudoin had commented, 'My accusers altered the facts for their own political ends.' He had marked the letter 'personal' and sent it to the man's private address, but the restriction was ignored, and parts of it were published in *La Patrie*, the newspaper for which Cinq Mars worked. On June 29, George Drew rose on 'a question of privilege and of major public importance', announced that an 'intolerable situation' had been created by the 'utterly unprecedented action' of the Speaker 'in impugning the motives of many honourable members', and demanded that Parliament be dissolved. M. J. Coldwell supported his proposal. The House of Commons was in full crisis once again.

When he rose to comment on the new situation, Beaudoin confessed that he had been 'greatly shocked' when he saw that extracts of his private letter had been published; 'as if I did not have enough trouble so far, I was certainly hoping that no other trouble would arise'. He had felt strongly about not being able to take part in the debate on the motion to censure his conduct, he explained. 'The worst criminal in this country, the man accused of spying, is asked before sentence is passed: Do you have anything to say?' He attempted to minimize the importance of the incident by employing the word 'distort' to translate the word *'fausser'* that he had used in his letter, instead of 'falsify',* the word Drew had employed. The Leader of the Opposition refused to be mollified by the apologetic tone of the Speaker or the semantic discussion; he repeated his demand for an election. In his capacity as Acting Prime Minister, C. D. Howe conceded in an unusually conciliatory tone that the incident was unfortunate, but argued that it was not serious enough to require the premature dissolution of Parliament. He would report the situation to the Prime Minister in London, he stated, and St. Laurent would certainly 'make such statements as seem appropriate to him'. Diefenbaker insisted that the charge of falsification should be withdrawn, and the Speaker seemed about to do so when a C.C.F. member interjected that he could not 'see the value of that at this time'. Beaudoin stiffened, his voice became more strained, and he stated that if a proper motion was made, giving the reasons why he should be removed from office, he would resign immediately. Social Credit leader Solon Low managed to reduce the tension somewhat by arguing that the Speaker had a right and a duty to express a private opinion, just as all other members had certainly done. The admonishment to the Speaker's tormentors was effective, and the matter was dropped.

The press did not allow the matter to rest there. The *Ottawa Journal* attacked the Speaker on June 30, erroneously accusing him of having written to the editor of *La Patrie*, and not to one of its correspondents, and a Montreal *Gazette* writer added the further charge of tampering with Hansard, since the presiding officer had followed the usual practice of inserting the reference to the authorities he had mentioned the previous Friday. Although both criticisms were unjustified, Beaudoin had had enough; on Monday, July 2, he informed Howe that he was determined to resign at once. The Minister of Trade and Commerce telephoned the Prime Minister in London to inform him of this latest development, and to warn that his presence might be required in

---

*The expression 'alter the facts' is still more accurate.

Ottawa shortly. When the House of Commons met after lunch, the Speaker announced that he was submitting his resignation, 'to take effect at the pleasure of the House', and expressed the hope that it be accepted 'as soon as possible'. In what he described as 'my farewell speech', he repeated, his voice unsteady from emotion, that his conscience was 'perfectly clear', and asked, 'if I may be deserving of a last favour', that 'an act of oblivion will be passed' on anything offensive or wrong done by him to any other member. In the hushed silence that followed the statement, Howe rose, and in his characteristic slightly hunched, head-down stance, expressed his appreciation for the Speaker's 'forbearance' in not pressing the matter in the absence of the Prime Minister. St. Laurent, he announced, would be back in his seat in Parliament on the following Monday. There was a moment of quiet; then the booming voice of Conservative J. H. Ferguson thundered through the Chamber. 'I believe that the Liberal government has crucified one of the finest men that was ever here. One of the finest young men who ever walked into the House of Commons has been put on the cross and crucified by this government.' The Liberals were equally convinced that their opponents were to blame. 'You will pay for that,' replied the deputy government whip, Dr. Pierre Gauthier. The other members remained still. Beaudoin continued to preside; the House went on to its normal business.

St. Laurent saw the Commonwealth conference through to the end, but his thoughts were more than ever in Canada, and he read and re-read the telegrams from Ottawa informing him of the new crisis. Shaking off the last remnants of his winter-time mood, he ordered a cabinet meeting for the afternoon of his return. In contrast to the pitiful figure slouched in his seat in Parliament a few weeks earlier, he stepped from the aircraft at Uplands Airport near Ottawa on Saturday morning, July 7, looking fresh and well groomed in a grey business suit, and every inch the Prime Minister. After shaking hands briskly with Howe and other members of the welcoming party, kissing a little girl presented to him by her father, and announcing that the Queen had accepted provisionally the invitation to open the Seaway, he climbed into his waiting limousine with Howe and drove towards

the city. At a meeting earlier in the week, the Minister of Trade
and Commerce informed him, the cabinet had reached the conclusion that Beaudoin's resignation would have to be accepted,
and that René Jutras, member for Provencher in Manitoba,
should become the new Speaker. Jutras had begun to prepare
himself for his new functions, the Governor General had been
informed of the situation, and the Senate had been asked to meet
on the following Tuesday so that the change could be made.
These were precautionary steps, however, and the final decision
had been reserved for the Prime Minister. At the beginning of
the pipeline debate, St. Laurent might well have gone along with
the tentative plan, but now he was clearly in command once
again, and he insisted on examining the whole problem before
taking a decision. While Beaudoin was not popular among his
fellow Liberals, and many of them resented the difficulties he had
caused them by his mistakes, many French-speaking members
were indignant at the treatment of one of their group, and the
dispute was taking on an ethnic character. Some Quebec members
also had reservations about replacing Beaudoin with a French-
speaking Canadian from another province. While St. Laurent
took such considerations into account, they were of secondary
importance, and he was more impressed by the consequences to
Parliament of driving a Speaker out of office as a result of a bitter
partisan struggle. He decided that Beaudoin would have to set
aside his personal preferences and carry on his duties.

St. Laurent called Beaudoin to his office on Monday morning,
and told him plainly what course he felt he should follow.
Although the Speaker had made up his mind to leave, he was
desperately in need of moral support, and the prospect of having
the firm backing of the Prime Minister to complete his term of
office was decisive; taking new hope, he agreed to remain in his
post. As soon as the House of Commons met that afternoon, St.
Laurent rose quickly to his feet. He had given 'careful consideration' to the situation that had developed in his absence, he
declared in a firm tone, and had discussed it, 'as I am sure every
member would have expected me to do', with the Speaker. It was
not hard to understand the desire of a man who felt himself
unjustly accused, and who could not reply, to place himself on a

basis of equality with other members in order to explain his conduct. At the same time, as Prime Minister, he himself was responsible for the leadership of the House, and he did not intend to shirk that responsibility. He had to ask himself whether the newspaper incident was of 'sufficient gravity to justify the resignation of a Speaker who recently received an overwhelming vote of confidence from the House', and he had no 'hesitation in saying that I do not think so'. The publication of a personal letter was regrettable, but the opinion it contained did not make the author incapable of being an impartial and competent presiding officer. In the circumstances, St. Laurent stated deliberately, his confidence in the Speaker was unshaken, and he had asked him 'to subordinate his personal feelings' to his duty to Parliament and the country, and to continue in the office in which 'he has served with great distinction'. There was a moment of surprised silence; then the Liberals burst into a storm of applause. One opposition member called, 'The Liberals are yellow.' No one rose. The Speaker asked if there were any other motions. There was no answer. The Prime Minister stood up again, and proceeded to report on the Commonwealth conference. Commenting on the scene the following day, *Toronto Daily Star* columnist Peter Stursberg wrote that, in contrast with the earlier picture of 'a baffled old uncle sitting by while his nephews enforced closure and generally cut up rough, when the die is cast and the chips are down the Prime Minister takes over and changes the orders and reverses the decisions which his captains and commanders have made.'

When they had recovered from their surprise, the opposition tried once more. On July 11, Stanley Knowles raised a grievance against the Prime Minister himself. The government leader had added insult to injury by taking unto himself the prerogative of deciding who would be the Speaker for the balance of the Parliament, the C.C.F. member charged, and called for 'a new Parliament, that can measure up to what the Canadian people have a right to expect'. St. Laurent was in top form when he rose to reply. Standing perfectly erect, his eyes flashing, he looked straight across the floor at his critic. There might come a time when the member would 'not only have to think but be in a position to do what he thinks should be done,' he stated, 'but that time has not yet arrived.' Some members had been taking the attitude that

> it was not the supporters of the Government who had the right to make decisions . . . and that, whenever there was any suggestion put before the House with which the members of the Opposition did not agree, it was wrong, unconstitutional, and a contempt of Parliament not to take into account their views instead of taking into account the views of the majority sent here by the Canadian people. . . . It is not by any accident that the party of which I have the honour to be the leader at the present time has been in office now for twenty-one years and plans to continue in office for several years longer.

The other Liberals could hardly contain themselves for delight as they observed the fiery performance; their desk-banging was deafening. Tackling Knowles on his own ground, St. Laurent commented that 'the honourable gentleman has been posing, and with some justification, as an expert on the rules and precedents of parliamentary institutions', but even those who were not so expert knew that Beaudoin had not vacated his office formally. Having ascertained that the Speaker was willing to have his duty to Parliament and to the country regarded as higher than his natural desire to be able to meet the criticisms levelled against him, the Prime Minister explained, he had merely announced that the presiding officer was not going to take any further action. If Knowles did not share his view concerning the support still existing in the House of Commons for the present Speaker, he could make a motion to remove him from the Chair, 'and he will see'.

Donald Fleming replied to the Prime Minister the following day for the official opposition. In the harshest attack of the entire struggle, he described St. Laurent's speech as 'a bald bare-faced declaration of dictatorship', and 'an act of supreme arrogance'. Constitutional rights, traditions of centuries, minority rights, guarantees of freedom, parliamentary liberties and privileges, had all been cast aside, he charged, and 'one-party government' had been all but achieved by the Prime Minister and a government 'with a totalitarian mind and purpose'. Before the time allowed for the debate expired, Walter Harris was just able to reply: 'No one in this Dominion of Canada believes the things he has said about the Prime Minister of Canada, and when the time comes he will find out.' The long wrangle that had begun over the pipeline, that had turned into a fight over the rights of Parliament, and had ended in personal attacks on both the Speaker and the Prime Minister, was over at last. St. Laurent's last statement was undoubtedly the best he had made during the entire session; in the words of Toronto *Globe and Mail* correspondent George Bain, he 'again sounded like a leader'. If it was the jaunt to London that had transformed him, the witty newspaperman remarked, perhaps the best thing the opposition members could do to defend themselves in the future would be to steal his airplane.

# 15

## The Suez Crisis

The remaining weeks of the session were an anticlimax. The new federal-provincial tax-sharing formula was approved after a short debate, with only the Social Credit members proposing amendments to it. In contrast to his forceful performance during the pipeline debate, George Drew was strangely quiet; in late July he fell ill with a bout of influenza, complicated by a dental infection. Two weeks before the end of the session he was obliged to accept his doctor's advice and leave on a holiday. He was never to sit in Parliament again. Louis St. Laurent, on the other hand, was in excellent form. After the session ended on August 14, he tackled his holidays with the same enthusiasm that he was again displaying for his prime ministerial functions. When he appeared at the annual meeting of the Canadian Bar Association in Montreal in early September, he joked about the pipeline debate almost as if it had been merely a vigorous match between sportsmen. He was shaken by the death of John Hackett on September 15, followed three days later by that of Adélard Godbout, but he took the blows in his stride, whereas a few months earlier they might have had far more serious consequences. That same month, his first great-grandchild was born. That happy event and the disappearance of his oldest friend emphasized the irreversible break with the past.

Seeking to reassert his authority, he displayed an interest in new projects and a determination to supervise the activities of his cabinet colleagues that were in strong contrast to his conduct of the previous winter. When he learned that a construction project was being delayed in Quebec City because three federal government departments were quarrelling over their respective areas of jurisdiction, he summoned the three ministers and deputy ministers to his East Block office and lectured them in a language that left them speechless; within a few days, the argument was settled and the project authorized. Planning the next and final session of Parliament before the general election, he called in Walter Gordon to discuss the progress of his Royal Commission on Economic Prospects, agreed after several years of hesitation to the formation of a Canada Council, and began negotiations with the National Conference of Canadian Universities to devise a way of distributing grants to universities that would circumvent Duplessis's objections to federal aid in that field. In a radical departure from past practice, he let the other political parties know that the election would be held the following June 'so that they may not be taken by surprise'. When he received the news that George Drew was seriously ill in a Toronto hospital, St. Laurent wrote at once to Mrs. Drew, suggesting that they consider taking a house near his in St. Patrick, in order to assure the Leader of the Opposition of the best possible conditions for a 'speedy and complete restoration to his usual vigour'. On learning a few days later that Drew had been persuaded by his doctors to resign the Progressive Conservative Party leadership, he telephoned him at the hospital and offered him a senatorship, or, if he preferred, some other post that would enable him to continue his service to Canada. Touched, but also surprised, by the unprecedented gesture, Drew asked that the matter be postponed until he could make a proper decision.

At a press conference on September 28, his first in over a year, Louis St. Laurent was both the understanding grandfather and the stern parent who brooked no questioning of his authority. The trade deficit with the United States did not worry him as much as it did some people, he replied to one questioner, as the imports were a reflection of Canada's development program, and of the need for capital goods and materials for that purpose. He also disagreed with those who saw a danger of the country being taken over by American capitalists; Canadians themselves were making about 80 per cent of current investments, and they would gradually become the owners of much of the foreign capital. In his view, the problems facing Canada were the result of a record level of growth and prosperity, and that was a pretty happy situation. On other topics, he was more sensitive. He had been 'a little bit shocked', he confessed, to read newspaper reports of his offer to George Drew of a senatorship; such stories were not going to be helpful in providing a way for the retiring Conservative leader to continue his service to the public. One Liberal senator who had been interviewed that morning 'did not seem very happy over the suggestion', commented one newspaperman. St. Laurent bridled, and snapped:

> But it so happens that it is not the Liberal Senator who makes the appointments to the Senate. Here, I said that I felt that it would be a tragedy if George Drew, at the age of sixty-two, was debarred from the possibility of public service, and I meant it, and as long as I am going to be in a position to have anything to do that could prevent that from happening . . . I am going to do it, no matter what any Liberal Senator has to say about it.

He was also annoyed that the press had learned of the expulsion of a Soviet diplomat from Canada several months earlier for engaging in espionage activities, and that a federal civil servant had been dismissed in connection with the same incident. When the news broke, the government had issued a statement, declaring that no harm had been done, and that the matter was closed. The *Globe and Mail* had condemned the government's attitude as 'McCarthyism'. 'Now, I want to repeat here that I am the one who took the responsibility for making the public statement,' he declared when the matter was raised at the press conference; there had been no damage to national security, and 'we did not think that what happened here was worth making an international incident about.' Asked if any other diplomats were under suspicion, he glared at the questioner and retorted, 'I am not going to deal with what we suspect. There is a limit to just how much you can pry into my mind. When I do things, I am responsible for them, but when I think, until I come to some conclusion, I am responsible only to my own conscience.' Although the press conference was marked by several brisk exchanges, it ended on a cordial note. Would he take into account the health of reporters in planning the next campaign? inquired one correspondent with an obvious allusion to the Prime Minister's fine condition. He allowed himself to relax into a more genial role. 'Well, I could give a lot of reporters a pretty good run just now,' he replied with a smile. His audience agreed. 'If the Prime Minister feels as perky in the campaign as he did in his office,' wrote one correspondent the next day, 'the Opposition [and reporters] are in for a heap of trouble.'

In the pleasant Indian summer, St. Laurent gave the impression of appreciating life to the full. After spending most of one Saturday morning in his office, he strolled over to the entrance of the Centre Block, where a group of young Montreal folk dancers, Les Plumes au Vent, were preparing a special outdoor performance. Standing under the Peace Tower, he watched them go through their numbers, then told them that they should go on television so that other Canadians could enjoy their talent as well. (The following Monday he followed up his comment with a letter to C.B.C. Chairman Davidson Dunton; the suggestion was adopted.) Following their performance, the troupe of children moved off, and he was left waiting for his car in the bright autumn sun. Noticing a little Chinese girl among the tourists who were wandering about, he went over to her, sat down on the stone steps, took her on his knee, and chatted with her.

Determined to maintain his improved health, St. Laurent adopted a practice of having a daily swim at the Château Laurier hotel on the way home from work. The management inquired whether the public should be excluded while he was in the pool in order to ensure greater privacy, but he insisted that they should not be inconvenienced on his account. With his usual punctuality, he could be seen walking down Wellington Street about six o'clock every evening in the company of a secretary who doubled as swimming companion, chatting about the day's activities and his plans for the future. In the water, he worked his way systematically up and down one side of the pool, supporting himself on the rail with one hand, and paddling with the other. Hardly believing their own eyes on recognizing the distinguished head above the surface, some fellow bathers swam over, stuck out a hand, and introduced themselves. As reports of his daily dip spread, the pool became crowded with people eager to say they had shared the swimming-pool with their Prime Minister.

With his advancing years, St. Laurent required less sleep than previously, and awoke before dawn every morning, but he forced himself to remain in bed until the staff of the residence was up, in order to allow them to have a proper night's rest. For the same reason, he refrained from arriving at the office before nine o'clock. Occasionally, he walked part of the way to Parliament Hill to take some exercise and to fill in the time.

During the autumn of 1956, the principal preoccupation in Ottawa, as in most other capitals of the world, was the Suez crisis. For many months, St. Laurent and Pearson had been observing with anxiety the growing tension in the Middle East. Under strong American pressure, the British government had agreed in 1954 to withdraw its troops from Egypt, and to recognize the Suez Canal as an integral part of that country, although it continued to be operated by the Suez Canal Company. President Nasser, in turn, had recognized that the great waterway was of international importance, and pledged himself to assure perpetual freedom of navigation on it. The arrangement was part of a plan devised by John Foster Dulles to establish a basis for peace in the Middle East compatible with American interests, including a balance between the military power of Egypt and Israel. In 1955, however, the Egyptian revolutionary leader went outside the American sphere of influence and made a huge purchase of arms, including MIG jet aircraft, from Soviet Russia. Preoccupied with maintaining United States influence in the area, Dulles accepted the rebuff and offered to pay a major share of the cost of a huge dam at Aswan on the Nile River; Nasser appeared to be getting the best of both worlds, and his confidence rose accordingly.

When Prime Minister Eden called at Ottawa in February 1956 following a visit to Washington, he reported to the Canadian cabinet that he had urged the Americans to take a strong and united stand with Great Britain and France in the Middle East; otherwise Nasser, whom he considered a sort of Egyptian Mussolini, would be impossible to restrain. The sympathy of the Canadian ministers was clearly on Eden's side, for, like the British, they had serious reservations about some of the policies being pursued by the American Secretary of State. At the same time, they were still sensitive to opposition charges in Parliament that they were aggravating tension in the Middle East by selling arms to both Israel and Egypt, particularly since their declared policy was to reduce the possibilities of conflict there through the United Nations, and a Canadian officer, General E. L. M. Burns, was in command of the U.N. force supervising the truce between Egypt and Israel. The Canadian position was made more difficult shortly after the British Prime Minister's visit when the government received a request from Israel to purchase twenty-four jet fighter aircraft. Members of Parliament soon learned of the request and, changing their attitude abruptly, the Progressive Conservatives pressed the government to accede to it. During the weeks of the pipeline debate, St. Laurent replied frequently in response to questions in the House of Commons that the matter was still under consideration.

At the Commonwealth conference in late June and early July, the situation in the Middle East was discussed, and St. Laurent had returned home 'somewhat reassured' by what he had heard in London concerning relations between Israel and her neighbours. 'We all recognize that the situation there is dangerous,' he stated in the House of Commons on July 9, but the danger had become 'a little less acute' as a result of attempts by United Nations Secretary General Dag Hammarskjöld to mediate between Israel and her neighbours. At the same time, he had not been able 'to get anything from the conference' that would enable the government to meet the Israeli request for fighter aircraft. The government's principal concern, he repeated, was to avoid doing anything that might aggravate the tense situation in the Middle East. In the third week of July, the situation was altered radically when Dulles, annoyed at Nasser's action in recognizing Communist China and signing a huge barter deal with the Peking régime, withdrew the American offer to assist in building the Aswan dam.

The Egyptian President responded on July 26, the third anniversary of his régime, by seizing the Suez Canal and telling the United States at a mass rally, 'Americans, may you choke to death on your fury!' In London, Eden reacted in turn with equal forcefulness. If the Western powers did not take a stand against Nasser at once, he warned in a telegram to President Eisenhower on July 27, their influence in the Middle East would be lost. 'We must be ready, in the last resort,' the British Prime Minister declared, 'to use force to bring Nasser to his senses.' The message concluded: 'I have this morning instructed our chiefs of staff to prepare a military plan accordingly.'

At the same time that Eden announced to Eisenhower his determination to use force if necessary in the Middle East, he sent word to the other Commonwealth prime ministers, informing them that Great Britain planned to call a conference of maritime nations to establish a common front against Egypt. St. Laurent received the message when he arrived at his office on Saturday morning, July 28. As he read the dispatch, his interest turned to uneasiness, and then to annoyance. Its tone and content were in such marked contrast to the reassurances he had received in London earlier in the month that he had the impression of not having been kept fully informed. That was Britain's perfect right if she considered it necessary in the international interest; what was less acceptable in view of the principle of prior consultation among Commonwealth members in matters of common interest was that Canada's endorsement of the new British policy was taken for granted. Eden not only did not invite Canada to take part in the meeting, but concluded his message with the words: 'I know I can count on your joining us in expressions of concern and indignation.' St. Laurent was sensitive to the suggestion that his country's support could be taken for granted; to him it seemed to indicate that the British still thought of Canada as a colony whose leaders would cry, in Meighen's words, 'Ready, aye, ready', at the first command from London.

He was still studying the text when Pearson entered the office, and he tossed it across the desk with the comment: 'See what he wants? Canada should express indignation because Nasser has grabbed the Suez. What do you think?' 'We will certainly have to take a hard look at that,' the Minister for External Affairs replied. Pearson was more concerned over another sentence in the message. 'We believe that we should seize this opportunity of putting the canal under proper international control in permanent arrangement.' That was the first intimation received in Ottawa that the use of force was being contemplated.

When the House of Commons met later that same morning, the Progressive Conservative spokesman on external affairs, John Diefenbaker, made it clear that his party's sympathy was firmly with the United Kingdom. He urged the government 'to join with Britain in condemnation of what has taken place as a perversion of an international contract, and also indicate to Britain and the other nations Canada's agreement with the stand which they are taking to meet this situation'. To St. Laurent, the suggestion revealed once again that the Tories were not yet ready to recognize that Canada could have a foreign policy of her own. In replying to Diefenbaker, Pearson agreed that the seizure of the canal constituted a 'violation . . . of an international convention' and was 'of course, to be condemned' but avoided endorsing the British position by giving the assurance that views were being exchanged with governments 'probably more concerned [than Canada] with this matter'.

As the session of Parliament drew to a close, the official opposition maintained the pressure on the government to line up solidly with the United Kingdom, Diefenbaker denouncing Nasser's 'truculent attitude', describing him as the 'dictator of Egypt', and comparing him with Hitler and Mussolini. While St. Laurent largely shared that opinion of the Egyptian leader, he was convinced that to meet force with force, except under the aegis of the United Nations, would alienate the leaders of neutral nations such as India, and would give Soviet Russia a pretext to intervene still further in the Middle East. Just before Parliament adjourned on August 3, St. Laurent read into Hansard a statement by representatives of the United States, British, and French governments, announcing a conference of users of the Suez Canal 'to establish operating arrangements under an international system' consistent with 'legitimate Egyptian interests'. Although Canada had not been invited to attend, he added, the government 'would be kept in the closest possible touch', and he was informing Sir Anthony Eden that it 'supports strongly the objectives of the conference as stated in this communiqué'. Diefenbaker continued to insist that Canada should be represented at the meeting to give 'a degree of support . . . to the United Kingdom in this hour of great stress and difficulty'. Pearson could only point out that Canada had not been invited.

The initial reaction of St. Laurent and Pearson, that the crisis had far wider implications than the control of the Suez Canal, was borne out by subsequent messages that arrived in Ottawa. Returning on August 4 from a quick visit to London, Dulles told the Canadian Ambassador in Washington, Arnold Heeney, that the British had reached 'the calm and deliberate decision' that they could not allow Britain to be at the mercy of a man like Nasser 'even though the calculated risk of their decision is nuclear war'. The Deputy Secretary of State, Robert Murphy, described the situation to Heeney in still more vivid terms: 'The British and French mean business. Regardless of the legal position of the canal, they are determined to get it back and place it under international control. Nasser will resist, and God knows where the mess will end. Perhaps you people in Canada can do something to urge caution on them.' The conversation was reported at once to Ottawa.

Opinion among members of the Canadian cabinet was divided concerning the call for a conference of users of the canal. Several members shared the Progressive Conservative view that they should stand by the mother country, if only to avoid giving the official opposition an opportunity to accuse them of making Canada, in Diefenbaker's words, 'a mere tail on the American kite'. St. Laurent was still sensitive about Eden's diplomatic *faux pas* in taking Canada for granted; more important, he felt that the military action evidently being planned by the United Kingdom and France was both legally and morally wrong, and politically irresponsible, and that the best service Canada could render those countries was to dissuade them from such an act of folly. Already the Commonwealth countries were divided on the issue, Australia and New Zealand lending unqualified support to Great Britain, while India, Pakistan, and Ceylon were showing signs of aligning themselves with President Nasser. Even more serious from the Canadian viewpoint, the United States and the United Kingdom were likely to disagree openly in the event of an invasion of the Suez Canal area, and Anglo-American co-operation was the single most important consideration in Canadian foreign policy. In brief, the Commonwealth, the North Atlantic Treaty Alliance, the Anglo-American unwritten pact, and the United Nations itself, were being placed in jeopardy. At the conclusion of the cabinet meeting, St. Laurent gave Pearson wide liberty to do whatever possible to avoid such a catastrophe, and promised him his full support.

Throughout the summer and autumn, St. Laurent observed the gathering storm through the diplomatic dispatches, news reports, and briefings from Pearson and his staff. The 'users' conference was held in London in mid-August, and while several nations soon withdrew, eighteen others agreed on a proposal for international control of the Suez Canal. Dulles was asked to lead a delegation to Cairo to present the plan to Nasser, but he declined, and Prime Minister Menzies of Australia accepted the assignment. Shortly after the group arrived in the Egyptian capital, President Eisenhower declared in a press conference that the United States could not 'in any circumstances' support the use of force in settling the dispute. Encouraged by the statement, Nasser rejected the 'users' proposal.

Worried by the increasing tension, Norman Robertson, High Commissioner in London, called on Lord Home, British Secretary of State for Commonwealth Affairs, and asked him directly: 'Is it your intention to proceed with an attempt to humiliate and replace Nasser?' 'The possibility can't be washed out,' the other man replied circumspectly, and countered with a question of his own: 'If we have to use force, would we have the approval of Canada?' Robertson answered: 'In my opinion, no.' A short time later, he was more categorical. 'We sympathize with your predicament,' he told Sir Ivone Kirkpatrick, senior staff member of the Foreign Office; 'we even support your concern that the canal operations should be insulated against the political whims of any one nation. But we cannot support, nor even approve, any resort to force [for that purpose].' In London on September 3, Pearson discussed the situation with Foreign Secretary Selwyn Lloyd, and urged him not to resort to force except under the authorization of the United Nations; a few days later he repeated his argument before the NATO Council in Paris. During the NATO meeting Lloyd commented to Pearson almost casually that 'if things drag on, you know, Israel might take advantage of the situation to move against Egypt. . . . They'd probably win, Nasser would go, and most of our troubles would be solved for us.' 'Ingenious idea,' the Canadian minister replied, 'but it won't work. A few Arab leaders are sitting tight on the fence now. An Israeli attack would unite them all behind Nasser. I hope you won't do any urging in that direction. The repercussions would be terrible.'

Anxious to avoid a situation in which the British and French would appear to be taking the law into their own hands, and even using the Arab-Israeli conflict for their own purposes, Pearson sought to place the dispute before the United Nations. Even if the Soviet Union used its veto in the Security Council, he argued before members of the NATO Council in private session, the weight of a majority opinion would be valuable for subsequent negotiations; more important, it would align the British, French, and Americans on a common approach to the problem. He instructed Heeney to find out how the United States would regard an Anglo-French resolution to the Security Council; Dulles opposed the suggestion, accusing the British of trying to impose their will on Egypt and manoeuvre the Security Council into appearing to support them. The American Secretary of State had devised a new plan of his own, the creation of a new body called the Suez Canal Users' Association that would operate the canal, and he had just obtained the very reluctant agreement of the British and French to join it. The Canadians were convinced that it would never become operative, particularly since the United States had announced that it would not use force if Egypt refused to co-operate. On September 23, the first cracks in Anglo-American solidarity appeared when Eden ignored the American viewpoint and sent a letter to the President of the Security Council, asking that Egypt's seizure of the Canal be inscribed on the agenda; France joined in the request, but the United States refused to be associated with it.

While the British government was under heavy pressure from the United States and Canada not to resort to force, it was exposed to equally heavy pressure from the French to do so. Already involved in a war with the Arabs, in Algeria, where the National Liberation Front was receiving aid from Egypt, Premier Guy Mollet and Foreign Minister Christian Pineau were just as anxious as Eden to unseat Colonel Nasser. Throughout 1956, French aircraft, tanks, and other military supplies were shipped secretly to Israel, and in early September the French and Israelis drew up a joint plan of attack on Egypt. Following a series of meetings in Paris and London between the British and French leaders in the last week of September and early October, Eden accepted a plan on October 3 to undertake a joint military action against Egypt in concert with the Israelis. Unknowingly, the Canadian government contributed to the plan on September 21 by agreeing, under strong Israeli pressure and after being advised by London and Washington that there would be no objection to the step, to grant a permit for the export of the twenty-four jet fighters to Israel. In announcing the decision, St. Laurent declared that 'assurances have been received from the government of Israel that the interceptors in question will be used solely for defence against aggression.'

As was generally expected, the Security Council meeting proved abortive, the Soviet Union imposing its veto on a proposal to have shipping tolls on the Suez Canal paid to the Users' Association. Eden decided that the time had come for more forceful action; on October 16, he flew to Paris to arrange the co-ordinated Israeli-French-British military operation. According to the plan that was drawn up in the French capital, the Israelis were to attack first, and the other two countries were to appear to be reacting to an Israeli-Egyptian war by intervening to protect the canal. The D-day was set for November 1 for the Israelis, with the Anglo-French landings to take place five days later. On October 24 a document setting out the agreement was signed in Paris by Israeli Prime Minister Ben Gurion, Pineau, and Patrick Dean of the British Foreign Office. On October 29, Israeli paratroops were dropped twenty-five miles from the Suez Canal; at 4:15 p.m., London time, on October 30, Britain and France issued an ultimatum to both Israel and Egypt to cease fire and withdraw ten miles from the waterway.

The British-French-Israeli operation was prepared in the greatest possible secrecy, neither the United States nor the other Commonwealth countries being given a hint of it. The Commonwealth high commissioners in London were informed of the terms of the ultimatum at the same time as it was delivered, and messages were also dispatched by Sir Anthony Eden to the prime ministers; however, news reports, based on Eden's statement to the House of Commons at 4:30 p.m., reached North America first. St. Laurent learned of the sensational development first through an Ottawa newspaper. Still in an aggressively confident mood, the Canadian Prime Minister read the press report and reacted with indignation and alarm, realizing that all the time that he and Pearson had been working to maintain western unity, and to prevent Britain and France from being charged with violating international law, the two countries had been plotting in secret the very course of action against which Canada and other friendly countries had advised them. While he could understand their concern over Nasser's conduct, the decision to take matters into their own hands smacked, in his view, of old-style imperialism; worse still, the deliberate decision not to take their friends into their confidence made a mockery of the much-vaunted system of consultation among members of the Commonwealth. Even the timing of the military action seemed unfortunate. Since October 20, reports had been leaking out of Hungary of a popular uprising; the free world was observing with a mixture of anxiety and hope the first serious attempt to throw off the Communist yoke in eastern Europe, and the reported use of Soviet troops to suppress it was being widely condemned; an equally blatant aggression by the British and French in Egypt could only make a mockery of Western protests and seriously jeopardize the possibilities of assisting the Hungarian people to regain their freedom.

When Eden's message arrived a short time later, it did nothing to assuage the Canadian Prime Minister's feelings. It repeated Israel's claim that Egypt was the aggressor, and the fiction that Britain and France were merely concerned with stopping the fighting between Israeli and Egyptian troops, as well as ensuring the safety of the Suez Canal. Although Israeli troops had not yet reached the waterway, and the Canal Zone had been recognized as part of Egyptian territory, both sides were being ordered to cease hostilities and withdraw from its banks; otherwise, military action would be taken 'to compel the offender to conform'. If the British Prime Minister's argument was – to say the least – misleading, the conclusion of the message was bound to irritate. He knew, declared Eden, that he could count on Canadian understanding and support, and would continue to keep St. Laurent closely informed of developments.

St. Laurent had sent for Pearson as soon as the news report arrived, and delivered himself of a blast of indignation against the British and French. The Minister for External Affairs returned to his office to see what additional information he could find, but was summoned back shortly by his still more concerned leader, who tossed Eden's message across the desk at him, with the comment 'Tell me how I ought to answer this.' Pearson was equally disturbed by its contents, but remained calm. 'I agree he presumes a bit,' he conceded, 'but let's look at it from the British side. They couldn't very well tell us, the Americans, or anyone else in advance, because if they had we would have stopped them. And they're in no mood to be stopped.' The two men agreed that each should prepare a draft reply, and that they would compare them before raising the matter at a cabinet meeting later in the day.

Putting aside all other business, St. Laurent went to work, setting down in words his feeling of indignation and his sense of having been betrayed; Pearson suggested some changes to make the tone somewhat softer, expressing more regret than indignation over the turn of events, and looking ahead for a possible way out of the critical situation. To this end, he proposed to reject Canada's association with the British and French action and to work for a solution within the terms of the United Nations Charter. That was the proposal made in the Council Chamber at the end of the busy afternoon. Several ministers, more preoccupied with the domestic political scene than St. Laurent and Pearson, were alarmed at the prospect of an open disagreement with the United Kingdom at such a crucial moment in history.

Walter Harris's first reaction was that such a move would cost the Liberals forty seats in Ontario at the next election; Robert Winters frowned as he thought of the effect it would have on the Atlantic provinces. When the Minister of Finance raised his objections to the proposed reply, St. Laurent commented impatiently, 'You're just talking with your blood.' Harris refrained from remarking that the same could be said of the Prime Minister. The discussion continued for some time, and it was then agreed that work would go ahead on a more definite text. St. Laurent spent the evening trying to devise a statement that would reconcile the opposing points of view without sacrificing what he considered the principles of proper international conduct. In a highly agitated state of mind, he telephoned Harris at least eight times during the evening, and even arranged a three-way telephone conversation with Pearson, before completing the task about midnight.

In Washington, President Eisenhower had been taken equally unawares by the British and French ultimatum, and his reaction was similar to the Canadian Prime Minister's. Although he was in the final phase of an election campaign that was scheduled to end on November 6, he had sent a series of messages across the Atlantic and to the Middle East in recent days, expressing concern about the reports of imminent fighting, and urging restraint on all sides; for ten days before the Israeli attack, however, no communications on the subject were received from London or Paris. When he learned on October 29 of the Israeli attack, Eisenhower called in the British *chargé d'affaires*, and reminded him in blunt terms that the United States had signed a pledge in 1950 to support the victims of any aggression in the Middle East. Seeing the crisis in the context of the cold war, he declared, 'We plan to get to the United Nations the first thing in the morning – when the doors open, before the U.S.S.R. gets there.' His annoyance and concern were increased later that same evening when he learned that the British Ambassador to the United Nations, Sir Pierson Dixon, refused to join in placing the matter before the United Nations with a view to taking action against Israel, and that the British considered the tripartite agreement of 1950, guaranteeing assistance against aggression, 'ancient history and without current validity'.

On October 30, United States Ambassador Henry Cabot Lodge placed before the Security Council a resolution calling on Israel to withdraw behind the 1950 armistice line, and asking all members of the United Nations to refrain from giving her aid until she did so. The British delegate pleaded for a modification of the resolution in order that he and the French delegate could support it, but his request was brushed aside, and Lodge urged that a vote be taken as soon as possible. The Soviet Union and five other members supported the Americans; Australia and Belgium abstained; the British and French used their veto for the first time, and against the United States!* Later in the day, they used it a second time, on a somewhat similar Soviet resolution; on that occasion, the United States abstained. At the end of the Security Council meeting, the Yugoslav member called for an emergency session of the General Assembly under the terms of the 'Uniting for Peace' resolution that had been designed by the Western nations in 1950 to circumvent a Soviet veto relating to the Korean War.

The Canadian cabinet met on Wednesday morning, October 31, to approve the government's reply to Sir Anthony Eden. Since the previous meeting, the Security Council had met, Nasser had rejected the British and French ultimatum, the Royal Air Force had dropped leaflets over the Port Said area to warn the population of an imminent air attack, and British and French troops were reported to be moving towards Egypt from bases in the Mediterranean Sea. In London, opposition leader Hugh Gaitskell condemned the joint venture as 'an act of disastrous folly that we shall regret for years'. Jawaharlal Nehru denounced it in equally forceful terms. The British veto had not improved St. Laurent's humour, reminding him of the discussions at San Francisco in 1945, when Canada had opposed the rule of unanimity in the Security Council, and the Americans and British had given

*The United States, the United Kingdom, and France had all voted 'no' on numerous occasions, but only France, of the Western powers, had voted 'no' in isolation.

solemn assurances that they would use the veto only as a last resort to prevent abuses of the Charter. The votes against the United States resolution made a mockery of that assurance, for Britain and France were clearly acting to save the remnants of their prestige as world powers, and doing so in direct violation of the United Nations Charter.

In the circumstances, the final draft of St. Laurent's telegram to Eden was surprisingly mild and conciliatory, regretting that Britain should have acted without prior consultation, but expressing understanding of the reasons for doing so. At the same time, on the basis of available information, the Canadian government could not endorse the military actions of either Israel, the United Kingdom, or France; it was, therefore, suspending all shipments of arms to Israel, and would shape its course in conformity with its obligations under the United Nations Charter. While he and his colleagues were 'never unmindful . . . of the very special relationship of close friendship and intimate association' of Canada with the United Kingdom, and 'the vital importance of the Suez Canal to the economic life of the United Kingdom', three aspects of the situation were causing them particular anxiety. The first was the effect of Eden's decisions upon the United Nations, of which the United Kingdom had been such a staunch and steady supporter; taking military action while the Security Council was seized of the matter was most regrettable, as was the vote itself on the American resolution. There was also a danger of a serious division within the Commonwealth over the British action that might 'prejudice the unity of our association'. And finally, there was the 'deplorable divergence of viewpoint and policy between the U.K. and the U.S.A.'. Anglo-American co-operation and friendship was the surest foundation for a peaceful world, St. Laurent remarked, and it would be a tragedy beyond repair if that basis were to disappear, or even be weakened; it was difficult for a Canadian to consider anything, except Canada's national survival itself, as more important. He concluded the message by saying that, while he had no desire to add to the heavy burdens already being borne by Sir Anthony, he felt he should explain frankly, and as a friend, the concern of the Canadian government over the tense situation.

The text was approved by the whole Canadian cabinet with relative ease, considering that it marked a fundamental change in Canadian foreign policy, and was certain to have serious repercussions on the domestic political scene. Only Agriculture Minister Gardiner expressed serious doubt about it; the last of the Mackenzie King school of Liberals, he commented that the Middle East conflict was no business of Canada's, and that she should keep out of it entirely. When the message reached London the next morning, it created consternation; Sir Anthony Eden had really assumed that Canada would back him up in the hour of need, regardless of legal and political niceties. The assumption was another in the growing list of British miscalculations. Still, the shock and disappointment were not sufficient to stop the course of events; shortly after the message from Ottawa arrived, the Royal Air Force began to attack Egypt's airfields. The latest development kindled St. Laurent's anger anew.

Except for an expression of 'regret' by the Minister for External Affairs on October 30 that Britain and France had 'found it necessary to take action while the Security Council was discussing the matter', the government gave no indication of its attitude to the Canadian public until the reply to Eden was dispatched. Nevertheless, to the reporters who crowded into the corridor between the Prime Minister's Office and the Privy Council Chamber, St. Laurent's displeasure was evident. Asked by one of them if he shared Pearson's 'regret', he turned on the questioner, his eyes flashing, and snapped that he was 'having nothing further to say about that'. When a decision had been taken by the government, he would let it be known; in the meantime, he was not going to reveal what might be running through his own mind. He did announce that the permit to export the twenty-four fighter planes to Israel had been suspended.

By the time the Canadian cabinet met again on Thursday morning, November 1, the international situation had deteriorated still further. Nehru had condemned the Royal Air Force attacks on Egyptian airfields as a 'naked aggression'; a former Indian governor general recommended that India leave the Commonwealth, and urged Pakistan and Ceylon to do so as well. British and French troop landings in the area were clearly imminent, Nasser had ordered ships sunk in the Suez Canal to block the waterway and had presumably appealed to Russia for help, and United States warships were reported to be patrolling the possible invasion route in the eastern Mediterranean. In New York, the General Assembly of the United Nations was scheduled to meet that afternoon, and Canada's two mother countries were bound to be severely condemned by a large majority of members. Pearson had telephoned to London and Washington the previous evening to see if the British and American governments could be persuaded to support a proposal for a United Nations force; just before the cabinet meeting, word was received from both capitals that the two governments welcomed the proposal as an eventual or ultimate solution, but considered it too complicated to serve their respective interests in the immediate future.

The corridor of the East Block was already crowded with newspapermen as St. Laurent made his way to the Privy Council Chamber at eleven o'clock. To be obliged to elbow his way through the crowd and run a gauntlet of questions every time he emerged from his office was a source of annoyance to him at the best of times; in the tense situation, it aggravated his already bad mood. Australia had indicated support of the latest British and French move, one reporter called out as he moved through the milling group of men, their pencils and cameras at the ready. 'That is their affair,' the Prime Minister barked. 'We have no criticism or commendation to make of what other governments choose to do. We have made no decision where Canada stands.' Was the crisis on the cabinet agenda? another reporter ventured. 'That is our business,' he was told bluntly. 'We'll deal with that in the proper order.' He disappeared behind the swinging doors leading to the Council Chamber, then suddenly reappeared, shouting: 'It's too bad you can't come in and tell us how to do it, but we are the ones responsible to Parliament and the Canadian public.' Before the newsmen could recover from their astonishment he was gone again. As they dispersed, someone suggested that 'Uncle Louis' be renamed 'Louis the Terrible'.

In cabinet, Pearson outlined the most recent developments and submitted two guide-lines as the basis for Canada's attitude. First, he suggested, everything possible should be done to avoid Britain and France's being arraigned before the United Nations on charges of conspiring to commit an act of war against a weak and sovereign state. Second, a way must be found of imposing the authority of the United Nations in the Middle East through the creation of an international police force. If at all possible, the British and French troops, about to land in the canal zone, should be incorporated into such a force in order to get those two countries back on the side of legality. Because of the divergence of views within the cabinet, the minister was careful not to ask for detailed and specific instructions from his colleagues; it was simply agreed that he should fly to New York immediately, and see what he could do to extricate the British and French from the impossible situation into which they were plunging deeper and deeper by the hour. He was to consult the Prime Minister by telephone if a decision had to be taken, and the other ministers would be on hand if another cabinet meeting was required. Pearson left the Council Chamber early in order to fly to New York for the meeting of the General Assembly that was scheduled to begin later that same afternoon. When St. Laurent emerged, he was in a more relaxed mood, and told the tenacious newspapermen that he hoped Canada would not have to take a position on the United States resolution that was to be discussed in New York that evening.

Pearson arrived at United Nations headquarters too late to have his name placed on the list of speakers, but he began immediately to consult his many friends, and particularly the members of the British and American delegations. In an impromptu conference with Dulles during the dinner recess, he urged the United States Secretary of State to cease his insistence on an early vote, or at least to accept an amendment providing for some sort of 'negotiating machinery' rather than simply condemning America's closest allies. Engaged in a game of one-upmanship with the Soviet Union, Dulles was determined to go on record at once as condemning the aggressors. Asked in turn whether he would support the United States resolution, Pearson said that he had not yet received instructions from Ottawa, but that he had hoped personally for a more constructive proposal.

'We're interested in helping Britain and France,' he stated frankly. 'I would like to make it possible for them to withdraw with as little loss of face as possible, and bring them back into re-alignment with the United States.' 'That's not possible at this time,' Dulles replied. 'They've damaged the whole cause of freedom by placing us in an inferior position morally to the Communists. We could be having a showdown with Russia right now over this Hungary situation but for their actions.' He appeared even less interested than the British in a United Nations force, Eden having at least offered to hand over control of the area to such a unit once the military situation was stabilized.

By the time Pearson telephoned St. Laurent shortly before ten o'clock that evening, he had abandoned hope of transforming into a United Nations force the British and French units approaching Egyptian territory, and was casting about for a more acceptable alternative. In order to maintain his freedom of action to put forward a proposal for a United Nations force with maximum chance of acceptance, he recommended to the Prime Minister that Canada abstain from voting on the American resolution. If the British and French could be persuaded to accept such a Canadian plan, he explained, 'they can be seen to be complying with the United Nations wishes and thereby upholding the Charter. That way they're off the hook.' 'Can you persuade the Assembly to go along?' St. Laurent asked somewhat dubiously. 'We'll try,' came the reply. The Prime Minister said that he would consult some of their cabinet colleagues and call back. After a series of telephone calls to ministers' residences, he advised Pearson to go ahead.

The vote on the American resolution was taken about 3 a.m. on the morning of November 2; sixty-five nations supported it, five were opposed, and six, including Canada, abstained. As soon as the result was announced, Pearson took the rostrum to explain the Canadian position. He regretted the use of military force in the Middle East, he stated, but he also regretted that there had not been time, before a vote was taken, for consideration of 'the best way to bring about that kind of cease-fire which will have enduring and beneficial results'. He would have liked to see in the resolution a provision authorizing the Secretary General to make arrangements for a United Nations force 'large enough to keep these borders at peace while a political settlement is being worked out'. The British delegate himself, Pearson recalled, had mentioned the possibility of such a step a few hours earlier, and he would be glad to recommend Canadian participation in 'a truly international police force'. Having achieved his purpose of placing the United States squarely on the side of anti-colonialism, Dulles rose at 4 a.m. and endorsed the Canadian proposal as a logical extension of his own. His country would be 'very happy indeed', he stated, 'if the Canadian delegation would formulate and introduce . . . a concrete suggestion along the lines Mr. Pearson has outlined'.

The next step facing the Canadian statesman was to persuade the United Nations Secretary General that the plan would work. Dag Hammarskjöld had been shocked and dismayed at the violation of the United Nations Charter by two permanent members of the Security Council. Filled with gloom and foreboding, he was convinced that the Canadian proposal had little chance of success. Taking advantage of their personal friendship, Pearson insisted that the obstacles could be overcome; as dawn was about to break, he received support for his argument in the form of a telephone call from Norman Robertson in London, informing him that the British government was becoming worried about the proportions of the crisis, and thought that the Canadian proposal held the most promise of a way out of the predicament. Hammarskjöld agreed to give it a try; despite his late start, the Canadian minister had done a good night's work.

Louis St. Laurent learned of the latest development first thing next morning, and arranged for Pearson to report to cabinet at 4 p.m. Although he was sure of the Prime Minister's support, the Minister for External Affairs was not at all certain that all his colleagues would go along with his proposed action. For that reason, when he appeared back in the Council Chamber after being flown up from New York in an R.C.A.F. plane, he restricted himself to a general statement, rather than entering into details at this time and asking for specific instructions. The Canadian delegation was trying to keep Britain and France from being branded as aggressors, he explained, and was working on a resolution that would not only give them an opportunity to withdraw from their impossible situation, but would also point the way to a general peace settlement in the Middle East. When Pearson had finished, there was some discussion, but St. Laurent did not allow it to continue for long. As the meeting broke up, Pearson and St. Laurent chatted for a moment in the corner of the Council Chamber; the Minister for External Affairs said that he intended to go back to New York and introduce a resolution at the earliest possible moment concerning the establishment of an international peace force. 'Do as you think best,' he was told. 'I will support you here.'

On Saturday morning, November 3, an increasingly worried Sir Anthony Eden telephoned St. Laurent from London to ask if Canada intended to propose the creation of a United Nations force, and, if so, to suggest that British and French troops 'continue our operations under the United Nations flag'. The Canadian Prime Minister was sceptical of the chances that such a step would be accepted in New York, but he was pleased to learn of the British change of attitude, and agreed to discuss it with Pearson in New York. Eden urged that if the British and French troops could not be accepted as part of a United Nations unit they should at least be allowed to hand over their positions to a United Nations authority as soon as their initial objectives had been accomplished. The two men discussed the crisis for half an hour across the Atlantic Ocean, and while the conversation did not completely dispel the effects of their recent disagreement, they did decide to work together in solving the crisis. Most important of all, with communications between the British and American governments all but non-existent, they succeeded in re-establishing a precious link between the two sides of the Atlantic.

When St. Laurent reported the telephone conversation to Pearson, including the suggestion that the British and French forces be placed under the United Nations flag, the Minister for External Affairs was emphatic that there was no possibility of getting approval for their participation in a United Nations police action. Told that Sir Anthony could see no other way out of the situation, he agreed to try to meet the British at least part way. At a cabinet meeting that same morning, St. Laurent outlined a plan for at least some of the British and French troops to be integrated into a United Nations force, since they were the most readily available; such a step would assure the co-operation of the two governments in bringing about a cease-fire. One way or another, he argued, an early cessation of the military adventure was imperative. By asserting his leadership, he obtained the agreement of his colleagues to the formation of an international police force in two stages, first by adding British and French units to the existing United Nations Truce Supervisory Organization under the command of General Burns, and, subsequently, by creating a more permanent force composed of troops from other nations, including Canada, which could keep the peace between Israel and her neighbours while a political settlement was being negotiated.

In New York, Pearson maintained an equally busy pace. In a telephone call to Norman Robertson that same morning, he asked the High Commissioner to inform the British government that Canada was going to present a resolution calling for the creation of a United Nations force, but to warn that there was no hope of approval by the General Assembly if the British and French invasion units landed before the vote was taken. 'It's vitally important that they slow down now to give us a chance,' he stressed. Despite French objections, Robertson was successful in obtaining the undertaking that was asked for, provided that the vote was taken by the following evening, London time. In the meantime, Pearson was carrying on negotiations with Henry Cabot Lodge on the text of the resolution he proposed to make. The Americans accepted the general principle implied, but refused categorically to agree to any provision to use British and French troops as part of a United Nations force. A vague but very meaningful reference in the draft resolution to using 'military forces immediately available' was therefore dropped.

The task of devising a course of action acceptable to all the non-Communist nations was a gigantic one, and it was nearly midnight on Saturday, November 3, before Pearson had a draft resolution ready to show to the Secretary General. While he had failed to persuade India to act as co-sponsor, Norway and Colombia had agreed to join with Canada in placing it before the General Assembly, and even to supply troops as part of the police force. Hammarskjöld was still pessimistic.

'It won't work,' he stated flatly. 'We'll never get a force going in time to stop the British and French.' The Canadian minister had made his preparations well, and was able to meet the Secretary General's objections. The British had sent further word through Robertson that no landings would take place until Monday evening, provided the United Nations acted quickly to set up an international force. Furthermore, Nasser had indicated through the Indian delegation that he would accept American, Canadian, and Scandinavian troops on Egyptian soil as part of a truce unit. There was also the possibility of using the United States Sixth Fleet if that was really necessary. Hammarskjöld brightened; he could see the way ahead. Pearson made a quick telephone call to St. Laurent to tell him that all was ready, and obtained his final approval; then he entered the Assembly hall.

The resolution proposed by Pearson called on the Secretary General to submit a plan within forty-eight hours 'for the setting up, with the consent of the nations concerned, of an emergency United Nations force to secure and supervise the cessation of hostilities'. To ensure the support of the Asian and African delegations, he moved it concurrently with a nineteen-member Afro-Asian resolution, calling for a cease-fire within twelve hours; he had agreed to vote for it in return for their endorsement of his plan. Lodge spoke in favour of the Canadian proposal, describing it as containing 'a real hope of meeting the very grave emergency that confronts the world'. The voting took place at 2 a.m. on Sunday, November 4; Pearson's resolution was carried by fifty-seven votes to none, with nineteen abstentions, the latter including Britain, France, the Soviet bloc, Egypt, Israel, Australia, and New Zealand. Immediately afterwards, the Afro-Asian resolution was adopted by fifty-nine votes to five, with twelve abstentions; keeping his part of the bargain, Pearson voted 'yes'.

While Canada's Minister for External Affairs was being showered with congratulations and expressions of appreciation from representatives of other governments, including the United Kingdom, for what was described as one of the most skilfully organized diplomatic manoeuvres in United Nations history, messages of outrage poured into the Prime Minister's Office in Ottawa at the 'betrayal' of the mother country. Former Prime Minister Arthur Meighen summed up the views of many English-speaking Canadians in a statement to the press, declaring that Eden deserved the support of the Commonwealth 'in his endeavour to maintain Britain's honour and her place in world affairs', and that it was 'highly unfortunate that here in Canada . . . we have been providing ammunition for . . . critics of the Eden government and its policies'. History was to prove the St. Laurent government right on the international plane, but wrong on the level of domestic politics; the 'betrayal' of Britain was to cost the Liberal Party many votes, and almost certainly a majority of seats in Parliament, in the next election.

In a carefully prepared radio broadcast delivered on Sunday evening, November 4, the Prime Minister tried to soothe the ruffled feelings of his fellow citizens and to explain Pearson's conduct. He and his colleagues believed that Israel's relations with her neighbours, and the future of the Suez Canal, had to be solved 'by peaceful negotiations under the aegis of the United Nations', St. Laurent declared, and they regretted that the Israelis, the British, and the French had resorted to force in seeking to impose a solution. In order to open the way for a settlement through the United Nations, Pearson had put forward a plan for the creation of a special international force, and the government was ready to recommend Canadian participation in it, if it was thought that Canada could play a useful role. The crisis of recent days had strained the Western alliance and the bonds of the Commonwealth more than any other event since World War II, but if the opportunity could be used 'to dissipate the black cloud which has hung over the Middle East these many years, the present danger and strain may prove to have been a price worth paying'. He referred as well to the 'grave and tragic events' in Hungary, where the Soviet Union, encouraged by the British and French aggression in Egypt, had ordered tanks into action against the insurrectionists. For the first time since 1945, there had been a 'real hope' in recent months that some countries in that area might secure some independence from Moscow; a form of national Communism had appeared in Poland, and the new Soviet leaders had declared their readiness to re-negotiate their relations with the nations of eastern Europe on the basis of equality and non-interference in their neighbours' affairs. However, following the uprising on October 20, the 'gallant and unarmed people of Hungary' had been crushed by Soviet armed might, and the Soviet Union had imposed its veto on a United States resolution at the United Nations condemning its interference in the internal affairs of Hungary. The one encouraging aspect of the events of the recent past had been the 'almost unanimous action of the nations of the world in endeavouring to implement their obligations' under the United Nations Charter. Finally, in a hardly veiled reply to reports of dissension within the cabinet over the Suez crisis, St. Laurent assured his listeners that all the ministers had been 'in full agreement at all times as to what should be done and what could be said and when it should be done and when it could be said'. If parliamentary approval was required of the government's action, he was sure that it would be given 'in no uncertain terms'.

While Louis St. Laurent strove to assure Pearson of full support at home and maximum freedom of action in New York, events in other parts of the world continued to move forward at a rapid pace. Fearing that Eden was wavering before the growing criticism of his government at home and abroad, French Foreign Minister Pineau made two quick trips to London during the week-end to insist that no change be made in the military plan. Eden, increasingly worried, was indeed considering other alternatives, and had hoped that Pearson's resolution might open the way for a change of strategy. On Sunday, however, a telegram from Hammarskjöld made it clear that British and French troops could not be accepted as part of the United Nations force; Eden had to choose between cancelling the whole military operation and proceeding as scheduled; he stiffened and plunged ahead. British and French paratroops were dropped into Port Said early on Monday morning, November 5.

St. Laurent called in the Acting United Kingdom High Commissioner in Ottawa that same day and asked him to inform Sir Anthony Eden that, in the Canadian view, further delay in complying with the wishes of the United Nations would be dangerous. About noon he received a telegram from the British Prime Minister, telling him that the agonizing decision to go ahead with the military operation had been taken, and expressing the hope that St. Laurent would understand the importance of protecting the Suez Canal. He warmly welcomed the Canadian initiative in New York to establish a United Nations force, and expressed his personal indebtedness to Pearson 'for the skill and energy with which he has sponsored this idea'. At the same time, he pointed out that it would take several days to set up the force, and argued that in the meantime it was imperative to create the conditions under which such an international force could take over the responsibility of halting the fighting between the Israelis and the Egyptians. Once again, he committed the diplomatic blunder of announcing a decision directly opposed to Canada's view, and then concluding the message by expressing confidence that he could rely on her support.

A meeting of the Canadian cabinet had been called for that Monday afternoon to consider the advisability of calling a special session of Parliament to authorize Canadian participation in a United Nations police force. St. Laurent consulted Pearson by telephone on the latest message from London, then submitted it to his colleagues, together with a proposed reply. The tone of the latter was stiffer than that of the one sent a few days earlier, but still did not exceed the bounds of courtesy. 'I think we have a sympathetic understanding of your and France's position,' it ran, 'but we still regret you found it necessary to follow the course you are taking.' Unfortunately, it continued, the events in the Middle East had cloaked with a smoke-screen the renewed brutal international crimes of the Soviet Union in Hungary, and had allowed the Russians to claim that they, too, were acting merely to restore order in the face of the inability of local authorities to do so. Although such attempts to draw a parallel between the two crises were not valid, the text went on, the apparent disregard of the United Kingdom and France for the United Nations Charter and their refusal to adhere to decisions of United Nations bodies were a handicap in attempts to use world opinion as a check on the outrageous conduct of the men in the Kremlin. Canada was also much concerned about the reactions of the Asian members of the Commonwealth, and her efforts had been directed in recent days to finding some workable solution of the situation in the Middle East that would minimize the damage to the Commonwealth and the Western alliance. 'We will continue to do our best to be of whatever assistance we can in a positive way,' St. Laurent concluded, 'but I would not wish to leave with you the impression that as seen from here the situation appears other than tragic.' The other ministers approved the message, and also the Prime Minister's recommendation to summon Parliament to meet on November 20.

Meanwhile, the crisis was approaching its peak. Late on Monday evening, Eden and Mollet received messages from Premier Bulganin, warning that London and Paris lay under the threat of Soviet missiles, and declaring that Soviet Russia was 'fully determined to crush the aggressors . . . through use of force'. At the same time, the Soviet Union asked the United States to join with it in using sea and air power to expel the aggressors from the Middle East. In Port Said, the paratroopers captured their initial objectives quickly, and began pushing inland. The local Egyptian commander agreed to surrender, but before negotiations were completed, loudspeakers in Cairo proclaimed that London and Paris had been bombed, that Russian help was on the way, and that World War III had begun. Informed that reinforcements would arrive in a matter of hours, the Egyptian troops resumed the fight. The British and French land forces reached Port Said at dawn on Tuesday, November 6, and began moving ashore.

In London, the pressure on Eden was becoming unbearable. In addition to the threats from Moscow, and the condemnation from Commonwealth and other capitals, a large sector of the British public was expressing vehement opposition to the military operation. More serious still, the Bank of England announced a serious run on the pound, and an urgent call to Washington by the Chancellor of the Exchequer, Harold Macmillan, had brought the answer that a loan was conditional on a cease-fire being announced by midnight on November 6. A message from New York gave the British Prime Minister the opening he needed so desperately; Hammarskjöld and Pearson, he was informed, had completed their report on the formation and composition of the international police force; its approval by the General Assembly was merely a matter of form. Sir Anthony gave in. 'I am cornered,' he telephoned to Mollet in Paris. 'I can't hang on. I'm being deserted by everybody.' The French Premier pleaded, tears in his eyes, for a few more hours to enable the troops to reach the Suez Canal, but to no avail. Norman Robertson was summoned to the British House of Commons and informed that the cease-fire would take effect one minute before midnight as Washington had demanded.

In announcing the decision to Robertson, Sir Anthony Eden expressed his gratitude to St. Laurent 'for Canada's steadying influence in the councils of the United Nations', and requested him to take the initiative in having the canal cleared as soon as possible. St. Laurent was elated when he received the good news, and telephoned Washington to assure President Eisenhower that the British were going to co-operate with their friends once again. It was election day in the United States, but Eisenhower was far more preoccupied with the international situation than with domestic politics; he had been as relieved as the Canadian Prime Minister to learn of the British decision, and had already spoken with Eden for the first time since the beginning of the crisis. 'Things are encouraging,' the President told St. Laurent in a new mood of optimism. 'Never have I seen action on the part of a government that excited me more than the rapid way you and your government moved into the breach with your proposal for a United Nations force to go to Suez. You did a magnificent job, and we admire it.' The sun was breaking through the war clouds at last.

Throughout the critical period, the relations between St. Laurent and Pearson were a near-perfect example of team-work; they consulted by telephone several times a day, discussing each new development, and co-ordinating every move. No foreign minister ever had a more helpful and understanding prime minister; no government leader ever had a more loyal or zealous colleague. While St. Laurent continued to be impatient in his relations with the press, no shadow of disagreement marred his dealings with Pearson or hampered their joint actions. At Pearson's suggestion, he sent a very cordial message to Nehru, that was obviously designed to keep the Indian leader from breaking openly with the Commonwealth. 'In these difficult days . . . India has never been far from my mind,' he wired. 'I hope that our friendship has given me some understanding of, and sympathy for, India's position in the present Middle East crisis, and I know that you appreciate our situation here.' The two countries shared the same objectives of restoring peace in that troubled area, and of achieving, under the auspices of the United Nations, a permanent settlement of the dispute. 'It is my earnest hope,' he declared, 'that none of us will be diverted from our common purpose and our long-term interests by the unhappy events which have led to the present crisis in the affairs of the world.'

In one of his frequent encounters with the press corps, St. Laurent described as 'ridiculous and completely without foundation' a speculative article that he had thought in recent days of withdrawing Canada from the Commonwealth. 'Such an idea,' he scoffed, 'or anything resembling it, has never crossed my mind.' He reacted with equal indignation to a story emanating from London that he had 'sharply rebuked' Sir Anthony Eden in one of his communications to London; he had never had anything but 'frank and friendly communications' with the British Prime Minister over the crisis.

Although he had less opportunity to influence the course of events there, St. Laurent was also very concerned about the fighting in Hungary. In fact, his annoyance with the British and French had been heightened by his sense of frustration at the inability of the Western nations to come to the assistance of the insurrectionists. When the tension in the Middle East had subsided, he sent a message to Premier Bulganin, expressing Canada's 'horror' at the suffering of the Hungarian people 'as a result of their efforts to obtain the freedom to choose their own type of government'. 'In the name of humanity' he pleaded with the Soviet leader to use his influence to alleviate the suffering, and allow 'competent international agencies and organizations' to supply food and care to the needy. Predictably, the plea was rejected in less conciliatory terms than those that the Canadian Prime Minister had employed.

Canadians were seriously divided over the Suez crisis. A Gallup poll indicated that 43 per cent of the population approved of the British and French action, 40 per cent opposed it, and only 17 per cent had no definite opinion. A majority of citizens in Ontario and the Maritimes felt that the government had let the mother country down, and damaged the Commonwealth, by taking an independent stand. Their dissatisfaction increased when it was learned that a famous Canadian regiment, the Queen's Own Rifles, had been moved all the way from Calgary to Halifax, and was about to board the aircraft carrier *Magnificent*, en route for the Middle East, when word was received that Egypt was objecting to Canadian infantry as part of the United Nations Emergency Force. President Nasser feared that in their British-type uniforms, and proclaiming their allegiance to the Queen of England on their shoulder badges, they would be indistinguishable from the British invaders, and would be subjected to harassment by the Egyptian people. General E. L. M. Burns, who had been chosen to command the United Nations force, solved the difficulty in a matter of hours by suggesting that Canada's contribution be made in the form of technical and other supporting units, which were needed with equal urgency, and would not have the same direct contact with the population. The change in plans meant that the Queen's Own Rifles had to return almost across the continent to their barracks in Calgary. Their national pride wounded, many Canadians agreed with the *Globe and Mail*'s description of the incident as 'The U.N. Police Farce' and with the *Calgary Herald* editorial that summed up Pearson's role at the United Nations as providing 'a face-saver for the Soviet puppet-dictator in Egypt . . . [and] a rank disservice in the cause of peace'.

When Parliament met in special session on November 26, it was asked to provide funds for the United Nations Emergency Force, and to enable the immigration to Canada of some of the refugees who were streaming out of Hungary to Austria following the repression of the uprising in their country. Speaking as Acting Leader of the Opposition, Earl Rowe made a strong defence of the British and French action in the Middle East, and suggested that the government had been more ready to place its trust in President Nasser than in Sir Anthony Eden. 'The United States committed a series of blunders . . . ,' he declared, 'which finally left the United Kingdom and French governments with no alternative but to bring force to bear in the Middle East, if their interest in that vital area was not to be given up in the face of rising Soviet power there.' The Canadian government, in his view, appeared to have been 'influenced almost exclusively by the Administration in Washington'. He rejected as mere political propaganda the praise that Pearson had received for his part in solving the crisis.

> Let not the Government believe it can any longer deceive the Canadian people by creating a halo around the Secretary of State for External Affairs. Unfortunately, Mr. Speaker, no one knows better than he does that the actions of our Government and the claims to fame of our Foreign Minister have yet to create any practical results in the Middle East crisis.

Turning to the Prime Minister, the veteran Tory charged that his reported 'angry note' to Eden had 'probably done a great deal of harm to the unity and harmony and trust that are essential to the maintenance of a vital alliance with a tried and trusted friend'. Even on its Hungarian policy, the government was condemned; the proposal to spend a million dollars to bring refugees to Canada, Rowe scoffed, was a sort of 'conscience money' it was offering because it had failed to take 'any other real action of positive value'. Breaking for the first time since World War II with the practice of presenting a common front on foreign policy, he moved an amendment to the Speech from the Throne, regretting that the government had

> followed a course of gratuitous condemnation of the action of the United Kingdom and France which was designed to prevent a major war in the Suez area . . . weakly followed the unrealistic policies of the United States . . . placed Canada in the humiliating position of accepting dictation from President Nasser . . . [and] failed to take swift and adequate action to extend refuge to the patriots of Hungary and other lands under the cruel Russian yoke.

Although he had firmly resolved to maintain his equanimity during the emergency session, St. Laurent was nettled by the charges levelled against the government, and particularly by the

Louis St. Laurent and President D. D. Eisenhower on a golf cart;
near Atlanta, Georgia, December 1956.

Louis St. Laurent and Sir Anthony Eden; Uplands Airport, Ottawa, February 1956.

Louis St. Laurent and cabinet colleagues (except L. Chevrier) shortly before their resignation, June 21, 1957. Left to right: G. Prudham, W. Harris, J. J. McCann, L. S. St. Laurent, C. D. Howe, J. G. Gardiner, P. Martin; *second row*: R. Campney, L. B. Pearson, H. Lapointe, R. Pinard, S. Garson, M. Gregg, R. Macdonald; *back row*: P. Hellyer, J. W. Pickersgill, R. Winters, J. Sinclair, J. Lesage, G. Marler.

Louis St. Laurent and leadership candidates L. B. Pearson (left) and Paul Martin (right), at the Liberal leadership convention; Ottawa Coliseum, January 1958.

attempt to belittle Pearson's accomplishment. Just before Parliament met he had invited Rowe to his office and briefed him as fully as possible on the whole situation; he had gained the impression that the acting Progressive Conservative leader understood the government's position, and that the official opposition would support its proposals. Obviously, between the time of the interview and the meeting of Parliament, someone had succeeded in altering the policy of the Progressive Conservative Party. The debate was soon to reveal the probable authors of the change. When he rose to reply to Rowe, the Prime Minister was so eager to rebut the criticism that he forgot to congratulate the mover and seconder of the Speech from the Throne. The attack on Pearson was 'in strange contrast' with the compliments paid to him in other countries, he commented. He rejected hotly the charge that Canada had been 'humiliated' by Nasser, or that the government had indulged in 'gratuitous condemnation' of Britain and France. Some blame had to be placed on those two countries and on the Israelis, he insisted, for taking the law into their own hands. 'These gentlemen who utter these high-flown phrases seem to forget that the nations of the world signed the Charter of the United Nations and thereby undertook to use peaceful means to settle possible disputes and not to resort to the use of force.' He struggled to keep from saying more, but the need to speak his mind fully was too great; drawing a deep breath, he plunged on.

> I have been scandalized more than once by the attitude of the larger powers, the big powers as we call them, who have all too frequently treated the Charter of the United Nations as an instrument with which to regiment smaller nations and as an instrument which did not have to be considered when their own vital interests were at stake. I have been told, with respect to the veto, that if the Russians had not insisted upon it the United States and the United Kingdom would have insisted upon it, because they could not allow the smaller nations to deal decisively with questions which concerned their vital interests.

'Why should they?' interjected someone from across the floor. With the sense of relief of a man unburdening himself of a grievance of long standing, the Prime Minister threw back his shoulders defiantly, reddened, and retorted: 'Because the members of smaller nations are human beings just as are other people; because the era when the supermen of Europe could govern the whole world is coming pretty close to an end.'

'Throwing Canada to the slaughter-house,' jeered one Conservative in reply.

St. Laurent's use of the word 'supermen' was unpremeditated, and the burst of anger lasted only a few seconds, but the damage was done; he had lent further weight to the charge of taking sides against the mother country. He proceeded with his speech, denying again that he had sent a 'blistering reply' or given 'gratuitous advice' to Eden, but reading into the record a telegram from the British Prime Minister, who insisted that, in accordance with the usual practice, the messages exchanged by the two government leaders should not be published. In an attempt to counter the criticism of callousness and inaction in the face of the Hungarian uprising, he also read his message to Premier Bulganin, and a reply just received, in which the Soviet leader complained of his 'one-sided, tendentious and unobjective information' about developments in Hungary and the Soviet role there. 'Reactionary forces', with active outside support, had tried to establish a Fascist régime, the Soviet leader stated, and 'patriotic forces' in Hungary had asked for Soviet assistance to defend the 'people's democratic régime'.

By the time St. Laurent had reached the conclusion of his remarks, he had recovered his good humour and gracious manner, but the Progressive Conservatives refused to be appeased by his soothing words. When C.C.F. leader Coldwell expressed disapproval of British policy, he was asked if he could not say one decent word about the country in which he was born. His remark that every Canadian could be 'proud and happy' over Pearson's achievements was answered with a blunt interjection: 'They are not.' There was much more to come. If Earl Rowe was able to arouse St. Laurent's temper, Howard Green could whip him into a state of near-fury. Taking the floor that same evening, the Vancouver member pointed a long bony forefinger at the cabinet benches, and declared that the government did not have the 'backbone' to stand with the United Kingdom because 'they were so busy currying favour with the United States'. The Prime Minister had 'lumped the United Kingdom and France and Russia in his condemnation', Green charged.

> I suppose he considers that all the supermen are in the Canadian government. If they are not all in the Canadian government then I presume the opinion of this same Prime Minister is that they are in the United States government. . . . I suppose the Prime Minister of Canada sneers at Sir Winston Churchill as a superman and includes him in his nasty, biting remarks. . . . The Uncle Louis kissing babies went out the window this afternoon; so smug; so full of self-righteousness; so hypocritical.

In the view of the Tory member, Israel had been perfectly justified in attacking Egypt since she was about to be attacked herself, Britain 'had a perfect right to occupy the canal zone', and Britain and France had succeeded, at 'tremendous risk' in preventing not only 'a Russian-dominated Middle East', but also 'a major war'. The two countries had 'never been aggressors and are not aggressors on this occasion', he declared vehemently, yet the Prime Minister had the 'effrontery' to compare their actions with the actions of the Russians in Hungary. The Canadian government had become merely the 'United States chore boy' and the Prime Minister had proved himself a better friend of President Nasser, 'this tinpot dictator', than of the United Kingdom and France. 'It is time,' Green declared in a climax of indignation, 'that Canada had a government which will not knife Canada's best friends in the back.' Half unbelieving, half outraged, St. Laurent tried to protest against the 'entire misconstruction' and 'distortions', but Green silenced him with the added charge that 'the Prime Minister is again attempting to prevent free discussion in this House'.

On the following day, Pearson tried to put the government's record before Parliament in more balanced perspective. 'Our policy with regard to this matter . . . was to try to stop the fighting through the United Nations,' he declared. 'How could we follow any other course without betraying our obligations under the Charter?' He rejected Green's charge that Canada had been a mere 'chore boy' of the United States, and recounted his attempts in New York to avoid the formal condemnation of Britain and France as aggressors, to restore communications between the Western allies, and to hold the Commonwealth together. 'Our purpose was to be as helpful to the United Kingdom and France as we possibly could be', he declared, and 'that attitude has been appreciated in London even if it has not been appreciated by my honourable friends opposite.' The presentation of the Minister for External Affairs did succeed in reducing the tension and acrimony of the debate, and the session was concluded in a single week. Rowe's motion was defeated by the combined strength of the Liberal, C.C.F., and Social Credit groups. Just before the adjournment, St. Laurent tried once again to counteract the effects of the more violent outbursts, including his own, by declaring in his most reasonable manner that the government's policy had been designed to preserve the Commonwealth and the Western alliance. 'We felt that to do that we had to speak our considered views frankly to all our friends, in no "blistering" terms . . . but in frank terms', he explained; Canada was not required to feel, in every instance, that 'everything done by every one of our allies was the wisest course and decision that could be taken'. The debate was over in Parliament, but it was to continue throughout the country, and to figure in the next general election.

International affairs accounted for only one part of St. Laurent's schedule during those busy weeks of late 1956. Some provincial premiers were still unhappy over the new tax-rental arrangements, Premier Flemming of New Brunswick complaining that Ottawa was being unduly tight-fisted, and Premier Frost expressing disappointment that a larger share of the main tax fields had not been left to the richer provinces. The new plan to distribute federal assistance to Canadian universities through the National Council of Canadian Universities was also encountering resistance. Although the arrangement had been worked out in close co-operation with Dr. Edward Hall, president of that organization, and had the personal support of every university rector in Quebec, Maurice Duplessis was reported to be determined to prevent the distribution of federal funds to universities in that province. As soon as St. Laurent was convinced that the university authorities themselves all approved of the plan, and were ready to assume responsibility, through their organization, for the distribution of federal funds, he decided to go ahead. He made the proposal formally at the National Conference on Higher Education in Ottawa on November 12. In a carefully prepared statement, he pointed out that the federal government had the 'absolute right to levy indirect taxes for any purpose, and the power to impose direct taxes provided that they are intended for the Consolidated Revenue Fund of Canada'. With Parliament's approval, it could use such money to 'offer gifts or grants to individuals, institutions, provincial governments or even to federal governments'; that was a royal prerogative which was not in any way restricted by the constitution. In discussing that point in relation to unemployment insurance, he recalled, the current Chief Justice of the Supreme Court of Canada, Patrick Kerwin, had declared that Ottawa could even impose 'restrictions and conditions' on such gifts, leaving the proposed recipient free 'to decline the gift or to accept it subject to such conditions'. The Privy Council had supported that interpretation of the Canadian constitution. St. Laurent argued that just as Parliament had been able to make provision for family allowances, equalization payments to provinces, and technical and vocational training, just as Quebec made grants to educational institutions in other provinces, so by the same token it was possible for the federal government to offer grants to universities, bursaries to students, or other forms of financial assistance in all fields of culture. 'In other words,' he asserted, 'these problems are a matter of national cultural policy in respect of which the federal government also has responsibilities.'

The government of Canada had been involved in cultural activities ever since Confederation, and for over forty years, grants to universities and scholarships had been distributed through the National Research Council, as well as a number of government departments. It was the first time, however, that a spokesman for the national administration had proclaimed a 'national cultural policy', and outlined the legal basis for such an innovation. The step would have been taken several years earlier except for the opposition of Maurice Duplessis and fears in Ottawa about the consequences for national unity of a conflict with him on that subject. After eight years as Prime Minister, it was clear that St. Laurent would never obtain the Union Nationale leader's consent to such an initiative, and that he must either resign himself to doing nothing, or go ahead regardless of the reaction in Quebec. Convinced that the national interest required him to act, St. Laurent had taken the decision to proceed. 'That man and that situation cannot last forever in Quebec,' he commented to one university administrator, and if necessary, the funds earmarked for Quebec universities could be held in trust in Ottawa until time or an awakening public opinion brought about a change of government in Quebec. Coupled as it was with the announcement that the long-awaited Canada Council would be set up, and endowed with a hundred-million-dollar fund, the plan announced by the Prime Minister was received by the university administrators gathered in the Chateau Laurier ballroom with happy enthusiasm. Duplessis countered at once by forbidding Quebec universities to accept the money from the federal treasury. The pains taken to overcome his opposition by eliminating any possibility of federal interference in the distribution or granting of the funds were in vain.

Three days after his important statement of cultural policy, St. Laurent observed his eighth anniversary as Prime Minister at a banquet in his honour in Toronto. In excellent form, and with a twinkle in his eye, he expressed the hope that his hosts had not chosen to mark that anniversary with such éclat because he might not reach a more 'outstanding' one. The crowd roared with delight at the unlikelihood of such a prospect. In 1946, he recalled, he had been about to return to Quebec, when Mackenzie King had told him, in the words of a Negro sergeant, that 'de war may be ovah, but de duration am just beginning'. 'Well, ten years later, the duration still doesn't seem to be over as far as my own career is concerned,' he commented, 'and, unless the Canadian people decide to the contrary, it looks at the present time as though it will last for a while yet.' The possibility of the electorate sending him back to Quebec against his will seemed remote, even to St. Laurent himself.

# 16

---

## The Last Campaign

Although he became too busy during the Suez crisis for his daily swim, Louis St. Laurent continued to pace himself carefully, sleeping regular hours, following a simple diet to keep his stomach in order, and reducing his smoking to a few cigarettes a day. In order to avoid another bout of fatigue during the winter, or, worse still, during the election campaign that was to follow, he was persuaded to take a holiday in Florida during the first part of December. Increasingly reluctant to remain away from his office for more than a few days, he accepted only on the grounds that the time spent would be a good investment for the future.

Even outside the country, he found ways of combining pleasure and public business. Jawaharlal Nehru had agreed to visit Washington shortly before Christmas, after refusing several invitations because of his annoyance over American military aid to Pakistan and other aspects of Dulles's Asian policy. When he received the news, St. Laurent recalled his own meetings with the Indian leader and with President Eisenhower, and speculated hopefully on the immense benefits in the field of East-West relations if the two men succeeded in establishing a basis of understanding. During his years in public life he had come to feel strongly that personal discussions between men in positions of responsibility were the most effective means of resolving differences, and that even ideological considerations were not insurmountable obstacles to men of good will. In view of his excellent personal relations with both Nehru and Eisenhower, he wondered what he could do to make the occasion a success. The solution was both simple and ingenious; Eisenhower was spending a few days at a golf course near Atlanta, Georgia; it was arranged that St. Laurent should call there on his return journey to Canada so that he and the President could play a round together, and have a chat about matters of common interest.

The game was pleasant as well as fruitful. St. Laurent was paired with the local golf pro, while Eisenhower played with Madeleine O'Donnell, who had been holidaying with her father in Florida. If the Canadian Prime Minister was no match for the President as a sportsman, he could hold his own as they rode from tee to tee on a two-seater battery-powered golf cart. He commented later with amusement:

> I found . . . that a game of golf with one of those electric go-carts was about the best way to have an international conference, because you are getting off the go-cart quite frequently for only a couple of minutes but for time enough to reflect on what has been said up to that moment and . . . what is going to be said when you get back on. . . .

The conversation ranged widely over current Canadian-American problems, and international relations in general. As the game proceeded, St. Laurent got around to the principal purpose of his visit. Three years earlier in New Delhi, he recalled, he had tried to reassure Indians about American policies in Asia, and had urged Nehru to make a real effort to get to know and understand the President; now, he was making the same appeal to Eisenhower. The two men were probably the most influential statesmen in the free world at the moment, he declared. The Indian leader was a statesman of whom all Asians were proud, and he had an influence on their thinking, even if they could not all agree fully with him; he was just as anti-Communist as the President himself, although in India there were not the fears of Communism that Senator McCarthy and others were expressing in the United States. It should not be forgotten, St. Laurent argued, that the North American continent was not the only background against which one should appraise the attitude of other peoples. Eisenhower had developed a strong liking for his guest, and respected him for both his reasonable approach to public issues and his mastery of the topics they discussed. He listened carefully to St. Laurent's views, and indicated his agreement with them; St. Laurent felt that the day was well spent. No communiqué summed up the results of the meeting, and not even the final golf score was announced. The perfect host, President Eisenhower declared that St. Laurent and the golf pro had won, but the Canadian Prime Minister made no such claim. 'I was no worse than usual,' he told a reporter on arriving back in Ottawa that same evening. '[But] when I manage to break a hundred, I'll announce it myself.'

Shortly after St. Laurent's return to the capital, a Progressive Conservative convention picked John Diefenbaker over Donald Fleming and Davie Fulton as the new Tory leader. In a sense, the decision marked the victory of a man over his own party. The Saskatchewan lawyer had failed in two previous bids for the leadership, and had almost reconciled himself to never achieving his childhood ambition of becoming Prime Minister, when Drew fell ill. It remained to be seen whether his evangelical style of oratory, combined with the tactics of a criminal lawyer, would suffice to counterbalance the prestige and popularity of Louis St. Laurent. Since he was far from popular in Conservative circles in Ontario, practically unknown in the Atlantic provinces, and had not been able to win more than his own seat for his party in Saskatchewan, there seemed little cause for concern in Liberal circles. Recalling Diefenbaker's advocacy of conscription, his fervent declarations of loyalty to the United Kingdom, and charges that he had once joined in preventing Roman Catholic nuns from teaching in public schools in Saskatchewan, Quebec Liberals were almost pleased by the choice, and looked forward to dealing with him on the hustings. St. Laurent himself was neither concerned nor relieved. As opposition critic of the Department of Justice, and then of the Department of External Affairs, Diefenbaker had given him some difficult times, but there was a degree of respect and even admiration between the two men, based in part on their respective accomplishments in the legal profession. As soon as the decision of the convention was announced, St. Laurent wired his congratulations to the new party leader. Privately, he expressed doubts whether the proven ability of the new Leader of the Opposition as a criminal lawyer qualified him to direct the affairs of the nation. 'It is not enough to win a decision of not guilty in running the country,' he remarked, as he prepared for the coming contest.

As the year 1956 drew to an end, preparations went ahead for the last session of the twenty-second Parliament, called for January 8, and for the election that was to follow immediately. Once again, the Liberals were going to run on their record; they would 'tell the people of Canada . . . what has been accomplished', the Prime Minister declared, 'so the electors may judge for themselves if their decisions in 1945, 1949, and 1953 were in the best interest', and if a new mandate was warranted. The emphasis was to be put on economic growth, and the report of the Royal Commission on Canada's Economic Prospects, completed in mid-December, was to outline the goals for the future. Walter Gordon and his fellow commissioners predicted that by 1980 Canada's population would reach twenty-six and a half million, the gross national product would be seventy billion dollars, and personal incomes almost three thousand dollars per person. Such were the benefits, it was to be implied, of a further period of Liberal government. The Liberal objective was to convince the electorate that the government was not only the most efficient team of administrators in the country's history, but vigorous enough to continue in office for a further period.

Just before Christmas, Prime Minister Nehru and his daughter, Indira Gandhi, arrived in Ottawa for a two-day visit. The Indian leader was much more satisfied with his talks in Washington than on his first trip there in 1949, and was pleased with the consideration shown him by President Eisenhower. When he remarked that there were still important differences of viewpoint between India and the United States, St. Laurent reminded him with a smile of his own comment that the terrestrial globe looked very different to someone sitting on the north pole from the way it looked to someone on the equator. His point was well illustrated by the weather in the Canadian capital; still wearing a white cotton cap and jodhpurs, to which he had added warmer western clothes, Nehru looked at least as much out of his element in the snow and biting wind as St. Laurent had done under the Indian sun. The Canadian Prime Minister did not miss the opportunity to repeat to his friend the North American view of the international situation, just as he had received instruction in the Asian point of view in New Delhi three years earlier. Canadians did not feel that Soviet agression was likely, he stated, but if it did occur, the target would more likely be the United States than India, and any attack on the Americans would be made across Canada; thus the national interest of Canada was to block that possible path, or, at least, to make certain that anyone who tried to use it would suffer as much damage as he might be able to inflict. True to the pacifist teachings of Mahatma Gandhi, Nehru replied that military alliances merely added to international tension by encouraging warlike attitudes. As long as a potential aggressor had the capacity for nuclear attack, St. Laurent countered, North America's only protection was to be able to retaliate in kind, and with equal effectiveness; the tension of which the Indian leader complained was necessary as a deterrent against the use of the new and terrible instruments of destruction. As on previous occasions, the meeting did not produce complete agreement on all points, but the exchange did contribute to the goal of both men, the broadest possible basis of understanding between East and West.

For the second time since St. Laurent had become Prime Minister, the opening of Parliament coincided with the threat of a railway strike. This time, the disagreement centred on the fate of the locomotive firemen whose jobs had been eliminated by the introduction of diesel engines; Labour Minister Gregg and Canadian Labour Congress President Claude Jodoin proposed a seven-man commission to study the problem, but Canadian Pacific Railway President Norris Crump rejected the plan as a mere stop-gap. Anxious to avoid the charge of strike-breaking, the government let the work stoppage take effect, and the entire Canadian Pacific Railway network was brought to a halt. The transportation tie-up did not distract the government from its plan to present an image of competence and confidence. Except for some additional emphasis on the Commonwealth to counter the recent charges of being anti-British, the Speech from the Throne read by Governor General Massey on January 8, 1957, was not inspired particularly by immediate political considerations. Even John Diefenbaker made his début as Leader of the Opposition in a relatively moderate key, although he accused his opponents, with his particular gift for phrase-making, of 'resolute inaction' in dealing with the railway strike, trade, and other matters.

St. Laurent made a casual, chatty, reply to the criticism, chiding the new Tory leader for apparently reverting to R. B. Bennett's policy of 'blasting' a way for Canada into the world's markets, and commenting that he preferred the tone that had marked his golf game with President Eisenhower. His references to the strike were equally conciliatory; he enjoyed 'pretty good personal relations' with both sides, and felt that they realized he was trying to bring about the 'best kind of an outcome'. Even his references to Maurice Duplessis were made in a tone of sorrow rather than anger. Referring to Diefenbaker's call for a study of municipal problems, he warned that since municipalities fell under provincial jurisdiction, some people would assert, if the proposal was adopted, that Ottawa was aiming to destroy the Catholic religion and the French language in the Province of Quebec. Nothing could be 'more silly, more groundless', but any further steps in building a Canadian nation would have to be taken 'in such a way that we will not frighten anyone with the bugaboo that the religion and the language of my own race in the province of Quebec are going to be taken away from them'. He had generous words for George Drew, and for Sir Anthony Eden, who had just been forced by poor health and the public reaction to the Suez fiasco to resign the prime-ministership of the United Kingdom. 'We must do everything required of us in order to have the personal satisfaction that we have done our best,' he remarked, in referring to the two distinguished careers that had been ended abruptly, 'but having done that we should not feel that we should have been able to manage the affairs of the world.' When a man had done his best to perform his duty, he should be prepared to accept whatever happened as 'part of a general design . . . that is attributable to a power infinitely greater and wiser than any one of us.' The advice was sound, but St. Laurent was to discover before the year ended how difficult it was to follow.

The Prime Minister's patient and conciliatory approach proved highly effective. Working steadily behind closed doors, he persuaded the parties to the railway dispute to accept an investigation by a commission of three judges, assuring them that any conclusion would be considered merely advisory in character, and would lead to further negotiations. When he announced in the House of Commons, on January 11, that the rail services would be resumed 'forthwith', his supporters pounded their desks with delight, realizing that an embarrassing situation had been turned into a political success. On the same day, he wrote to President Eisenhower, recalling their agreement on the Augusta golf course in December that the economies of their two countries were closely interrelated, and that care should be taken by each to avoid adopting policies that would have an adverse effect on the other. Although the President had given assurances that the United States surplus wheat disposal program would be administered with that consideration in mind, he pointed out, serious injury was being done to Canadian producers and consequently to the prosperity of both countries. The letter was well received in Washington, a report soon arriving back in the Canadian capital that Eisenhower had given firm instructions that the United States should behave as a good neighbour, and avoid as far as possible any actions that would interfere with Canadian trade.

By careful self-discipline, St. Laurent managed to avoid falling prey either to the fatigue that had assailed him in previous winters or to the displays of bad temper that also made him vulnerable to opposition attack. Pleased to have re-established his authority as head of the government, he no longer looked forward to returning to Quebec. 'What would I do if I went back?' he asked one visitor, pointing out that his family had long since grown up, some of his closest friends had died, and that he would have difficulty in resuming his law practice. On his seventy-fifth birthday, Stanley Knowles suggested jokingly that he had earned a respite from his heavy duties. 'I feel that I shall be

happier as long as I do not have to reach the point where retirement would be the wisest decision to make,' he replied. '. . . I
think the greatest satisfaction that we get out of life now is that
of doing useful work to the best of our ability.' Diefenbaker
pointed out that he was only the second prime minister to reach
his seventy-fifth birthday in office; Solon Low wondered if he had
found the fountain of eternal youth. Liberal strategists spared no
effort to persuade him that his rightful place was at the party
helm for as long as his health allowed. His work schedule could
be greatly reduced, they argued, and his share of the election
campaign limited to a few television speeches and appearances
in the principal cities. When a younger member of the team
mentioned that the Liberal Party needed some kind of an election
program, he was told: 'St. Laurent will be seventy per cent of the
campaign. What do we need a program for if we have him?'

The Prime Minister's seventy-fifth birthday was made the
occasion by the Liberals for a mammoth party in Quebec City.
Supporters and admirers from as far away as Yellowknife, Northwest Territories, and Twillingate, Newfoundland, gathered in
the old city to pay tribute to the man whom one Conservative
newspaper, the Vancouver *Province*, described as 'Mr. Canada'.
C. D. Howe introduced him at a fourteen-hundred-seat banquet.
'I sometimes hear it said that Prime Minister St. Laurent carried
on where Mackenzie King left off,' the normally dour minister
commented. 'I have heard him referred to as a second Laurier.
These are meant as tributes to our Prime Minister. But to me, he
stands in the shade of no man, living or dead.' Caught by surprise
at the eloquent tribute, the guests were silent for a moment, then
rose to their feet as one man to endorse the testimony; tears filled
St. Laurent's eyes. A huge cake was piped to the head table, and
a cry went up for him to blow out the mass of candles in a single
puff. They proved to be too many for him, and he puffed at them
several times, leaning over the cake and smearing his dinner
jacket with icing in the process. His wife wiped off the sticky
substance, scolding him gently for being so awkward. The crowd
roared with pleasure.

Predictably, his speech was devoted mainly to the theme of
national unity. He endorsed a statement made by Laurier in 1894,

criticizing those who believed that there should be established on the shores of the St. Lawrence River a small French state. 'As for me, gentlemen,' his predecessor had declared, 'I do not want any small republic such as San Marino or Monaco . . . my ambition is to be the citizen of a great country.' National unity was 'the basic condition of our existence and of our progress as a nation,' St. Laurent continued. '. . . I do not think we have any other choice.' Addressing himself in particular to his fellow citizens in Quebec, he suggested pointedly in French that it was

> perhaps time that we . . . stopped wondering with too much anxiety about our future; it will be what we ourselves make of it by our work, our perseverance, our confidence that there is a place for us in the Canadian nation, that we are capable of filling that place, and that it is a place which is growing larger and is becoming more and more assured as the nation expands.

French-speaking Canadians were proud of their forebears, he declared. 'Let us have the backbone to stand erect as they did, and our descendants will be able to add us to the long list of those of whom they in their turn may be proud.' They were forthright words, and the words of a leader who not only gave advice, but preached by his example. He concluded his address with a quotation from Robert Browning:

> Grow old along with me,
> The best is yet to be. . . .

Quite apart from the fact that it was out of character for him to quote poetry, the choice of lines (not his own) was unfortunate, since they drew attention to the fact that he was beginning his fourth quarter of a century. Image-makers and speech-writers notwithstanding, however, the birthday party was a success.

In late March, the Canadian Prime Minister was given another opportunity to play a personal role in international diplomacy. The new British Prime Minister, Harold Macmillan, was scheduled to meet President Eisenhower in Bermuda for the first top-level talks between their countries since the Suez crisis. St. Laurent was delighted to learn of the meeting, and sent an invitation to Macmillan to visit Ottawa during his trip; Macmillan suggested instead that St. Laurent join him in Bermuda immediately after Eisenhower's visit. The counter-proposal was accepted.

The Bermuda meeting was held on March 25 and 26, with Pearson and Howe also in attendance. Macmillan and Foreign Secretary Selwyn Lloyd were anxious to draw the curtain on the events of the previous autumn, and the Suez crisis received only brief mention. Financial and trade problems were the principal British concern. The United Kingdom government was weighing the advantages and disadvantages of entering the European Common Market, and was searching for a formula that would prevent Britain from being shut out of the important continental market, while at the same time maintaining the Commonwealth trade pattern under British leadership, and assuring access to the hard currencies based on the American dollar. St. Laurent and his colleagues were generally favourable to British entry into the Common Market, feeling that an economically strong and integrated Europe would be the most effective possible answer to the threat of Communism, and would constitute a still larger market for Canadian produce. At the same time, they realized that if the new economic unit was surrounded by high tariffs, countries such as Canada would be excluded from their principal markets. The British leaders gave the assurance that if they did decide to enter the Common Market, they would insist that the tariffs should not apply to raw materials and foodstuffs, the principal commodities supplied to the United Kingdom by other Commonwealth countries. Macmillan realized that the negotiations might well break up on that account, and was already considering an alternative plan for a free-trade area outside the Common Market in the event that his insistence on only a modest tariff proved unacceptable. The most concrete result of the Bermuda meeting was an agreement to sell large quantities of Canadian uranium to the United Kingdom as fuel for a projected series of atomic energy power stations. At the conclusion of the talks, Macmillan found an opportunity to tell the press that, contrary to reports circulated during the Suez crisis, 'the service Mr. Pearson gave to finding good solutions and helping us at critical moments was one of a most remarkable kind and will always be remembered by us with gratitude'. The statement was in marked contrast to those of Canadian Conservatives, who were still insisting that Canada had stabbed the mother country in the back.

Walter Harris's pre-election budget, delivered on March 15, was, like the man himself, responsible, well balanced, and cautious. Faced with conflicting advice from the Department of Trade and Commerce on the one hand, urging an expansionist budget to stimulate the economy, and from his own officials on the other, arguing that the increase in the supply of credit should be restrained for a while longer to prevent inflation, he finally opted for the second point of view, even though it was bound to be less popular. The Minister of Finance had already made his decision when C. D. Howe informed him that the current economic boom was drawing to an end, and that the 'tight money' policy of the Bank of Canada would increase the downward trend. He decided that it was too late to begin the whole budget over again, and that expansionist measures could be introduced in the autumn if Howe's predictions proved accurate. Closely related to the government's monetary policy was its spending program. The opposition parties were demanding an increase in social welfare payments, and pressure was particularly strong to raise by ten dollars the forty-dollar a month universal old age pension. In private, many Liberal members of Parliament, uneasy over the criticism being levelled at the government in other fields, urged Harris to put an end to the long series of budget surpluses, reduce taxes, and increase all social welfare payments, including family allowances. Caught between his responsibility for the nation's financial stability and his party's political interests, the unhappy minister compromised; he cut taxes a mere $50 million, edged up old age pension payments by six dollars a month to correspond to the increase in cost of living since 1949, added a dollar on family allowances, and made proportionate increases in other welfare payments. That done, he was still able to predict a surplus of $152 million for the coming fiscal year. The carefully conceived solution pleased no one. The conscientious Minister of Finance was denounced by his opponents as 'six-buck Harris'; far from increasing his party's chances of re-election, he had diminished them.

While the attitude of the Minister of Finance was not shared by all members of the cabinet, it was strongly endorsed by the Prime Minister, who was determined that no attempts should be made to bribe the electorate with its own money. Every proposal submitted to him was examined from the points of view of the public interest and of administrative feasibility just as at any other time. The plan agreed upon at the federal-provincial conference to provide hospital and diagnostic services was introduced to Parliament, the government offered to build a series of thermal plants in the Maritimes, and the Canada Council was set up with a hundred-million-dollar initial fund. On the other hand, James Gardiner was unable to persuade him to proceed with the South Saskatchewan dam project, and several other attractive proposals were also rejected. As a result the impression was enhanced that the government was sitting on stacks of money, but was indifferent to the needs of the population, or at least insensitive to public opinion. As a matter of fact, the public-opinion polls were pleasantly reassuring. The results of a survey published on April 27 indicated that 47 per cent of the electorate supported the Liberals, only 1 per cent less than in February, while the popularity rating of the Progressive Conservatives remained steady at 32 per cent. The C.C.F. and Social Credit supporters made up only 11 and 9 per cent, respectively, of the population. Even in Diefenbaker's home territory of western Canada, the Liberals were leading the Tories by 32 to 20 per cent. Most encouraging of all, 74 per cent of the persons interviewed considered that Louis St. Laurent was doing a good job as Prime Minister. On the assumption that the party in power usually gains in strength during an election contest, there seemed, indeed, little cause for concern. Most Liberals assumed that the government would be returned with between 150 and 160 seats, compared to 173 in 1953. Shortly before Parliament was dissolved on April 8, Earl Rowe questioned the Prime Minister about the attitude he intended to adopt at the Commonwealth conference that had been called for late June; only when the Liberals burst out laughing did the Progressive Conservative member add that he was not certain who would be attending the meeting. St. Laurent's staff made reservations for him to sail for London on June 20, and he himself wrote to the new Prime Minister of Ghana, Kwame Nkrumah, to say that he hoped to have the pleasure of meeting him there.

St. Laurent finished the session in excellent form, and announced that the election would be held on June 10, just as he had indicated publicly the previous autumn; the contest was being organized like any other phase of the public's business. Following his usual policy, only essential appointments to the public service were made after the dissolution of Parliament, and instructions were given to take only routine administrative decisions until the Liberals or some other party had received a new popular mandate. The large number of Senate vacancies were left unfilled, and only one retiring Liberal member of Parliament received an appointment.* Even a minimum of cabinet changes were made. Having almost completed the task of constructing the St. Lawrence Seaway, Lionel Chevrier rejoined the cabinet as President of the Privy Council, filling a vacancy caused by the retirement of Secretary of State Roch Pinard. Almost grudgingly, and certainly too late, the Toronto area was given its first cabinet representative in the St. Laurent administration. The appointment went to thirty-three-year-old Paul Hellyer, who moved up from the post of parliamentary assistant to Associate Minister of National Defence. A change was considered in the cabinet representation for Alberta where many Liberals were demanding that George Prudham be replaced by the colourful and dynamic mayor of Edmonton, William Hawrelak. The suggestion appealed to St. Laurent because of the opportunity it afforded of giving one of the largest ethnic groups in the country, the Ukrainian Canadians, a representative in the cabinet, but he had a strong sense of loyalty towards his colleagues, and was determined that Prudham should not appear to have been dismissed. Hawrelak was nominated as the Liberal candidate in Edmonton East, and Prudham declined to run again, but at his request the cabinet change was postponed until after the election. Two other long-overdue appointments were postponed, one to give Prince

*Maurice Boisvert, appointed to the Income Tax Appeal Board.

Edward Island cabinet representation, the other to replace the former Postmaster General, Alcide Côté, who had died nearly two years earlier.

The official opening of the Liberal campaign was scheduled to take place in Winnipeg on April 29. That decision, too, was motivated in large part by non-political considerations. The suggestion had been made that the Prime Minister should deliver his first speech in the Canadian Arctic, and throw out to the younger generation the challenge of northern development, just as Laurier had inspired his contemporaries with the vision of building western Canada. The plan was dismissed because of the expense and fatigue of such a long flight. The trip to Manitoba could be made at no cost, it was argued, since the railway companies did not charge to haul the Prime Minister's special car, and he could rest during the two-day journey.

Louis St. Laurent had two basic considerations in mind as he boarded the train in Ottawa's Union Station on the evening of April 27. He was determined to show himself to as many people as possible so that they could judge for themselves whether he was too old to be given a new mandate, as some of his opponents were suggesting, and he was equally determined to make no promises simply for the purpose of winning votes. There would be Liberals along the campaign trail who would argue that an appointment here, or a construction project there, would mean an extra seat, he told one of his aides as he settled into one of the easy chairs in the lounge section of the car. If the requests merited consideration on purely administrative grounds, they were to be forwarded to Ottawa for consideration by the appropriate department; if not, they were to be ignored. In high spirits at the prospect of a trans-Canadian tour, the aide asked facetiously: 'But, sir, aren't you afraid of creating a precedent in Canadian politics?' The Prime Minister flushed, and retorted angrily, 'Well, that's the way it's going to be as long as I'm around. . . .' The younger man interrupted to assure him that he was only joking.

The Winnipeg meeting was not a success. The weather was still cool, and there was still little interest in the election. The political climate in Manitoba was equally unpropitious for the

Liberals. Over the previous years, the *Winnipeg Free Press* had been criticizing the government on many counts, accusing it of departing from the principles of Liberalism. Farmers were annoyed at having been refused advances on farm-stored grain, and even the Liberal Premier Douglas Campbell had felt obliged to attack the federal administration to shore up his own crumbling political fortress. As a result, the auditorium was only partially filled, and only the persons who had come to heckle showed any appreciable spirit.

St. Laurent's speech was designed as a report on the government's stewardship over the previous four years; it read like an auditor's report, replete with numerous statistics, and was delivered in a similar manner. The record of growth was certainly an impressive one, and the period warranted the description of 'the best ever experienced in Canada'. 'No government in Ottawa could take the credit for the great things that Canadians have done and are doing,' the Prime Minister declared, 'but the present government has certainly helped,' and the record gave 'solid assurance that a Liberal administration is well qualified to give dynamic direction to Canadian progress in the years immediately ahead.' He answered the principal charges of his opponents good-naturedly, but without attacking them in turn, or even mentioning them by name. Parliament was, and would remain, supreme, he declared, 'regardless of what our disappointed opponents may say'. The gas pipeline – 'this tremendous venture' – had been started despite great resistance, and 'after a debate nearly as long as the pipeline itself and quite as full of another kind of natural gas'. The reference to the pipeline debate produced a few cries of 'closure' and 'guillotine', and shouts of 'supermen' and 'what about the farmers?' were hurled at the stage, but they did not distract him seriously from his course. For the future, St. Laurent suggested the slogan: peace, prosperity, and social security. The good times would continue, he predicted, and there was no reason 'for any part of Canada, for any citizen of Canada, to fail to share in the good life that a kindly Providence has put within reach of our hearts and of our hands'. Strangely, the speech made no direct reference to his greatest theme of national unity; it no longer seemed an issue, but rather an accomplished fact. St. Laurent concluded by reading an editorial from the *Winnipeg Free Press* that warned of the 'grave dangers' to Canadian Liberalism of another four years in power, but argued that the risk had to be taken 'in the national interest' because of the 'superiority of the present government, compared with any possible group or grouping which might take its place'. It was damningly faint praise. As the train rolled on across the prairies that night, the Liberal campaign had been started officially, but, in fact, it had not yet begun to move.

The meetings in Edmonton and Calgary were hardly more inspiring, but Vancouver, true to its tradition of colourful and lively politics, was the scene of a much more interesting performance. Hecklers were numerous, and several had to be expelled by the police to maintain a semblance of order. Nonplussed at first, St. Laurent soon rose to the challenge, and replied heatedly to the interjections. The day he spent in Vancouver was a long and strenuous one, including visits to several parts of the city to satisfy the different factions within the party, and the Prime Minister was extremely tired when he was escorted aboard a private yacht at midnight for the overnight trip to Vancouver Island. The next day he drove from Nanaimo to Victoria along the Malahat Drive, which was rough and dusty because of the construction work in progress, and arrived in the British Columbia capital with hardly enough time to glance over his notes before the evening meeting. The text was a good example of how not to conduct a political campaign. Conceived as his principal statement on Canada's foreign policy, it had been prepared by career diplomats in the Department of External Affairs, who had protested vigorously against any attempt to adapt it to the needs of the political hustings. As a result, it resembled a diplomatic 'position paper', and was carefully designed to avoid saying anything that could possibly be considered as breaking new ground. In the most pro-British part of Canada, it did attempt to soothe ruffled feelings over Canada's role in the Suez crisis by repeating that the government had sought to save the Commonwealth and to prevent a split between the United Kingdom and the United States. The emergence of Ghana as the first black African member of the Commonwealth was hailed as a significant event, and

Canada's role was described as that of a respected, objective intermediary, 'with a constructive role to play in the development of peace and progress in the free world'. The message was undoubtedly right in content, but it was wrong for those particular circumstances. As soon as the meeting was over, the local candidate telephoned to Pearson to rush over as soon as possible and repair the damage by making a more appropriate and stirring speech.

The day following the Victoria meeting was Sunday, and St. Laurent was taken salmon fishing in Brentwood Bay. He caught nothing, but the weather was pleasant, and he was able to obtain a few hours of much-needed relaxation. The train trip back across the Rocky Mountains was also restful, and he was feeling fresh and cheerful when he arrived in Saskatoon on May 7. Asked how he felt about the contest, he remarked that he was 'as optimistic as I was in 1953'; in the parts of the country he had visited, he expected an increase in Liberal seats. What about rumours that he would retire soon after the election? one reporter wanted to know. 'Tommyrot,' he snorted, 'I'm wearing the hat I wore in the 1953 campaign. I got it cleaned for this one. And I'm going to send it back and have it cleaned for the next one.' The meeting in Saskatoon took the form of a lunch-box picnic in the local arena. Citizens had been asked to bring their own food and join the Prime Minister for a mid-day meal before listening to his speech; for him and the other dignitaries, however, linen-covered tables had been arranged at the front of the vast hall, and they were served a proper meal. A local cartoonist described the invitation: 'You are invited to have lunch (bring your own) . . . and I hope you will remember on which side your bread is buttered.' Once again, the arrangements backfired.

Inevitably, the subject of the South Saskatchewan dam was raised during his western tour. 'There has been no decision,' St. Laurent replied sharply when questioned at Regina airport. 'I'm sure that this project offers many benefits but I'm not prepared to give a definite answer until I can tell Parliament that I'm certain the nation would get more out of it than it would put into it.' That evening he was more specific. Agriculture Minister Gardiner had long favoured the project, he declared in a major address, but the other ministers were not yet convinced that it was 'something that it would be proper to undertake as a national project'. The proposal would continue to be examined 'on its intrinsic merit', and he would recommend that it be undertaken 'when we are assured that such indirect benefit would put back into the national economy more than what was taken out in interest and amortization charges'. The whole question, he argued, should not, and would not, be used by him as 'election bait'. Since the other three parties had endorsed the project, and all candidates in Saskatchewan, including the Liberals, were in favour of it, St. Laurent's attitude seemed to many westerners to smack more of stubbornness than of administrative efficiency, or at least to prove once again that eastern Canadians had little understanding of the west.

Until he boarded the T.C.A. aircraft to return to Ottawa, St. Laurent maintained his jovial 'Uncle Louis' image, only occasionally allowing a heckler to provoke him into a show of temper. On the way east, however, he exploded. Glancing through the morning paper, he read an assertion by Solon Low that Canada had threatened to leave the Commonwealth during the Suez crisis if British troops were not withdrawn within a specified time. The Prime Minister was 'going to be forced to reveal the telegram' to Eden containing the threat, the Social Credit leader had asserted. Since he had denied the charge in Parliament, and had stated there that Eden refused to allow the exchange of messages to be published, St. Laurent was first indignant, and then enraged. By the time he arrived in the capital at 10 p.m., he could hardly contain himself. Striding out of the aircraft, he made his way straight towards a knot of waiting newspapermen, took one by the lapel, and read the report to him. 'This statement amounts to a downright lie,' he declared to the astonished man. His oath as a privy councillor prevented him from making the telegram public, he went on, but there were forty or fifty other privy councillors from both major parties, and if one were designated by Low, he would show him the message; that person would be able to ascertain that there had been no threat, and 'that should deal with this ridiculous assertion'. The Liberal campaign was beginning to warm up at last.

John Diefenbaker opened his campaign in Toronto's Massey Hall with a very considerable assist from Leslie Frost. The Ontario Premier did not know Diefenbaker well, and did not think the westerner had a serious chance of winning the election, but he was still anxious to obtain a further $100 to $150 million in tax revenues; Oakley Dalgleish, editor of the *Globe and Mail*, persuaded him that he would strengthen his own hand at the new federal-provincial conference if he supported the federal wing of the Progressive Conservative Party. Accordingly, Frost appeared on the platform with Diefenbaker, and declared that a Progressive Conservative victory would mean an extra $100 million for Ontario. St. Laurent read the report of the meeting with a sense of disappointment, not because he objected to Frost supporting his national leader, but because the Ontario Premier had always insisted that federal-provincial relations should be kept out of politics, and because they had been in such close agreement in the past.

The Liberals also had cause for concern about another of Diefenbaker's supporters. Dr. Merril Menzies, a brilliant young economist with special knowledge of wheat marketing, had been executive assistant to Minister of Justice Stuart Garson for several years, but had left Ottawa after becoming frustrated at what he considered the government's lack of receptiveness to new ideas. In the autumn of 1956, he wrote a forty-page analysis of the current political and economic situation in Canada, arguing that the Liberals were mesmerized by 'the cult of the gross national product', and had become so preoccupied with statistics that they failed to realize that some parts of the country were not doing so well as others. The government was assuring prosperity and a welfare state, he pointed out, 'but the Canadian people want more than this. They ask for vision in their statesmen, a sense of national purpose and national destiny. . . . Without a vision the people (and the nation) perish.' There was nothing in the paper that Menzies and his friends in other ministers' offices had not said aloud many times; the difference was that in 1956 the ideas fell into John Diefenbaker's hands and he accepted them. When the Tory leader began his campaign, Menzies was with him as his principal speech-writer. Also on the team were Allister Grosart and Dalton Camp, two of the most competent public relations experts in Canada.

From the outset, Diefenbaker put on a stirring performance. Canadians, he charged, were being overtaxed, and it was time 'to take the unrepentant tax-masters off the backs of the Canadian people'. He cited St. Laurent's reference to the British as 'supermen' as an indication of Liberal arrogance, referred to the pipeline debate as evidence of his opponents' 'shocking contempt' of Parliament, and declared fervently: 'I am one of those who believe that the party has a sacred trust. . . . It has an appointment today with destiny, to plan and build for a greater Canada . . . to lay the foundations of their nation for a great and glorious future.' The effect on the press corps was inspiring; bored by the one-sidedness of national politics and the cautious efficiency of the federal administration, they were at last given something exciting to write about, and many of them pictured the Progressive Conservative leader alternately as the underdog fighting valiantly against overwhelming odds, and David doing battle with an over-aged Goliath.

One area in which the Liberals appeared at first glance to have a clear advantage was Quebec. Even though his opponents there still insisted that he was 'more Stephen than Louis', and he was inclined to lecture French-speaking Canadians about their narrow nationalism, he was a native son, and the province was proud of him. John Diefenbaker, on the other hand, was unknown there and spoke excruciatingly bad French, and Duplessis was known to have no liking for him. Liberal organizers underestimated one significant factor, the feeling of animosity harboured by the Union Nationale leader against the only man capable of challenging his power. The by-elections of 1955 had demonstrated that his organization could counteract St. Laurent's personal influence without his even appearing in public; he decided to teach the Prime Minister a lesson by knocking out a few of the Liberal candidates.

Louis St. Laurent opened the Quebec portion of his campaign in his own constituency on May 13. The Capitol Theatre, chosen for the occasion, was not large, but Quebec City residents were convinced that the result of the election was a foregone conclusion, and the room was filled only by the desperate last-minute efforts of local organizers, and at considerable expense. In comparison to most political meetings in Quebec, it was hardly an exciting affair. The Prime Minister recalled that it was nearly sixteen years since Mackenzie King and the late Cardinal Villeneuve had persuaded him to go to Ottawa. He had no desire to equal Laurier's record of service to the constituency, but he might be tempted to equal Lapointe's, who had been the federal member for Quebec East for twenty-two years. He was happy to continue the work of those two great men; in fact, he confessed, 'I wonder what I would do if I ceased to be Prime Minister.' He wanted to go on as long as possible serving the cause of 'the dynamic unity of Canada'. He called it that because, in his view, Canadian unity would never be static, but rather 'the fruit of a continuous effort'. The Liberal Party, he declared, was the only possible instrument of that unity, since it alone was a 'truly national' party, with 'principles equally acceptable to all the population of Canada'.

As the campaign progressed, St. Laurent abandoned more and more his prepared texts, and chatted with his audiences like a neighbour calling on a Saturday afternoon. The important thing was not to make statements of policy, he explained apologetically to one overworked speech-writer, but to give people a chance to see him and to judge for themselves whether he was likely to be able to lead them for another four years. If they did feel he was still sufficiently alert and competent for the job, they would vote for him; if not, no quantity of prepared statements would persuade them to do so. As a result of that attitude, his speeches became largely a long and disjointed series of anecdotes, interspersed with comments on newspaper articles and on statements by his opponents. He ended invariably with a lecture on the benefits of the Canadian democratic system, and a reminder that if the audience did not feel the Liberals could do the best job for them over the next four years, it was their duty to vote for some other party. But, he would add, with a shrug of his shoulders, as he gathered up his papers and started to move away from the rostrum, 'I don't know where you will find anyone who can do any better.'

The Prime Minister's television appearances were undoubtedly the weakest aspect of his campaign. He had adapted well to radio broadcasting on first entering public life, but he took a dislike to television on the grounds that programs were carefully prepared performances similar to stage shows and that they did not present a true-to-life picture of the politician. He considered teleprompters and make-up theatrical devices designed to deceive the public. In vain, his advisers tried to convince him that a teleprompter would enable him to communicate his views more effectively to his fellow citizens, and that make-up merely corrected the effects of the strong studio lights, which accentuated wrinkles and blemishes not visible under normal conditions. Becoming adamant, he threatened at one point to use the aids, but to begin his appearance by explaining that he was using a teleprompter and wearing grease-paint, so that no one would be able to feel he was trying to create a false impression. He made three television broadcasts during the campaign, but read his text with scarcely a glance at the camera, and he looked much older than usual. Liberal Party strategists concluded that he was right to use the new medium as little as possible and to concentrate on showing himself personally to as many voters as he could.

By mid-May, it was evident that some of the cabinet ministers were in serious difficulties. Walter Harris was widely criticized for the meagre increase in the old-age pension, and was meeting strong opposition in his own constituency of Grey-Bruce in rural Ontario, traditionally a Conservative stronghold. In the Maritimes, Robert Winters and Milton Gregg encountered resentment because that region was falling behind other parts of Canada in terms of economic growth; the refusal to construct the South Saskatchewan dam was an albatross around Gardiner's neck in his province, and Stuart Garson was denounced in Manitoba for the government's failure to deal with the huge wheat surpluses. C. D. Howe was a favourite target of opposition attack, and such 'Howe-isms' as 'What's a million?', 'Who can stop us?', and 'Nuts', were repeated across the country to illustrate the charge that the government was autocratic and callous. On the prairies he was held responsible for the refusal to pay cash advances on farm-stored grain. In rural Manitoba in May, the Minister of Trade and Commerce told one heckler to go away and make his speech when his own party organized a meeting; the man turned out to be the president of the local Liberal association. Faced with one burly individual who complained that the farmers were starving to death, Howe poked his finger into the man's bulging stomach and remarked, 'It looks to me like you've been eating pretty well under a Liberal government.' One meeting was so disorderly that he left the hall early and returned to his hotel.

John Diefenbaker's meetings, in contrast, were increasingly well attended, and he handled his audiences like a musician playing his favourite instrument. The Progressive Conservative leader's appeal was almost entirely emotional, and he switched back and forth between good humour, indignation, mystical idealism, and appeals to self-interest with great dexterity. Catch-phrases such as 'and Howe' after every criticism of the government, 'those supermen of Europe whose days are about over', and references to Canada being 'allied at the United Nations with Russia', almost invariably provoked a strong response. When he spoke in Vancouver on May 24, the auditorium was filled to overflowing, and in the awed tones of a prophet evoking a miracle, he declared, 'I think tonight across Canada something is happening, I think the Liberal Party is now realizing Canada is aroused as it has not been aroused in many years.' His speech was interrupted by applause and laughter over forty times. That same evening, Louis St. Laurent was drawing an audience of only four hundred people in his home town of Sherbrooke.

As the half-way mark of the campaign was reached, some Liberals were beginning to become concerned, and while few conceived that defeat was possible, they decided to step up their efforts. Realizing that the size of the old age pension increase had been a political mistake, Walter Harris suggested to St. Laurent that the figure be increased by four dollars, making a total pension of fifty dollars a month. The Prime Minister rejected the suggestion almost scornfully, declaring that the matter had been decided weeks earlier on the basis of all available facts, and that those facts had not changed. He was prepared to take the consequences of the decision announced in the budget. In a television broadcast on May 20, St. Laurent described as 'just plain ridiculous' the 'Tory election promise to spend more and tax less', and invited Canadians 'to commission us to go on doing our best, under all circumstances, and for all the people, and to stick to our "no nonsense – no promises" program'. Speaking in Ottawa on May 27, he dealt for the first time in detail with the pipeline debate. Two months before the debate began, Diefenbaker had promised to block the project, the Prime Minister recalled, 'and this is one promise that they kept'. The debate had gone on for a whole month, he reminded his audience, and covered nearly a thousand pages of Hansard; no responsible government could allow a minority group to prevent members of Parliament from expressing their views on a bill by their votes, 'so we applied a rule that exists in every parliament, closure'. Then on 'Black Friday – certainly a black Friday in the history of the Tory and Socialist parties', they turned in their desperation on the Speaker himself. 'They were so afraid that the majority will would prevail that they were ready to destroy the reputation of Canada's first commoner to prevent that from happening.' St. Laurent's reply to the charges of the other parties was an effective one, but there were two disadvantages; first, it came very late, and secondly, it meant that the Liberals were fighting on ground that was not of their choosing.

The Ottawa meeting was marked by a still more serious tactical error. Hoping to sow dissension within the Tory ranks, Liberal strategists persuaded the Prime Minister to draw attention to the fact that Progressive Conservative advertisements gave prominence to the name and picture of their new leader, but that in most instances the only reference to the party itself was the mandatory one in very small letters at the bottom of the page identifying the organization that paid the bill. Apparently, it was more accurate to speak of the Diefenbaker party than the Progressive Conservative Party, St. Laurent joked; the Tory slogans seemed to be saying in effect, 'now is the time for all good Diefenbakers to come to the aid of their party'. The ghost-written comment proved to be too clever by half; when Conservative organizer Grosart read it the next morning, he realized that the Prime Minister had simply drawn attention to the slogan Grosart himself was promoting: 'It's time for a Diefenbaker government.'

The newspaper report of St. Laurent's speech was dispatched to Progressive Conservative speakers across the nation with instructions to draw attention to the new party image.

On Monday, June 3, St. Laurent began his final week of campaigning with two meetings the same evening in Montreal, one in predominantly English-speaking Notre Dame de Grâce, the other in the huge Show Mart in the centre of the city. The Liberals in Notre Dame de Grâce were badly divided and many gave only half-hearted support to the candidate that had been chosen; hecklers were more in evidence than usual. Beginning to tire after five weeks and fifteen thousand miles of campaigning, the Prime Minister was depressed at the atmosphere of the gathering. 'I am finished, they don't want anything more to do with me,' he commented to Lionel Chevrier and Roch Pinard as the three men were driven to the second meeting. 'They don't want a French Canadian in Ontario any more.' The two ministers tried in vain to reassure him. The second meeting almost turned into a riot. Despite careful screening at the door, a large group of troublemakers succeeded in entering the Show Mart, and formed into a solid bloc about half-way down the hall, in order to create a disturbance at a given signal. Accustomed to such forms of political warfare in Quebec, the Liberals had taken the precaution of hiring a phalanx of their own. When St. Laurent was well launched into his speech, the trouble-makers began to jostle and shout, but they found themselves hemmed in on all sides, and within seconds they were moved towards the door and onto the street. With only a momentary break as the crowd turned towards the scene of the commotion, St. Laurent carried on with his speech.

The leaders of both principal parties spent the last days of the contest in Ontario, the critical fighting ground of the campaign. The Prime Minister's tour continued to have the character of a royal progress, Diefenbaker's that of a messianic crusade. Their paths crossed in Woodstock on June 6, where St. Laurent spoke to two hundred people at mid-day, the Progressive Conservative leader to an overflow audience of a thousand the same evening. Staff members of the Prime Minister's team who attended both meetings were shocked at the contrast. Diefenbaker was late, and frequent progress reports were given to the audience, depicting him making his way through hordes of enthusiastic admirers anxious to see his face and touch his hand. After more than an hour, the atmosphere was tense with expectancy, and suddenly the message boomed forth: 'He is here!' When the long, lean figure appeared, he was met by a roar of welcome. Diefenbaker was smiling happily, obviously enjoying himself, and his performance was of high calibre. While his statements were sometimes outrageous, the audience enjoyed every minute of the meeting and it seemed probable that anyone who dared to interrupt would be mobbed.

The Liberals reserved their greatest effort for a mass meeting in Toronto's Maple Leaf Gardens on the last Friday of the campaign. On hand were Walter Harris, aware that he would likely be defeated personally but putting on a bold front, C. D. Howe, in trouble in his riding as well, L. B. Pearson, Paul Hellyer, and a stage full of other party dignitaries. Over ten thousand people were packed into the sports stadium, and a sea of red and white photographs of the Prime Minister, fixed on sticks, waved gaily as he mounted onto the platform. There was some booing, but it only added spice to what seemed certain to be a happy evening. Howe, Harris, and Hellyer spoke first, then St. Laurent advanced to the microphone. He had just begun to hit his stride when a fifteen-year-old lad stepped out of the crowd with a poster bearing the Prime Minister's picture in his hand, walked a dozen steps up to the podium, muttered a few unintelligible words, and tore up the poster before St. Laurent's face. The seventy-five-year-old leader stared, open-mouthed and uncomprehending, at the spectacle; the crowd watched in hushed silence. Then the chairman of the meeting, fearing a direct attack on the Prime Minister, rushed forward to seize the wrongdoer; he only succeeded in pushing him backwards, and the boy fell down the steps, striking his head on the cement floor, and knocking himself unconscious. A horrified gasp rose from the crowd as the figure lay, crumpled and alone, a few feet below the Prime Minister of Canada. St. Laurent continued to stare at the scene, as if in a state of shock. In a matter of a few seconds, which seemed like hours, the young man was surrounded by attendants, and within a few minutes he was able to stand up and be escorted out of the hall.

The first reaction over, the crowd turned its indignation upon the men on the platform; the incident appeared to prove the charges of the other parties that the Liberal oligarchy was so remote from the people that it could not be approached with impunity. As soon as the disorder had subsided sufficiently, St. Laurent resumed his speech, referring in a tone of regret to the 'unfortunate incident', provoked by the 'ill-advised youth', but he too was clearly shaken and was unable to regain his earlier enthusiasm. The crowd, for its part, was no longer interested in his remarks; all minds were on the lad, and wondering what was the extent of his injury. He had stolen the Prime Minister's final show.

While the estimate of Liberal losses had been increased by analysts in recent days, there still did not seem to be any serious possibility that the government would be defeated. In fact, the last public-opinion poll, released on June 7, reported that 48 per cent of the electorate would vote Liberal and 34 per cent Progressive Conservative, suggesting a slight reversal of the recent anti-government trend. *Maclean's* Magazine had already sent to press its post-election editorial, beginning: 'For better or for worse, we Canadians have once more elected one of the most powerful governments ever created by the free will of a free electorate.' Nevertheless, St. Laurent was still uneasy, and rather than relax on the last Saturday and Sunday before the voting as had been planned originally, he continued to campaign in the Quebec City area, in an effort to assist Hugues Lapointe and other Liberal candidates reported to be in trouble.

On June 10, election day, he was up early as usual, still feeling reasonably fresh and vigorous, cast his ballot early, and passed the day calling on party workers in his constituency. By seven p.m. he was installed in front of the television set in his living-room with most of his family and a few close friends. The news was bad almost from the outset. In Newfoundland, where Smallwood was supposed to have absolute control, Progressive Conservative candidates were leading in both St. John's ridings. In Nova Scotia and New Brunswick, Robert Winters and Milton Gregg were trailing their opponents, and by nine o'clock it was evident that they would be beaten. St. Laurent observed the results with outward calm, saying little, but when Gregg conceded defeat, he telephoned the Minister of Labour to express his disappointment. 'They have just got tired of seeing us around,' he told Gregg despondently. In Quebec, Jean Lesage took an early lead, but Hugues Lapointe was running behind his Progressive Conservative opponent, who was known to have strong Union Nationale support. When the results from Ontario began to arrive, it was revealed that Howe, Harris, and Hellyer were all going down to defeat. It looked like a rout. The political forecasters had all been wrong; John Diefenbaker, who at times seemed alone in believing he could win, had been right. When Chubby Power called at the St. Laurent residence at 11 p.m., the little group was ready to admit that the government would have to resign. About midnight, Louis St. Laurent, shaken but still determined to carry out his responsibilities to the letter, appeared in the C.B.C. television studio in the Château Frontenac Hotel, and stated that while the result of the contest was still uncertain, the necessary action would be taken as soon as all the returns were available. He looked dazed, and, for the first time in a year, a tired old man.

By the following morning, the people's verdict was clear; the Progressive Conservatives had won 112 seats, the Liberals 106, the C.C.F. 25, the Social Credit group 19; and there were one Independent Liberal and two Independent winners. On the other hand, the Liberals had received 42.3 per cent of the total vote compared to 39 per cent for the Progressive Conservatives. Two of the principal artisans of the Tory victory were Leslie Frost and Maurice Duplessis. By his personal endorsement of John Diefenbaker, the Ontario Premier had contributed to the 8-per-cent shift in the vote there, and the resultant increase in Progressive Conservative seats from 33 to 61. In Quebec, the Union Nationale organization had been the main factor in the election of 11 Progressive Conservatives and Independents. Premiers Robert Stanfield of Nova Scotia and Hugh John Flemming of New Brunswick deserved considerable credit for the results in the Maritimes. But above all, the victory was a personal achievement for John Diefenbaker. By his inspiring oratory, he had exploited issues of the Liberals' making and convinced a sufficient proportion of the electorate that there was, in fact, an alternative to the twenty-two-year-old Liberal administration. A post-election survey was to reveal that, of the persons who abandoned the Grits, 5.1 per cent did so because of the Suez crisis, 38.2 per cent because of the pipeline debate, 26.7 per cent because of the inadequate increase in the old-age pension, and 30 per cent because it was 'time for a change'. They were all points that the political maverick from western Canada, who had become the Tory party leader almost by default, had argued with great skill in every corner of the land.

Louis St. Laurent's first and only reaction to the popular verdict was to hand over the reins of power to John Diefenbaker as promptly and in as orderly a fashion as possible. That was his firm intention when he arrived in Ottawa on June 12, accompanied by his daughter Madeleine, and called a cabinet meeting to discuss the situation. Other Liberals, including some ministers, had greater difficulty in accepting the situation. The voters had merely wanted to express some minor grievances, and give the government a warning, but not to upset it, they argued; the Liberals still had the confidence of a majority of the electorate; they should heed the warning, and carry on. Convinced that the small parties would not support the Tories, James Gardiner felt particularly strongly that Parliament should be called, a program of legislation introduced, and the new members allowed to decide on the next step; by that time, he reasoned, Canadians would have had an opportunity to realize their mistake and would insist that the proven team remain in office. St. Laurent was unconvinced. Personally, he had no desire to give the impression of clinging to office for the sake of power; he had often declared that he would be happy to return home when his period of service was over. Above all, he was determined to do the right thing, regardless of political or personal considerations. One of the most important factors to be taken into account, in his view, was the Commonwealth conference scheduled to begin on June 26; Canada could not be effectively represented by a prime minister whose authority to speak for the Canadian people was in serious doubt. If a new group of men was to take over the responsibility of running the country, he insisted, then the national interest required that they do so as soon as possible. An indication from the C.C.F. and Social Credit leaders that they would support a Diefenbaker government until another election could be held strengthened his feelings in that regard.

On his first day back in the capital, St. Laurent telephoned Diefenbaker in Prince Albert, Saskatchewan, congratulated him on his achievement, assured him that he was going to do whatever the public interest required, and suggested that he fly down to discuss the situation. He firmly opposed a request that a Liberal caucus be held to decide the course to be adopted; the decision whether he should attempt to remain in office was one for which he had to take the sole responsibility, he replied to one such suggestion. By the time John Diefenbaker arrived in the East Block on June 14, beaming with happiness, St. Laurent's mind was made up. He received the Progressive Conservative leader with his usual courtesy, chatted cordially about the campaign, and informed him that he was prepared to resign as soon as it was convenient to him; his only concern, St. Laurent stressed, was to ensure a smooth and efficient transfer of power. Since the vote of the members of the armed forces had not yet been reported, and a decision before that was done would appear to ignore their views, he suggested that the formal announcement be delayed until the following Monday. Diefenbaker accepted the plan, and acknowledged the helpful attitude with gratitude.

On Monday, June 17, the service vote was received; while it was largely favourable to the Liberals, it gave them only one additional seat. The cabinet met after lunch for two hours to examine the situation a final time, and to tidy up the last ends of outstanding business. Afterwards, John Diefenbaker was asked to come over from the Centre Block, where he was already planning his cabinet. He and St. Laurent chatted briefly, then the Prime Minister left for Rideau Hall to recommend that Diefenbaker be asked to form a government. St. Laurent entered the Governor General's residence with the same brisk purposefulness that he had displayed since arriving back in Ottawa five days earlier. When he reappeared half an hour later, he was still smiling, but he looked tired. The tremendous weight of responsibility that he had borne for fifteen and a half years was gone from his shoulders; he had taken the first important step towards becoming a free man again. At the end of the afternoon the Prime Minister's Office released his final statement as head of the government. Although no party would have a clear majority in the new Parliament, St. Laurent announced, the Progressive Conservative Party appeared to have the largest number of elected members; in the circumstances, he had decided that the proper course was to resign. Before doing so, he had assured the Progressive Conservative leader that he would extend 'full co-operation . . . so that the Queen's government can go on without interruption'. He had also told Diefenbaker that he felt the Liberal members would not attempt to prevent the new government from carrying through Parliament the program it had placed before the people as 'we feel that the growth and prosperity of the country should not be endangered by instability of government which would come from irresponsible obstruction'.

There were still a few details to be attended to before St. Laurent could return to Quebec. He had to move to an office in the Centre Block in order to assume his new duties as Leader of the Opposition, a twenty-two-year accumulation of files had to be disposed of, and a small staff selected to assist him in his new functions. Among the matters awaiting his attention was a letter from Solon Low, recommending Arthur Meighen as the man who should examine the controversial exchange of telegrams with Sir Anthony Eden; all that had become unimportant, and the letter was filed. Messages had to be sent to Harold Macmillan, Nehru, and the other prime ministers he had planned to see in a few days, and there were hundreds of letters and telegrams from both political friends and foes to be acknowledged. One was particularly gratifying. 'Since the election returns became public, I have followed with admiration the calm, dignified and courageous manner in which you accepted the unpalatable results,' wrote a Justice of the Supreme Court. 'You were splendid in office, but magnificent in defeat.' Governor General Massey was later to describe the transfer of power as a model of constitutional propriety.

On Friday, June 21, Louis St. Laurent addressed a caucus of the newly-elected Liberals, and outlined plans for the party's first period in opposition since 1935. The policy would be to put on the record the Liberal achievements of the past twenty-two years, he stated, and to make the new government produce the legislation it had promised. At the end of the day, he climbed into a private railway car for the last time, and set off for St. Patrick.

In the pleasant surroundings of the lower St. Lawrence, Louis St. Laurent began gradually to relax. Packages of mail and newspaper clippings continued to arrive from Ottawa, but none of the matters was urgent, and he had free time on his hands for almost the first occasion in his adult life. Friends and admirers sent him messages of appreciation for his service to Canada. Nehru wrote from London to express his 'affectionate regards', to tell him how much he had been influenced by their 'association and . . . friendship', and to assure him of a welcome in India at any time. As the weeks passed, and the continuous tension of recent years gave way to a sense of fatigue, the letters of praise seemed to him like generous attempts to excuse his failure. Rather than accept the invitations of his sons and daughters to join them on the golf course or at the swimming-pool, he withdrew after breakfast to the sun-room, and read the newspapers, or, most of the time, just stared into space. Increasingly weary and despondent, he began to feel that he had been a failure, that the great goal he had set himself of ensuring Canadian unity was a mere mirage, and that the country was as divided as when he had entered public life. He was convinced that many English-speaking Canadians had voted against the Liberals because he was a French-speaking Catholic; and he knew that he had been condemned by some in his own province as a traitor to his race. Equally worrying to him was the fact that Mackenzie King had handed him a party that was well organized, cohesive, and dynamic, and that, after some initial victories, he had led it to defeat. Sitting in his armchair and gazing out across the broad St. Lawrence River, he asked himself over and over where he had failed, what mistakes he had made, and what he should do to redress his errors. Should he have asserted his leadership more vigorously? Should he have tried to be more of a politician? Should he have clung to office as the more politically minded Liberals urged him to do? Had he been naïve to think that it was possible to treat all Canadians alike, whatever their origin, their language, or their province? By mid-August his health was becoming a matter of serious concern to the other members of the family as he continued to torture himself with doubts and self-recrimination, but he refused to consult a doctor. When he was urged to resign the Liberal leadership, he replied angrily that he had got the party into trouble, and that he had an obligation to lead it out again; he was not going to abandon the ship while it was in difficulties.

In the press, speculation had begun about a possible successor. Walter Harris, previously the heir apparent in many minds, was not only defeated but stood condemned by public opinion for having refused to grant a larger pension increase. Brooke Claxton and Douglas Abbott had been gone from the political scene for three years; Robert Winters was already beginning a new career in private business; Lionel Chevrier was a French-speaking Catholic, and the Liberal Party could not have two such leaders in a row. The two most likely candidates were L. B. Pearson and Paul Martin, but the first had shown little interest in domestic politics, and the second had not been popular with all of his cabinet colleagues. To add to St. Laurent's distress, James Sinclair was quoted as having said that a convention would be held soon to pick a new Liberal leader, and a member of the Ontario Young Liberal Association announced that he would raise the subject at a meeting to be held in Presqu'île, near Kingston, in September. St. Laurent interpreted the reports as added proof of his failure, and as an indication that he was to be cast aside without having had the opportunity to redeem himself.

When a brief trip to Ottawa in August did nothing to improve the worried man's spirits, the other members of the family decided that some drastic action was required. Renault and his brother-in-law, Dr. Mathieu Samson, spent a week trying to persuade him to resign, but he clung tenaciously to the argument that it was his duty to carry on, or at least to meet the Liberal caucus, and face his responsibility for the party's defeat. In desperation, they decided that the only solution was to prove to him that he was not indispensable. All the family had a deep admiration and affection for Pearson, and they knew that he would be strongly urged to contest the leadership when it became available. At the beginning of September they persuaded St. Laurent to send for him to discuss the situation. When Renault made the call, he asked Pearson to bring along Lionel Chevrier, who had been elected in Montreal-Laurier constituency, in order to avoid the impression that an English-speaking Canadian had come down and demanded the old man's resignation. Realizing the delicacy of his situation as a possible leadership candidate, the former Minister for External Affairs was only too happy to comply with the suggestion.

Mathieu Samson and Renault met the two men at the railway station in Quebec City at noon on September 3, and explained the situation to them during the drive to St. Patrick. They arrived late in the afternoon, and while they found the former Prime Minister looking older and tired, they were received by him and his wife with the usual courtesy. After a pleasant dinner, Jeanne St. Laurent and her sister-in-law, Lora, withdrew, and the men turned their attention to the purpose of the visit. Louis St. Laurent began the discussion by announcing at once that he agreed that he was no longer physically able to carry on as leader of the Liberal Party. Three questions were troubling him, he explained: would he be considered to be letting the party down if he resigned? Should he not go to Ottawa and face his colleagues before making a decision? And would the announcement of his retirement not be difficult to reconcile with a remark he had made to the press a few days earlier that he was going to carry on? The other four men spent the evening endeavouring to reassure him on all three points. They also spoke of the future leadership of the party, and St. Laurent asked Pearson for an assurance that he would agree to place his name before a leadership convention. Anxious to put the worried man at ease, Pearson gave the commitment that he would stand, if and when the top post in the party became vacant. Finally, it was decided that Pearson should draft an appropriate statement, announcing the former Prime Minister's intention to resign.

Pearson spent a good part of the night working on the draft.

He showed it to Chevrier at breakfast, and the latter approved it with one or two minor changes. At ten o'clock they presented it to St. Laurent, who read it over two or three times, and then declared that it was just right. There remained to be decided the matter of releasing it to the public. St. Laurent felt he should go to Ottawa, meet the press there, and submit himself to questions, or in his own words, 'face the music'. The others finally succeeded in convincing him that this was not necessary, and that the news release could be made in his absence from the office of the Leader of the Opposition. He was also concerned about his former colleagues learning of the decision through the news media; it was arranged that the staff in Ottawa should telephone them in advance of the announcement. When all his objections had been met and the arrangements made, Louis St. Laurent brightened noticeably; his wife and sister were radiant with relief and happiness, and served a regal meal to celebrate the occasion. Late in the afternoon of September 5, the statement was released:

> After careful consideration and in the light of medical advice . . .
> I have come to the conclusion that I no longer have the vigour
> and energy required to lead the party through a general
> election. . . . Health permitting, however, I will be happy to
> continue to serve as leader of the Liberal Party pending the
> choice of my successor at the convention which will, no doubt,
> soon be held. My regret at having to make this decision is
> equalled only by my conviction that it is the right one and that
> any other would not be fair to the party through which I have
> had the honour – and there can be no greater – to serve my
> country for so many years.

In response to the announcement, tributes and expressions of regret once again flowed in from across Canada and abroad. The news of his decision was received at Presqu'île just as a draft resolution was being circulated, calling for a leadership convention within six months. The proposal was quickly dropped, and replaced by a telegram of regret at the announcement, declaring him for good measure 'the greatest living Canadian'. C. D. Howe, already beginning a new business career, wrote to say that he was relieved at the news. 'The young men of the party must take on that job of reorganizing and rebuilding,' he commented, 'and perhaps the sooner they get at it the better.' One of St. Laurent's political opponents, Charlotte Whitton, described him in a newspaper column as 'a very great Canadian and a courtly Christian gentleman'. Ottawa would say *au revoir* with real regret, she stated, to 'the chevalier St. Laurent'.

A final stint of duty had still to be accomplished and once again Louis St. Laurent rose to the occasion. In late September, he returned to Ottawa and took up his duties as Leader of the Opposition. Declining the use of the residence provided for the occupant of his new post, he moved into a small suite in the Château Laurier. On October 11, three days before the opening of the new Parliament, he spoke to the Liberal caucus, outlining the tactics to be adopted during the first session. The Liberals should not offer any 'irresponsible obstruction' to the new administration, he declared. That did not mean that they should remain silent or refrain from questions and constructive criticism, but they should take care not to give the government an excuse for an election until its program had been placed before Parliament and debated properly. In short, the Liberal policy was to play for time to reorganize under a new leader.

In accordance with arrangements made by St. Laurent the previous spring, the Queen arrived in Canada in early October, and read the Speech from the Throne that marked the opening of the new Parliament. The message announced many of the measures that the Liberals had refused to carry out in recent years, including the South Saskatchewan dam, assistance to the Beechwood power project in New Brunswick, cash advances on farm-stored grain, and a larger old-age pension. Although he looked somewhat out of place on the Speaker's left, St. Laurent discharged his new functions with careful propriety, seconding the choice of the new Speaker and a resolution of 'loyalty and love' to Her Majesty, and leading off for the opposition in the Throne Speech debate. He had been disappointed in the results of the election, he confessed, but the Liberal Party accepted them 'loyally, without hesitation, in what we believe is the true spirit of our parliamentary system'. The ease with which the change of government had taken place would, he hoped, give many Cana-

dians 'a deeper faith in the strength of our parliamentary traditions and our parliamentary institutions'. He teased the new
ministers gently for statements some of them had made that they
had found little change necessary in their respective departments,
and he made one or two minor criticisms, but in a tone that made
it evident that he had no heart to lead an attack on the new
administration. The official opposition would not obstruct the
government in carrying out its election promises, he stated, and
the ministers would have no excuse for any failure to carry out
their program. When John Diefenbaker rose to reply, he referred
to St. Laurent twice as 'the Prime Minister'. The slip was reveal-
ing: despite the election result, the two men seemed to be on the
wrong sides of the Chamber.

Throughout the session, St. Laurent's attendance in the House
of Commons was even more regular than as Prime Minister, but
he spoke only when it was absolutely necessary, and then in short
prepared statements. Most of the time, he slumped in his front
row seat, reading and fingering his moustache, and looking, in the
words of one observer, 'like a collapsed effigy of himself'. Although
he appeared to be well, the strain of forcing himself to do his duty
to the last was beginning to have its effects; his stomach was giving
him pain again despite a strict diet, and a prostate condition was
poisoning his system. Fresh ideas and new challenges had no
appeal for him. In an effort to encourage him to look ahead, an
aide recalled Laurier's statement that as long as there were problems to be solved, there would be a need for a Liberal Party in
Canada, and remarked that Canada's urban areas offered un-
limited challenge to reformers. St. Laurent replied impatiently,
'There will always be people who need better housing, no matter
who is in power.'

The Liberal convention was held from January 14 to 16, 1957,
in the Ottawa Coliseum, where St. Laurent had received the
leadership nine and a half years earlier. Except for a Protestant
minister from Manitoba with no serious support, there were only
two candidates, Lester Pearson and Paul Martin, and the former
was a clear favourite from the outset. His chances had been even
further enhanced shortly before Christmas when he received the
Nobel Peace Prize for his contribution towards resolving the Suez

crisis. Although the St. Laurents favoured the former Minister for External Affairs, they observed an attitude of strict neutrality during the contest.

Louis St. Laurent made his final speech as party leader on the first evening of the meeting; his words were carried by television across the nation. 'In my own heart, I feel nothing but appreciation to my fellow citizens for the popular support we received in all three elections,' he declared, and the deepest gratitude for the loyalty and support of his fellow Liberals. Nor was he bitter about the party's defeat. 'As a Liberal I have always believed in the capacity and judgement of the ordinary people. And I carry that belief to the point of believing that when we do not carry the judgement of the people, the fault is in ourselves and not in the people. When that happens it means we need to get closer to the people.' He concluded his political career, as he had begun it, and as he had conducted it, on the theme of national unity.

> As I said in 1948, our nation was planned as a political partnership of two great races; it was planned by men of vision, of tolerance, as a partnership in which both of the partners would retain their essential characteristics, their religion, their language, their culture. To realize that plan, to make it work, has always required and still requires a practical recognition in government of the partnership of those two historic races.

In the previous ten years, the Canadian people had realized, more than ever before, that national unity was an essential foundation of effective action by government, and the large measure of unity attained in Canada had made possible the greatest period of development in the country's history. But, he warned, national unity was not just the absence of friction between Canadians of different races, religions, and regions; Liberal policies had created 'a positive unity based upon social security and social justice which have brought us closer to the ideal of equality of opportunity and have made Canadians realize more than ever before that it is good for us and our families that we are Canadians'. The words were Louis St. Laurent's political epitaph; they were also a chart bequeathed to his successors.

The reception given to the retiring leader was the most moving of the entire convention; for the moment, the delegates put aside their preoccupation with choosing a new chief and a new program, and revelled in the reflected glory of the man who had led them in the hour of their greatest triumphs. Faced with an uncertain future, they rejoiced in the accomplishments associated with his name, and identified themselves with the qualities of honesty, patriotism, and high-mindedness that had marked his leadership of the Liberal Party. Even in defeat, he was the most respected man in Canada. Unhappily, he alone refused to recognize that fact. Convinced that he had been unequal to their trust, and had failed in the highest duty ever asked of him, he interpreted the accolades as designed to assuage his feelings and give him the opportunity of a graceful exit to oblivion. He stepped down from the highest elective office in the land, after nine and a half years of fame and praise, as humble and unassuming as when he was a storekeeper's son in the Eastern Townships.

Throughout the convention, St. Laurent fulfilled his role with the thoroughness and punctuality that were part of his nature. Only after Pearson was chosen to succeed him did he allow himself to relax. Immediately, the signs of accumulated years of fatigue became evident. A winter rain was falling as he prepared to leave the Coliseum, late in the evening of January 16, to return to the hotel. He was helped into his coat, but his black Homburg had disappeared from the improvised cloakroom. Fretting to be off, he paced up and down, restless and bewildered, while friends and members of the family tried to dissuade him from going out bare-headed into the storm. Suddenly he was a helpless, spent, old man. After a few minutes, the missing hat was discovered and he was able to leave.

On the following Monday, he had to go through the final emotional experience of handing over the position of Leader of the Opposition to Pearson. He had enjoyed the fellowship of the House of Commons, he confessed with a note of regret; 'though we do differ on many occasions . . . each one is endeavouring to do that which he thinks is in the best interests of his fellow citizens, and that is our only justification for occupying places in this

House.' For a brief moment, he revealed something of his inner turmoil:

> Of course, we do all make mistakes, but I hope the mistakes can always be overlooked, if not forgotten, as generously as they have been this afternoon. . . . That being so, I can say to those who are much younger than I that there is a great satisfaction, in spite of our human frailties, in the feeling that as members of this House one can have the opportunity to be of some service to this great country.

When the tributes were over, Pearson rose to make his first speech as party leader. He was in a difficult position. A supply motion had been called for that day, and he had the usual opportunity of proposing a non-confidence motion. If he did so, he would offer Diefenbaker the opportunity to dissolve Parliament, and the near-certainty of obtaining a large majority in a new election. If he did not, he would be accused of cowardice, and his fighting speech in accepting the leadership a few nights earlier would appear to have been a mere sham. He compromised; after making a vigorous attack on the government, he argued that it was not in the public interest to have a second election at the moment, and demanded that the Tories 'submit their resignation forthwith', implying that the Liberals should be returned to their rightful places to the right of the Speaker. Cries of derisive laughter from the Progressive Conservative benches greeted the proposal, and Pearson realized even before he resumed his seat that he had made a terrible mistake. John Diefenbaker spent the next two hours cutting the proposal, and the new Leader of the Opposition, to ribbons.

Louis St. Laurent spoke once more in the House of Commons, in his capacity as Liberal spokesman on federal-provincial relations. At a conference in November, the new federal government had offered to increase the provinces' share of direct taxes, and to grant further assistance to the Atlantic provinces. Still holding himself erect, and speaking in calm, measured tones, he indicated that the official opposition would support the measure. On February 1, 1958, his seventy-sixth birthday, Parliament was dissolved, without the government having been defeated. The next day he went home to Quebec. By the time the election campaign began, his family had taken him away to Florida. As his friend and successor went through the darkest hours of his career, Louis St. Laurent was too ill and exhausted to be of any assistance to him.

The reaction to the election defeat lasted for over a year. The accumulated fatigue, accentuated by a sense of failure, produced in St. Laurent a feeling of lethargy and uselessness that prevented him from either resuming his long-abandoned law practice or enjoying a well-earned retirement. He refused to write his memoirs, insisting that he had done nothing worth recording. He did not feel that he could plead before the courts again, since he had recommended the appointment of most of the judges, and was afraid of placing them in an embarrassing position by having to decide for or against his clients. When he was summoned to Ottawa in 1941, he had been putting together a lucrative portfolio of directorships; at seventy-six years of age and in poor health, he felt it was too late to build up his personal income again, and his pension as a former member of Parliament was a mere three thousand dollars a year. The advice he had received from his mother, and repeated on so many occasions, that a man can only do his best, and let Providence see to the rest, brought no comfort in his hour of greatest need. Although he was home in Quebec City at last, his family were unable to comfort him. Thus, the man who had been a father-figure to a whole generation of Canadians was dispirited and alone.

Two developments helped to stir St. Laurent out of his unhappy state. In the spring of 1959, he was at last persuaded to have a complete medical examination. The doctors at the Boston hospital he visited informed him that a prostate operation was several years overdue and convinced him, not without some difficulty, to have it performed. It was a complete success. He was already beginning to feel better when Renault, who was not only head of the family law firm but also vice-president of the Canadian Bar Association, suffered a second heart attack. Jean-Paul having emigrated to Florida after being defeated in 1958, Louis St. Laurent was needed again. Reacting as he had always done to the call of duty, he resumed his place as head of the family and the firm, and was soon filling both roles again with much of his old vigour and enthusiasm. He accepted several directorships and became chairman of the board of one of the biggest cement firms in Canada. He also agreed to serve as president of the Canadian Heart Foundation, a public service he carried out with his usual devotion. By the summer of 1961, he began to feel, in his own words, that perhaps the Canadian people had forgiven him for his faults and shortcomings. Asked by a shoe salesman one day what was the secret of his good health and spirits, he answered chipperly: 'Get defeated in an election!' That same summer, he allowed the Canadian Broadcasting Corporation to interview him for a series of television programs. Sitting under the trees beside his St. Patrick residence, he recalled with pleasure his years in office. 'It's difficult to admit,' he commented in conclusion, 'but it always gives one satisfaction to speak of oneself.' The wounds of 1957 were healing, and he was finding peace.

On occasion, St. Laurent broke his silence and agreed to speak in public. At a mammoth Liberal rally in Ottawa in January 1961, he paid tribute to C. D. Howe, who had died suddenly of a heart attack a few days earlier, and he threw his prestige once more behind the Liberal cause. In his address, he praised the new government in Quebec under his former protégé, Jean Lesage, who, he declared, had 'put the isolation of Quebec behind him', and was 'exploring the new frontiers of the Canadian nation'. When he proposed a resolution of confidence in Lester Pearson, it was impossible to determine which man received the more enthusiastic demonstration of support and loyalty. In November 1961, he delivered a lecture at Sir George Williams University in Montreal. Against the background of the new separatist movement in Quebec, he appealed once again for 'a genuine spirit of national unity in Canada'. His message was the same one that he had been preaching for several decades, he commented, but it still remained his greatest aspiration. He welcomed the new ferment at work in the province of Quebec, not merely as the effervescence of a few 'angry young men', but 'as evidence of a deeper concern about many aspects of our social institutions and a more realistic concept of every individual's personal responsibility to make his or her contribution to meet, courageously and fruitfully, the challenges of changing conditions'. At the same time, he was as convinced as ever that the separation of Quebec from the rest of Canada was not a 'panacea' that would cure all the ills blamed on Confederation; nor would answers to the serious problems still to be solved between the two principal ethnic groups of Canadians be found by 'dogmatic pronouncements'. He regretted that almost a century after Confederation, there still was not real equality of opportunity for all young Canadians in the national economy, and attributed that unfortunate situation to the fact that bilingualism had not yet become accepted as a positive factor in the individual and collective life of Canadians. He suggested that the Canadian government make it known that, 'as a matter of national policy . . . after a certain number of years . . . it would be a required qualification for aspirants to high posts in the . . . federal civil service to be able to use both of our official languages'. If that were done, 'bilingualism in the top levels of our governmental and large industrial and business undertakings would soon, and without any noticeable hardship to anyone, become a practical as well as a legal characteristic of our Canadian society'. The new problems, and the rapidly changing conditions, did not alter his belief that 'it did in fact enter into the decree of Providence that our two main races and those who have joined us in this great land should henceforth live in peace and harmony and form one federated state on the basis of that absolute equality asserted by Sir John A. Macdonald and Sir Wilfrid Laurier'.

By the time Louis St. Laurent celebrated his eightieth birthday in February 1962, Renault was well again, and assuming his duties as head of the law firm. He was also president of the Canadian Bar Association, and making his own speeches on the advantages to Canada of having a legal system based on two of the greatest schools of jurisprudence in the world. The plan that father and son had laid so carefully half a century earlier had been carried out, to the letter. Louis St. Laurent had also regained his confidence and buoyancy. 'You can say that on my eightieth birthday I'll be just as optimistic about Canada as I was on my twenty-first,' he told a reporter the day before he celebrated that anniversary. In 1965 the firm moved into a new skyscraper office building directly opposite his residence on Grande Allée; he continued to put in a day's work as senior counsel. In an interview in late 1965 he stated:

> For the future of Canada it would be very necessary for Quebec to remain a part of Canada; for Quebec to separate would be a serious decrease in our family. I don't think that without Quebec Canada would have any standing in the family of nations; and certainly Quebec alone would have no standing in the family of nations.

The years of retirement from public life were happy ones for Jeanne St. Laurent. In Quebec City and, during the summers, at St. Patrick, she was able to devote all her time to her home and family. As in the first years of their married life, Louis St. Laurent spent as many evenings as possible with her, reading, playing cards, and now, watching television. They often received visits from their children, grandchildren, and the growing number of great-grandchildren, and kept in close touch with them by telephone. But, though she was the younger of the two by several years, Jeanne St. Laurent's health began to fail in the 1960s, and after an illness of several months she died on November 14, 1966, in the house they had designed and built together more than half a century earlier.

Louis St. Laurent continued to spend his days at the law office, at directors' meetings, or, occasionally, at public functions. In December 1966, a few weeks before his eighty-fifth birthday, he attended the launching in Montreal of a new Canadian ice-breaker that was to bear his name. It was a touching and symbolic ceremony. Surrounded by members of his family and former cabinet colleagues, including Prime Minister Pearson, Minister of Transport J. W. Pickersgill, and Walter Harris, he waved to the crew on deck as the vessel moved down the slip and into the waters of the St. Lawrence River. His public service was over, but men whom he had trained, and inspired by his personal and public conduct, were carrying on the government of Canada, and serving the ideals that had guided him for so long. Like the C.C.G.S. *Louis S. St. Laurent*, the Canadian ship of state would bear his mark for many years to come.

## APPENDIX I

## The Mackenzie King Ministry
### December 10, 1941, to November 15, 1948*

PRIME MINISTER

The Right Honourable William Lyon Mackenzie King

| Composition of Ministry, December 10, 1941 | | Appointed | Retired |
|---|---|---|---|
| President of the Privy Council | Rt. Hon. William Lyon Mackenzie King | Oct. 23, 1935 | Nov. 15, 1948 |
| Secretary of State for External Affairs | Rt. Hon. William Lyon Mackenzie King | Oct. 23, 1935 | Sept. 3, 1946 |
| Minister of Mines and Resources | Hon. Thomas Alexander Crerar | Dec. 1, 1936 | Apr. 17, 1945 |
| Minister of Justice and Attorney General | Hon. Louis Stephen St. Laurent | Dec. 10, 1941 | Dec. 9, 1946 |
| Minister of Public Works | Hon. Pierre Joseph Arthur Cardin | Oct. 23, 1935 | May 12, 1942 |
| Minister of Finance and Receiver General | Hon. James Lorimer Ilsley | July 8, 1940 | Dec. 9, 1946 |
| Postmaster General | Hon. William Pate Mulock | July 8, 1940 | June 8, 1945 |
| Minister of Trade and Commerce | Hon. James Angus MacKinnon | May 9, 1940 | Jan. 18, 1948 |
| Secretary of State of Canada | Hon. Pierre François Casgrain | May 10, 1940 | Dec. 14, 1941 |
| Minister of National Defence | Hon. James Layton Ralston | July 5, 1940 | Nov. 1, 1944 |
| Associate Minister of National Defence | Hon. Charles Gavan Power | July 12, 1940 | Nov. 26, 1944 |
| Minister of National Defence for Air | Hon. Charles Gavan Power | May 23, 1940 | Nov. 26, 1944 |
| Minister of National Defence for Naval Services | Hon. Angus Lewis Macdonald | July 12, 1940 | Apr. 17, 1945 |
| Minister of Pensions and National Health | Hon. Ian Alistair Mackenzie | Sept. 19, 1939 | Oct. 12, 1944 |
| Minister of National Revenue | Hon. Colin William George Gibson | July 8, 1940 | Mar. 7, 1945 |
| Minister of Fisheries | Hon. Joseph Enoil Michaud | Oct. 23, 1935 | Oct. 5, 1942 |
| Minister of Labour | Hon. Norman Alexander McLarty | Sept. 19, 1939 | Dec. 14, 1941 |
| Minister of Transport | Hon. Pierre Joseph Arthur Cardin | July 8, 1940 | May 12, 1942 |
| Minister of Munitions and Supply | Hon. Clarence Decatur Howe | Apr. 9, 1940 | Dec. 31, 1945 |
| Minister of Agriculture | Hon. James Garfield Gardiner | Oct. 28, 1935 | Nov. 15, 1948 |
| Solicitor General | Vacant | Oct. 23, 1935 | Apr. 17, 1945 |
| Minister of National War Services | Hon. Joseph Thorarinn Thorson | June 11, 1941 | Oct. 5, 1942 |
| Minister without Portfolio | Hon. Raoul Dandurand | Oct. 23, 1935 | Mar. 11, 1942 |

*Ministry formed October 23, 1935

## Changes in Composition of Ministry December 10, 1941, to November 15, 1948

| Office | Minister | From | To |
|---|---|---|---|
| Secretary of State for External Affairs | Rt. Hon. Louis Stephen St. Laurent | Sept. 4, 1946 | Sept. 9, 1948 |
| | Hon. Lester Bowles Pearson | Sept. 10, 1948 | Nov. 15, 1948 |
| Minister of Mines and Resources | Hon. James Allison Glen | Apr. 18, 1945 | June 10, 1948 |
| | Hon. James Angus MacKinnon | June 11, 1948 | Nov. 15, 1948 |
| Minister of Justice and Attorney General | Rt. Hon. James Lorimer Ilsley | Dec. 10, 1946 | June 30, 1948 |
| | Rt. Hon. Louis Stephen St. Laurent (Acting Minister July 1–Sept. 9, 1948) | July 1, 1948 | Nov. 15, 1948 |
| Minister of Public Works | Hon. Joseph Enoil Michaud (Acting Minister) | May 13, 1942 | Oct. 5, 1942 |
| | Hon. Alphonse Fournier | Oct. 6, 1942 | Nov. 15, 1948 |
| Minister of Finance and Receiver General | Hon. Douglas Charles Abbott | Dec. 10, 1946 | Nov. 15, 1948 |
| Postmaster General | Hon. Colin William George Gibson (Acting Minister) | June 9, 1945 | Aug. 28, 1945 |
| | Hon. Ernest Bertrand | Aug. 29, 1945 | Nov. 15, 1948 |
| Minister of Trade and Commerce | Rt. Hon. Clarence Decatur Howe | Jan. 19, 1948 | Nov. 15, 1948 |
| Secretary of State of Canada | Hon. Norman Alexander McLarty | Dec. 15, 1941 | Apr. 17, 1945 |
| | Hon. Paul Joseph James Martin | Apr. 18, 1945 | Dec. 11, 1946 |
| | Hon. Colin William George Gibson | Dec. 12, 1946 | Nov. 15, 1948 |
| Minister of National Defence | Hon. Andrew George Latta McNaughton | Nov. 2, 1944 | Aug. 20, 1945 |
| | Hon. Douglas Charles Abbott | Aug. 21, 1945 | Dec. 11, 1946 |
| | Hon. Brooke Claxton | Dec. 12, 1946 | Nov. 15, 1948 |
| Minister of National Defence for Air | Vacant | Nov. 27, 1944 | Nov. 29, 1944 |
| | Hon. Angus Lewis Macdonald (Acting Minister) | Nov. 30, 1944 | Jan. 10, 1945 |
| | Hon. Colin William George Gibson | Jan. 11, 1945 | Dec. 11, 1946 |
| Minister of National Defence for Naval Services | Hon. Douglas Charles Abbott | Apr. 18, 1945 | Dec. 11, 1946 |
| Minister of Veterans' Affairs | Rt. Hon. Ian Alistair Mackenzie | Oct. 13, 1944 | Jan. 18, 1948 |
| | Hon. Milton Fowler Gregg | Jan. 19, 1948 | Nov. 15, 1948 |

| Position | Name | | |
|---|---|---|---|
| Minister of National Health and Welfare | Hon. Brooke Claxton | Oct. 13, 1944 | Dec. 11, 1946 |
| | Hon. Paul Joseph James Martin | Dec. 12, 1946 | Nov. 15, 1948 |
| Minister of National Revenue | Hon. James Angus MacKinnon (Acting Minister) | Mar. 8, 1945 | Apr. 17, 1945 |
| | Hon. David Laurence MacLaren (Acting Minister) | Apr. 18, 1945 | July 29, 1945 |
| | Hon. James Angus MacKinnon (Acting Minister) | July 30, 1945 | Aug. 28, 1945 |
| Minister of Fisheries | Hon. James Joseph McCann | Aug. 29, 1945 | Nov. 15, 1948 |
| | Hon. Ernest Bertrand | Oct. 6, 1942 | Aug. 28, 1945 |
| | Hon. Hedley Francis Gregory Bridges | Aug. 29, 1945 | Aug. 10, 1947 |
| | Vacant | Aug. 11, 1947 | Aug. 13, 1947 |
| | Hon. Ernest Bertrand (Acting Minister) | Aug. 14, 1947 | Sept. 1, 1947 |
| | Hon. Milton Fowler Gregg | Sept. 2, 1947 | Jan. 18, 1948 |
| | Hon. James Angus MacKinnon | Jan. 19, 1948 | June 10, 1948 |
| | Hon. Robert Wellington Mayhew | June 11, 1948 | Nov. 15, 1948 |
| Minister of Labour | Hon. Humphrey Mitchell | Dec. 15, 1941 | Nov. 15, 1948 |
| Minister of Transport | Hon. Clarence Decatur Howe (Acting Minister) | May 13, 1942 | Oct. 5, 1942 |
| Minister of Reconstruction | Hon. Joseph Enoil Michaud | Oct. 6, 1942 | Apr. 17, 1945 |
| | Hon. Lionel Chevrier | Apr. 18, 1945 | Nov. 15, 1948 |
| Minister of Reconstruction and Supply | Hon. Clarence Decatur Howe | Oct. 13, 1944 | Dec. 31, 1945 |
| | Rt. Hon. Clarence Decatur Howe | Jan. 1, 1946 | Nov. 15, 1948 |
| Solicitor General | Hon. Joseph Jean | Apr. 18, 1945 | Nov. 15, 1948 |
| Minister of National War Services | Hon. Léo Richer LaFlèche | Oct. 6, 1942 | Apr. 17, 1945 |
| | Hon. James Joseph McCann | Apr. 18, 1945 | Jan. 18, 1948 |
| Minister without Portfolio | Hon. James Horace King (Leader of Government in Senate) | May 26, 1942 | Aug. 23, 1945 |
| | Hon. Wishart McLea Robertson (Leader of Government in Senate) | Aug. 29, 1945 | Nov. 15, 1948 |

## The St. Laurent Ministry
### November 15, 1948, to June 21, 1957

PRIME MINISTER

### The Right Honourable Louis Stephen St. Laurent

THE MINISTRY

| | | Appointed | Retired |
|---|---|---|---|
| President of the Privy Council | Rt. Hon. Louis Stephen St. Laurent | Nov. 15, 1948 | Apr. 24, 1957 |
| | Hon. Lionel Chevrier | Apr. 25, 1957 | June 21, 1957 |
| Minister of Trade and Commerce | Rt. Hon. Clarence Decatur Howe | Nov. 15, 1948 | June 21, 1957 |
| Minister of Agriculture | Rt. Hon. James Garfield Gardiner | Nov. 15, 1948 | June 21, 1957 |
| Minister of Mines and Resources | Hon. James Angus MacKinnon | Nov. 15, 1948 | Mar. 31, 1949 |
| | Hon. Colin Gibson | Apr. 1, 1949 | Jan. 16, 1950 |
| Secretary of State of Canada | Hon. Colin Gibson | Nov. 15, 1948 | Mar. 31, 1949 |
| | Hon. Frederick Gordon Bradley | Apr. 1, 1949 | June 11, 1953 |
| | Hon. John Whitney Pickersgill | June 12, 1953 | June 30, 1954 |
| | Hon. Roch Pinard | July 1, 1954 | June 21, 1957 |
| Minister of Labour | Hon. Humphrey Mitchell | Nov. 15, 1948 | Aug. 2, 1950 |
| | Hon. Paul Joseph James Martin (Acting Minister) | Aug. 3, 1950 | Aug. 6, 1950 |
| | Hon. Milton Fowler Gregg | Aug. 7, 1950 | June 21, 1957 |
| Minister of Public Works | Hon. Alphonse Fournier | Nov. 15, 1948 | June 11, 1953 |
| | Hon. Walter Edward Harris (Acting Minister) | June 12, 1953 | Sept. 16, 1953 |
| | Hon. Robert Henry Winters | Sept. 17, 1953 | June 21, 1957 |

| Office | Name | | |
|---|---|---|---|
| Postmaster General | Hon. Ernest Bertrand | Nov. 15, 1948 | Aug. 23, 1949 |
| | Hon. Gabriel Edouard Rinfret | Aug. 24, 1949 | Feb. 12, 1952 |
| | Hon. Alcide Côté | Feb. 13, 1952 | Aug. 7, 1955 |
| | Vacant | Aug. 8, 1955 | Aug. 15, 1955 |
| | Hon. Roch Pinard (Acting Minister) | Aug. 16, 1955 | Nov. 2, 1955 |
| | Hon. Hugues Lapointe | Nov. 3, 1955 | June 21, 1957 |
| Minister of National Defence | Hon. Brooke Claxton | Nov. 15, 1948 | June 30, 1954 |
| | Hon. Ralph Osborne Campney | July 1, 1954 | June 21, 1957 |
| Associate Minister of National Defence | Hon. Ralph Osborne Campney | Feb. 12, 1953 | June 30, 1954 |
| | Vacant | July 1, 1954 | Apr. 24, 1957 |
| | Hon. Paul Theodore Hellyer | Apr. 25, 1957 | June 21, 1957 |
| Solicitor General | Hon. Joseph Jean | Nov. 15, 1948 | Aug. 23, 1949 |
| | Hon. Hugues Lapointe | Aug. 24, 1949 | Aug. 6, 1950 |
| | Vacant | Aug. 7, 1950 | Oct. 14, 1952 |
| | Hon. Ralph Osborne Campney | Oct. 15, 1952 | Jan. 11, 1954 |
| | Hon. William Ross Macdonald (Leader of Government in Senate) | Jan. 12, 1954 | June 21, 1957 |
| Minister of Transport | Hon. Lionel Chevrier | Nov. 15, 1948 | June 30, 1954 |
| | Hon. George Carlyle Marler | July 1, 1954 | June 21, 1957 |
| Minister of National Health and Welfare | Hon. Paul Joseph James Martin | Nov. 15, 1948 | June 21, 1957 |
| Minister of Finance | Hon. Douglas Charles Abbott | Nov. 15, 1948 | June 30, 1954 |
| | Hon. Walter Edward Harris | July 1, 1954 | June 21, 1957 |
| Minister of National Revenue | Hon. James Joseph McCann | Nov. 15, 1948 | June 21, 1957 |
| Minister of Veterans' Affairs | Hon. Milton Fowler Gregg | Nov. 15, 1948 | Aug. 6, 1950 |
| | Hon. Hugues Lapointe | Aug. 7, 1950 | June 21, 1957 |
| Minister of Fisheries | Hon. Robert Wellington Mayhew | Nov. 15, 1948 | Oct. 14, 1952 |
| | Hon. James Sinclair | Oct. 15, 1952 | June 21, 1957 |
| Secretary of State for External Affairs | Hon. Lester Bowles Pearson | Nov. 15, 1948 | June 21, 1957 |

| | | | |
|---|---|---|---|
| Minister of Justice and Attorney General | Hon. Stuart Sinclair Garson | Nov. 15, 1948 | June 21, 1957 |
| Minister of Reconstruction and Supply | Hon. Robert Henry Winters | Nov. 15, 1948 | Jan. 17, 1950 |
| Minister of Resources and Development | Hon. Robert Henry Winters | Jan. 18, 1950 | Sept. 16, 1953 |
| | Hon. Jean Lesage | Sept. 17, 1953 | Dec. 15, 1953 |
| Minister of Northern Affairs and National Resources | Hon. Jean Lesage | Dec. 16, 1953 | June 21, 1957 |
| Member of the Administration and Minister without Portfolio | Hon. Wishart McLea Robertson (Leader of Government in Senate) | Nov. 15, 1948 | Oct. 13, 1953 |
| | Hon. James Angus MacKinnon (Senator) | Apr. 1, 1949 | Dec. 13, 1950 |
| | Hon. William Ross Macdonald (Leader of Government in Senate) | Oct. 14, 1953 | Jan. 11, 1954 |
| Minister of Mines and Technical Surveys | Hon. James Joseph McCann | Jan. 18, 1950 | Dec. 12, 1950 |
| | Hon. George Prudham | Dec. 13, 1950 | June 21, 1957 |
| Minister of Citizenship and Immigration | Hon. Walter Edward Harris | Jan. 18, 1950 | June 30, 1954 |
| | Hon. John Whitney Pickersgill | July 1, 1954 | June 21, 1957 |
| Minister of Defence Production | Rt. Hon. Clarence Decatur Howe | Apr. 1, 1951 | June 21, 1957 |

# APPENDIX II

## Provincial Administrations Dec. 10, 1941, to June 21, 1957

| Years of Ministry | Premier | Date of Appointment | Party |
|---|---|---|---|
| **ALBERTA** | | | |
| 1935–1943 | William Aberhart | September 3, 1935 | Social Credit |
| 1943– | E. C. Manning | May 31, 1943 | Social Credit |
| **BRITISH COLUMBIA** | | | |
| 1933–1941 | T. D. Pattullo | November 15, 1933 | Liberal |
| 1941–1947 | John Hart | December 9, 1941 | Coalition |
| 1947–1952 | Herbert Anscomb | December 29, 1947 | Coalition |
| 1952 | Byron Johnson | January 18, 1952 | Coalition |
| 1952– | W. A. C. Bennett | August 1, 1952 | Social Credit |
| **QUEBEC** | | | |
| 1939–1944 | Adélard Godbout | November 8, 1939 | Liberal |
| 1944–1959 | Maurice Duplessis | August 30, 1944 | Union Nationale |
| **MANITOBA** | | | |
| 1922–1943 | John Bracken | August 8, 1922 | United Farmer<br>Progressive<br>Coalition |
| 1943–1948 | S. S. Garson | January 8, 1943 | Coalition |
| 1948–1958 | D. L. Campbell | November 7, 1948 | Liberal |
| **NEW BRUNSWICK** | | | |
| 1940–1952 | J. B. McNair | March 13, 1940 | Liberal |
| 1952–1960 | H. J. Flemming | October 8, 1952 | Conservative |

| Years of Ministry | Premier | Date of Appointment | Party |
|---|---|---|---|
| NEWFOUNDLAND | | | |
| 1949– | Joseph R. Smallwood | April 1, 1949 | Liberal |
| NOVA SCOTIA | | | |
| 1940–1945 | A. S. MacMillan | July 10, 1940 | Liberal |
| 1945–1954 | Angus L. Macdonald | September 8, 1945 | Liberal |
| 1954 | Harold Connelly | April 13, 1954 | Liberal |
| 1954–1956 | Henry D. Hicks | September 30, 1954 | Liberal |
| 1956– | Robert L. Stanfield | September 20, 1956 | Conservative |
| ONTARIO | | | |
| 1934–1942 | M. F. Hepburn | July 10, 1934 | Liberal |
| 1942–1943 | G. D. Conant | October 21, 1942 | Liberal |
| 1943 | H. C. Nixon | May 18, 1943 | Liberal |
| 1943–1948 | George Drew | August 17, 1943 | Conservative |
| 1948–1949 | T. L. Kennedy | October 19, 1948 | Conservative |
| 1949–1961 | Leslie M. Frost | May 4, 1949 | Conservative |
| PRINCE EDWARD ISLAND | | | |
| 1936–1943 | Thane A. Campbell | January 14, 1936 | Liberal |
| 1943–1953 | J. Walter Jones | May 11, 1943 | Liberal |
| 1953–1959 | A. W. Matheson | May 25, 1953 | Liberal |
| SASKATCHEWAN | | | |
| 1935–1944 | W. J. Patterson | November 1, 1935 | Liberal |
| 1944–1964 | T. C. Douglas | July 10, 1944 | Co-operative Commonwealth Federation |

# References

CHAPTER 1  CALL TO DUTY

6  15  J. W. Pickersgill, *The Mackenzie King Record*, Vol. 1, 1939-44, University of Toronto Press, Toronto, 1960, p. 284.

7   8  Interview with Mr. Justice R. Ouimet.

34  J. W. Pickersgill, *op. cit.*, p. 288.

8  14  Interview with Mme Renée Vautelet.

9   5  J. W. Pickersgill, *op. cit.*, p. 290.

19  *Loc. cit.*

11  5  J. W. Pickersgill, *op. cit.*, p. 291.

26  *Ibid.*, p. 293.

12  18  Interview with W. Turnbull.

26  *Ibid.*

32  J. W. Pickersgill, *op. cit.*, p. 293.

16  11  Interview with the Hon. P. Sévigny.

18  *Time* Magazine, Sept. 12, 1949.

17   3  Interview with Mr. Justice W. Scott.

23  J. W. Pickersgill, *op. cit.*, p. 294.

31  *Loc. cit.*

18  27  Montreal *Gazette*, Dec. 11, 1941.

CHAPTER 2
EASTERN TOWNSHIPS BOY

21  30  L. S. Channell, *History of Compton County, 1692-1896*, Cookshire, Quebec, 1896, p. 11.

22  30  *Le Progrès de l'Est*, June 12, 1875.

38  *Ibid.*, Feb. 23, 1877.

25  29  Interview with Miss A. Gillard, Compton Academy.

27  16  Interview with Miss Lora St. Laurent.

28  31  Statement, Jan. 29, 1951.

30   2  Interview with resident of Compton, November 1963.

34  19  Interview with Mr. Justice Rolland Millar.

35  20  *Annuaire du Séminaire*, 1895.

36  22  Interview with Father Léon Marcotte.

39   2  Manuscript in possession of Miss Lora St. Laurent.

21  *Régistres de l'Académie St-Barthélémi*, Oct. 6, 1898.

36  *Ibid.*, Jan. 5, 1899.

40  28  *Régistre des Chroniques du Séminaire*, 1901.

41   5  *Le Progrès de l'Est*, Jan. 16, 1900.

42  23  C.B.C. interview.

## 544    LOUIS ST. LAURENT

*Page Line*
**45** 35 Sherbrooke *Daily Record,*
Oct. 1, 1904.
**46** 4 Recalled by Théo. Paquet.
**48** 2 Sherbrooke *Daily Record,*
Nov. 24, 1904.
**50** 2 *Ibid.,* June 20, 1904.
3 Quoted in *ibid.,* June 21, 1904.

CHAPTER 3    UP THE LADDER

**52** 30 *Liberty* Magazine, March 1956.
**53** 12 Recalled by St. Laurent.
**55** 3 *La Patrie,* Jan. 29, 1950.
**56** 15 Recalled by St. Laurent.
**57** 1 Recalled by St. Laurent.
**58** 13 Interview with the Hon.
Antonin Galipeault.
**61** 4 Recalled by St. Laurent.
31 Recalled by St. Laurent.
**68** 30 Interview with Mr. Justice
W. Scott.
**69** 6 Interview with Warwick
Chipman.
**70** 3 Ernest Lapointe Papers, J.-F.
Pouliot to Lapointe, Nov. 22,
1938.
**71** 29 R. A. Olmstead, *Decisions of
the Judicial Committee of the
Privy Council,* Vol. 2, p. 255ff.
**72** 18 A.C.P., 1928, p. 187.
**74** 36 *Ibid.,* 1937, p. 377.

CHAPTER 4    IN PUBLIC VIEW

**82** 16 *Report of the Proceedings of
the Canadian Bar Association,*
1920.
**83** 32 Address to the Empire Club of
Toronto, Nov. 25, 1920.
**84** 11 Toronto *Globe,* Nov. 26, 1920.
24 *Le Soleil,* Oct. 23, 1925.
30 *Ibid.,* July 8, 1926.
**85** 13 *Ibid.,* Sept. 10, 1926.
**86** 25 *Ibid.,* June 5, 1929.
34 *Report of the Proceedings of
the Canadian Bar Association,*
1929.
**88** 12 *Le Soleil,* Oct. 4, 1929.
**89** 18 *Report of the Proceedings of
the Canadian Bar Association,*
1930.
35 *Ibid.*
**90** 24 *Report of the Proceedings of
the Canadian Bar Association,*
1931.

*Page Line*
**92** 5 *Report of the Proceedings of
the Canadian Bar Association,*
1932.
**93** 7 *Le Borroméen,* Sherbrooke,
September 1933 (St. Charles
Seminary publication).
**94** 2 *Winnipeg Free Press,* May 16,
1935.
14 *La Nation,* first edition, Feb.
15, 1936.
16 *Ibid.,* Feb. 22, 1936.
20 *Ibid.,* Dec. 16, 1937.
23 *Le Soleil,* Dec. 20, 1937.
37 *Le Borroméen,* September
1938.
**95** 8 *Report of the Royal Commission on Dominion-Provincial
Relations,* Ottawa, 1940.
**96** 9 *Transcript of Proceedings of
Royal Commission on Dominion-Provincial Relations,*
Library of Parliament, Ottawa.
26 *Winnipeg Free Press,* Dec. 1,
1937.
**97** 6 *Ibid.,* Dec. 13, 1937.
8 *Ibid.,* Dec. 8, 1937.
10 *Ibid.,* Dec. 14, 1937.
36 *Le Soleil,* Jan. 7, 1938.
**99** 11 Interview with Mr. Justice
Boisvert, Sherbrooke, Quebec.
20 *Le Soleil,* May 13, 1938.
**100** 3 *Transcript of Proceedings of
Royal Commission on Dominion-Provincial Relations,* Library of Parliament, Ottawa.
**103** 6 *Le Soleil,* Sept. 25, 1939; Oct. 5,
1939.
20 *Ibid.,* Oct. 6, 1939.
26 *Ibid.,* Oct. 10, 1939.
**104** 25 *Ibid.,* June 2, 1939.
32 Letter dated May 5, 1941.
36 *Le Soleil,* June 26, 1941.
**105** 12 *Loc. cit.*

CHAPTER 5    CONSCRIPT

**106** 2 J. W. Pickersgill, *op. cit.,*
p. 306ff.
**108** 4 *Ibid.,* p. 303.
18 *Ibid.,* pp. 294-5.
**109** 15 *Le Soleil,* Dec. 13, 1941.
**110** 27 *Ibid.,* Dec. 23, 1941.
**111** 37 *Ibid.,* Jan. 13, 1942.
**112** 14 J. W. Pickersgill, *op. cit.,*
p. 313ff.

*Page Line*

35  *Le Soleil*, Jan. 22, 1942.

113  1  *Ibid.*, Jan. 27, 1942.

8  J. W. Pickersgill, *op. cit.*, p. 342.

114  1  *Le Soleil*, Feb. 3, 1942.

115  7  *Ibid.*, Feb. 4, 1942; *Montreal Star*, Feb. 2, 1942; Quebec *Chronicle-Telegraph*, Feb. 5, 1942.

19  *Le Soleil*, Feb. 5, 1942; Quebec *Chronicle-Telegraph*, Feb. 5, 1942.

117  29  Pamphlet dated Feb. 6, 1942.

119  1  *Le Soleil*, Feb. 10, 1942.

15  J. W. Pickersgill, *op. cit.*, pp. 348-9.

120  33  C.B.C. broadcast, March 24, 1942.

121  1  *Le Soleil*, April 18, 1942.

18  J. W. Pickersgill, *op. cit.*, p. 364.

22  *Ibid.*, p. 365.

122  33  *Ibid.*, p. 377.

37  *House of Commons Debates*, June 10, 1942, p. 3236.

123  8  *Ibid.*, June 15, 1942, p. 3333.

18  J. W. Pickersgill, *op. cit.*, p. 382ff.

33  *H. of C. Debates*, June 16, 1942, p. 3389ff.

125  15  J. W. Pickersgill, *op. cit.*, p. 390.

24  *H. of C. Debates*, June 16, 1942, p. 3389.

28  *Globe and Mail*, June 19, 1942.

36  J. W. Pickersgill, *op. cit.*, p. 397ff.

126  25  *H. of C. Debates*, June 5, 1942, p. 3094.

27  J. W. Pickersgill, *op. cit.*, pp. 404-5.

35  *H. of C. Debates*, July 10, 1942, p. 4096.

127  10  *Ibid.*, July 13, 1942, p. 4134.

19  Quoted in *ibid.*, July 28, 1942, p. 4870.

128  4  *New World*, December 1942.

129  28  J. W. Pickersgill, *op. cit.*, pp. 442-4.

130  11  *Ibid.*, p. 445.

131  4  Address to the Canadian Club of Quebec, Oct. 21, 1942.

11  Ottawa 'Morning' Citizen, Oct. 30, 1942.

26  *Le Droit*, Nov. 19, 1942.

29  André Laurendeau, *La Crise de la Conscription, 1942*, Les

*Page Line*

Editions du Jour, Montreal, 1962, p. 138.

33  *Ibid.*, p. 82.

132  14  *H. of C. Debates*, June 23, 1943, p. 3930.

18  Vancouver *Province*, July 9, 1943.

26  *H. of C. Debates*, July 5, 1943, p. 4355ff.

133  10  *Ibid.*, p. 4361.

12  *Ibid.*, pp. 4365-7.

134  12  Resolutions of the Advisory Council, Sept. 27 and 28, 1943.

22  Address to the Montreal Reform Club, Nov. 13, 1943.

135  11  Address to the Kiwanis Club of Hull, May 21, 1943.

136  1  *H. of C. Debates*, July 11, 1944, p. 4748ff.

26  *Ibid.*, July 25, 1944, p. 5350ff.

137  26  *Ibid.*, July 31, 1944, p. 5677.

28  C.B.C. broadcast, Aug. 9, 1944.

138  3  *H. of C. Debates*, July 5, 1944, p. 4531ff.

28  *Le Devoir*, March 25, 1944.

30  *Ibid.*, March 30, 1944.

139  11  A. Laurendeau, *op. cit.*, p. 149.

CHAPTER 6  CONSCRIPTION

142  3  Interview with C. G. Power.

10  For the most competent analysis of the conscription crisis of 1944, see R. MacGregor Dawson, *The Conscription Crisis of 1944*, University of Toronto Press, 1961.

146  14  Montreal *Gazette*, Nov. 6, 1944.

25  *Globe and Mail*, Nov. 8, 1944.

149  28  *H. of C. Debates*, Nov. 22, 1944, p. 6504ff.

152  11  *Ibid.*, Nov. 23, 1944, p. 6515ff.

153  5  *Winnipeg Free Press*, Nov. 25, 1944.

154  34  *H. of C. Debates*, Dec. 1, 1944, p. 6735.

156  1  *Ibid.*, Dec. 5, 1944, p. 6830.

12  *Ibid.*, Dec. 6, 1944, p. 6858ff.

157  34  *Montreal Star*, Dec. 7, 1944.

36  Quebec *Chronicle-Telegraph*, Dec. 7, 1944.

158  1  *Globe and Mail*, Dec. 7, 1944.

24  Address in Quebec City, Nov. 29, 1946.

*Page Line*
159  33  *Ottawa Journal,* Feb. 26, 1945.
     35  *Globe and Mail,* Feb. 27, 1945.
160   1  *Ottawa Citizen,* Feb. 28, 1945.
163  14  Address to the Club Richelieu, Montreal, March 5, 1949.
164   1  C.B.C. broadcast, May 8, 1945.
     24  *Ottawa Citizen,* April 26, 1945.
166   4  C.B.C. broadcast, May 23, 1945.
      9  *Le Soleil,* May 26, 1945.
167   2  Address by W. L. Mackenzie King, Montreal, June 3, 1945.

CHAPTER 7   THE BRAVE
POST-WAR WORLD

170  12  C.B.C. interview, 1961.
     31  *Globe and Mail,* July 28, 1945.
     36  *Dominion-Provincial Conference on Reconstruction,* Ottawa, 1945.
172  17  For further details, see I. Gouzenko, *This Was My Choice,* J. M. Dent & Sons (Canada) Ltd., Toronto, 1948.
     36  *Globe* Magazine, April 28, 1962.
173  24  C.B.C. interview, 1962.
176   6  *H. of C. Debates,* Oct. 16, 1945, p. 1185ff.
     36  *Ibid.,* Oct. 22, 1945, p. 1334.
177  28  *Ibid.,* Nov. 13, 1945, p. 2090.
     31  *Ibid.,* p. 2096.
178  27  *Ibid.,* Nov. 23, 1945, pp. 2453-61.
     35  *Ibid.,* Dec. 4, 1945, p. 2923.
179   4  *Ibid.,* Dec. 5, 1945, pp. 2998-9.
     16  *Ottawa Journal,* Dec. 12, 1945.
     18  *The Printed Word,* December 1945.
181  10  *Montreal Star,* Jan. 18, 1946.
182  28  Press release, Feb. 15, 1946.
184  31  *H. of C. Debates,* March 14, 1946, p. 3.
185   1  *Ibid.,* March 18, 1946, p. 33.
     14  *Ibid.,* March 19, 1946, p. 88.
     15  *Ibid.,* p. 88ff.
186   2  *Ibid.,* March 21, 1946, p. 138.
     12  See *Dominion-Provincial Conference on Reconstruction,* Ottawa, 1946.
188   1  *H. of C. Debates,* May 28, 1946, p. 1930ff.
     24  *Ibid.,* June 6, 1946, p. 2228ff.
     34  *Ibid.,* June 18, 1946, p. 2616ff.
190  12  *Ibid.,* June 20, 1946, p. 2687ff.
     20  *Ibid.,* p. 2695.
191   3  *Montreal Star,* June 20, 1946.

*Page Line*
17  *H. of C. Debates,* June 21, 1946, p. 2712ff.
194  12  *Ibid.,* Aug. 31, 1946, p. 5750.
197  23  *Montreal Star,* Oct. 29, 1946.
     38  *Ottawa Citizen,* Nov. 26, 1946.
198  18  Text of Mackenzie King and St. Laurent addresses.
200  25  *Montreal Star,* Dec. 2, 1946.
     27  For example, the *Ottawa Journal,* Dec. 9, 1946.

CHAPTER 8
RE-CONSCRIPTED

203   6  'Foundations of Canadian Policy in World Affairs', Gray Lecture, University of Toronto, Jan. 13, 1947.
204  16  *H. of C. Debates,* March 3, 1947, p. 967.
     38  *Ibid.,* p. 975.
205  36  Address to the Canadian Institute of International Affairs, Quebec City, May 31, 1947.
215   3  C.B.C. interview, 1962.
217  29  Address to the Ottawa Branch of the United Nations Association, Sept. 8, 1947.
     33  R. A. Spencer, *Canada in World Affairs 1946-9,* Oxford University Press, Toronto, 1959, p. 81.
     36  *Ibid.,* p. 85.
219   2  *Ibid.,* pp. 96-7.
     23  Address to the Chamber of Commerce, Quebec, Oct. 7, 1947.
220  12  *Toronto Daily Star,* Nov. 6, 1947.
226  12  *Ottawa Journal,* Jan. 23, 1948.
     15  Address to the Manitoba Liberal Association, Jan. 22, 1948.
227  30  Quoted in the *Ottawa Journal,* Jan. 28, 1948.
228   3  *H. of C. Debates,* Feb. 6, 1948, p. 940ff.
     15  *Ibid.,* Feb. 6, 1948, p. 977.
229  33  *Ibid.,* March 17, 1948, p. 2303.
230  15  Address to a joint meeting of business and service clubs, Kitchener, Ontario, March 24, 1948.
     22  *H. of C. Debates,* April 29, 1948, p. 3438ff.

*Page Line*

30  *Winnipeg Free Press*, May 1, 1948.

35  Quoted in the *Lethbridge Herald*, May 20, 1948.

231  34  British United Press report, March 5, 1948.

232  11  *Le Progrès de Terrebonne*, April 30, 1948.

234  19  Article by Stuart Keate, *Maclean's* Magazine, Sept. 1, 1948.

37  Notes for a speech in Quebec City, July 15, 1948.

235  11  *Le Soleil*, July 19, 1948.

14  Montreal *Gazette*, July 22, 1948; *Toronto Daily Star*, July 26, 1948.

19  *Montreal Star*, July 21, 1948.

25  *Maclean's* Magazine, Sept. 1, 1948.

31  *Toronto Daily Star*, July 29, 1948.

236  16  *Ottawa Citizen*, Aug. 5, 1948.

237  18  *Proceedings of the National Liberal Convention*, 1948, p. 203.

27  *Ibid.*, pp. 207-12.


CHAPTER 9 'UNCLE LOUIS'

241  2  L. G. Bernard, 'The Mantle of Sir Wilfrid', in *Extension*, August 1949.

242  38  Léopold Archer in *Action Catholique*, Aug. 3, 1963.

245  7  Quebec *Chronicle-Telegraph*, Aug. 20, 1948.

18  Address on International Day at the Canadian National Exhibition, Toronto, Sept. 7, 1948.

246  3  Toronto *Globe*, Nov. 10, 1936.

6  *Toronto Daily Star*, Aug. 10, 1944.

9  *Everybody's Weekly*, Sept. 30, 1944.

13  Montreal *Gazette*, April 16, 1948.

26  *Ibid.*, Aug. 20, 1948.

252  14  C.B.C. broadcast, Nov. 15, 1948.

29  *Le Soleil*, Dec. 6, 1948.

253  9  Regina *Leader-Post*, Dec. 8, 1948.

18  *Maclean's* Magazine, Sept. 15, 1948.

*Page Line*

254  29  *H. of C. Debates*, Jan. 26, 1949, p. 11.

255  4  *Ibid.*, Jan. 28, 1949, p. 47ff.

21  *Ibid.*, p. 57ff.

257  15  Montreal *Gazette*, Feb. 3, 1949.

24  *H. of C. Debates*, Feb. 3, 1949, p. 199.

28  C.B.C. broadcast, Feb. 3, 1949.

258  6  *H. of C. Debates*, Feb. 8, 1949, pp. 358-9.

14  Minutes of press conference, Feb. 12, 1949.

259  15  Bill Henry in *Los Angeles Times*, Feb. 15, 1949.

32  Toronto *Star Weekly*, Sept. 8, 1951.

260  2  Address in Windsor, March 12, 1949.

25  Montreal *Gazette*, Feb. 28, 1949.

28  *H. of C. Debates*, Feb. 28, 1949, p. 949.

262  11  *H. of C. Debates, and Appendix*, April 1, 1949, p. 2276ff.

264  9  *Ottawa Citizen*, April 12, 1949.

14  C.B.C. broadcast, April 7, 1949.

29  *Le Droit*, April 12, 1949.

265  20  Quoted by G. Bain, *Globe Magazine*, April 14, 1962.

34  *Calgary Herald*, April 19, 1949.

266  3  Montreal *Gazette*, April 25, 1949.

7  Address to the Manitoba Educational Association, April 20, 1949.

22  *Winnipeg Free Press*, April 18, 1949.

267  16  P. Gordon-Walker, 'Canada Shapes the Commonwealth', in *New Commonwealth*, Dec. 21, 1953, pp. 646-7.

38  *Le Soleil*, April 29, 1949.

268  17  C.B.C. radio broadcast, May 9, 1949.

38  *Toronto Daily Star*, May 11, 1949.

269  9  Beland Honderich in *Toronto Daily Star*, May 11, 1949.

270  28  *L'Autonomiste*, June 10, 1949.

34  Vancouver *News Herald*, June 27, 1949.

271  7  Address in Owen Sound, Ontario, June 1, 1949.

36  *Ottawa Citizen*, June 24, 1949.

*Page Line*

272    7    Toronto *Telegram*, June 25,
              1949.
       20   *Edmonton Journal*, June 25,
              1949.
       28   C.B.C. broadcast, June 24,
              1949.
       35   *Canada Weekly*, July 15, 1949.
273    11   *Saskatoon Star-Phoenix*,
              June 28, 1949.
       15   C.B.C. broadcast, June 27,
              1949.

CHAPTER 10
POSITIVE NATIONALISM

274    6    *Montreal Star*, July 30, 1949.
       17   London *Economist*, July 2,
              1949.
275    28   *Montreal Star*, Aug. 6, 1949.
277    38   *H. of C. Debates*, Sept. 23, 1949,
              p. 196.
278    11   *Ibid.*, Sept. 27, 1949, p. 282.
       15   Letter to St. Laurent, Sept. 21,
              1949. Printed as Appendix to
              *H. of C. Debates*, Oct. 24, 1949.
       29   Address to National Conven-
              tion of Young Liberals, Oct. 13,
              1949.
279    29   *H. of C. Debates*, Oct. 24, 1949,
              p. 1102ff.
281    12   *Proceedings of the Constitu-
              tional Conference*, Jan. 10-12,
              1950, p. 10.
283    27   *Ibid.*, p. 106.
       33   *Toronto Daily Star*, Jan. 29,
              1950.
284    24   *H. of C. Debates*, Feb. 16, 1950,
              p. 2.
       28   *Ibid.*, Feb. 20, 1950, p. 49.
       37   C.B.C. broadcast, March 21,
              1950.
285    31   Address to the Canadian Club
              of Toronto, March 27, 1950.
287    4    For example, the Montreal
              *Gazette*, Jan. 30, 1950.
289    27   Address at St. Louis University,
              June 6, 1950.
290    6    *H. of C. Debates*, June 7, 1950,
              p. 3301ff.
292    17   *Ibid.*, June 26, 1950, p. 4116.
293    5    *Ibid.*, June 28, 1950, p. 4251.
       21   *Ibid.*, June 30, 1950, p. 4459.
295    6    *Toronto Daily Star*, July 10,
              1950.
       29   B. Hutchison, *The Incredible*

*Page Line*

              *Canadian*, Longmans, Green
              and Company, Toronto, 1953,
              p. 444.
296    3    C.B.C. broadcast, July 23, 1950.
297    16   For St. Laurent's account, see
              *H. of C. Debates*, Aug. 29,
              1950, pp. 11-13.
298    15   *H. of C. Debates*, Aug. 30, 1950,
              p. 31.
       36   *Ibid.*, Sept. 6, 1950, p. 343.
299    8    *Le Devoir*, Sept. 12, 1950.
       11   *H. of C. Debates*, Sept. 14,
              1950, p. 719.
       18   *Proceedings of the Constitu-
              tional Conference* (Second
              Session), Sept. 25-8, 1950.
301    23   Address to the Canadian
              Industrial Preparedness
              Association, Montreal, Oct. 6,
              1950.
       33   *Hamilton Spectator*, Nov. 24,
              1950.
302    12   *Proceedings of Federal-
              Provincial Conference*,
              Dec. 4-7, 1950.
305    6    *Ottawa Journal*, Dec. 30, 1950.
       17   Address to the Canadian Club,
              Jan. 8, 1951.
306    19   Final Communiqué published
              in N. Mansergh, *Survey of
              British Commonwealth Affairs,
              1939-52*, Oxford University
              Press, London, 1958, p. 752.
307    18   L. Chevrier, *The St. Lawrence
              Seaway*, Macmillan Company
              of Canada, Toronto, 1959,
              p. 42.
308    6    *The Proposed South Saskat-
              chewan River Development
              Project*, Regina, Saskatchewan,
              Nov. 20, 1949.
       16   *Montreal Star*, March 18, 1950.
       22   *Le Devoir*, July 10, 1950.
       29   *H. of C. Debates*, Feb. 1, 1951,
              p. 24.
309    3    *Ibid.*, p. 26ff.
       26   *Ibid.*, Feb. 20, 1951, p. 499ff.
310    1    *Ibid.*, March 1, 1951, p. 805.
311    36   *Ibid.*, March 15, 1951, p. 1281ff.
312    3    *Ibid.*, March 16, 1951, p. 1134.
       17   *La Tribune* (Sherbrooke),
              Jan. 12, 1951.
       22   *H. of C. Debates*, Feb. 26, 1951,
              p. 692.

*Page Line*

25 *Le Devoir*, March 7, 1951.
313 6 Address to the Reform Club of Montreal, April 21, 1951.
17 Toronto *Star Weekly*, March 3, 1951.
37 *H. of C. Debates*, May 21, 1951, p. 3253.
314 14 *Ibid.*, June 14, 1951, p. 4097.
20 *Ibid.*, June 28, 1951, p. 4807.
315 28 Eye-witness account.
316 13 Toronto *Telegram*, July 16, 1951.
30 Reproduced in the St. Thomas *Times-Journal*, Aug. 30, 1951.
32 *Ottawa Citizen*, Aug. 28, 1951.
317 20 Press statement, Sept. 6, 1951.

CHAPTER 11
EXTENDED MANDATE

318 12 C.B.C. broadcast, Sept. 4, 1951.
320 9 *Globe and Mail*, Sept. 29, 1951.
31 *H. of C. Debates*, Oct. 9, 1951.
321 12 *Ibid.*, Nov. 8, 1951, pp. 851-2.
35 *Ibid.*, Dec. 20, 1951, p. 2254.
322 9 *Ibid.*, Dec. 28, 1951, p. 2449.
323 23 Press conference, Ottawa, Jan. 25, 1952.
324 33 Quebec *Chronicle-Telegraph*, April 24, 1952.
325 31 *H. of C. Debates*, April 9, 1952, p. 1419ff.
326 10 *Ibid.*, April 28, 1952, p. 1635.
327 12 *Ibid.*, June 28, 1952, p. 3901.
26 *Ibid.*, July 2, 1952, p. 4093.
330 15 *Le Droit*, July 8, 1952.
22 *Ottawa Citizen*, July 12, 1952.
331 15 Address in Trail, B.C., Sept. 1, 1952.
21 Address to the Chamber of Commerce, Prince Rupert, B.C., Sept. 7, 1952.
35 Address to the Canadian Club of Hamilton, Sept. 12, 1952.
332 12 Address to the Advisory Council of the National Liberal Federation, Oct. 28, 1952.
333 14 *H. of C. Debates*, Nov. 24, 1952, p. 19ff.
30 Reproduced in *H. of C. Debates*, Dec. 15, 1952, p. 737ff.
334 5 *H. of C. Debates*, Dec. 15, 1952, p. 736.

*Page Line*

23 *Ibid.*, p. 743.
31 *Ibid.*, p. 712ff.
335 18 *Ibid.*, p. 639ff.
336 24 *Ibid.*, Dec. 17, 1952, p. 829.
338 38 *Ibid.*, Jan. 29, 1953, p. 1473.
339 6 *Toronto Daily Star*, Jan. 30, 1953.
16 *H. of C. Debates*, Feb. 3, 1953, p. 1565ff.
340 18 *Ibid.*, p. 1568.
341 10 *Ibid.*, p. 1577ff.
342 3 *Ibid.*, Feb. 16, 1953, p. 1950.
12 *Rapport de la Commission d'Enquête sur les Problèmes Constitutionnels*, Province de Québec, 1956 P.V.
344 1 *H. of C. Debates*, Feb. 20, 1953, p. 2277.
11 *Ibid.*, March 26, 1953, p. 3316ff.
27 *Ibid.*, March 18, 1953, p. 3071.
31 *Ibid.*, May 7, 1953, p. 4923.
345 4 *Ibid.*, March 9, 1953, p. 2775.
22 *Ibid.*, April 23, 1953, p. 4265.
31 *Ibid.*, April 29, 1953, p. 4509.
347 33 Address to the National Press Club, May 8, 1953.
350 1 St. Laurent Papers. Report of press conference, June 12, 1953.
25 Montreal *Gazette*, June 20, 1953.
32 C.B.C. broadcast, June 22, 1953.
351 27 *Toronto Daily Star*, June 24, 1953.
37 *Winnipeg Free Press*, April 15, 1953.
352 14 Address in Saint John, N.B., June 30, 1952.
19 C.B.C. broadcast, July 9, 1953.
34 Address in Edmonton, Alberta, July 13, 1953.
353 3 Appendix to address in Regina, Sask., July 14, 1953.
354 3 *Windsor Star*, July 21, 1953.
18 C.B.C. broadcast, Aug. 7, 1953.
20 *Ottawa Journal*, July 14, 1953.
23 Toronto *Telegram*, June 30, 1953.
28 Mac Reynolds in the Vancouver *Sun*, July 10, 1953.
355 8 C.B.C. broadcast, Aug. 7, 1953.
17 Quoted in the *Ottawa Journal*, Aug. 4, 1953.

*Page Line*

CHAPTER 12
WORLD STATESMAN

**358** 21 *H. of C. Debates*, Nov. 12, 1953, p. 2.
33 *Ibid.*, Nov. 13, 1953, p. 24ff.
**359** 24 *Ibid.*, Nov. 16, 1953, p. 42ff.
**361** 9 C.B.C. broadcast, Feb. 2, 1954.
32 Press conference, Bonn, Feb. 10, 1954.
**362** 12 Press conference, Karachi, Feb. 18, 1954.
25 *Ottawa Journal*, Feb. 22, 1954.
31 *Loc. cit.*
**363** 8 Address to the Parliament of India, Feb. 23, 1954.
**364** 16 Remarks by Prime Minister Nehru, Feb. 23, 1954.
**365** 13 Press conference, New Delhi, Feb. 24, 1954.
**367** 13 Interview with the author, July 1961.
37 *H. of C. Debates*, March 18, 1954, p. 3099ff.
**368** 33 British United Press report, March 8, 1954.
**369** 6 Press conference, Tokyo, March 11, 1954.
30 Press conference, Rockcliffe Airport, March 17, 1954.
**370** 1 *H. of C. Debates*, March 18, 1954, p. 3099ff.
31 *The Canadian Liberal*, Spring 1954, pp. 30-1.
**371** 6 *H. of C. Debates*, March 25, 1954, p. 3322ff.
**372** 14 *Ibid.*, April 6, 1954, p. 3722ff.
16 *Ibid.*, April 13, 1954, p. 4031.
21 *Ibid.*, April 14, 1954, p. 4077ff.
26 *Ibid.*, May 3, 1954, p. 4355.
**373** 6 *Ibid.*, May 4, 1954, p. 4380.
**374** 24 *Ibid.*, June 23, 1954, p. 6533.
**375** 16 Press conference, Ottawa, July 1, 1954.
20 Saint John *Telegraph-Journal*, Oct. 19, 1954.
**376** 14 Statement by Donald Gordon, Aug. 16, 1954.
24 Statement by Frank Hall, Aug. 18, 1954.
**377** 14 Address to Chambre de Commerce des Jeunes, June 1954.
19 *Action Catholique*, July 3, 1954.

*Page Line*
23 *Maclean's* Magazine, Jan. 1, 1955, p. 7.
32 Toronto *Telegram*, Sept. 14, 1954.
36 *Loc. cit.*
**378** 5 Address at the Quebec Reform Club, September 1954.
**380** 22 Address at Valleyfield, Quebec, Sept. 26, 1954.
**382** 11 *Notre Temps*, Oct. 2, 1954.
13 Robert LaPalme in *Le Devoir*, Oct. 2, 1954.
**383** 9 *Maclean's* Magazine, Jan. 1, 1955, p. 7.
**384** 16 Press conference, Montreal, Oct. 5, 1954.
33 *Toronto Daily Star*, Oct. 9, 1954.
**386** 15 Toronto *Telegram*, July 14, 1954; *Winnipeg Tribune*, Sept. 14, 1954.
**388** 25 N. Mansergh, *Documents and Speeches on Commonwealth Affairs 1952-62*, Oxford University Press, London, 1963, pp. 415-16.

CHAPTER 13 VULNERABLE

**390** 6 *H. of C. Debates*, Feb. 17, 1955, p. 1231.
21 *Ibid.*, March 1, 1955, p. 1630.
**394** 31 Press release, Ottawa, March 17, 1955.
**395** 4 Calgary *Albertan*, March 16, 1955.
15 *Federal-Provincial Conference, 1955. Preliminary Meeting*, Ottawa, April 26, 1955.
**397** 8 *H. of C. Debates*, March 10, 1955, p. 1904ff.
14 *Ibid.*, p. 1907.
26 *Ibid.*, June 7, 1955, p. 4513.
**398** 3 *Ibid.*, June 13, 1955, p. 4683.
24 *Ibid.*, June 28, 1955, p. 5376ff.
**399** 1 *Ibid.*, June 29, 1955, p. 5382.
23 *Ibid.*, June 7, 1955, p. 4509.
**400** 11 *Ibid.*, July 4, 1955, p. 5623.
15 *Ibid.*, p. 5642.
**401** 15 Quoted in *Liberal Newsletter*, July 1955.
**402** 33 *H. of C. Debates*, July 11, 1955, p. 5937ff.
**403** 33 *Ibid.*, July 20, 1955, p. 6448ff.
**404** 28 *Windsor Star*, July 29, 1955.

*Page Line*

407 16 Address before Legislative Buildings, Regina, Sept. 5, 1955.
409 1 *Proceedings of Federal-Provincial Conference*, 1955.
413 19 Appendix to *H. of C. Debates*, Jan. 11, 1956, p. 23ff.
   36 *H. of C. Debates*, Jan. 10, 1956, pp. 2-3.
414 8 *Ibid.*, Jan. 19, 1956, p. 34ff.
   14 *Ibid.*, p. 45ff.
415 26 *Ibid.*, Feb. 1, 1956, p. 763.
419 10 Toronto *Telegram*, April 24, 1956.

CHAPTER 14
THE TRANS-CANADA PIPELINE

420 16 *H. of C. Debates*, May 25, 1956, p. 4338.
421 3 *Ibid.*, March 15, 1956, p. 2164ff.
422 11 *Ibid.*, p. 2171ff.
424 4 *Ibid.*, May 4, 1956, p. 3571.
425 16 *Ibid.*, May 8, 1956, p. 3663ff.
426 3 *Ibid.*, May 14, 1956, p. 3864.
   38 *Ibid.*, May 15, 1956, p. 3911.
427 3 *Ibid.*, p. 3938.
   9 *Ibid.*, p. 3949.
   24 C.B.C. interview, May 16, 1956.
   30 *Globe and Mail*, May 18, 1956.
428 4 *H. of C. Debates*, May 17, 1956, p. 4025.
   35 *Ibid.*, May 22, 1956, p. 4173ff.
430 13 *Ibid.*, May 24, 1956, p. 4302.
431 25 *Ibid.*, May 25, 1956, p. 4365.
   31 Montreal *Gazette*, May 25, 1956.
432 24 *H. of C. Debates*, May 30, 1956, p. 4464.
   37 *Ibid.*, May 31, 1956, p. 4503ff.
433 24 *Ibid.*, p. 4517.
435 30 *Ibid.*, June 1, 1956, p. 4537.
439 14 *Ottawa Citizen*, June 2, 1956.
440 3 *H. of C. Debates*, June 4, 1956, p. 4653ff.
441 38 *Ibid.*, June 7, 1956, p. 4821.
442 36 Toronto *Telegram*, June 2, 1956.
445 3 *H. of C. Debates*, July 9, 1956, p. 5764.
   21 *Ibid.*, June 29, 1956, p. 5330ff.
447 4 *Ibid.*, July 2, 1956, p. 5553ff.
448 36 *Ibid.*, July 9, 1956, p. 5763.
449 27 *Toronto Daily Star*, July 11, 1956.

*Page Line*

30 *H. of C. Debates*, July 9, 1956, p. 5852ff.
450 30 *Ibid.*, July 10, 1956, pp. 5863-4.
451 10 *Globe and Mail*, July 12, 1956.

CHAPTER 15
THE SUEZ CRISIS

453 34 Text of press conference, Sept. 28, 1956.
457 30 *H. of C. Debates*, July 9, 1956, p. 5765.
458 4 H. Finer, *Dulles over Suez*, Quadrangle Books, Chicago, 1964, p. 56.
   9 *Ibid.*, pp. 63-4.
   30 T. Robertson, *Crisis: The Inside Story of the Suez Conspiracy*, McClelland and Stewart, Toronto, 1964, p. 74.
   38 *Ibid.*, p. 74.
459 10 *H. of C. Debates*, July 28, 1956, p. 6607.
   27 *Ibid.*, July 31 and Aug. 1, 1956.
   37 *Ibid.*, Aug. 3, 1956, p. 6919.
460 15 T. Robertson, *op. cit.*, p. 82.
   22 *Loc. cit.*
   29 *Ibid.*, p. 83.
461 23 *Ibid.*, p. 87.
   29 *Ibid.*, pp. 87-8.
   38 *Ibid.*, p. 92.
462 8 *Ibid.*, p. 101.
463 22 Press release, Sept. 21, 1956.
465 5 T. Robertson, *op. cit.*, p. 181.
   22 *Ibid.*, p. 182.
466 33 D. D. Eisenhower, *Waging Peace*, Doubleday, New York, 1965, p. 73.
467 34 J. Eayrs, *The Commonwealth and Suez*, Oxford University Press, Toronto, 1964, p. 172.
468 21 T. Robertson, *op. cit.*, pp. 182-3.
469 21 *Globe and Mail*, Oct. 31, 1956.
   27 *Ibid.*, Nov. 1, 1956.
   37 J. Eayrs, *op. cit.*, p. 194.
470 27 Montreal *Star*, Nov. 1, 1956.
472 4 T. Robertson, *op. cit.*, pp. 188-9.
   24 *Ibid.*, p. 189.
   37 J. Eayrs, *op. cit.*, pp. 317-20.
473 12 T. Robertson, *op. cit.*, p. 192.
474 11 *Ibid.*, p. 199.
   16 *Ibid.*, p. 200.

*Page Line*
**475** 24 *Ibid.*, pp. 202-3.
33 *Ibid.*, p. 215.
**476** 5 *Ibid.*, p. 220.
22 J. Eayrs, *op. cit.*, p. 279.
28 T. Robertson, *op. cit.*, p. 223.
**477** 10 *Globe and Mail*, Nov. 5, 1956.
18 C.B.C. broadcast, Nov. 4, 1956.
**479** 9 T. Robertson, *op. cit.*, p. 250.
28 *Loc. cit.*
**480** 16 *Ibid.*, p. 252.
**481** 5 H. Finer, *op. cit.*, p. 429.
15 T. Robertson, *op. cit.*, p. 266.
28 D. D. Eisenhower, *op. cit.*, pp. 92-3.
**482** 7 T. Robertson, *op. cit.*, p. 272.
17 *Ottawa Citizen*, Nov. 6, 1956.
23 *Ottawa Journal*, Nov. 8, 1956.
33 *H. of C. Debates*, Nov. 26, 1956, pp. 24-5.
**483** 4 J. Eayrs, *Canada in World Affairs, Oct. 1955 to June 1957*, Oxford University Press, Toronto, 1959, p. 186.
26 *Globe and Mail*, Nov. 21, 1956.
29 *Calgary Herald*, Nov. 12, 1956.
**484** 5 *H. of C. Debates*, Nov. 26, 1956, p. 12ff.
**485** 14 *Ibid.*, p. 19ff.
**486** 33 *Ibid.*, p. 30ff.
**487** 1 *Ibid.*, p. 40ff.
33 *Ibid.*, Nov. 27, 1956, p. 51ff.
**488** 21 *Ibid.*, Nov. 29, 1956, pp. 174-5.
**489** 6 Address to the National Conference on Higher Education, Nov. 12, 1965.
**490** 28 Address in Toronto, Nov. 15, 1956.

CHAPTER 16
THE LAST CAMPAIGN

**492** 21 *H. of C. Debates*, Jan. 9, 1957, p. 31ff.
**493** 13 *Toronto Daily Star*, Dec. 12, 1956.
**496** 9 *H. of C. Debates*, Jan. 9, 1957, p. 25ff.
**497** 13 *Ibid.*, Jan. 11, 1957, p. 154.
**498** 4 *Ibid.*, Feb. 6, 1957, p. 871.
21 *Vancouver Province*, Feb. 1, 1957.

*Page Line*
**27** Canadian Liberal, Second Quarter, 1957, p. 23ff.
**37** Address for Seventy-fifth Anniversary Banquet, Quebec, Feb. 2, 1957.
**501** 2 Press conference, Bermuda, March 26, 1957.
**507** 17 *Ottawa Journal*, May 8, 1957.
29 *Saskatoon Star-Phoenix*, May 7, 1957.
37 Regina *Leader-Post*, May 8, 1957.
**508** 3 Address at Regina Armouries, May 7, 1957.
37 *Ottawa Journal*, May 9, 1957.
**509** 33 J. Meisel, *The Canadian General Election of 1957*, University of Toronto Press, 1962, p. 43.
**510** 6 *Ibid.*, p. 45.
**511** 13 Address in the Capitol Theatre, Quebec, May 13, 1957.
**513** 7 *Winnipeg Free Press*, May 20, 1957.
23 Peter Newman, *Renegade in Power: The Diefenbaker Years*, McClelland and Stewart, Toronto, 1963, p. 53.
**514** 4 C.B.C. broadcast, May 20, 1957.
6 Address in the Ottawa Coliseum, May 27, 1957.
**517** 24 *Maclean's* Magazine, June 22, 1957.
**519** 9 J. Meisel, *op. cit.*, p. 273.
**521** 12 Press release, June 17, 1957.
**525** 28 Press release, Sept. 5, 1957.
**526** 6 *Ottawa Citizen*, Sept. 13, 1957.
34 *H. of C. Debates*, Oct. 16, 1957, p. 41ff.
**527** 19 P. Newman, *op. cit.*, p. 63.
**528** 6 Address to the National Liberal Convention, Jan. 14, 1958.
**530** 9 *H. of C. Debates*, Jan. 20, 1958, p. 3503.
31 *Ibid.*, Jan. 27, 1958, p. 3852.
**532** 29 Address, 'National Unity in Canada', Sir George Williams University, Nov. 9, 1961.
**533** 38 *Montreal Star*, Jan. 31, 1962.
**534** 9 *Globe and Mail*, Oct. 1, 1965.

# Index

553

558  LOUIS ST. LAURENT

125, 128, 129, 138, 196, 240, 273, 511; illness and death of, 2, 6, 7, 9; relationship with Mackenzie King, 5, 6, 7; attitude to St. Laurent as successor, 7; conscription, 6, 94, 103, 106-8, 110, 120
Lapointe, Hugues, 120, 167, 244, 443; conscription, 155-6; Solicitor General, 275; Minister of Veterans' Affairs, 296, 517, 518
Laurendeau, André, 131, 138, 139, 159
Laurier, Robert, 117
Laurier, Sir Wilfrid, 7, 33, 34, 40, 41, 45-6, 80, 97, 112, 125, 205, 212, 213, 215, 232, 243, 251, 334, 433, 498, 511, 533
Léger, Jules, 263
Leiterman, Douglas, 439
Lemieux, Sir François, 86
Lesage, Jean, 188, 192, 437, 443, 532; Minister of Resources and Development, 357, 372; Minister of Northern Affairs and National Resources, 412, 518
Liberal Party, 298; in Quebec provincial politics, 45-8, 94, 138, 330, 376ff.; in federal politics, 84-5, 88, 94, 103, 112, 117, 134-9, 256-7, 328, 341, 376, 380; *1945* election, 160, 163-7, 326; leadership, 180, 205, 210-16, 224-5, 227, 235-40, 316, 374-5, 400-1, 522ff.; political principles and program, 237-9, 241-2, 268, 280, 332, 348, 355, 418-19, 494, 505, 509, 528; *1949* election, 268-73; *1953* election, 343-5, 348, 350-5; *1957* election, 494, 502, 504ff.
Lie, Trygve, 180
Lloyd, Selwyn, 462, 500
Lodge, Henry Cabot, 467, 475
Low, Solon, 188, 309, 446, 498, 508, 521

MacArthur, Douglas, 300-1
McCann, J. J., 436, 442; Minister of War Services, 161; Minister of National Revenue, 172, 399, 403-4
McCarthy, D. L., 126-7
McCarthy, Joseph, 289, 492

McCartney, Gordon, 384-5
Macdonald, Angus, conscription, 107, 121, 144, 147, 148, 149, 150, 160, 173; Premier of Nova Scotia, 281-2
Macdonald, Sir John A., 17, 33, 212, 251, 291, 433, 533
Macdonald, Ross, 323
MacDougall, John, 436, 441
McGeachy, J. B., 97
McInnis, Angus, 194
Mackay, R. A., 95, 209
Mackenzie, Ian, 141, 175, 193, 225
Mackintosh, W. A., 297
McLaren, D. L., Minister of Revenue, 161, 169
McLarty, N. A., 160
McLaughlin, R. S., 80
*Maclean's* Magazine, 253, 355, 517
MacLennan, Hugh, 355
MacMahon, Frank, 423, 426
Macmillan, Harold, 480, 499-501, 521
McNaughton, General A. G. L., 172; conscription, 143-54, 159, 169
McPhail, Agnes, 132
Maltais, Abbé A., 36-7, 40, 41
Manning, Ernest, 330, 391, 406, 421
Mao Tse-tung, 285-7, 371, 387
Marcotte, Léon, 36, 43, 268
Marler, George, 276; Minister of Transport, 374-5
Martin, Abraham, 20
Martin, Paul, Secretary of State, 161; Minister of National Health and Welfare, 200, 357, 374; and Liberal leadership, 215-16, 236, 237, 523, 527-8
Masaryk, Jan, 228
Massey, Vincent, 254, 307, 320, 322, 385; Governor General, 308, 323, 496, 521
Massey Commission, *see* Royal Commission on the Arts, Letters and Sciences
Matheson, W. A., Premier of Prince Edward Island, 411
Mayhew, Robert, Minister of Fisheries, 263, 330-1; Ambassador to Japan, 332, 368
Meighen, Arthur, 84, 85, 108, 112,